John Lynch

Professor of Latin American History in the University of London

The Spanish American Revolutions 1808-1826

Second Edition

 W · W · Norton & Company · NEW YORK · LONDON

Library of Congress Cataloging-in-Publication Data
Lynch, John, 1927–
    The Spanish American revolutions 1808–1826.
    (Revolutions in the modern world)
    Bibliography: p.
    Includes index.
    1. Latin America—History—Wars of Independence,
1806–1830. I. Title. II. Series: Revolutions in the
modern world (New York)
F1412.L96 1986   980'.02   86-2390

                ISBN 0-393-02349-4
                ISBN 0-393-95537-0 PBK.

W. W. Norton & Company, Inc., 500 Fifth Avenue, New York, N.Y. 10110
W. W. Norton & Company Ltd., 10 Coptic Street, London WC1A 1PU

        6 7 8 9 0

Contents

PREFACE IX

PRINCIPAL PERSONAGES XIII

GLOSSARY OF SPANISH TERMS XXV

1 The Origins of Spanish American Nationality ... 1
   (i) *The new imperialism* ... 1
   (ii) *American responses* ... 7
   (iii) *Incipient nationalism* ... 24

2 Revolution in the Río de la Plata ... 38
   (i) *Merchants and militia* ... 38
   (ii) *The May revolution* ... 52
   (iii) *Buenos Aires and the interior* ... 58
   (iv) *Rivadavia and the new economy* ... 71
   (v) *Estancieros and the new society* ... 80

3 Revolution Against the Río de la Plata ... 89
   (i) *Independence of Uruguay* ... 89
   (ii) *Paraguay, the impenetrable dictatorship* ... 105
   (iii) *The war of guerrillas in Upper Peru* ... 118

4 Chile, Liberated and Liberator ... 128
   (i) *The Patria Vieja* ... 128
   (ii) *San Martín and the army of the Andes* ... 139
   (iii) *From O'Higgins to Portales* ... 141
   (iv) *The beneficiaries* ... 151

5 Peru, the Ambiguous Revolution 158
   (i) *Royalists and reformists* 158
   (ii) *The rebellion of Pumacahua* 165
   (iii) *San Martín and the liberating expedition* 172
   (iv) *The protectorate* 180
   (v) *The Guayaquil interview* 185

6 Venezuela, the Violent Revolution 191
   (i) *From colony to republic* 191
   (ii) *War to the death* 199
   (iii) *The revolution lives* 207
   (iv) *New masters, old structures* 219

7 Liberation, a New Site in Colombia 228
   (i) *The grievances of a colony* 228
   (ii) *Liberation of New Granada, conquest of Quito* 236
   (iii) *Colombia, one nation or three?* 249
   (iv) *The liberal society* 258

8 The Last Viceroy, the Last Victory 267
   (i) *Peru, reluctant republic* 267
   (ii) *Bolivia: independence in search of a nation* 279
   (iii) *'America is ungovernable'* 291

9 Mexico, the Consummation of American
   Independence 295
   (i) *Silver and society* 295
   (ii) *The insurgents* 306
   (iii) *The conservative revolution* 319
   (iv) *New mule, same rider* 326
   (v) *Central America: independence by default* 333

10 The Reckoning 341
   NOTES 357
   BIBLIOGRAPHICAL ESSAY 411
   INDEX 439

Maps

1   South America 1800–30   6
2   Southern South America and Peru   62
3   Gran Colombia   208
4   Mexico and Central America 1824   308

Preface

THIS BOOK ATTEMPTS to present a modern history of the revolutions for independence in Spanish America. The subject is large, the setting vast, but I hope that my interpretation does justice to the preoccupations of participants and the interests of readers as well as to the demands of space. I have sought to establish the character of the revolutions, to identify the forces which made and opposed them, the social groups who profited and suffered from them, and the economic environment in which they developed and had their being. As the revolutions culminated in national diversity rather than American unity, I have found it necessary to proceed by regions, without, it is hoped, neglecting the continental movement of events. I have adopted a predominantly Spanish American vantage point, seeing the revolutions as creators of the American nations rather than dissolvents of the Spanish empire, and concentrating on the 'internal' history of independence in preference to its international aspects. These are my priorities, and to those who have others I can only say, here is my story and this is the evidence.

I am grateful to Professor Jack P. Greene of The Johns Hopkins University who invited me to write this book for the series 'Revolutions in the Modern World' and who has helped me with his valuable advice. I am grateful also to Donald S. Lamm of W. W. Norton & Company, Inc. for his expert editorial assistance. I wish to thank Dr David Robinson for help with the maps; these have been provided by Miss Valerie Tassano of the Cartographic Unit, Department of Geography, University College, London, to whom grateful acknowledgment is made. I am indebted to Dr Joseph Smith for research in the Public Record Office, London.

University College, London

J.L.

Preface to the Second Edition

THE PRESENT EDITION has been revised to take account of recent research and the development of the subject. I have not sought to alter the structure or identity of the book, but parts of each chapter have been re-written, and there is a new bibliographical essay. The most extensive changes will be found in the first chapter and the last, those concerned with origins and aftermath, on which probably the most interesting new work has been done. A section on Central America has been added, reflecting perhaps changing perceptions and filling, I hope, a previous gap.

Institute of Latin American Studies
University of London

J.L.

Principal Personages

ABASCAL Y SOUSA, José Fernando de (1743–1821). Viceroy of Peru in the years of crisis 1806–16; an uncompromising defender of empire, opponent alike of Spanish liberalism and American independence.

ALAMÁN, Lucas (1792–1853). Mexican statesman and historian; son of a wealthy mining family in Guanajuato; sympathetic towards Spanish values and social structure but a supporter of political independence in 1821; his conservatism was tempered by a strong interest in economic development.

ALVEAR, Carlos de (1789–1852). Argentine-born officer in Spanish army who returned from Europe at same time as San Martín to serve cause of independence, first in a military capacity, then as supreme director 1815; exiled to Brazil.

ALZAGA, Martín de (1756–1812). Wealthy, self-made Spanish merchant in Buenos Aires; focus of royalist resistance first to liberalizing viceroy Liniers 1808–9, then to independent regime from 1810; executed for conspiracy in 1812.

ARTIGAS, José Gervasio (1764–1850). Gaucho caudillo in the Banda Oriental who led the first Uruguayan movement for independence against Spain, Buenos Aires and Portugal; a nationalist, an extreme federalist, and to some extent a populist; defeated by Portuguese invaders in 1820, he spent the rest of his life in enforced exile in Paraguay.

BELGRANO, Manuel (1770–1820). Creole intellectual who used his position as secretary of the consulado of Buenos Aires (1794) to promote cause of economic development of Río de la Plata; played a leading role in the May revolution and subsequently as a general of the patriot army, commanding unsuccessful expeditions to Paraguay 1810–11 and to Upper Peru 1812–13.

BOLÍVAR, Simón (1783–1830). The greatest of the liberators; son of a wealthy Venezuelan family, educated in an enlightened environment, widely travelled, he transcended class and national interests and sought the liberation of all peoples and all countries in Spanish America; personally responsible for the liberation of Venezuela, New Granada, Quito and Peru; an inspired soldier, an informed political thinker, his generous liberal instincts were gradually eroded by the violence and anarchy of the new societies and the disintegration of the new states; he died of tuberculosis on his way into exile, despairing of Spanish America's capacity for stability and progress.

BOVES, José Tomás (1782–1814). Asturian *émigré* and adventurer who became royalist caudillo in eastern Venezuela and led the llaneros in the violent counter-revolution of 1814 until his death in battle.

BUSTAMANTE, Carlos María de (1774–1848). Mexican lawyer, patriot, and historian of the revolution; an outspoken liberal, he joined the insurgents in 1812, and was imprisoned during the counter-revolution; supported Iturbide's independence movement in 1821 but subsequently imprisoned for congressional activities.

CABALLERO Y GÓNGORA, Antonio (1723–96). Spanish Churchman, Bishop of Mérida 1775–8, Archbishop of Bogotá 1778–9, Viceroy of New Granada 1782–9, and Archbishop of Córdoba 1788–96; a conservative in Church and state who ruled New Granada with integrity but exclusively in the interests of Spain.

CALDAS, Francisco de (1771–1816). Scholar and patriot; leader of the New Granadan Enlightenment and supporter of independence; executed during the Spanish counter-revolution of 1816.

CANTERAC, José de (1787–1835). Chief-of-staff of royalist army in Peru in last years of Spanish rule.

CARRERA, José Miguel (1785–1821). Officer son of a powerful Chilean family who joined the revolutionary army in Chile in 1810 and became military dictator 1811–14; although he fought and fled with O'Higgins at Rancagua, he remained a stubborn and conspiring enemy of the Chilean liberator until his own execution in Argentina 1821.

CASTELLI, Juan José (1764–1812). Creole lawyer who played a leading role in the May revolution in Buenos Aires both as a theoretician and as an activist; less successful in leadership of expedition to Upper Peru from which he returned to trial and disgrace.

CHARLES III (1716–88). Enlightened King of Spain who presided over the administrative, economic and military reform of the Spanish empire and strengthened metropolitan control.

CHARLES IV (1748–1819). King of Spain from 1788 until his forced abdication in 1808; his own ineptitude combined with the influence of his wife María Luisa and her favourite Manuel Godoy brought Spanish government into great disrepute, not least in Spanish America.

COCHRANE, Thomas, Tenth Earl of Dundonald (1775–1860). British naval officer, brilliant but difficult, recruited to command the Chilean navy, which he used to clear the Pacific of Spanish naval power, escort the liberating expedition to Peru and enhance his own fortune.

DORREGO, Manuel (1787–1828). Argentine statesman; after military service in the revolutionary cause in the Río de la Plata and exile in the United States he became provisional governor of Buenos Aires and, in 1827, governor; a *porteño* federalist, he was assassinated by unitarians.

ELÍO, Francisco Xavier de (1767–1822). Spanish Governor of Montevideo 1807–9; organized ultra-Spanish junta in 1808 in opposition to Viceroy Liniers and all forms of liberalism; in 1811 was viceroy without a viceroyalty, beset by Artigas and by Buenos Aires.

EGAÑA, Juan (1769–1836). Peruvian by birth, Chilean by choice; an intellectual precursor of independence and political activist from 1810; an eccentric conservative, a prolific and prolix writer, chief author of the unworkable Chilean constitution of 1823.

FERDINAND VII (1784–1833). Son of Charles IV, whom he succeeded briefly in 1808 before he too was forced to abdicate by Napoleon; some of the early revolutionaries in Spanish America claimed to rule in name of Ferdinand VII but soon dropped this mask, especially after his restoration in 1814 when he imposed a savage despotism and sought to recover his American possessions by force; hated by liberals, he was a disappointment to conservatives when, in 1820–3, he was forced to accept constitutionalism, thus undermining the remnants of royalism in America.

FRANCIA, José Gaspar Rodríguez de (1766–1840). Paraguayan lawyer who emerged as the strong man of Paraguay's independence; hostile to Buenos Aires, in reaction to whose claims he sealed off Paraguay; implacable towards Spaniards and creoles, paternalist towards Indian masses, established state control of the economy.

FREIRE, Ramón (1787–1851). Chilean patriot and officer who became leader of the liberals in opposition to O'Higgins; supreme director 1823–6, president 1827; regime notable for anarchy and growing conservative resistance, culminating in Freire's defeat and exile.

GÁLVEZ, José de (1720–87). Spanish administrator, inspector-general in New Spain, Minister of the Indies, Marquis of Sonora; a reformer, closely associated with the creation of intendant system and other imperial changes.

GUADALUPE VICTORIA (Manuel Félix Fernández) (1785–1842). Mexican revolutionary, one of the few who kept alive the cause of Hidalgo and Morelos; went underground during counter-revolution; joined Iturbide's independence movement 1821 without conviction; president 1824–9.

HIDALGO Y COSTILLA, Miguel (1753–1811). Mexican revolutionary, priest of Dolores, a man of advanced ideas who led the first Mexican revolution, a violent social protest in which Indian hordes threatened creoles as well as Spaniards and provoked a counter-revolution by forces of law and order;

defeated and executed by creole-Spanish forces but regarded in Mexico as father of Mexican independence.

HUMBOLDT, Alexander von (1769–1859). German scientist and traveller; his observations in Venezuela, Cuba and Mexico were acutely recorded in works which remain the most enlightened sources of information and comment on the Spanish empire in the years around 1800.

ITURBIDE, Agustín de (1783–1824). Mexican officer and landowner who fought on royalist side against the social revolution of Hidalgo and Morelos; when Spain went liberal led Mexico into independence 1821; his social and political conservatism expressed in his form of government, an empire and himself emperor; forced by republicans into abdication and exile 1823, tried to return 1824, captured and shot.

LA MAR, José de (1778–1830). Creole officer (born Cuenca), first in service of Spain, then, having delivered Callao to San Martín, in that of liberator 1821; highly regarded by Bolivar but proved to be hostile to Colombian presence in Peru; President of Peru 1827–9.

LA SERNA, José de (1770–1831). Last Viceroy of Peru; commander-in-chief in Upper Peru and Peru; a liberal, he replaced absolutist viceroy Pezuela in coup of January 1821; negotiated with San Martín but remained an imperialist; defeated at battle of Ayacucho and surrendered to the liberators.

LAVALLEJA, Juan Antonio (1784–1853). Uruguayan patriot and military leader who activated the second independence movement when he left Buenos Aires for the Banda Oriental (19 April 1825) at the head of a revolutionary force, the 'immortal thirty-three'.

LINIERS, Santiago (1753–1810). French naval officer in Spanish colonial service; organized successful resistance of Buenos Aires to British invaders 1806–7; a liberal viceroy 1807–9, partial to creoles but royalist enough to be shot for counter-revolution in August 1810.

LUNA PIZARRO, Francisco Javier de (1780–1855). Peruvian priest and republican, not entirely consistent in his attitude towards independence, but in general liberal in politics, hostile to foreign intervention in Peru and to militarism.

MARIÑO, Santiago (1788–1854). Patriot leader in Venezuela, the 'liberator of the east'; hostile to Bolívar but collaborated in the end and was chief-of-staff at battle of Carabobo; a powerful militarist in the post-independence period.

MILLER, William (1795–1861). British officer, commissioned captain in army of the Andes October 1817, lieutenant-colonel 1820, brigadier-general 1823; outstanding military service in Peru followed by appointment as governor of Potosí 1825.

MIRANDA, Francisco de (1750–1816). Venezuelan revolutionary and 'precursor' who in his long exile in United States, France and Britain vainly sought international aid for liberation of Spanish America; led an abortive expedition to Venezuela 1806; returned in 1810 to work with Bolívar for independence; given dictatorial powers April 1812 but capitulated to royalists in July, for which arrested by Bolívar and handed over to enemy; died in a prison in Spain.

MONTEAGUDO, Bernardo de (1785–1825). Argentine revolutionary who advocated hard line towards Spain and Spaniards; with San Martín's army in Chile and in Peru, where appointed minister of war then of foreign affairs; closely associated with policy of San Martín and proposals for monarchy, but unpopular with Peruvians and driven out in July 1822; assassinated in Lima 1825.

MONTEVERDE, Juan Domingo (1772–1823). Spanish naval officer who from western Venezuela led royalist forces which defeated the first republic; established reign of terror and personal dictatorship which tarnished Spanish cause and was ended by Bolívar's second republic in 1813.

MORELOS, José María (1765–1815). Mexican revolutionary, priest, and guerrilla who took over leadership of first social revolution after execution of Hidalgo; sought to rescue revolution from anarchy and indiscriminate violence, and, without abandoning radical social objectives, to widen its political base; creoles did not respond and, after an initially brilliant and subsequently faltering military campaign, Morelos was captured and executed; one of the most inspired, most radical and most tragic of the American revolutionaries.

MORENO, Mariano (1778–1811). Creole lawyer and revolutionary who played a leading role in pre-independence politics in Buenos Aires and in the May revolution; stood for absolute independence and for strong line against counter-revolution; editor of *Gaceta de Buenos Aires*; a radical and unitarian, resigned from governing junta December 1810 when conservative provincial delegates admitted; accepted diplomatic mission to England but died on voyage in March 1811.

MORILLO, Pablo (1778–1837). Spanish general, veteran of Trafalgar and Peninsular war; in 1815 commanded expedition of ten thousand sent by Ferdinand VII to crush the American revolution; a tough professional soldier, vigorously reimposed Spanish rule in Venezuela and New Granada; his merciless policy towards insurgents counter-productive and not altogether to his liking; signed armistice with Bolívar in November 1820 and took opportunity to return to Spain.

NARIÑO, Antonio (1765–1823). Colombian precursor and revolutionary; liberal republican; imprisoned and exiled before and during war of independence; a centralist amidst federalist anarchy, appointed President of Congress of Cúcuta by Bolívar 1821.

O'HIGGINS, Bernardo (1778–1842). Chilean liberator; son of Ambrosio O'Higgins, Irishman in Spanish colonial service, and a Chilean mother; educated in England where influenced by Miranda; already converted to independence in 1810 and in 1813 patriot commander-in-chief; after defeat of Rancagua 1814 regrouped with San Martín in Mendoza; his revolutionary record rightly rewarded when he became supreme director of liberated Chile; his regime an enlightened despotism, but his radical liberalism and lack of political sense made him vulnerable; forced to abdicate 1823 and spent rest of life in Peru.

OLAÑETA, Pedro Antonio de (died 1825). Spanish merchant who became royalist general and commander in Upper Peru; an absolutist, he opposed American liberation and Spanish liberalism, and was eventually defeated by Sucre in April 1825, when he died fighting.

O'LEARY, Daniel Florence (1801–54). Irishman, enlisted in 1817 for service in Venezuela, and from time of spectacular invasion of New Granada served close to Bolívar; 1820 became an *aide-de-camp* to the liberator, accompanying him thereafter in Venezuela, Quito, Peru , Upper Peru and Colombia; special missions to Chile, Bogotá, Venezuela and Antioquia; author of *Memorias*, the richest contemporary narrative of the northern revolution.

PÁEZ, José Antonio (1790–1873). Venezuelan caudillo, product of the llanos and leader of the llaneros in the war of independence; uneasy relationship with Bolívar, took Venezuela out of the union of Gran Colombia, becoming first President of Republic of Venezuela 1830; one of most successful caudillos of the revolution, starting from nothing and becoming one of greatest landowners in Venezuela.

PEZUELA, Joaquín de la (1761–1830). Spanish general who after commanding counter-revolution in Upper Peru became Viceroy of Peru in 1816; an absolutist, he fought a losing battle against both San Martín and the liberals in his own ranks; deposed by a royalist military coup in January 1821.

PIAR, Manuel (1782–1817). Venezuelan mulatto, successful revolutionary commander in the east; influential among the people of colour, whom he tried to mobilize against Bolívar; executed by the liberator for treason and as a warning to racialists.

PORTALES, Diego (1793–1837). Chilean businessman turned politician, who harnessed forces of conservatism against liberals and anarchy and was the inspiration behind the conservative government of 1830.

PUEYRREDÓN, Juan Martín de (1777–1850). Argentine revolutionary and statesman; appointed supreme director by Congress of Tucumán 1816; provided essential backing for San Martín's expedition to Chile.

PUMACAHUA, Mateo (1740–1815). Peruvian Indian, cacique, royalist, who led his followers against rebellion of Tupac Amaru and subsequent disturbances; disillusioned, he changed sides and became military commander of Cuzco revolution of 1814; abandoned by creoles and pursued by royalists, he was caught and executed.

RIVA AGÜERO, José de la (1783–1858). Wealthy Peruvian with long record of independist sympathy and briefly President of Peru 1823, but little military capacity or political sense; ambiguous attitude towards foreign aid and ready to collaborate with Spain rather than with Bolívar.

RIVADAVIA, Bernardino (1780–1845). Argentine revolutionary and statesman, a practitioner of enlightened reform, first during the triumvirate of 1811–12, then as minister in the Rodríguez administration 1820–3 and president 1826–7; his plans of economic development and uncompromising unitarian policies alienated powerful interests and he was forced to resign in July 1827, to spend most of remaining years in exile.

RIVERA, José Fructuoso (c 1784–1854). Uruguayan caudillo who fought under Artigas, submitted to Brazilian occupation, but rejoined the revolution 1825 and played a leading military role in its success; first President of Uruguay 1830.

ROSAS, Juan Manuel de (1793–1877). Argentine caudillo, land-owner, and leader of private gaucho army; a Buenos Aires federalist, he opposed Rivadavian liberalism and unitarianism, and ended both when he became Governor of Buenos Aires 1829–32, dictator 1835–52.

ROZAS, Juan Martínez de (1759–1813). Chilean revolutionary, born in Mendoza; family connections and public career in Chile gave him great influence among creoles; an independist in 1810, member of governing junta 1810–11, of congress 1811, and of Concepción provincial junta 1811–12; exiled to Mendoza 1812 where he died.

SAAVEDRA, Cornelio (1759–1829). Argentine militia officer who came to the fore during the British invasions of 1806–7 and provided the military force behind the May revolution 1810; became president of the governing junta; too conservative for Moreno and other radicals and suffered temporary eclipse, though appointed chief-of-staff of army in 1816.

SALAS, Manuel de (1754–1841). Distinguished Chilean intel-lectual and educationist who sought reform and development of Chilean economy; member of 1811 and 1823 congresses; exiled to Juan Fernández during counter-revolution of 1814–17.

SÁNCHEZ CARRIÓN, José (1787–1825). Peruvian patriot and theoretician of independence; a liberal republican, he was a minister in Bolívar's administration in 1824 and in the Peruvian government in 1825.

SAN MARTÍN, José de (1778–1850). Great liberator, soldier and statesman; born in remote Misiones (Argentina); after service in Spanish army returned to Buenos Aires 1812 to join the revolution, leading it from Argentina across the Andes to Chile and up the Pacific to Peru, a strategy conceived and executed by his own military genius; in Peru he faltered, seeking a political solution and miscalculating Peruvian commitment to independence; after much frustration he left the field clear for Bolívar 1822, retiring to Europe where he ended his days.

SANTA ANNA, Antonio López de (1794–1876). Mexican caudillo who led revolt against Iturbide 1822, the first of many opportunist political interventions which took him to presidency and dictatorship.

SANTA CRUZ, Andrés (1792–1865). Mestizo from Upper Peru who fought for Spain before he fought for independence; then served under San Martín and Bolívar; President of Bolivia 1829–39.

SANTANDER, Francisco de Paula (1792–1840). Colombian patriot and general, promoted by Bolívar; Vice-President of Gran Colombia 1821–8, when he showed his great administrative talents and uncompromising liberalism; on personal and political levels little sympathy between him and Bolívar and relations deteriorated; in exile 1828–32; President of New Granada 1832–7.

SUCRE, Antonio José de (1795–1830). Venezuelan officer, Bolívar's most talented and faithful commander; after service in Venezuela and New Granada he reached his greatest powers of leadership in Quito, Peru and Upper Peru; first President of Bolivia 1826–8 where he sought to establish enlightened administration; assassinated in southern Colombia by political enemies.

TORRE TAGLE, Fourth Marquis of (1779–1825). Peruvian aristocrat, governor of Trujillo; declared for San Martín and independence in 1820, but politically devious and sought to subvert Bolívar's position; returned to royalist allegiance and died during siege of Callao.

TORRES, Camilo (1766–1816). Colombian precursor and revolutionary whose *Memorial de agravios* became a classical statement of colonial grievances; a federalist, anti-Nariño but pro-Bolívar; executed during counter-revolution.

TUPAC AMARU, or José Gabriel Condorcanqui (1740–1781). Peruvian Indian, cacique and revolutionary; led a great Indian rebellion against Spanish administration 1780, captured and executed in Cuzco.

Glossary of Spanish Terms

administradores de pueblos civil administrators of Guaraní communities after expulsion of Jesuits.

albocracia white rule.

alcabala sales tax.

alcalde mayor district officer, comparable to a *corregidor*.

alteza Highness (title).

arribeños highlanders, regiment of creole militia in Buenos Aires.

artiguismo federal doctrine or movement of Artigas; *artiguista*, follower of Artigas or of his policy.

audiencia high court of justice with administrative functions.

aviador financier.

ayuntamiento town council, or *cabildo*.

Banda Oriental 'the east shore', i.e. of the river Uruguay and the Río de la Plata, equivalent to the modern Uruguay.

blancos de orilla poor whites.

boga boatman, in present context on the river Magdalena.

bonos bonus in national property, vouchers or bonds for this.

caballero gentleman.

cabildo town council, or *ayuntamiento*; *cabildo abierto,* a *cabildo* augmented with selected citizens for an extraordinary meeting.

campesino peasant.

canarios people of Canary Islands, emigrants from Canaries in Venezuela.

castas   racially mixed groups, between Spaniards and Indians.

caudillo   regional chieftain, leader, dictator.

champan   pole-boat on river Magdalena.

chapetón   South American nickname for a European-born Spaniard.

cholo   Peruvian mestizo, near-Indian, non-community Indian.

coca   coca, narcotic which formed part of staple diet of Andean Indians.

colonos   labourers occupying land in return for service; Indian farmers.

comuneros   members of a 'commune', supporters of a popular revolt.

comunidad   community, settlement of free Indians enjoying communal use of land.

consulado   merchant guild and commercial court.

corregidor   district officer with administrative and judicial authority.

coyote   a mixed-blood with mestizo and mulatto ancestry, a dark mestizo.

criollo   creole, a Spaniard born in America.

Cuerpo de Blandengues   cavalry corps employed as rural patrol and anti-rustling force in Banda Oriental.

cuzqueños   inhabitants of Cuzco.

delegado   delegate, representative.

donativo   contribution, forced loan.

encomienda   grant of Indians, especially as tribute payers; *encomendero*, holder of an *encomienda*.

estancia   large landed estate or ranch; *estanciero*, owner of *estancia*, rancher.

estanco   tobacco monopoly.

estanqueros   hard-line conservatives in Chile who resented loss of *estanco* to the state.

federales   federalists.

fuero   corporate privilege or right giving possessor protection of his corporation's jurisdiction and courts; *fuero eclesiástico*, *fuero militar*, clerical and military immunity from civil jurisdiction.

gachupines   nickname in Mexico for European-born Spaniards.

gaucho cowboy; *gauchos malos*, gaucho bandits or outlaws; *gauchos vagabundos*, vagrant gauchos unattached to any ranch.

gente de color coloured people.

godos pejorative name for Spaniards in America.

golpe de estado coup d'état; *golpista*, supporter of a *golpe*.

grandes cacaos nickname for wealthy owners of cacao plantations in Venezuela.

grito proclamation, especially of independence.

guayaquileños people of Guayaquil.

hacienda large landed estate; *hacendado*, owner of *hacienda*.

hato cattle ranch (Venezuela).

honderos Indians armed with slings.

indio Indian

infame infamous, vile.

inquilino tenant farmer, especially in Chile, holding land in return for labour services; *inquilinaje*, such a status or tenancy.

jueces comisionados judge-commissioners.

junta committee, board; *juntas provinciales*, provincial juntas; *juntista*, supporter of junta movement in Spain and America 1808–10.

juzgado court, tribunal.

latifundia large landed estate.

letrado lawyer or person with a legal training.

limeño inhabitant of Lima.

mayorazgo entail, entailed estate.

mestizo person of mixed white and Indian blood; *mestizaje*, miscegenation.

mita Quechua word meaning 'turn'; conscription of Indian labour for public or private work, especially in mines of Upper Peru; *mitayos*, Indians so conscripted.

montoneros guerrillas.

morenista follower of Mariano Moreno.

obraje workshop or factory, especially textile.

o'higginistas political adherents of Bernardo O'Higgins in Chile.

olañetistas followers of General Olañeta in Upper Peru.

orejones 'big-ears'; Indian caste of Inca Peru; herdsman or plainsman of northern South America.

paceños inhabitants of La Paz.

palenque commune or colony of fugitive slaves.

pardo mulatto, of mixed white and Black descent, free coloureds; *pardocracia*, pardo rule.

pastusos people of Pasto.

patria native land, fatherland; *patriotas* patriots.

Patria Vieja the old fatherland, name given to a country's first, if temporary, independence.

patricios patricians, regiment of creole militia in Buenos Aires.

patronato right of presentation to ecclesiastical benefices; royal or state authority over the Church.

pelucones 'big-wigs', nickname for conservatives in Chile.

peruanidad Peruvianness, sense of Peruvian identity.

pipiolos 'novices', nickname for liberals in Chile.

poder moral 'moral power' in Bolívar's constitution, as distinct from executive or legislative power.

pongo domestic servant of a land-owner, drafted from among tenants occupying land in return for services, in South American Andes; *pongaje, pongueaje*, forced domestic service thus rendered to a land-owner.

porteño of Buenos Aires; an inhabitant of Buenos Aires.

presidio prison, fortress.

provinciano provincial, partisan of provincial autonomy.

pueblo bajo common people, lower orders.

pueblo de indios Indian community or village.

querencia lair, home ground, especially of a fighting bull.

quiteños inhabitants of Quito.

regidor town councillor, member of a *cabildo*.

reglamento provisorio provisional regulation or ordinance.

repartimiento forced distribution of credit and goods to Indians by *corregidores*.

republiqueta mini-republic, guerrilla enclave.

resguardos reservations, Indian community lands, especially in Colombia.

residencia judicial review of an official's conduct at end of his term of office.

saladero meat-salting plant.

tertulia   social gathering, literary *salon.*

tierras baldías   crown lands, unoccupied or available for public use.

unitarios   unitarians (political), as opposed to federalists, especially in Argentina.

yanacona   tenant in Andean America holding land in return for labour service or, in coastal areas, in return for payment in money or kind.

yerba mate   maté, Paraguayan tea; *yerbales,* maté plantations.

zambo   a Black-Indian mixed-blood; *zambo prieto,* a dark *zambo.*

The Spanish American Revolutions
1808-1826

Second Edition

ONE *The Origins of Spanish American Nationality*

(i) THE NEW IMPERIALISM

THE REVOLUTIONS FOR independence in Spanish America were sudden, violent and universal. When, in 1808, Spain collapsed under the onslaught of Napoleon, she ruled an empire stretching from California to Cape Horn, from the mouth of the Orinoco to the shores of the Pacific, the site of four viceroyalties, the home of seventeen million people. Fifteen years later she retained only Cuba and Puerto Rico, and new nations were already proliferating. Yet independence, precipitated though it was by external shock, was the culmination of a long process of alienation in which Spanish Americans became aware of their own identity, conscious of their own culture, jealous of their own resources. This growing *conciencia de sí* caused Alexander von Humboldt to observe : 'The creoles prefer to be called Americans. Since the Peace of Versailles, and in particular since the year 1789, they are frequently heard to declare with pride, "I am not a Spaniard, I am an American", words which reveal the symptoms of a long resentment'.[1] They also revealed, though still obscurely, the existence of divided loyalties, for without disavowing the sovereignty of the crown, or even ties with Spain, Americans had begun to question the basis of their allegiance. Spain itself fed their doubts, for in the twilight of empire Spain became not less but more imperialist.

Spanish America was subject in the late eighteenth century to a new imperialism; its administration was reformed, its defence reorganized, its commerce revived. The new policy was essentially an application of control, which sought to increase the colonial status of America and to heighten its dependency. Yet imperial reform planted the seeds of its own destruction: its reformism whetted appetites which it could not satisfy, while its imperialism mounted a direct attack on local interests and disturbed the delicate balance of power within colonial society. But if Spain now sought to create a second empire, what had become of the first?

By the end of the seventeenth century Spanish America had emancipated itself from its initial dependence on Spain.[2] The primitive imperialism of the sixteenth century could not endure. Mineral wealth was a wasting asset, and invariably engendered other activities. American societies gradually acquired an identity of their own, developing further sources of wealth, reinvesting in production, improving their subsistence economies in foodstuffs, wines, textiles and other consumer goods. As the inequity, shortages and high prices of the Spanish monopoly system became more flagrant, the colonies extended economic relations between themselves, and intercolonial trade developed a buoyancy of its own, independent of the trans-Atlantic network. Economic growth was accompanied by social change, by the formation of a creole elite of landowners and others, whose interests did not always coincide with those of the metropolis, least of all in their pressing claims to property and labour. The creole was a Spaniard born in America. And while the colonial aristocracy never acquired formal political power, it was a force which bureaucrats could not ignore, and Spanish colonial government became in effect a compromise between imperial sovereignty and settler interests.

The new balance of power was first reflected in the notorious diminution of treasure returns to Spain. This was a consequence not merely of recession in the mining industry but also of re-distribution of wealth within the Hispanic world. It meant that the colonies now appropriated more of their own production, and employed their capital in their own administration, defence and economy. Living more for itself, America gave less to Spain. Shift of power could also be seen outside the mining sector, in the development of plantation economies in the Caribbean and northern South America, which sold their products direct to foreigners or to other colonies. The expansion of economic activity in the colonies denoted an investment pattern – American capital in the American economy – which, though modest in its propor-tions, was outside the trans-Atlantic sector. America developed its own shipbuilding industry, in Cuba, Cartagena and Guaya-quil, and acquired an overall self-sufficiency in defence. Military and naval defence in Mexico and Peru were financed out of the local treasuries, and this activated not only shipyards, copper-foundries and arms workshops, but also secondary supply bases servicing these industries. The decline of mining, therefore, was not necessarily a sign of economic recession : it could indicate greater economic development, a transition from a narrowly based economy to one of greater variety.

As Mexico's first mining cycle drew to a close, about the middle of the seventeenth century, the colony reorientated its economy towards agriculture and livestock and began to supply more of its own needs in manufactured goods. The hacienda, the great landed estate, became a microcosm of Mexico's economic self-sufficiency and of its growing independence. But the hacienda could generate further activity, for it needed to import some con-sumer goods and it provided raw materials for the colony's own production. At the same time an increasing proportion of govern-ment income in Mexico remained in the colony or its dependencies for administration, defence and public works, which meant that Mexico's wealth now sustained Mexico rather than Spain. It is assumed too readily that because a colony is not behaving as a colony it is therefore declining, that because it is not exporting a public and private surplus to the metropolis, participating in the trans-Atlantic trade, consuming great quantities of monopoly im-ports, therefore it is depressed. But these can be signs of growth, not depression. Peru always remained more 'colonial', less 'developed' than Mexico, and its mining capacity survived longer. But to supply the mining settlements the colony created an agricultural economy which developed a prosperity of its own. Peru never became so self-sufficient in manufactures as it did in agriculture. But numerous workshops, the notorious *obrajes*, employing forced labour and owned by the state or private enterprise, produced for the lower-class market or for particular needs. For the rest, Peru did not necessarily rely on imports from Spain : she had surplus capital and a merchant marine, and she could satisfy many of her consumer needs within America, particularly from Mexico, and from Asia. And remittances to Spain dropped spectacularly. Between 1651 and 1739, 30 per cent of the income of the Lima Treasury was invested in defence of the viceroyalty and its dependencies; a further 49.4 per cent was expended on viceregal administration, salaries, pensions, grants and purchase of supplies for the mining industry; and only 20·6 per cent was remitted to Spain. The bulk of the Peruvian revenue, therefore, was spent in Peru. The colony had become in some degree its own metropolis.

Historiography is familiar with the concept of informal empire, of outside economic control, as applied to Latin America in the national period. But was not Spanish America in a state of informal emancipation in the colonial period, or more precisely in the late seventeenth and early eighteenth centuries? It is true that the imperial power continued to exert its bureaucratic control; it is also true that the colonies did not declare their independence during the War of the Spanish Succession, when the metropolis was helpless. Apart from the fact that the political and ideological environment of the early eighteenth century was not propitious for a colonial liberation movement, Spanish Americans had little need to declare formal independence, for they enjoyed a considerable degree of *de facto* independence, and the pressure upon them was not great. A century later the situation was different. Then the weight of imperialism was much heavier, precisely as a result of the renewal of imperial control after 1765. Provocation occurs not when the metropolis is inert but when it is active.

The self-sufficiency of the American colonies was appreciated by contemporaries, particularly by the Spanish authorities. This was a recurring theme of the developmental literature of the eighteenth century, which sought a way to bind the Spanish American economy more closely to Spain. And this was the obsession of so many viceroys and other officials, seen in their frantic advice that economic dependence should be increased as a basic condition of political union. These views were reflected in 1790–91 by Gil de Taboada, Viceroy of Peru, who rejoiced in the increase of trade and lowering of prices which followed the commercial changes decreed by Charles III, especially the notable rise of imports into the colony and the consequent damage to Peruvian industries. 'The security of the Americas', he announced, 'must be measured by the extent of their dependence on the metropolis, and this dependence is founded on their need of consumer goods. The day they can supply all their needs themselves, their dependence will be voluntary.'[3]

To reverse the first emancipation of Spanish America – this was the object of the new imperialism of Charles III. The policy carried some risks: to disturb the balance of forces in the colonies might undermine the fabric of empire. But in so far as they were appreciated, the risks were regarded as acceptable. For colonial reform was part of a larger design to create a greater Spain, a vision shared by Charles III and his enlightened ministers, and brought to life in a movement of reform which sought to rescue Spain from the stranglehold of the past and to restore her power and prestige. Reform was given impetus by disastrous defeat at the hands of Britain in the Seven Years War, and from 1763 Spain made a supreme effort to redress the balance in Europe and in the Americas. A national reappraisal was undertaken. The ruling elite – a select group of intellectuals, economists, prelates and bureaucrats – canvassed various measures: equitable taxation, industrialization, expansion of overseas trade, improvement of communications, a programme of internal colonization, projects for the disentailing of estates and Church property, the ending of the pasture privileges of the powerful sheep-breeders in favour of arable farming, and many other proposals for economic development. The quasi-official economic societies were an important focus of reform, attached as they were to pragmatic solutions rather than abstract speculation and aiming essentially at the prosperity of the country by applied science. Not all of these plans were brought to fruition, but in the course of his

MAP I

SOUTH AMERICA
1800-30

Km.
0   400   800   1200

reign (1759–88) Charles III led Spain in a political, economic and cultural revival, and left the nation more powerful than he had found it. Government was centralized, the administration overhauled; agriculture was made to increase its yield and industry to expand output; overseas commerce was promoted and protected.

What did reform mean for Spanish America? Creole elites were by now well established throughout America, based on vested interests in land, mining and trade, on enduring ties of kinship and alliance with the colonial bureaucracy, and on a strong sense of regional identity. The weakness of royal government and its need for revenue had enabled these groups to develop effective forms of resistance to the distant metropolis. Offices were bought, fiscal bargains made, trade restrictions ignored. The traditional bureaucracy reflected these conditions, bending to pressure and avoiding conflict, constituting in effect not the agents of imperial centralisation but mediators between Spanish crown and American subjects. The Bourbons had a different concept of empire. Their government was absolutist, their taxation non-negotiable, their economic system strictly imperial.[4]

(ii) AMERICAN RESPONSES

The second conquest of America was first of all a bureaucratic conquest.[5] After a century of inertia, Spain at last laid hands on America. New viceroyalties and other units of administration were created. New officials, the intendants, were appointed. New methods of government were tried. These were not merely administrative and fiscal devices : they also implied closer supervision of the American population. The intendants were instruments of social control, sent by the imperial government to recover America.[6] During the age of inertia colonization had meant different things to different interests. The crown wanted America governed without expense. Bureaucrats wanted a well-paid job. Merchants wanted produce for export. Indian peasants wanted to be left alone. Many of these interests were irreconcilable; yet they were in fact resolved by an expedient of startling simplicity.

At some time in the early seventeenth century, in a period of great economic crisis, the crown virtually stopped paying a salary to its key officials in America, the *alcades* corregidores, the district officers of the Spanish empire. Toward they were allowed to raise an income by breaking the law, becoming in effect pure merchants, trading with the Indians under their jurisdiction, advancing capital and credit, acquiring equipment and goods, and exercising an economic monopoly in their districts.[7] Very few officials possessed initial capital to stimulate such economic activity. On route to their posts, therefore, they signed contracts with merchant capitalists – in Mexico City, for example – and entered into commercial partnership with these so-called *aviadores*.[8] The merchants guaranteed a salary and expenses to ingoing officials, who then forced the Indians to accept advances of cash and equipment in order to produce an export crop or simply to consume surplus commodities. This was the infamous *repartimiento*, a device which forced the Indians into financial dependence and debt peonage. In this way the different interest groups were satisfied. The Indians were forced into producing and consuming; royal officials received an income; merchants gained an export crop; and the crown saved money on salaries. But the price was high in other ways. It diminished imperial control over local policy and interests; the empire was administered by men dependent not on government salaries but on trade and the financiers of trade. And it reduced the Indians to a form of servitude from which they could not escape. The system was extensive in Mexico, in Oaxaca, Zacatecas and Yucatán; and in Peru, where it was practised with particular violence, it helped to cause the Indian rebellion of Tupac Amaru in 1780.

The system had its defenders. According to the author of *El Lazarillo de ciegos caminantes*, 'if it were absolutely forbidden to supply the Indians with clothes, mules and iron for farm tools, they would be ruined within ten years and would let themselves be eaten by lice, so lazy is their temperament and so prone are they to drunkenness'.[9] But it outraged the Spanish reformers of the eighteenth century. In the interests of rational and humane administration they abolished the entire system by royal decree. The Ordinance of Intendants (4 December 1786), a basic instrument of the reconquest, ended repartimientos and replaced corregidores and alcaldes mayores by intendants, assisted by sub-delegates in the *pueblos de indios*. This was in Mexico. In Peru too the repartimientos were abolished and the intendant system imposed (1784).[10] The new legislation introduced paid officials; and it guaranteed the Indians the right to trade freely with whom they wished. They could now refuse to work on the haciendas or on any land not their own and to pay debts not freely contracted. Above all, landowners and financiers were restricted in their use of labour; the crown interposed its sovereignty between private enterprise and the Indian sector.[11]

Spanish liberals were not popular in America. Colonial interests found the new policy inhibiting and they resented the unwonted pressure from the metropolis. Peruvians believed that land and trade depended on the old system. As the author of *El Lazarillo* explained, 'When the Indians are indebted to the cor-regidor ... then the hacendado finds labourers and the shop-keeper moderately priced textiles. The Indians have the same quality as mules in that they are ruined by very hard work but become torpid and almost useless with too much idleness.'[12] In Peru the repartimientos reappeared, as the subdelegates sought to increase their income, the landowners to retain their grip on labour, and the merchants to re-establish old consumer markets.[13] In Mexico, too, powerful groups were alerted, and the new officials were gradually persuaded to resume the old methods.[14] After a brief experiment, therefore, Bourbon policy was sabotaged within the colonies themselves; and in Mexico a local elite would eventually reach for political power in order to prevent, among other things, a repetition of liberal legislation. Absolute control over labour was too important to be relinquished.

As the Bourbons strengthened the administration, so they weakened the Church. In 1767 they expelled the Jesuits from America, some 2,500 in all, many of whom were creoles and were thus deprived of their homelands as well as their missions. No reason was given for the expulsion, but it was essentially an attack on the semi-independence of the Jesuits and an assertion of imperial control. For the Jesuits possessed a great franchise in America; they also enjoyed independent economic power through their ownership of haciendas and other forms of property and their successful entrepreneurial activities. Spanish Americans regarded the expulsion as despotism against their compatriots in their own countries. Of the 680 Jesuits expelled from Mexico about 450 were Mexicans; their life-long exile was a cause of great resentment not only among themselves but also among the families and sympathizers whom they left behind.[15] But this was only the preliminary round of a long struggle with the Church.

An essential theme of Bourbon policy was opposition to corporate bodies enjoying special status and privilege. The greatest example of privilege was the Church, whose religious mission in America was supported by two powerful foundations, its *fueros* and its wealth. Its fueros gave it clerical immunity from civil jurisdiction and were a closely guarded privilege. Its wealth was measured not only in terms of tithes, real estate and liens on property, but also by its enormous capital, amassed through donations of the faithful, capital which made the Church the largest spender and lender in Spanish America. This complex of ecclesiastical interests, another focus of independence, was one of the principal targets of the Bourbon reformers. They sought to bring the clergy under the jurisdiction of the secular courts, and in the process they increasingly curtailed clerical immunity.[16] Then, with the defences of the Church thus exposed, they hoped to launch a major attack on its property. The Church reacted strongly. While the clergy did not challenge Bourbon regalism, they bitterly resented the infringement of their personal privilege and immunity. They therefore resisted Bourbon policy, and were supported in many cases by pious laymen. The lower clergy, whose fuero was virtually their only material asset, were permanently alienated, and it was from their ranks that many of the insurgent officers and guerrilla leaders were to be recruited. As the great priest-revolutionary Morelos proclaimed to the Bishop of Puebla : 'We are more religious than the Europeans.'[17]

Another focus of power and privilege was the army, but here the metropolis had to proceed more warily. Spain had neither the money nor the manpower to maintain large garrisons of regular troops in America, and she relied chiefly on colonial militias, which from the mid-eighteenth century were expanded and re-organized. To encourage recruits, they were admitted to the *fuero militar,* thus giving creoles, and even mixed races, the

privileges enjoyed by the Spanish military, in particular the protection of military law. As imperial defence came to depend
more on local militias, as even the regular colonial army became
increasingly Americanised, so Spain designed a weapon which
might be turned against her.[18] The risk to security was soon
evident. In Peru the Indian rebellion of 1780 called into question
the efficiency and the loyalty of creole and mestizo units, and
Spain subsequently acted to strengthen imperial control. The
role of the militia was reduced in favour of the regular army.
Senior officers in both forces were now invariably Spaniards; and
the *fuero militar* was restricted, especially among non-whites. In
Mexico too the militia had its critics. Viceroy Revillagigedo
thought it folly to give weapons to Indians, Blacks and other
castes, and he doubted the loyalty of creole officers. It became
rare for a creole to obtain a senior commission, and Mexicans
learnt that access to military promotion, as well as civil office,
was increasingly restricted.[19]

While Spain sought to apply greater bureaucratic control, so
she was concerned to reassert closer economic control. The object
was not only to undermine the position of the foreigners but also
to destroy the self-sufficiency of the creoles, to make the colonial
economies work directly for Spain, to syphon off the surplus of
production which for so long had been retained within America.
From the 1750s great efforts were made to increase imperial
revenue. Two devices were particularly favoured: the extension
of a state tobacco monopoly and the direct administration of the
alcabala (sales tax), previously farmed out to private contractors.
The alcabala was a classical Spanish tax, a sturdy transplant from
the peninsula. Now its level was raised – in some cases from 4 to
6 per cent – and its collection more rigorously enforced. While
the colonies were thus made to yield a greater quota of taxation,
they were not consulted either about revenue or expenditure. In
the past there had been no major objection to the raising of
revenue for expenditure within America, on public works, roads,
social services and defence. But now the intention was to divert
this to metropolitan interests, in particular to make taxpayers in
America subsidize Spain's wars in Europe. From about 1765
resistance to taxation was constant and sometimes violent.[20] And
as, from 1779, Spain began to turn the screw more tightly to

finance its war with Britain, so opposition became more defiant; in Peru in 1780 creole riots were overtaken by Indian rebellion; and in New Granada in 1781 mestizo taxpayers – the *comuneros* – surprised the authorities by the violence of their protest. Less spectacular but more relentless opposition came from the *cabildos*, or town councils, the only institutions in which creole interests were represented. Here too the hands of Bourbon control were imposed, as the new intendants stirred the municipalities from their previous inertia. The finances of the cabildos were improved and their energies directed to public works and services. But the price of these gains was high: as royal agents subjected the cabildos to ever-closer supervision, so, from the 1790s, they provoked in them an unexpected opposition, and councillors began to claim the right not only to raise revenue but also to control expenditure.

The planners sought to apply the new fiscal pressure to an expanding and a controlled economy. Between 1765 and 1776 they dismantled the restrictive framework of colonial trade and abandoned centuries-old rules. They lowered tariffs, abolished the monopoly of Cadiz and Seville, opened free communications between the ports of the peninsula and the Caribbean and its mainland, and authorized intercolonial trade.[21] And in 1778 'a free and protected trade' between Spain and America was extended to include Buenos Aires, Chile and Peru, in 1789 Venezuela and Mexico. All this, combined with the extension of a free slave trade from 1789, permission to trade with foreign colonies from 1795, and in neutral vessels from 1797, greatly expanded trade and navigation in the Spanish Atlantic. But to what extent did it benefit Spain? The average annual value of exports from Spain to Spanish America in the years 1782–96 was 400 per cent higher than in 1788, and there seems little doubt that the metropolis profited from the receipt of greater surpluses from the colonies, public and private, and from better export opportunities for Spanish goods.[22] Yet, in spite of the formal exclusion of foreigners from imperial trade, Spain still relied on the more advanced economies of western Europe for goods and shipping, and even for permission to keep the routes open. Much of the Cadiz trade to America was a re-export trade in foreign goods. In 1778 foreign products amounted to 62 per cent of registered exports to America, and they were also ahead in 1784, 1785 and 1787. Thereafter the share of national goods improved and in the whole period 1782–96 they averaged 52 per cent. But these were predominantly agricultural goods. National industry did not respond to the colonial market, Spain did not become a developed metropolis.

Spanish America experienced revival and recession under free trade. During 1782–96 the average value of American exports to Spain was more than ten times greater than that of 1778.[23] Mexico accounted for 36 per cent of these, followed by the Caribbean (23 per cent), Peru (14 per cent), the Río de la Plata (12 per cent), and Venezuela (10 per cent). Treasure exports, at 56 per cent, continued to dominate the trade, and of these about one-quarter were crown revenues. But agricultural exports, tobacco, cacao, sugar, cochineal, indigo and hides, accounted for 44 per cent. This indicates that marginal regions — the Río de la Plata and Venezuela — and neglected products — agropastoral goods — were now brought into the mainstream of the export economy. But Americans also learnt that they were still subject to a monopoly, still deprived of market options, still dependent on Spanish-controlled imports.

There was, moreover, a basic flaw in *comercio libre*. The American economy could not respond quickly enough to external stimulus. It remained essentially underdeveloped and starved of investment, open to imports but short of exports. The result was predictable – an outflow of bullion, one of the few American products for which there was a constant world demand. In one year alone, 1786, Peru was flooded with twenty-two million pesos worth of imports, compared with its previous annual average of five million.[24] The markets of Peru, Chile and the Río de la Plata were saturated, and while this lowered prices for the consumer, it ruined many local merchants and drained the colonies of their money.[25] From all South America cries arose that the metropolis restrain itself. No doubt these were the squeals of monopolists unable or unwilling to readjust to competition and lower prices, and impervious to consumer interests. But other complaints were genuine and desperate: they were the out-cries of local industries, the textile *obrajes* of Quito, Cuzco and Tucumán, the hardware of Chile, the viniculture of Mendoza.

Soon even the ponchos and stirrups for the gauchos of the pampas would come from England. This was the crucial problem – colonial industries unprotected, European manufactures flooding in, and the local economies unable to earn them through increasing their own production and exports. Bourbon economic policy thus increased the colonial status of Spanish America and intensified its underdevelopment. The economic dependence – the 'colonial heritage' – of Spanish America had its origin not in the age of inertia but in the new imperialism.

American manufactures and products which duplicated European imports were deprived of essential protection by Bourbon policy. The Río de la Plata was an example. The textiles of Tucumán receded before imports through Buenos Aires. The wine industry of Mendoza was crippled by a combination of heavy taxes and competition from Spain. Mendoza complained of 'tyrannical taxes', of its status as 'feudatory of Buenos Aires', and requested Spain to halt the export of its own wine to the Río de la Plata.[26] The request was inevitably rejected, for it struck at the foundations of the imperial economy. Even when Spain could not apply her monopoly effectively, especially during the Napoleonic wars and the British-imposed blockade, foreign merchants penetrated to perpetuate dependency. Mexico, with a rising population, agricultural prosperity and a mining boom, was an economic success in the later eighteenth century. Its silver production rose continuously, from five million pesos in 1762 to a peak of twenty-seven million in 1804.[27] By 1800 Mexico produced 66 per cent of the world's silver output, and Spanish America contributed 90 per cent of total world production.[28] Mexico was now a source of considerable revenue to Spain, sending a surplus of over 6·5 million pesos a year in the period 1800 to 1810. But Mexico's own prospects of development were severely limited and her few existing industries found themselves in imminent jeopardy. By 1810 textiles in Querétaro and Puebla, a growth industry in the eighteenth century, were in recession, hit by regional difficulties and competition from imported cloth. This was the meaning of the new imperialism. As Viceroy Revillagigedo observed to his successor in Mexico in 1794: 'It should not be forgotten that this is a colony which must depend on its mother country, Spain, and must yield her some benefit because of the protection it receives from her; and thus great skill is needed to cement this dependence and to make the interest mutual and reciprocal; for dependence would cease once European manufactures and products were not needed here.'[29] The function of America was to produce raw materials. Bolívar himself described it : 'Do you wish to know what our future was? We were mere consumers, confined to the cultivation of indigo, grain, coffee, sugar, cacao and cotton; raising cattle on the empty plains; hunting wild game in the wilderness; mining in the earth to produce gold for the insatiable greed of Spain.'[30]

Spanish policy created a dilemma of interests between agricultural exporters and local manufacturers, a conflict between free trade and protection which was transferred almost intact to the new republics. While industry vainly demanded protection, agriculture sought greater export outlets than Spain would allow. America was still debarred from direct access to international markets, still forced to trade only to Spain, still deprived of commercial stimulus for production. In Venezuela the great creole landowners, lords of vast haciendas, owners of numerous slaves, producers of cacao, indigo, tobacco, coffee, cotton and hides, were permanently frustrated by Spanish control of the import-export trade. The intendant of Caracas, José Abalos, concluded that 'if His Majesty does not grant them the freedom of trade which they desire, then he cannot count on their loyalty'.[31] In 1781 the Caracas Company, the chief instrument of monopoly, lost its contract, and in 1789 *comercio libre* was extended to Venezuela. But the new breed of merchants were still Spaniards or Spanish-orientated creoles, and their control of the trans-Atlantic trade enabled them to exert a stranglehold on the Venezuelan economy, to underpay for exports and overcharge for imports. Creole landowners and consumers demanded more trade with foreigners, denounced Spanish merchants as 'oppressors', attacked the idea that commerce existed 'solely for the benefit of the metropolis', and agitated against what they called in 1797 'the spirit of monopoly under which this province groans'.[32]

The Río de la Plata, like Venezuela, underwent its first economic development in the eighteenth century, when an incipient cattle interest emerged, ready to expand the export of hides and other animal products to the markets of the world. From 1778 the Cadiz merchant houses with capital and contacts secured firm control of the Buenos Aires trade and interposed themselves between the Río de la Plata and Europe. But in the 1790s these were challenged by independent *porteño* (Buenos Aires) merchants, who procured slave trade concessions and with them permission to export hides. They employed their own capital and shipping, and they offered better prices for hides than did the Cadiz merchants, freeing the *estancieros* from the grip of monopoly.[33] The ranchers formed a third pressure group, small as yet and undistinguished, but allies of the creole merchants against Spanish monopolists. These porteño interests had spokesmen in Manuel Belgrano, Hipólito Vieytes, and Manuel José de Lavardén. Belgrano was secretary of the *consulado*, or merchant guild, which he made a focus of liberal economic thinking. Lavardén, son of a colonial official, man of letters, successful rancher, whose essential moderation added force to his views, reduced the economic programme of porteño reformers to a demand for four basic freedoms: to trade directly with all countries, thereby obtaining imports from the cheapest source; to own an independent merchant marine; to export the products of the country without restriction; to expand livestock and agriculture by land distribution on condition that the recipient worked the grant.[34] The coherence of this programme can be misleading. Economic interests in America were not homogeneous: there was conflict between and within the various colonies. And emancipation was not simply a movement for freedom of trade. But if there was a universal ideal, it was desire for a government which cared for American interests yet limited itself to protecting liberty and property. Americans were increasingly sceptical of the possibility of procuring this from Spain.

The second conquest of America was reinforced by continuous waves of immigration from the peninsula, as bureaucrats and merchants flocked to the colonies in search of a new world, a world fit for Spaniards, where they were still preferred in the higher administration, and where *comercio libre* had built-in safeguards for peninsular monopolists. The decree of 1778 was the signal for renewed immigration and a new process of control. Cadiz firms and their subsidiaries moved into the south Atlantic trade, and to Buenos Aires went the Anchorena, Santa Coloma, Alzaga, Ezcurra, Martínez de Hoz, agents of commercial conquest and precursors of the Argentine oligarchy.[35] In Mexico generation after generation of peninsulares renewed the Spanish presence.[36] During the period 1780–90 the level of immigration from Spain to America was five times as high as that of 1710–30.[37] Spanish Americans had a distinct, if exaggerated, impression that their countries were being invaded by shiploads of *gachupines* and *chapetones* their derisive nicknames for peninsulares. And the reconquest brought not only more immigrants but a new type of immigrant. Whereas in the sixteenth and seventeenth centuries the majority of Spaniards who went to America were from central and southern Spain, the new conquistadores came from the north, from Cantabrian Spain, hard, ruthless and parsimonious men, true products of their patria.[38] The Mexican statesman and historian, Lucas Alamán, described these immigrants as he remembered them. The majority were young men of humble origin who came to 'make America' and were assigned to a relative or friend already established, under whom they served a business apprenticeship. It was a harsh and grinding service; working hours were long, supervision by the patrón was exacting, and living was frugal, as the trainee had his earnings saved for him, perhaps married into the firm or was eventually given his arrears of salary with interest to start out on his own. The products of the system came to form a serious and successful entrepreneurial class, active in commerce and mining, and constantly reinforced from the peninsula, for the creole sons did not usually follow their father's vocation, preferring the life of the landed aristocracy. Alamán recorded the culmination of this success story: 'With wealth and marriage into respectable families came prestige, municipal offices and influence, which sometimes unfortunately gave them absolute predominance.'[39] From this point of view the revolution for independence can be interpreted as an American reaction against a new colonization, a defence mechanism set in motion by a new Spanish onslaught on commerce and office.

Spain did not trust Americans for positions of political responsibility; peninsula-born Spaniards were still preferred in higher office as well as trans-Atlantic commerce. Some creoles possessed large fortunes, based principally on land and in some cases on mines. But the majority had only a moderate income; they were struggling hacendados, managers of estates or mines, local businessmen; or they scraped a living in the liberal professions, including the overcrowded legal profession. First-generation creoles felt the greatest pressure, for they were immediately challenged by a new wave of immigrants. To the creole, therefore, office was a need not a bonus. During the first half of the eighteenth century creoles were allowed to purchase offices, and by the 1760s the majority of judges in the *audiencias* of Lima, Santiago and Mexico were creoles, linked by kinship or interest to the local elite.[40] Then came a Spanish reaction: the metropolis began to reassert its authority, reduce creole participation in government, and break the links between bureaucrats and local families. Higher appointments in the Church, the administration, and the military were restored to Europeans in an effort to de-Americanise the government of America. In the period 1751– 1808, of the 266 appointments in audiencias only 62 went to creoles, compared with 200 to peninsulares. In 1808 of the 99 officials in the colonial tribunals only six creoles had appointments in their own regions, and nineteen elsewhere.[41] The crown acquired a new imperial government, but frustration among Americans mounted. In Peru, New Granada and Mexico creoles made explicit demands for appointments: they wanted a share, or a majority, or an absolute monopoly of offices, and they wanted them in their homelands. So the traditional antagonism between the two groups was aggravated by the new colonization. As Humboldt observed: 'The lowest, least educated and un- cultivated European believes himself superior to the white born in the New World.'[42] In the Río de la Plata Félix de Azara reported that mutual aversion was so great that it often existed between father and son, between husband and wife. In Mexico Alamán was convinced that this antagonism was the cause of the revolution for independence:

This preference shown to Spaniards in political offices and ecclesias- tical benefices has been the principal cause of the rivalry between the two classes; add to this the fact that the Europeans possessed great wealth, which, although it may have been the just reward of effort and industry, excited the envy of Americans and was considered as so much usurpation from them; consider that for all these reasons the Spaniards had obtained a decided preponderance over those born in the country; and it will not be difficult to explain the increasing jealousy and rivalry between the two groups which culminated in hatred and enmity.[43]

American expectations, nurtured during the age of inertia, were thwarted by the new imperialism. The set-back was uncompromising yet unreal, granted the demographic superiority of the creoles. There was an obvious difference between the first conquest and the second. The first was a conquest of the Indians; the second sought to control the creoles. This was a losing battle, for the creoles constantly increased their numbers. In the sixteenth century, about 1570, there were 115,000 to 120,000 whites in Spanish America, just over half of whom were born in Spain. At the beginning of the nineteenth century in a total population of 16·9 million there were 3·2 million whites, and of these only 30–40,000 were peninsulares.[44] This minority could not expect to hold political power indefinitely. In spite of increased immigration, the facts of population were against them: the creoles now dominated the peninsulares by some 99 per cent. In these terms independence had a demographic inevitability and was simply the overthrow of a minority by the majority. But there was more to it than numbers. The social hostility of Americans towards the new immigrants had racial undertones. The peninsulares were pure whites, with a sense of superiority born of their colour. Americans were more or less white; in fact many of them were dark with thick lips and coarse skin, rather like Bolívar himself as described by his Irish-born aide, General O'Leary.[45] They resented the Spanish super-whites and desperately wanted to be regarded as whites themselves. Humboldt observed this race consciousness: 'In America a more or less white skin determines the class which a man occupies in society.'[46] This explains the obsession with minute definition of racial gradations – *zambo prieto* was seven-eights Negro, one-eighth white – and the anxiety of suspect families to prove their whiteness even by litigation, having sometimes to be satisfied with the court's declaration that 'they may be regarded as white'.

Colonial societies were composed, in varying proportions, of a great mass of Indians, a lesser number of mestizos, and a minority of whites. The Indian base of this vast pyramid was extensive in Peru, Mexico and Guatemala, less so in the Río de la Plata and Chile. But almost everywhere the Indians were a conquered people, forced into an inferior status, subject to the tribute and to personal and public services. Throughout Spanish America, but especially in northern South America and coastal Peru, the Negro slave was an added element, from whom descended free Negroes and mulattos, sometimes called *pardos* or *castas*. The status of the pardos was even worse than that of the other mixed group, the mestizos, who were the offspring of Spanish-Indian unions. The pardo was despised for his slave origin and his colour; discriminatory legislation debarred him from all white status symbols, including education; he was confined to *oficios bajos y serviles* in the towns and to peon-type labour in the country; and his ancestry in the union of white and Negro was regarded as so monstrous that it was compared to the nature of the mule, hence the term mulatto. A Spaniard might marry a mestizo but rarely a mulatto; the mulattos and Indians were regarded as inferior beings with whom even social proximates like poor whites and mestizos did not wish to marry.[47] Racial distinctions formed a part, though not an exclusive part, of class definitions.[48] 'Colonial social stratification was based on a graduated series of positions, openly called castes by colonial officials, which were determined by racial, economic and social differences.'[49] Whatever the degree of racial and cultural factors in determining social structure, colonial society was marked by rigid stratification; it was a caste society, though without religious sanction and with at least the possibility of movement. It was this possibility which alarmed the whites.

The creoles were intensely aware of social pressure from below, and they strove to keep the coloured people at a distance. Race prejudice created in Americans an ambivalent attitude towards Spain. In parts of Spanish America slave revolt was so haunting a prospect that the creoles would not lightly leave the shelter of imperial government. This was a major reason why Cuba remained aloof from the cause of independence. On the other hand Bourbon policy introduced an element of social mobility. The pardos were allowed into the militia, which gave them access to fueros, status and wealth, to an extent which many whites did not enjoy. They could also buy legal whiteness through purchase of *cédulas de gracias al sacar*. By law of 10 February 1795 dispensation from the status of pardo was offered for a sum of 1,500 reales de vellón, lowered in 1801 to 700 reales.[50] Successful applicants were authorised to receive an education, marry whites, hold public office and enter holy orders. This mobility was encouraged by the imperial government for reasons of its own. The reasons were not entirely fiscal, for the device did not have great revenue potential; nor were they purely humanitarian. The policy was basically a recognition of changes in society. Pardos were increasing in numbers yet suffered gross injustice; it was necessary to offer them space and release tensions. The policy also reflected perhaps the economic thinking of the metropolis and its attitude towards aristocratic power and independence. To increase social mobility would be to reinforce the white elite by an economically motivated and ambitious class; this would simultaneously undermine traditional ideals of honour and status and enhance entrepreneurial values. Whatever the motive, the result was to blur the lines between whites and castes and to enable many who were not clearly Indian or Black to be regarded as socially and culturally Spanish. The irony was that this liberal attack on seigneurial values ended by invigorating them, with the result that they were bequeathed to the independent states in yet more extreme form.

For the whites reacted sharply to these concessions. Their concern could be seen in a growing exclusiveness and sharpened sensitivity about race. In the Río de la Plata, according to Concolorcorvo, the principal families of Córdoba 'are very tenacious in observing the customs of their forbears; they do not allow the slaves or even the free coloureds to wear anything except their working dress, though this is quite coarse.' In parish churches whites and castes had separate registers for births, marriages and deaths, which made the Church in effect one of the guardians of racial purity; indeed it was the practice of the whites to have their children baptized at home, in the belief 'that to be baptized in church was a mark of Indians and mulattos'.[51] In New Granada the creoles regarded the terms mestizo, mulatto and zambo as insulting, and clung to their privileges as important class distinctions, at a time when the crown was increasingly critical of fueros and anxious to reduce them. The courts were flooded with requests for declarations of whiteness, the petitioners rejecting allegations that 'he is no more than a poor mulatto', and seeking certificates 'that he does not belong to the class of mestizos or have any other defect'.[52] Equally the mestizos sought to be declared mestizos, not Indians, and thereby free from tribute and better placed to profit from social mobility and the possibility of passing for white. But it was Venezuela, with its plantation economy, slave labour force and numerous pardos – together forming 61 per cent of the population – which took the lead in rejecting the social policy of the second empire and established the climate of the revolution to come.

The Venezuelan aristocracy, a relatively small group of white landowners and merchants, fiercely resisted the advance of the *gente de color*, rejected a new slave law, protested against the *cédulas de gracias al sacar*, and opposed popular education. According to the cabildo of Caracas, the laws of the Indies 'do not intend the pardos to live without masters, even though they are free'.[53] These issues came to a head in 1796, when improved status was granted to a pardo doctor, Diego Mejías Bejarano; he was dispensed from the 'status of pardo', and his children were permitted to dress like whites, marry whites, obtain public office and enter the priesthood. The cabildo of Caracas protested against what it called this 'amalgamation of whites and pardos', and concluded:

The great numbers of pardos in this province, their proud and arrogant nature, their stubborn determination to gain equality with the whites, demands as priority policy that Your Majesty keep them always in a certain dependence and subordination to the whites, as they have been until now; otherwise they will become intolerable in their insolence, and very soon they will seek to dominate those who have hitherto been their lords.[54]

The policy would lead, they insisted, to 'subversion of social order, a system of anarchy, and will cause the ruin and loss of the states of America, whose people have to live here and suffer the dismal consequences of this policy'. The crown repudiated these arguments and ordered its law officers to apply the cédula. But when, in 1803, Mejías tried to enter his son in the University of Caracas, the latter resisted, on the grounds that this would 'ruin the university for ever, submerging it in the deep abyss of barbarism and confusion, where the pardos would spread the pernicious seed of their ideas of equality and predominance'.[55]

In Mexico, too, the social situation was explosive, and the whites were always aware of the simmering resentment of the Indians and castes. Alamán described the Mexican Indians as 'an entirely separate nation; all those who did not belong to them they regarded as foreigners, and as in spite of their privileges they were oppressed by all the other classes, they in turn regarded all the others with equal hatred and distrust'.[56] In 1799 Manuel Abad y Queipo, Bishop Elect of Michoacán, analyzed the deep cleavage in Mexican society:

The Indians and castes are employed in domestic service, agriculture, the menial side of commerce, the crafts and trades. In other words they are servants, menials or labourers employed by the upper class. Consequently between them and the Spanish class there is the conflict of interests and the hostility which invariably prevails between those who have nothing and those who have everything, between vassals and lords. To some extent these conditions are prevalent all over the world. But in America it is worse, for there are no gradations between classes, no mean; they are all either rich or poor, noble or vile.[57]

The pent-up anger of the Mexican masses exploded in 1810 in a violent social revolution, which proved to the creoles what they had long suspected, that in the final analysis they themselves were the guardians of social order and the colonial heritage.

The creoles, therefore, lost confidence in Bourbon government and began to doubt whether Spain had the will to defend them. Their dilemma was real. They were caught between the imperial government and the mass of the people. The government allowed them privilege but not the power to protect it; the masses resented privilege and might be tempted to destroy it. In these circumstances, when the monarchy collapsed in 1808, the creoles could not allow the political vacuum to remain unfilled: they had to move quickly to anticipate popular rebellion. They then had to seize the opportunity of independence not only to take power from Spain but, above all, to prevent the pardos from taking it. Bolívar was appalled by the dilemma, aware that it survived independence: 'A great volcano lies at our feet. Who shall restrain the oppressed classes? Slavery will break its yoke, each shade of complexion will seek mastery.'[58]

Meanwhile the advance of the Bourbon state, the curbing of creole participation, the increase of taxation did not go unchallenged. Resistance to government innovation and abuse of power found expression in protest and rebellion, culminating in the revolts of 1780–81 in Peru, New Granada and Venezuela.[59] These were not so much popular movements as temporary coalitions of social groups, which the creoles first led and then, alarmed by the pressure from below, abandoned. They were not 'antecedents' of independence. The rebels appealed rather to a past utopia when bureaucratic centralisation and tax oppression were unknown. While they did not anticipate independence, they nevertheless helped to undermine loyalty to Bourbon rule. They demonstrated that the traditional formula of protest, 'Long live the King, down with bad government', was obsolete, discredited not least by the Bourbons themselves, whose policy of centralisation invalidated the old distinction between king and government and made the crown directly responsible for the actions of its servants. The rebels characterised the Spanish authorities as outsiders and the Americans as claimants to their own countries. In this sense they were a further stage in the development of colonial self awareness, a defense of American interests against those of Spain.

(iii) INCIPIENT NATIONALISM

Political power, social order: these were the basic requirements of the creoles. But even had Spain been able and willing to guarantee their needs, the creoles would not have been satisfied for long. The demands for office and security expressed a deeper awareness, a developing sense of identity, a conviction that Americans were not Spaniards. This presentiment of nationality could only find satisfaction in independence. At the same time as Americans began to disavow Spanish nationality they were also aware of differences among themselves, for even in their pre-national state the various colonies rivalled each other in their resources and their pretensions. America was too vast a continent and too vague a concept to attract individual loyalty. Men were primarily Mexicans, Venezuelans, Peruvians, Chileans, and it was in their own country, not America, that they found their national home. This sense of identity, of course, was confined to the creoles, and even they were conscious of an ambiguity in their position. As Bolívar recalled:

We are neither Europeans nor Indians, but a mixed species midway between aborigenes and Spaniards. Americans by birth and Europeans by law, we find ourselves engaged in a dual conflict, disputing with the natives for titles of ownership, and at the same time struggling to maintain ourselves in the country of our birth against the opposition of the [Spanish] invaders. Thus our position is most extraordinary and complicated.[60]

In so far as there was a nation it was a creole nation, for the castes had only an obscure sense of national identity, and the Indians and Negroes none at all.

Conditions in the colonial period favoured the formation of regional units distinct from each other. Spanish administrative divisions provided the political framework of nationality. The empire was divided into administrative units – viceroyalties, captaincies general, audiencias – each with a bureaucratic machine and a chief executive. These divisions, based on existing pre-Spanish regions, further promoted regionalism and a sense of local loyalty. And after 1810 they were adopted as the territorial framework of the new states, under the principle of *uti possidetis*, or, as Bolívar expounded it: 'What has come to be recognized as a principle of international law in America, namely, that the republican governments are founded within the boundaries of the former viceroyalties, captaincies general, or presidencies'.[61]

Nature reinforced the divisions imposed by man. America was a conglomeration of countries. Was there not a world of difference between the pampas of the Río de la Plata and the altiplano of Upper Peru, between the Chilean countryside and the plantations of coastal Venezuela, between the agricultural economy of New Granada and the mining zones of Mexico and Peru, between the gaucho, the llanero, the cholo and the inquilino? The difficulties of communications further separated the various colonies from each other. The Bourbons improved the roads, postal services and maritime communications of the empire, but natural obstacles, the formidable rivers, plains and deserts, the impenetrable jungles and mountains of America, were too great to overcome. Journeys were long and slow. It took four months by sea from Buenos Aires to Acapulco, and the return was even slower.[62] The journey by land from Buenos Aires to Santiago, crossing pampas and cordillera, took two tiring months. Anyone rash enough to travel from Buenos Aires to Cartagena by land faced a journey by horse, mule, wagons and river transports via Lima, Quito and Bogotá, and it took nine months. Regional isolation helped to stifle American unity and to promote particularism.

Regionalism was reinforced by economic divisions. Some colonies had agricultural and mineral surpluses for export to others and they broke through the legal barriers to intercolonial trade. When these barriers were formally removed, from 1765, the imperial government encouraged inter-American trade, but could not effect economic integration. Chile resented its dependence on Peru, virtually the only market for its wheat. Buenos Aires competed with Lima for the market of Upper Peru.[63] Peru bitterly resented the loss of Potosí to the Río de la Plata in 1776 and objected to the obligation to provide mita Indians for continued operation of the mines.[64] Buenos Aires in its turn became a kind of metropolis, controlling river communications, channelling all trade to itself, and arousing the resentment of its satellites, the Banda Oriental and Paraguay. These economic rivalries had a dual significance. First, viceroys and other officials, Spaniards as well as creoles, took up the regionalist position of their colony and supported it against rivals. Secondly, while it might appear that colonial nationalism first showed itself less against Spain than against other colonies, in fact the colonies learnt the lesson that their economic interests had little chance of an impartial hearing from the imperial government, that the rivalries of the various regions were an inevitable consequence of colonial rule, and that they needed independent control over their own destinies. And after 1810 each country would seek its individual solution and attempt to resolve its economic problems by establishing relations with Europe or the United States without reference to its neighbours.

Incipient nationalism also received a degree of political expression. This was the meaning of the irrepressible American demand for office, a demand which probably reflected more concern with patronage than with policy. But it was further evidence of a growing assumption – that Americans were different from Spaniards. In 1771 the cabildo of Mexico City asserted that Mexicans should have exclusive right to office in their own country. Americans, they claimed, were educated and qualified for office, and had a prior right over Spaniards, who were foreigners in Mexico. True, Spaniards and Mexicans were subjects of the same sovereign and as such members of the same body politic, but, they argued, 'as far as appointments to offices is concerned European Spaniards must be counted as foreigners here, for they are liable to the same objections which all peoples bring against the employment of foreigners'.[65]

What were the intellectual sources of the new Americanism? The ideas of the French *philosophes*, their criticisms of contemporary social, political and religious institutions, were known to Americans though they were not accepted indiscriminately. The literature of the Enlightenment circulated in Spanish America with comparative freedom. In Mexico there was an audience for Newton, Locke and Adam Smith, for Descartes, Montesquieu, Voltaire, Diderot, Rousseau, Condillac and D'Alembert. Readers were to be found among viceroys and other officials, members of the professional and business classes, university personnel and ecclesiastics. The inundation reached its height in the 1790s, and it was now that the Mexican Inquisition began to move, alarmed less by religious heterodoxy than by the political content of the new philosophy, which it regarded as seditious, 'contrary to the security of states', full of 'general principles of equality and liberty for all men', and in some cases a vehicle for news of 'the frightful and damaging revolution in France'.[66] But the new intellectual movement was not an issue which divided creoles from Spaniards, nor was it an essential ingredient of independence. To possess a book was not necessarily to accept its ideas. American readers were often inspired by nothing more than intellectual curiosity; they wanted to know what was happening in the wider world; they resented official attempts to keep them ignorant; and they welcomed contemporary ideas as instruments of reform, not destruction. It is true that some educated creoles were more than reformers; they were revolutionaries. In northern South America Francisco de Miranda, Pedro Fermín de Vargas, Antonio Nariño, and the young Simón Bolívar were all disciples of the new philosophy, ardent seekers after human liberty and happiness. In the Río de la Plata Viceroy Avilés observed 'signs of a spirit of independence', which he attributed precisely to excessive contact with foreigners.[67] Manuel Belgrano was widely read in the thought of the Enlightenment. Mariano Moreno was an enthusiastic admirer of Rousseau, whose *Social Contract* he edited in 1810 'for the instruction of young Americans'. These men were true precursors of independence; yet they were a small elite and undoubtedly ahead of creole opinion. The mass of Americans had many objections to the colonial regime, but these were pragmatic rather than ideological; in the ultimate analysis the greatest threat to the Spanish empire came from American interests rather than European ideas. To suppose that the thought of the Enlightenment made revolutionaries of Spanish Americans is to confuse cause and effect. Some were already dissenters; for this reason they sought in the new philosophy further inspiration for their own ideals, intellectual justification for the revolution to come. While the Enlightenment had an important role in Spanish America, therefore, this role was not primarily a 'cause' of independence. Rather there was a movement of ideas from the Enlightenment via the revolutionary movement into the new republics, where they became an essential ingredient of Latin American liberalism.[68] And in the final reckoning Americans received from the Enlightenment not so much new information and ideas as a new approach to knowledge, a preference for reason and experiment as opposed to authority and tradition. This was a potent if intangible challenge to Spanish rule.

The Enlightenment was brought into sharper focus by the revolutions in North America and France. Of these two great liberating movements the French model had less appeal to Spanish Americans. Their reaction was based not on ignorance but on interest. Spanish government, it is true, attempted to prevent French news and propaganda from reaching its subjects, but the barriers were breached by a flood of revolutionary litera-

ture in Spain and in America. Some read the new material out
of curiosity. Others instinctively recognized their spiritual home,
embracing the principles of liberty and applauding the rights of
man. Equality was another matter. Situated as they were between
the Spaniards and the masses, the creoles wanted more than
equality for themselves and less than equality for their inferiors.
In 1791 the French island colony of Saint Domingue was engulfed in a ferocious slave revolt, and in 1804 Negro and
mulatto generals proclaimed a new and independent state,
Haiti. As violence spread from Haiti to the slave compounds of
Venezuela, white property owners rejected with horror revolutionary doctrines which could so inflame their dependants. The
more radical the French revolution became and the better it was
known, the less it appealed to the creole aristocracy. They saw it
as an archtype of extreme democracy and social anarchy; and
even liberals like the Mexican José Luis Mora came to believe that
Spanish America had nothing to learn from the French revolution, which had attacked, not promoted, individual liberty and
civil rights. As for Napoleon, the instigator .of crisis in the
Hispanic world in 1808, to Americans he stood not for national
interests but for French imperialism.

The influence of the United States was more benevolent and
more enduring. In the years before and after 1810 the very
existence of the United States excited the imagination of Spanish
Americans, and its embodiment of liberty and republicanism
placed a powerful example before their eyes. The works of Tom
Paine and Franklin, the speeches of John Adams, Jefferson and
Washington all circulated in Spanish America. Many of the precursors and leaders of independence visited the United States
and saw free institutions at first hand; Bolívar respected Washington and admired, though never uncritically, the United
States, 'land of freedom and home of civic virtue', as he described
it. Economic relations forged further bonds. United States trade
with Spanish America, first with the Caribbean then, after the
disintegration of the Spanish monopoly during the Napoleonic
wars, with the Río de la Plata and the Pacific coast, was a
channel not only of goods and services but also of books and
ideas. Copies of the Federal Constitution and the Declaration of
Independence, conveniently translated into Spanish, were carried

into the area by United States traders whose liberal views coincided with their interest in developing a market free of the Spanish monopoly. After 1810, before disillusion with their powerful neighbour prevailed, Spanish American statesmen looked north for guidance. Constitutions in Venezuela, Mexico and elsewhere would be closely modelled on that of the United States, and many of the new leaders — though not Bolívar — would be profoundly influenced by North American federalism.

The influence of the United States, like that of Europe, is difficult to measure. If it played only a secondary role in the political education of Spanish Americans, it was still significant, for, like the Enlightenment, it helped to open their minds. This new vision they now applied to their own environment. In the course of the eighteenth century Spanish Americans began to rediscover their own land in a uniquely American literature. Their patriotism was American, not Spanish, regional rather than continental, for each country had its own identity, observed by its peoples and glorified by its writers. Creole intellectuals in Mexico, Peru and Chile expressed and nurtured a new awareness of patria and a greater sense of exclusiveness, for as the *Mercurio Peruano* observed, 'it interests us more to know what is happening in our own nation'.[69] Among the first to give cultural expression to 'Americanism' were the creole Jesuits expelled from their homelands in 1767, who became in exile literary precursors of American nationalism.

To some extent it was a literature of nostalgia. The Chilean Jesuit Manuel Lacunza imagined himself eating his favourite Chilean dishes, while Juan Ignacio Molina thirsted for the sparkling water of the cordillera. The Mexican Juan Luis Maneiro implored the Spanish king to allow him to die 'en patria suelo':

> Quisiéramos morir bajo aquel cielo
> Que influyó tanto a nuestro ser humano.[70]

But the patriotism of the American Jesuits went beyond personal sentiment. They wrote to dispel European ignorance of their countries, and in particular to destroy the myth of the inferiority and degeneracy of man, animal and vegetable in the New World, a myth propagated by a number of anti-American works of the mid-eighteenth century. Buffon claimed that American immaturity could be seen in the puma, which was more cowardly than the lion; De Pauw alleged that the Mexican Indians could only count up to three; Raynal referred to American decrepitude and even censured America for the 'excessive altitude of the Peruvian mountains'.[71] In reply the exiles described the nature and history of their countries, their resources and qualities, producing in the process works of scholarship as well as of literature. Juan Ignacio Molina, the Chilean Jesuit, wrote a major study of the geography and history of Chile, its mineral, vegetable and animal resources, whose scientific spirit caught the attention of Europe. Molina had a distinctly pro-creole bias and he defended his fellow Americans for the progress which they had made despite lack of opportunity and education. He was also Indianist in his sympathies. Deploring the universal ignorance about Chile, he remarked, 'the nature, customs and beautiful language of its ancient inhabitants remain unknown, as are their remarkable efforts in defence of their liberty, in battles stretching from the beginning of the conquest to the present day'.[72]

The most eloquent and perhaps the most scholarly of all the exile writers was Francisco Javier Clavijero, who compared his native Mexico to the heavenly Jerusalem of Holy Scripture.[73] Clavijero's nostalgia masked a more serious intent. He sought to provide an exact study of Mexico, especially of its prehistory, and in the process to refute De Pauw. He himself was a creole, born in Veracruz in 1731, and as a youth he learnt the Indian languages. His *Historia Antigua de México*, therefore, first published in 1780–1, was a history of ancient Mexico written in a scientific spirit by a qualified Mexican, in order, as he put it, 'to make himself useful to his patria'. He underlined the differences between Mexico and Spain, especially the ethnic differences. He argued that a more homogeneous Mexican nationality could have been formed by means of complete *mestizaje*: 'There is no doubt that the policy of the Spaniards would have been wiser if, instead of taking European women and African slaves to America, they had intermarried with the Mexicans alone and thus formed a single nation.'[74] Clavijero's work circulated not only in Europe but also in Mexico, where the rector of the university promoted its distribution. And it was continued by Andrés Cavo, who extended the story into the colonial period.[75] Cavo prefaced his study with the hope 'that this history undertaken out of love of my native land may be received with favour by those of my nation'. And he too considered the problem of nationality: 'If after the conquest there had been widespread intermarriage between the two nations, which the Mexicans would have welcomed, then in the course of time out of two nations a single nation would have been formed.'[76]

The literature of the Jesuit exiles belonged to Spanish American rather than Spanish culture. And if it was not yet a 'national' literature, it contained an essential ingredient of nationalism, awareness of the patria's historical past. But the significance of the Jesuit works lay less in their direct influence than in the way they reflected the thinking of other less articulate Americans. The Jesuits were simply interpreters of regionalist sentiments which had already taken root in the creole mind. And when the creoles themselves expressed their patriotism it was usually more optimistic than that of the exiles. The pre-independence period saw the emergence of a literature of hyperbole, in which Americans glorified their countries, extolled their resources, and praised their peoples. No doubt there was something pretentious about these works; their patriotism was exaggerated; and their knowledge of other parts of the world was not impressive. But they represented a natural reaction against European prejudice and an important stage in American cultural development.[77]

In Buenos Aires the *Telégrafo Mercantil* described the Río de la Plata as 'the richest country in the world'. Manuel de Salas described Chile as 'without doubt the most fertile land in America and the most propitious for human happiness', summing up the thought of a whole generation of creoles such as José Antonio de Rojas and Juan Egaña, who paid lyrical tribute to their country and affirmed their patriotism in literature. And by 1810 the word *patria* was coming to mean Chile rather than the Hispanic world as a whole.[78] In New Granada the botanist and patriot Francisco José de Caldas – he was shot by the Spaniards in 1816 – eulogized the environment, the mineral resources, the animal life of his country, and concluded 'there is no place better situated in the Old World or the New than New Granada'.[79] The Economic Societies, which in the 1780's spread from Spain to America, were another vehicle of Americanism. Their function was to encourage agriculture, commerce and industry by study and experiment, and while they were reformist rather than revolutionary they sought American solutions to American problems. A patriotic and anti-Spanish note was struck in the Quito Society's *Primicias de la cultura de Quito,* edited by Francisco Javier Espejo, who spent years rebutting European prejudices about America and wrote in the *Primicias* of a 'nation' which was 'American'.[80]

In Peru the works of doctors José Manuel Dávalos and Hipólito Unánue entered the controversy against De Pauw and acclaimed the natural assets of the country.[81] They went to extraordinary lengths. The mulatto doctor Dávalos claimed that 'there is a place in Peru called Piura where syphilis disappears simply through the salubrious influence of the climate', and that the balmy breezes of Miraflores automatically cured chest complaints. The Academic Society of Lima was founded to study and promote the interests of Peru, and in particular to produce a new periodical, the *Mercurio Peruano.*[82] The latter was frank in its patriotism: 'We love Peru because it is right to do so, because of our natural inclinations, and because of its particular character.' A precondition of patriotism was knowledge, so the *Mercurio* was concerned almost exclusively with Peru: 'Love of the patria makes us detest that vice of preferring foreign defects to our own, and helps us to follow the dictates of natural reason, preferring our own to foreign good.'[83] But Peruvianism contained diverse elements, conservative as well as radical, and conflicting notions of patria: some saw it as compatible with imperial unity; others believed that it could only be fulfilled in independent nationality.

Mexican nationalism was less ambiguous. In the second half of the eighteenth century a group of Mexicans deliberately undertook an analysis of the condition and the prospects of their country. Some like Clavijero, wrote primarily for a foreign audience. Others such as José Antonio Alzate Ramírez and Juan Ignacio Bartolache were inspired by a desire to teach their own compatriots, and this they did in a series of periodicals, including the *Gaceta de Literatura de México* and the *Mercurio Volante*.[84] These described the resources, flora and fauna, climate, agriculture, mines and commerce of Mexico, in order to instruct Mexicans in their own assets and culture and to demonstrate to them that they were as rational as Europeans. Their Americanism was uninhibited and employed terms such as 'la nación', 'la patria', 'nuestra nación', 'nuestra América', 'nosotros los Americanos'. The *Gaceta de Literatura* used the phrase 'nuestra Nación Hispano Americana' as early as 1788. While this was a cultural rather than political nationalism, and did not immediately seek to destroy the unity of the Hispanic world, yet it prepared men's minds for independence by showing that Mexico had independent resources. Mexico's wealth, human talents, military strength, these were the qualities emphasized by Jesuit and creole writers and assumed by their public.[85] They were also applauded by a number of foreign observers, notably by Alexander von Humboldt, whose scientific and political works gave Mexicans renewed confidence in their country and perhaps an inflated idea of its potential. As Lucas Alamán subsequently remarked: 'The writings which he published while still in Mexico, and later his *Ensayo Político sobre la Nueva España,* made known this important dominion to Spain itself, to all the nations whose attention he aroused, and to the Mexicans, who formed an extremely exaggerated idea of the richness of their country, and imagined that if it were only independent it would become the most powerful nation in the world.'[86] It was an irresistible conclusion: if Mexico had great assets, it needed independence to realize them.

In order that loyalism should diminish and Americanism grow a further factor was needed, the factor of opportunity. This came in 1808 when the crisis of government in Spain in effect deprived the colonies of a metropolis. The end was quick though the preceding agony prolonged. Before the final catastrophe Spain endured two decades of national humiliation, as Charles III's programme of reform and revival gave way to renewed decline and a new dependence. Startled by the French revolution, helpless before the power of France, Spain lurched from crisis to crisis. As leadership declined from the standards of Charles III and his enlightened ministers to those of Charles IV and his favourite, Manuel Godoy, government survived by improvisation. From 1796 Spain was dragged through France's wars against Britain in a satellite role, forced to subsidize its imperial neighbour and to sacrifice its own interests. Colonial trade was the first victim. The British navy blockaded Cadiz and cut the transatlantic route. To supply colonial markets and preserve for itself some returns, Spain allowed neutrals to trade with America, by decree of 18 November 1797. This was revoked eighteen months later but the revocation was ignored and neutral vessels continued to trade into Veracruz, Cartagena and Buenos Aires at a time when Spanish vessels simply could not make the crossing. The Spanish trade monopoly came to an effective end in the period 1797–1801, and the economic independence of the colonies was brought inexorably closer. After a brief respite during the peace of Amiens (1802–4), the renewal of war with Britain accelerated the decline of imperial trade. A series of naval reverses, culminating in Trafalgar, deprived Spain of an Atlantic fleet and further isolated her from the Americas. Imports of colonial products and precious metals slumped, and in 1805 exports from Cadiz declined by 85 per cent from those of 1804. The demise of Spain's American trade coincided with a desperate British thrust to compensate for the closure of European markets by Napoleon's continental blockade, and there was a new urgency to British contraband trade. Spanish policy was under pressure from various groups, from the central government dependent on colonial revenue, from agricultural and industrial exporters in the trading regions demanding a monopoly market, and from the colonies anxious to maintain trade and supplies. To satisfy as many interests as possible the Spanish government again authorised a neutral trade and from 1805 neutral shipping dominated the Spanish Atlantic, contributing 60 per cent of the total imports of Vera Cruz in 1807 and 95 per cent of exports, of which silver constituted 80 per cent. The future of Spain as an imperial power was now in the balance. The economic monopoly was lost beyond recovery. All that remained was political control, and this too was under increasing strain.

When, in 1807–8, Napoleon decided to destroy the last shreds of Spanish independence and invaded the peninsula, Bourbon government was divided against itself and the country defenceless against attack. In March 1808 a palace revolution forced Charles IV to dismiss Godoy and to abdicate in favour of his son, Ferdinand. The French then occupied Madrid, and Napoleon induced Charles and Ferdinand to proceed to Bayonne for discussion. There, on 5 May 1808, he forced both of them to abdicate and in the following month proclaimed Joseph Bonaparte King of Spain and the Indies.

In Spain the people began to fight for their independence and the liberals to plan for a constitution. Provincial juntas organized resistance to France, and in September 1808 a central junta was formed, invoking the name of the king and, from Seville in January 1809, issuing a decree that Spanish dominions in America were not colonies but an integral part of the Spanish monarchy with rights of representation. But as French forces penetrated Andalucía the junta was driven into a corner and in January 1810 it dissolved, leaving in its place a regency of five instructed to summon a Cortes (Parliament) which would represent both Spain and America. Spanish liberals were no less imperialist than Spanish conservatives. The Cortes of Cadiz produced the constitution of 1812 which declared Spain and America a single nation. But while Americans were granted representation they were denied equal representation, and while they were promised reform they were refused freedom of trade.

What did these events mean to Spanish America? The two years after 1808 were decisive. The French conquest of Spain, the collapse of the Spanish Bourbons, the implacable imperialism of Spanish liberals, all delivered a profound and irreparable shock to relations between Spain and America. Americans were faced with a crisis of political legitimacy. They could not have the Bourbons; they did not want Napoleon; they did not trust the liberals. Whom then should they obey? And how should power be distributed between imperial officials and local elites? Once autonomous decisions were taken upon these issues, independence quickly gathered momentum. It swept across the subcontinent in two great movements. The southern revolution gained a slight lead in time, advancing from the Río de la Plata, across the Andes to the Pacific. The northern revolution, more closely harassed by Spain, veered from Venezuela to New Granada and back to its birthplace. Both converged on Peru, the fortress of Spain in America. And in the north Mexican insurgency followed a course of its own – frustrated social revolution, prolonged counter-revolution, and successful conservative revolution – demonstrating in microcosm the essential character of Spanish American independence.

TWO *Revolution in the Río de la Plata*

MERCHANTS AND MILITIA

INDEPENDENCE CAME EASILY to the Río de la Plata, and if man secured it nature prepared it. The youngest of the great viceroyalties spanned the southern continent from Tierra del Fuego to Upper Peru, from the Atlantic to the Andes. Immense distances separated its peoples not only from Spain but also from each other. Córdoba was five hundred miles from Buenos Aires, Salta twelve hundred miles, and settlements were isolated from settlements by vast pampas, rivers and mountains. Underpopulated, the colony was inevitably underpoliced, and allegiance to the metropolis rested less on military sanction than on habits of inertia and obedience. But habits were changing. Rediscovered in the eighteenth century, the Río de la Plata was at once stimulated by imperial reform and thwarted by imperial control.

On the eve of independence the territory of the future Argentina, some 1 million square miles, contained about four hundred thousand people under Spanish jurisdiction, some 53 per cent of whom lived in the Andean provinces and 47 per cent in the great plains of the littoral.[1] This hierarchical society was acutely conscious of social differences. At the top the whites or near-whites, 38 per cent of the whole, monopolized offices, property and privilege, and carefully preserved their position against the encroachments of other races. Miscegenation came less through the Indian than through the Negro. Indians there were – the docile inhabitants of the northern littoral and the north-west – who came into peaceful contact with the colonists. But many more, perhaps as many as three hundred thousand, lived outside colonial jurisdiction. These were the wild and implacable warriors of the endless pampas and the savage Chaco. So *mestizaje* was promoted chiefly through the Negroes, the *mala raza* of colonial society; imported as slaves to work in houses, haciendas and workshops, the Negroes were the stock from whom came mulattos, zambos and other castes, the whole comprising 32 per cent of the population. The extraordinary increase of the castes in the course of the eighteenth century alarmed the whites and bred in them a new awareness of race. They became more concerned with law and order, more sensitive of social status, and more repressive towards the coloured classes. As the *Telégrafo Mercantil* remarked in 1801, the castes, 'debased simply by their status and birth, are denied admission to the primary schools, in order to prevent their associating with children of Spaniards'.[2] And in Catamarca a mulatto was whipped 'for having been discovered to be able to read and write'.[3]

United in its attitude to race and colour, white society was deeply divided in its other interests. The colonial system rested upon a balance of power groups – the administration, the Church, and the settler class. The administration possessed political though little military power, and derived its prestige from the sovereignty of the crown and its own bureaucratic function. Secular sovereignty was reinforced by the Church, whose religious mission was backed by jurisdictional and economic power. But the greatest economic power lay with the settlers, property owners in town and country, comprising a minority of peninsulares and a greater proportion of creoles. Although the large cattle estate was growing in importance, the greatest source of wealth and prestige was still foreign trade, and the merchant took precedence socially over the estanciero. This favoured the Spaniards over the creoles, as the former dominated the trans-Atlantic trade. And their numbers grew from the 1770s when the liberalization of trade drew a further wave of immigrants to the developing colony. This new conquest of the Río de la Plata reinforced the position of the peninsulares in the colonial economy and in the cabildo of Buenos Aires. But it was a hollow victory.

The new immigrants reached the Río de la Plata at a time when relations between the major power groups were changing. The administration itself was the first to disturb the balance. Enlightened absolutism enlarged the function of the state at the expense of the private sector and ultimately alienated the local ruling class. The expulsion of the Jesuits, the extension of royal patronage and control, and the secularization of many ecclesiastical revenues gave the state greater power over the Church. Simultaneously the administration advanced on the secular front. The establishment of the new viceroyalty in 1776 and the intendant system in 1782 expanded the institutional framework of the colony and introduced a horde of new officials to manage the resources of the state, the Church and the municipalities. While this development enhanced the status of Buenos Aires, it reduced the independence of the local elite who regarded the new viceroys and intendants as dangerous despots.

Overshadowed by the bureaucracy, the peninsulares were also threatened by the creoles, who came to constitute a new source of power based on military capacity. What enabled the creoles to realize a vital but hitherto dormant asset, their numerical superiority? In 1806 a British expeditionary force from the Cape of Good Hope crossed the south Atlantic, entered the Río de la Plata, and on 27 June occupied Buenos Aires. From the British point of view the operation was a minor episode in the long war against France and Spain, in an area which might develop into a useful outlet for British exports. But in the Río de la Plata itself the British invasion had far-reaching consequences. The invaders underestimated the will and the ability of the people of Buenos Aires to defend themselves. While the Spanish viceroy, the Marquis of Sobremonte, fled to the interior and the wealthy citizens of Buenos Aires sought the shelter of their country houses, the lower classes and many of the younger generation took to the streets, anxious to assert themselves and to confront the English. A Spanish merchant reported, 'the streets were full of Negroes, mulattos and young men, fearless and ready to face death'.[4] The propertied classes had to organize this mass, in the interests of their own security as well as the country's defence. Creoles and Spaniards made a united war effort, but it was creole numbers which counted. Their regiments, known as *patricios* and *arribeños*, were larger and more numerous than those of the peninsulares, and eventually totalled some eight thousand men.[5] At the same time they chose their senior officers by election, thus converting their military organization into a kind of democracy.[6] Led by Santiago Liniers, a French officer in the Spanish service, this volunteer army attacked the British force on 12 August, defeated it, and took its commander and twelve hundred troops into captivity.

Liniers, the hero of the reconquest, now became military governor of Buenos Aires. He was popular with the creoles but not with the Spaniards, who regarded him as a demagogue and would have preferred to keep the war effort under their exclusive control. But Liniers' authority was confirmed when, on 3 February 1807, reinforcements from Britain captured Montevideo. The incompetent Sobremonte now met swift retribution. The audiencia decreed his suspension and arrest, and Liniers was made acting captain-general. This action had revolutionary significance. As Mitre put it: 'For the first time the American colonies witnessed the deposition and imprisonment of the legal representative of the sovereign.'[7] They also witnessed a vivid example of self-defence. Crossing the River Plate from Montevideo, the nine thousand strong British force under General Whitelocke advanced on Buenos Aires, evaded Liniers, and reached the streets of the capital. There they were trapped in the defences organized by Martín de Alzaga, a Spanish merchant and senior magistrate of the cabildo. Whitelocke promptly capitulated and, with indecent haste, agreed to evacuate Montevideo. His military conduct was condemned in England as 'extravagently incapable and criminal', and so it was. But his withdrawal was basically correct: 'I shall evacuate a province which the force I was authorized to calculate upon could never maintain, and which from the very hostile disposition of its inhabitants was in truth not worth maintaining.'[8]

The British invasions taught a number of lessons. They showed that Spanish Americans were unwilling to exchange one imperial master for another. They also exposed gaping holes in Spain's southern empire, its fragile administration, its feeble defences. It was the local inhabitants, not Spain, who had defended the colony. The creoles in particular had tasted power, discovered their strength, and acquired a sense of identity. 'The great victory of Buenos Aires', wrote Mitre, 'had a resounding impact on the world, and above all in the hearts of Americans, who were now made conscious of a force which had been previously unknown. They were given a new sense of nationality.'[9] Cornelio de Saavedra, the creole militia leader, spoke of 'the merit of those born in the Indies . . . not inferior to European Spaniards', and pointed out that 'Buenos Aires accomplished this memorable and glorious defence with its own sons and its own people alone'.[10] And power once acquired was not to be relinquished. After the British withdrawal the peninsulares sought to restore the old equilibrium. They pressed Liniers to disband the creole troops, offering to provide garrisons at their own cost until Spain should dispatch regular troops. Liniers, who was now temporary viceroy, resisted this pressure, and the creole militia thus became a new source of power in the colony and a new irritant to the Spaniards.

While the weakness of Spain in America brought the creoles into politics, the crisis of Spain in Europe gave them a further opportunity to advance their interests. In March 1808 Charles IV abdicated in favour of his son Ferdinand. This was rapidly followed by the French occupation of Madrid, the departure of both Charles and Ferdinand to Bayonne where Napoleon forced them to renounce their sovereign rights, and the proclamation of Joseph Bonaparte as King of Spain and the Indies. The news of these unbelievable events reached Buenos Aires in July 1808, and on 17 August Viceroy Liniers issued an ambiguous decree advising the people to await events.[11] The provinces in the persons of the intendants loyally proclaimed Ferdinand, while the intendants themselves remained faithful to viceregal authority. But this attitude was unreal. Ferdinand was in custody and did not in fact rule Spain. How then could he rule in America? The so-called junta central, constituted at Aranjuez on 25 September 1808 and subsequently transferred to Seville, governed in the name of Ferdinand vii, though by what legal right and with what popular support few could agree. In Buenos Aires the junta central was recognized by the authorities but rejected by an incipient revolutionary party who sought more autonomous solutions. The revolutionaries were not agreed upon tactics. A group of intellectuals composed of Manuel Belgrano, Juan José Castelli, Hipólito Vieytes, Nicolás Rodríguez Peña and Antonio Luis Beruti, favoured a non-violent revolution. They believed they could secure this by a transition to independence under the auspices of a new and constitutional monarchy, now available in neighbouring Brazil in the vigorous if unlovable person of Princess Carlota of Portugal, wife of the prince regent and sister of Ferdinand vii. Carlota had arrived in Brazil in January 1808, a refugee with the rest of the Portuguese royal family from Napoleon's onslaught; in August she proclaimed herself Regent of Spain and the Indies and laid claim to rule in Buenos Aires in the name of her brother.[12] But the porteño revolutionaries were deceived in their hopes. Carlota was a malicious and unstable woman, and also an absolutist. When she saw that the objectives of the creoles were different from hers she denounced them as subversive to the viceroy.

Meanwhile the peninsulares had also lost faith in the metropolis, but they drew their own conclusions. They conspired to depose Liniers and establish a governing junta which would restore the old balance of power and continue their monopoly of political and commercial privilege. Their leader was Martín Alzaga, an influential member of the cabildo and one of the heroes of the reconquest. Like many recent immigrants, Alzaga started life a poor boy from northern Spain, so Basque that he could hardly speak Castilian. He entered the merchant house of Santa Coloma, advanced to trading on his own account, and soon became one of the wealthiest merchants in the Río de la Plata.[13] Alzaga and his associates detested Liniers, his French origins, his toleration of foreigners, his frankly pro-creole position.[14] They regarded him as an unscrupulous despot who promoted favourites, sanctioned large-scale contraband and fined the small offenders. They associated him with a faction of socially inferior creoles whom he cultivated to insure himself against the political risks of the time; and they held him responsible for aggravating relations between Spaniards and creoles and for causing 'the contempt in which all European Spaniards are held'.[15]

This was in Buenos Aires. In Montevideo the ultra-royalist governor, Francisco Javier Elío, suspecting the equivocal policy of Liniers, repudiated the viceroy's authority and charged him with treason. On 21 September 1808 a *cabildo abierto*, or open town council, supported Elío's action and established in the name of Ferdinand VII a governing junta composed entirely of Spaniards. This was precisely the system which Alzaga and the peninsulares sought to establish in Buenos Aires. They planned their *golpe* for 1 January 1809, the day on which the cabildo chose its membership for the coming year. Protected by Spanish troops, a carefully packed cabildo abierto chose a governing junta comprising European Spaniards and demanded the resignation of Liniers. But the creole troops, led by Saavedra, came to the viceroy's rescue, and the superior military balance enabled him to crush his opponents.[16] Alzaga and the other leaders of the conspiracy were exiled to Patagonia, though they were soon brought back by Elío.

The conspiratorial movement in Buenos Aires was a Spanish reaction to the new distribution of power in the Río de la Plata, an attempt by propertied peninsulares to restore the old order and procure exclusive power for themselves. The leaders – Martín de Alzaga, Estéban Villanueva, Olaguer Reynals, Juan Antonio de Santa Coloma and others – were the richest men in Buenos Aires, 'the most respected in the community and from the principal families'; and they dominated the cabildo.[17] 'They were accustomed', Saavedra subsequently remarked, 'to regard the sons of the country as their dependants and to behave as if they were conquistadores'. Faced with the loss of Spain in Europe, 'they proposed the idea of forming another Spain in America in which they and the many whom they hoped would emigrate from Europe would continue to rule and dominate'. The creole reaction was unmistakable: 'The spirit of rivalry against them increased in us, especially when we were left in no doubt that the object of their plans was simply that, although

Spain might be lost in Europe, Spaniards would continue to rule and dominate in America.'[18]

The golpe of 1 January 1809, and its failure, propelled the colony further along the road to revolution. At a critical juncture imperial unity broke and creoles witnessed Spaniards struggling with Spaniards for political power. Before the Spanish position was attacked from without it was subverted from within. The failure of the coup virtually eliminated the peninsulares as a focus of power: their cabildo was discredited, their leaders were dispersed, and their troops disbanded. Their property and commerce too were in jeopardy, as one of their merchants lamented. 'This man', remarked Santa Coloma of Liniers, 'has caused us great harm, more so than the English, and if the junta central does not do something, all the wealthy subjects of this capital will be put at risk.'[19] But while the peninsulares lost, the administration did not win. On the contrary, it was exposed for what it was, effete, isolated, and dependent on the creoles for support. And the creoles rallied round Liniers not to defend the administration but to thwart the peninsulares. So the real victors were the creole militia, those regiments first recruited at the time of the British invasions, young men from all social groups, officers elected chiefly from the upper class, and all strongly motivated by *criollismo*. This was a new political force, and its power grew still further with the disbandment of the Spanish regiments. Liniers subsequently treated the creole forces with marked respect. He had little option. The breakdown of communications with Spain, and Spain's inability to provide troops during the Napoleonic war, kept the regular garrison in the colony starved of reinforcements. In Buenos Aires in May 1810 it numbered only 371 as against 2,979 creole militia.[20] The distribution of power had been decisively readjusted. A new elite had emerged.

While the strength of the creoles lay in their military capacity, they also had strong ideological resources. The military sector – Cornelio de Saavedra, Juan Martín de Pueyrredón, Martín Rodríguez, the Balcarce, Viamonte and others – tended to come from propertied families, and their commitment to independence was accompanied by conservative social values. But among the creoles there was also an identifiable intellectual group, graduates, lawyers, doctors, clerks and priests, an incipient middle sector, influenced by the Enlightenment, and directly or indirectly products of the recent growth of the colony. They came from a lower social group than the military: Belgrano and Castelli were sons of Italians; Moreno and Vieytes sons of modest Spanish immigrants; Larrea and Matheu were Catalans. And they had to work for a living, as minor bureaucrats or professional people. They were more interested in ideas than in arms, and while they did not question the existing social structure they tended to be more radical in their thinking, supporting enlightened reform, the *Semanario de Agricultura* and other newspapers; and having failed to secure a constitutional monarchy they came to stand for outright independence. Military and intellectuals were not mutually exclusive groups. Indeed some of the military were radical in their thinking, and some of the intellectuals were traditionalists.[21] But they represented two tendencies within the creole ranks, and the division was to be apparent in the early years of the independent republic. On one issue, however, there was no marked division. Neither of the creole groups represented a particular economic interest. Rather they all favoured a greater liberalization of the economy.

The dominant economic interest in the Río de la Plata was commerce, not agriculture. The absence of really large estancias, the division of the land into numerous holdings and their vulnerability to Indian raids, the existence of a number of small and weak producers at the mercy of the porteño buyers, all these factors prejudiced the rural producer in the Buenos Aires hinterland and strengthened the merchants' grip on the economy. Poorly educated, living little better than the gauchos around them, impeded by restricted commerce which kept the value of hides low, the estancieros, who were generally creoles, were socially inferior to the merchants, who were usually Spaniards.[22] The rural production of Buenos Aires was not primarily orientated towards export; in any case cattle and hides were more abundant in the superb grasslands of the Banda Oriental, Entre Ríos and Corrientes. Buenos Aires province tended to specialize in arable farming, but production was retarded by price and export controls. The big merchants of Buenos Aires therefore made their profits not by exporting the products of the country but by importing manufactured goods for a consumer market stretching from Buenos Aires to Potosí and Santiago in exchange for precious metals. In the late colonial period cattle products accounted for only 20 per cent of the total export trade of Buenos Aires; the other 80 per cent was silver. The economy of the Río de la Plata was ready to expand beyond the restrictive framework of the colony. Its first period of growth followed the reorientation of empire which made Buenos Aires a new port of entry for trade into South America and attached to it the mining area of Upper Peru; to a lesser degree it was also stimulated by the development of cattle-raising for export. With valuable export commodities – silver and hides – Buenos Aires favoured this monopoly. But many creole merchants, active in the export of hides, in the slave trade and in shipping, wished to liberalise and expand trade, as did the estancieros.[23] Neither of these groups represented the economic thinking of the interior, of Córdoba, Mendoza and Tucumán, where industries and agriculture supplying local markets relied on colonial protection. The only spokesman for these interests were in fact monopolists like Alzaga, who argued that the producers of the interior needed the protection given by the mercantilist system: 'The people of the interior form a single whole with the capital, and their common good ought to be preferred to the particular interest of some individuals in the capital.'[24] The expanding economy of the littoral should have provided for the interior a good market. But the littoral preferred to buy British. And this too Spain sought to stop.

The economic problems of the Río de la Plata had worsened since 1796 and the onset of the long war with Britain. The common good ought to be preferred to the particular interest of some individuals in the capital.'[23] The expanding economy of the littoral should have provided for the interior a good market. But the littoral preferred to buy British. And this too Spain sought to stop.

The economic problems of the Río de la Plata had worsened since 1796 and the onset of the long war with Britain.[24] The British naval blockade cut exports from Buenos Aires from five and a half million pesos in 1796 to less than half a million in 1797. The permission to trade with foreign colonies granted in 1795 was supplemented from 1797 by permission to trade in neutral shipping, measures which Spain was forced to concede simply to keep some routes open and preserve a measure of legal and taxable trade. But by 1802 these concessions had widened the rift between those who wanted freer trade and those who defended the old monopoly. In any case, wartime shortages – and war was renewed in 1804 – made the Río de la Plata a tempting target for foreigners. While the British navy blockaded Cadiz, British exports supplied the consequent shortages in the colony. In the period 1804–7 hides and other products piled up again in the warehouses awaiting export, while the consumer market was starved of imports. British merchants began to push their way in with yet greater persistence, partly through the invasions of 1806–7, when the colony was given a lesson in British trade practices, but chiefly by more orthodox methods, by licensed trade in neutral vessels, by re-export from Brazil, and by sheer contraband.[25] In 1808 fifty-four recorded vessels left Buenos Aires, forty-two for foreign colonies (chiefly Brazil), and only two for Spain.[26] In the same year, when Britain became an ally of Spain against Napoleon, British commerce was tolerated in Buenos Aires and Montevideo, and by 1809 Santa Coloma was describing Buenos Aires as 'an English colony'. British stocks left behind after the military evacuation managed to penetrate via local merchants and hacendados to the most distant parts of the viceroyalty, with the connivance of Liniers. The creoles wanted more, and the prolonged debate between liberal and monopoly interests entered a new stage. With the viceroy dependent on their support, the creoles agitated for commercial reforms. Belgrano, secretary of the consulado urged the opening of ports to British trade if only as a means of bringing revenue to the impoverished administration. Admiral Sir Sidney Smith, commanding the British naval station in South America seconded these efforts with the suggestion to Liniers that he open ports 'for mutual convenience and regional benefits, raising revenue from a tolerated commerce'. In fact Liniers was tolerant. Between November 1808 and November 1809 at least thirty-one British vessels traded illegally at Buenos Aires, landing goods to the value of more than £1·2 million.[27] And Liniers seemed ready to grant even a legal trade when he was removed from office by a distrustful junta central, and his successor reached Buenos Aires in July 1809.

The last viceroy of the Río de la Plata, Baltasar Hidalgo de Cisneros, was a naval officer, veteran of Trafalgar. At Buenos Aires, he reported, he found 'two formidable parties', the Spaniards and the creoles, great political disorder, a variety of opinions on the future of Spain, and 'intimations of independence'.[28] The Spaniards regarded him as their deliverer; the creoles accepted him with polite reserve. He arrived with 'orders against the admission of foreign ships in the river'.[29] But he was aware of the pressures for freer trade, the advice of liberals like Belgrano and Castelli, the superior military power of the creoles, and the need for more revenue.[30] When, in August 1809, two English merchants applied for permission to sell their cargo, the viceroy sought the advice of the cabildo and consulado, and appointed a commercial committee to resolve the issue.

The cabildo, dominated still by peninsulares, continued to oppose in principle any concessions to foreigners, but conceded that trade with foreigners was a necessary evil. And the consulado agreed. Not so the monopolists. Fernández de Agüero, attorney for the merchants of Cadiz, went direct to the viceroy to oppose this innovation, which he argued was illegal, detrimental to the Spanish merchant marine, conducive to what he called 'luxury, libertinage and corruption', and harmful to the agriculture and industry of the interior. So the conventional argument had a sting in its tail: 'Our interior provinces are going to suffer intensely from the entry of English goods into our ports; they will suffer inevitable ruin and perhaps even ignite among themselves the fires of division and rivalry.'[31] This was a telling, indeed a prophetic, argument, and in order to counter it the landowners of the east and west banks of the Río de la Plata commissioned Mariano Moreno, a young creole lawyer, to put the case for open trade. This he did in his celebrated *Representación de los Hacendados* (31 September 1809).[32] Moreno went beyond the argument of immediate fiscal advantage and demanded freedom of trade as vital for the welfare of the people of the Río de la Plata. He argued that it was right for the country to import what it needed, thus lowering consumer prices, and to export its own surplus, thereby presenting the farmer with a larger market.

'There are truths so obvious that it insults the intelligence to attempt to prove them. Such is the proposition that this country should freely import the goods which it does not produce or possess and export its own abundant products which are being wasted for lack of outlet'.[33] The influence of the *Representación* has been extensively debated.[34] The ideas of economic liberalism which it expressed had long been current in creole circles, especially in the writings of Belgrano. It was essentially a tract for the times, tactically useful but to some degree tendentious in argument. Against all the evidence it maintained that freer trade would not damage local industry: 'The cloths of our own provinces will not decline, because the English can never provide them so cheap or of such quality as ours.' In fact the English demonstrated that ponchos made in Yorkshire could easily undersell the local product. So the dilemma remained, and the clash of interests between the littoral and the interior would be inherited by the independent republic.

In November the commercial committee recommended a limited trade with allied and neutral nations, and the advice was immediately implemented. The results were predictable. The administration gained, as contraband was replaced by open commerce and customs revenue relieved the Treasury.[35] Consumers gained by cheaper and better quality goods, and some local merchants working with the British also gained. But the peninsular merchants and their importers in Buenos Aires, unable to compete with the British, suffered heavy losses and in some cases ruin. This further weighted the balance of power against the peninsulares.[36] Alzaga – Cisneros had restored him to Buenos Aires – led the Spanish monopolists in an effort to salvage the remnants of their business. In fact there were still restrictions – foreigners could only consign to Spanish merchants and duties were high – and British merchants regarded the concession 'as nearly tantamount to a prohibition'.[37] But the innovators were on the move and the monopolists on the retreat. 'The economic emancipation of Buenos Aires was determined before its political emancipation began.'[38]

The first move towards political independence was made not in Buenos Aires but in Upper Peru. The crisis of imperial government in 1808 reverberated also in this distant corner of the viceroyalty, and here too the administration was first subverted from within. In Chuquisaca, the capital of this silver province, rival factions of Spaniards disputed for power in the vacuum created by the fall of the monarchy.[39] On 26 May 1809 the audiencia imprisoned the president-intendant and, like Elío in Montevideo, took over the government.[40] Soon disorder spread from Chuquisaca to La Paz, but with this difference, the rising in La Paz was genuinely American in personnel and objectives. Exploiting the cracks in imperial administration, the revolutionaries came out into the open, and on 16 July they captured the barracks, deposed the intendant and the bishop, and formed a governing junta under the presidency of a mestizo soldier, Pedro Domingo Murillo. A 'plan of government' was drawn up by a radical priest, José Antonio Medina, and on 27 July the junta issued a proclamation asserting: 'Now is the time to organize a new system of government, founded upon the interests of our country which is downtrodden by the bastard policy of Madrid. . . . Now is the time to raise the standard of liberty in these unfortunate colonies.'[41] The revolt was frankly radical, seeking autonomy for Upper Peru from Buenos Aires as well as from Spain. The plan of government criticized Spain's commercial monopoly; it deplored Upper Peru's economic dependence on Buenos Aires; and it announced an end to remittances to Buenos Aires.[42] It also found a place for the Indians, providing for a 'congress representative of the rights of the people', in which Indians would be represented, in order to convince them that the revolutionaries desired nothing more than 'their deliverance and happiness'.[43]

In the event social and racial issues split the movement. The rebellion drew its leadership from two groups, creoles like Gregorio and Manuel García Lanza, and mestizos like Juan Manuel de Cázeres and Murillo himself. While mestizos provided the rank and file of the insurgents, the military command was bitterly disputed. It was won by Pedro Indaburu, a creole who despised his rival Murillo and really identified with peninsulares. Meanwhile rebellions of a more popular kind in Santa Cruz de la Sierra and Toledo remained isolated from the main movement. These divisions and the refusal of most creoles to join forces with mestizos enabled the viceregal authorities to crush the rebellion. Expeditions from the Río de la Plata and Peru converged on the rebels, overthrew the junta in October 1808 and imposed a reign of terror throughout the province. Upper Peru was not yet ready for independence. The mining economy, the dominance of the hacienda, the large Indian and mestizo populations, and traditional links with Lima, all made this a conservative society, imbued with seigneurial values, and inhibited the creoles from committing themselves to a revolutionary movement which might subvert the existing order. They preferred Spanish rule to mestizo revolution.

In Buenos Aires, on the other hand, the social environment was different, and here the creoles were confident enough of their own strength to discard inhibitions.

(ii) THE MAY REVOLUTION

By 1810, when the armies of Napoleon engulfed the Iberian peninsula, the balance of social forces in Buenos Aires had changed. The administration had lost ground during the British invasions and the ambiguous rule of Liniers. The Church had been reduced by regalism. The wealthy Spanish class had been defeated in the abortive coup of January 1809. This left the way open to the two creole groups, the military and the intellectuals, who possessed the arms and the ideas to take the initiative. On 13 May 1810 an English vessel brought to Montevideo news that French armies had occupied Andalucía and entered Seville. The junta central had fled to Cadiz and dispersed, providing for a council of regency to be established in its place.[44] This was the opportunity awaited by the revolutionaries.[45] A creole underground movement was already in being, and its plans were prepared. Belgrano, Castelli, and Nicolás Rodríguez Peña – these were its leading members. And they had won over the senior officers of the militia, whose forces had been thwarted in the past by Spanish prejudice and were now fired by the prospect of future promotion.[46] So the revolution was initiated, on 18–19 May, by military action. Cornelio Saavedra, commander of the *Patricios*, and his militia colleagues pressed the cabildo and the viceroy to call an open meeting of the town council, a cabildo abierto. Saavedra, who was determined to destroy the authority of the viceroy, overcame the latter's opposition by placing him under virtual house arrest. At the same time, to impress the cabildo, an armed band of about six hundred young activists were mobilized under the leadership of two radical creoles, French and Beruti. These were the spearhead of the revolution, the nearest approach to popular forces; they controlled the streets, and they constituted in effect the 'people' who congregated in the main square. On 21 May a general congress was summoned and on 22 May it met. The intention of its authors was simple – to depose the viceroy and erect a new government. It was a representative assembly only in a limited sense. A cabildo abierto was a traditional device which summoned only the urban elite – officials, ecclesiastics, and propertied citizens. The population of Buenos Aires was over fifty thousand, of whom over eleven thousand would be adult males and thus potential voters.[47] But according to Viceroy Cisneros the revolutionaries numbered only three thousand, and the hard-core militants in the main square were no more than six hundred. To the congress only 450 people were invited; of these 251 accepted and actually attended. The others were deterred by rain, by disapproval, or by fear. The main square was dominated by French's militants, who frightened off many Spaniards and turned back others. Of the 251 who made their way into the cabildo, all were substantial citizens, as even creole accounts were proud to acknowledge. There were 70 officials and ecclesiastics, 25 lawyers and professional men, 59 merchants, 59 military, and 21 ordinary citizens.[48]

If this was a select it was also a divided assembly. In the opening debate the cabildo itself took a middle position, counselling caution, rejecting violence, and reminding the assembly of the existence of the interior provinces: 'Your deliberations will be frustrated if they do not conform to the law and to the general consent of all those peoples.'[49] Conservatives could scarce believe what they heard. Did a Spanish cabildo speak of 'consent'? There followed a noisy and confused debate, which revealed the widening gulf between supporters and opponents of the viceroy. Bishop Benito de Lué y Riega defended the viceroy as the representative of royal sovereignty and took the Spanish position to its logical if insane conclusion: 'As long as there remains a single member of the junta central, and if he were to arrive on our shores, we ought to receive him as the representative of the king.'[50]

This was more than the revolutionaries could tolerate. Saavedra declared that 'there is no doubt that it is the people who confer authority or power'. But it was Castelli, the hard and impatient creole advocate, who led the radical opposition with an eloquent speech and a powerful thesis. The government of Spain, he argued, was now extinct; as for the former junta central, it was illegal in origin and without power to transfer authority to a regency. The absence of legitimate government caused 'a reversion of sovereignty to the people of Buenos Aires', who could now install a new government.[51] The doctrine of the reversion of sovereignty was not a new one, nor was it exclusive to any one school of political thought, scholastic or modern. The formula was in frequent use at the time, and not only by the creoles; in Buenos Aires it had been invoked by the Spanish conservatives in January 1809; and it was similar to the doctrine on which the junta movement in Spain was based. For a colony, however, this was a revolutionary doctrine. If the imperial government was extinct, the empire enjoyed *de facto* independence. This was basic change, far more decisive than would be the establishment of legal independence.

The revolutionaries were now masters of the assembly, as well as of the plaza outside. And they began to press their views. Castelli proposed a motion of outright independence, and although this was not accepted, the creole majority insisted on public, not secret, voting on the position of the viceroy. The voting yielded a decisive majority in favour of change. The small group of senior officials voted unanimously for the viceroy. The clergy were not so sure : the bishop and six religious voted for the viceroy, but sixteen priests voted for a new government. The wealthy upper sector was also divided. This group consisted of merchants and other citizens, seventy-nine in all, not one of whom was described as a hacendado; landholding had not yet attained the social power of commerce. The majority of the big merchants defended the continuation of the *status quo*, though many others favoured revolutionary change. And on both sides there were people of great wealth and status. In the whole of this group twenty-nine were for the viceroy, fifty against. The military sector was more homogeneous. Of the sixty present only ten defended the viceroy, almost all of them peninsulares; the rest, led by Saavedra, mostly officers of the militia formed during the British invasions, voted for a change of government. The intellectuals were almost all revolutionaries; nineteen lawyers and four doctors were against the viceroy and only one in favour. The division of voting was not entirely on Spanish-creole lines, but it was clear that the revolutionary position had greater support from creoles and the conservative position from Spaniards. According to the Spanish merchant Santa Coloma, Spaniards and Americans held basically different ideas, born of a sense of superiority in the first and of resentment in the second.[52] A British naval observer was impressed by another difference, 'the great power, which is the troops, being in the possession of one party'.[53] This creole military power was soon deployed.

The debate lasted beyond midnight; then the assembly adjourned until the following afternoon. In the meantime it was resolved that the viceroy should relinquish his office and that authority should reside temporarily in the cabildo, pending the formation of a governing junta. The cabildo, however, had not yet learnt the facts of power. It cancelled the adjourned meeting of the assembly, and on 24 May appointed a junta of four, including Castelli and Saavedra but retaining the deposed viceroy as president.[54] This junta did not conform to the new balance of power in Buenos Aires.

Late in the evening the regiment of *Patricios*, now en masse, with a great proportion of the inhabitants, went to the houses of the different officers of the cabildo and declared that, if an alteration was not immediately made in the junta that was formed, by excluding the late viceroy, they would teach them the way to shed blood.[55]

The menace was now explicit. Saavedra advised Cisneros to quit. The revolutionaries presented a petition bearing 409 signatures, most of them creole military, demanding the establishment of an acceptable junta. On 25 May the cabildo yielded, and the patriot junta was proclaimed. Saavedra was president, Belgrano and Castelli were among the members, and Moreno was one of the two secretaries. In this second junta the administration and the Spanish conservatives were eliminated, and power was effectively divided between the military and the intellectuals.

This was a creole revolution, accomplished by an elite who spoke for the people without consulting them. 'Where are the people?', asked a cabildo official on 25 May from a balcony overlooking the plaza. Only a few had assembled, those allowed into the square by the regiment of *Patricios*. The nearest approach to a popular element were the few hundred activists led by French and Beruti who constituted an armed mob dominating the streets. But there was a limit to popular mobilization.[56] Like most revolutions, it was initiated by a minority who sought to mobilize — and manipulate — a majority. The problem for the revolutionary leaders was to mobilize the masses as allies against political opponents and against Spain, without admitting them to power. As Juan Cruz Varela subsequently wrote in his periodical *Centinela* (4 August 1822): 'We repeat, the revolution against Spain was the work of four men who, impelled by honour and patriotism, put themselves at the head of enormous masses of timid and servile people, preoccupied with their own interests.' And this was the way the leaders wanted it, both before and after the revolution.

If the events of 25 May were not 'democratic', were they even revolutionary? Did not the *juntistas* invoke the name and authority of the sovereign king, Ferdinand vii? Did not the creole elite lack ideological and group cohesion? These signs of political continuity and conservatism were more apparent than real. The formal deference to Ferdinand was a convenient device, a temporary tactic. By assuming the 'mask of Ferdinand' the patriots hoped to make capital out of the remnants of royalist sentiment in the people of the Río de la Plata, to avert a Spanish counter-revolution, and to secure the support of Britain, Spain's powerful ally. Moreover, it involved no great commitment, no real sacrifice, to invoke the sovereignty of a man who was no longer sovereign, to defer to a ruler who did not rule, to speak for a crown that was in captivitiy. The mask of Ferdinand was quickly torn off when, after the defeat of Napoleon, Ferdinand was restored to power, indeed to despotism, in Spain. Then the creole revolutionaries had to admit that they did not want him. The periodical *El Censor* explained the situation.

In 1810 we only wished to preserve freedom against foreign domination. . . . But the Spaniards began to make war on us and tried to
impose despotism on America. We still placed all our hopes in
Ferdinand. But these hopes were destroyed when he actually reached
the throne, for he waged bloody war against America. And we began
to detest so unjust a king.[57]

Saavedra placed the break even earlier and he did not doubt that
it was decisive:

The deposition of the viceroy and the consequent creation of a new
American government were, for all to see, the blows that broke the
dominion exercised by the kings of Spain for almost three hundred
years in this part of the world.[58]

Moreno had no inhibitions. As secretary of the junta his declared
aims were 'to destroy the oppressive administration, to promote
a new and unprecedented government activity'.[59]

This was a revolution directed precisely against the administration which then held power. Spanish officials were removed,
and the viceroy and judges of the audiencia shipped off to the
Canary Islands. This policy was soon extended to all Spaniards
known or suspected to be hostile to the junta. They were barred
from public office and from election to the Assembly; they were
subject to 'violence and unprecedented oppression', arrested,
expelled, and in some cases executed.[60] In Córdoba there was
resistance. The former viceroy, Santiago Liniers, with the intendant and the bishop planned a counter-revolution, and they had
contact with the Spanish authorities in Upper Peru. The junta
struck hard: an expeditionary force crushed the resistance,
captured the leaders and shot Liniers and the intendant.[61] This
was in August 1810. In January 1811 the junta created a
Committee of Public Safety, to search out opposition and to
receive denunciations against counter-revolutionaries.[62] And in
1812 the new government suppressed the last and most formidable conspiracy against creole rule; its leader, the irrepressible
Martín Alzaga, and forty others were executed in Buenos Aires.
This strategy of terror to save the revolution strongly suggests
that the junta considered itself permanently independent of
Spain – and of the Spanish crown. For the changes wrought
were so substantial and the link with the crown was so tenuous

that a restoration of royal sovereignty was hardly conceivable. The May revolution was thus more than an extension of the resistance and junta movement in Spain, more than a bid for self-government under the crown. It was the revolt of a colony, led by radical and violent revolutionaries, whose loyalty to a captive king cannot be taken seriously. And in Buenos Aires few contemporaries would have accepted for long a distinction between independence of Spain and independence of the Spanish crown. In short, the *de facto* change was so revolutionary that it is relatively unimportant whether the insurgents deceived themselves or others with the 'mask of Ferdinand'.

(iii) BUENOS AIRES AND THE INTERIOR

The new government came under two immediate pressures, divisions within the revolutionary ranks and opposition from the regions. Two days after its installation the junta invited the other provinces of the Río de la Plata to send deputies to the capital. It also prepared an expeditionary force to spread the revolutionary message to the interior and to impose its authority over the whole of the former viceroyalty. For its authority was not freely accepted. In the eyes of the other regions the May revolution was itself a regional movement, not necessarily favourable to their own political and economic interests. The claims of the junta were not acceptable to the Banda Oriental, to Paraguay, or to Upper Peru, and these regions opposed force with force.[63] Their opposition to Buenos Aires was at first Spanish-inspired, but this soon gave way to a more widely based resistance from which emerged nations – Uruguay, Paraguay and Bolivia – independent of Spain and of the Río de la Plata. This was on the periphery. In the core of the area, the territory which became modern Argentina, the regions did not secede outright. Most of them gave qualified recognition to the junta and accepted its invitation to send deputies.[64] But they reserved their freedom of action, for they suspected that Buenos Aires wished to monopolize the fruits of revolution. To some degree these reservations reflected differences of political opinions as to the future organization of the area. Some saw the Río de la Plata as a single entity with Buenos Aires its capital. Others argued that separation from

Spain left each province master of its own destiny, a destiny which might include association with Buenos Aires, but in freedom not subservience. These were not simply differences of political theory. They reflected also deep economic divisions.

The Río de la Plata was constructed on the basis of regional economies, each facing different ways. In the north-west the Andean provinces of Salta, Tucumán, Jujuy and Catamarca profited from their proximity to Upper Peru, for whose mining economy they produced food, livestock and pack animals; they also possessed a few primitive industries – sugar, textiles and transport equipment – which survived on protection from outside competition. In the far west, where stony plains gave way to the fertile foothills of the western cordillera, the provinces of Mendoza, San Juan and La Rioja were orientated towards Chile as well as towards the Río de la Plata; this region practised subsistence agriculture, together with wine and brandy production which, if protected, could sell profitably throughout southern South America. The mid-west, Córdoba and San Luis, consisted of hilly and semi-arid prairie lands; here the regional economy was saved from stagnation by the production of coarse textiles and the supply of draft animals for Upper Peru. The provinces of the interior thus earned good profits in the mining sector, and it was these earnings rather than those of the littoral which accounted for the export of silver through the port of Buenos Aires in the late colonial period. The littoral provinces themselves formed a fourth group consisting of Buenos Aires, Santa Fe, Entre Ríos and Corrientes. Much of this was pampa country, a flat expanse of natural grassland, barely 10 per cent of which was settled by Europeans; but this proportion was growing as livestock farming expanded at the expense of the Indians, and the littoral economy became increasingly orientated towards the European market through the port of Buenos Aires. These economic divisions were accompanied by social differences. The interior was the home of conservatism. The large hacienda, with its Indian and mestizo labour force and its seigneurial values, was more firmly planted in the north-west and far west than in the littoral, where to a large extent the gaucho was still untamed and the land unclaimed. Provincial conservatism sought to preserve an economic structure which gave local products protection against the open trade policy of Buenos Aires. And socially it stood for hierarchy, for a patrón-peon relationship, as against the more mobile society of Buenos Aires and the relative freedom of the pampas. The revolution was also under pressure from within, as liberal and conservative factions struggled for control. Saavedra, president of the junta, headed the conservatives, while Moreno led those who desired radical political and social reforms and sought a unified as well as an independent Argentina. It was the reformists who first moved ahead. They secured the appointment of Castelli as a kind of commissar to the army of the north, and Belgrano as commander of the expedition to Paraguay, while Moreno directed from Buenos Aires internal policy and foreign relations. But the liberal intellectuals overreached themselves. The admission of conservative provincial deputies into the junta represented a serious defeat for Moreno, who resigned and accepted a diplomatic mission to Great Britain; he died on voyage in March 1811. In April 1811 Saavedra's faction instigated a riot in Buenos Aires which resulted in the banishment of Moreno's supporters in the administration. The new regime subdued the revolution and established a reinforced Committee of Public Safety which pursued radicals as well as royalists.[65]

But the conservative *golpe* was short-lived. The military disaster of Huaquí in June 1811 which lost Upper Peru to the revolution ruined the reputation of Saavedra and the unwieldy junta. By September 1811 the young *morenistas* were making a comeback. Grouped in the Sociedad Patriótica and meeting in the Café Marco, they continued to work for an uncompromisingly liberal revolution. Under popular pressure the junta was forced to establish a new executive, a triumvirate consisting of Manuel Sarratea, Juan José Paso, and Martín Pueyrredón, while the junta itself was transformed into a legislative chamber. The driving force behind the triumvirate was its young secretary, Bernardino Rivadavia, a ruthless administrator and bearer of pure liberal doctrine. He gave the new government a purpose and a programme, and sought to establish what he regarded as 'the limit to which its liberal principles ought to extend'.[66] He laid the foundations of a new education system, produced a generous definition of civil rights, and inaugurated an anti-slave trade policy.[67] In the interests of enlightenment the government was ruthless with its opponents. It abolished the Committee of Public Safety, now an instrument of reaction not of revolution; it brought back the victims of Saavedra's regime; and it dismissed Saavedra himself. Resistance was swept aside. There was in fact mounting rivalry between porteño leadership and provincial sentiment, between the triumvirate stimulated by Rivadavia and the junta activated by the *provincianos*. The triumvirate resented the legislative claims of the junta and rejected any limitations on its sovereignty. So the junta had to go, and when, on 7 December 1811, the various victims of the new regime tried to stage a military coup, they were savagely suppressed. Later in the same month the government ordered the provincial deputies back to their provinces, calling them traitors to the patria. Finally, in January 1812, it dissolved the *juntas provinciales*. This was the reign of porteño centralism and liberalism; it was the American version of enlightened despotism.

Rivadavia's 'oligarchy of intellectuals' soon lost support among important sections of the people. New men were entering the revolution. On 9 March 1812 the English merchantman *George Canning* arrived at Buenos Aires, carrying on board José de San Martín, Carlos de Alvear, and other returning *émigrés*. San Martín, a creole from Yapeyú in the distant province of Misiones, was a talented soldier, a young veteran of service in the peninsula; he immediately set to work to give the revolution a new military corps, the Granaderos a Caballo. Alvear, who had also seen military service in Spain, added further strength to the military sector. Bernardo de Monteagudo, a man of many principles and few scruples, attacked the Triumvirate from the other wing.[68] As co-editor of the *Gazeta de Buenos Aires* he turned this newspaper into an organ of radical views. He himself was an advocate of extreme democracy; fanatically anti-Spanish, he exhorted his fellow Americans to 'exterminate the tyrants'.[69] The administration replied to criticism by muzzling the private press and allowing the publication only of official news. It provided for a general assembly, but gave a majority of seats (33 out of 44) to Buenos Aires and effective control to the central government.[70] And when the assembly began to claim more power as representative of the people and the provinces,

MAP 2

SOUTHERN SOUTH
AMERICA AND PERU

Km.
0   400   800   1200

Rivadavia dissolved it and at the same time curbed the cabildo. At this point the enemies of the triumvirate – the new revolutionaries, the assembly and the provincials – began to fight back, and on 8 October 1812, with the slogans of independence, constitution and democracy, 'a powerful army faction' led by Alvear and San Martín overthrew Rivadavia's government and installed a second triumvirate.[71]

The second triumvirate summoned the people to elect delegates to a general constituent assembly. But this simply advanced the conflict between centralists and provincialists a stage further. From the Banda Oriental the gaucho caudillo, José Artigas, strongly influenced by the constitutional thought and practice of the United States, instructed his deputies to demand an immediate declaration of independence and the establishment of a federal system of government in which each province would retain its sovereignty. Other delegates, representing a more national or at least a more centralist outlook, prevented the artiguistas from being admitted to the assembly. So the congress which opened its sessions on 31 January 1813 contained irreconcilable groups, each of which put forward opposing constitutional plans. The result was that the Constituent Assembly of the United Provinces of La Plata produced neither unity nor a constitution.[72]

Soon the new government was further demoralized by setbacks at home and on the fighting fronts. In September 1813 royalist reinforcements reached Montevideo from Spain; in November Belgrano was defeated at Ayohuma and his rabble army was swept ignominiously out of Upper Peru; in Europe, meanwhile, the prospects of Spain and her allies showed distinct improvement. In the subsequent panic there were many who advocated accomodation with Spain, even to the point of surrender. In mid-December Manuel de Sarratea, who had been appointed to seek British mediation, requested the good offices of Britain for peace 'at almost any price short of unqualified submission to Spain' on the basis of British protection against reprisals.[73] Even Alvear, who had returned to the Río de la Plata 'full of ideas of liberty and independence', subscribed to these defeatist views.[74]

This failure of nerve was only temporary. In the first place, the Spaniards themselves were the worst enemies of reconciliation: they refused to offer suitable terms to the insurgents or to speak of anything but unconditional return to colonial status. From Montevideo they 'make no secret of the exemplary punishments they mean to inflict on Buenos Aires whenever they can reconquer it'.[75] So after the reinforcement of the royalist garrison in Montevideo, Buenos Aires in turn began to harden its policy towards Spaniards, herding them into the interior and taxing them ever more heavily.[76] Secondly, the defeatists were challenged from within the revolution by a hard core who advocated absolute independence and who on this issue at least followed Monteagudo and Artigas. Gradually the government began to recover its nerve. San Martín was appointed to the stricken army of the north. The unwieldy triumvirate was abolished, and central government was consolidated in the hands of a single executive, Gervasio Antonio Posadas, who held office from 31 January 1814.

Posadas was styled Supreme Director of the United Provinces of the Río de la Plata. In fact the provinces were not united and Posadas did not govern them. He had little authority outside Buenos Aires, and even within the capital effective power lay in the hands of Alvear, commander-in-chief of the military forces in the area. The revolutionaries were no nearer to creating an Argentine state, the provinces no nearer to recognizing the sovereignty of a central government or the leadership of Buenos Aires.[77] What were the obstacles to unity?

Local caudillos and municipal oligarchies defied Buenos Aires and claimed autonomous or federal status for their provinces. At its worst this was a crude struggle for political power; at its best it represented a kind of regional democracy. It was provoked in part by the intransigence of Buenos Aires, whose only response to resistance was to send armies of punishment and occupation, such as the expedition to Santa Fe in 1815 which alienated that province for years to come.

Each province aspired to independence and sovereign power, and as, instead of resorting to measures of negotiations and conciliation, Buenos Aires has always repelled these pretensions by force and treated those who advanced them as rebels and traitors, she has been considered by the inhabitants of the interior as unjustly usurping a dominion to which nothing entitles her, and her authority has been resisted by arms whenever a fair opportunity offered.[78]

A policy of compulsion, applied to the whole of this gigantic region, needed great military force, immeasurably more force than Buenos Aires possessed. This was a major flaw in the policy, and a further obstacle to unity. The porteño armies had already suffered a number of punishing defeats. After the euphoria of the victories of Tucumán (21 September 1812) and Salta (20 February 1813), Belgrano's defeat in Upper Peru with the loss of three thousand men and desertion of many others, reduced the government to despair. Buenos Aires not only lost stature in the eyes of the provinces, it also lost the means of imposing its will on the provinces. Moreover, defeat in the north and resistance from the interior served to intensify factionalism and power struggles within the porteño government, with the result that its own weakness and disunity became an added hindrance to unification.

Buenos Aires in fact was an object of revulsion, not attraction. In January 1815 Posadas resigned, overcome by sterile disputes with provincial caudillos and insubordinate military. Into his place stepped the ambitious Alvear, and for four months he maintained a precarious hold in Buenos Aires. But in the course of 1815 Santa Fe and Córdoba announced their independence of Buenos Aires, opened their own customs houses, and began to manage their own affairs.[79] In the Banda Oriental Artigas ruled without reference to Alvear and headed a loose federation of Uruguay and its riverine neighbours. The army of the north rejected the new director as politically unreliable and incompetent. And in the far west, where San Martín was grouping his forces and training them for the liberation of Chile and Peru, Alvear's decrees went unheeded. In Buenos Aires itself Alvear conjured with three lines of policy – reconciliation with Spain, association with Portugal, and 'a secret offer of these provinces to the British government'.[80] All of these ideas, especially that of a British protectorate, were totally unreal and simply underlined the bankruptcy of Alvear's policy. His tenure of office was soon cut short. In April 1815 troops who had been sent against Artigas mutinied and fraternized with the enemy, while in the capital the cabildo led an uprising against the director and formed a provisional government. Was it surprising that to provincials Buenos Aires had become synonymous with chaos?

Provincial defiance of Buenos Aires had an economic basis. Just as Buenos Aires tried to impose its own revolution on the whole region, so it sought to apply a single economic policy. Dimly perceived in 1810, by the 1820s it was clear beyond all doubt that the interests of the port and those of the provinces were irreconcilable.[81] In these terms, the caudillos represented essential regional interests.

Who profited by the revolution of 1810? Overseas trade was the first interest to benefit. The revolution advanced the process of price competition by removing the last vestiges of Spanish monopoly. Stimulated by the opportunity of better prices for exports and by access to the cheapest markets for imports, foreign trade increased in volume and the balance of payments improved.[82] Thus the consumer benefited, and even more the merchant class, especially the new foreign merchant. Secondly, the prospects of the cattle industry improved, now that it had direct access to larger markets for its hides and other animal products. Land appreciated in value; cattle owners and meat producers began to increase their profits. For Buenos Aires and the littoral provinces, therefore, the revolution of 1810 seemed to be fulfilling its expectations. The provinces of the interior, on the other hand, suffered grave recession. The primitive industries of Córdoba, Mendoza, Salta and Tucumán – textiles, vinculture and sugar – made from local sources of raw materials and sold in local and regional markets, had been protected by the Spanish colonial monopoly; now they were exposed to intense competition from cheaper and better goods from Europe and Brazil imported under the open trade policy of Buenos Aires, at the very time when other outlets in Chile and Peru were cut off by the wars of independence.[83] The revolution, therefore, brought no economic advantage to the interior provinces; it brought stagnation and population decline. Their only defence was the cost and the difficulty of transporting goods from Buenos Aires across the great plains and hills into the interior. This isolation helped to preserve the old social structure of the provinces, and it prevented their integration with the littoral into a national economy. Domingo Faustino Sarmiento, the liberal statesman and intellectual, equated urban Buenos Aires with civilization and the rural interior with barbarism. Yet he believed that provincial prospects could be improved: 'From poor inland cities, with small populations, they might in ten years be converted into great centres of civilization and wealth, if under the protection of an able government, they could devote themselves to removing the slight obstacles in the way of their progress.'[84] In fact the obstacles to progress were far from slight and with the exception of Rivadavia, who sought to improve overland transport and river navigation, porteño politicians had no policy for removing them.

If the interior provinces were to salvage any prosperity from the revolution, they would have to protect their economies against foreign competition by fiscal barriers or outright prohibition. But protection conflicted with the free trade interests of Buenos Aires, because higher duties would reduce trade, raise prices and perhaps wages, to the detriment of employers, ranchers, hide producers and merchants. To impose protection, therefore, the provinces needed political power and a degree of independence. This was the basic conflict: Buenos Aires versus the interior, centralization versus states rights, *unitarios* versus *federales*. But this conflict was rendered more complex by two further factors. First, Buenos Aires was opposed not only by the interior but also by the littoral, by the provinces of Santa Fe, Entre Ríos and Corrientes, whose economic resources and potential were similar to those of Buenos Aires, and who wanted freedom of trade and direct access to the sea by the rivers Uruguay and Paraná. Buenos Aires interposed itself between the littoral provinces and their foreign markets, and sought to keep the rivers closed to foreign trade, even though this raised transport and middlemen costs for the littoral. Indeed Buenos Aires behaved like a new colonial power; like the old metropolis it wished to have one port of entry and exit for the whole country. Therefore, as Buenos Aires fought to monopolize the economic gains of the revolution, the provinces had to defend their standards of living. A second complicating factor was that Buenos Aires itself was divided between unitarians and federalists. Here the federalists were those who wished to preserve the revenues from foreign trade for the province of

Buenos Aires instead of sharing them with a larger state. This was the point of view of the estancieros, who saw an exclusive customs revenue as a means of avoiding an income or land tax upon themselves. Unitarian policy, on the other hand, appealed to a group of intellectuals who had a development plan for the whole country and to merchants, especially foreign merchants, who wanted a large common market, untrammelled by provincial tariffs.

By 1816 the united provinces seemed to be on the verge of dissolution. This was the worst year since the revolution began. San Martín referred to the risk of utter ruin in 1816: 'I fear this not from the Spaniards, but from domestic discord and our lack of education and judgment ... it was a moral impossibility that we should organize ourselves properly; we are very young, and our stomachs are too weak to digest the food they need.'[85] Santa Fe and Córdoba were in open revolt. A Portuguese army was advancing from Brazil to occupy the Banda Oriental. In Upper Peru a Spanish army was assembling to carry the war into Tucumán.[86] To fortify the country in the midst of its agony, and to reassure the provinces, the government of Buenos Aires called a new congress, to meet at Tucumán in the interior, and delegates assembled in March 1816.[87] But there was still no national union. The artiguista provinces – Uruguay, Entre Ríos, Santa Fe, Corrientes and Córdoba – were conspicuously absent.[88] Many of the other provinces were represented, if that is the right word, by porteños or by pro-porteño provincials. Even the deputies from Buenos Aires were split, with monarchists and federalists striking discordant notes. The monarchists, some of whom advocated the restoration of the royal Incas, were too frivolous to be taken seriously. The Buenos Aires federalists, however, represented an identifiable interest: they argued that Buenos Aires should cease struggling against the facts of disunity and, with its superior resources, confine itself to being an independent province like the others. The firmest line was imposed on the congress from without, by San Martín and Belgrano, who wanted a declaration of independence as an indispensable preliminary to renewing the war effort against Spain.

On 3 May 1816 the delegates elected Juan Martín de Pueyrredón the 'Supreme Director of the State', and on 9 July they declared 'the independence of the United Provinces of South America'.[89] On 3 August, in an effort to contain the civil war in the littoral, congress issued a decree demanding respect for its authority and threatening death to those who promoted rebellion or caused public disorder.[90] These bold words masked real insecurity. As the advance of the Spanish army from Upper Peru threatened Tucumán, congress moved to Buenos Aires, where it could also give closer attention to military operations against the forces of Brazil. But in Buenos Aires too it was threatened – by the federalists. Pueyrredón, showing the mailed fist that was never far from unitarian policy, exiled the most distinguished spokesman of provincial interests, Manuel Dorrego, an able and cultivated army officer. Meanwhile congress continued its search for the elusive constitution, and eventually produced the Constitution of 1819 for the 'United Provinces of South America'. This provided for a strongly centralized government headed by a director who was to be chosen by congress, and it blatantly favoured the province and city of Buenos Aires. The provinces were alerted : some of them declared their independence while others prepared to join Artigas. In this way a number of small republics emerged, their independent governments sustained by local economic interests.

The caudillo of Santa Fe, Estanislao López, declared in August 1819 : 'We wish to form a small republic in the heart of our territory.'[91] He sought to secure free navigation of the rivers and to draw revenue from provincial-based customs duties. In fact López never established his independent republic and he gradually became reconciled to a larger national structure. But across the river Paraná, in Entre Ríos, Francisco Ramírez, a yerba maté merchant, came nearer to success.[92] Entre Ríos was a zone of new colonization, an expanding livestock area, with an estanciero class which controlled local office and the militia, while the economy of the province was dominated by the merchants of Buenos Aires. The conflict between artiguismo and Buenos Aires brought war to Entre Ríos and made Ramírez a provincial caudillo, representing the interests of the local ruling class. In 1820 he founded the Republic of Entre Ríos (which also included Corrientes) with its own customs houses for direct trade with Europe. In the event, Ramírez did not have the political ability to rule an independent state and the experiment was short-lived. But it was not unique. In the north-west the separatist movement produced the Federal Republic of Tucumán, created in 1819 by Bernabé Aráoz, Governor of Tucumán. The new state comprised the provinces of Tucumán, Catamarca and Santiago del Estero, and its constitution stated that Tucumán was 'a free and independent republic', with a president who had powers to nominate provincial governors. But the logic of separatism was not yet complete. For the other provinces did not want governors nominated from Tucumán. Santiago del Estero resisted, asserted its own independence, and was immediately attacked by its new metropolis. Martín Güemes, caudillo of Salta, went to the assistance of Santiago, admonishing Aráoz, 'you have no right to attack this people, even on the pretext that it has proclaimed its independence, since it has the same right to do this as you have to make your province a republic'.[93] And his forces also went to liberate Catamarca from Tucumán's rule. Güemes, guardian of the northern frontier, was concerned chiefly with the effect of civil war on the war effort against Spain. Yet the proliferation of republics was not finished. On 17 January 1820 Córdoba declared its independence; on 30 January 1821 it adopted a constitution which vested executive power in a 'governor of the republic' and legislative power in a congress. On 1 March 1820, exercising what it regarded as 'the sovereignty of the people', La Rioja proclaimed its 'provisional independence' from Córdoba until a general congress under federal form should determine 'the form of government'.[94] Thus La Rioja began its autonomous existence under a notorious caudillo, Facundo Quiroga, the Tiger of the Pampas.

The instinct of the unitarians was to fight back. José Rondeau, successor of Pueyrredón as supreme director, sought assistance from the forces of San Martín and Belgrano. This he was denied, and the military impotence of the unitarians was now starkly revealed. Rondeau marched with inadequate forces against the *montoneros* of López and Ramírez and was defeated at the battle of Cepeda (1 February 1820). Backed by his gaucho cavalry, Ramírez scattered the directorate, the congress and every vestige of central authority. All that remained was the government of Buenos Aires province. This government was forced to conclude with the triumphant caudillos the first of a series of inter-provincial pacts, the Treaty of Pilar (23 February 1820), which recognized the jurisdiction of the provinces in a vague federal structure.[95] More significantly, it established freedom of river navigation – at least for the shipping of the riverine provinces – indicating the concern of the littoral merchants for their independence and their trade. In abandoning the pretence of heading a unitary state, Buenos Aires became totally disorientated. It even had to endure intimidation by the provinces. In March 1820 Ramírez's montoneros pressed on the outskirts of Buenos Aires to 'persuade' Juan Ramón Balcarce to give way to the federalist Manuel Sarratea as Governor of Buenos Aires.[96] But Buenos Aires's problems were not so simply solved. In the course of this fateful year government changed hands on an average once a fortnight. Eventually elections were held in[97] Buenos Aires province, and in September 1820 the Junta of Representatives chose as governor Martín Rodríguez one of the heroes of the reconquest. In July 1821 Rodríguez appointed Bernardino Rivadavia his minister of government and foreign affairs. Peace gave this government a new freedom of manoeuvre.

(iv) RIVADAVIA AND THE NEW ECONOMY

The anarchy of 1820 had a cathartic effect in Buenos Aires; it purged the past and forced men to think of a new future. After ten years of violence and frustration political independence was assured. But had living conditions improved, had the economy developed? A society at war with an enemy and with itself had few resources left for creative effort. Now that the national framework was shattered, Buenos Aires was able to concentrate on itself and to create in its own province a viable society. In time perhaps the part would be able to convert the whole, spreading enlightenment by example, making the province a centre of attraction and of nationhood. Meanwhile, with a semblance of peace, its leaders could turn to economic problems, to the development of agriculture and industry, and to the promotion of education and useful knowledge.

The Rodríguez administration was inspired by Rivadavia, now forty-one years old and recently returned from abroad. A child and an apostle of the Enlightenment, Rivadavia possessed the most original political mind of his generation. He was strongly influenced by Jeremy Bentham, whom he had met in London and corresponded with in the years 1818–22, and whose works he began to translate.[98] The influence of Bentham could be seen throughout Rivadavia's policy, especially in his legislative programme, his plan for a house of representatives, his determination to reform social abuses, to assure civil rights and liberty of the individual, to promote public works and welfare, to implement ecclesiastical reform. Bentham himself had reservations about Rivadavia's constitutional thinking, especially about the excessive power he would allow to the executive at the expense of the legislature. But Rivadavia's concern for human progress, and his belief that this could be promoted by legislation, reflected the teaching of his master. Rivadavia had no doubts about his own political virtue. According to an English observer, General William Miller;

In Rivadavia there is an affectation of superiority, and a hauteur exceedingly repulsive; but these are counterbalanced by a strength and capaciousness of mind, combined with a high degree of political courage, which places him far above every other South American in the character of a statesman.[99]

Rivadavia was an impatient and intolerant liberal. He had waited almost ten years for the opportunity to realize his political vision. And his views were the same now as when he had first formulated them during the triumvirate. Independence, he had argued, could not in itself secure liberty

... as long as error and ignorance dominate the people's destiny, and as long as the sciences are neglected in favour of commitment to war, necessary though that is. . . . We will triumph over the last remnants of our oppressors : but having overcome them, we still have to triumph over ourselves, to know who we are, what we have and what we need, and to throw off the absurd preoccupations which we have inherited. The zeal of the government would count for nothing if it did not strive to accomplish this salutary renewal, giving the people new institutions which would spread enlightenment in every field of public welfare.[100]

To start with, Rivadavia sought to introduce new educational institutions, and his programme of reform included experiments with the Lancasterian, or monitorial, school system. But he was more interested in the development of higher education for an elite. The University of Buenos Aires had been planned since 1816 under the supervision of the priest Antonio Saenz. But it was actually brought into existence by Rivadavia, who, with the anarchy of 1820 still fresh in his mind, explained in the edict of establishment (9 August 1821): 'Now that the peace and tranquility of this province have been restored, one of the first duties of the government is to take up again the subject of public education.'[101]

Rivadavia also took up the subject of the Church. Although he was a practising Catholic, his mind was chiefly formed by secular and humanist values, and these led him beyond existing public opinion. The revolution had from the beginning tended to look with suspicion upon the temporal power of the Church and to favour religious freedom; and without disestablishing the Church it had brought in its wake substantial *de facto* toleration. It is debatable whether Rivadavia needed to do more. But within a few months he began to take action. In November 1821 the government curtailed the movement of clerics in and out of the province of Buenos Aires; and in May 1822 it threatened to expel from the province any religious who preached against ecclesiastical reform. The key measure was the Law of Reform of the Clergy (21 December 1822).[102] This suppressed the ecclesiastical fuero and the tithe; it provided for the state to support previous charges on the tithe, including the seminary; it suppressed some religious orders and confiscated their property; and it curtailed the membership and the establishments of other religious orders. These measures aroused violent opposition from some Catholics. One of the centres of resistance was the conservative cabildo of Buenos Aires, which was opposed to religious toleration, especially in education. For this and other reasons the cabildo was abolished. The religious policy of Rivadavia was doctrinaire, provocative to his enemies, and irrelevant to his main programme, which was to secure a viable economic structure for the new state.

The basic interest of Rivadavia was economic development.[103] His plan of modernization comprised the development of industry, agriculture and transport; the federalization of Buenos Aires and its customs house; the promotion of immigration and land distribution; and a plan of colonization which he promoted in London. The principles behind these reforms were those of liberal economics. The state limited itself to providing the conditions in which individuals could pursue their own interests, which were also regarded as the interests of the state. A law of 4 September 1821 declared the inviolability of private property; and taxation was placed under the control of the legislature, a reform applauded by the foreign merchant community.[104] But the Rivadavia administration was faced with the classical dilemma of liberals: to achieve their objectives they had to use illiberal methods, to emphasize authority and strong government, because they had to enforce their reforms against popular resistance. They appealed to the upper classes, especially to merchants and intellectuals. For the lower classes they had little to offer except hard work, a campaign against drunkenness, and a labour policy of exceptional severity.[105] Vagabonds were described as 'an unproductive class, a deadweight, harmful to public morals and a cause of social disorder'.[106] They were ordered to be conscripted into the army or assigned to public works. These measures were difficult to implement. A year later the administration again expressed horror at the alleged idleness 'of the rural peons, which reaches such an extreme that not only have they no wish to improve their own fortune but they even withhold the labour they owe their masters'.[107] A further decree was issued, obliging the rural population to carry identity cards and certificates of employment; otherwise a peon caught out of his estancia would be put in the army for two years or sent to labour in public works.

The porteño liberals argued that while the country had great natural resources, these needed to be exploited by factors which the country lacked – capital, labour and technical skill. So they proposed to enlarge profits in order to give incentive, and to attract capital and technical skill from abroad by opening the country to foreign trade, foreign investment, colonization and immigration. Meanwhile, to prepare the way, they funded the public debt and restored public credit; a 6 per cent bond issue was established to satisfy the claims on the government, including those of military officers demobilized in 1821, 'a numerous and very clamorous party'.[108] The tax system was reformed in order to substitute an income and land tax for export and import duties. In Rivadavia's view, two institutions above all were necessary to assemble financial resources – banks and joint stock companies. These in turn needed the cooperation of foreign capital. On 2 February 1825 a commercial treaty with Britain was signed on the basis of equality and freedom of opportunity. This formalized a relationship which already dominated the Argentine economy and on which Rivadavia's entire programme depended.[109]

In 1812 the triumvirate had opened the port of Buenos Aires to world trade and allowed foreigners to own property and to trade on equal terms with nationals: high protective tariffs operating since 1809 had been replaced by lower revenue tariffs and export controls abolished. The British were the first to take advantage of these opportunities, providing a source of consumer goods from the industrial revolution and a market for the exports of Buenos Aires. Soon the British had a substantial stake in the Buenos Aires economy. Between November 1811 and July 1813 they exported about 5½ million dollars in specie from Buenos Aires as a return on trade.[110] By 1813 communications with the interior were open and the demand for British goods rose accordingly. The British brought pressure to bear to keep permission to export specie at low duties and objected to having to use 'native consignees or commission agents'.[111] The average annual value of imports into Buenos Aires in 1814–19 was £1½ million sterling, of which four-fifths was on British account and comprised chiefly British manufactures. As mining output did not keep pace with commercial expansion, most of the returns were now in hides, tallow, furs and wool, and jerked beef.[112] But this early success was not sustained. The Pueyrredón administration was less sympathetic to British interests than its predecessors; it was reluctant to allow export of bullion and in 1818 it attempted – though unsuccessfully – to impose a forced loan of 150,000 dollars on the British community.[113] The British condemned this regime for its 'profligacy, venality, tyranny, and corruption'.[114] And worse was to come. The anarchy of 1819–20 seriously depressed trade, and British goods to the value of £1 million sterling piled up unsold in Buenos Aires. As for the interior, the British always found it difficult to penetrate there directly, for local traders and estancieros kept the retail trade in their own hands, and the civil wars hampered all economic activity. For the British, therefore, the Rodríguez administration did not take office a day too soon.

The economic plan of Rivadavia revived British faith in Argentina and renewed British enterprise. In June 1822 Britain opened its ports to ships of Spanish America, a foretaste of diplomatic recognition. The trade of Buenos Aires now underwent striking expansion, thwarted only by a primitive monetary and credit system. The Rodríguez administration, therefore, authorized a private company composed largely of British merchants to establish the Bank of Discount of the Province of Buenos Aires (20 June 1822), with a projected capital of 1 million dollars, though it began operations in September with much less.[115] British entrepreneurs now swarmed into the Río de la Plata to direct the economic development of the new state, now apparently in the throes of a second revolution. They sold cheap good-quality goods, especially textiles and hardware, offering long credit at low interest rates, backed by the London money market and competitive freightage. They exported hides and indeed controlled the export trade 'on their own account and in their own vessels'.[116] They moved into production, buying land in the littoral provinces and exploring again the economic possibilities of the interior. In January 1824 John Parish Robertson (who already held shares in the bank), in association with Félix Castro, a Buenos Aires merchant, contracted with the Rodríguez government to negotiate a loan of £1 million in Europe. They employed the House of Baring, who marketed bonds at 85 per cent; the government of Buenos Aires would get no more than £700,000, Barings £30,000, and Robertson and Castro no less than £120,000.[117] Rivadavia assumed that this loan could be used to finance further economic growth, which in turn would facilitate repayment; but war and economic recession intervened, and Buenos Aires suspended payments in 1827. Meanwhile the British had forged ahead. By 1824 there were some three thousand British residents in Buenos Aires, and the British consul-general, Woodbine Parish, estimated that half the public debt and most of the best property were in British hands.[118]

In April 1824 Juan Gregorio de las Heras succeeded Rodríguez as governor; and Rivadavia resigned and departed for London to promote the diplomatic and economic interests of his country as he saw them. The new administration was still controlled by the unitarians and it continued the economic policies of its predecessor. This meant that it continued to depend on the British. For their part the British favoured the idea of a unitary state with a strong central government, for they wanted a commercial treaty and they preferred a large market to a series of provincial trade barriers. Woodbine Parish was anxious to avoid what 'might possibly be construed by other parties into an undue interference' in internal political affairs, but he followed the proceedings of the congress of 1824 with great interest and was present at unitarian meetings held to discuss constitutional issues.[119] Argentina, of course, was far from becoming a British colony. Freedom of trade was the best policy for the new state and responded to the balance of interests within the country; it stimulated production, especially livestock production, and it favoured the consumer; and Argentina's future growth lay in the influx of foreign capital and immigration.

Nevertheless, Rivadavia's great plan, the first economic experiment of independence, ended in failure. Who were the culprits? Were they the porteño estancieros, defenders of their province's interests and followers of the caudillo Rosas, 'who applied the knife of the gaucho to the culture of Buenos Aires'?[120] Or were they the perfidious British who allegedly subverted a number of financial schemes essential for the success of the Rivadavia plan? The trouble began with the regime itself, that 'brilliant but artificial' government, as Sarmiento called it, so full of ideas, so lacking in judgment. It tried to do too much too quickly. Many of its ideas were out of touch with Argentine reality and seemed to ignore the sheer size of the country, its intense regionalism, its vast emptiness. Rivadavia brought Europe to America, to quote Sarmiento again, and sought 'to accomplish in ten years what elsewhere had required centuries'. But the Rivadavia plan, so daring in conception, was destroyed by internal contradictions. How could Argentina industrialize? Capital investment had nothing to work on : there were no raw materials for industry, no coal or iron, and the domestic market was not large enough. Silver mining looked more promising, or was made to look promising by the exaggerated propaganda of Rivadavia himself, and it proved irresistable to foreign capital. With the encouragement of the Buenos Aires government a joint stock company, the Río de la Plata Mining Association, was launched in London in December 1824, to exploit the mines of La Rioja.[121] The project was a failure. The company found that the government of La Rioja had granted concessions to the same mines to a rival concern, the Famatima Mining Company, and that provincial interests resented the presumption of Buenos Aires in granting concessions in territory outside its jurisdiction. But the major obstacles were common to both companies – the cost of transport to this distant sub-Andean mining zone, the shortage of suitable labour, and the prospect of poor returns on a large investment.

Rivadavia also sought to attract British capital to immigration and agricultural colonization, and several hundred poor and bewildered British labourers were shipped to the alien shores of the Río de la Plata. But these projects also failed. Colonization involved capital investment with no immediate returns. The government could not afford to pay for the transport and settling of immigrants, and private estancieros were not willing to raise their own production costs by sharing the expense of an operation which might bring socially disruptive elements to the pampas. Yet the Rivadavia plan depended on an increase of rural production. The government was not really interested in arable agriculture and thought mainly in terms of livestock expansion. The best cattle areas had been the Banda Oriental, Entre Ríos and Corrientes, provinces which were now lost to Buenos Aires. The province of Buenos Aires itself was in the early stage of cattle development and it still needed to expand further south against Indian territory. Rivadavia helped it to realize its potential by a major land distribution policy.[122] But, ironically, in furthering the interests of the estancieros, Rivadavia strengthened his political enemies. After 1825–6, when the expensive and disruptive war against Brazil was alienating all the economic interests, Rivadavia faced the particular hostility of the land-owners of the province, who rejected his unitary policy.

Rivadavia and the unitarians at first resigned themselves to the facts of Argentine life – to the caudillos of the provinces and the federalists of Buenos Aires – and confined their policies to the province of Buenos Aires, which they regarded as the incipient nation of Argentina. But Rivadavia was haunted by the vision of a united and centralized Argentina; this was also the ideal economic unit for which he wished to plan. His tragedy was that he reached for these ideals too soon; he was fifty years ahead of his time. The congress of 1824, an instrument of porteño centralism, was used by Rivadavia to erect a facade of national institutions. This congress decided in favour of a state called the 'United Provinces of the Río de la Plata', and, on 7 February 1826, Rivadavia was named president under a unitary constitution. With the passage of the law of the federalization of the city and port of Buenos Aires the process of unification seemed complete. These measures were unacceptable to the federalists and the provinces; the latter refused the ratify the constitution, recalled their delegates from the congress and withdrew from the 'treaty of association'.[123] The federalist position had its supporters in Buenos Aires. The big estancieros of the province believed that Rivadavia's unitary regime discriminated against the rural districts, that the burden of taxation was weighted against the country in favour of the city, that provincial interests would be further hit by a national organization, that in short they would lose their privileged position. For political centralization meant federalization of the city of Buenos Aires, which would deprive the province of Buenos Aires of a large part of its territory and about half its population; it also meant nationalization of the customs revenues, and this in turn would force the provincial government, stripped of its most important income, to impose new taxes and increase old ones. So the rural interest bitterly resisted Rivadavia's attempt to impose an income tax and land tax.

In spite of his fanatical liberalism Rivadavia was essentially a man of peace, unlike many of the hard-line unitarians. Bowing to the opposition of provincial caudillos and porteño federalists, he stepped down from the presidency in July 1827 and retired to poverty and exile. The congress now declared its own dissolution and the provinces reverted to their pristine dissociation. Manuel

Dorrego, leader of the federalist politicians, assumed the duties of governor of the reconstituted province of Buenos Aires. This was the first of two important victories of porteño federalism. The second was the election in 1829 as Governor of Buenos Aires of Juan Manuel de Rosas, powerful estanciero and caudillo of the pampas. Thus, as Sarmiento argued, 'the provinces had their revenge on Buenos Aires when they sent to her in Rosas the culmination of their own barbarism'.[124]

Rivadavia's own explanation of the disorder of independence was that its causes lay 'not in principles nor in the system; the causes are the disproportion between the population and the territory, the lack of capital, the ignorance and social imperfection of individuals, and the legacies of the colonial regime and war of independence'.[125] He did not appreciate the changing pattern of power. The Rivadavia group consisted essentially of intellectuals, bureaucrats, professional politicians, 'career revolutionaries', who did not represent a particular economic interest or social group. He appealed to entrepreneurial interests, it is true, but these were dominated by the British, and the British, for all their influence, did not constitute a power base within Argentina. His enemies on the other hand possessed real power; the estancieros were a strong political base, rooted in the country. And the fact remains that federalism responded to basic economic interests and stood for immediate economic returns — southward expansion against Indian territory, growth of the cattle industry, and booming exports, the profits of which were to remain in the province instead of being absorbed into a national economy. Such a system favoured rural society in general. But the chief benefits went to the estancieros. These were the new men of the revolution.

(v) ESTANCIEROS AND THE NEW SOCIETY

While independence brought commercial expansion to the Río de la Plata, it did not create a native merchant elite. The entrepreneurial function previously exercised by the Spaniards was taken over by the British, and the merchants of Buenos Aires could not compete with these new invaders. They were handicapped from the beginning by the financial policy of their own government. The chief source of revenue was the customs, and this could not be raised for fear of damaging overseas trade and alienating the powerful British interest. So to meet the mounting cost of war against Spain and against Brazil the government had to rely on voluntary and forced loans.[126] The greatest burden inevitably fell on those least able to defend themselves, first the Spaniards then the native merchants. These groups endured ten years of more or less forced exactions, while the British, backed by the royal navy, put up a successful resistance to arbitrary taxation. But the British enjoyed other and more powerful assets over their local rivals. Porteño merchants did not have expert contacts in Rio de Janeiro, London and Liverpool; they did not have direct access to the factories of Lancashire, Yorkshire and the midlands; they did not possess capital resources to finance imports or to secure the principle export commodity, the products of the cattle industry, with which the British soon established dominant relations. This inferiority deterred new entrants to commerce and drove existing members out, forcing them into alternative investments. Unable to compete in a British-dominated commerce, the local ruling class sought outlets in another expanding sector of the economy, the cattle industry.[127]

The estancia became a large-scale unit of production working for the export market and, in time, a great source of capital accumulation. From 1820, when relatively peaceful conditions improved incentives for investment, until about 1850 the province of Buenos Aires underwent a great cattle boom.[128] Anyone with a modest amount of capital to employ found a unique conjunction of circumstances assuring good returns – abundance of fertile and watered grassland in the pampas, an expanding industrial demand for hides in Europe and outlets for jerked beef in the Americas, the technical simplicity and low cost of live-stock farming, and its moderate labour requirements. Buenos Aires province profited from the absence of competition from its economic rivals. From 1813 Santa Fe, Entre Ríos and Corrientes were devastated by their wars of secession, while the Banda Oriental was ruined by the Brazilian invasion of 1816. Porteño capital took advantage of this new opportunity and found a highly profitable outlet in cattle ranching. Pasture began to expand at the expense of arable farming and the province soon came to depend on imported grain. In the 1820s a livestock estancia yielded returns of 31·4 per cent on investment, compared to the 25 per cent return on arable farming.[129] Territorial expansion took the place of technical improvement of existing land. The new frontier policy pushed back territorial limits and claimed vastly more land for exploitation. Powerful hacendados like Rosas directed the expansion southwards against Indian territory. And government played its part when Manuel J. García, Minister of Finance, introduced the system of emphyteusis – from 1822 in Buenos Aires province, and in other provinces by the Constituent Congress in 1826.[130] This measure authorized public land, sale of which was prohibited without special permission of the legislative and because it was pledged as security against foreign and internal debt, to be rented out for twenty years at fixed rentals. Thus the government simultaneously put land to productive use and satisfied the needs of farmers and cattlemen. No one imagined that this was agrarian reform. There was no limitation of the area that a landowner might acquire in emphyteusis, and the land commissions which administered distribution were dominated by estancieros. From 1824 to 1827 a number of huge individual grants were made – 6½ million acres to only 112 people and companies, of whom ten received more than 130,000 acres each. By the 1830s some twenty-one million acres of public land had been transferred to five hundred individuals. This was a crucial stage in the growth of latifundism. It may have been intended that emphyteusis remain dependent on the state, which actually owned the land and took the rent, but the state was not strong enough to sustain its role against powerful landed interests, and under Rosas these acquisitions were simply transferred into freehold.

The combination of British commercial competition, investment opportunities in ranching, and the favourable agrarian policy of the government, persuaded many Buenos Aires merchants to move from commerce to land. The existing hacendado class – neither numerous nor notable before the revolution – was thus reinforced by distinguished recruits from urban society, the Anchorena, Santa Coloma, Alzaga, Saenz Valiente, most of whom acquired immense concessions under emphyteusis.[131] And in the rush for land politicians and military were not far behind, nor were the ubiquitous British, who invested returns from trade in cattle estates and meat processing plants.[132] In this way Argentina's landed oligarchy, the new ruling class, came into being. With economic and political power, the estancieros also acquired military power. The revolutionary government, fighting on two fronts, the Andes and the littoral, could not afford to station regular troops in the countryside, so the militia took their place. The militia was based on the big ranches; it was commanded by the estancieros, officered by ranch officials, and manned by peons. The *Colorados del Monte* of Rosas were only the more spectacular example of a local militia which had become in effect a private army.

As the state became weaker through civil war and federalist resistance, the estancia grew stronger, and landowners came to dominate the state, providing a kind of stability. Argentina became little more than a conglomeration of estancias. And as the estanciero class dominated the apparatus of the state, so it was able to discipline the labour force on the estancias.

The gaucho, a product of mestizisation was traditionally a free man on horseback. Skilled in cattle work on the pampas, fiercely independent and attached to no particular ranch, a valuable recruit for any war against the Indians, he lived a nomadic and semi-delinquent existence on a diet of yerba maté, beef and bread.[133] In the new estancia economy these *gauchos vagabundos* had to be tamed and tied to employment. Judges were at the service of the estancieros to condemn criminals and unruly peons into the army for frontier service, an example which helped to discipline those who remained on the estancia. The law attacked nomadism, and the marginal population of the countryside had to carry identity cards and certificates of employment or suffer the alternatives of military service and hard labour. The proprietor had other controls. Low wages and financial advances kept the peon in permanent indebtedness, as also did credit in the estancia store. Control was total and acquired seigneurial characteristics; the peon was allowed no existence, no economic activity, independent of the master. The instructions for the management of estates drawn up by Rosas for his overseers prohibited employees from even rearing poultry or hunting ostriches, because the sale of these products in the urban market would give the peon a degree of independence of the estanciero.[134] Thus, in spite of his fiery and stubborn resistance, the once nomadic gaucho was inexorably reduced to a hired ranch hand, attached like a peon to his master's estancia.

The fate of the gaucho was symptomatic of the revolution. The new order employed the old social structure, adapting it to its own needs without significantly modifying it. The Indian policy of the revolution was enlightened, but it confined itself to providing freedom, not welfare. The Indians were declared equal to creoles before the law. On 8 June 1810 the revolutionary junta informed the Indians of Buenos Aires that they would not henceforth be excluded from white regiments, since both Spaniards and Indians 'are equal and always ought to remain so'.[135] On 1 September 1811 the junta suppressed the Indian tribute in the United Provinces including the interior, and on 17 October 1811 General Pueyrredón declared the Indians of Peru released from tribute and from ecclesiastical charges. On 12 March 1813 the General Assembly ratified and amplified the decree of 1 September 1811, abolishing *encomienda* (grant of Indians), *yanaconazgo* (Indian serfdom) and all personal services, including parish services. Finally, the constitution of 1819 summed up all these provisions and assured the Indians complete civil liberty and equality. In practice, however, the servile and depressed conditions of the Indians did not improve. Numerically, of course, the problem did not reach the proportions of that in Bolivia and Peru. Argentina's pure-blooded Indian communities were concentrated in the sub-Andean provinces and the remoter parts of the littoral, where they practised subsistence agriculture outside the national economy. Where the Indians entered the white economy it was as labourers in the sugar plantations of the north-west or as rural peons. The most intractable Indian problem was that of the hostile warrior hordes of the southern frontier. Argentina had to fight these Indians and in the course of the nineteenth century to defeat and disperse them, in order to remove the last obstacle to the southward and westward expansion of the estancias.

The slave policy of the revolution was also theoretically enlightened.[136] In the colonial period the Negro slave in the Río de la Plata was generally a domestic servant, or an artisan working at a rudimentary industry for a master who regarded his purchase as an investment on which he wanted a return.[137] So there were powerful interests to overcome in ending slavery. The first stage was the abolition of the slave trade. Basing itself on liberal and humanitarian principles, the triumvirate issued decrees on 9 April and 14 May 1812 prohibiting the slave trade to and within the United Provinces, 'that our ports should not be contaminated by a trade as shameful as it is reprehensible'.[138] An illegal slave trade survived, due to the proximity of Brazil and the device of introducing slaves into the country under the guise of servants, to be subsequently traded. But by the Anglo-Argentine Treaty of 1825 both parties undertook to cooperate in the complete suppression of the slave trade.

Slavery itself was another matter, and it long survived the revolution. To mitigate the institution a number of measures were taken in 1813. The Constituent Assembly decreed (2 February) the so-called *libertad de vientres*, whereby all slave offspring born on and after 31 January 1813 were declared free. A second decree (4 February) declared free all slaves introduced into the United Provinces from that date. A third measure (6 March) elaborated further provisions for the education of former slave children and their integration into free society, but it also assigned the limits of freedom: all children of slaves who were born free were to remain in the household of the master until they were twenty years of age; for the first fifteen years they were to give unpaid service to their masters, and for the remaining five years they were to work for a wage of one peso a month. These laws were applauded by contemporaries as enlightened, and the *Gazeta de Buenos Aires* exhorted Negroes not to be discouraged:

Africans, do not complain if some of you continue still in oppressed conditions. The barbarous laws which afflicted whites and Negroes in these tyrannized lands still cause you this great evil. Although the Spaniards no longer rule here, having once made you slaves they have deprived you perhaps for ever of the great benefit of being free.[139]

According to this argument freedom was not something which could be acquired by decree alone; in any case it conflicted with another right, the property rights of those who had invested in slaves. These were convenient doctrines for property-owning whites; and even those anti-slavery laws which were passed at the centre were thwarted in their application by federalism. At the end of the colonial period there were over thirty thousand slaves out of a population of four hundred thousand, or about 8 per cent. But the incidence of slavery was greatest in the towns. In 1810 there were 11,837 Negroes and mulattos in Buenos Aires, or 29.3 per cent of the total population of 40,398, and over 77 per cent of the Negroes were slaves. In 1822 of the 55,416 inhabitants of Buenos Aires, 13,685 or 24.7 per cent were Negroes and mulattos; six out of ten Negroes were still slaves, as were three out of ten mulattos.[140] Where slaves were not in domestic service, they were mainly to be found in manual trades and in industry, which tended to make these occupations unacceptable to whites and thus reinforced regressive social and economic attitudes. And although the number of slaves greatly diminished, slavery was not totally extinct until it was expressly prohibited for the whole of Argentina in the constitution of 1853.[141]

Slaves – and also free Negroes and mulattos – were needed in the revolutionary armies. But conscription was not necessarily an instrument of emancipation. On 31 May 1813 the Assembly approved a plan proposed by the executive to raise a corps of Negro slaves. This was the first of a series of measures which obliged masters to sell to the state a certain number of slaves for service in the army. In 1813 this device brought into existence Battalions 7 and 8, composed of over a thousand slaves from Buenos Aires; in Córdoba 105 slaves were bought by the state in 1813. In 1816 further corps of slaves were raised: Buenos Aires recruited 576 slaves whom the state bought from 357 Spanish proprietors, the latter usually being more vulnerable than American proprietors. From these transactions the slave benefited least: he procured his freedom only after five years service, and he was paid less than the white soldier.[142] Thus the 'emancipation' of slaves in return for military service meant a change of masters rather than immediate freedom. And their new masters did not always appreciate their fighting qualities. General Belgrano, commander of the second Argentine expedition to Upper Peru, remarked that 'the Negroes and mulattos are a rabble, as cowardly as they are bloodthirsty . . . the only consolation is that white officers are on the way'.[143] San Martín, on the other hand, went out of his way to recruit Negroes in the conviction that 'the best infantry soldier we have is the Negro and mulatto'. Former slaves were a large part of San Martín's army of the Andes – 1,500 out of 5,000 – and of Sucre's army which completed the liberation of Peru at Ayacucho. General Miller, who had been second-in-command of the 8th or 'Black' Battalion of Buenos Aires in San Martín's army, recorded:

> The privates of the Battalion No. 8 were Creole Negroes, and had been for the most part in-door slaves previously to the commencement of the revolution, when, by becoming soldiers they obtained their freedom. They were distinguished throughout the war for their valour, constancy, and patriotism. . . . Many of them rose to be good non-commissioned officers.[144]

There was a price to be paid for this kind of freedom. The Negro infantry of the patriot armies suffered heavy casualties, and conscription usually led not to freedom but to death. If the Negro population of the Río de la Plata declined in the period of independence it was partly because it was a victim of war.

While the prospects of Indians and Negroes were little enhanced by independence, those of the mestizos and pardos were hardly better. In the Río de la Plata the pardos had increased rapidly in numbers in the course of the eighteenth century; in the province of Córdoba they came to form, with slaves, half of the population.[145] Their growing numbers caused a white reaction. In spite of the ideals of liberty and equality proclaimed by the May revolution and the Assembly of 1813, the creoles were reluctant to share the fruits of independence with the coloured classes. In the colonial period the pardos were not only excluded from municipal office but did not even have the right to elect white candidates. This discrimination survived into the independence period and pardos were denied the right to vote for deputies to the General Constituent Assembly in December 1812. And in the province of Córdoba the great majority of them were excluded from full civil rights until the 1850s. Education, too, long remained closed to pardos. It was not until 1829 that the provincial government of Córdoba decreed educational equality in primary schools and specifically declared that 'the doors of public education shall be open to all the sons of pardos'.[146] But the pardos were still excluded from higher education; it was 1852 before the provincial government decreed equality of opportunity in the University of Córdoba 'sin distinción de linajes'.[147] Ironically it was in the army that the pardos, like the slaves, first enjoyed a measure of equality and could make their way up the officer scale, though preference was given to white officers even in pardo regiments. More commonly pardos were confined to the socially depressed manual trades and industries.

The revolutionary leaders were rarely conscious of a need for social change, and they tended to think almost exclusively in political terms. Condemned to inaction in 1814, San Martín retired to an estancia outside Córdoba and brooded on the stagnation of the revolution: 'This is a revolution of sheep, not of men.' A peon came to complain that the Spanish overseer of his estancia had beaten him. San Martín was indignant, but it was a nationalist rather than social indignation. 'What do you think? After three years of revolution, a *maturrango* [Spaniard] dares to raise his hand against an American!'[148]

THREE *Revolution Against the Río de la Plata*

REVOLUTION BRED FURTHER revolution, and independence fed upon itself. While the interior of the Río de la
Plata challenged the unitary policy of Buenos Aires, the
periphery provinces came to reject any association with the new
state and to seek their own political solutions. The success of
Uruguay, Paraguay and Bolivia in asserting their independence
was in part a measure of their isolation behind rivers, deserts and
mountains, and of the inability of Buenos Aires to focus sufficient
military force upon them. But it stemmed ultimately from a conviction that their interests could not be accommodated in the
United Provinces and needed self-determination. In pursuit of
this goal the greatest ordeal was endured by Uruguay.

The Banda Oriental, the 'eastern bank' lying between the river
Uruguay and the Atlantic, was an underpopulated and barely
urbanized country, whose greatest asset was the fertile and
watered soil of its undulating plains, making it in the colonial
period the richest reserve of livestock in the whole of the Río de

la Plata. It contained little more than forty thousand people in 1810, many of them nomadic gauchos of mestizo and mulatto stock, whose main activity was the hunting of wild cattle.[1] In the course of the eighteenth century, land and people came under increasing control. The expansion of the livestock industry gave birth to a new and powerful landed class, drawn in part from local interests and in part from recent and vigorous immigrants from northern Spain; these groups were enriched by land grants which carved up the country into a series of great estancias based on gaucho and slave labour. The Durán, Martínez de Haedo, Alzáibar, Viana, Arias, Villanueva, Rivera and García de Zúñiga, these were some of the new aristocracy, owners of truly vast estates, patriarchal and self-sufficient.[2] Rural development also drew more merchants to the province, many of them peninsulares, who became exporters of hides and salt beef, shippers, and slave-traders. The merchants tended to exploit the rural producers and to introduce an element of Spanish-creole antipathy. But there was not a sharp cleavage of interests between commerce and land: many merchants invested in land, and a number of successful estancieros spread their assets into hide-processing, *saladeros* (salt beef plants), shipping and commerce.[3]

In the Spanish imperial system the Banda Oriental had a triple significance, strategic, political and commercial. Its strategic importance lay in its commanding position at the entrance to the river Plate, where it could control traffic in and out of this great river complex. It was, moreover, a buffer between Brazil and the Río de la Plata, and therefore an object of intense competition between Portugal and Spain. On the Spanish side it was of particular interest to Buenos Aires, primarily as a source of livestock and of revenue therefrom, being regarded 'as a sort of large ranch leased to Buenos Aires'.[4] The situation of the Banda Oriental, and its empty northern frontier, also invited Portuguese intervention – rustlers in search of cattle, traders looking for outlets – and this forced Spain to provide for the province. The Portuguese Colônia do Sacramento, founded in 1680 on the north bank of the river Plate, was a smuggling centre as well as an imperial outpost, and became an active threat to Spanish interests. Spain replied by founding Montevideo in the 1720s. This was a defence base which eventually gave a capital to the area. Defence was further strengthened in 1776 by the creation of the viceroyalty of the Río de la Plata and the removal of the Portuguese from Colônia. Viceregal status enhanced the position of Buenos Aires and made it more sensitive to the growing power of Montevideo. The latter had become a vital link in imperial defence and an important centre of administration; inevitably it had also become the capital of the Banda Oriental and acquired a political identity. It now had its own governor, though he was subordinate to the governor of Buenos Aires and, from 1776, to the viceroy. The commercial role of Montevideo kept pace with its political growth. Even during the closed-port regime its contraband activity siphoned off trade from Buenos Aires and aroused the resentment of Spanish merchants there. But the growth of legitimate trade from 1778, when Montevideo could participate in the benefits of *comercio libre*, brought much greater prosperity to the port and hostility from Buenos Aires. Montevideo now enjoyed direct trade with Spain and intercolonial trade in the Americas; it acquired its own customs house and Treasury officials.[5] Indeed Montevideo had natural advantages over Buenos Aires in competing for European and American markets : it had a harbour, it was nearer the Atlantic and therefore the first port of call, and it had a hinterland rich in exportable produce from estancia and saladero. Buenos Aires was acutely conscious of this competition and strove to reduce it; while the acquisition of a consulado in 1794 advanced its own monopolist claims, Buenos Aires denied all concessions to Montevideo and even refused to authorize port improvements there.[6] The exploiting, 'colonial' policy, it appeared, came to the Banda Oriental not directly from Spain but from Buenos Aires. Montevideo looked to the imperial power to protect it from the sectional interests of the immediate metropolis across the river. And demands for commercial concessions were accompanied by demands for administrative autonomy : in 1807 Montevideo requested that as a reward for damages suffered and services performed during the British invasions it should be assigned an intendancy and a consulado, that is an administrative unit and an economic institution separate from Buenos Aires.[7] This request was not granted, but in 1808 the Governor of Montevideo, Francisco Xavier Elío, was made governor of the whole of the Banda Oriental, a new and expanded office. Meanwhile, after six months of British occupation and trade, Montevideo was reluctant to return to satellite status under Buenos Aires and the monopolists across the river.

The rivalry between Buenos Aires and Montevideo, therefore, had a long history and derived from a clash of interests. It was almost inevitable that in 1808 each should react differently to news of the crisis of government in Spain and that latent rivalry should flare up into open hostility. Montevideo under Elío, 'an Old Spaniard thoroughly attached to the cause of the mother country', immediately recognized the rights of Ferdinand vii and Spain, while in Buenos Aires Liniers hesitated.[8] On 6–7 September Elío demanded the removal of Liniers. In conjunction with the Portuguese demand for the cession of the Banda Oriental to Brazil, this gave Buenos Aires the impression of treachery.[9] So mutual suspicion prevailed, Montevideo believing that Liniers was going to sell out to France, and Buenos Aires that Elío was a tool of Portugal. When Liniers tried to depose Elío, Montevideo resisted, held a cabildo abierto, and this turned itself into a governing junta under Elío, following the Spanish example. In this way Montevideo asserted its loyalty to Spain – and its emancipation from Buenos Aires. Hostilities between the two ports began at sea, as each sought to blockade the other and to compete for British trade.

The revolution in Buenos Aires could not be Montevideo's revolution. There was a brief and superficial reconciliation between the two rivals in 1809 with the arrival of a new viceroy, Cisneros, but he was more acceptable in royalist Montevideo than in dissident Buenos Aires. And he soon lost the support of Montevideo by dismissing the uncontrollable Elío. He never had the support of the creoles in Buenos Aires and he was deposed by them in May 1810. But Montevideo refused to accept the May revolution. In the first place, it came in the wrong form. The Buenos Aires revolutionaries requested Montevideo to recognize *their* junta. But why should the people of Montevideo be excluded from the reversion of sovereignty claimed by Buenos Aires? Why should they not decide for themselves? Having long sought freedom from Buenos Aires, why should they now submit?[10] So Montevideo rejected the request and decided to recognize the Council of Regency in Spain. The only way it could secure independence of Buenos Aires, it seemed, was by loyalty to Spain. This was the creoles' dilemma. For them loyalty to Spain was only a means to an end, emancipation from Buenos Aires. But it meant that Montevideo and the Banda Oriental were put under the government of Spanish partisans when elsewhere in the Río de la Plata the independence movement was growing in momentum. When this happened the creoles in Montevideo found themselves in a false position. At this point resistance to Buenos Aires was a victory for the royalist rather than the creole party in Montevideo.

There were some who realized this, among them José Gervasio Artigas, a gaucho caudillo, whose career hitherto had been a curious mixture of personal lawlessness and official law-enforcing. Artigas was born to a landowning and military creole family in Montevideo, and started life as a wild leader of *gauchos malos,* a rustling and smuggling gang operating near the Brazilian frontier.[11] On the strength of his expert knowledge he then joined an official Spanish force, the *Cuerpo de Blandengues* organized to rid the country of outlaws and smugglers. This experience was valuable in extending his knowledge of the countryside, the northern frontier, and Portuguese penetration. By 1810 he was a man of some stature in the Banda Oriental and a recognized gaucho leader. In February 1811 he joined the independence movement in Buenos Aires, and the junta gave him a small force to help revolutionize the Banda Oriental.

By now the political front in the Banda Oriental had broken. And divisions were widened by two important factors. First, the heavy cost of administering the country as a separate province and a Spanish base had to be met from increased taxes on property and trade. This caused a reappraisal. One particular financial device provoked great resentment among the estanciero class. The government in Montevideo ordered all ranchers to prove title to their land : those who were unable to do so had to pay the purchase price of their estate or have it auctioned as royal property.[12] Secondly, the pressure on the Banda Oriental was increased when Elío returned as viceroy at the beginning of 1811. To enforce the government's financial policy the interior had to be held down by Spanish troops. The Banda Oriental now looked precisely what it was, an occupied colony.[13] This was not autonomy. And in February, with indecent haste, Elío declared war on Buenos Aires.

This was the spark which fired the real independence movement in the Banda Oriental. Political opposition had already been prepared by groups of intellectuals, lawyers and clergy, inside and outside Montevideo. But the backbone of the revolution lay in the countryside, where estancieros and their gaucho followers rose to join Buenos Aires in opposition to Spanish authority. In the remote south-west corner of the province a small gaucho army under rural caudillos assembled and raised the *grito de Asencio* (26 February 1811), the rallying cry of the revolution. The movement spread rapidly throughout the province and was reinforced from outside : Belgrano sent troops from the remnants of his abortive expedition to Paraguay; Buenos Aires sent a force under José Rondeau.[14] And Artigas, crossing from Entre Ríos with his own detachment, came to command the vanguard of the patriot forces; these defeated the Spaniards in a major engagement at Las Piedras and began to press on Montevideo.

The power base of Artigas's movement was the estanciero class, the majority of whom, directly or indirectly, supported the revolt of 1811. The Durán, García de Zúñiga, Barreiro, Gregorio Espinosa, and many others brought in their peons and their resources to the revolutionary cause and sustained it in the years to come. They had their own reasons for doing so; this was their answer to the heavy tax demands of Montevideo for the war against Buenos Aires and to the new review of land titles which the Spanish authorities sought to impose. But self-interest coincided with the interests of their province and with the patriotism of their leader. They trusted Artigas because of his own estanciero origins and because of his military success before 1811 in bringing law and order to the countryside, a cause which was also their own. From the merchants of Montevideo, however, Artigas received little support; Spanish by nationality and by sympathy they supported the royalist cause in the expectation of monopoly rewards. For the moment they had little option. Montevideo was the focus of Elío's power; here he retained his grip and from here he kept command of the sea, which enabled him to receive supplies and reinforcements and to harry Buenos Aires. And to recover his position by land he gambled on another possibility – cooperation with Portugal.

Portugal's objectives in the Río de la Plata were intelligible, if crude. Overtly she simply wished to restore stability to the area in order to prevent revolutionary unrest subverting her own position in Brazil. In reality Portugal wanted to exploit instability in order to extend Brazil to the shores of the river Plate and add great wealth and power to her empire. Elío mistook propaganda for truth. Cornered in Montevideo, he believed he could call in Portugal to subdue the insurgents on behalf of her ally Spain, and then persuade her to leave afterwards.[15] He gravely miscalculated. In the second half of 1811 a Portuguese army advanced southwards, penetrated deeply into the Banda Oriental and showed every sign of staying. Predictably this produced diverse reactions from the patriots in Buenos Aires and those in the Banda Oriental. Buenos Aires preferred to preserve the province intact even under Elío as long as Portugal did not procure it. Artigas and his revolutionaries regarded this as selling out to Elío and the Spanish royalists; they wanted the Spaniards as well as the Portuguese ejected. Nevertheless, fear of Portugal caused Montevideo and Buenos Aires to come to terms in an armistice treaty (20 October 1811), uniting both and handing over all the Banda Oriental to Elío, as a preliminary to joint efforts to prize out the Portuguese. And Artigas was not consulted.

This armistice did one thing for Artigas: it made clear that there was no place for him nor independence for his province in the policy of Buenos Aires, and that provincial interests were quite distinct from those of Buenos Aires. So it taught a valuable lesson for the future. For the present, what could be done? Artigas, who had recently been acclaimed by his followers *Jefe de los Orientales*, undertook to withdraw across the river Uruguay to Entre Ríos. It was a memorable withdrawal, a triumph in defeat. Artigas marched out of his homeland with four thousand troops. He was followed in addition by four thousand civilians, fearful of Spanish reprisals and Portuguese brutality, people who sought independence in exile, leaving behind a scorched earth and an empty countryside.[16] This great

Exodus of the Oriental People had profound significance in the history of Uruguay. It was an exercise if not of popular at least of provincial sovereignty, an announcement in effect that the Banda Oriental preferred secession to subordination and would serve neither Spain nor Buenos Aires. Yet this act of defiance would have remained an empty gesture had it not been identified with a leader who had a purpose and a policy. The Exodus gave Artigas the unmistakable stature of a leader, the head of an independent people, the guide in whom thousands of Orientals put their trust. After this any relationship with Buenos Aires would be one of equality: the Orientals would take assistance offered to equals but not orders given to inferiors.[17] The Orientals of the Exodus, in short, were the nucleus of an independent nation.

The Portuguese army, needless to say, did not share these sentiments. It was not disposed to withdraw from the Banda Oriental, and neither Buenos Aires nor Montevideo could force it to do so. The only power capable of influencing Portuguese policy was Great Britain, the ally on whom Portugal depended for survival in the war against France. Britain was also an ally of Spain and had to support the Spanish position in the Río de la Plata by keeping the Portuguese in check, partly to preserve the anti-French alliance, partly to protect British trade in the area. The British foreign secretary, Castlereagh, made it clear that he wanted 'the unconditional evacuation of all the Spanish American possessions' by the Portuguese, and this strengthened the hand of Lord Strangford, the British minister in Rio de Janeiro, in dealing with the Portuguese government.[18] He forced the Portuguese to accept armistice terms with Buenos Aires and to take their forces out of the Banda Oriental. In this instance, as in others, British interests coincided with those of the patriots. For the Banda Oriental itself was not included as a party to the armistice; the Portuguese evacuation, therefore, opened the way for the return of the patriots. But they soon found that they did not have the field to themselves and that they were still challenged by the forces of Buenos Aires. In 1813 both the artiguistas and the porteños were besieging Spanish-held Montevideo. It was an uneasy alliance.

In Buenos Aires the centralists were in command, and it was

they who controlled the Constituent Assembly of the United Provinces which met early in 1813. This organization ordered the Banda Oriental to recognize its sovereignty and send representatives. The Orientals objected. Artigas himself was strongly influenced by the constitutional experience of the United States; he was also aware of the implications of porteño centralism for local economies. He therefore advocated self-determination for individual provinces; these would be allied in no more than a loose confederation, which in time perhaps might develop into a real federation.[19] But the starting point was provincial autonomy. The other provinces of the littoral shared these sentiments and aligned themselves with Artigas. As he was more articulate than the other caudillos and already led a liberation movement, he became the recognized spokesman of provincial resistance to porteño centralism. He and his Oriental associates gave notice of their position in the *Instructions* which were debated in local congress and issued to the deputies of the Provincia Oriental to the Constituent Assembly.[20] These took a more militantly anti-Spanish line than did Buenos Aires: they demanded a formal declaration of independence for the United Provinces and made such a declaration for the Provincia Oriental. But the crucial issue was political organization. The *Instructions* asserted the independent sovereignty of the Provincia Oriental, which would keep all powers not expressly delegated to a federal government; and they further demanded separate governments for *all* the provinces.

The *Instructions* of 1813 projected a system in which the provinces would have full sovereignty; this would include economic autonomy and also the power to raise their own armies. The federal framework would be extremely weak, and the central government stripped of any means of controlling the provinces. This was not true federalism. It would have reduced the Río de la Plata to an agglomeration of mini-states ruled by petty caudillos and stagnating in their own inadequacy, as indeed it became in the years of anarchy 1819–20. Argentina's future did not lie in this direction – nor in that of rigid centralism. The attitude of Buenos Aires was not encouraging. The Constituent Assembly refused to accept the Oriental deputies. This seemed to confirm the entire thesis of Artigas. He now withdrew from the siege of Montevideo and, while Buenos Aires declared him an outlaw, he turned his attention to consolidating provincial independence and arousing the whole of the littoral in war with Buenos Aires. Montevideo surrendered to the land and sea forces of Buenos Aires in June 1814. But with Artigas in open opposition and with elements in Montevideo cooperating with the revolution outside, what could Buenos Aires do in the Banda Oriental? Alvear considered that a new monarchy or a British protectorate was preferable to federalist anarchy; but these desperate and fruitless plans only underlined the political bankruptcy of the porteño regime.[21] Alternatively it could abandon an untenable position, evacuate Montevideo and turn it over to Artigas. This it did in February 1815.

In 1815, therefore, Artigas at last ruled the Provincia Oriental, the *Patria Vieja* as it came to be called.[22] In the same year the littoral provinces of Santa Fe, Entre Ríos and Corrientes, together with Córdoba, grouped themselves into a so-called Federal League and recognized Artigas as Protector of the Free Peoples, the leader of the armed struggle against Buenos Aires.[23] The 'protectorate' in fact was never more than an uneasy assemblage of local caudillos, each looking over his shoulder at his neighbour as well as at Buenos Aires. And it was only in the Provincia Oriental that Artigas really governed. Even there he had little to govern. After five years of war the province was almost a desert. Armies had marched back and forth across the country; royalist, patriot and Brazilian forces had lived off the land, occupying ranches, sacking property and hunting livestock. 'Immense quantities of cattle were killed to raise a revenue upon the hides, and more were destroyed in the gratification of the appetites and private interests of officers and soldiers.'[24] Proprietors took refuge in the towns and labour was dispersed. Arable farming was insufficient to feed the population, which eventually came to depend on imports of foreign grain. But trade too was depressed and yielded little either in revenue or in foreign earnings. Montevideo had been cut off from the interior, and in wartime conditions production in the interior had receded.

Artigas sought to repair the destruction of war and to develop his country anew. He wanted to promote the economy of the whole of the Río de la Plata on the basis of freedom of trade for the provinces in general and for the Provincia Oriental in particular. This included commerce with Britain. In 1815 Commodore William Bowles, commander of the British naval station, requested trading facilities for British merchants, and Artigas opened the ports of Montevideo and Colonia on condition that foreign merchants traded only in the ports, not in the interior, and consigned their goods to native middlemen. An active British trade developed from which the protectorate drew supplies and revenue on a scale which seemed to warrant the signing of a convention (2 August 1817) between Artigas and local British officials. This admitted 'to a free commerce all English merchants', regulated the commerce, and granted the English better fiscal terms than those enjoyed by other foreign traders. Although the British government did not give its authorization, Artigas circulated the regulation in his ports and a mutual trade developed on this basis.[25] But Artigas was interested in the distribution of wealth as well as in its creation.

The social policy of the regime had distinctly radical undertones. Federalism in itself, of course, had social implications. Provincial resistance to centralism had to be paid for : this sometimes meant taxes on property-owners and in any case military depredations on property and produce. There were also problems of recruitment. The caudillos, like Buenos Aires itself, would try to attract Negro slaves to their forces by offering a kind of emancipation. Artigas too appealed to the slaves, in southern Brazil as well as in his own province. This further alarmed people of property :

There is no doubt a considerable fermentation has been excited amongst the slaves by his proclamations and the encouragement he holds forth, and it is extremely probable very many of them will escape and join his army. . . . The general feeling amongst people of property and any consideration, not only on this side of the Plata but on the opposite one, is against Artigas, whose popularity, although considerable, is entirely confined to the lower orders of the community and arises from those very causes which make him most dreaded by the higher, namely his not only permitting but encouraging every excess and disorder amongst his followers.[26]

In 1815 Artigas issued a *Reglamento provisorio*, a plan for promoting agricultural settlement by granting land to those who were willing to work it, with preference to Negroes, zambos, Indians, and poor whites, all of whom could 'be granted estancia lots, if with their work and probity they are inclined towards their own happiness and that of the province'. The source of the grants was to be unoccupied marginal land and land confiscated from *emigrados, malos europeos y peores americanos,* that is from royalists. No doubt there were urgent economic reasons for land development, and these can also be seen in Artigas's decrees forcing vagabonds to work and urging estancias back into production, all of which were attempts to reassemble labour and capital. But agrarian reform was also a social investment, the work of a populist caudillo. The formation of great estates in the eighteenth century had concentrated property in the hands of a few, raised the price of land, and impoverished the dispossessed population who were unable to acquire or to afford land. It was for these that Artigas legislated in 1815, and there is evidence that numerous grants of land and cattle were made.[28] The programme was reformist rather than revolutionary, but even this was calculated to alarm the estancieros, especially the absentee landlords in Montevideo. And the agrarian radicalism of Artigas could be expected in time to alienate the very class on which any political movement depended. In any case, from 1816 Artigas had to subordinate his schemes to military necessity. The young and heroic Patria Vieja was brought to a brutal end by a new wave of Portuguese invaders.

The Portuguese in Brazil had never reconciled themselves to the enforced withdrawal from the Banda Oriental in 1812. They were still ready to extend their frontiers to the Río de la Plata and they were still powerful enough to do so. Indeed they now had even greater assets than in 1812. The end of the war in Europe released a powerful division of veteran troops under General Carlos Frederico Lecór for service in America. Simultaneously it became clear to the Portuguese that they had little to fear from Buenos Aires. By now the porteño centralists welcomed any opportunity to destroy Artigas and his federalists, and Pueyrredón had no scruples over conniving with Brazil against the common enemy.[29] The pretext was almost a formality : Artigas had incorporated into the Provincia Oriental part of the province of Misiones claimed by Portugal. Declaring Artigas a 'disturbing influence', the Portuguese invaded in August 1816.[30] Lecór's superior forces advanced inexorably southwards by sea and land, promising the Orientals peace and prosperity as part of a greater Brazil. Artigas, outnumbered and outfought, was forced to surrender Montevideo in January 1817 and to concentrate his effort in the interior; there he conducted a stubborn guerrilla campaign.

Artigas had to fight on two fronts. While the centralists of Buenos Aires acted in collusion with his enemies in the Banda Oriental, they also sought to subvert his position in the littoral. By a combination of armed force and diplomacy Buenos Aires strove to lure the caudillos away from the federal league. The military approach was a fiasco. The wild montonero cavalry and gaucho guerrillas of Santa Fe and Entre Ríos fought off the porteño armies and took the offensive against Buenos Aires, defeating the centralists at Cepeda (1 February 1820).[31] These victories contrasted vividly with the misfortunes of the protector himself. The Portuguese inflicted a decisive defeat on his forces at Tacuarembó on 22 January 1820, and Artigas with the remnant of his forces had to retreat across the Uruguay into Entre Ríos. Positions were now reversed; victory against Buenos Aires enhanced the stature of the federalist caudillos and placed them beyond Artigas's control. After Cepeda, López and Ramírez were powerful and independent leaders, arbiters of policy in the littoral; and they had no more wish than Buenos Aires to become involved in Artigas's war with Brazil. Artigas was not a party to the interprovincial Pact of Pilar, and in the subsequent discussions he was 'seldom mentioned'.[32] He now had to endure the bitter logic of provincialism as his own provincial colleagues withdrew from the federal league. Soon the caudillos were openly hostile, and the Protector of the Free Peoples was left with the support of only Corrientes and Misiones.[33] Ramírez accepted arms from Buenos Aires and savagely turned on his former ally, defeating him in battle, and driving him into the wilderness of northern Corrientes. On 5 September 1820 Artigas crossed the river Paraná into Paraguay in search of a temporary refuge. The dictator Dr Francia insisted that the asylum be permanent. Artigas never returned to the outside world, and he died in Paraguay thirty years later.

While the provinces of the Río de la Plata fought ruinously among themselves, the Portuguese forces of occupation secured their grip on the conquered territory. In July 1821 an Oriental congress subservient to the new regime voted the incorporation of the Provincia Oriental into the Portuguese empire as the Estado Cisplatino, and in the following year this became a province of independent Brazil under the relatively enlightened, if absolutist, rule of General Lecór. He had the support of many of the wealthier estancieros, alarmed perhaps by the later populism of Artigas, reassured by the seigneurial social values of Brazil, and relieved by the return of law and order to the country-side.[34] He had even greater support from the merchants of Montevideo who welcomed the return of stability and prepared to profit from his open-port policy. These golden years of the Estado Cisplatino were marred by only two things – the endur-ing, if dormant, claim of Buenos Aires to the territory, and the survival of a resistance movement among the Orientals themselves.

Artigas was a victim of his own ideals, destroyed by the very provincialism he had helped to create. But in his homeland he left a programme and a nucleus of an independence movement, and these could not be destroyed. Juan Antonio Lavalleja, an officer of Artigas and a veteran of the patriot wars, was the first to revive the idea of liberation. After an unsuccessful attempt to raise a revolt in Tacuarembó, he escaped to Buenos Aires and there he formed a revolutionary organization in exile. News of Ayacucho (December 1824), the last great victory of Bolívar's army, released a torrent of nationalist fervour in Buenos Aires; for now the Provincia Oriental was the only part of Spanish South America under foreign domination. While Buenos Aires pre-pared to wage war on Brazil, the Orientals themselves struck the first blow. A band of volunteers led by Lavalleja, the Thirty-Three Orientals, crossed the river Plate in small boats on 19 April 1825 and landed near Colonia to activate the latent resistance movement in the interior. The patriots projected some kind of autonomy not yet defined : their reliance on the support of Buenos Aires prevented them from speaking of absolute independence. The expedition of the Thirty-Three was privately financed by a group of Buenos Aires estancieros led by the Anchorena. Was this an investment for the future? Did the porteño ranchers still aspire to control a competitor? The porteño government itself had clear objectives. From October 1825 it began to finance and support the patriots, not for independence but for reunion with the United Provinces. In spite of its political ambiguity, the revolution soon dominated the countryside, drawing its support in the beginning from the gauchos and smaller estancieros; soon Brazilian rule was confined to the towns, and Lavalleja became governor of the Provincia Oriental. Brazil retaliated by declaring war on the United Provinces in December 1825.

Thus by the end of 1825 there were three forces in the Provincia Oriental: Brazil fought to preserve its new dominion; Buenos Aires to incorporate the area in the United Provinces; and the Orientals to gain self-rule within an Argentine confederation. Two factors changed this situation in favour of absolute independence for Uruguay. In the United Provinces the centralist constitution of 1826 which produced the presidency of Rivadavia was a facade and a provocation.[35] It was rejected by the provinces and by the federalists of Buenos Aires itself. And it ruthlessly exposed the pretensions of the porteño centralists – and their weakness. Rivadavia had to withdraw his forces from the Provincia Oriental in order to confront the federalists at home. When he lost the struggle for power at the centre, provincial autonomy gained momentum. Fructuoso Rivera, son of one of the richest landed families in the Provincia Oriental, seized the opportunity to strike out for complete independence. Rivera was a former officer of Artigas and after the collapse of the Oriental war effort had submitted to the Portuguese in 1820. Now, early in 1828, he recruited a guerrilla force from the Provincia Oriental and the littoral, advanced along the river Uruguay and conquered Brazilian Misiones. At last the Orientals had something to bargain with.

Meanwhile Brazil and the United Provinces had exhausted their military resources and fought themselves to a standstill. The result was a stalemate; the balance of power was too evenly divided between these two countries for either to win a clear victory. For lack of alternatives, therefore, the Provincia Oriental emerged as a nation independent of both its larger neighbours. The vehicle of independence was British mediation which began in 1826 and reinforced the military efforts of the patriots. As in 1812 Britain had 'motives of self-interest, as well as of benevolence' in seeking a peace formula.[36] The war was crippling British trade in the south Atlantic and merchants were suffering severe losses from the Brazilian blockade of Buenos Aires and the spread of privateering. And politically Canning attached a curious importance to preserving at least one monarchy in the Americas by saving Brazil from herself and from her republican neighbours. Britain had considerable influence over the governments both in Rio de Janeiro and in Buenos Aires, but she had not been able to prevent war and she found it difficult to restore peace. In 1826 Canning sent Lord John Ponsonby to seek a solution.[37] He advised pragmatism and avoidance of discussion of 'abstract legitimate right', for, as he saw it 'the value of Montevideo to each party consists less, perhaps, in the positive benefit which they may expect to derive from it themselves, than in the detriment which they apprehend from its being in possession of the opposite party.'[38] Canning contemplated the possibility of independence for Montevideo but not with any great confidence. But Ponsonby was soon convinced that the Orientals were ready for independence : 'It is an undisputed fact that the Orientalists dislike being subject to Buenos Aires *only less* than being subject to Brazil, and that independency is their dearest wish.'[39] By the end of October 1826 Ponsonby had persuaded Buenos Aires to allow him to approach Brazil with a formula of independence, though he could not offer a British guarantee of the existence of the new state. With the Emperor of Brazil, however, he had no success at all, and in November Canning instructed Ponsonby to stand back and allow the passage of time to bring the belligerents to their senses, 'when the events of the war may have sickened and exhausted both parties'.[40] It was sound advice. In the course of 1828 Ponsonby was able to exploit the military impasse and bring the two powers to the peace table on the basis of independence for the Provincia Oriental.

By now the Orientals outside Montevideo and Colonia were

in fact free and self-governing. So it was a recognition of existing facts when Brazil and the United Provinces signed a peace treaty (27 August 1828) declaring the independence of the Provincia Oriental.[41] In 1830 the Oriental State of the Uruguay acquired its first constitution, which at once completed and fulfilled the struggle for independence.[42] Past political records – actions as well as opinions – were declared annulled; this apparently generous amnesty was a piece of class legislation, for it was intended to benefit those upper sectors who had collaborated with Buenos Aires or Brazil. In other respects too this so-called liberal constitution was a socially conservative document which fell far short of the ideals of Artigas. It provided for representative government, but only a small sector of society was represented. Certain categories, including those who had born the burden of active service in the wars of independence, were specifically excluded from the franchise: peons, ranch hands, paid labourers, common soldiers, and vagabonds – a term sufficiently vague to cover the entire gaucho population – were all denied the right to vote. To be a deputy or senator a man had to be a property owner with capital of four thousand or ten thousand respectively, or to have a profession, occupation or office which produced an equivalent income. In 1842 less than 7 per cent of the population of Montevideo and even less in the countryside voted in the national elections. Having ensured its control of the state, the ruling class of Uruguay then arranged that the state should have little to do. The various liberties enshrined in the constitution of 1830, freedom of commerce, of opinion, of the press, the abolition of entail and of ecclesiastical and military fueros, all these classical liberal measures created a *laissez-faire* system which meant little to the mass of the people. And no more was heard of the agrarian reform initiated by Artigas. Only in the abolition of the slave trade and the ending of slavery could be noticed a faint echo of the precursor's ideals.

(ii) Paraguay, the Impenetrable Dictatorship

Paraguay, like Uruguay, repudiated the authority of Buenos Aires, first and very briefly in support of Spain, then more vigorously in assertion of its own independence. This was a very rapid movement, and Paraguay was in effect a sovereign state from 1811 without the long ordeal by battle endured by Uruguay. But whereas Uruguay used its independence to create a liberal state, dominated by the landed and merchant aristocracy, Paraguay acquired a pseudo-populist dictatorship under the sinister Dr Francia.

Situated more than a thousand miles up river, Paraguay was naturally isolated by its remoteness and its great river boundaries. The economy was fairly primitive, being based upon subsistance agriculture and a few export crops. These were drawn from rich natural resources, tobacco, sugar and honey, and above all the *yerba mate,* the tea leaf which grew in abundance in the extensive *yerbales* in the vicinity of Villa Real and which had a market in many parts of South America.[43] But in spite of its assets Paraguay's economy was floundering in the late colonial period. In good years the province exported as much as three hundred thousand arrobas of yerba, and never less than two hundred thousand. Yet this was far below the productive capacity of the province, for in the face of crippling taxes there was no incentive to more intensive cultivation: first the product went to Santa Fe whence it was distributed to Buenos Aires, Tucumán, Potosí, Peru and Chile, taxed all the way from post to post, by provincial as well as by alcabala taxes.[44] At the same time tobacco production, like the rest of agriculture, was retarded by primitive technique and failed to capture available markets.[45] Analyzing the economy of Paraguay in 1798, Intendant Lázaro Rivera drew a vivid comparison between the potential wealth of the province and the evidence of poverty which he saw on all sides. Out of a population of about a hundred thousand more than five thousand were living below subsistence level and only a minority above it. Seeking an explanation, he drew attention to yet another factor impeding economic development – the shortage of manpower, aggravated by the antiquated military system with which the province was burdened. Surrounded by hostile and predatory Indians, the region had to be kept in a constant state of defence. But instead of provision of regular garrisons, all the settlers were subject to militia service, a suitable system for pioneering days but wasteful in a period of potential growth.[46]

The Paraguayan ruling class was a rural class, owners of

estancias, producers of maté, tobacco and hides, officers of the provincial militia; speaking Guaraní as well as Spanish, they were the patriarchal leaders of this docile and largely mestizo people, of the smaller farmers of the interior, the artisans, muleteers and peons, wage-earners and dependants.[47] These creoles had a strong local sentiment, born of isolation, administrative detachment, and local interests. Their grievances against the metropolis were various: they resented the burden of militia service, the anti-creole prejudice in the distribution of offices, the rigid control and restriction of the economy. Peninsulares dominated commerce and the bureaucracy. Paraguay, like many other parts of the empire, received an increasing influx of Spanish immigrants in the course of the eighteenth century, especially in the last decades when *comercio libre* attracted many entrepreneurs and imperial reform provided more jobs in the bureaucracy. The Spaniards formed an urban class and came to dominate the cabildo of Asunción, which had been traditionally the mouthpiece of local interests. In 1810 this cabildo was more royalist than the intendant himself. And it was utterly incompatible with incipient creole nationalism.

Paraguayan regionalism faced two ways, one towards Brazil, where Paraguay defended at its own cost and from its own resources the Paraná frontier against Portuguese encroachments, transforming an imperial duty into a local cause; the other towards Buenos Aires, whose administrative and economic domination Paraguay greatly resented.[48] As an intendancy within the viceroyalty of the Río de la Plata, Paraguay was subject from the 1780s to much greater administrative intervention from Buenos Aires. And Paraguay's vital exports depended on the river passage which was taxed and controlled by Buenos Aires. So Paraguay was even more of a colonial dependency of Buenos Aires than was the Banda Oriental, for Paraguay had no alternative outlet. For all these reasons the creoles had no wish to exchange the dominion of Spain for the even closer rule of Buenos Aires.

Revolutionary propaganda circulated in Asunción from 1809, but it was the May revolution in Buenos Aires which forced Paraguay to reach a decision. In cabildo of 26 June, Intendant Bernardo de Velasco summoned a cabildo abierto to decide upon relations with the junta of Buenos Aires. This was held on 24 July and was attended by about two hundred of the more prominent citizens. It decided to swear obedience to the Council of Regency in Spain, to maintain fraternity with Buenos Aires without recognizing its authority, and to take measures for the military defence of the province.[49] With characteristic folly the porteño revolutionaries decided to force the issue. They sent a small expedition under the command of Manuel Belgrano. The former consulado secretary was more at home in the office than on the battlefield. He advanced into the province convinced that he brought liberty to the Paraguayans, that only a few royalists opposed the May revolution, and that the leaders of resistance should be executed.[50] All these were basic miscalculations. About five thousand Paraguayans took up arms to resist absorption by Buenos Aires and defend their national identity; and they vindicated their claims at the battles of Paraguarí (9 January 1811) and Tacuarí (9 March), where they overwhelmed Belgrano's army of seven hundred.[51] In the first of these encounters the intendant took to flight and the Spanish forces dispersed; but the ill-armed Paraguayan cavalry came to the rescue under creole officers, reproducing the master-peon relationship of the estancia, and it was they who decided the issue. For the rest of the campaign operations continued under the command of creole officers, and it was a Paraguayan, Manuel Atanasio Cabañas, who signed the armistice with Belgrano. In their military repudiation of Buenos Aires the Paraguayans also in effect emancipated themselves from Spanish control and experienced the advantages of self-government. The first to realize this was Intendant Velasco himself, who sought Portuguese assistance from Brazil in an attempt to recover lost ground. But he failed. Paraguay was safe from Spain because Viceroy Elío in Montevideo was unable to overcome Buenos Aires; and the royalists in Asunción, being an urban group, lacked any popular support in the countryside.

The initiative now rested with the creole ruling class leading their armed people.[52] They controlled the grass-roots of independence in the provinces, while in Asunción they had an apparent ally in the creole cabildo official and lawyer, Dr José Gaspar Rodríguez de Francia.[53] It was they who directed the revolution of 14 May 1811 and produced the declaration of independence on 17 May – independence of Buenos Aires as well as of all foreign powers.[54] On 9 June they deposed Velasco. And they dominated the General Congress which met in Asunción during 1–20 June; there they defined their policy. Mariano Antonio Molas, patriot spokesman, proposed that integration with Buenos Aires should be accepted only on terms of equality as part of a larger American confederation; this was approved by a large majority. Meanwhile, the congress asserted, 'this province will govern itself', and so it created an independent *junta superior gubernativa*. Even more explicit was the note of 20 July 1811 drawn up by Francia and sent by the junta to the authorities in Buenos Aires; this expressed support for a confederation provided that it was founded on complete equality of the parts.[55] And on 12 October 1811 Paraguay signed a treaty with Buenos Aires which freed its commerce of old impediments and paid lip service to ideas of federation.

The junta was headed by an estanciero, Fulgencio Yegros, and included another estanciero, Pedro Juan Cavallero, and the rising Dr Francia. It lasted only two years, during which it vainly tried to define a national policy and to implement liberal principles This liberal government was the last expression of the colonial ruling class. For the estancieros had no organization and, once independence was won, they had no policy. Francia twice withdrew from the junta, alleging that some of its members were planning to sell out to Buenos Aires. Without him the junta was headless; he was almost the only politician of talent and education in the whole of Paraguay. During his absence he began to seek a kind of power base by cultivating unaligned landed proprietors but particularly the smaller estancieros and farmers of the interior and the peasants of the countryside.[56] According to the young Scots entrepreneur, John Parish Robertson, who first met Francia during the latter's absence from the junta in 1812, his preparations were careful and calculating.

He encouraged the aspirations of men who had hitherto never dreamt of obtaining power; he was all meekness and condescension to the *lower*, all hauteur to the *higher* classes of society. His plan was to imbue the country-people with a feeling that they were misgoverned by a few ignorant men devoid of merit, and to insinuate if *he* should once come back to power how different it would be. He represented to them that the object of the revolution had been to overthrow the aristocratic pretensions of Old Spain; whereas it was now apparent that these pretensions were only superseded by others more odious, because they were set up by men whom they know to be no more than their equals, some of them their inferiors.[57]

But there was a further explanation for Francia's rise to power. The burning political issue was Paraguay's relation with Buenos Aires; this was the major problem of independence, the real test of Paraguay's nationhood. It was now apparent that Francia alone among the revolutionaries possessed the necessary political acumen to deal with the pressing and devious approaches of Buenos Aires and to cope with its experienced and clever politicians. Francia thus became identified with a policy and a following. In seeking political support from alternative social groups, and in demonstrating his hard-line policy towards Buenos Aires, Francia outmanoeuvred the other members of the junta both before and after the Congress of 1813. This assembly chose Francia as one of two consuls of the Republic of Paraguay who were to share executive power between them. And it offered nothing to Buenos Aires, whose envoy returned home empty-handed, 'without union, without alliance, without treaty'.[58] Subsequent communications from Buenos Aires were returned unopened.[59]

The second consul, Yegros, was an ignorant and illiterate estanciero, utterly incapable of competing with Francia, who called him 'such an animal, such a fool'.[60] Francia summoned another congress in 1814. This too he prepared and indoctrinated. He insisted that a large number of deputies be called from all parts of the country, most of them from the lower classes. He made himself personally acquainted with the humblest deputies, cultivating, flattering, using them : 'The Indian alcalde, the small farmer, the cattle-grazier, the petty shopkeeper, the more wealthy merchant, and the substantial hacendado, all became his prey.'[61] Seven-eighths of the country votes were for Francia, and congress made him 'Supreme Dictator of the Republic' for five years.[62] Ostensibly this was simply to place power in the hands of a single executive, as most of the new nations did in the revolutionary period; and the office was apparently limited, first by a congress, which was supposed to meet once a year, and secondly by the resolution that there should be a judicial power outside the executive and that the dictator should establish an independent judiciary as soon as possible. But this was a facade : congress had no power, and to leave the appointment of the judicial power to Francia was to invite him to keep it for himself, which was precisely what he did.[63] Not content with the prospect of five years dictatorship, Francia pressed the Congress of 1 June 1816 into appointing him 'Perpetual Dictator' for the rest of his life, and into resolving that congress would only assemble 'when the dictator requires it'; and so it was dissolved, not to meet again for a quarter of a century.[64]

Dr Francia, *el Supremo,* ruled Paraguay absolutely from then until his death in 1840 at the age of seventy-four. This long term of personal rule marked the extinction of the colonial ruling class, the estancieros, as a political force, while Francia appealed *a la chusma* – to the populace. In 1820 the traditional aristocracy made a last, despairing bid for survival, and lost. A conspiratorial movement, allegedly in collusion with Ramírez, Francia's caudillo enemy in Entre Ríos, was discovered and savagely suppressed. The leaders were imprisoned, tortured, in some cases executed, their families harrassed, their property confiscated. Those who survived this reign of terror vegetated in rural isolation, impoverished by the country's stagnation, excluded from public affairs, and cut off from any communication with the outside world.

Francia was undoubtedly the most bizarre of the new Spanish American dictators. A Paraguayan creole, he was educated at the University of Córdoba del Tucumán. There he took a doctorate in theology, a strange qualification for one who, on his return to Asunción, practised law and gradually ceased to practise religion. In Asunción he also began to occupy himself with municipal affairs and to acquire a reputation of incorruptibility. When the revolution began he was in middle age, a bachelor, tall and sombre, usually to be seen with a cup of maté in one hand and a cigar in the other. He was an aloof and solitary character, a harsh ruler, an implacable and vengeful enemy, a man who never forgave or forgot. His rule was personalist and centralist, and the machinery of his government rudimentary. The dictator was not only head of state but also principal civil servant, for Paraguay suffered, as he lamented, from 'a dearth of men qualified for office'.[65] His minister of finance and secretary of state were little more than clerks. His officials outside the capital — *subdelegados* and *comandantes* — could neither initiate action nor deviate in the slightest degree from his instructions. The *jueces comisionados* who administered each village and the *administradores de pueblos* who collected taxes had even less scope for initiative. Rival institutions, already weak, were systematically stripped of any vestige of power. The Church was abused and abased. The victim of Francia's growing aversion to religion, it lost its fueros, its tithe, its schools, control over appointments, and all contact with Rome. It was deprived of power and influence and reduced to an instrument of state control. The army too was Francia's creature. In this case he did not so much control an existing institution as create a new one to his own specifications. He moulded the army into a kind of praetorian guard, an anonymous and politically silent force which produced no leader and developed no identity. Francia was its only leader; it was he who supervised the recruitment, training and equipment of this force, and fixed its optimum strength at about three thousand. The army was supplemented by a crude but effective espionage network covering the whole country, so that it seemed that one half of Paraguay was spying on the other. There were, of course, no media of communications; neither newspapers nor books were published, and people even needed permits to travel from one part of the country to another. This was Francia's regime, and it was based less on the support of any one class than on the absence of alternatives. The Spanish entrepreneurial class had been broken by the revolution for independence. The native ruling class had been destroyed by its own ineptitude and the dictator's superior skill. The mass of the population, the bland and docile Guaraní people – unorganized farmers and apolitical peasantry – were passive spectators of Francia's rise to power, content to follow and to yield. His spurious populism made no impact on the social structure and attracted no positive class allegiance to his rule.

This grotesque system could only be preserved by keeping

Paraguay in total isolation, immune from comparison with the rest of mankind. Francia hermetically sealed his country against the outside world. Paraguayans were unable to send or receive correspondence, forbidden to trade or to travel. Diplomatic exchanges with other states ceased. No one could enter or leave the country without the personal permission of the dictator, grudgingly given and easily revoked. Foreigners caught in the trap, especially after 1820, remained in Paraguay year after year, dead to the rest of the world. The French naturalist, Aimé Bonpland. was held for eight years; Artigas never returned to his native Uruguay. The policy of isolation was first imposed from 1813 as a political device; then, from 1820, it became economic and total. How can it be explained?

Isolation was originally a defence mechanism against Buenos Aires. The porteños refused to recognize Paraguay's independence, and it was only their own poverty and anarchy which prevented them from attempting to conquer the new state. If Francia distrusted Buenos Aires, his distrust of Buenos Aires's rivals among the provincial caudillos was only slightly less, and for this reason he kept out of all federal entanglements. Francia was also concerned to protect Paraguay from ideas as well as from intervention. He wanted to avoid the contagion of democracy and liberalism emanating from Buenos Aires and other revolutionary provinces which might undermine his own dictatorship. He believed that Spanish America was not ready for free institutions. He explained to John Parish Robertson that he kept Paraguay isolated 'from contamination by that foul and restless spirit of anarchy and revolution' in the rest of South America in order to preserve 'order, subordination and tranquility'.[66] In the early years of his rule, however, Francia did not seek or plan economic isolation. On the contrary, he looked for commerce with Europe, particularly with Britain.[67] He wanted British vessels to trade directly with Paraguay and to keep the river open. 'Your countrymen', he told Robertson who was already trading on a small scale, 'shall traffic in manufactures and munitions of war, and shall receive in exchange the noble products of this country.'[68] In 1814 he loaded Robertson with specimens of Paraguayan tobacco, tea, sugar and cloth, and told him to present them at the bar of the House of Commons and announce that the ruler of Paraguay wished to sign a treaty of commerce and alliance.[69] In fact Robertson got no further than Buenos Aires, and on a subsequent visit to Paraguay was peremptorily expelled. By then prison bars had gone up around Paraguay.

Paraguayans lived by trade, but their life-line was fragile. Nature placed them in an inland cul-de-sac at the end of the river system. They were at the mercy of the down-river powers, which could intercept their shipping and prevent their trading freely with American and European markets. Buenos Aires in particular was in a position to monopolize entry and exit and to exert a new economic imperialism over the Río de la Plata. Independence gave the porteños their chance; they now sought to make Buenos Aires the new metropolis of the great river complex and to usurp the customs revenue of the entire littoral. Paraguayans, on the other hand, claimed freedom of navigation of the river Plate and its affluents the Paraná, Paraguay and Uruguay, and sought unrestricted access to the sea. When this was denied them they were confirmed in their desire for independence. Buenos Aires, in turn, could think of no other way of reducing the rebels than blocking river traffic and strangling their economy. The porteños proceeded to deny Paraguay the right to trade and navigate freely by its natural outlet, the river Paraná; they taxed Paraguayan exports in the Buenos Aires customs house; and in 1817 they prohibited the import of Paraguayan tobacco.[70] In these circumstances Francia emerged as a champion of national economic interests. He soon found that Buenos Aires was not the only threat to these interests. As a consequence of separatism and civil war in the littoral the banks of the Paraná were infested by a number of hostile caudillos, all of whom began to prey on Paraguayan trade. In Corrientes, Entre Ríos and Santa Fe each ruler claimed the right to detain Paraguayan shipping and if necessary to arrest the crew, fine the captain and tax the cargoes. And they automatically confiscated any arms destined for Francia.[71] The dictator was deeply outraged: petty caudillos were attempting to make Paraguay their permanent tributary, holding her to ransom by blockade and harassment. He declared in 1823: 'Neither Buenos Aires, nor Corrientes, nor Santa Fe, nor Entre Ríos have observed or respected the law of nations; on the contrary, they have constantly violated it . . . like pirates and thieves.'[72]

Francia had few options. But he was wiser than his enemies, the porteños and the caudillos, for he appreciated that he could not win a war outside his own province. In default of force, therefore, he established from 1822 the rule of isolation: 'Because of these infamous, inhuman, arbitrary and barbarous procedures, nothing will enter Paraguay from Corrientes until freedom of navigation is established.'[73] This was the key to Francia's policy. Independence had been won from Spain; he could not tolerate that his country should now become a colony of a new metropolis. By blocking and taxing Paraguay's trade with the outside world, he argued, Buenos Aires held Paraguay

in the most abject and infamous dependence; the limit has been reached when every petty town and port on the route to Buenos Aires vilely exploits Paraguay's inertia and tolerance and seeks to establish the practice of forcing Paraguayan vessels to stop and pay tribute on the pretext that they have a right to transit dues, in denial of free navigation and as though they were sovereign masters of the river Paraguay.[74]

To free Paraguay from economic dependence on the rest of the littoral Francia imposed a twofold policy – economic autarchy and use of alternative outlets. Self-sufficiency was a drastic solution for a country of agriculturalists and exporters. It meant reducing Paraguay to a virtually subsistence economy. To close all outlets for exports would certainly hurt producers and merchants. But it would also lower the living standards of the mass of the people. It was no coincidence that this uncompromising policy was imposed only after 1822 when, having overcome conspiracy and resistance, Francia possessed absolute power. Self-sufficiency implied not only a subsistence economy but also a state-controlled economy.

Francia directed the Paraguayan economy in every detail. Farmers were assigned a production quota of grain and cotton which they had to fulfil in order to substitute for imports. The dictator established a government monopoly of yerba maté. He also planned and completed the diversification of agriculture from yerba, tobacco and sugar to rice, maize, cotton, vegetables and hides.[75] The state not only controlled the activity of private estancias but also entered directly into production on the extensive public lands at its disposal. These were assembled from various sources. The crown lands of the colonial period covered almost half of Paraguay and had never been exploited. To these had been added the lands of the Jesuit missions after the expulsion of the order in 1767. And Francia himself annexed the lands of the religious orders and the estates of political delinquents. Francia was the first Paraguayan to make this state land productive, partly by letting out a portion at moderate rents on condition of actual production, partly by developing estates operated directly by the state. These estancias de la patria, as they were called, became efficient units of production; they specialized in livestock – cattle, horses and mules – and successfully ended Paraguay's dependence on livestock imports from Entre Ríos.[76] While agriculture underwent distinct improvement under Francia, industry lagged far behind. The dictator promoted a few primitive industries, notably textiles, but these were inevitably handicapped by lack of capital and skilled labour. Some labour was found among the Indians of the former Jesuit missions; Francia brought the civil administrators of these communities under strict government control and forcibly recruited the Indians for cotton manufacture and public works.

The modest success of Francia's agricultural programme could not save the Paraguayan economy from rank stagnation. The country reverted to a subsistence level unknown since the early colonial period. Paraguay had the capacity as well as the need to export. Yet Francia persisted in his policy, refusing to negotiate with Buenos Aires, until isolation seemed to become an end in itself, a morbid introversion which took Paraguay out of the mainstream of Spanish American development. In the process Paraguay irretrievably lost valuable markets such as Chile and Peru where it had been the principal supplier of maté and tobacco. And it lost the Buenos Aires market in maté to Brazil, whose product was inferior but available.[77] Woodbine Parish, the British consul-general in Buenos Aires, made overtures to Francia in 1824–5 with the object of reopening commercial links; the dictator expressed a willingness to trade as soon as the river was open and a hope that Britain would help to open it by enforcing freedom of navigation.[78] But this was impossible, and he knew it. He also knew that isolation could not remain absolute: even Francia's economy needed an escape valve, especially as agricultural production was improving. There was a faint trickle of trade with Argentina through Pilar de Ñeembucú. But the principal outlet was the port of Itapúa in Misiones on the river Paraná, where a regulated trade with Brazil and Brazilian merchants was permitted.[79] Brazil responded with some enthusiasm, seeking as it did an understanding with Paraguay against the common enemy Buenos Aires. From 1822, therefore, a mutual trade developed between Paraguay and Brazil; in 1824 a Brazilian envoy, Correa da Cámara, was received by Francia and became consul. Paraguay exchanged sugar, maté, tobacco and other agricultural products against manufactured goods.[80] But this trade, lacking specie and credit facilities, was little more than barter and no substitute for free commerce with traditional markets in Spanish America.

Paraguay had secured independence and nationhood but at a cruel price. Francia's economic system held down living standards and impeded social change. Conditions were against the emergence of a middle sector. The entrepreneurial function in Paraguay had been fulfilled by Spaniards; ruined by taxation, isolation and political pressure, these now took refuge among the estancia class, while the embargo on foreign trade prevented their replacement by a new commercial group. In the rural sector denial of export outlets frustrated the development of commercial, as distinct from subsistence, agriculture, and deprived Paraguay of an estanciero class comparable to that in the rest of the littoral. The demise of the commercial and landowning groups did not mean the advancement of lower sectors. Francia has been subsequently credited with coming to power as the leader of a social revolution, the saviour of the Guaraní peasantry against the landed aristocracy.[81] In fact social reform was alien to the dictator's mentality, and he did nothing to disturb the basic structure of society. Negro slavery survived until 1869, and slaves were owned not only by private proprietors but also by the government on the state estancias. Paraguay even lagged behind other Spanish American states in outlawing the slave trade. Indian servitude and forced labour continued in Misiones on the secularized land of the former Jesuit missions, where government agents put the Indians to work or hired them out to private landowners. Elsewhere peonage endured and no one planned an agrarian revolution. It is true that Francia de-hispanicised Paraguayan society, expelling many peninsulares and terrorising the rest. He even issued a decree prohibiting Spaniards from marrying whites, restricting them to Indians, mestizos and mulattos in a policy of enforced mestizisation.[82] But this did not prevent the survival of a creole elite, politically crushed but clinging grimly to the remnants of a primitive social structure.

(iii) THE WAR OF GUERRILLAS IN UPPER PERU

Buenos Aires had a vital stake in Upper Peru. Up to the May revolution this mining province in the distant Andes had been, like the Banda Oriental and Paraguay, part of the viceroyalty of the Río de la Plata. When Buenos Aires revolted Lima moved quickly to claim its ancient patrimony and, with the eager co-operation of local colonial officials, to reintegrate it into the royalist stronghold of Peru. Buenos Aires refused to accept this secession and made the liberation of Upper Peru one of the essential objectives of the revolution. Politically Upper Peru was a challenge to the ideals of 1810. Economically its silver production had become an important item in the overseas trade of Buenos Aires. And strategically it was an obvious springboard for Spanish counter-insurgency operations. The porteños had allies among the patriots in Upper Peru, and believed it would be a simple matter for a liberating expedition to join with the politicians of the towns and the guerrillas of the mountains in a concerted campaign to drive out the Spaniards.

Yet Upper Peru was not an easy terrain for a war of liberation. The failure of the revolution of 1809, the reluctance of the creole aristocracy to subvert the social order in a population where they were vastly outnumbered by Indians and mestizos, the military resources and resourcefulness of the viceroy in Lima, all made it difficult for the forces of liberation to secure Upper Peru. But the revolutionary cause had one asset. This mountain corner of the Hispanic world was made by nature for irregular warfare.

And independence was first expressed as guerrilla resistance to royalist armies of occupation.

The guerrillas of Upper Peru, the montoneros of the peaks, deserts and jungles, assembled spontaneously in bands of various sizes, and were held together less by military discipline than by a common, and sometimes temporary, purpose and by allegiance to a successful caudillo. Individuals contributed arms and horses, or acquired them in action, and expected a return from operations. And for supplies they lived on the country, drawing an income from voluntary or forced exactions on the towns and villages they controlled, from crops such as *coca* which were taken and traded, from estates whose pro-royalist proprietors had fled to the towns, and from the Indians who were forced to yield services and foodstuffs.[83] Each valley, each mountain, each village had its partisan group and its petty caudillo, who made their locality a minor zone of insurrection, a *republiqueta*, where local patriotism burgeoned into local independence. There were six major foci of resistance, each under the command of a senior guerrilla chief.[84] In the north, on the shores of Lake Titicaca, the priest Ildefonso de las Muñecas operated out of Ayata, and menaced the route from Lower Peru. In the central zone there were two extensive republiquetas. Juan Antonio Alvarez de Arenales commanded a band based on Mizque and Vallegrande, harassing communications between Cochabamba, Chuquisaca and Santa Cruz; the other, the republiqueta of Ayopaya hidden in the mountains and jungles between La Paz and Cochabamba, fell under the violent rule of Miguel Lanza after bloody disputes for the leadership. In the south, covering the route from Argentina over which the liberating armies passed, lay the republiqueta of José Vicente Camargo. The capital itself, Chuquisaca, was screened by another partisan group, that of Manuel Ascensio Padilla. And in the far east lay the extensive republiqueta of Ignacio Warnes, based on Santa Cruz de la Sierra and providing the ultimate refuge of all the guerrillas.

These mounted resistance fighters played only a limited role in the war of independence. Numerically the guerrillas were never very strong, and even the principal groups comprised only a few hundred men each. But they exposed some of the gaps in Spanish defences. They dominated communications between towns and immobilized the enemy. They pinned down royalist forces and diverted them from other theatres of war. And until 1816 they frustrated effective Spanish control of Upper Peru and forced the authorities to mount a major campaign against them. This the guerrillas were not equipped to resist and, with the exception of the Ayopaya band which fought on until 1825, they were destroyed in 1816 by the Spanish security forces, their leaders killed and their bands scattered. They were thus not a decisive force for independence in 1825. This was predictable, for the guerrillas were not strongly motivated politically. They had no programme and their activities were not geared to a war of independence. It is true that the mass of the guerrillas fought for independence, but not necessarily national independence; they fought for independence of Spanish law and order, of political and fiscal control. The montoneros were a mixture of nonconformists, adventurers and delinquents, seizing the opportunity of metropolitan weakness to fight private and local wars in which booty was an important object. The military individualism of the caudillos precluded concerted action against the Spanish forces, and tactically individual bands were often ready to do a deal with the enemy. While they lacked a clear social programme, the guerrillas were more than bandits and they appealed unequivocally to the popular sectors. They were not an Indian movement. The caudillos and officers were creoles of middle and lower rank, and their immediate followers were mestizos. They regarded the Indians as allies, though not perhaps as equals, recruiting them when they could and drawing on their services, but rarely integrating them into the guerrilla ranks. When they used them as combat troops it was as auxiliaries in separate units, crudely armed with lances, slings and cudgels and liable to disperse after a given engagement. But normally they used the Indians as a kind of service corps, producers of food, transporters of goods and equipment; the guerrillas in effect continued the system of taking tribute and forced labour from the Indians, as did the liberating armies from Argentina. The Spaniards, of course, exacted similar services and their record was not much better than that of the creoles, but as they did not dominate the countryside they had less access to the Indian population.[85]

The guerrillas spoke of fighting for the patria, but this did not yet mean the nation. Patria in Upper Peru simply meant freedom and was accompanied by nominal acknowledgment of the revolutionary movement in the Río de la Plata, where freedom already existed. But Buenos Aires was over a thousand miles away and perhaps distance made its authority more acceptable. Even when its armies reached out to Upper Peru the guerrillas at first regarded them as senior allies and collaborated with them. But this sentiment of allegiance did not survive the early years of the revolution, when it became clear that the porteño armies aimed not only to liberate Upper Peru but also to attach it in a subordinate position to Buenos Aires, when they behaved like depredators rather than allies, and when they finally retreated in ignominious defeat. Then the political orientation of Upper Peru would turn away from Buenos Aires towards self-determination.

The first of the liberating expeditions, or 'auxiliary armies' as they were called, arrived in a blaze of glory. Having wiped out a pocket of royalist resistance in Córdoba and carried the revolution to Salta and Tucumán, it proceeded to Upper Peru in October 1810, pushing its way through the spectacular passes of the Andes into the altiplano. There, on 7 November, it defeated a royalist force at Suipacha, a victory which opened the gates of Potosí to the revolution; soon the whole of Upper Peru – Chuquisaca, Cochabamba, Oruro and La Paz – battered but unbroken by the repression of 1809, declared for the revolution. It was a premature triumph. The liberating army, nominally commanded by a porteño soldier Antonio González Balcarce, was in fact under the direction of a political commissioner, the humourless and fanatical Castelli, who knew Upper Peru from his student days at the University of San Francisco Xavier in Chuquisaca but was otherwise out of touch with reality. He claimed to offer freedom and military assistance, but his proclamations, cast in language of extravagant pomposity, masked a hard and cruel purpose. He initiated a rule of terror which soon alerted even the patriots.[86] Royal officials were shot, Spaniards penalized, and the patriots treated as mere provincials. Audiencia President Vicente Nieto, Intendant Francisco de Paula Sanz, and General José de Córdova were shot without trial in the main square of Potosí, in spite of local pleas for clemency and for no other crime than being royal officials. Castelli then asserted himself politically. He personally appointed officials and remodelled the administration, regardless of local interests, and he promised death to anyone who opposed or even criticized. Meanwhile the auxiliary army was on the rampage, plundering the country, terrorizing anyone who stood in its way and many who just stayed at home, and behaving suspiciously like an army of occupation. While Castelli and his forces were making the Upper Peruvians think twice about 'liberation', the royalist army under General José Manuel de Goyeneche was regrouping on the other side of the river Desaguadero. Castelli, as lacking in military ability as he was in political judgement and obsessed with the illusion of advancing upon Lima itself, walked into a trap and was defeated at Huaqui (20 June 1811), if 'defeat' it was, for the patriot army simply disintegrated at sight of the enemy and fled with very few casualties. As a contemporary remarked, this was 'a disgraceful event in which the enemy became the victor without winning any victory'.[87] The behaviour of the auxiliary army was even more discreditable in retreat than in attack; and in Potosí the people rose up and massacred one unit, causing more casualties than the battle of Huaqui. Having helped themselves to the contents of the Casa de Moneda (mint), the 'liberators' retreated in disorder into Salta. So in the eyes of Upper Peruvians the first expedition brought them nothing and took their silver. Castelli was recalled to stand trial in Buenos Aires where he died less than a year later in disgrace.

The royalists too overreached themselves and were defeated in their invasion of the Río de la Plata at the battle of Salta (20 February 1813). In the euphoria of victory the porteños dispatched a second expedition to Upper Peru in 1813, this time under General Belgrano. The new commander and his forces were a better advertisement for Buenos Aires than their predecessors, but militarily they were just as vulnerable. And they were confronted by an able and experienced Spanish general, the recently arrived Joaquín de la Pezuela, who briskly brought Belgrano to two battles and defeated him each time.[88] Again, adversity brought out the worst in the porteños. Belgrano himself was responsible for the monstrous, though happily abortive, plan of blowing up the Casa de Moneda in Potosí and with it presumably the entire city centre, 'a barbarous project whose fulfillment would have done more damage to the credit of the revolution than to the enemy'.[89] Again the royalists over-estimated their own prospects by invading Tucumán, and again they were defeated, this time by the newly appointed San Martín. But San Martín had no desire to retrace the disastrous steps of Castelli and Belgrano. He was already convinced that the way to Lima lay not north through Upper Peru but west via Chile and the Pacific. And he left his command of the army of the north in order to effect his great strategy.

Meanwhile command of the third expedition to Upper Peru in 1815 fell to General José Rondeau, a second-rate soldier and something of a fool. He had the best chance of all the liberators, for the guerrilla leaders had intensified their operations and were pinning down the security forces, while the Spaniards themselves had been forced to divert some of their units to deal with the rebellion of Pumacahua in Peru.[90] But Rondeau had no control over his troops; they plundered on a scale unprecedented even among the liberating expeditions, and when they were not looting they were drinking. Pezuela outmanoeuvred Rondeau with effortless precision and annihilated the third auxiliary army on the plains of Sipe Sipe on 29 November 1815.

Sipe Sipe confirmed the Spanish reconquest of Upper Peru. Rondeau had virtually no army even for retreat. Only the guerrillas remained, and they now lost confidence in Buenos Aires. They also began to lose the war, for the royalists followed up their victory by mounting an anti-insurgency campaign, and success enabled them to use Upper Peru as a base for incursions into Salta and Tucumán. But in the long run Sipe Sipe also helped the Upper Peruvians to discover their own identity. With the collapse of military assistance from Buenos Aires, the resistance movement in Upper Peru ceased to defer to its senior ally and began to develop a growing self-awareness and an incipient sense of nationality. 'After Sipe Sipe', Mitre remarked, 'the enlightened classes of Upper Peru were determined to form a nation apart.'[91] As for Buenos Aires, apart from a minor raid under Colonel Aráoz de la Madrid in 1817, this was the last attempt to strike northwards. From now on San Martín's strategy prevailed, and revolutionary policy looked westwards to Chile and the Pacific.

Monteagudo, with characteristic extremism, attributed the defeat of Castelli to 'the crime of lenity', to excessive toleration of royalists. He was wrong. The porteño armies of the north, hastily raised and relying to some extent on mestizos recruited in Upper Peru itself, were easily demoralized by defeat at the hands of Spanish regular troops. Their higher command, civilians turned soldiers, did not bear comparison with the royalists. The Spanish army in Upper Peru, a skilled and experienced body, reinforced after 1815 by troops from other theatres of war in Europe and America, was simply the outer bastion of Spain's great fortress in America, the viceroyalty of Peru. Its commanders were experienced professional officers. General Pezuela, conservative, absolutist and military-minded, relentlessly destroyed organized resistance in Upper Peru, and was rewarded after Sipe Sipe by appointment as viceroy. His principal colleagues in Upper Peru were General Juan Ramírez who crushed the rebellion of Pumacahua and later became president of the audiencia of Quito, and Colonel Pedro Antonio de Olañeta, a hard-headed businessman from Salta, a fanatical royalist who fought for the Spanish cause until his death in battle in 1825. Compared with this successful team, the porteños were amateurs, their officers incompetent, their ranks split by the factional politics of Buenos Aires. Yet the adverse balance of military power was not the only cause of their defeat. Their position in Upper Peru was already undermined before the battles of Huaqui and Sipe Sipe : it was undermined by their own reputation. They bore the unfortunate stigma of social reformers.

A revolution in Upper Peru could not ignore the Indians.[92] The revolutionaries of La Paz in 1809 had sought to appeal to the Indian masses and to mobilize them, though in a vague and insincere way. According to Viceroy Abascal, the *paceños* attempted 'to engage in their unworthy cause the innocent natives of the country, exploiting their very rusticity and ignorance'.[93] The porteño armies of the north also addressed themselves to the Indians : this was the policy established by the junta in Buenos Aires. The object was to end Indian servitude and to convert the Indians into salaried workers and consumers. Castelli was instructed to 'conquer the will of the Indians', and in his progress through Upper Peru he halted in Indian villages to explain revolutionary policy, proclaimed the message of freedom brought by the May revolution, gave interviews to caciques, and raised them up from their prostrate obeisances, saying 'all that is finished now, we are all equal'.[94] Castelli issued instructions for enfranchizing the Indians according to a decree of the junta that in each intendancy they should elect a deputy of their own to a general congress. From Charcas he delivered a manifesto to counter what he described as a fraudulent proclamation of Viceroy Abascal which had offered the Indians education, honours and offices. 'I have a great interest in your welfare,' declared Castelli, 'not only personally but as a matter of policy', and he gave an undertaking that the junta of Buenos Aires 'will regard you always as brothers and equals'.[95] On 25 May 1811, among the Inca ruins of Tihuanaco, he celebrated the anniversary of the May revolution with a parade of his troops, firing of guns and blowing of trumpets; and before the concourse of Indians whom he had summoned he issued a decree suppressing abuses, exempting the Indians from charges and tributes, distributing lands, establishing schools and declaring 'the Indian is equal to any other national'.[96]

These declamatory promises did not automatically win the Indians to the revolutionary cause, nor did they go unchallenged by the royalists; these, too, addressed themselves to the caciques and argued that the revolution held nothing for their people. While he was regrouping at the Desaguadero, General Goyeneche made much propaganda among the indigenous population over Castelli's failure to fulfil his promises; and he was able to secure if not the support of the Indians at least their neutrality and the bonus of intelligence reports on the patriot forces. When the first auxiliary army was defeated and forced into disorderly retreat, it pillaged the lands of Indians in its path, who were easily persuaded by the royalists to cut off stragglers. The royalists could usually find Indian allies, as they did in 1811, when they used Pumacahua and three thousand of his followers to suppress the rebellion of cacique Juan Manuel Cázerez in the province of La Paz.[97] But neither side won the war of words for the soul of the Indian. Apolitical and largely ignorant of the issues involved, the Indians were never reliable allies. When they were not dragged in as the beasts of burden of the wars of independence, they remained passive spectators, rightly divining that the revolution offered them little more than did the colonial regime.

Without gaining the confidence of the Indians, the patriots said enough to frighten the creole aristocracy. Belgrano was more cautious than Castelli and forbade his army to contravene the local 'usos y costumbres', that is the existing social structure. But this attempt to reassure the creoles was frustrated when he too indulged in pro-Indian demagogy in order to procure provisions and support; and he did in fact receive the alliance of the Indian caudillo Baltasar Cárdenas. Belgrano reiterated that the intention of the Buenos Aires government was to liberate the Indians from servitude and forced labour, including agricultural duties and the mining mita.[98] Again, this was not implemented, nor was there time to do so. Society could not be changed overnight by mere decree. It was easy for the agents of Buenos Aires to proclaim Indian emancipation in a country which was not their own, but without the agreement of local creoles such a policy was meaningless. The most powerful social groups in Upper Peru reacted strongly to the Indian policy of the auxiliary armies. The mine-owners believed that the liberation of the Indians and in particular the suppression of the labour mita threatened their social predominance and economic prospects. They joined the counter-revolution with arms and money. The landed proprietors, too, abhorred the egalitarianism shown towards Indians, mestizos and mulattos, and resented the threat to their labour supply. After Sipe Sipe the Upper Peruvian aristocracy were openly royalist and supported the security forces against the partisans, whom they feared and hated. When the Spaniards wiped out the guerrillas in 1815–6, the field was left clear for the creole ruling class, who remained loyal to Spain until it was obvious that the Spanish cause was doomed. It was into their hands, not to the porteños or the guerrillas, that the independence of Upper Peru fell.

Meanwhile the guerrillas fulfilled an important role even in their death throes. It was to destroy them that Viceroy Pezuela reinforced the army of Upper Peru, thus diverting troops – some 3,500 – from use in Chile and Peru. The failure to reinforce General Marcó's army in Chile in anticipation of San Martín's trans-Andean expedition was due in large part to this decision to augment the army of Upper Peru.[99]

FOUR *Chile, Liberated and Liberator*

CHILE WON INDEPENDENCE later than the Río de la Plata but sooner than Upper Peru. Remote from the great foci of revolution in the subcontinent, the colony lay under the menacing shadow of royalist Peru, within range of viceregal arms and ships. Yet Chile's sense of identity was more developed than that of Upper Peru and its ruling class less fearful of revolution. Society was racially homogeneous. The people numbered no more than eight hundred thousand, over half of them mestizos, with a powerful creole elite of land-owners, merchants and mine-owners.[1] While they heavily out-numbered the twenty thousand Spaniards, the creoles faced little demographic pressure from the coloured sectors. Negroes, zambos and mulattos amounted to only twenty thousand, of whom about five thousand were slaves employed mainly in domestic service.[2] And the Indians were a military rather than a social problem, concentrated as they were – some hundred thousand of them – beyond the river Bío-Bío and forming in effect an independent and hostile state.

This mestizo society was enclosed within the narrow central valley between the Andes and the Pacific; Coquimbo marked the desert frontier to the north, and the Bío-Bío the Indian frontier in the south. Economic activity was based on the production and sale of agricultural goods, chiefly livestock extracts and grain for the Peruvian market, while a small copper output found a market in Buenos Aires and Europe. In a limited economy of this kind *comercio libre* was not a major issue. Geography, not monopoly, restricted Chile's prospects and kept her remote from the major shipping routes. Colonial monopoly was relaxed under the later Bourbons; access to international markets was easier and foreign manufactures were in greater supply. Chile's difficulty was to earn enough to pay for expanding imports; failure to do so meant that the market was glutted, bankruptcies were frequent, local industry declined, and precious metals flowed out of the country.[3] At the close of empire the Chilean economy needed freedom, but not free trade; rather it needed freedom to impose its own protection, to arrange its own taxes, to control its own growth. Above all, in accordance with the political economy of the Enlightenment, it wanted freedom to expand, to develop resources neglected by the metropolis, to earn more by producing more.[4] Demands of this kind, however, were made chiefly by intellectuals who spoke only for themselves. Chile lacked a strong entrepreneurial class capable of representing business interests or challenging the preponderance of the landed gentry.

The social structure was built around land, owned by the fortunate few, worked by the miserable many. The landed proprietors of the central valley were the dominant social group, headed by some two hundred creole families, strengthened by entrants from commerce and mining, secure in their property and status, and spilling over into other occupations.[5] In the course of the eighteenth century the great livestock estancias underwent further expansion through the development of arable agriculture. The haciendas, as they were now called, were commercial enterprises producing for the livestock and grain markets of Pacific South America.[6] They were exploited directly by the hacendados, managed by an administrator, while the proprietor himself lived in Santiago, looking after his legal interests and returning to the hacienda at harvest or slaughter time. The great haciendas came to monopolize almost all the land of the central valley, and they now entered a period of notable stability lasting until about 1850. The growth of arable farming and of grain export to Peru increased the demand for labour. Negro slaves were expensive, and a hacienda would employ only a few as domestics or artisans. The hacienda preferred to hire its labourers, to reduce them to the status of tied dependants, to allow them plots of land in return for payment in money or in kind, but increasingly in return for personal labour on the hacienda. These were the *inquilinos*, no longer tenants but serfs, products of increased commercialization and 'cerealization' of agriculture in the eighteenth century, and victims perhaps of growing class consciousness.[7] The inquilinos were drawn largely from the mestizos, and to a smaller degree from the castes and poor whites. They were worse off than slaves, for these were at least employed in household or semi-skilled work; and after independence, while slavery was abolished, the inquilinos were subject to more closely defined and more onerous labour services. Meanwhile their standard of living was painfully low : 'Nothing is more common than to see the same hands which have harvested rich crops, and in the same fields, held out to beg alms and bread. . .'.[8]

It was logical that the creole aristocracy, masters of the countryside, should aspire to be masters too of their country. In the first place, in an age of rising taxation, they needed political power to protect their economic interests. For fifty years before 1810 the creoles maintained constant opposition to imperial taxation, reaching a peak of hostility to the wartime demands of 1805–6.[9] In other respects the creole elite adapted easily to Bourbon policy. They desired, of course, access to office and privilege, but they preferred to acquire these through infiltration of the bureaucracy rather than confrontation. The key to political success was membership of a family alliance, a kinship group, a faction, which linked creoles and peninsulares, enabling Spain to coopt many Chileans and the latter to influence the administration.[10]

Yet political differences were growing. Behind the opposition to taxation and the claims to office lay a new sense of Chilean identity.[11] As this grew in strength it was directed first against the nearest manifestation of foreign power, Peru. A victim of its geographical remoteness and dearth of export commodities, Chile was utterly dependent on the Peruvian market for the sale of its grain. The superior influence, wealth and power of Peru enabled it to force down prices, usually with viceregal support. Chileans resented their satellite status and fought against it.[12] First, Lima lost its traditional monopoly of the trans-Atlantic trade and of the Pacific coastal trade, and in 1795 the Chileans acquired their own consulado. In 1778 Chile was promoted in status from province to captaincy-general, and in 1798 it won administrative independence of Peru. By 1810 Chile had virtually emancipated itself from Peruvian tutelage; in the process it had grown in maturity and further heightened its self-awareness.

Regional self-consciousness was expressed and nurtured in Chilean literature. Among the first literary exponents of this spirit were Chilean Jesuit exiles such as Felipe Gómez de Vidaurre and Juan Ignacio Molina, who wrote with pride of their homeland, its human and natural resources, its history and institutions. These Jesuit writings made articulate an incipient sense of nationality which had already taken root in Chilean minds. A whole generation of creoles, Manuel de Salas, José Antonio de Rojas, Juan Egaña, paid literary tribute to their country and affirmed their patriotism in stylish if exaggerated prose.[13] After a long period of development the growth of Chilean identity was suddenly quickened by events. The crisis of 1808–10 forced the creole leaders to act like nationalists, and by 1810 the concept of patria was coming to mean Chile alone rather than the whole Hispanic world.[14] As early as 1811 the Chilean journalist Camilo Henríquez regarded the existence of independent nationality as proven : 'In the present circumstances [Chile] should be considered as a nation. . . . Everything impels her to seek her security and happiness on her own.'[15] Bernardo O'Higgins believed that national identity was self-evident, that Chile was emancipated by its age and maturity. These sentiments, of course, were not shared by the lower classes, who with no stake in the nation had no sense of nationality. Many of them fought on the royalist side, and these O'Higgins harangued in frankly nationalist terms : 'Do not forget that you are Chileans, our brothers, from the same homeland and with the same religion, and that you have to be free in spite of the tyrants who are deceiving you.'[16]

Incipient nationalism undermined the basic assumptions of Spanish rule and loosened the bonds between the Chilean ruling class and their sovereign. When, in 1808, the sovereign was deposed by Napoleon, the fabric of empire began to fall apart. After recent experience of good government, Chile was then under the despotic rule of Governor Francisco Antonio García Carrasco, whose clumsy policy in the next two years aggravated the crisis.[17] Ruling with the support of a Spanish faction and in narrowly Spanish interests, he quickly alienated the creole aristocracy. His reaction to the May revolution in Buenos Aires was to apply yet further repression, and, to set an example, he imprisoned three well-known and respected creoles. Anxious for their lives and property, the Chilean aristocracy were prepared to intervene, and the cabildo of Santiago sought to depose the governor by force. In order to preserve some measure of control, the audiencia itself deposed Carrasco (16 July 1810) and replaced him by a Chilean, Mateo de Toro Zambrano, Conde de la Conquista, a wealthy and harmless octogenarian, who was manifestly a front for the aristocracy.[18] But rearguard action could not stem the flood of more radical solutions or the pressure of their chief advocate, the cabildo of Santiago, which had become a vehicle of creole reformist ideas.[19] A great political debate developed, and it was argued that the Spanish people had no sovereignty over America, Spanish juntas no validity, and Spanish officials no credentials. A cabildo abierto was summoned (18 September 1810), a governing junta established, and provision made for calling a national congress. The junta was composed of upper-class creoles and Spaniards, and in giving the creoles five out of seven seats it reflected a new balance of power. Otherwise it was not a noticeably radical body, representing rather a mixture of 'tradition and reform'.[20]

Santiago thus followed the example of Buenos Aires. And it did so in a torrent of overt loyalism to Ferdinand vii. But what did this mean, and how long could it last? Could Spanish officials survive without a source of authority? Was not *de facto* separation a revolutionary situation in itself? There were roughly two answers to these problems, reformist and revolutionary. The reformists wanted to end colonial oppression and economic restriction and to establish home rule within a Spanish framework; they therefore demanded a congress and a constitution. The revolutionaries went further : for them loyalty to Ferdinand was no more than a mask behind which they shielded their real intent – the end of colonial rule in any form and the complete independence of Chile. The justification was nothing less than a statement of popular sovereignty. The anonymous author of the *Catecismo político cristiano* (1810), a prolonged argument for independent institutions and republican government, maintained that in the event of the government's dissolution by the death or imprisonment of the king, 'authority returns to the people from whom it came', and these alone have the right to form a new government.[21] In 1810 the revolutionaries were a minority. Future independists like Juan Egaña and Manuel de Salas still stopped short of outright commitment, José Antonio de Rojas and Juan Martínez de Rozas led those who sought true liberation; but perhaps the least equivocal revolutionary was Bernardo O'Higgins.

Bernardo was the son of Ambrosio O'Higgins, an Irishman in the Spanish colonial service who, at the time of Bernardo's birth in 1778, was intendant of Concepción, and subsequently Governor of Chile and Viceroy of Peru. Bernardo was taken from his Chilean mother and received much of his education in England. There, in 1798, under the influence of Miranda, he was converted to the cause of independence and became 'nourished in the liberal principles and love of liberty which at that time burned too fiercely in the hearts of European youth'.[22] He returned to Chile in 1802 to take over the hacienda Canteras which he inherited from his father, and to live the life of a rich landowner, a leader of southern society. In 1810 he joined the party of Martínez de Rozas in Concepción, raised a militia force for the junta, and prepared to leave the seclusion and the security of his hacienda. In 1811 he became deputy for Los Angeles to the national congress in Santiago.[23] O'Higgins entered revolutionary politics with some reluctance, preferring the life of a farmer; but the decision once taken was absolute. He was convinced that the movement of 1810 was a revolution and that it must be maintained. He wrote to his Argentine friend

Terrada: 'Since the 25 of May your sole object has been independence from Spain and the establishment of republican institutions. But in Chile neither your uncle nor Rozas nor I have dared to declare openly that this has been our real aim from the beginning of our revolution.'[24]

O'Higgins expressed the viewpoint of a hard core of revolutionaries in Santiago and Concepcíon. But how was this minority able to mobilize a majority? How did the revolutionaries convert the reformists? In the first place, rule by Spain meant in effect rule by Peru, which in the circumstances of 1810 naturally became the base of Spanish power in South America. Chile could not tolerate rule by this alien and traditionally hostile neighbour. Secondly, the revolutionaries were undoubtedly right and were proved right by the Spaniards themselves. No Spanish government would offer home rule or equal status; neither liberals nor absolutists had any policy for America other than unconditional surrender to imperial authority. There was thus no place for reformism, and in the years after 1810 the reformists were thrown into the arms of the revolutionaries and helped to form a larger body of *patriotas*. But these still had to win over the rest of Chilean society, which was deeply divided over the great political issues of the day.

Between 1810 and 1814 Chile was an incipient nation with government and institutions of its own. Without a formal declaration of independence it eased its way out of the Spanish empire, engaged in political discussion, experimented with representative government, and acquired the habits of independence. This was the Patria Vieja, the old fatherland which pioneered the way to nationhood. The junta of 1810, dominated by the experienced creole official Juan Martínez de Rozas, inaugurated a series of liberal reforms, including the decree of 21 February 1811 opening Chile's ports to international trade, a decree which, whatever its practical effects, was certainly an exercise in autonomy.[25] The audiencia, a focus of pro-Spanish interests, was dissolved. And the provisional constitution of 1812 stated that 'no decree issued by any authority or tribunal outside the territory of Chile will have any effect'. The progress of revolution, however, did not appeal to all sectors of Chile's ruling class, and it would be a mistake to regard the landed aristocracy as a united group or party. O'Higgins identified three sections: the *godos*, who were Spanish and creole royalists; the *indiferentes*, who occupied a noncommittal position in the centre; and the *patriotas*, who stood for outright independence.[26] The meeting of the national congress from 4 July 1811, Chile's first outlet for opinion, brought these divisions into the open. The assembly was dominated by the conservative wing of the landed aristocracy led by the Larraín family, and the radicals of the Rozas faction found themselves outnumbered. Congress began to apply the brakes on political change, and formed a second executive junta to its own liking. In these circumstances Rozas and the radicals withdrew to Concepción where they set up a provincial junta and sought to preserve the revolution. But congress in turn was outmanoeuvred, for it was first purged then dissolved by a newcomer to the revolutionary scene, José Miguel Carrera, a twenty-six year old veteran of the peninsular war.

Carrera returned to Chile convinced that 'the age of American independence has arrived and no one can prevent it'.[27] He was backed by a powerful landed and military family who regarded Chile almost as a private concern, and he was fired with ambition for personal power. This he procured by a virtual *coup d'état* (15 November) with independence as his object but little more, for he had no political programme. But he did have a greater military following than any of his rivals and this enabled him to confront Rozas in the first half of 1812 and to have him deported. The field was now clear. In a sense Carrera answered to the revolution's need of a military caudillo; it had not had time to develop robust institutions of its own and was faltering for lack of leadership. Carrera provided this. He was able to control the patriot army, and to give the revolution the military organization which it needed; and as an aristocrat he reassured, if only for a time, the creole ruling class. He also enjoyed some general support, and his regime had faint populist undertones. But these were deceptive. For a man who claimed that 'the people have never been heard', Carrera was singularly reticent in voicing their needs.[28] Nevertheless, under his direction the revolution gained a new political momentum – and new recruits, especially in the fields of journalism and propaganda. And it was now, in the pages of the *Aurora de Chile*, that Camilo Henríquez sounded the basic claims and hopes of the Chilean revolution. But it was almost inevitable that a military caudillo should provoke rival factions among the aristocracy. One opposition group centred around the Larraín's, a powerful and extensive family network. And the 'constitutional' wing of the revolution looked to O'Higgins, who in the south was the political heir of Rozas. Finally, while he disrupted the revolution at home, Carrera also invited royalist retribution from Peru.

By the beginning of 1813 Viceroy Abascal was convinced that the Chilean patriots were aiming at independence and that they did not command mass support. He therefore sent a small force under Brigadier Antonio Pareja to crush the insurgents and force them to submit unconditionally to Spanish rule. The Chileans were not strong militarily, they were weakened by internecine strife, and they possessed no naval power. So the Spanish expedition was able to disembark in the south, take Concepción, and advance northwards up the central valley where it was joined by many Chilean sympathizers, making this a civil war. Military stalemate induced further opposition to Carrera, who, in spite of his dictator's power, proved incapable of defeating the royalists. The opposition placed its hopes in O'Higgins, who had already distinguished himself in a number of minor engagements, and offered him the leadership. But O'Higgins still preferred to follow rather than lead; arguing that change of command would endanger the war effort, he vacillated badly before he eventually (9 December 1813) accepted appointment as commander-in-chief.[29] He had little to command, and the hiatus had weakened the patriot position. Abascal struck again, sending in a second force to stiffen the Chilean royalists early in 1814. O'Higgins was a novice compared with his professional opponents; he was forced to cede Talca and to fall back on a brittle defensive. He was glad to accept an armistice (3 May 1814) under which Chile was to have some autonomy and open trade in return for accepting the Spanish Constitution of 1812 and the sovereignty of Ferdinand vii. But the patriots had little to bargain with, weakened as they were by civil war between the forces of O'Higgins and Carrera, who had managed to reinstate himself as head of government in Santiago. Abascal repudiated the armistice and dispatched a third wave of reinforcements under General Mariano Osorio; these consisted of veteran troops fresh from the peninsular war, and they were of course a united force. O'Higgins and Carrera, on the other hand, could not reintegrate their forces in time effectively to confront the royalists. The latter won a decisive victory at the battle of Rancagua (1–2 October 1814), where in spite of O'Higgins's heroic efforts, the revolutionaries suffered a major disaster and lost the majority of their forces.[30]

After Rancagua, O'Higgins and Carrera fled across the Andes to Mendoza, while Osorio entered Santiago in triumph, boasting to the Viceroy of Peru that his enthusiastic reception convinced him that 'the caudillos of the insurrection and their deluded followers had never ruled men's hearts; Rancagua will cause their name to be remembered with horror for all time'.[31] He dismantled the Patria Vieja and restored the pre–1810 order. But he could not restore the pristine political innocence of Chile. The Patria Vieja had been the forum of a great ideological debate, and it was in these years that 'the political consciousness of the ruling creole elite in Chile was largely transformed'.[32] Theorists like Juan Egaña and Camilo Henríquez elaborated the pure liberal doctrines of sovereignty of the people, representative government, written constitutions, rights of liberty, security, property and equality. And what the ideologists of independence left undone the Spaniards themselves completed. For they followed up their victory at Rancagua with a policy not of reconciliation but of repression. The military campaigns of 1813–4, unsuccessful for the creoles in the short term, had actually served the cause of independence by widening the gulf between patriots and royalists. This was the first miscalculation of Viceroy Abascal. The second was the counter-revolution. In 1815 Osorio was succeeded as governor by Francisco Casimiro Marcó del Pont, who immediately imposed a reign of terror on the beleaguered country.[33] Creoles were hauled before special courts to prove their loyalty. Revolutionary leaders were imprisoned on the island of Juan Fernández while their trials dragged on endlessly. Property was confiscated, houses were destroyed, forced loans exacted. This indiscriminate repression, falling on creoles of all political views, made Spanish rule an object of universal revulsion. The degrading experience of

1814–17 alienated the vast majority of Chileans from Spanish rule and brought the desire for independence to a peak.[34] In the countryside guerrilla bands began to operate and to infiltrate the towns. And across the Andes a great liberating army was being formed.

(ii) SAN MARTÍN AND THE ARMY OF THE ANDES

Rancagua was part of a pattern of defeat. The years 1814–16 were years of depression for the whole revolutionary movement in South America. With the end of the peninsular war and the restoration of Ferdinand vii Spain began to strike hard in America. In the north General Morillo's army crushed the Venezuelans and New Granadans. In Upper Peru the royalists threw back the last porteño army of liberation and appeared poised to descend upon Tucumán. In Chile the counter-revolution was dominant. By 1816, as a British observer noted, 'it was impossible for appearances to be more unfavourable to the revolutionary cause'.[35] But on the ruins of the first revolution the liberators created a second surge of emancipation, and this became a pincer movement on a vast continental scale, converging on Peru from north and south. The northern movement was led by Bolívar, the southern by San Martín.

In January 1814 San Martín was appointed commander of the battered army of the north. He briskly set to work to improve the defences of Tucumán, and it was now that he began to show that organizing ability which became the key to his military success.[36] It was now, too, that he became convinced of the folly of the northern strategy of the revolution. In April he was granted permission to retire to Córdoba for health reasons and he relinquished command of the army of the north. In August he requested and received from the Posadas administration the governorship of Cuyo, and at the beginning of September he set up his headquarters at Mendoza. He had left the army of the north; he now had to create the army of the Andes. His strategy was based on the thesis that the South American revolution could not be secure until the heart of Spanish power in Peru had been destroyed; that the northern route to Peru was closed; and that the way ahead was by a gigantic flanking movement, across the Andes to Chile, then up the Pacific in a seaborne invasion of Peru. After Rancagua this presupposed that Chile too would first have to be liberated, and in 1815 San Martín estimated that he would need an expeditionary force of four thousand.[37] These plans coincided with the interests of the Chilean revolution and appealed to O'Higgins and most of the Chilean *émigrés*.

As he approached his fortieth year, San Martín left a vivid impression on his English friend, Commander William Bowles, who described him as 'tall, strongly formed, with a dark complexion and marked countenance. He is perfectly well bred . . . simple and abstemious.'[38] Bowles noted that he was liberal in his instincts, knowledgeable and widely read, with a fanatical devotion to work, yet without personal ambition or aquisitiveness. To his troops he was a hard disciplinarian, but he earned their allegiance through his care for their welfare. As a soldier he had two great qualities, the ability to think and plan on a large scale, and a positive genius for organization. He now needed all his resources of mind and will, for he had to prepare his trans-Andean expedition in the face of two appalling obstacles – the creeping anarchy which threatened to engulf the whole of the Río de la Plata, and a paralyzing poverty in the public sector. Yet from late 1814 he began to translate his vision into reality, converting Mendoza into a military as well as a civil headquarters, and making Cuyo in effect into a separate province isolated from the anarchy surrounding it and geared economically and psychologically to the demands of war.[39]

The greatest problem, perhaps, was financial, for the United Provinces had insufficient revenue for even ordinary expenditure, and its economic position was precarious until the 1820s. Cuyo itself, with a population of some forty-three thousand, had a relatively healthy economy based on agriculture and livestock, with commercial production of wines and fruits. San Martín and his officials directed this regional economy to the continental war effort. They expanded agricultural production, set up an arms industry, reformed the incidence and administration of taxation, and drew a revenue from customs, sales tax, municipal dues, donations, forced loans, sale of public lands and confiscation of royalist property.[40] Cuyo in general and Mendoza in particular responded generously, and gradually the army of the

Andes began to take shape. Regular troops from the Río de la Plata were the nucleus of this force; and fifteen hundred Negro slaves served in return for future freedom.[41] San Martín established a security screen to prevent the infiltration of royalist spies, put out patrols in the cordillera, and personally reconnoitred the mountain passes to test the routes his army would take. And he organized his own intelligence service, procuring regular details of royalist plans in Chile, and spreading alarm and confusion among the enemy through agents across the Andes.

Amidst the continental collapse of the independence movement, Cuyo became a cradle of resistance and resurgence. The political front, however, was still unstable. Behind him San Martín needed strength and security; but the Río de la Plata was divided, with Buenos Aires weak and the provinces unhelpful. Was there any authority? Would there be any support? In 1816 prospects began to improve, if only temporarily. The Congress of Tucumán met in March; this produced a declaration of independence, a revival of revolutionary purpose, and a favourable director, all indispensable preliminaries for the war effort.[42] On his way back to Buenos Aires, Director Pueyrredón stopped in Córdoba for a meeting with San Martín; there he learnt the plan in detail, agreed on the trans-Andean expedition, and promised all possible help. San Martín could now complete his preparations. And having secured the political front behind him, he also planned ahead for the government of Chile. His relations with O'Higgins were already good. After a period in Buenos Aires the Chilean leader joined San Martín's headquarters in February 1816; the two liberators became close collaborators.[43] San Martín was determined that O'Higgins should head the government of Chile upon liberation, partly because O'Higgins was a national leader, partly because he himself wished to remain mobile for the invasion of Peru. And Pueyrredón supported this proposal.[44]

By the end of 1816 all was ready – an army of five thousand, a vast quantity of equipment and supplies, and thousands of mules. At the last minute San Martín fed false information concerning his proposed routes to the Pehuenche Indians, who commanded the southern passes of the Andes and who, as he rightly guessed, would sell it to General Marcó. Then, from

9 January 1817, the liberating army began to move out of Mendoza.[45] The first enemy was the towering Andes, a monstrous barrier separating the plains of Argentina from the valleys of central Chile, crossed by only a few precipitous passes at heights between nine and twelve thousand feet, and never before traversed by a force of this size. San Martín sent his main army through the central passes of Los Patos and Uspallata, and smaller detachments via the northern and the southern routes. They accomplished one of the greatest feats of the revolutionary wars, equalled only by Bolívar's march to Boyacá, and unsurpassed not only for its courage and endurance but also for its superb timing which brought each section of the army to its right place at the appointed time. On reaching Chile the army regrouped, quickly penetrated through the central region towards Santiago, and on the plains of Chacabuco defeated the royalists (12 February 1817) and entered the capital.

The victory of Chacabuco was indispensable but not decisive. While San Martín travelled to Buenos Aires to seek supplies and ships for the invasion of Peru, the royalists were allowed to regroup in the south around the naval base of Talcahuano, and all the efforts of an expedition led by O'Higgins failed to prize them out. Indeed under General Osorio they again penetrated northwards through the central valley, defeated San Martín at Cancha Rayada on 19 March 1818, and threatened Santiago. With little time to spare San Martín just managed to concentrate his forces and defeat the royalist army on the plains of Maipo outside Santiago (5 April 1818), a victory which, in San Martín's words, 'decided the fate of South America'.[46] Although the war on the southern frontier continued for some years to come, the royalist cause was on the retreat. The Chileans were now sovereigns of their own land, and O'Higgins was supreme director.

(iii) FROM O'HIGGINS TO PORTALES

San Martín saw Chile as politically apathetic but ready for a lead. 'Liberated, they want only proper models and an established government, which latter they anxiously desire.'[47] O'Higgins gave them an established government, and for the next five years he himself dominated it. He was a pragmatic politician, who believed that independence had to be consolidated by strong government, if necessary at the expense of representation, in order to stem the post-independence anarchy so dreaded by all the South American liberators. As the army of the Andes entered Chile he declared 'we will establish order with liberty'.[48] He was conscious that he assumed absolute power, and he believed that this met the needs of the situation and the desire of the people.[49] His ideal, as expressed in 1814, was 'a genuinely paternal government, proceeding from the unanimous choice of a free people'.[50] In the Constitution of 1818 there was an advisory senate nominated by himself, but no place for an elected congress. The Constitution of 1822 provided for two houses, the lower house to be elected, but the executive was still virtually absolute. Yet O'Higgins still regarded himself as a liberal, in objectives if not in methods.

O'Higgins sought absolute power not only to repel anarchy but also to implement radical reform against vested interests. He was convinced that if necessary people must be forced to be free and happy, and he was known to say of the poorer sectors, 'if they will not become happy by their own efforts, they shall be made happy by force, by God they *shall* be happy'.[51] This is the voice of enlightened despotism. Like Rivadavia in Argentina, O'Higgins was strongly influenced by the philosophy of the eighteenth century, and for him, as for Rivadavia, government was an exercise in applied enlightenment. He too was concerned about moral and material improvement, about education, cultural progress, and economic development. In other respects he differed from Rivadavia, being more *simpático*, a pleasant and uncomplicated man, 'modest and simple, and plain in his manners', as Maria Graham recorded.[52] He was politically honest, even innocent, and perhaps too diffident. Was there a paradox about O'Higgins? Was he personally too weak to measure up to his ideal of strong government? It is probably true that he trusted others too easily and his own judgement too little. At least this was the view of British observers such as Lord Cochrane and Maria Graham. But General Miller expressed it in a different way: 'His errors of judgement are forgotten in the recollection of the goodness of his heart.'[53]

The first task was to liquidate the past, to eliminate royalists, to create a national army, and to raise a revenue for the new government. O'Higgins's policy of repression towards Spaniards and royalists was understandable after Marcó's treatment of Chileans and in view of the enemy foothold in the south, an expensive breach in the defences of the new state. He confiscated all royalist property. And on 12 February 1818, from Talca, he issued the Proclamation of Independence, a declaration of national sovereignty for the attention of Spain – and for the ears of politicians in Argentina.[54]

O'Higgins was not a *laissez-faire* liberal. He believed that state intervention was necessary to change social and economic conditions. In his view economic improvement depended on raising cultural standards. He therefore sought to extend and enhance education, in order to produce professional and scientific experts and a skilled working class. Yet he was interested not only in the education of an elite but also in that of the under-privileged; and in introducing the Lancasterian system into Chile he spoke of the need to expand 'the instruction of all classes but especially the poor'.[55] He identified other prerequisites for economic development, such as better transport, new immigration, and reform of the tax structure.[56] The Maipo Canal, begun during the colonial regime, was finally completed under O'Higgins, thus opening up the central region by better transport. His tax policy seems to have been radical in intent if not in accomplishment. Some reforming economists advocated a direct tax on capital invested in real estate and other forms of tangible property. In 1817 O'Higgins decreed a direct tax of this kind on rural property, as well as a tax on the incomes of public employees, though no record exists that these taxes were in fact collected.[57] In all probability they were simply resisted by the powerful landed interest.

The social policy of O'Higgins had distinctly egalitarian tendencies. 'I detest aristocracy, such is my nature; beloved equality is my idol.'[58] These views were reflected in his public policy. He attacked the outward trappings of aristocracy, abolishing by decree all titles of nobility as 'relics of the feudal system'.[59] The measure had chiefly symbolic value, for there were only twelve aristocratic titles in Chile. The same can be said of his policy towards entail of landed property. By decree of 5 June 1818 he sought to abolish *mayorazgo* (legally binding entail), which, rightly or wrongly, was regarded as an essential prop to the social and economic dominance of the aristocracy, and which O'Higgins saw as 'one of the abuses established by the feudal government', incompatible with 'the liberal system'.[60] The decree had no effect, and in December 1819 it was suspended by the senate. Mayorazgo was an emotional issue, its significance exaggerated by both sides. The practice had developed only from the end of the eighteenth century and on a small scale; by the mid-nineteenth century there were no more than seventeen mayorazgos in the whole of Chile.[61] But O'Higgins saw them as a badge of aristocracy rather than an obstacle to efficient land use. His radicalism was liberal rather than social in its inspiration. He attacked mayorazgo not because he was an agrarian reformer but because he was opposed to privilege. Even these limited objectives, however, alerted and alarmed the aristocracy.

O'Higgins also aroused the suspicions of the Church. In general his ecclesiastical policy assumed that the state should protect the Catholic Church as the official religion, at the same time as it respected the liberty of conscience of foreign Protestants.[62] It was a small enough concession, and he regretted 'the want of religious toleration, or rather, the very small measure of it which, considering the general state of things he had been able to grant, without disturbing the public tranquility'.[63] Without satisfying the liberals, he provoked the Church, for he considered that he had inherited the Spanish *patronato*. And he used ecclesiastical jurisdiction, partly to eliminate royalist clergy, partly to assert state sovereignty, and partly to control the public actions of the clergy. While he did not abolish the ecclesiastical fuero, his use of the patronato damaged his standing with the Church.

As an active reformer O'Higgins was bound to provoke factional opposition. But he laid himself open to more general criticism by a lapse of political judgement combined with ineptitude in economic affairs. His appointment of José Antonio Rodríguez Aldea as minister of finance in 1820 brought into the administration a controversial figure, a man resented as an ex-royalist and soon suspected of being corrupt. Rodríguez Aldea alienated the commercial sector by using his office for private profit. He speculated in consumer goods, witheld export permits from Concepción in order to favour the interests of Valparaiso in which he had a stake, and awarded monopolies to himself and his friends. His economic policy, if such it can be called, consisted in imposing restrictions and increasing taxes. He was especially resented in the south, an underdeveloped area of Chile, where continual warfare retarded the economy, used up manpower, and impoverished the whole region. The southern front was a running sore in O'Higgin's regime, at a time when he had to support a second front in Peru. Chile's share of financing the liberating expedition to Peru was more than its primitive economy could endure and imposed a great burden on its people. O'Higgins, like his country, was a victim of the war in the Pacific.

But the fundamental weakness of O'Higgins was that he represented ideas, not interests; like Rivadavia, he possessed no power base for his rule. His regime rested on political principles and the support of some intellectuals; further, in the beginning, he benefited from the strength of San Martín, the army, and the expedition to Peru. But San Martín passed on, Chile's external role diminished, and the force of revolutionary ideology waned. Meanwhile the basic source of political power remained the landed aristocracy, and among them O'Higgins had no base. Indeed he appeared to attack their interests and he was never disposed to consult them. Thus his relations with the senate deteriorated. In 1820 the senate compiled instructions to govern San Martín's rule in Peru, including the type of constitution to be adopted, one which would not alter the status of slaves. These instructions encroached on the sovereignty of O'Higgins, not to mention that of San Martín and Peru, and O'Higgins rightly refused to transmit them.[64] From then on the senate blocked him all the way, especially on finance. He drew a moral from the experience, as he ruefully wrote to San Martín : 'When men who are selected and supposedly friends present so disagreeable an aspect, what can one expect from those who are indifferent and elected by the unbridled multitude?'[65] The senate tried to reduce to three years the terms of intendants and governors, to submit them to *residencia* (investigation), and to allow cabildos to present candidates for appointment. O'Higgins angrily threw out the idea as encroaching on his power, and in January 1822, arguing that very few senators actually performed senatorial duties, he decided that the senate should be suspended and its duties transferred to the supreme director. The senate refused to accept this and demanded that the supreme director provide for the election of all governors and intendants. Again O'Higgins rejected the proposal, but in May he convoked a convention to prepare a constitution, a convention for which he himself controlled the 'elections', and to which he made clear his own constitutional preferences, namely that a strong executive should take preference over representative government. A constitution was produced in October 1822, a sound enough instrument but the occasion of a final crisis. O'Higgins assumed that he would continue as supreme director – and possibly for another ten years. The opposition regarded this as the last straw.[66]

The intendant of Concepción, General Ramón Freire, led a revolutionary movement against the capital. In the north Coquimbo also declared against O'Higgins. The revolt of the provinces encouraged conspiracy in the capital itself. On 28 January 1823 O'Higgins agreed to abdicate and to transfer power to a national junta. And soon he went into exile in Peru where he divided his time between Lima and his hacienda of Montalván, and in Peru he died in 1842. In a sense O'Higgins had ruled in a vacuum, devoid of social support. So as soon as he made political mistakes his enemies pounced. Yet O'Higgins's egalitarian ideas, temporarily frustrated, would find a more sympathetic audience among later generations. Although he was overtly amicable towards O'Higgins, Bolívar privately described him as 'a stupid despot, abhorred generally for his cruelty and bad administration'.[67] This was a gross injustice. O'Higgins was a great Chilean and a great American. With his departure, and that of San Martín, Chile began to look inwards upon itself and to forsake its international role in the liberation of the north.

The fall of O'Higgins, accomplished as it was by the revolt of the provinces against the capital, destroyed national unity. So in addition to producing a new supreme director, General Freire, the opposition had to reassemble the country. Representatives of the three provinces signed on 30 March 1823 an 'Act of Union' which reunited the provinces on the basis of equal provincial representation in a senate and prepared for a new constituent congress. A congress met and constitution was produced, the work of Juan Egaña, an eccentric intellectual who used Chile as a laboratory to test his political ideas. These were chiefly obsessed by virtue, morality and elitism, which, converted into constitutional language, spawned a conservative, absolutist and pretentious document. Compared to this the political thinking of O'Higgins was a model of moderation. Within a year Egaña's brain child had to be destroyed, hated by liberals as authoritarian, and suspected even by the conservative aristocracy because of Egaña's aversion to elected assemblies.

Chile was now left with a supreme director and a congress. The latter, as empty of ideas as it was full of factions, presented a deplorable example to the nation and was dissolved by default: the provinces began to withdraw their deputies and establish their own assemblies. Concepción did so in April 1825, Coquimbo in May. Freire struck a solitary blow for national unity in his successful expedition to the south; there he forced the royalists in Chiloé to capitulate (18 January 1826) and brought Chile's war of independence to a close. On his return to Santiago he summoned a new congress, and he himself gave way to a succession of presidents. In the months that followed Chile reverted politically to a state of nature, glorified by the name of federalism. This was fed by local and provincial sentiment; reaction against the strong centralism of O'Higgins and the presumption of Santiago; liberal ideological hostility to strong central power and admiration of the constitution of the United States. But federalism is too sophisticated a word to describe the anarchy, disorder and military insubordination over which a series of fleeting presidents presided. It was an appalling price to pay for liberty. 'Chile has reached the depths of national humiliation . . .', wrote O'Higgins to San Martín, 'the country is null and void in all its parts, without troops, credit, resources, or union.'[68] But in the end Chile purged itself of extreme federalism by the sheer inconvenience of it. In 1828 yet another congress met and produced yet another constitution, a balanced, liberal instrument, striking a mean between centralism and provincialism, but sounding a warning note to conservatives in its abolition of mayorazgos. President Antonio Pinto was a tolerant ruler, who operated the constitution wisely and stood for moderation and conciliation. He represented the mainstream of Chilean liberalism, with its insistence on individual liberty and equality, freedom of speech, representative government, restraint on the executive, and abolition of privilege. At the same time he sought to reassure the conservatives by appointing Francisco Ruiz Tagle as finance minister, and General Joaquín Prieto as commander of the army of the south, the first a conservative, the second an O'Higginist. But it was too late. The whole liberal movement was tarnished by the anarchy of the years 1824–9, the excesses of federalism, and the failure to govern effectively. By the time the moderates rallied around Pinto and began to restore stability the enemies of liberalism had already begun to concentrate their forces. The political conflict grew more bitter, and by the late 1820s a struggle for power was being waged if not by parties at least by groupings.[69] The liberals, or *pipiolos* ('novices'), were fought by an emerging conservative movement.

The conservatives were composed of roughly three groups, all of whom were alienated or repulsed by the liberal governments of 1824–9.[70] The *pelucones* ('big-wigs') were the traditional landed aristocracy. They were joined by the *estanqueros*, so called because their leader, Diego Portales, businessman turned politician, had been deprived of the *estanco* (tobacco concession) by the liberal congress of 1826; they stood for a hard-line government, centralist and absolutist. The third group were the *o'higginistas*, who simply wanted the restoration of O'Higgins. During the Pinto regime the conservatives were rallied by Portales, who put the estanqueros at the head of the movement with the simple aim of destroying liberalism. As the conservatives came together, the liberals began to fall apart. Ruiz Tagle broke with Pinto; and Prieto decided to join the growing movement around Portales. In the elections of 1829 the liberal congress gave the vice-presidency to a liberal candidate, although he did not have an absolute majority. This gave the conservatives the pretext which they wanted, and crying out against liberal illegality they revolted against the government. The revolt was a union of powerful forces. The pelucones disliked the abolition of mayorazgos in the constitution of 1828 and Pinto's anticlericalism. The estanqueros abhorred the widespread disorder and insecurity. Both wanted strong centralized government, arguing that liberal policies were out of harmony with the social realities of Chile and were too bland towards lawlessness and disorder. The revolt came from conservative bases in the provinces. Concepción revolted in October 1829 and named Prieto its intendant. Maule and then Coquimbo declared for Prieto.[71] At the end of October troops under Manuel Bulnes advanced north on Santiago; outside the capital they were joined by Portales, Manuel Rengifo and other conservative leaders. In January 1830 they controlled the capital; from February they extended their control to the rest of the country; and at the battle of Lircay (17 April 1830) they ended the civil war. Lircay also brought to an end Chile's revolution for independence. The victors now came into their own.

The new rulers abolished the acts of the liberal congress of 1829. In March 1830 José Tomás Ovalle became puppet president, and in April Portales took the key ministries; these he retained until 1831 when he stepped down from power but not from influence.[72] His philosophy of government was summed up in his well-known dictum, 'the stick and the cake, justly and opportunely administered, are the specifics with which any nation can be cured, however inveterate its bad habits may be.'[73] Uncompromisingly conservative, paternal and pragmatic, this was Portalian government, and this was the fulfilment of independence. And the new order was institutionalized by the Constitution of 1833.[74] In effect the new constitution was a presidential charter. While it did not entirely deprive congress of power, it gave preponderence to the president : it gave him great emergency powers, the right to veto and thus to delay any law, power to appoint provincial intendants, and the possibility of holding office for two terms, that is for ten years. Congress was left with power to approve the budget, taxes and the armed forces annually. But congress, of course, represented primarily the aristocracy, for the franchise was confined to literate property-owners. In theory the constitution established equality before the law – 'in Chile there is no privileged class' – but in practice it perpetuated privilege. Indeed two notorious privileges were inscribed in the constitution. While, as good civilians, the legislators abolished the military fuero, they preserved the ecclesiastical fuero, in order to ensure Church support, and they restored mayorazgo, in order to placate the great landowners.[75] The Constitution of 1833 preserved property and privilege; it simultaneously reflected the social structure and perpetuated it. The conservative regime also sought economic development, though not by state intervention. The government was expected to balance its budgets, to economize, and to limit its role to providing conditions of order and stability in which private enterprise could operate.

(iv) THE BENEFICIARIES

Economic independence was not a burning issue in 1810. Chile enjoyed increasing opportunities for trade in the last decades of the colony, more than her primitive economy could exploit.[76] The most urgent problem of the governing junta was to defend the revolution against the counter-blow which would undoubtedly come from Peru. In October 1810 it took steps to form a patriot battalion, to purchase arms in England, and to establish a munitions factory. In December it decreed an expansion of infantry, cavalry and artillery. But how could these vital defence measures be paid for? It was suggested by some, though not usually by merchants, that freedom of trade would yield the necessary revenue. From his estancia at Canteras O'Higgins urged on the junta 'the necessity of two measures directed to raising the people from their lethargy and making them take an interest in the revolution: the convocation of a congress and the establishment of freedom of trade'.[77] These ideas were not welcome to all merchants. Many of the old Spanish monopolists argued that open trade and increased imports would worsen balance of payments, hit local industries, and introduce poor quality goods, epidemics and heresy.[78] And most merchants resisted change. Even Egaña's *Plan of Government* (1810) advocated freedom of trade only in so far as the local economy would benefit.[79] But the junta, influenced by revolutionary ideology, decreed freedom of trade on 21 February 1811, arguing that 'all men have certain imprescriptible rights given to them by their Creator to procure their happiness, prosperity and welfare'.[80] This immediately opened the ports of Chile to trade with friendly and neutral nations. It was an important step forward, though in view of previous opportunities not a spectacular one. But it was an essential part of the political break with Spain. And it was protectionist.

The decree of free commerce of 1811 was not a statement of economic liberalism and it did not subscribe to free trade. Its aim was to free Chile from colonial restriction and monopoly, to give her freedom to trade with the rest of the world – and freedom to impose her own tariffs. In Chile principles of free trade and *laissez-faire* were regarded as more suitable for developed economies than for pre-industrial ones. Until the 1830s economic ideas were predominantly neo-mercantilist, and they assigned the state a positive role in the development of a national economy through education, protection of new industries, and social policies for the poor and unemployed.[81] The decree of free commerce placed a duty of 30 per cent on all imports and authorized whatever prohibitions on imports 'that are considered suitable to the development of the country's industry'. Subsequent tariffs were high, rising to $36\frac{1}{2}$ per cent in 1821–3, then falling to 27 per cent. These tariffs were both protectionist and revenue-raising. A revenue tariff was a characteristic feature of a society dominated by landed proprietors who diverted taxation away from property towards the consumer. 'We are all liberals', the minister of finance told his critics in 1822, 'in all that does not tend to ruin us.'

High tariffs, of course, were a deterrent to overseas trade.[82] But they did not prevent Chile from falling under the influence of foreign, particularly British, interests. Free commerce attracted large numbers of British merchants, especially from 1817–8, many of whom were more interested in trading in the larger and more profitable market of Peru. For independence and war broke direct trade and navigation between the new state and royalist Peru. Chile did not at first possess sufficient naval power to blockade the enemy coast, and the British moved in to do a brisk trade carrying Chilean grain to Peru; they also re-exported British manufactures from Chile, using the latter as an entrepôt where they could keep their goods until the prices were high in the Lima market. From Chile's point of view this trade had three disadvantages. It fortified Spanish power and popularity in Peru by supplying abundant consumer goods and thus preventing wartime shortages; it provided a cover under which the British sold war supplies to the royalists; and it diverted grain from the home market to seek higher prices in Peru. Some of the war planners urged the government to prohibit the trade.[83] But O'Higgins was unable to comply, for contraband would always defeat prohibition, and the export of grain was one of the few ways in which Chile could improve her foreign earnings. So Chile continued to trade with the enemy. And British trade with Lima could never be completely stopped, even when the Chilean navy attempted to enforce a blockade.[84]

British trade with Chile itself took root in the 1820s, when consular missions were established at Valparaiso, Coquimbo and Concepción, and British merchants crowded into these and other ports. Chile exported wheat, jerked beef, hides and tallow from Concepción (Talcahuano), copper, gold and silver from Coquimbo. She imported most of her manufactured goods from Britain and British India, and some flour from the United States. But Chile was not as important to Britain as was Buenos Aires, for, apart from gold and silver, there were few desirable returns; wheat, copper, hemp and hides were not suitable for speculation at so great a distance.[85] But British merchant capital came to exercise an important role in financing Chilean copper mining. British advances helped to free the miner from the more onerous credit relations which the Spanish and Chilean financiers had imposed, by paying more for the copper and offering him better credit terms.[86] This cut out competition from other capitalists and tied the miners to good buyers. The British had two advantages over local capitalists. They could operate on a large scale, getting hundreds of mines under their credit control, which enabled them to pay better prices to the miners.[87] They also had the advantage of working with their colleagues the British importers, who in turn gave them credit facilities for purchasing copper for export against their imports. The average annual export of copper from 1817 was sixty-one thousand quintals, three-quarters of which went to Calcutta.[88]

Chile was the first of the new Spanish American nations to raise a loan in the London money market. The agent, Antonio José de Irisarri, contracted with Hullet Brothers in 1822 for

£1 million to finance part of the enormous cost of the liberating expedition to Peru. As Chile's independence and stability were still uncertain, her credit rating was not high. Bonds were placed at 70 per cent of their face value; Irisarri took a commission of 2 per cent, Hullet 1·5 per cent; the interest was 6 per cent, and amortization 1 per cent. This left the Chilean government with 67·5 per cent, some £675,169 only, the service of which was £60,216.[89] Irisarri purchased merchandise with much of the proceeds; part of this was lost in the shipwreck of the *Voltaire*, and the rest depreciated in value before being resold. The Chilean government did not possess the knowledge or the experience to use this money wisely or to service it correctly. To defray the principal and interest, it granted the firm of Portales, Cea and Company (20 August 1824) the *estanco*, or monopoly of importing and selling tobacco and related commodities. But the company was unable to earn enough to service the debt, and after two years the contract was annulled. The monopolists liquidated the business favourably to themselves, but the resentment aroused by the cancellation drew Portales into politics as leader of the political faction known as the estanco.[90] This was a political rather than economic or social pressure group.

The Chilean revolution was not a struggle between different social classes or groups. There was no rival power to challenge the landed aristocracy, who monopolized the landed wealth of the country, formed the social ideal to which all Chileans aspired, produced from within its ranks the intellectual, merchant and professional groups, and dominated the military power. This was important. The rural militia, a semi-feudal organization of landowners and their retainers, although not always thrown directly into the revolution, was always there as a latent threat or restraint.[91] Certain caudillos, first Carrera then O'Higgins, might be tolerated for specific objectives, the first to provide military organization, the second a stable administration, but they would be destroyed as soon as they threatened to become an independent power. The social homogeneity of Chile's ruling class, however, did not engender political unity. The aristocracy were more agreed on what they wanted to prevent than on what they wanted to promote. They wanted a strong but not an absolute president, a congress with power enough to represent their interests in case the president threatened them, but not enough to cause anarchy. Above all they wanted respect for the rights of property and preservation of social stability. Within these terms, however, there was a range of political beliefs and behaviour, the fruit of ideas rather than of interest. The aristocracy were not unanimous even in overthrowing O'Higgins, and in the years following they enlisted in various factions. The anarchy of 1823–9 was not a struggle between two different classes, for the liberals came from the same social sector as the conservatives. Neither Freire nor Pinto were hostile to the aristocracy. Their administration contained people who were socially indistinguishable from the post-Portales governments, namely a mixture of status aristocrats and professional administrators.[92]

Independence and subsequent political change, therefore, took place within the existing hierarchical structure and did not fundamentally disturb it. Indeed standards of living now diverged more widely, for while free commerce lowered the price of consumer goods for everyone, it was the upper sectors who could benefit most from this, having greater purchasing power and being the producers of an expanding export. These differences were noted by an English observer:

The peasant's station in society had not been materially changed by the subversion of the Spanish authority; while that of his landlord was essentially altered in almost every point. . . . In Chili, while the peasant remains nearly as before, his superior has gained many advantages. He has obtained political independence; he is free, and secure in his person and property; for the first time in his life, he has a share in the government of his country; he may aspire to the highest offices of profit or distinction; the value of his property is enhanced by the market which has been opened to carry off its produce; and he feels no reserve in displaying his wealth, or in expressing his opinions; in short, he is in possession of civil liberty.[93]

The extent to which civil liberty was shared with the mass of the people cannot easily be measured. The Indians were not automatically allies of the new rulers during the war of independence or submissive subjects afterwards.[94] The pampa Indians of the eastern Andes, the nomadic and warlike Pehuenches, kept a strict neutrality, not well inclined towards either party.[95] The Araucanians, or the great majority of them, were also neutral, though by no means aloof, being equally hostile to both patriots and royalists. After the battle of Maipo the Spanish commander, General Sánchez, crossed the Bío-Bío and fell back on Araucanian territory where he had already won over several caciques and now managed to obtain exceptional permission to take his troops through Arauco to Valdivia. The 'royalist' guerrilla leader, Benavides, was left among the Araucanians with a few other terrorists to preserve hostility against the patriots, and although the latter crossed the Bío-Bío several times to attempt to destroy these depredators, they always returned with heavy losses and without success.

They cared not on which side they fought, provided they were instrumental to the destruction of either, as they considered both parties their natural enemies. Perhaps Benavides is indebted for a part of his popularity with the Indians to his hatred of the very Spaniards he served, as evinced by his shooting or hanging, under different pretexts, every respectable Spanish officer sent from Valdivia to assist him.[96]

O'Higgins sought to win over the Araucanians by improving the legal position of the Indians in Chilean society. He decreed that they were no longer to have a different status from the whites; they were equal to others, 'Chilean citizens, free like the other inhabitants of the state'; they were free from tribute, and free 'to obtain political and military appointments according to their aptitude'.[97] But the Araucanians remained obdurate enemies of the new state, difficult and expensive to contain. And military operations against them would be ineffective unless followed up by intensive colonization. This was the object of O'Higgins's project – unfulfilled – for Irish colonization south of the Bío-Bío, which drew the British consul in Peru to warn:

The barrier of the brave Irish against this savage horde, and the sort of commitment of Great Britain to give a protection to the settlers, would undoubtedly be a very desirable object for the Chile government; but the poor Irish peasant . . . will soon find that he must hold the ploughshare in one hand and the sword in the other to defend his industry and life.[98]

The emancipators had more success with the Negro slaves. Slavery was not significant either in numbers or as a work force.

Chile had no plantation economy with massive labour requirements, and there were no more than five thousand slaves, working principally as domestics and artisans for propertied Chileans. But the revolutionaries regarded the institution as a moral outrage and a badge of colonialism, and they soon said so. The first anti-slavery measure was introduced by the national congress of 1811 after it had been purged by Carrera. On the initiative of the humanitarian intellectual Manuel de Salas, and with the argument that slavery was 'opposed to the Christian spirit, to humanity, and to good customs', congress passed a law (11 October 1811) abolishing any slave trade into Chile, and declaring free the children born of slaves in Chile and any slave introduced into the country and staying for six months.[99] There was much opposition, especially from royalists and conservative politicians, who argued that this measure would subvert the social order and encourage older slaves to rebel. For the moment, therefore, reform went no further, though under the influence of the new law some slave owners – Carrera among them – voluntarily freed their slaves. And on 29 August the junta decreed immediate freedom for all slaves aged thirteen upwards who enlisted in the army, the owner to be indemnified by half the monthly pay of the soldier. This was largely ineffective, for the masters prevented their slaves from leaving and the slaves themselves were not always anxious to exchange a civilian master for a military one. In any case the royalist restoration abruptly annulled all the anti-slavery measures of the patriot government.

O'Higgins resumed the reform policy of the Patria Vieja, though not the policy of offering freedom in return for military service.[100] The Constitution of 1818 re-established *libertad de vientres*, and the Constitution of 1822 declared that 'all Chileans are equal before the law without distinction of rank or privilege', though this did not take effect, for O'Higgins fell in January 1823 and with him his constitution.[101] The advent of the liberal regime reopened the struggle between the abolitionists, inspired by the distinguished liberal José Miguel Infante, and those who defended slavery as inviolable private property and whom Infante described as 'assassins who dare to kill only slaves'.[102] He exaggerated, for in Chile the slaves were not an agricultural labour force vital to the economy but indoor servants, most of them now old, and numbering about four thousand in all. On 24 July 1823 a law abolishing slavery was promulgated, but absolute enforcement was held up, and a group of owners organized a petition to the senate, allegedly signed by two hundred slaves, who claimed that 'the opinion of the slaves has not been heard', extolled their masters and conditions, and argued that 'we do not want this justice, nor this liberty ... for us liberty would mean loss of welfare and security'.[103] The senate ignored this spurious document. And Egaña's constitution of December 1823 declared in article 8, 'in Chile there are no slaves'. This was the end of slavery, and abolition was confirmed in the constitutions of 1828 and 1833.[104]

Abolition was a great moral victory, but had only limited social significance and virtually no economic consequences. And the end of slavery, small in scale as it was, must be considered in relation to the perpetuation of other and greater forms of servitude, particularly *inquilinaje*. Independence did nothing to modify the dominance of the hacienda, its monopoly of land and control over labour; there the *inquilinos* remained, a captive work force bound to their master, to whom they owed labour service in return for a small plot of land.[105] And while the Indian was equal and the Negro free, race remained an essential ingredient of class consciousness and an important test by which Chileans judged each other for many generations to come.[106]

FIVE *Peru, the Ambiguous Revolution*

(i) ROYALISTS AND REFORMISTS

Peru was inhabited by diverse races split by latent antagonism; even the whites were divided, according to whether they were Europeans or Americans. Peru was also the heart of royalist reaction, and for fifteen years she held the revolution in check. Peru was the Carthage of San Martín and had to be destroyed. So it was that in 1820 the liberating armies from the north and from the south converged upon her.[1]

ON THE EVE of the revolution Peru had a population of just over one million.[2] The Indians (58 per cent of the total) and mestizos (22 per cent) were concentrated in the Andean region, where they practised subsistence agriculture and provided labour for mines, obrajes and haciendas. Negro slaves formed some 4 per cent of the population, and free coloureds about the same; but in Lima and the coastal valleys, where commercial agriculture and a plantation economy demanded a more mobile labour force, Negroes and pardos predominated among the non-Spanish population. The whites totalled less than 13 per cent of the whole and were to be found chiefly on the coast, with a sizable concentration also in Cuzco. But race was not the only determinant of status. Peru was split too by deep social and economic divisions. The ruling elite, of course, Spaniards and creoles alike, were inevitably white. But not all the Indians were culturally Indian. As Concolorcorvo pointed out, it was sufficient for an Indian to wash, cut his hair, wear a clean shirt and get a useful job to pass for a *cholo* : 'If he serves his Spanish master well, the latter dresses him and puts him in shoes, and in two months he is known as a mestizo.'[3] The mestizos themselves were not a single social group; depending on their education, work, way of life, they could approximate to whites or to Indians. The mulattos and other castes suffered even worse discrimination than the mestizos : they were forbidden to dress as whites, to live in white districts, to marry whites, and they had their own churches and burial grounds.[4] But even the coloured people were not immutably classified by race; economic advancement could secure them white status either by 'passing' or by purchase of a certificate of whiteness. So there were cultural as well as racial determinants, though this did not lessen the divisions in Peruvian society or dilute its seigneurial values.

The Peruvian aristocracy – an aristocracy of land, office and trade – clung fanatically to their power and privilege. Their conservatism was induced not only by nostalgia for past status but also by fear of future disorder. The propertied classes of Lima were terrified by 'the licentiousness of the populace and the coloured people of this city and its environs, who exceed the whites by a third or a fifth and who are arrogant, insubordinate and lawless'.[5] The elite preferred security to change and were not prepared to risk their social predominance for the sake of independence. They were inspired less by loyalism than by fear of social upheaval and the collapse of law and order. Even the Peruvian liberals sought reform, not revolution. Intellectuals like José Baquíjano, Toribio Rodríguez de Mendoza, Hipólito Unánue, and the writers of the *Mercurio Peruano,* who imbibed the thought of the eighteenth-century Enlightenment, condemned the obscurantism and intolerance of the old regime, and advocated liberty and equality, did so within the existing structure.[6] The growing sense of *peruanidad* was also limited by an innate caution.[7] In fact Peruvian liberals held conflicting ideas of patria. A few believed that it could be fulfilled only in independent nationality. But the majority saw it as compatible with the ideal of imperial unity: 'Uniformity of religion and language, similarity of customs and the ties of blood, these are and always will be the guarantees of the indissoluble union of both Spains.'[8] And this union was regarded as the safest guarantee against anarchy.

The Peruvian liberals, therefore, did not produce an independence movement. Prisoners of their society, they demanded no more than political reform and equality for creoles within the colonial framework. Their spokesmen were the cabildos, drawn suddenly into the limelight in 1808 by the collapse of imperial government. In 1809, responding to the decision of the central junta that they should assist in the election of a deputy to be sent to Spain, the cabildos of Peru chose José de Silva y Olave, rector of the University of San Marcos. His instructions were issued by the cabildo of Lima and they summarized the demands of the creoles at this moment, demands which revealed as much conservatism as liberalism.[9] They criticized the intendants for abuse of power and oppression of the cabildos; and they sought the restoration not only of the corregidores but also of the infamous repartimientos (forced sale of goods to the Indians), arguing that the suppliers of the corregidores had been deprived of a market. They demanded the abolition of monopolies, which raised the price of mercury, tobacco and other commodities, and a lowering of taxes, especially the alcabala, or sales tax; and they demanded freedom of trade. Finally, they expressed resentment of the meagre career prospects of creoles – 'farmers, clerics or lawyers' – and they insisted that Americans should be given at least half a share in the government of America.

This manifesto revealed the acute concern of the creoles over their living standards. The economy was suffering from past neglect and a current crisis.[10] Peru's traditional supremacy in South America had been based on two vulnerable assets – a monopoly of the trans-Atlantic trade and of the export of bullion. From its own production the colony earned little. Agriculture was retarded by shortage of capital and labour and by the poverty of the local market; in good years it supplied the needs of Peru and Upper Peru, while the latter was also a market for the coarse textiles of the obrajes. But these were secondary activities, subordinate to the trade monopoly and possession of the Upper Peruvian mines. The economy's structural defects were now aggravated by a new depression. Peru was the victim of the imperial reforms of 1776–8, which simultaneously deprived it of Upper Peru and of the commercial monopoly.[11] Subverted by its own metropolis, Peru was then hit by the wars in which the metropolis was so grievously involved, first in 1779–83, then almost continuously from 1793, wars which not only increased taxes but also deprived Peru of export markets and of vital imports. In time of peace, with the loss of the silver provinces, Peru found it increasingly difficult to earn its imports. In 1777–86 exports amounted to five million pesos a year against imports of eight million pesos a year. After the loss of Upper Peru the colony's foreign trade dropped from four to five vessels to Spain a year, to three vessels of five hundred tons only.[12] Foreign trade was sustained by silver exports, which in 1785–89 amounted to 88 percent of total exports.[13] Lower Peru increased its silver output in the late eighteenth century through improved draining techniques, diversion of capital from Potosí, a ready supply of free labour, and the support of the mining tribunal. Registered silver rose from 246,000 marks in 1777 to a peak of 637,000 marks in 1799 (a mark was worth 8 pesos 4 reales), maintaining a high level until 1812.[14] But if this minor boom mitigated the effects of economic depression it could not reverse it. And the situation worsened after 1808 when war and revolution in Spanish America further disrupted commercial activity. Many Peruvians now thought that their interests were being ignored, and, if the views of the cabildo of Lima may be taken as representative, they increased their demands for freedom to trade directly with foreigners, including those in Asia, and they renewed their opposition to imperial taxation.[15] For Peru's role as a royalist stronghold had to be paid for, and Viceroy Abascal raised his tax demands to the point where they really hurt. At the same time Abascal was horrified by demands for freedom of trade: 'It would be tantamount to decreeing the separation of these dominions from the mother country, since, once direct trade with foreigners was established on the wide basis which they demand, the fate of European Spain would matter little to them.'[16] But how complete was the Peruvian conversion to economic freedom? Was there not an ambiguity in the creole position even here? The American revolution implied economic freedom for Peru's rivals: Buenos Aires and to some extent Chile could now improve their position in the markets of Upper Peru and of Peru itself. This caused some economic interests in Peru to think twice before deserting the cause of Spain and monopoly. And their caution was confirmed when Viceroy Abascal rescued Upper Peru from the clutches of Buenos Aires and re-annexed it to Lima. This vindicated at least one of Peru's claims. Economic arguments, therefore, were no more decisive than political ones. Peruvians were still not convinced that the hour of revolution had come. They still sought reform, not independence, from Spain, and from 1808 they were encouraged in their expectations by the emergence of a liberal regime in the peninsula.

The creoles were the key to the situation, in Peru as elsewhere in Spanish America; with their numerical superiority over the Spaniards, they could promote or prevent political change. In Peru, it is true, the Spanish presence both in the bureaucracy and in the private sector was more powerful than in the Río de la Plata or Chile. 'Lima has been the refuge for most of the Old Spaniards driven from Buenos Aires and Chile, and, independent of this, Peru, from being considered the principal viceroyalty, has many more natives of Spain in proportion to the other provinces.'[17] But without creole support Viceroy Abascal could not have held Peru, much less launched the counter-revolution against neighbouring provinces.[18] Within a few years, of course, creole opinion would be less complacent: the restoration of Ferdinand VII in 1814 shattered hopes of reform within a Spanish framework. By that time, however, it was difficult to challenge the military power built up by Abascal or to stem the counter-revolution which was sweeping over the subcontinent. In 1808–9, on the other hand, Spain's military position in Peru was not strong: Abascal had only one regular regiment in Lima (under fifteen hundred strong) and smaller detachments in the interior.[19] The militia had a nominal strength of forty thousand, though its real strength was inferior and its quality suspect. But in the final analysis it was upon the allegiance of the creole militia that Abascal had to rely.

The viceroy himself was perhaps the greatest asset to the Spanish cause in Peru. José Fernando de Abascal had an instinct for leadership and authority which he had displayed ever since his arrival in Lima in 1806. In the crisis of imperial government he kept his nerve and reacted to the revolution with great energy and determination, a solitary but self-confident defender of empire. He quickly transformed Peru into a powerful base for Spanish defences in South America and then took the offensive against the insurgents. In 1809 he dispatched troops under José Manuel de Goyeneche to crush the rebellion in Upper Peru; in the following year he re-annexed the province to his viceroyalty and began to organize its defence against the forces of Buenos Aires. Next he moved against the revolution to the north of Peru : he stiffened royalist resistance in Guayaquil, Cuenca and Popayán, and sent a punitive expedition against Quito.[20] In 1811 he assigned three hundred thousand pesos to the royalists in Montevideo, and in 1813 he sent an invading force into Chile. These measures weighed heavily upon Peruvian taxpayers and crippled the Peruvian Treasury. But Abascal was impervious to criticism. And he acted entirely on his own initiative. As he himself explained : 'These complex, extraordinary and violent adversities demand remedies of a similar kind, beyond the powers of viceroys, whose authority has been gradually eroded.'[21] He deplored the weak governments in Spain – the central junta, the council of regency, the cortes – and he had nothing but contempt for their liberalism, losing no opportunity to sabotage it whenever it was applied to Peru. Abascal never understood the new spirit animating America; he failed to identify the real causes of the American revolution and mistakenly attributed every manifestation of revolt to a conspiracy emanating from Buenos Aires. His contemptuous language towards Americans betrayed a fundamental lack of sympathy with the people he had to govern and did great moral damage to the Spanish cause. He described Quito as 'an imbecile country', its citizens as 'motivated by malice'.[22] His decree re-annexing Upper Peru to Lima (13 July 1810), spoke of Americans as 'men born to vegetate in obscurity and abasement'.[23]

To make his viceroyalty a counter-revolutionary base Abascal had to preserve stability at home. Rebellions in Peru tended to be southern-based and of Indian origin, as in Huánuco in 1812 when an Indian rising against oppressive subdelegates developed into a creole-led anti-Spanish movement. These factors alone were sufficient to place the Lima elite alongside the viceroy in suppressing them.[24] The greatest threat to Abascal's policy came not from Peru but from Spain, where successive regimes in the years 1808–13 hopefully exported liberalism – of a kind – to America. In 1809 each cabildo in Peru was allowed to play a part in selecting a deputy to join the central junta as representative of Peru. In 1810 the council of regency summoned a cortes for 24 September; again the Peruvian cabildos were called upon to elect deputies, and they were informed 'your destinies no longer depend upon viceroys, governors and ministers; they are now in your own hands'.[25] Sentiments like these tended to subvert Abascal's authority, without even possessing the merit of sincerity. For the Spanish liberals did not support equality of representation in the cortes: this would have enabled Americans, superior in numbers, to outvote the peninsulares. The seven Peruvian deputies to the cortes of Cadiz supported the American demand for greater representation, but cautiously, lest the franchise be extended to Indians, mestizos and castes.[26] The growing claims of the free coloureds in Peru and elsewhere to equality of status and opportunity alarmed the creole upper classes. Spaniards in the cortes were able to play upon this racial prejudice in order to exclude the great mass of the castes from citizenship and franchise and thus to diminish American representation. And they had the support of the Peruvian deputies who sought to ensure that the Indians could neither elect nor be elected, citing 'the grave disadvantages which equality of this sort would have, notably in Peru'.[27] This was the true voice of Peruvian liberalism.

Cautious though it was, Spanish constitutionalism was too radical for Abascal. From the second half of 1812 he was forced to implement a series of reforms designed to placate creole opinion – dismissal of unpopular officials, appointment of more creoles to offices, abolition of Indian tribute and mita, and freedom of the press – most of which deeply offended his conservative instincts. He was also obliged to apply the constitution of 18

March 1812, including the abolition of sale of office, the abolition of the old hereditary cabildos and their replacement by annually elected bodies, and the election of deputies to the Spanish cortes.[28] The new constitutional cabildos were elected on a restricted franchise and they were far from revolutionary; but while they did not bring true devolution of power from the metropolis to the colony, they were another element of instability and made the viceroy's task more difficult. Abascal detested the constitution of Cadiz; he regarded it as a 'monstrous deformity' which usurped the authority of the king and introduced 'revolutionary principles of democracy, impiety and irreligion'.[29] He went through the motions of applying the constitution in Peru without relinquishing his own power, and he and his officials worked to frustrate the ambitions of the new cabildos. Why did the creoles of Peru not break the restraints imposed by Viceroy Abascal and overcome the last obstacle to liberal reform? Was it that they needed Abascal, or someone like him, as a barrier to social revolution and a restraint on Indian violence?

(ii) The Rebellion of Pumacahua

The Peruvian whites, 140,890 in a population of 1,115,207 (1795), were always conscious of the superior numbers of Indians and mestizos and of the volcano in their midst. Between 1708 and 1783 Peru experienced at least 140 uprisings, most of them Indian in origin, violent yet futile protests against various forms of servitude: excessive demands for tribute, taxes and tithes; the reparto and the mita; and the hated corregidor, the personification of all abuses.[30] Most of these movements were unexceptional, part of the normal pattern of race relations in Peru. But two rebellions shook the colony to its foundations. The first, in 1780, was a desperate affirmation of classical Indian grievances, aggravated by two particular forms of exploitation, the raising of the alcabala to 4 per cent in 1772 and to 6 per cent in 1776, and the establishment of internal customs posts to ensure collection. These Bourbon expedients weighed heavily on Indian producers and traders and served to alienate the middle groups of Indian society and to nurture a rebel leadership. The leader was Tupac Amaru, an educated cacique, whose extended family networks and links with regional trade and transport gave the whole movement a coherent chain of command and a source of recruitment.[31] Beginning near Cuzco in November 1780, the rebellion soon spread to a great part of southern Peru, then in a second and more radical phase to the Aymara provinces of Upper Peru.

Tupac Amaru declared war to the death against the Spaniards and he appealed to the creoles to join with the Indians 'to destroy the Europeans', and he claimed to stand for 'the protection, preservation and tranquility of the creoles, the mestizos, zambos, and Indians, for they are all compatriots and equal sufferers from the oppression and tyrannies of the Europeans'.[32] The appeal was unsuccessful, as it was bound to be, granted his social policy. Tupac Amaru promised to free slaves, a tactical manoeuvre, to be sure, for he referred only to those who joined his forces and there were hardly three hundred Negroes in the whole of Cuzco.[33] Even so, it was alarming. His views on property were also suspect, and his followers attacked white towns and their inhabitants indiscriminately. Appalled by the magnitude and violence of the rising, creoles soon made common cause with Europeans in suppressing it. The suppression was cruel. The Indian leaders were sadistically executed, their people terrorized. Indian property was sacked and confiscated; and for many years to come foodstocks were low and labour resources diminished among the Andean communities.

Indian risings sought immediate relief, not permanent political change. They could not be genuine independence movements. They lacked ideas, organization and military resources. Two particular obstacles frustrated their chances of success. There was, of course, no solidarity among the non-whites; the coloured militia of the coast helped to suppress the rebellion of 1780–1 and they formed part of the royalist forces after 1809. But the Indian cause was even divided against itself. During the rebellion of Tupac Amaru at least twenty caciques, motivated in part by personal and tribal rivalry, kept their people loyal to the crown, and subsequently received rewards and pensions.[34] The most distinguished of these was Mateo Pumacahua, descendant of the Incas and cacique of Chincheros, a man of substance and property, who not only fought against Tupac Amaru but participated in the savage repression afterwards. Pumacahua and his people remained loyal to Spain during the first years of the American revolution and even served in punitive expeditions to Upper Peru. At the request of Viceroy Abascal in 1811 Pumacahua and his followers sacked rebellious La Paz; they ruthlessly attacked the Indians of Sicasica, Cochabamba and Oruro, leaving devastation in their wake. Pumacahua was rewarded with further titles and offices; he was promoted to the rank of brigadier and then appointed, although temporarily, president of the audiencia of Cuzco.[35] But these tended to be empty dignities and fell below expectations. Pumacahua and other royalist caciques seem to have sought from the colonial government recognition of their sovereignty, or a degree of sovereignty, over the Indians of Peru, in order to bring about by peaceful reform the improvement which Tupac Amaru sought by revolution. But these were vain hopes and those who held them received nothing for their loyalism.

Indian rebellions lacked a further condition essential for independence – creole leadership. The creoles were committed to the existing economic structure, which was based upon Indian labour in the mines, haciendas and workshops. And overwhelmingly outnumbered as they were, they hesitated to put themselves at the head of an Indian movement which they might not be able to control. Their rejection of Indian aspirations strengthened their position in relation to the Spaniards. For it was obvious to the colonial authorities that Spanish defences against Indian rebellion depended on the cooperation of creoles and mestizos. For these reasons the rebellion of Tupac Amaru, while it heightened the social conservatism of the creoles, also enhanced their political pretensions and their bargaining power.

A successful Indian movement, therefore, would depend upon Indian unity and creole alliance. In 1814, in Cuzco, these conditions briefly prevailed, and for once Indian and creole rebellion coincided. By now Pumacahua had broken with the colonial government. The Spaniards had refused to tolerate his appointment as president of the audiencia of Cuzco and had procured his replacement. For him this was final proof that he and his people had been used by the Spaniards and had received nothing in return.[36] He now retired, disillusioned and apparently broken – he was seventy-four – to his hacienda at Urquillos. Meanwhile the cause of Indian reform had made little progress. After the rebellion of 1780–1 the repartimientos had been officially abolished, and the corregidores replaced by intendants and subdelegates, who were expected to provide better administration in the Indian sector. But in fact the repartimientos soon reappeared, and the new subdelegates were no improvement on the old corregidores.[37] In 1811 the cortes of Cadiz abolished the Indian tribute and in 1812 it suppressed the mita and personal service. Again, legislation was incapable of effecting social change, and the reforms were frustrated by vested interests in Peru. Some of their opponents were to be found even in the Church, which also depended upon Indian labour; the Bishop of Maynas protested to the Spanish authorities against measures which he regarded as highly impolitic.[38] By 1814, therefore, Indian conditions were little better than in 1780.

The creoles too had reached a new stage of alienation. Expectations had been raised by the promise of liberal reforms from the Spanish constitutionalists, reforms which threatened to subvert the absolute power of viceregal government and give the creoles a greater share in decision-making. These hopes were especially strong in southern Peru where a growing sense of grievance and identity posed a threat to the dominance of Lima and a challenge to the colonial authorities, raising the spectre of regional secession.[39] In Cuzco the audiencia, focus of Spanish and bureaucratic interests, continued to control the administration, but was faced with mounting opposition from creole 'constitutionalists', who demanded the application of liberal reforms and of the constitution of 1812. Once they procured a new cabildo, the reformists disputed control of Cuzco with the audiencia. The latter replied by imprisoning the creole leaders. But on the night of 2 August 1814 the prisoners escaped, rallied their supporters and promptly imprisoned the majority of the Spanish faction in the city.

The rebels needed greater military support than could be supplied by creoles and mestizos alone. They therefore recalled Pumacahua from retirement and offered him first place in a triumvirate nominated to govern the city. Their real object was to recruit Pumacahua's Indian followers, together with his financial and moral support, for, as a royalist observer noted, 'he had decided ascendancy over the Indians, people of humble station, as he himself was an Indian who had been promoted to the rank of brigadier for his services to the crown in the time of the rebel Tupac Amaru'.[40] Some of the leading rebels aimed at independence from Spain and from Lima. Others who supported the movement were reformists, seeking the dismissal of unacceptable officials, greater opportunities for creoles, the application of the constitution of 1812, and an end to the war against the insurgents of Upper Peru, a war for which Cuzco had to pay.[41] They were too late: constitutionalism was almost dead, and Abascal refused to negotiate. This helped to separate reformists from revolutionaries. The latter now had to fight and to rally the support of the Indian masses, while moderates began to have second thoughts. The creole military leader, José Angulo, incorporated into his forces thousands of Indians loyal to Pumacahua, and sent out three expeditions, one south to Puno and La Paz, another north to Huamanga and Huancavelica, and a third south-east to Arequipa.[42]

The expedition against Puno and La Paz attracted further Indians and mestizos on route. Puno was taken without resistance, but La Paz became a blood bath. The Spanish garrison was slaughtered; and the Indians, 'accompanied by the populace of the city', as Abascal recorded, mercilessly attacked Europeans, pillaged their property and sacked their houses.[43] A reign of terror prevailed until a small but powerful Spanish force under General Juan Ramírez was detached from the army of Upper Peru for counter-insurgency duty. Ramírez attacked strongly, recaptured La Paz and Puno, and drove back the rebel masses. Meanwhile, Pumacahua himself had led the attack on Arequipa. His horde of twelve thousand undisciplined and inexperienced Indians overwhelmed the royalists and captured the town on 10 November. But news of the approach of Ramírez caused the Indian leader to fall back, and in reprisal for Spanish atrocities he ordered a number of prisoners to be shot without trial, including the Intendant of Arequipa, José Gabriel Moscoso.[44] Pumacahua was now a marked man. He appealed to Ramírez to negotiate, but the Spaniard replied 'my bayonets will put down your arrogance'.[45] Defeated in battle in March 1815, Pumacahua was hunted down relentlessy and was finally betrayed to the royalist forces by *cholos*, former rebels anxious to redeem themselves. He was executed at Sicuani in the presence of his own Indians in May 1815.

The creole revolutionaries of 1814 had no policy for the Indians and in their proclamations they barely referred to their brothers in arms. On the northern expedition Manuel Hurtado de Mendoza appealed to the Indians and creoles of Castro-virreina to drive out the Spaniards.[46] But many creoles preferred Spanish rule to Indian rebellion. The creoles of Lima and the coast, of course, remained aloof, but so did many in Cuzco itself. The wealthy were the first to withdraw, reluctant to contribute the 'voluntary' donations which the rebel leaders had to levy. An anonymous chronicler observed that all property-owners, creole and European, were soon convinced that 'the revolution and the war are directed against all who have property to lose'.[47] The Intendant of Arequipa exhorted his people to be thankful to their 'liberators' who had freed them from the threat presented by

... thousands of Indians, mobilized with the object of removing these provinces from the rule of Ferdinand VII, best of sovereigns; then, in satisfaction of their hatred towards the other races, they would exterminate all the other non-Indians of this hemisphere. If this assertion appears exaggerated, direct your imagination towards the village of Sicuani, where the ungrateful and infamous Pumacahua developed his horrifying plans, designed to exterminate every white, beginning with those of Arequipa.[48]

In Cuzco, therefore, a royalist reaction ended the revolution, and by mid–1815 the leading rebels had all been executed. A royalist view of the rebellion remarked on the dominance of creole motivation and saw Indian participation as a matter of delinquency rather than ideology :

All those who have lived any length of time in the Americas will have noticed the hatred which in general the Spanish creoles nurture in their hearts against the Europeans and their government. This anti-pathy is much less marked in the Negroes and Indians, for it can be truthfully said that these direct their hatred more towards the creoles. This is not to deny the support which both Negroes and Indians have given to the rebellion, for their addiction to robbery, pillage, assassination and every kind of disorder make them amenable to its ideas and readily enlists them in its ranks. The creoles have never been able to reconcile themselves to the wealth and offices which the Europeans have secured by their industry and application. . . . These considerations are not important in the case of Indians and Negroes, because the crass ignorance and servile abasement of both castes have prevented them from raising their desires to the point of thinking that they could gain either wealth or office.[49]

Basically the creoles shared this view of the Peruvian masses. And the memory of Indian rebellion haunted them for many years to come. Indian pressure, therefore, far from hastening independence, brought out the latent conservatism of the creoles and persuaded them to accept Spanish rule until a more favourable opportunity occurred. And this was provided not by Peruvian initiative but by the armies first of San Martín then of Bolívar.[50] Meanwhile the liberal experiment came to an abrupt end. Ferdinand VII was restored to power in May 1814. He immediately annulled the constitution of 1812 and began to reimpose absolutism. The effects were soon felt in Peru, during the rebellion of 1814, when Abascal cheerfully dismantled the last remnants of reform, and then, once the *cuzqueños* were crushed, restored the old order from a position of strength.

For the next five years Peru remained a royalist base, internally secure but subject to increasing pressure as the American revolution approached its borders. The bureaucracy itself was subject to great strain. In mid–1816 Abascal retired from office, aged but unbowed, leaving a viceroyalty which he regarded as 'the greatest among the countries of America, because of its constant and incomparable role during the ten years of my afflicted government'.[51] His successor, Joaquín de la Pezuela, an Aragonese officer who had organized the counter-revolution in Upper Peru, shared Abascal's conservative principles but lacked his clarity of mind and singleness of purpose. Within a year of taking office he allowed himself to be outmanoeuvred at great distance by San Martín; failing to keep pace with the military thinking of the liberator, he continued to concentrate his forces in Upper Peru and did not anticipate the greater threat to the royalist position in Chile.[52] His judgement was soon challenged by his own colleagues, particularly by a group of new officers released for service in Peru at the end of the Napoleonic wars –

General José de la Serna, commander of Upper Peru from November 1816, Colonel Jerónimo Valdés, his chief-of-staff, and General José Canterac who brought further reinforcements to Upper Peru in 1818. These veterans of the peninsular war represented a new and younger school of political and military thinking. They were not absolutists but liberals who believed that the American revolution was a consequence of Spanish intransigence, that the colonies could only be held by a more liberal policy, and that the vehicle of this should be the constitution of 1812. And as experienced soldiers they despised Pezuela's irresolution. Spanish unity in Peru was beginning to crack.

Pezuela's preoccupations grew in the course of 1817–18. San Martín's victory in Chile pushed back the royalist frontier in the south, and even sparked a conspiratorial movement in Lima itself, ineffectual but a sign of growing patriot strength.[53] The viceroy found it difficult to increase the royalist forces; he lacked revenue and the cabildos refused to cooperate.[54] In 1818 he was pessimistic : 'Loyalists are apathetic; the cholos and Indians are not favourably disposed to the king; and the mass of the slaves are without exception supporters of the rebels, from whom they hope to obtain their freedom.'[55] His political position was further weakened in 1820 when the Spanish army at Cadiz mutinied and forced Ferdinand VII to restore the constitution of 1812. In due course Pezuela was instructed to apply the constitution in Peru, to restore the elected cabildos, and to implement yet another version of Spanish liberalism. Confusion followed : the Peruvian aristocracy were alienated; the people were not impressed; Pezuela dragged his feet; and the cabildo of Lima constitutionalized itself. The only pattern was instability, which was the last thing Pezuela wanted in his own camp. San Martín had just landed near Pisco at the head of a liberating expedition.

(iii) SAN MARTÍN AND THE LIBERATING EXPEDITION

In 1820 San Martín was ready to embark upon the last stage of his grand strategy.[56] It was a costly strategy, and from Chile in particular it demanded great sacrifices. To clear the south Pacific of Spanish sea power, an indispensable preliminary, Chile had to create a navy from nothing, to buy ships and equipment, to recruit personnel, to find an admiral.[57] The ships and crews were obtained in Britain and the United States. And a famous British naval officer, Thomas Cochrane, the future Earl of Dundonald, assumed command of the new squadron – seven warships in all – in November 1818. Cochrane was a man whose liberal sentiments were overshadowed by an intense interest in money and status. Like the rest of his countrymen who fought for the insurgents in Spanish America, he was a mercenary; but he was also a first-class professional sailor, an experienced administrator, and the possessor of an international reputation. Although he did not work well with San Martín, he gave victories as well as prestige to the revolutionary cause. He captured Valdivia (3–4 February 1820), Spain's strongest naval base in the Pacific; and he established such a powerful command of the sea that the Chilean squadron was able to intercept reinforcements from Spain, to destroy Spanish trade in the south Pacific, and to impose a blockade on the Peruvian coast.[58]

The liberation of Peru could give Chile long-term gains – political security and the emancipation of a market. In the meantime it was a crippling burden on an economically under-developed country. To provide an army was expensive enough. But to create and sustain sea power was one of the costliest operations any state could undertake. In February 1819 Chile and Argentina signed a treaty of alliance in which each undertook to contribute half the forces and finances needed to invade Peru. But Argentina, who had borne the main burden of the trans-Andean expedition, could not repeat this effort in the Pacific; financial disputes strained relations between the two countries to breaking point, and eventually Buenos Aires managed to send not the five hundred thousand pesos promised but about three hundred thousand and the rest in war materials.[59] Chile had to dig deep into its meagre resources. Ordinary revenue – taxes on agriculture, mining production and trade – was not sufficient, nor was it sufficiently augmented by extraordinary devices such as confiscation of royalist property and forced loans; and O'Higgins got virtually no financial help from the parsimonious senate, representing the landed aristocracy. The root difficulty was the stagnant economy, after eight years of war and revolution with consequent loss of labour and capital. On the other hand freedom of trade from 1811 had attracted a number of foreign merchants to the ports, and many of these were now making good profits from trade with royalist Peru. Yet the government's attempt to raise a forced loan of three hundred thousand pesos met with much resistance; British merchants in particular refused to pay. Lacking resources of its own the government was forced to rely on private enterprise. The navy alone cost seven hundred thousand pesos; this could only be raised by costly contracts with foreign merchants for loans against the customs revenue and in return for a share of the prize money which the warships would earn. And the contract to transport the liberating army to Peru was consigned exclusively to a private company.[60] By August 1820 the contractors had assembled sixteen transports, most of them prizes taken by privateers.

On 20 August the expedition set sail from Valparaiso – 4,500 troops, escorted by seven warships manned by sixteen hundred seamen; the latter included about six hundred foreigners, and the captains were either British or American.[61] San Martín had the advantage of surprise and the option of various landing points. Pezuela had a long coastline to defend; he had no intelligence on the enemy's destination and no prospect of reinforcements from Spain after the army revolt in Cadiz in January 1820. But the liberators too had their problems. When the expedition arrived off the coast of Peru, Cochrane wanted to land near Callao, engage the royalists immediately, and occupy the capital. Instead San Martín landed at Pisco and there he remained for six weeks. These bitter differences between San Martín and Cochrane were the product not only of personal incompatibility, but also of conflicting strategic concepts. Cochrane believed that it was necessary to destroy Spanish power and that it was possible to do so. San Martín too sought an absolute victory in Peru, 'to destroy for ever Spanish dominion in Peru and to place the people in the moderate exercise of their rights, this is the essential objective of the liberating expedition'.[62] But the methods which he envisaged were more complex than those of Cochrane; they were subtle and possibly unique in the American revolution. San Martín believed that a foreign liberating expedition could not in fact liberate Peru, that liberation needed the cooperation of Peruvians and should be secured as much as possible by Peruvians, with the minimum of violence. 'He has always expressed the greatest anxiety to prevent if possible any revolution in Lima which might occasion bloodshed and calamity.'[63] And San Martín himself declared : 'My soul would never be satisfied with a victory obtained at the cost of spilling American blood; I desire a peaceful victory, fruit of irresistible necessity.'[64] The political vehicle of such liberation would be monarchy, a further reason why the viceregal structure should not be entirely destroyed.

San Martín had a long record of monarchist sentiment, confirmed by his observation of anarchy in the Río de la Plata and by the hitherto fruitless search for political stability.[65] He held a pessimistic view of human nature, especially of American nature, its ignorance, its proneness to factionalism and violence unless restrained by strong government. So the monarchy which he sought was not a decentralized or constitutional monarchy. He told an English observer in Buenos Aires in May 1817 that Chile had more need of 'a monarchical than a republican form of government'.[66] And to his friend the Earl of Fife he argued that revolution and war had induced a yearning for peace, stability and firm government, that 'democratical notions have lost 90 per cent among the leading men, in this state no less than in the United Provinces'.[67] In a conversation with Commodore William Bowles at Valparaiso in February 1818 he put forward 'the idea of dividing South America amongst the principal European powers, and forming such a number of kingdoms as might provide for a prince of each royal house', and he particularly desired British mediation to this effect.[68] He sought, unsuccessfully, to have these ideas accepted in Chile in 1818–19. But it was in Peru that he saw his best chance, and there he was prepared to negotiate with the royalists for a monarchic settlement of the war.

Was San Martín ready to compromise with Spain? Did he plan to found a Pacific empire and make himself emperor? In fact he was a staunch independist, devoid of personal ambition, and moved primarily by the desire to avoid social upheaval. As reported by Bowles, he was convinced that the early revolutionary governments in America were unduly dependent on popular opinion and conciliatory to popular forces: 'The lower orders have thus obtained an undue preponderance and are beginning to manifest a revolutionary disposition dangerous in any country but more particularly in this, where want of education and general information is so strongly felt.' The danger was greatest in Peru, 'where the unenlightened part of the community are so numerous (particularly the slaves and Indians) and at the same time so formidable'.[69] The situation was rendered even more explosive by the prevalence of irresponsible demagogues thrown up by the revolution, 'visionaries, agitators, adventurers ... patriots, true, but more harmful than all the chapetones together'.[70]

San Martín, therefore, went to Peru as a true liberator, to wage a war not of conquest but of opinion, a war for the minds of Peruvians, a war between reason and bigotry, between freedom and tyranny. Rather than engage the enemy immediately, he preferred to wait for the Peruvian patriots to join his forces. His tactics could be defended on military as well as political grounds; his own army was not large, under five thousand, and it faced royalist forces, which, including reinforcements from Cuzco and Upper Peru, militia as well as regular units, totalled about twelve thousand. Viceroy Pezuela could not immediately exploit his military superiority, for he was tied by instructions from the new liberal regime in Spain to seek a pacification. San Martín responded promptly to his overtures; he sent commissioners to a peace conference at Miraflores (25 September 1820) and agreed to an eight-days armistice.[71] But there was no basis for a settlement, for while the royalists were reassured by San Martín's conservatism, they could not accept his insistence on independence, even in the form of an independent Spanish monarchy in Peru. The liberator then prepared to put his military plan into operation. A detachment under General Arenales penetrated into the sierra, with the object of moving northwards parallel to the coast and cutting Lima off from the interior. San Martín took the main force beyond Lima, first to Ancón (1 November) then to Huacho, seventy miles north of Callao, thus interposing his army between the capital and the agricultural region of northern Peru. His intention was to blockade Lima by land and sea, and thus to avoid the need of direct assault.

This cautious strategy was deeply resented by many of San Martín's officers, not least by Lord Cochrane, who controlled the seas and provided the naval cover for the move to Ancón. Naval forces were too expensive to keep inactive; and Cochrane wanted to destroy the remnants of Spanish naval power in Callao and simultaneously to attack Lima. He was incapable of influencing San Martín's policy by land, but on 4 November 1820 in a striking naval action brilliantly organized and bravely executed, he cut out the *Esmeralda*, a 44–gun frigate, under the very batteries of Callao, and thus captured the best Spanish warship in the Pacific, 'a death blow to the Spanish naval force in that quarter of the world'.[72] But San Martín continued to await the dissolution of the enemy forces and the rising of the Peruvian patriots. He believed that his mere presence was a disintegrating factor, that patriot recruits were swelling his forces while the viceregal army suffered desertion and demoralization.[73] 'How could the cause of independence', he asked, 'be advanced by my holding Lima, or even the whole country, in military possession? ... I wish to have all men thinking with me, and do not choose to advance a step beyond the gradual march of public opinion.'[74] Was he right?

The proximity of the liberating expedition and the consequent reaction of the royalists caused many Peruvians to re-think their position. A growing number of municipalities declared independence, first Supe in April 1819, then in the following year the cabildos of Ica, Tarma and Lambayeque. In November 1820 San Martín wrote to the Intendant of Trujillo, the Marquis of Torre Tagle: 'Public opinion hardens and declares itself more openly, for it sees that I scrupulously fulfil my promises to respect the rights, offices and property of those who are not enemies of the cause which I am charged to sustain and promote', and he called on Torre Tagle to join the cause of independence. Would it be prudent and just, he asked, 'to struggle against the torrent of events and the demands of justice, against the will of the people and the dictates of necessity?'[75] Torre Tagle, a creole aristocrat, was not a convinced independist, and he would have preferred autonomy within a Spanish framework. But reassured by San Martín's political moderation and bias towards monarchy, he led the cabildo of Trujillo in a declaration of independence on 29 December 1820.[76] The example was soon followed by Piura and other towns of the north. By May 1821 the whole of northern Peru had declared for independence and under the leadership of the creole elite began to supply men and money to San Martín at a time when he badly needed both. In the south the campaign waged by the English officer William Miller between March and May 1821 served to divert enemy forces from central Peru. And in the interior Arenales defeated a royalist detachment at Pasco. None of this was conquest, but it kept the enemy at full stretch.

As San Martín tightened his stranglehold on Lima, tension in the Spanish ranks added further credibility to his thesis of revolution without war. Desertions multiplied, and in December 1820 the entire battalion of Numancia, about 650 strong, passed over to the liberating expedition. Pezuela's conduct of the war, his vacillation, loss of Chile and defeats in Peru drew angry criticism from his own army and led to a palace revolt. A group of higher officers at Aznapuquio deposed the viceroy (29 January 1821) and replaced him by General José de la Serna. This military golpe, although condoned by Madrid, impaired Spanish legitimacy in Peru without earning military dividends. La Serna and his colleagues failed to exploit their military superiority over San Martín, preferring instead indecisive negotiations which further confirmed the liberator's argument.[77] Negotiations opened at Punchauca on 4 May 1821 and on 2 June San Martín himself met Viceroy La Serna. Again it was San Martín's monarchism which attracted the interest of the royalists. He proposed first that Spain should recognize the independence of the Río de la Plata, Chile and Peru; secondly, that a governing junta should be formed, composed of a nominee of the viceroy, another of San Martín, and a third of the Peruvians; thirdly, that two commissioners should be sent to Spain to notify the king of the declaration of independence and to invite him to place a prince of the royal family on the throne of Peru, on condition that the new sovereign accept the constitution. Again, the Spaniards rejected independence, the talks ended in deadlock, and hostilities were resumed.[78] According to subsequent explanation, San Martín was aware that Madrid would never ratify such a treaty, and his real object was to compromise the royalist commanders, thus leaving them no alternative to uniting with him.[79] But Punchauca taught a more significant lesson than this. It was another vindication of the revolutionaries, another sign that Spain, liberal or absolutist, had nothing to offer America.

In Lima the position of the royalists was now insecure, blockaded as they were by sea and surrounded by an increasingly hostile public. On 6 July 1821 La Serna evacuated the capital – but not Callao – and took his troops into the interior. In spite of the urging of Cochrane, San Martín still made no move to destroy the viceroy's disorganized army, which was able to regroup in the sierra.[80] On 12 July San Martín entered Lima, promising full protection to all inhabitants. On 15 July a cabildo abierto representing upper-class citizens declared for independence. This was officially proclaimed on 28 July and power was given to San Martín.[81] Patriotism was not the only explanation of these events. The transfer of Lima was accompanied by incipient social violence and by creole fear 'that the slave population of the city meant to take advantage of the absence of the troops, to rise in a body and massacre the whites'.[82] These fears were exaggerated, for the slaves of Lima, being mainly domestic servants, were not accustomed to concerted action. But patriots and royalists alike looked to San Martín to protect them from social disorder, and after the departure of the viceroy leading citizens invited the liberator to take over promptly in the interests of law and order. According to an English observer, 'it was not only of the slaves and of the mob that people were afraid; but with more reason of the multitude of armed Indians surrounding the city, who, although under the orders of San Martín's officers, were savage and undisciplined troops . . .'.[83] San Martín therefore came to the rescue of Lima, with the collaboration of those who in the circumstances placed security above royalism. Not all subscribed to this position and many suffered for their beliefs. Many others hid their true convictions, signing the declaration of independence out of fear or under duress. This was not a true gauge of Peruvian opinion or a sure guide for San Martín. No doubt the fall of Lima vindicated his strategy of non-violence. But only to a degree. For Lima was not the whole of Peru, and there was no evidence that the interior could be secured by similar methods, or that the royalist forces would retreat indefinitely. Yet he was still not prepared to engage them.

Independence could not be secure as long as Callao remained in royalist hands. It would be difficult to take by force. But San Martín did not even prevent the royalists from reinforcing it.

On 10 September a large Spanish force from the interior under General José Canterac marched past Lima unmolested and entered Callao. There it remained only a few days before shortage of provisions forced it to retire into the interior taking the treasure with it. And again San Martín declined to attack, arguing that 'the risks of a battle would not benefit the patriot cause'.[84] There was now a storm of criticism and protest: 'His loss of popularity may be said to take its date from that hour.'[85] And his popularity was not restored when the fortress of Callao surrendered a few days later, without San Martín having risked the loss of his untried army in an engagement with veteran troops.[86] The acquisition of Callao confirmed the patriots' dominance of the coast and opened their sector to foreign shipping. San Martín mistakenly believed that the war was over. Cochrane was convinced that it had still to be fought. He had now lost two of his warships and had neither supplies nor pay for the rest. Yet San Martín argued that this was a Chilean navy and therefore a charge on Chile not Peru. This was virtually to dismiss the Chileans from the war of Peruvian liberation. And it remained to be seen whether San Martín could instil a comparable sense of responsibility in the Peruvians themselves. Meanwhile, before his squadron disintegrated for lack of pay, Cochrane took the law into his own hands and seized government funds at Ancón to pay his crews. This was the end of collaboration between the two men. Ordered to quit Callao, Cochrane took his force out of the liberator's service in order to pursue his own campaign against Spanish shipping in the Pacific.

(iv)   The Protectorate

The independence of Peru was declared on 28 July 1821, and on 3 August San Martín became protector with supreme civil and military power.[87] He appointed Juan García del Río minister of foreign affairs, Bernardo Monteagudo minister of war, and Hipólito Unánue minister of finance. And he immediately launched a substantial reform programme. On 12 August he decreed that the children of slaves born in Peru from 28 July 1821 should be free.[88] A decree of 15 August declared that all naval and military personnel on the liberating expedition from

Valparaiso should be considered to be in the service of Peru and entitled to a pension. A resounding decree of 27 August abolished the Indian tribute, and forbade the name of Indian to be applied to the aborigines; they were henceforth to be called Peruvians, a name previously confined to those born of Spanish parents and their descendants. And on the following day he abolished the mita and every kind of compulsory labour service to which the Indians had been subjected.[89] Yet these noble sentiments remained purely legislative statements as long as the Peruvian creoles made no effort to apply them.

The reverse side of San Martín's Peruvian policy was his anti-Spanish programme. Towards the end of 1821 all unmarried Spaniards were ordered to leave the country and to forfeit half their property; and within a few months this policy was extended to married Spaniards. As peninsulares were thus forcibly expelled, their property was confiscated not to half the amount but in its entirety. Contemporaries attributed this hard line to the baleful influence of Monteagudo, the protector's closest political associate. 'The whole of these arbitrary measures were carried into effect during the nominal administration of Torre Tagle; and it was generally believed, that their offensive and cruel execution originated with the prime minister, Monteagudo.'[90] The influence of Monteagudo pervaded Peruvian politics in other directions. This radical of the Río de la Plata became a monarchist in Peru and reinforced the political ideas of the liberator. Monteagudo argued that Peru could not aspire to democracy because of its hierarchical traditions, deference to authority, lack of education, maldistribution of wealth, and social structure.[91] Now, in November 1821, San Martín entrusted García del Río and an English entrepreneur James Paroissien with a secret mission to Europe to offer the crown of Peru to a European prince, to secure European recognition of Peruvian independence, and to negotiate for a loan.[92] Another measure consonant with monarchy was the foundation of a new Peruvian aristocracy. In October 1821 San Martín established a new honour, the Order of the Sun, modelled upon the Legion of Honour in France, with pensions attached to first-class membership. And on 19 December property valued at five hundred thousand dollars was granted to twenty general and field officers of the liberating army as a reward for past services.[93]

In the interior, of course, San Martín's writ did not run. There the Spaniards still held power, though they were squandering their assets by their brutality and terrorism. Patriots were shot and property was confiscated at the caprice of the commanding officers. The people of Ica had to endure the sadistic rule of Colonel Santalla, whose circular order dated 19 July 1821 declared: 'The landed proprietors of this valley will deliver up three hundred horses and mules at the house of the Marques of Campo Ameno, within the peremptory and precise time of *four hours*, taking them from any person who may have them, without any exception whatever; it being understood that, in failure hereof within the said term, the defaulters will be immediately shot, their houses pillaged and burned, their estates ravaged, and their families put to the sword.'[94] The town of Cangallo near Huamanga was burnt to the ground; the viceroy issued a decree (11 January 1822) that the walls of the houses should be destroyed and that the name of Cangallo should henceforth disappear from the map. Many other villages and estates in the vicinity of Tarma were victims of Spanish incendiarism.[95] Thus in Peru, as elsewhere, the Spaniards were the worst enemies of the Spanish cause. Their savage and costly counter-revolution increased the revulsion against imperial rule and extended the patriot cause. When the patriots were able to impose sufficient power and security, then property-owners would openly declare themselves.

The montoneros, the guerrilla bands operating in central Peru between 1821 and 1824, were not Indian irregulars or populist forces. They were creoles and mestizos of middle rank and modest fortune whose property and families had suffered at the hands of royalists and who then sought vengeance.[96] They were joined by delinquents, by bandit chiefs and their followers such as those of the notorious Quirós, 'wearing long beards and dressed in the most grotesque manner', who used guerrilla operations as a means of personal plunder.[97] Guerrilla leaders sometimes practised forced conscription in the zones of their command, evidence of lack of popular recruits and perhaps of their own indifference to local problems. Yet the montoneros filled an important role in the patriot war effort. Until mid-1821 they attacked communications between the interior and the coast, cutting supply lines into the capital. During the retreat of the royalists from Lima in July 1821 the montoneros were well placed to harass the enemy and cut off stragglers. It was San Martín's failure to second their efforts that perhaps lost him the chance to hasten the end of the war.[98] Operating in bands of fifty to a hundred each, most of them from a base at the town of Reyes, the montoneros maintained guerrilla operations in the region between the central sierra and the coast, attacking and disappearing, preying on royalist communications, and keeping the army under Canterac constantly on the alert. This was a Peruvian contribution to the war of independence, led by such men as Francisco Vidal, Ignacio Ninavilca, Gaspar Huavique, and the Argentine officer Isidoro Villar, whom San Martín made commander-in-chief of the guerrillas of the sierra. But it could not be a decisive contribution. They themselves lacked cohesion; interest and motivation differed widely between men and between groups. Some communities in guerrilla territory refused to support the cause of independence. Many guerrillas were in the war solely for plunder. Others were forced into collaboration with the enemy in order to protect the lives of their families or neighbours. And dissension between guerrilla chiefs, or between these and patriot officers, often arose out of regional, racial or political rivalries. Some of the Argentine and Colombian military referred to the Peruvians contemptuously as *cholos, indios* or *peruleros.*

The Peruvian economy could not be totally geared towards the war effort. Military operations damaged the economy of the central zone, at a time when the people had to provide recruits and supplies for the guerrillas and the patriot army. The revenue of the patriots at the beginning of the war was minute. When they entered Lima there was not a peso in the Treasury. The mines were occupied by the enemy. Commercial and industrial activities had been hit by the siege imposed on the capital. So the government had recourse to forced loans from merchants. In 1822 a group of English merchants, including John Parish Robertson, were forced to make a loan of seventy-three thousand pesos, repayable on the customs but without interest.[99] Loans and taxes gave the government a revenue of 2·8 million pesos in the period 1 August 1821 to 31 July 1822. But this fell far short of expenditure, and to some extent the patriot forces had to live off the land. Economic help from the towns and villages for the patriot cause began with the first expedition of General Arenales to the central sierra and continued during the second expedition in 1821. But cooperation was not always forthcoming, and some areas resented the army's demands for cattle, foodstuffs and personnel.

The *reglamento provisional de comercio* (28 September 1821) provided for freedom of trade, and suppressed interior customs; but it placed a protective tariff (20 per cent) on imports in order to help local industries.[100] But the war dislocated trade and reduced production, while it also disrupted communications. The ranchers of Cajatambo, Huamalies, Junín and other areas were ruined through lack of buyers; the farmers of Conchucas, Huánuco and Huaylas were deprived of transport (mules and muleteers) to take their products to the consumer markets, while demand itself was suffering. The mines had entered a period of rapid decline. Operations were disrupted by the flight of proprietors, technicians, labour and capital, by the shortage and cost of mercury, and by the devastation of the mining support regions. When the patriots took possession they strove to increase output, and the silver mines of Cerro de Pasco were one of the few sources of revenue which they possessed; but these were still vulnerable to royalist attack and plunder. Economic disorder and the flight of private capital – exported sometimes with the help of the British navy – led to the creation of a bank to issue paper money. The Banco Auxiliar was established in 1821 to provide finance for the war effort and for the new administration at a time when the patriots found it almost impossible to impose new taxes or increase old ones; a further function was to supply a circulating medium in paper money to compensate for lack of silver.[101] But this development could not disguise the fact that many Peruvians expected immediate returns from independence without investing in it, and that the protectorate rested on fragile economic foundations.

(v) THE GUAYAQUIL INTERVIEW

Political opposition to San Martín was growing in Peru. While his monarchism appealed to some Peruvians such as Torre Tagle, it alienated many others. The liberal wing of the Peruvian political movement had done virtually nothing to win independence; but now it sought to impose its views on the independent state. Whereas previously the liberals had sought to reform though not to subvert the colony, now they worked to control the new Peru and destroy its creator. They saw San Martín as an obstacle who had to be removed. The new regime gave them greater freedom and opportunity to propagate liberal constitutionalism than the colony had done. Manuel Pérez de Tudela proclaimed republican principles. The priest Francisco Javier Luna Pizarro worked behind the scenes to undermine monarchcal plans.[102] And Sánchez Carrión returned to the fray, launching polemical tracts advocating liberalism and republicanism.

While they frustrated San Martín's political plans, the Peruvians also witheld the military help which he needed to end the war. In the vicinity of Lima San Martín had an army of eight thousand, with an effective strength of five thousand; competently led, it could have engaged the royalist forces, no more than five thousand strong, with some chance of success. But the patriot army lacked cohesion. Rivalry between Argentines, Chileans and Peruvians blunted its fighting edge, and many of the local officers were loathe to embark on active service.[103] San Martín himself, hampered by the material at his disposal, made a number of inept appointments in Peru, and many military commands were given to propertied creoles not because they were qualified but simply because they had declared for independence. There was an understandable lack of military zeal, and officers preferred the pleasures of Lima to the hazards of the sierra. Meanwhile Lima became resentful of this unemployed army and of the financial burden which it imposed.[104] And the viceregal forces remained intact. How could San Martín escape from this stalemate? How could he solve his political problems and end the military impasse? Leaving Torre Tagle in executive command, he went to Guayaquil to confer with the great liberator of the north, Simón Bolívar. Yet he could expect no simple solution there. Association with Bolívar raised more problems than it solved: it brought into question the whole basis of military collaboration; it exacerbated the issue of monarchy versus republicanism; and it introduced a new problem, the status of Guayaquil.[105]

Guayaquil was a naval base, a shipbuilding centre, and a major port. Strategically and commercially it was indispensable to the revolution. Late in 1820 Guayaquil declared its independence, formed a new government and opened its port to foreign trade. To which of its larger neighbours should it be joined? San Martín wanted it for Peru, though he acknowledged its right to decide its own political future. Bolívar claimed it for Colombia on the ground that the presidency of Quito had belonged to the viceroyalty of New Granada, and he did not regard the matter as negotiable. At the end of 1821 San Martín had some bargaining power, for Bolívar was floundering in Ecuador and needed the help of the division seconded by San Martín under the command of Colonel Andrés Santa Cruz. But Bolívar continued to treat Guayaquil as his, and after the decisive victory at Pichincha in May 1822, which won Quito for the northern revolution, he entered Guayaquil in person with his army behind him. He approached the interview with San Martín, therefore, from a position of superior strength. His letters of 17 and 22 June 1822 repeated his wish to meet San Martín and expressed his willingness to lead his army into Peru. In a letter of 13 July San Martín accepted the offer and made his way north. By now his position had been eroded. He had lost ground in Peru and he needed more from Bolívar than Bolívar needed from him. San Martín sought three things: the annexation of Guayaquil to Peru, the assistance of Colombian troops to bolster his own forces and defeat the Spaniards, and the acceptance of a monarchical constitution for the new states. As he approached Guayaquil it must have been obvious that he was the proposer, Bolívar the disposer.

The meetings were held on 26 and 27 July.[106] San Martín was realist enough to see that nothing could be done to reverse Bolívar's occupation of Guayaquil. And Bolívar made it clear that there could be no European monarchy in America. So San Martín's basic aim was reduced to securing Bolívar's military support, in the form either of a large auxiliary force or of an army under Bolívar himself. He even offered to serve with his own army under Bolívar. But Bolívar rejected these proposals. He needed his army at the time for internal security in Colombia. He doubted whether San Martín would really take orders from a younger man or whether San Martín's army would accept such an arrangement. And he regarded San Martín's military policy as impractical and irresolute. So the interview was fruitless. San Martín retired in angry frustration, convinced that Bolívar either doubted his sincerity or was embarrassed by his presence in the revolution. He believed that Bolívar was superficial, vain and ambitious, but he also had the honesty to recognize that this was the man to win independence, a man who would crush anyone in his way, not only the Spaniards but if necessary San Martín himself. So the leader of the southern revolution decided to withdraw and leave the way open for Bolívar to conquer Peru for independence.

When San Martín returned to Lima he found that his protégé Monteagudo had been overthrown in a conspiracy organized by Luna Pizarro, that his closest Peruvian collaborator Torre Tagle was under severe attack, and that he himself had lost the support of the Peruvian ruling class.[107] He was now more than ever convinced that the time had come to leave Peru. On 20 September, before the first constituent congress of Peru, he resigned his power. The same night he left Lima, and the next day he sailed for Chile, thence to Europe and a long exile until his death in 1850.[108] Contemporary criticism of San Martín concentrated on his alleged inertia in the conduct of the war in Peru; his despotic expulsion of the Spaniards in Lima; and his desertion of the cause of independence by premature retirement. To each of these charges there was a reply. San Martín frankly sought to revolutionize, not to conquer, Peru. His severity towards Spaniards was necessary in the interests of security, at a time when the royalist army was undefeated. And his retirement was realistic, for he had lost influence in Peru. All his tactics were consistent with his avowed policy. The policy perhaps was open to question , but Bolívar too was to find Peru a difficult case. At the end San Martín pointed to a new danger in Spanish America, that soldiers might destroy constitutions; in an age of military golpes he set a rare example of restraint. And he was generous in defeat. In 1826, when the liberation of Peru was complete, he acknowledged that 'the successes which I have gained in the war of independence are really inferior to those which General Bolívar has won for the American cause'.[109]

Congress gave executive power to a junta – three nonentities who had no policy and no solution to the continuing conflict between conservatives and liberals. Conditions were ripe for military intervention. In February 1823 the Peruvian army leaders forced congress to replace the junta by José de la Riva Agüero. The new president of the republic came from the highest ranks of the colonial aristocracy and represented the enduring power of the Peruvian ruling class. His friend Santa Cruz, a prime mover in the golpe, was rewarded with the command of the Peruvian army. Colonel Agustín Gamarra was appointed chief-of-staff. And Colonel Ramón Herrera was appointed minister of war.[110] 'It is remarkable', observed William Miller, 'that these four persons, occupying the highest offices in the state, should have held commissions from the King of Spain for some time after San Martín had made good his footing in Peru, and at a period eleven years subsequent to the commencement of the revolution.'[111] Miller was possibly less than just to Riva Agüero : his record of independist sympathies was perhaps more convincing than that of his colleagues. But there was an ambiguity in his position, as there was among the entire Peruvian aristocracy. Jealous of their privileges and conscious of the underprivileged masses beneath them, they were primarily concerned neither with the survival of Spanish rule nor with the winning of independence but with the degree of power and control which they would have in any regime. In the period between the departure of San Martín and the arrival of Bolívar the Peruvian aristocracy briefly enjoyed an exclusive control over that part of their country which San Martín had liberated. But they proved incapable of ruling or of winning the war. They could not even agree among themselves on basic objectives. Riva Agüero was convinced that Peru could not win independence by its own effort because of the concentration of Spanish power there; so he sought the assistance of Bolívar.[112] Otherwise he was politically inept and, even worse, a military failure. The Spaniards were allowed to recapture Lima in June 1823. Riva Agüero and congress fled to Callao. There congress deposed the president in favour of Bolívar's envoy, General José Antonio de Sucre; and the ex-president moved defiantly to the northern town of Trujillo where he began to re-group his following. Amidst increasing disorientation Peru desperately needed the saving hand of Bolívar.

SIX *Venezuela, the Violent Revolution*

(i) FROM COLONY TO REPUBLIC

VENEZUELA WAS PART plantation, part ranch. People and production were concentrated in the valleys of the coast and the llanos of the south. Dispersed among the great plains of the interior and the western shores of Lake Maracaibo, hundreds of thousands of cattle, horses, mules and sheep formed one of the country's permanent assets and provided immediate exports in the form of hides and other animal extracts. The commercial plantations produced a variety of export crops, tobacco from Barinas, cotton from the valleys of Aragua, coffee from the Andean provinces. In the 1790s, after a century of economic expansion, these products accounted for over 30 per cent of Venezuela's exports. But the mainstay of the economy was cacao; produced in the valleys and mountain sides of the central coastal zone, cacao expanded until it came to form over 60 per cent of total exports.[1] This was the world of the great latifundia, whose labour was supplied by an ever-expanding slave trade and by tied peons who were often manumitted slaves. Venezuela was a classical colonial economy, low in productivity and in consumption.

Alexander von Humboldt observed that the Venezuelan aristocracy were averse to independence, because 'they believed that in revolutions they would run the risk of losing their slaves'; and he argued that 'they would even prefer foreign domination to rule by Americans of a lower class'.[2] The social structure was indeed subject to great stress. Around 1800 the population totalled 780,000, of whom about 60 per cent lived in the Bishopric of Caracas. There, out of a total of 427,205, the whites numbered 108,920, or 25.5 per cent, the vast majority of them creoles. The mass of the population consisted of Blacks and pardos, who together formed 61.3 per cent of the whole. Pardos numbered 163,275 (38.2 per cent), and free Blacks 34,463 (8 per cent). There were 64,462 slaves (15 per cent), though these were in greater concentration in the coastal region (26.2 per cent).[3]

The whites were not a homogeneous group. At the bottom swarmed the *blancos de orilla*, artisans, traders and wage-earners, who merged into the pardos and were identified with them. These poor whites had little in common with the great latifundistas, the *grandes cacaos*, owners of land and of slaves, producers of the colony's wealth, commanders of the colony's militia. Land was their base, and land their ambition. Original grants had grown in various ways, legal and illegal, until they formed vast holdings, held on a family or clan basis, and spreading out from the Caracas valley to the rest of the province, north-west to Coro and south to the llanos, into the western valleys and the eastern zones.[4] By the middle of the eighteenth century 1·5 per cent of the population of Caracas monopolized all cultivable and grazing land in the province, though the areas under actual cultivation were very small, perhaps under 4 per cent of the whole.[5] At the end of the colonial period the landed aristocracy, the majority of them creoles, comprised 658 families, totalling 4,048 people, or 0·5 per cent of the population. This was the group who monopolized land and mobilized labour. Its members usually lived in town houses and were active in such institutions as Spanish practice opened to them, the cabildos, the consulado, and the militia. 'Almost all the families whose friendship we enjoyed in Caracas', reported Humboldt, 'the Uztariz, the Tovares, the Toros, had their base in the beautiful valleys of Aragua, where they were proprietors of the richest plantations.'[6]

The landed aristocracy were imbued with a deep class consciousness, born of their close clan ties and sharpened by conflict with Spaniards on the one hand and pardos on the other. As producers of commercial crops for export the latifundists wanted to place their products directly in the world market and to procure imports from the cheapest sources. They therefore resented control of overseas trade by Spanish monopolists, who bought exports cheaply and sold imports dearly. This conflict of economic interests between landowners and merchants reinforced the political antagonism between creoles and Spaniards; and joint representation in the consulado of Caracas, far from assuaging hostility, only focused it more clearly.[7] Venezuelan producers were forced to evade monopoly restrictions: in one way or another, via the metropolis or via contraband, the expanding output of the plantations reached the consumer markets of the world; and for at least 50 per cent of its imports the colony depended on non-Spanish suppliers. Growth brought to the colony many new immigrants, above all Canarians, poor but ambitious men who soon controlled the Venezuelan end of trade with Spain and the interior. The new peninsulares also encroached on the political preserves of the Venezuelan elite. With the backing of the crown they advanced to share cabildo posts with Venezuelans and to dominate the newly created audiencia. The frustration of creoles was the more acute as they felt themselves threatened by the socio-racial policy of the metropolis.

The pardos, or free coloureds, were branded by their racial origins; descendants of Negro slaves, they comprised mulattos, zambos and mestizos in general, as well as blancos de orilla whose ancestry was suspect. In the towns they were artisans and an incipient wage-labour group; in the country they engaged in subsistence farming and cattle enterprises or they were a rural peonage. With the free Negroes they formed almost half the total population; their numbers were particularly noticeable in the towns, scenes of acute social tension, 'the constant struggle, the daily collision, the agelong conflict of castes, oppression met by profound and implacable hatred'.[8] The pardos were not a class but an indeterminate, unstable and intermediary mass, blurring at the edges downwards and upwards. But whatever they were, they alarmed the whites by their numbers and aspirations. The creoles went over to the offensive and opposed the advance of the *gente de color,* protested against the sale of whiteness, resisted popular education, and petitioned, though unsuccessfully, against the presence of pardos in the militia.[9] They regarded it as unacceptable 'that the whites of this province should admit into their class a mulatto descended from their own slaves'. They argued that this could only lead to the subversion of the existing regime: 'The establishment of militias led by officers of their own class has given the pardos a power which will be the ruin of America; incapable of resisting invasion by a powerful enemy, and as there are sufficient whites for the task of controlling the slaves and maintaining internal order, they serve only to enhance the arrogance of the pardos, giving them an organization, leaders and arms, the more easily to prepare a revolution.'[10] In short, the creoles resented imperial policy towards the pardos: it was too indulgent; it was 'an insult to the old, distinguished, and honoured families'; it was dangerous 'to enfranchise the pardos and to grant them, by dispensation from their low status, the education which they have hitherto lacked and ought to continue to lack in the future'. The creoles were frightened men; they feared a caste war, inflamed by French revolutionary doctrine and the contagious violence of Saint Domingue.[11]

These forebodings were intensified by horror of slave agitation and revolt.[12] Again the creole aristocracy lost confidence in the metropolis. On 31 May 1789 the Spanish government issued a new slave law, codifying legislation, clarifying the rights of slaves and duties of masters, and in general seeking improvement of conditions in the slave compounds. The creoles rejected state intervention between master and slave, and fought this decree on the grounds that slaves were prone to vice and independence and were essential to the economy. In Venezuela – indeed all over the Spanish Caribbean – planters resisted the law and procured its suspension in 1794.[13] The following year both reformers and reactionaries could claim to have proved their point when a Negro and pardo revolt convulsed Coro, the centre of the sugar-

cane industry and the base of a white aristocracy so class conscious that 'the families of notorious nobility and purity of blood
live in terror of the day that one of their members should surpris-
ingly marry a *coyote* or zambo'.[14] The revolt was led by José
Leonardo Chirino and José Caridad González, free Negroes who
were influenced by the ideas of the French revolution and the
race war in Saint Domingue. They worked on the slaves and
coloured labourers, three hundred of whom rose in rebellion in
May 1795 with the proclamation of 'the law of the French, the
republic, the freedom of the slaves, and the suppression of the
alcabala and other taxes'.[15] They occupied haciendas, sacked
property, killed any landowners they could lay hands on, and
invaded the city of Coro. This was an isolated and ill-equipped
rebellion and was easily crushed, many of its followers being shot
without trial. Yet it was only the tip of a constant underlying
struggle of the Negroes against the whites in the last years of the
colony, when slave fugitives frequently established their own
communes, remote from white authority.

The creole elite was conditioned by disorder. Another subversive movement, slowly building up from 1794, recruiting
pardos and poor whites, labourers and small proprietors, and led
by Manuel Gual and José María España, came to the surface in
La Guaira in July 1797. The conspiracy stood for 'liberty and
equality' and the rights of man, and it had a plan of action for
taking power and installing a republican government. Its programme included freedom of trade, abolition of the alcabala and
other taxes, abolition of slavery and of Indian tribute, and distribution of land to the Indians; and it pleaded for harmony
between whites, Indians and coloureds, 'brothers in Christ and
equal before God'.[16] This was too radical for creole property-
owners, many of whom collaborated with the authorities in suppressing the 'infamous and detestable' movement and offered to
serve the captain-general 'not only with our persons and
haciendas but also by forming armed companies at our own
cost'.[17]

Until the last years of the colonial regime the creole aristocracy
saw no alternative to the existing power structure and they
accepted Spanish rule as the most effective guarantee of law,
order and hierarchy. But gradually, between 1797 and 1810,

their loyalism was eroded by shifting circumstances. In an age of increasing instability, when Spain could no longer control events either at home or abroad, the creoles came to appreciate that their social pre-eminence depended on gaining an immediate political objective – to take exclusive power instead of sharing it with officials and representatives of a debilitated metropolis. The Venezuelan economy, moreover, was a victim of the European wars which engulfed Spain and which exposed even more glaringly the flaws of colonial monopoly – the great shortage and high cost of manufactured goods and the difficulty of getting the colony's products to foreign markets. Contraband was the only safety valve, but contraband too could become a form of monopoly in the hands of the English or the Dutch and was not a permanent alternative to freedom of trade. The creoles believed that the Spanish monopolists were determined to retain control at all costs and even after 1810 they were convinced that the various expeditions bringing 'pacification' to Venezuela were simply agents of Cadiz interests. In the Spanish view, of course, none of these issues were negotiable: it was this intransigence which persuaded a majority of the creoles that their interests could only be secured by absolute independence. Their determination was reinforced by a growing realization that they themselves were better guardians of the existing social structure than was the metropolis.

Political objectives were focused more sharply from July 1808 when news of the French conquest of Spain reached Caracas. While the Spanish bureaucracy dithered, a group of leading creoles presented a request for the establishment of an independent junta to decide the political position of Venezuela.[18] The authorities clamped down on the movement, imprisoned or exiled its authors, and quickly made propaganda among the pardos and lower classes that creole power would be harmful to them. And they survived attempts to depose Captain-General Vicente Emparán on 14 December 1809 and 2 April 1810. But they could not control events in Spain. There the central junta dissolved itself at Cadiz in February 1810 in favour of a regency. Why should Americans accept these manoeuvres? The question was asked in all the Spanish colonies. But Venezuela heard the news first and Venezuela took action on 19 April 1810. The captain-

general still refused to collaborate in the creation of an autonomous junta, so the revolutionaries took matters into their own
hands. While young activists mobilized a crowd in the main plaza
of Caracas, the cabildo met independently of the Spanish authorities and it was joined by creole revolutionaries representing
various interests.[19] They deposed and deported the administration and the audiencia, and made the cabildo the nucleus of a new
government of Venezuela, the *Junta Conservadora de los
Derechos de Fernando VII.*[20]

The junta represented the creole ruling class, but this class did
not speak with one voice. It was divided between conservatives
and radicals, between autonomists who wanted home rule under
the Spanish crown and independists who demanded an absolute
break with Spain.[21] At first the conservatives were in the ascendancy, and it was they who forbade the entry of the veteran
revolutionary, Francisco de Miranda, a man whose family was
socially suspect, the conspirator of 1797, the 'traitor' of the
abortive invasion of 1806, the deist and anti-clerical.[22] The
early legislation of the junta was a version of liberal self-interest:
it abolished export duties and the alcabala on essential consumer
goods; it decreed freedom of trade; and it proscribed the slave
trade (though not slavery). It then held elections in all the towns
under its rule, on a franchise restricted to adults (minimum age
twenty-five) owning not less than two thousand pesos in movable
property. The national congress met on 2 March 1811, thirty-
one deputies from seven provinces, all from great landed families
and the majority favouring the 'autonomist' position. Congress
replaced the junta by a new executive consisting of three rotating
members, an advisory council, and a high court.

Miranda was allowed into Venezuela in December 1810
assisted by the influence of Simón Bolívar. These men were the
leaders of a small radical group who stood for absolute independence. They operated from within the *Sociedad Patriótica,* an
organization founded in August 1810 for 'the development of
agriculture and livestock', but soon transformed into a political
club and a pro-independence pressure group. The membership
of the society was almost as exclusive as that of congress itself,
though the creoles made a gesture towards democracy by allowing a number of pardos to attend meetings. The fact is that the

radicals no less than the conservatives stood primarily for the advancement of creole interests, but they believed that these could best be served by national independence. Bolívar himself proclaimed this view in congress in the session of 4 July 1811 : 'The Patriotic Society rightly respects the national congress; but equally congress ought to listen to the Patriotic Society, centre of enlightenment and of all revolutionary interests. Let us banish fear and lay the foundation stone of American liberty. To hesitate is to perish.'[23] It was a seductive call. Independence was declared on 5 July and the first Venezuelan republic was born.[24] It lived for one year.

The creole concept of the new society was revealed in the Constitution of December 1811, a constitution strongly influenced by that of the United States, scrupulously federal, weak in executive power, and hierarchical in its social values.[25] These had been first announced by congress in its declaration of the *Derechos del Pueblo* (1 July 1811): 'Citizens shall be divided into two classes, those with right of suffrage and those without.... The latter are those who do not have the property qualifications specified by the constitution; these shall enjoy the benefit of the law without participating in its institution.'[26] The constitution, it is true, established 'liberty, equality, property and security'. And it was egalitarian in the sense that it abolished all fueros and all legal expressions of socio-racial discrimination : 'The old laws which imposed civil degradation on one part of the free population of Venezuela known hitherto as pardos are revoked and annulled in all their parts.'[27] But legal inequality was replaced by a real inequality based on the franchise, which confined voting rights and therefore full citizenship to property-owners.[28] To the pardos, therefore, an illusion of equality. And the slaves remained slaves. The constitution confirmed the suppression of the slave trade, yet preserved slavery. The new rulers, indeed, ordered the establishment of a 'national guard for the apprehension of fugitive slaves; they shall patrol and search fields, haciendas, highlands and valleys; they shall enforce law and order among that sector of the population assigned to agricultural labour, preventing them from evading such labour through caprice, idleness, vices or other reasons prejudicial to the tranquility and prosperity of the country.'[29] The creole message was unmistakable, and it soon reached the Negroes and pardos.

Independence, then, simultaneously raised and frustrated expectations. So the Negroes fought their own revolution, that 'insurrección de otra especie' as a Spanish official described it. The royalists were quick to exploit the situation. The Archbishop of Caracas instructed his clergy in the plantation areas to preach to the slaves the advantages of Spanish government compared to rule by creole landowners.[30] Royalist agents moved through the coastal zone provoking and sustaining black insurrection. Creole leaders like Bolívar were appalled by this 'revolution of the Negroes, free and slave, this inhuman and atrocious people, feeding on the blood and property of the patriots, committing, especially in the village of Guatire, the most horrible assassinations, robberies, violence and destruction.'[31] The slaves, of course, were creatures of the society which bred or bought them, and they seem to have fought less for liberty than to enslave their masters; alternatively they massacred the whites and destroyed their property. This upsurge of racial violence alienated most creoles from the cause of abolition and many creoles from the cause of independence. The royalist ranks began to swell.

Royalist opposition to the first republic centred on Coro, Maracaibo and Guayana.[32] And in Valencia the pardos, frustrated by denial of full rights of citizenship, rose against the whites and vigorously repelled the forces of the Marquis of Toro until Miranda himself took command and reduced the town to capitulation (13 August 1811). While the royalists fought without pity and without scruple, the congressional leaders were victims of their own social prejudices; inflexible towards the coloureds, they were too lenient to the royalists and allowed many to escape and re-group.

The republic was already tottering on its narrow base when it suffered a series of external shocks. On 26 March 1812 a major earthquake struck Venezuela; from the Andes to the coast 'a strange roar was followed by the silence of the grave'. In Caracas, where destruction and casualties were heavy, Bolívar was seen struggling to rescue victims from the rubble and crying 'we shall fight nature itself if it opposes us'.[33] But they also had to fight the Church, for the catastrophe was exploited by royalist clergy who preached that this was God's punishment for independence. In the same month Captain Domingo Monteverde advanced out of Coro at the head of royalist troops reinforced from Puerto Rico. Soon, without even a major battle, he recovered the whole of western Venezuela. The republic reacted to these disasters by appointing Miranda commander-in-chief with dictatorial powers. But the aged revolutionary, a pompous and pedantic failure who lacked ideas and resolution, could not stem the tide of royalism which swept over the republic. On 3 May Monteverde entered Valencia with the connivance of the inhabitants. In the llanos the guerrilla leader Boves joined the royalist cause. At the beginning of July Bolívar lost Puerto Cabello. And Miranda completed the demoralization of the republic. He opened negotiations with Monteverde, and in return for a promise that patriot lives and property would be respected he capitulated on 25 July 1812. Bolívar and his associates were furious; they arrested Miranda at La Guaira before he could leave Venezuela and allowed him to be taken by the Spaniards. Meanwhile, as the *República Boba* died amidst angry recriminations, Monteverde entered Caracas in triumph and established what he called 'the law of conquest'. The conquering 'army' numbered less than three hundred.[34]

The first republic was shackled by the social structure of the colony. The royalists fought for the old order. The independists fought for creole supremacy. The pardos and slaves fought for their own liberation. So there were a number of movements and each confronted or exploited the other. These divisions created propitious circumstances for the restoration of royal power.

(ii) WAR TO THE DEATH

Monteverde was an unprincipled and ambitious demagogue. The ink was hardly dry on the capitulation when he began to jail patriots and confiscate their property. Soon the fortresses of Puerto Cabello and La Guaira were full of independists and of many who were mere suspects. The caudillo based his rule on upper-class creoles, royalist clergy, and his upstart compatriots, the *canarios;* many personal scores were settled and much property changed hands. But this military dictatorship was not an unmitigated blessing to Spain. It alienated the legitimate

Spanish bureaucracy and outraged moderate royalists by its greed and cruelty.[35] And the counter-revolution bred its own destruction. On the one hand it furthered the formation of national consciousness among creole victims. At the same time, once the mask of racial benevolence was removed, it became clear to pardos and slaves that royalism held nothing for them. They had not fought the aristocratic republic simply to substitute new oppressors. The slaves rebelled once more; at Curiepe they armed themselves with staves, machetes and knives and marched on La Guaira. The pardos of the coast conspired in November 1812 in a vain attempt to overthrow the dictatorship. Bands of insurgent llaneros, peons and other marginal groups continued guerrilla action, inspired by an enduring hatred of white property-owners. These half-brigands, half-revolutionaries were no asset to the economy; they preyed upon the country and terrorized the population. Yet they performed two essential services to the cause of independence. They provided a source of recruits for the republican forces when the patriot leaders renewed the struggle. And their survival demonstrated to the creoles that restoration of royal power was no guarantee of social order.

Those republican leaders who managed to escape Monteverde's dragnet fled to the Antilles or New Granada, or they went underground. Bolívar himself made his way to Cartagena, and there he reviewed the situation.

Simón Bolívar was a product of the creole aristocracy, born (24 July 1783) to one of the richest and most powerful families in the colony, owners of cacao haciendas, cotton plantations, cattle ranches, sugar mills, various houses in Caracas, and of course a large number of slaves.[36] He began his adult life with a large personal fortune in capital and property, and he was a leading member, if not representative, of the land-owning class. This was the interest for whom he spoke when he denounced the servitude of Americans, their exclusion from office and trade, their role as producers of raw materials and consumers of Spanish manufactures.[37] But Bolívar towered above his class in knowledge, judgement and ability. His liberal education, wide reading, and extensive travels in Europe heightened his innate idealism and opened his mind to new horizons, in particular to English political virtues and to the thought of the European enlightenment. Hobbes and Locke, the encyclopedists and *philosophes*, especially Montesquieu, Voltaire and Rousseau, all left a deep impression upon his mind and gave him a life-long devotion to reason, freedom and order. Allied to his own originality, these external influences endowed his thought with an intellectual quality and ideological richness rare among Americans, particularly among men of action. Bolívar also stood apart from his class in his acute political sense. He saw that the strategy of emancipation would have to be changed, that victory could not be won without greater popular support. His ancestors had bequeathed to him a trace of Negro blood, seen perhaps in his dark complexion and thick lips. He freed his own slaves, offered freedom to all who joined the patriot forces, and promised the llaneros land taken from the enemy. Although he never gained mass support for emancipation, yet he expanded the movement beyond the narrow base of the first republic. As for religion, it played little part in his life, and the traditional faith of Americans left him unmoved. According to O'Leary, his aide and confidante, Bolívar was 'a complete atheist' who believed only that religion was necessary for government.[38]

Bolívar's basic aim was liberty, 'the only object worth the sacrifice of a man's life'; and with this, equality – that is, legal equality – for all men, whatever their class, creed or colour. In principle he was a democrat and he believed that governments should be responsible to the people: 'Only the majority is sovereign; he who takes the place of the people is a tyrant and his power is usurpation.'[39] But Bolívar was not so idealistic to imagine that America was ready for pure democracy, or that the law could annul inequalities of nature and society. He spent his whole life developing his principles and applying them to American reality. The first stage of development took place at Cartagena, where, at the age of twenty-nine, he gave vent to his intellect and expounded his vision.

The 'Cartagena Manifesto', the first major statement of Bolívar's ideas, analyzed the failings of the first republic and probed its political assumptions.[40] The reasons for failure, he argued, lay in the adoption of a constitution ill-adapted to the character of the people, excessive tolerance towards the enemy, reluctance to recruit military forces, financial incompetence leading to issue of paper money, the religious fanaticism unleashed by the earthquake, and the factionalism which subverted the republic from within. Popular elections, he maintained, allowed the ignorant and the ambitious to have their say and placed government in the hands of inept and immoral men who introduced the spirit of faction. Thus, 'our own disunity, not Spanish arms, returned us to slavery'. Peoples so young, so innocent of representative government and of education, could not be immediately transformed into democracies; their system of government should not advance beyond social realities. He insisted on unity and centralization; a 'terrible power' was needed to defeat the royalists, and constitutional susceptibilities were irrelevant until peace and happiness were restored. This was the beginning of his permanent opposition to federalism, which he regarded as weak and complex, when America needed strength and unity. Bolívar also appealed for continental collaboration, and he wrote to the Congress of New Granada requesting assistance for the liberation of Venezuela. The recovery of Venezuela, he urged, was essential to the security of the American revolution. If royalism in Coro led to the fall of Caracas, could not counter-revolution in Venezuela endanger the whole of America? 'Coro is to Caracas what Caracas is to America.'[41]

Bolívar's military service in New Granada earned him credit with congress, and enabled him to secure a base on the border and to recruit an army of invasion. It was a small army – no larger than seven hundred – and its prospects depended upon striking at the heart of royalist power before Monteverde could concentrate his scattered forces. Bolívar therefore moved quickly out of New Granada along the shortest route to Caracas. Between May and August 1813, in a series of lightning strikes, he freed Mérida, Trujillo, Barquisimeto and Valencia. His victory was so complete that he was able to enter Caracas in triumph on 6 August and establish a virtual dictatorship.[42] While Bolívar was advancing from the west, Santiago Mariño, a minor caudillo of the east, was leading the liberation of Cumaná. With the exception of Maracaibo and Guayana, therefore, Venezuela was now in patriot hands. Bolívar had already been acclaimed liberator on his entry into Mérida on 23 May. And with military success behind him, he was in a position to dictate policy. He was determined to avoid the mistakes of the first republic. He spoke of 're-establishing the free forms of republican government', but he really wanted new and strong executive power; this he procured on 2 January 1814 when a representative assembly granted him supreme power. And in spite of the reservations of the Venezuelan aristocracy, who regarded him as a tyrant and sought to restrain him by reinforcing the cabildos and the judiciary, he established a hard-line revolutionary government and a policy of no mercy towards Spaniards.

The war of liberation in Venezuela was cruel, destructive and total. This was a measure of the insecurity felt by each side, neither of which held preponderance of power or could afford to allow the other to grow. Monteverde tried to tip the balance in his favour by terrorizing the population and allowing his subordinates to kill civilians as well as belligerents. The cruelty of the Spaniards was nowhere worse than at Maturín and no one more monstrous than the officer Antonio Zuazola, who burnt, mutilated and murdered indiscriminately, 'a detestable man' Bolívar called him, who destroyed even the foetus in the mother's womb 'with more impatience than the tiger devours its prey'.[43] Atrocities were committed by both sides, inevitably, but it was Monteverde who first applied 'the law of conquest'. In Bolívar's view the enemy was fighting an undeclared war of extermination, killing prisoners whose only crime was that they fought for freedom. He believed that the patriots were at a disadvantage and could no longer wage civilized war against the Spaniards. He therefore resolved upon a new policy – war to the death, pardoning only Americans, in order to give the patriots parity of menace. 'Our tolerance is now exhausted, and as our oppressors force us into a mortal war they shall disappear from America and our land will be purged of the monsters that infest it. Our hatred will be implacable, the war will be to the death.'[44] On 15 June 1813, in the celebrated decree issued at Trujillo, Bolívar made the position even clearer :

Any Spaniard who does not work against tyranny in favour of the just cause, by the most active and effective means, shall be considered an enemy and punished as a traitor to the country, and in consequence shall inevitably be shot. . . . Spaniards and Canarios, depend upon it, you will die, even if you are simply neutral, unless you actively espouse the liberation of America. Americans, you will be spared, even when you are culpable.[45]

The exception was significant. This was a civil war, in which Americans predominated on both sides. And Bolívar could not bring himself to wage war to the death on Venezuelans, even though they might be royalists: 'It is not right to destroy men who do not wish to be free.'[46] Nor was it feasible to do so. The Trujillo decree ruthlessly distinguished between Spaniards and Americans; it sought to cut through categories like royalism and republicanism and to make this a war between nations, between Spain and America. To this extent the decree of war to the death was an affirmation of Americanism, an expression of Venezuelan identity. More simply it aimed to terrorize Spaniards into submission and encourage creoles to support independence. In fact it did not accomplish either.

By the beginning of 1814 the second republic was established and appeared to be secure. Monteverde had been driven from the royalist base at Puerto Cabello, and further victories in the east and the west consolidated the revolution. But 1814 began with bloody battles and ended in bitter defeat. The reasons were familiar. The base of the second republic was no wider than that of the first. The cause of emancipation had not yet won the heart and minds of all Venezuelans: 'The greater part of the Spanish forces', reported O'Leary, 'were composed of Venezuelans, a matter of great bitterness to Bolívar. American blood was spilt by American hands.' And Bolívar confessed his humiliation 'that our conquerors are our brothers and our brothers triumph only over us'.[47] Divided among themselves, the creoles were also rejected by the mass of the people. They earned the suspicion of the lower classes in general and the opposition of two particular groups, the slaves and the llaneros. The slave rebellions of the first republic still haunted the minds of the Venezuelan aristocracy, who were not disposed to concede either manumission or reform. When the liberating army occupied Caracas in August 1813 it identified the slaves as a major focus of resistance and dispatched a punitive expedition against them. And hacendados pressed Bolívar to revive the national guard 'in order to pursue robbers, apprehend fugitive slaves, and preserve estates and properties free from all incursions'.[48] The slaves therefore continued their own autonomous struggle, independent of Spaniards and creoles alike. Race-conscious coloured forces fought on both sides, from opportunism not conviction. And they consistently singled out the whites of the opposing force for extermination. After an engagement with a royalist unit on 6 September 1813 a patriot officer reported: 'The death-roll [twenty-six] comprises whites, Indians and zambos, with only one Negro, and we have noticed that Negro casualties are invariably the least, a fact on which the government can reflect in the interests of our tranquility.'[49] The slaves could destroy but they could not win. Like the Negroes in general, they were unorganized and leaderless. Not so the llaneros.

In the south a new royalist leader rose to scourge the revolution – José Tomás Boves, an Asturian who had been attracted to Venezuela as a sailor and smuggler. After a brush with the law he retreated to the llanos and became a horse-dealer at Calabozo.[50] When the revolution began, the strong, cunning and sadistic Spaniard was already at one with his new environment, the great plains of Venezuela. This endless expanse of flat grassland, scorched by the sun in the dry season, and in the wet turned by torrential rain into fever-ridden swamps and lakes, was the home of a wild and warlike breed, a racial mixture from Indian, white and Negro stock, hardened by their savage surroundings and capable of great endurance on horseback. Insulted by the patriots in 1812, Boves became a caudillo of the llaneros and fashioned them into a powerful cavalry force. In the course of 1814 he led his mounted hordes against the republic, and on 15 June he routed the combined forces of Bolívar and Mariño at the battle of La Puerta, taking no prisoners and reducing the patriot ranks by about a thousand. Continuing his progress northward he entered Valencia on 10 July and on 16 July he was in Caracas; there he established a crude tyranny before moving on to Cumaná. As he extended the terror and the killing, so he personally supervised the massacre of men, women and children, moving about the carnage with his habitual, sinister smile.[51] He defeated the patriots in the east on 5 December in a battle in which he himself was killed by a lance thrust. Meanwhile, Boves and the llaneros had destroyed the second republic. What was the Boves attraction? How did he recruit his troops? Was he a genuinely populist caudillo, an agrarian reformer? In the Proclamation of Guayabal (1 November 1813) Boves decreed war to the death against his creole enemies and the confiscation of their property.[52] But the killing of prisoners was common to both sides. So was pillage. The decree simply meant that Boves, like other military leaders, royalist and republican, took property from the enemy to finance the war effort and pay his followers. His followers, it is true, were coloureds, and it was the property of whites which he promised them. A potent mixture of race and reward, therefore, animated the llaneros and gave Boves and other royalist caudillos their troops. But Boves himself was moved by military not social objectives. And while he distributed booty to his forces there is no evidence that he distributed land.[53] In the llanos agrarian reform was not an issue. The population was sparse, scattered over immense distances; and agricultural activity was limited. In the colonial period much of the cattle was 'free', that is wild and unappropriated. And the llaneros were not so much cattlemen as hunters. Here cattle rather than land was wealth, and it was to cattle rather than to land that the llaneros needed access. Over this cattle they had customary rights. But in 1811 the first republic issued its *Ordenanzas de llanos*, which sought to consolidate and protect incipient private property in the region.[54] The new laws imposed a fine and a hundred lashes on anyone who violated private property; this meant that there could be no hunting or rounding up of cattle except with the written licence of the owners of the land in question. The intention was to associate property in cattle with property in land, to eliminate common usages and to promote the extension of private property in the llanos, assigning cattle exclusively to stockmen and ranchers. On the pretext of pursuing bandolerismo, this was an assault on the traditional regime in the llanos and on the common rights long enjoyed by the llaneros.[55] At the same time the new laws sought to reduce the free llanero to the status of a semi-servile peon, forcing him to register, to carry an identity card, to belong to a ranch, dependent on the will of the patrón; anyone found without employment earned, on the second offence, a year's imprisonment, while cattle-rustling was assigned the death penalty.

It is not clear how far this legislation was applied. But its message was clear enough – it announced the agrarian policy of the republican leaders, of the land-owners and the ranchers. But the forces which they sought to contain exploded against them. This was the reason why the llaneros joined Boves against the republic – to fight for their freedom and their cattle. The republicans thus gave a bonus to their enemies. For Boves himself was no reformer. When he occupied Caracas he did so not as a guerrilla chief but as a man who represented royal power, a general who fought to destroy the republic in collaboration with hard-core defenders of the colonial order. He no longer distributed goods confiscated from the enemy; these were now sold for the royal Treasury and the war effort. And the profits went not to the dispossessed llaneros but to those who speculated in sequestered property, to royalist creoles and foreign merchants. Boves did not, in fact, attack private property as such; while he plundered republicans, he tried to protect royalist and Church property from his hordes. But whatever the objectives of Boves, the fact remains that the class hatred infusing the llaneros who followed him in the counter-revolution of 1814 horrified the creole aristocracy and confirmed their resolution to gain political power on their own terms.

At the end of 1814, however, this seemed a distant prospect. In July Bolívar left Caracas and retreated eastwards to Barcelona, followed by a mass of patriots fleeing in terror from the llaneros. At Carúpano, Bolívar and Mariño were actually arrested by two ambitious republicans, Piar and Ribas, but eventually, on 8 September, they managed to sail for Cartagena. All that remained of the revolution was a nucleus of guerrilla resistance.

(iii) THE REVOLUTION LIVES

In 1814 Ferdinand vii returned to Spain and restored a crass absolutism. For America too his policy was bankrupt of ideas and imagination. Here restoration meant reconquest and return to colonial status. On 16 February 1815 an expeditionary force

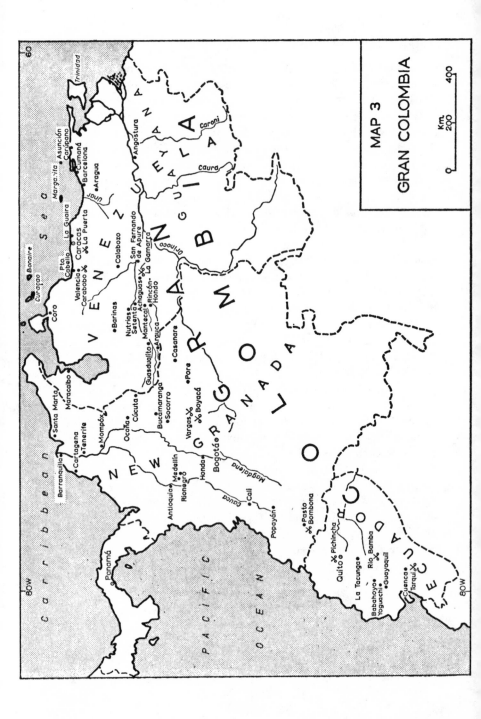

MAP 3

GRAN COLOMBIA

Km.
0   200   400

sailed from Cadiz under the command of General Pablo Morillo, a veteran of the peninsular war. Its original destination, the Río de la Plata, was changed in favour of Venezuela, the focal point of revolution and counter-revolution, from which New Granada could be reconquered, Peru reinforced, and the way opened to the Río de la Plata and Chile. In three centuries this was the largest expedition Spain sent to America – forty-two transports, five escorting warships and over ten thousand troops. But size exceeded morale. The reconquest of America was not a popular cause in Spain, and neither troops nor officers wished to risk their lives in America, least of all in Venezuela, where the environment and fighting were notoriously cruel.[56] They were soon in action and in the beginning numbers and professionalism prevailed. In April 1815 Morillo occupied Margarita before proceeding to the mainland. In May he entered Caracas, 'to forgive, to reward and to punish'. And in July he moved on to New Granada, where, in a brisk and uncompromising campaign, he completed the reconquest by October 1816.

The Spanish king spoke piously of mercy and reconciliation. But there had been too much carnage; creoles had lost lives and property; the pardos had advanced.[57] The clock could not be put back, and the counter-revolution imposed itself as a violent reconquest. Many patriots were punished; some were executed. And Morillo needed money and supplies. In 1815 he proceeded rapidly with the confiscation and sale of rebel property, rebels being defined widely enough to include leaders, supporters, passive followers and emigrants.[58] A *Junta de Secuestros* sold for the royal treasury almost 1 million pesos worth of property in 1815–16. Over 200 haciendas were confiscated, most of them in the coast and mountain valleys of the north, the property of a small elite comprising 145 individuals, among them the Tovars, Blancos, Toros, Machados and Palacios. Bolívar himself lost five estates and other properties valued at 80,000 pesos, the largest single confiscation made by the royalists, indicative of his total wealth of some 200,000 and his position as one of the richest men in Venezuela.[59] This was not the way to reconcile the Venezuelan elite. Here as elsewhere counter-revolution proved counterproductive.

In darkest exile Bolívar kept faith with the revolution. After six-months military service in New Granada he went in May 1815 to Jamaica. There he tried to interest Britain in the cause of independence. And there he wrote his famous Jamaica Letter (6 September 1815), a mordant attack on the Spanish colonial system, a criticism of the revolution's failure, and an expression of hope in the future.[60] He returned with yet greater urgency to his perennial theme – the need for strong, central government. Americans, he argued, were ill-prepared for freedom : 'We have been molested by a system which has not only deprived us of our rights but has kept us in a state of permanent childhood with regard to public affairs.' Political inexperience made it difficult for them to organize their independence or to benefit from liberal institutions. They set up popular juntas which in turn summoned congresses; these established democratic and federal governments; elections gave birth to parties, 'and parties led us back into slavery'. He concluded : 'Events in Tierra Firme have proved that wholly representative institutions are not suited to our character, customs and present knowledge.' The revolution needed power and unity. But first it needed a new foothold. Jamaica was no base for an invasion of Venezuela; and Cartagena had fallen to Morillo. So on 19 December 1815 Bolívar left Jamaica for Haiti. The president of this black republic, Alexandre Pétion, gave him substantial help in return only for the promise that the liberator would free the slaves in Venezuela.[61] The first invasion of the mainland (May-August 1816) was an ignominious failure. But a second expedition landed at Barcelona on 31 December 1816 and inaugurated what Bolívar called the third period of the republic. And this time the republic did not cling to the coast.

Bolívar led his men south into Guayana. This was a new and visionary strategy – to base the revolution deep in the hinterland, among the great plains of the Orinoco, impenetrable in their vastness, wide rivers and malarial swamps, a great barrier against defeat, a springboard for attack, and a source of wealth in their rich reserves of livestock.[62] But Bolívar had to fight on two fronts, against rivals within as well as royalists without, against civilians who disliked his militarism and military who disputed his strategy. Some of his former commanders, Santiago Mariño, Francisco Bermúdez and Manuel Piar, fired by particularist ambitions, were reluctant to recognize the command of a man whose grandiose plans had collapsed while they kept resistance alive in the east.[63] Of these republican caudillos General Piar posed the greatest threat to Bolívar, partly because of his military ability and partly because, a pardo himself, his ambition was coloured by an acute consciousness of race. According to a royalist chronicler, 'Piar was one of our most terrible enemies, adventurous, talented, and with great influence among the castes, to whom he belonged. He was thus one of the few Venezuelans who could inspire the greater part of the population.'[64] Piar had already begun to push back the royalists in Guayana when Bolívar joined him in April 1817 in the siege of Angostura. In July and August the royalists withdrew from the province, leaving Bolívar master of the Orinoco plains.[65] But was he master of the third republic? Piar was the test. Plotting against Bolívar, he sought to put himself at the head of the coloured population and to link up with Mariño's separatist movement in the east. He was hunted down, brought to trial and, on 16 October, shot as a conspirator, rebel and deserter. Bolívar calculated carefully in executing Piar. As O'Leary observed: 'General Mariño certainly deserved the same treatment as Piar, but he was less dangerous, and one example was sufficient.'[66] Piar's execution did in fact bring Mariño into line. But Bolívar's concern went deeper than this: in Venezuela racially divisive propaganda was too explosive to be tolerated. This was the danger of Piar.

The republic could no longer ignore racial problems or suppress popular forces. Bolívar himself, the most daring and idealist of the creoles, had long seen the need of fusing the creole, pardo and slave rebellions into one great movement. He considered himself free of racial prejudice; he fought for liberty and equality. This was the essence of independence: 'Legal equality is indispensable where physical inequality prevails.' The revolution would correct the imbalance imposed by nature and colonialism: previously 'the whites, by virtue of talent, merit and fortune, monopolized everything. The pardos, degraded to the most humiliating condition, had nothing. . . . But the revolution has granted them every privilege, every right, every advantage.'[67] So Bolívar denounced Piar – an unstable man who in other times disavowed his coloured mother and claimed noble birth – for inciting race war at a time when equality was already being granted to the coloured people; 'General Piar himself is an irrevocable proof of this equality.' The measured, gradual programme of reform under creole control was threatened by total subversion of the existing order, which, in the absence of ideas, experience and organization among the pardos, could only lead to anarchy. While it was essential to widen the basis of the revolution, this did not involve destroying the existing leadership: 'Who are the authors of this revolution? Are they not the whites, the wealthy, the aristocracy and even the militia chiefs? What principles have these caudillos of the revolution proclaimed? The decrees of the republic are eternal monuments of justice and liberalism . . . liberty even for the slaves who were previously the property of the same leaders.' And now Piar had sought to unleash a war against creoles 'simply because they had been born more or less white. According to Piar, a man's skin is a crime and carries with it the decree of life or death.'[68] The day after Piar's execution he asked the soldiers of the liberating army: 'Have not our arms broken the chains of the slaves? Has not the odious distinction between classes and colours been abolished for ever? Have I not ordered national property to be distributed among you? Are you not equal, free, independent, happy and respected? Could Piar give you more? No. No. No.'[69]

Bolívar was too optimistic, or perhaps too addicted to wartime propaganda. The problem of race was not so easily resolved. From 1815–16 growing numbers of pardos were incorporated into the army of liberation: they were needed to fill the gaps in the patriot ranks left by creole casualties and desertions; and they themselves were imbued with greater expectations from wartime social mobility. From now on the traditional structure of the republican army was transformed, and while the creoles retained military and political control, the pardos had greater opportunities for advance to higher ranks and offices. According to a royalist report of 1815, the pardos were now thoroughly militarized, their claims to equality sharpened by five years of war, and their animosity towards race-conscious creoles undiminished.[70] The crown was urged to turn this animosity to its own account. But it remained Spanish policy to rely, not on the pardos, but on Morillo's expeditionary force and the support of royalist creoles, in order to restore the colonial structure of society. To this extent Bolívar was right: the pardos had more to gain from the republican cause. But what had the slaves to gain?

Bolívar was an abolitionist. He regarded it as 'madness that a revolution for liberty should try to maintain slavery', and in one of his frankest speeches he called upon the Congress of Angostura (15 February 1819) to remove from Venezuela 'the dark mantle of barbarous and profane slavery'.[71] But Bolívar was also a military leader who needed recruits, and during the war he tied emancipation to conscription, offering Negro slaves manumission in return for military service. Decrees of 2 June and 6 July 1816 proclaimed the freedom of slaves on condition that they joined the republican forces.[72] The response was negative. Although Bolívar liberated his own slaves, few hacendados followed his example. The Venezuelan aristocracy did not embrace the republican cause in order to divest themselves of property; so the decrees of 1816 were unavailing, and the Congress of Angostura made little effort to apply them. The slaves themselves were hardly more enthusiastic. The liberator believed that 'the slaves have lost even the desire to be free'. The truth was that the slaves were not interested in fighting the creoles' war: 'Very few were the slaves who wished to accept liberty in exchange for the burdens of war.'[73] Nevertheless the policy of Bolívar helped to neutralize the slaves; they no longer actively fought the republic as they had done in 1812–14, and they gradually disappeared from the war as an autonomous movement. It was clear that Morillo had nothing to offer them and that, whatever the republic stood for, Spain stood unequivocally for the *status quo*. As the army of Morillo appeared more and more a colonialist force, so it lost the popular following which Boves had won and which Bolívar now sought to divert towards the republic. And Bolívar wanted the support not only of the pardos and the slaves but also of a third group, the llaneros.

In January 1817 Morillo returned to Venezuela, placed his forces astride the Andean provinces, and in August made his headquarters at Calabozo, the gateway to the plains. Bolívar was now bursting with premature optimism, impatient to take the offensive. In July he told the still enslaved province of Caracas of great republican victories: 'From the wide plains of Casanare to the mouths of the great Orinoco, victory has led our steps. Twenty glorious actions have assured the fate of Venezuela.'[74] Bolívar himself held Guayana. Mariño had freed much of Cumaná. In Maturín General Rojas kept the republican cause alive. General Monagas engaged the royalists at Barcelona. And in the south-west, in the Apure valley, José Antonio Páez fought as a republican caudillo of the llaneros. If Páez could be brought under Bolívar's command, the liberator would control a vast area from the Orinoco to the Andes. On 31 December 1817 Bolívar left Angostura and, in a spectacular march of three hundred kilometres, took his three thousand troops to the Apure plains. On 30 January 1818 Bolívar and Páez met for the first time.[75]

Páez was the complete antithesis of Bolívar. He came from Barinas in the west, son of a minor employee in a crown tobacco store; totally uneducated, illiterate, and unurbanized, reared in the sun, rain and ranges of the llanos, he began life as a simple, propertiless herdsman.[76] Yet through natural gifts of character and body Páez had become, by the age of twenty-seven, absolute lord of the plains. Built like an ox, bloodthirsty, suspicious and cunning, accompanied always by a giant Negro bodyguard, he was an unrivalled guerrilla leader, quick and resolute, expert in cavalry warfare and in fighting in tropical conditions. Páez was more llanero than the llaneros he led. These ferocious herdsmen of the plains, primitive and predatory, 'all badly clad and some almost in a perfect state of nudity', were creatures of their environment.[77] Bolívar never understood the llaneros. And Páez himself had no illusions about them: 'They lived and died like men who knew no other destiny than to struggle against the elements and the wild beasts.' They responded to no ideology and no principles, and the only way to hold them, as Boves had known, was by plunder: 'In the lower Apure', reported Páez, 'the only men to be found were execrable types; they formed bands to plunder the countryside, rob houses and commit crimes, and they were bold enough to drive off with five hundred horses and hide them without trace. A llanero chief has to cajole his soldiers with hard cash, otherwise they will ruin by their depredations the regions through which they pass.'[78] Now the republic offered them more than plunder. Páez promised a share of estates taken from the enemy, and Bolívar confirmed this policy in his decree of 1817, ordering land from national property to be distributed to the patriot troops.[79] In this way the new leaders abandoned the extreme agrarian policy of the first republic, and if they did not win the hearts of the llaneros they satisfied their stomachs.

Páez fashioned the llaneros into a savage yet disciplined lancer force. He accepted the sovereignty of Bolívar and in February contributed a thousand cavalry to a joint force of over four thousand. Bolívar moved north and forced Morillo to evacuate Calabozo; he then wanted to pursue the enemy towards Caracas. But Páez and his llaneros would not forgo the booty from a local action at San Fernando and they would not leave the Apure. Páez was essentially a local chieftain, an enemy of all subordination, who preferred his *querencia* in the south-west and could not see beyond the plains.[80] Bolívar learned to hold Páez and his warriors on a loose rein. But the first lesson was a bitter one. With depleted forces Bolívar was defeated by Morillo at the battle of Semen (16 March 1818), losing over a thousand infantry, much war material and his own papers.[81] Still retreating, the liberator was almost captured at Rincón de los Toros. On 2 May Páez was defeated at Cojedes, and Cumaná too was lost at this time. Once again the republicans were forced back to the south of the Orinoco.

Bolívar made Angostura a base from which to organize the republic and plan the liberation of Venezuela. He called a national congress (twenty-six delegates) which met on 15 February 1819 and to which he presented an outline of a constitution.[82] His Angostura Address embodied a kind of enlightened absolutism, enlightened in that he especially urged the abolition of slavery and distribution of land to the troops, absolutist in its constitutional thinking. He recommended the British constitution as 'the most worthy to serve as a model for those who desire to enjoy the rights of man and all political happiness compatible with our fragile nature'. But he reaffirmed his conviction that American constitutions must conform to American conditions, and that there could be no return to the debility of the first republic. Liberty and equality were still the essential objectives. But how could they be realized without sacrificing security, property and stability? He recommended a legislature with two chambers, one a house of elected representatives, the other a hereditary senate. The legislature should not usurp powers that properly belonged to the executive. And his executive, though elected, was powerful and centralized, virtually a king with the name of president. The judiciary should be independent. And to these three classical powers, Bolívar added a fourth of his own, the *poder moral*. This idea was badly conceived and met with no response from his contemporaries, but it was typical of his search for public virtue, goodness and enlightenment, values which he regarded as so important that they needed an institution to guard them. Was not the whole project anti-democratic? The hereditary senate, one of the most aristocratic of all Bolívar's projections, was an attempt to find stability between the extremes of tyranny and anarchy, but this transplanting of the English House of Lords to America – breaking his own 'American reality' principle – would simply have confirmed and prolonged the seigneurial social structure of Venezuela. The Congress of Angostura immediately elected Bolívar president of the republic, and in August 1819 it adopted a constitution embodying many of Bolívar's ideas, though not the hereditary senate or the moral power.[83] But the new constitution was pure theory, for the war had still to be won. And on the military front Bolívar had a new and exciting vision.

From August 1818 Bolívar turned his mind towards the liberation of New Granada[84] In that month he sent Francisco de Paula Santander to Casanare as governor and vanguard of a greater expedition. Casanare was a semi-desert, a poor and underpopulated province, but it was the sanctuary of New Granadan independence, it provided a nucleus of another army, and it could become the base for an invasion of New Granada. Bolívar's strategy involved great risks but promised rich returns. In Venezuela the revolution was at a standstill. In the Apure, it is true, Páez skilfully frustrated all Morillo's attempts to destroy him. And from Britain a legion of mercenaries arrived to strengthen the patriot forces. But the republic found it impossible to crush the royalists. Its army needed action and victories. Could these not be attained more easily in New Granada? The royalists there were more vulnerable, particularly exposed to a rapid invasion. Spanish rule – which meant in effect ten thousand troops, many of them Americans and disenchanted – was spread over a vast area between Cartagena and Quito and fully occupied with internal security. Even so, there were risks. Success depended on rapid penetration to the heart of Spanish power, and this too meant traversing great distances. And behind him Bolívar would leave a weak government and a number of semi-independent chieftains. Yet to switch the theatre of war from one country to another would have a magical effect and constitute in itself a rare moral victory. Bolívar could lure Morillo from Venezuela and, if the operation were successful, return to his homeland from a position of strength and with greater striking power. 'We will force Morillo either to evacuate Venezuela in order to defend New Granada, or alternatively to allow the latter to be entirely lost.'[85]

In March 1819 Bolívar once again left Angostura for the Apure, where he fought a gruelling campaign against Morillo. On 15 May he received news of Santander's success against the royalists in Casanare. This was the moment of decision. He announced the invasion of New Granada to his colleagues on 23 May in a council of war held in a simple cabin where the only seats were skulls of cattle bleached by the rain and sun of the plains.[86] There was much scepticism; and Páez proved to be uncooperative. But the caudillos had little to lose. All the risks were Bolívar's. And what alternatives had he? Would it not be suicidal to remain and winter in the llanos, his forces consumed by yellow fever and malaria? On 27 May 1819 the liberator left the Upper Apure to join with Santander and cross the Andes. He led his army to one of the unforgettable actions of the war of liberation, when all the obstacles of recent years – the disunity, the poverty, the social and racial conflict – were suddenly overcome by great feats of the human mind and great exploits of the human will.

The liberators crossed the Arauca and the plains of Casanare in the season of torrential rain, the land a spate of streams, rivers, lakes and swamps. 'For seven days', reported O'Leary, 'we marched in water up to our waists.'[87] This was only the beginning. After the junction with Santander the joint army of thirteen hundred infantry and eight hundred cavalry waded through further floods, a prelude to the ascent of the mighty

cordillera. Men bred in the plains now had to endure the towering Andes, suffering exposure, exhaustion and altitude sickness
as they crossed at a height of thirteen thousand feet by the tough-
est of all the passes, the bleak Páramo de Pisba. Men, animals
and equipment were lost in great numbers – a quarter of the
British legion died on the march – but by 5 July the exhausted
survivors began to reach the other side of the mountains at the
village of Socha, and local conscripts were forced at gunpoint
to fill the vacant ranks. Bolívar's leadership had brought them
through, and his inspiration now took them forward. The
liberator entered one of his greatest triumphs, winning battle after
battle, and crowning the campaign on 7 August with the victory
– in the event a relatively easy victory – of Boyacá, where the
royalist chief Colonel Barreiro and the remnants of his army were
taken prisoner.[88] On 10 August Bolívar entered Bogotá, to find
that Viceroy Sámano and his officials had fled. New Granada
was liberated, the royalists were scattered and their American
troops were incorporated into the republican army. Bolívar's
great act of faith was justified. He returned to Venezuela in
September, leaving Santander in charge of the newly liberated
country.

Victory in New Granada strengthened Bolívar's position on
two fronts – within the republic and against the royalists. He now
had advantage over caudillos and in congress. And on 17
December 1819 he won a victory for his constitutional ideas when
the Congress of Angostura decreed the union of Venezuela and
New Granada in the republic of Colombia. In the first half of
1820 Bolívar based himself in the region of Cúcuta on the border
between the two countries; backed by an independent New
Granada he rightly claimed to be fighting a war between nations.
But he could still not assemble enough troops and arms to fight a
decisive war; Páez would not operate out of the llanos; and
republican soldiers deserted in droves for lack of pay and food
in a country which could not support them. So Morillo continued
to dominate Caracas and the coastal highlands. At this point the
Spanish commander was dealt a second blow. The Spanish liberal
revolution of 1 January 1820, sanctioned by the army in Cadiz
which wished to avoid service in America, deprived him of reinforcements and subverted his political position; he was ordered

to negotiate with the patriots on the basis of recognizing a constitutional government in Spain. Although agreement was not reached between Morillo and Bolívar, a six-months armistice was signed on 26 November 1820.[89] The two men met on 27 November in Santa Ana; when Bolívar was pointed out to Morillo the Spaniard asked, 'What, that little man in the blue frock-coat and forage cap, riding a mule?'[90] The armistice was important for Venezuela: it legitimized the struggle; it ended the war to the death; and it forced Spain to recognize the existence, if not the legality, of the new state of Colombia. Even more important perhaps, it caused Morillo to retire to Spain, leaving the less resolute General La Torre in command and the security forces dispirited.

The armistice did not last six months. On 28 January 1821 Maracaibo revolted against Spain with republican connivance. Bolívar himself regarded the lull as a means of rearming. And in April he prepared to move, as a true liberator: 'This war will not be to the death, nor even a normal war. It will be a holy war, a struggle to disarm the enemy not to destroy him.'[91] Republican forces from the llanos, the Andes and Maracaibo converged upon the valley of Aragua, while Bermúdez advanced towards Caracas from the east in a diversionary tactic. The final confrontation came at Carabobo on 24 June 1821 when Bolívar, supported by Mariño and Páez, defeated the Spanish army.[92] Pockets of royalist resistance were then overcome at Maracaibo, Coro and Cumaná, and on 10 November Puerto Cabello surrendered. Meanwhile Bolívar entered Caracas on 29 June and after organizing civil affairs he departed for Bogotá on 1 August to take the revolution to the south. He was more than a Venezuelan. He was president of Colombia and a liberator with further freedoms to win. He left his respected colleague Carlos Soublette as vice president of Venezuela. But real power lay with Páez, who was inevitably given military command of the province. Bermúdez and Mariño were also appointed to high office. So the military caudillos entered their inheritance and took their reward.

(iv) NEW MASTERS, OLD STRUCTURES

The war of liberation left Venezuela a wasteland. For over ten years two fighting armies preyed upon her resources, consuming or destroying cultivation and livestock. In the absence of regular revenue, currency and supplies, pillage of all kinds was practised by both sides as a normal method of war : 'Towns were devastated and carved up indiscriminately; anyone with anything was robbed.'[93] The socio-racial environment made this a total war of uncontrolled violence, aggravated by conditions of misery and privation. The Consulado of Caracas reported in 1816 : 'The country has lost about eighty to a hundred thousand people in casualties and emigration; the haciendas of this province are either destroyed or decayed through repeated plunder by one side or the other.'[94] War consumption reduced livestock (cattle, horses, mules) from 4.5 million head in 1812 to 256,000 in 1823. Monteverde alone 'seized more than half a million pesos worth of cattle and mules from the herds of Americans'.[95] Flight of labour aggravated the situation, as slaves took to flight and peasants moved on. And there was a great flight of capital : royalists, creoles, and merchants of all persuasions sent their capital and treasures out of the country or resorted to hoarding. The valleys of Aragua, Tuy and Caracas, the region of Barlovento and the lowlands of Valencia, previously prosperous agricultural areas, were now scenes of desolation and depopulation, with nothing to export and hardly the means to supply the home market. Exports dropped sharply between 1810 and 1816, cacao from 120,000 fanegas a year to 30,000, coffee from 80,000 quintals to 20,000. And after the war agriculture remained depressed, in spite of the fact that 320,000 pesos of the Colombian loan was assigned as agricultural advances to Venezuelan producers.[96]

Inevitably the public Treasury was totally disorganized by the paralyzation of economic life, at a time when war and postwar needs increased expenditure. The tobacco revenue – the goose that laid the golden egg in Venezuela – was almost killed by over exploitation, falling from more than 1.2 million pesos to less than 300,000.[97] Customs were reduced by excessive contraband from the foreign Antilles. Money was in short supply, and measures to increase the circulating medium by issue of paper money and coinage of silver objects were hopelessly inadequate. In 1821–30 the bureaucracy and the army were paid in paper money or in bonds which lost 10 per cent whenever the owners could convert them into real money. The government deficit for 1825 was nine million pesos, and in that year the administration was living on the British loan.[98]

Independence freed Venezuela from the colonial monopoly and opened her to international trade. The new regime responded by reducing or reforming taxes, with the object of drawing maximum revenue from customs duties on imports. In view of the depressed economy, the limited internal market, and reliance on a narrow range of primary exports, freedom of trade served to increase Venezuela's dependence and perpetuate her under-development. The economy continued to rely upon exports of indigo, cotton, cacao, coffee, hides and tobacco, 70–80 per cent of which went to more developed countries.[99] But production suffered from lack of investment capital, shortage of labour, poor communications and low prices on the international market.[100] So Venezuela found it difficult to earn imported manufactures. Yet these were virtually the only manufactures which Venezuelans consumed, and most of them came from Britain.[101] In spite of the customs tariff, ranging from $7\frac{1}{2}$ to 36 per cent, foreign goods poured in and swamped primitive local industries. Rafael Revenga, the economist of the new regime, attributed the decadence of industry directly to

. . . the excessive import of many articles which were previously produced by poor families here. . . . Foreign soap, for example, has destroyed the various soap factories which we formerly had in the interior. And now we even take candles from abroad, retailed at eight per real, and the few that are still made in this country actually import their wicks from abroad. . . . It is notorious that the more we rely on foreign interests to supply our needs, the more we diminish our national independence; and our reliance now even extends to daily and vital needs.[102]

Revenga appreciated that Venezuela was not in a position to industrialize: 'Our country is essentially agricultural; it will develop mining before manufactures; but it must strive to diminish its present dependence on foreign powers.'[103]

The population growth of the late colonial period was temporarily halted and reversed. War to the death inevitably increased the death rate, and emigration added to the losses. The population of Caracas dropped from 50,000 in 1812 to 21,000 in 1814, that of Cumaná from 16,000 to 5,236 in the same period.[104] Venezuela lost 134,487 of its people between 1800 and 1816, and during the whole of the war an estimated 262,000. The total population fell from 800,000 in 1810 to little more than 700,000 in 1825.[105] Of this number 76 per cent was concentrated in the coastal and highland regions, 16 per cent in the llanos, and 8 per cent in Guyana. In the course of the war the white population, already a minority, was further reduced by casualties and emigration. The composition of the Venezuelan aristocracy was modified, as soldiers, merchants and adventurers profited from the hostilities to turn themselves into landed proprietors. As the colonial aristocracy was reduced in numbers and importance, the great estates passed into the hands of a new oligarchy, the successful caudillos of the war of independence, who acquired property which should in many cases have been assigned to the troops.

Bolívar wished to distribute confiscated and national land to the republican soldiers, whom he regarded as the people in arms.[106] A decree of 3 September 1817 confiscated for the republic the property of Spanish and American royalists. A month later, on 10 October 1817, he issued the 'law on the distribution of national property among the soldiers', and further decrees added further details.[107] It was to apply primarily to the troops who fought in the hardest years, 1814–21, and strictly speaking it was not a bonus but a basic payment to men whose service had never been regularly recompensed. It was a predictably hierarchical law; it established twelve ranks of recipient, ranging from general-in-chief to private soldier; a general received right to property worth twenty-five thousand pesos, a colonel ten thousand, a captain six thousand, a sergeant one thousand, and a soldier five hundred. Bolívar did not intend to break up big estates and create a number of minifundia; one estate could be granted to a group of beneficiaries. But his plans were frustrated by the combined action of legislators and officers. Congress decreed that soldiers be paid not in actual land but in *bonos*, vouchers entitling the holder to receive national land at a vague postwar date. Ignorant and impoverished soldiers were easy prey: the bonos were bought up by officers – such as Páez

– and civilian speculators at ridiculous prices, sometimes less than 5 per cent of the amount legally due; and in this way most of the soldiers were defrauded of their right to land. Bolívar protested and demanded that congress should implement the original law by assigning the troops not bonos but land.[108] Injustice angered him, and unrest disturbed him. The greatest trouble arose from dissatisfied llaneros, to be found in all ranks from caudillos to soldiers:

These are men who have fought for a long time; they believe that they deserve much, yet they feel humiliated and frustrated, and they have lost hope of gathering the fruit of what they have won by their lances. They are resolute, ignorant llaneros, who have never regarded themselves the equals of other men with more knowledge and better appearance. I myself, their leader for so long, still do not know of how much they are capable. I treat them with great consideration; yet even this is not enough to inspire in them the confidence and frankness which should exist among comrades and compatriots. You can be sure that we are over an abyss, or rather a volcano that is about to erupt. I fear peace more than war.[109]

The caudillos could look after themselves. But the mass of llaneros remained unsatisfied. In mid-1821 they were put on indefinite unpaid leave. Soon there was robbery and unrest in the Apure, while the successful landowners began to organize and extend their interests.

Independence reaffirmed the power of the land-owning class. The colonial aristocracy did not survive in its entirety, but its ranks were replenished by new, plebeian entrants. Estates confiscated by royalists were restored to their owners or descendants, while the republican government confiscated the property of its enemies. Some royalists, it is true, made a comeback, and a number of *émigrés* with influence in the government or in the courts recovered their estates at the expense of humbler candidates for land distribution. But the most successful republican caudillos acquired vast holdings from confiscated and national property, partly in their own right, partly by buying up the rights of their troops. Páez, Bermúdez, the Monagas brothers, Mariño and others became powerful hacendados and strengthened the political base of the landed class.[110] At San Pablo in the plains of Apure, Páez established an immense *hato*, or cattle ranch, where he lived like a primitive llanero. He told the British minister, Ker Porter, 'that he had purchased three estates, now forming the whole of what he called San Pablo, embracing an extent of forty leagues in circumference, and for which he had not paid more than about nine thousand dollars − £1,500'.[111] Páez also extended his properties into the centre-north, the homeland of the traditional oligarchy. From 1821 he began to appropriate lands in the valleys of Aragua and to transform himself into a northern hacendado with a new power base in the exporting sector.

The victory of 1821, therefore, produced a large-scale transfer of property and a new latifundist class, without significantly modifying the social structure. But the new masters were wiser in their day than their predecessors. While, in the south, they debarred the llaneros from property, they did not attempt to revive the draconian agrarian law of 1812 which had driven the llaneros under the banner of Boves. Páez decreed a new 'law of land-owners and ranchers in the llanos' (25 August 1828). This continued the policy of vindicating private property, prohibiting transit through estates without permission of owner or manager, and making rights over wild cattle depend on ownership of land. But the law was expressed in more moderate terms : smaller ranchers were allowed rights over cattle, and the llaneros were not subject to the degradation of forced labour or restriction of personal liberty.[112] Thus the llaneros were tamed and brought within the agrarian structure of the rest of the country.

Latifundists at the top, slaves at the bottom, the new Venezuela reproduced the essential features of the old. The slave trade was abolished in 1811, but slavery itself endured. Bolívar set an example. He liberated his own slaves, first on condition of military service in 1814 when about fifteen accepted, and then unconditionally in 1821 after Carabobo when over a hundred profited.[113] And he repeatedly pressed congress to decree abolition. He argued that the creole rulers and property-owners must accept the implications of the revolution, that the example of freedom was 'insistent and compelling', and that the republicans 'must triumph by the road of revolution and no other'.[114] But the delegates at Angostura were afraid to unleash the slaves into free society, and after 1821 proprietors brought an end to wartime manumission, small though this had been. The postwar Congress of Cúcuta passed a complex law of manumission (21 July 1821), allowing for liberation of adult slaves; but it lacked teeth and depended for its operation on compensation financed from taxes, including death duties, levied on property owners; and manumission was administered by local committees composed of the same class.[115] The Cúcuta law also provided for the freeing of all children subsequently born to slaves, on condition that each child worked for his mother's owner until the age of eighteen; this gave the land-owners a continuing supply of cheap and tied labour. Thus liberation was thwarted by fear of economic and social consequences. Negro revolts in Venezuela in 1824–7 and in Ecuador in 1825–6 prejudiced the prospects of emancipation. Persistent racial tension, including the revolt of the pardo Admiral Padilla in 1828, led even Bolívar to speak of the 'natural enmity of the people of colour' and to state that a Negro revolt was 'a thousand times worse than a Spanish invasion'.[116] Some observers believed that in 1827 he agreed with Venezuela's rulers not to press for abolition.[117] In face of the vested interest of the administrators of manumission and the widespread refusal to pay the taxes on which compensation depended, liberation was a slow and partial process, in which scores rather than hundreds were freed each year.[118] Government policy favoured gradual manumission and the peaceful integration of the slaves into society, while private interests did not wish to lose property without compensation. On 2 October 1830 congress published a new law of manumission which was actually worse than the Cúcuta law, for it decreed that the age required for manumission by freebirth would be twenty-one in place of eighteen; and in 1840 it became in effect twenty-five.[119] Gradually, however, the Venezuelan landowners began to appreciate that a slave was an expensive and uneconomical commodity, that a cheaper labour force could be procured by turning slaves into 'free' peons tied to the estates by harsh rental arrangements. In these circumstances the only reason for delay of emancipation until 1854 was the anxiety of the owners to procure maximum compensation.[120]

While the prospects of the Negroes were little enhanced by independence, those of the pardos were hardly better. They put up an intense struggle for equality with the creoles. Pardos were already free men, ready to use available avenues of advancement to acquire property and education. They were the most numerous and dynamic sector of society, about one-half of the population and increasing more rapidly than other sectors. They now sought freedom from the traditional restraints which law and society imposed upon them, and demanded opportunities hitherto reserved to creoles.[121] It was in the upper ranks of the pardos that frustration was most acute and the struggle for equality most insistent. Some of them were successful, and they gained access to education, offices, and social status: 'The first officers, and leading men, civil and military, are of this class.'[122] They thus came to have a vested interest in the revolution and grave suspicion of any constitutional change – towards monarchy, for example – that might revive their former status. But they made this ascent only by disavowing their class and becoming culturally white themselves, which meant that the most dynamic element in society worked not to dissolve the existing structure but to join it and profit from it. The fate of the mass of pardos was different. In numbers alone they were indispensable to the whites in the wars of independence, especially after 1815 when recruitment among pardos had to be increased in order to compensate for losses among creoles. So their claims could not be ignored. Their presence in the army gave them the chance of military promotion up to middle rank of the officer corps. And they gained legal equality, for republican law abolished all external signs of discrimination, seeing 'none but citizens in every class of inhabitants, whatever may be their origin or the tinge of their complexion'.[123] But the new rulers confined voting rights and therefore full citizenship to property-owners, so that inequality came to be based not on law but on wealth. The pardos wanted more than this. Bolívar himself warned : 'Equality before the law is not enough for the people in their present mood. They want absolute equality on both public and social levels. Next they will demand *pardocracia*, that they, the pardos, should rule. This is a very natural inclination which will ultimately lead to the extermination of the privileged class.'[124] The threat of pardocracia haunted Bolívar : he considered it as abhorrent as the *albocracia*, or white rule, which was 'absolute dogma' in Peru. And in the pessimism of his final years he feared that only excesses

could result from granting any political powers to pardos.
But the new rulers were careful to guard their inheritance,
and they defined the political nation as narrowly as they could.
In the aftermath of independence, around 1830, the population
of Venezuela was about 900,000, about half of whom were pardos
and free Blacks, over a quarter were whites, while slaves
amounted to about 15 per cent. Among the whites some 10,000
people — landowners, rich merchants and their families and
kinship groups — constituted the privileged elite, monopolising
power and institutions from the presidency down to the municipalities. Where they did not own land they controlled offices,
and they prolonged the wartime establishment of higher military
appointments which became mere sinecures, occupied by 'officers
whose only obligation is to collect their salaries'.[125] The Constitution of 1830 reflected their power. To be an elector a man had
to be twenty-one, literate, an owner of property yielding an
annual income of 200 pesos, or to have a profession or office or
'useful industry' yielding 300 pesos a year, or an annual salary
of 400 pesos.[126] This disfranchised the majority of pardos, whose
only recourse was protest and rebellion. The constitution was
reinforced by the caudillo, the strong man, who could control
the popular classes. Páez ruled with and for the elite and,
although he himself had come up through the ranks, he defined
the government of Venezuela as narrowly as the most tradi-
tionalist of his associates. In 1828, in an attempt to revive the
Venezuelan economy and rescue the country from depression,
Páez assembled a junta in Caracas: 'I brought together for this
purpose landowners, treasury officials, lawyers and merchants'.[127]
This was the political coalition which Páez led; it was also a
perfect description of the ruling class of Venezuela.

SEVEN *Liberation, a New Site in Colombia*

(i) THE GRIEVANCES OF A COLONY

NEW GRANADA, LIKE the rest of Spanish America, was a seigneurial society which enshrined the values of the mother country.[1] Great estates took root in the colony as the creole elite acquired land from the Indians, from crown grants, and in the eighteenth century from *tierras baldías*.[2] Yet the landed interest was not so dominant in New Granada as it was in Chile, Peru or Venezuela, and here it was outnumbered by an aristocracy of officials, merchants and professional people.[3] While large haciendas were typical of the regions of Santa Fe de Bogotá and Popayán, the cattle country of Tolima and the Llanos and to a lesser extent the sugar and cacao zones of the coast, their extension elsewhere was limited by the shortage of cheap labour, the essential basis of the latifundia. Forced Indian service and rural peonage were not developed to any degree, and the land was worked chiefly by free wage labour, supplemented by slaves, though these were not so numerous as in Venezuela. Indian numbers had been eroded not only by post-conquest mortality but also by extensive mestizisation. According to the census of 1778, in a total population of 826,550, there were

277,068 whites and 368,093 mestizos, the two groups comprising 80 per cent of the whole; Indians numbered only 136,753, or 15 per cent, and slaves 44,636, or 5 per cent.[4] Mestizisation was accompanied by the emergence of large numbers of resident farmers and *campesinos*, whom Viceroy Guiror called a 'middle class'. These mestizos, owners of small and middle-sized holdings, especially in the north-east, competed for land between the haciendas and the *resguardos* (Indian community lands).[5] And it was the latter which suffered : 'Most people of the middle class live dispersed in the country, in the vicinity and shelter of the Indian villages, using the resguardos of the Indians and small strips of land which helps them to eke out a bare subsistence.'[6]

New Granada was a conglomeration of regions, isolated from each other by mountains, jungles, plains and rivers, and kept apart by the poverty of communications. The most important urban centres – Bogotá, Honda, Tunja and Socorro – lay in the eastern belt, and here were concentrated about 485,000 or 60 per cent of the population. To the south and west lay the agricultural and pastoral areas of Popayán and the Valle del Cauca, together with the mining zone in the Pacific slopes of the Andes; this region had about 13 per cent of the population, including a high proportion of Indians and slaves. The coastal region of the north – its people 20 per cent of the whole, including many pardos – possessed fertile plains for livestock, not yet fully developed, and the country's seaports, Cartagena and Santa Marta, while Mompox was an entrepôt for imports and exports. Between the coast and the Cauca valley lay Antioquia, rich in minerals but poor in agriculture, a closely knit and dynamic society comprising about 6 per cent of the total.[7] Yet in spite of intense regionalism there was a degree of economic integration, seen in local specialization and active internal trade. Each region was more or less self-sufficient in agriculture, but some had particular assets which could be shared with the rest – manufactures in the eastern zone, silver and gold mining in Cauca and Antioquia, livestock in the plains of the Upper Magdalena and the eastern foothills of the cordillera, and commercial agriculture – cacao, sugar, tobacco, salt and flour – in various regions. Self-sufficiency was the keynote of the New Granadan economy. Settlement was concentrated in the interior, far from export outlets; most production was consumed within the colony; and although there was moderate export of cacao and to a lesser extent cotton, internal trade was more important than trans-Atlantic trade.[8]

It was gold, not agriculture, which earned New Granada its imports and produced what wealth the colony possessed. At the end of the colonial period the average annual produce of the mines was 4.5 million pesos.[9] The profits from mining and related activities were enjoyed almost exclusively by the colonial elite, the mine owners and hacendados associated with mines, the merchants who imported manufactured goods against gold, and the bureaucracy which was paid from taxation. These surpluses were employed not in the domestic economy but to pay for imported manufactures and slaves. Spanish *comercio libre* (combined with illegal trade to the free ports of the British West Indies) only gave added impetus to this pattern of trade. The result was that merchant capital flowed overseas and to the metropolis, though not necessarily to the royal treasury. Before 1790 New Granada, far from transferring public remittances to Spain, produced barely enough revenue to pay for its own administration and defence.[10] But the fiscal pressure was increasing, and it became clear to all that Spain's chief concern lay not in economic development but in satisfying the interests of the metropolis and those of the colonial elites.

Manufacturing activity in New Granada, especially in textiles, had reached a level of some importance to the local economy. While a few viceroys and officials encouraged this development as a means of avoiding the export of specie, its opponents were truer representatives of Spanish policy. Antonio Caballero y Góngora, the conservative archbishop and viceroy, considered agriculture and mining 'the appropriate function of colonies', while industry simply provided 'manufactures which ought to be imported from the metropolis'.[11] Another colonial official, Francisco Silvestre, expressed a similar viewpoint in 1789: 'It is vital to maintain this country's dependence by supplying its needs only from Spain; therefore it is not appropriate to allow manufacture of fine textiles in wool, cotton or silk, as is practised in Quito.'[12] The New Granadan textile industry, in fact, was limited to coarse products in wool and cotton for the lower-class market. The industry was sited in Cundinamarca, Boyacá, Pasto, above all Socorro; and it was organized, not in Indian obrajes, but in a more commercialized form of putting out, the entrepreneur supplying peasant weavers with raw materials and purchasing the finished product.[13] By the mid-eighteenth century New Granada was self-sufficient in textiles for the mass market and produced a surplus for export to other colonies; she also manufactured hides, leather goods, fibres, flour and chicha. These products suffered from the new competition introduced by *comercio libre*, as they were meant to do. For this was simply a particular application of Spanish policy. Any attempt to expand or improve industrial organization and output, or to aim at the luxury market, was frustrated by authority. Quito was one of the principal victims.

The future Ecuador had a population of 452,890 and a fragile economy.[14] Guayaquil possessed an export crop, cacao; but the temperate highlands were too far from outlets to develop commercial agriculture. Quito therefore specialised in manufacturing and became perhaps the largest textile centre in the Americas, producing superior as well as coarse cloth and exporting to a wide colonial market. Quito, which had slowly recovered from depression at the beginning of the century, was now the principal target of Caballero y Góngora's strictures against colonial industry, and he reported with satisfaction that its production was seriously impaired by the competition of *comercio libre* which introduced direct trade from Spain to the Pacific. The annual value of Quito's manufactures 'used to amount to more than a million and a half pesos; but with the new impulse recently given to overseas trade by *comercio libre,* these manufactures have declined to no more than six hundred thousand pesos'.[15] Again this was a new application of an old policy. It followed a notorious case: in the mid-eighteenth century a plan of the Count of Gijón and the Marquis of Maenza to expand the textile industry of Quito was frustrated by local officials acting on secret orders from Madrid.[16] In a manifesto of 1810 justifying independence various experiences of this kind were cited: 'Americans were allowed to do nothing. Lazo planted flax in Bogotá, the government prohibited it. Leyva cultivated vines in Sutatenza, the government pulled them up. Gijón financed the manufacture of cloths in Quito, the government destroyed both Gijón and his project.'[17]

The inflexibility of Spanish economic policy was increasingly resented and, as Spain endeavoured to force yet greater surpluses from the colony, resentment grew into rebellion. In 1781 a violent anti-tax movement erupted, provoked by the ruthless procedure of the regent and visitor-general Juan Francisco Gutiérrez de Piñeres, whose uncompromising demands contrasted sharply with traditional bargaining. The alcabala was increased to 4 per cent and taken out of farm into direct administration. Government monopolies were reorganised and prices increased. The tobacco monopoly had been progressively extended throughout the Spanish colonies from the 1750s; in New Granada it was the object of special hatred, accompanied as it was by restriction of tobacco production. The whole programme threatened to raise the price of foodstuffs and consumer goods and to increase the costs of industry. Even Caballero y Góngora was moved by the widespread distress: 'As they are bled white to pay today's taxes, they have no blood left to pay tomorrow's'.[18] The rebellion had its centre in the industrious but depressed provinces of Socorro and San Gil. In March 1781 the rebels refused to pay taxes, attacked government warehouses, drove out the Spanish authorities, and elected leaders. It was a popular and predominantly mestizo movement. A minority of Indians, encouraged by the example of Tupac Amaru and enraged by the invasion of the resguardos, added their support. But there could be little solidarity between Indian communities and land-hungry mestizos.[19] The core of the comuneros was a multitude of small farmers, the 'middle class' described by Viceroy Guirior, their expectations frustrated and their prosperity threatened by government monopoly and taxation. These were the people who marched in their thousands on Bogotá and who were with difficulty restrained by the leader, Juan Francisco Berbeo, and his creole associates, men of higher social pretensions who preferred to negotiate and reach a settlement with the government.[20] They demanded suppression of the tobacco monopoly and of various taxes; reduction of the alcabala from 4 to 2 per cent; administrative reform in favour of local self-government; better treatment for the Indians; and greater access to office for Americans, because 'nationals of this America should be preferred and privileged over Europeans'.[21] The authorities appeared to accept these demands, and they lured the creole leaders back into the fold. These indeed were glad to turn their backs on more radical elements who threatened to take the movement out of their control. And once the rebel coalition fell apart the authorities had little difficulty in crushing the remnants.

The comuneros were reformists rather than revolutionaries; they sought better opportunities and lowering of tax burdens, not the dissolution of empire. While a few provincial creoles supported the movement, the upper-class creoles of the capital remained aloof, indifferent to the interests of their inferiors. When, in 1809, the lawyer-revolutionary, Camilo Torres, issued his celebrated *Memorial de agravios*, he was not thinking of the comuneros; the equality which he claimed was equality with Spaniards not with mestizos. Yet the creole elite, or some of them, were politically more advanced than the comuneros. A group of revolutionaries – Pedro Fermín de Vargas, Antonio Nariño, José de Caldas, among others – were the nucleus of radical opposition potentially more dangerous to Spain than the social protest of the comuneros, though not yet robust enough to find expression in rebellion.[22]

Pedro Fermín de Vargas, an educated if eccentric creole, carried enlightenment to the point of subversion. From Zipaquirá, where he was corregidor, he fled abroad in 1791–2 in search of foreign aid for his revolutionary schemes. To finance his flight he sold his books to Antonio Nariño, a wealthy young creole of Bogotá.[23] Royal official, militia officer, Nariño was the owner of a large and heterodox library of encyclopedist literature; his intellectual hero was Benjamin Franklin, and his home was the centre of literary *tertulias*, which became in effect revolutionary cells. Nariño was introduced to the literature of the French revolution by a captain in the viceregal guard. In 1793 he translated into Spanish the French Declaration of the Rights of Man and printed it on his own press, only to see it destroyed before it could be published. The authorities regarded Nariño's action as subversive. They found him guilty of treason, confiscated his library, and condemned him to exile in a north African *presidio*; from 1797 to 1803 he was in prison in Bogotá, though he subsequently sought to recover his property through a show of loyalism. Nariño was a friend of Francisco de Santa Cruz Espejo, an Indian doctor and lawyer of Quito and another child of the Enlightenment. In a series of satirical publications Espejo denounced economic conditions in Quito and denounced Spanish rule as their cause. In 1795 he too was jailed on charges of subversion.

At a time when New Granada experienced unprecedented intellectual stimulus – the influence of the Botanical Expedition, an officially sponsored project for the classification of flora and fauna, the increase of education, books and newspapers, the development of political debate – many creoles became increasingly critical of Spain's role in America. How could this weak, impoverished metropolis initiate reform or invest in development? The Bourbons expressed paternal concern for their American subjects. The reality was a system of exceptionally harsh and unjust restrictions, commerce stifled by tariffs, agriculture by taxes, manufactures by monopoly, and the colony ruled by 'the most impolitic and anti-economic institutions that any government could possibly establish in America.'[24] On the eve of independence this was common criticism. There was as yet little agreement on economic objectives, no accepted order of priorities, no known equilibrium between agriculture and industry, free trade and protection. But the underlying assumption was clear – New Granada had a right to express its autonomy, take its own decisions and protect its own interests. And all were agreed that the estancos should be suppressed. In its Instructions for the deputy of New Granada to the central junta in 1809 the cabildo of Socorro demanded the emancipation of the Indians, distribution of the resguardos to members of the Indian communities, abolition of slavery, complete freedom of manufacture and trade, reform of taxation, and improvement of communications and education.[25] Vargas went further. He advocated not only absolute freedom of trade with other nations but also the adoption of a positive policy of industrial diversification, supported if necessary by government protection.[26] This did not mean that independence in New Granada was the expression of powerful economic interests or the outcome of coherent economic ideas. In 1810 attention was focused almost exclusively on the political issue of relations with Spain; the *Memorial de agravios* hardly mentioned the economy. The economic problem was seen as an aspect of the political problem : if the country was poor, backward and miserable, it was because of the restrictions imposed upon it by Spain. Only a political decision could change the system. This was first priority.

Critics of the imperial regime emphasized the odious discrimination against creoles and demanded a redistribution of power in their favour. 'Those who have been born in America believe that they have the exclusive right to inhabit it, to possess it, and to be owners of all its riches.'[27] Rivalry was most intense in Bogotá where the contrast between ruler and ruled was most glaring; and resentment was greatest among first-generation creoles, for those nearest to the Europeans were most conscious of their subordination to them. The Spaniards, of course, benefited from the normal instinct of subject peoples to rely on the metropolis against the pressure of local oligarchies : 'The Indians, the Negroes and the mulattos usually have a higher regard for the Europeans than for the creoles; so do the peasants, whom we call *orejones*'.[28] The creoles in turn guarded their status against the advance of the castes. They clung to their privileges as instruments of class distinction, at a time when the imperial government was increasingly critical of fueros. A contemporary official in New Granada noted the excessive creole appetite for nobility and titles : 'All privileged fueros should be suppressed; they only serve to multiply litigation and tribunals, and to hamper the administration of justice, to the detriment of the common good of subjects and of the royal justice.'[29] But the whites were all the more sensitive of their status when they saw it threatened by the pressure of the coloured masses and by the racial liberalism of imperial policy. The courts were flooded with requests for declarations of whiteness, for there was nothing more offensive than to be known as mestizo, mulatto or zambo. One petitioner would reject allegations that 'he is no more than a poor mulatto'; another would seek judgement 'that he does not belong to the class of mestizos or have any other defects'; and white families would take legal action to prevent any of their members marrying mestizos.[30] Equally mestizos sought declarations from the courts that they were mestizos, not Indians, in order to be free of tribute, to profit from social mobility, and to pass for white. The land-owners of New Granada were obsessed with the growing violence and independence of the slaves; they complained loudly of large-scale desertions; and they accused the authorities of indifference. In 1775 a proprietor in Socorro complained that 'masters now live in greater terror than slaves'.[31] The subsequent white reaction further embittered race relations. Between 1750 and 1790 slave rebellion was endemic throughout the viceroyalty and almost reached the proportions of civil war. Communes of fugitive slaves, the notorious *palenques*, armed and resistant to white sovereignty, with their own elected cabildos and chieftains, constituted enclaves of independence in the colony. The slave movement in Cartajó in 1785 had links with others in Cauca, Choco and Valle, their object 'to kill all the whites in Cauca'. In the hacienda San Bartolomé, property of Juan Martín de Setuaín near Mompox, the slaves revolted and formed a palenque in 1799; they resisted emisarries of the owners, declaring themselves 'ready to die rather than serve any white or submit to any white in that hacienda . . . and their machetes are always at the ready'.[32] By 1800 slave rebellion and independence, decline of the slave trade, and inability of the proprietors to invest in replacements, led to serious labour shortage and competition for slaves between land-owners and miners. This crisis of slavery also heightened the creoles' concern for law and order and further eroded their confidence in the imperial government.

(ii) LIBERATION OF NEW GRANADA, CONQUEST OF QUITO

The independence movement began in Quito, where a hard-line administration reacted strongly to the crisis of 1808 and arrested a number of its critics on charges of conspiracy. On 19 August 1809 the creoles rebelled against the president, the incompetent and decrepit Count Ruiz de Castilla, overthrew the audiencia, and formed a governing junta.[33] They emphasized, as justification, the discrimination practised against Americans, especially in recent years, and denounced the Spaniards as 'oppressors of the creoles and usurpers of their natural rights'.[34] They further declared: 'Quito has been treated by the Spaniards who monopolize its government as a recently conquered nation . . . the word *criollo* has been used as a term of abuse and contempt.'[35] This was not a popular movement. Quito mirrored the social structure of Peru, divided as it was between a small creole aristocracy and a mass of unassimilated Indians, its mestizo sector weaker than that of Venezuela and New Granada. The rebels of 1809 were a group of aristocrats and *letrados*; they had previously met in the hacienda of the Marquis of Selva Alegre; it was he who headed the first junta, while the Bishop of Quito was its vice president. They owed their initial success not to mass support but to aristocratic control of the local militia. They abolished the tobacco monopoly, lowered taxes and raised more troops; some offered their own contributions to the cause, others sought to sequester ecclesiastical property.[36] But they were still monarchists, acting, they asserted, in defence of the rights of Ferdinand VII. Selva Alegre himself was far from revolutionary; he insisted that Ruiz de Castilla be given safe conduct to his hacienda, and he wrote an ambiguous letter to the Viceroy of Peru, suggesting that the movement was a temporary expedient, pending the return to political legitimacy.[37]

Viceroy Abascal, the strong man of the empire, took Quito under his command. While Guayaquil imposed a blockade, royalist forces advanced from the coast and from Cuenca. The rebels capitulated, and on 28 October the junta surrendered power to President Ruiz de Castilla on terms of conciliation and reform. But as soon as reinforcements arrived from Lima, Guayaquil and Bogotá, Ruiz de Castilla broke his agreement and started repression. Over eighty rebels were imprisoned, and the old officials were restored.[38] Lives and property were now in jeopardy; royalist troops rampaged through the town. On 2 August 1810, when a group of patriots tried to rescue the prisoners, the occupying forces massacred more than sixty patriots and began a reign of terror. These sledgehammer tactics ended by making revolutionaries of the *quiteños*. A new junta was established on 22 September. The people had taken little part in the first revolution; but Spanish repression accomplished what creole exclusiveness ignored, and by October 1810 a second revolution was under way, with greater popular participation. The Lima troops had to be withdrawn and a general pardon was issued for all surviving patriots. But Viceroy Abascal still menaced, and the new president-elect, Molina, took orders from him. The quiteños decided not to accept the authority of Abascal or the appointment of Molina, but only that of their own junta; and the populace turned on the most hated members of the Spanish administration and killed them. Molina reported from Cuenca that the ideas prevalent in Quito were 'prone to revolution and independence'.[39] On 15 February 1812 a revolutionary congress promulgated a Constitution of the Free State of Quito. But the measure accentuated divisions within the revolutionary ranks, for many disliked its implications.[40] This was a major weakness. Unyielding factionalism, part personal, part ideological, in any case monarchists versus republicans, obstructed the Quito revolution. An even greater weakness was its failure either to liberate the other provinces or to attract them to its cause. The revolution thus lacked men and resources. Even during its second and more popular phase it did not secure the support of the Indian masses. On the contrary, many Indians supported the old regime and were recruited into the royalist forces from Cuenca; such were the cacique of Azoguez and his *honderos*. The Quito revolution could not survive without possession of Guayaquil and Cuenca. Through these bases the royalists channelled reinforcements, and when they closed in the insurgents had neither the power nor the unity to resist. General Toribio Montes advanced from the coast and on 8 November 1812 entered Quito. Once he had eliminated the rebel leaders, Montes imposed a policy of genuine reconciliation, and this was enough to reassure the mass of the people. So Spaniards continued to rule Quito, and it needed a combination of insurgency within and liberation from without to overthrow that rule in 1820.

The Quito rebellion received little direct support in New Granada. As news of the crisis in Spain reached Bogotá, from June 1808, Viceroy Antonio Amar y Borbón, a brusque old soldier, reacted positively enough within the limited means at his disposal. He took measures to recognize the interim Spanish authorities, to assuage hostility between Spaniards and creoles, and to fortify his sovereign-less administration.[41] But it was a losing battle. He was forced into alliance with hard-line peninsulares, and thus into confrontation with the creoles.[42] Troops were called from Cartagena, and Spanish officials were given armed escorts. On 5 September 1808 Amar summoned a junta of officials, ecclesiastics, and important citizens, a move which he soon regretted, for it identified Spanish and creole positions more clearly.[43] The creoles wanted a conciliatory policy towards the quiteños and the establishment of a ruling junta in Bogotá itself. But the viceroy sent troops against Quito, summoned reinforcements from Cartagena, and began to fill the jails with suspects.

Yet the Quito rebellion had repercussions in New Granada. An alleged conspiracy to kidnap the viceroy and establish an independent junta, headed by a triumvirate including Antonio Nariño and based on support of slaves and Indians, contained too many incompatible elements to be convincing, but the administration took it seriously enough to imprison Nariño.[44] The greatest menace was not conspiratorial but ideological. In September 1809 Camilo Torres, creole lawyer and assessor of the cabildo of Bogotá, presented an urgent political paper for dispatch to the central junta in Spain. The basic claim of the *Memorial de agravios* was 'equality, the sacred right to equality'.[45] This was a creole demand for equality with Spaniards; it said nothing of Indians and slaves; and it sought the creation of a local junta. While eleven creoles signed the document, the Spanish members of the cabildo refused to accept it, and the viceroy ordered its suppression. He believed, probably rightly, that a junta would be the first stage to independence. He preferred to place his confidence in the power of the army and the loyalty of the people.[46] The theory was soon tested.

Insurgency spread from the provinces. In May 1810 a small insurrection in the llanos of Casanare disturbed the viceroy's complacency. This was followed by a series of cabildo-led revolts against the corregidores, in Cali on 3 July, Pamplona on 4 July and Socorro on 9 July. Finally, in Bogotá itself, on 20 July 1810, the pent-up resentment of creoles against Spaniards – '*casi increible*' reported a contemporary periodical – exploded into rebellion when a Spanish merchant made a grossly insulting remark about Americans.[47] A group of revolutionaries, working through the cabildo, summoned a cabildo abierto, deposed the viceroy, and placed government in the hands of a supreme junta of government.[48] As for the military power of the royalists, this was quickly eroded. Amar's much vaunted forces were penetrated by revolutionary ideas and personnel and offered no serious resistance to the rebels. 'Military arms fell from their hands and passed into the hands of the people, and this was done without commotion and without violence.'[49] The royalist army was the least of the revolution's problems. It soon became clear that it was easier to overthrow the Spaniards than to organize the creoles.

The republic was immediately divided into centralist and federalist factions. Cundinamarca, the most important of the provinces, was a centralist base: in March 1811 it formed itself into the republic of Cundinamarca under the presidency of Jorge Tadeo Lozano, a weak nonentity possessed of little revolutionary fervour. He was replaced by Nariño in September 1811, but the problems remained. The other provinces refused to subordinate themselves to the rule of Bogotá. They grouped themselves into the Federation of New Granadan Provinces, its capital Tunja, and its first president Camilo Torres. And many cities, such as Cartagena, declared their independence of Bogotá as well as of Spain. These extreme federalist tendencies reflected in some degree predictable economic rivalries, between the coast, whose major asset was its control of exports and imports, and the production and consumer centres of the interior, between regions which wished to protect their own interests and the centre which threatened to subordinate the parts to the whole. Federalism was also an argument about offices and opportunities, and provincial oligarchies fought for control of their own assets. Whatever the cause, the result was anarchy. Nariño's newspaper, *La Bagatela,* lamented: 'Our revolution seems more like a lawsuit over lands than a political transformation to recoup our liberties.'[50]

The revolution now became self-defeating. Nariño was thwarted by a federalist-imposed constitution, the Act of Federation of the United Provinces of New Granada (27 November 1811), which saw the new republic as little more than an association of free, sovereign and independent states. A congress which met in October 1812 at Leiva presided only over confusion and disorder. The country was engulfed in civil war before it was even fully independent. Nariño vainly tried to impose a strong executive of his own. An expedition under General Antonio

Baraya was dispatched in March 1812 to subdue Tunja, its congress, and the congressional leaders Camilo Torres and Frutos Gutiérrez.[51] In June Nariño had to lead a further expedition to subdue Baraya as well as congress. The secretary of Baraya was a young officer, Francisco de Paula Santander, who later explained that 'the displeasure shown by the towns on being deprived of self-government and subjected to union with Bogotá, the protests of Pamplona and Casanare, the opposition of Cartagena and Antioquia to Bogotá, led Baraya to refuse to obey Nariño'. The expedition failed and Nariño returned to the capital which he then had to defend in turn against the forces of Baraya. When, in June 1813, the electoral college in Bogotá appointed Nariño dictator for life, he declared that 'our greatest present evil is partisanship and division. It is perfectly clear that Cundinamarca cannot last without congress and the help of the other provinces. We cannot go on divided as we are now.'[52] On 18 July 1813 independence was formally declared in Bogotá. It was an act of desperation.

The Spaniards simply had to wait for New Granadans to destroy each other. Royalist forces had already regained a foothold in the north, advancing along the river Magdalena to dominate Santa Marta and cut off Cartagena from the interior. In the south the royalist leader, Juan Sámano, was imposing a reign of terror in Pasto and Popayán and threatening to move on Bogotá. Towards the end of September 1813 Nariño led an expedition south to Popayán; he managed to push back the royalists into Pasto and to win a notable victory at Juanambú. But in Pasto he was confronted not only by an army but by a people, the fanatically royalist *pastusos,* who refused to accept defeat, re-grouped, and defeated the republicans on 11 May 1814. Nariño was captured and shipped off to Spain, and there he remained from 1816 to 1820, imprisoned in Cadiz.

Bolívar had already fought in New Granada in the first half of 1813, when he established a bridgehead for his return to Venezuela. Now, in 1814, he again needed New Granada in order to recover Venezuela. But he needed a united New Granada, and to secure this he was prepared to accept even federalist terms. At Tunja in November 1814 he was appointed Captain-General of the Colombia State Federation and set about defeating the 'rebellious' province of Cundinamarca.[53] On 9 December he took Bogotá and incorporated it into the federation. But the most urgent task was the security of the Atlantic coast, where the Spaniards possessed a vital bridgehead. He liberated Ocaña and Mompox, but before he could reach the last Spanish base at Santa Marta he was fatally diverted. The stubborn refusal of Cartagena to accept the authority of Bolívar or of any central institution, and the personal animosity of its commander, Colonel Manuel del Castillo, trapped the liberator in a civil war. While he fought to bring Cartagena into the mainstream of the revolution, the royalists were able to recover lost ground in the Magdalena valley and to open a gap through which the republic could be invaded. On 8 May 1815 Bolívar left New Granada, despairing of resolving its problems, and he went to Jamaica, defeated not by Spaniards but by Americans. 'In New Granada', he wrote, 'the excessive powers of the provincial governments and lack of centralization in the federal government have reduced that fair country to its present condition. For this reason its enemies, though weak, have been able to hold out against all odds.'[54]

Morillo landed his expedition at Santa Marta in July 1815. Cartagena maintained a suicidal resistance to a siege which lasted a hundred days, and was finally occupied on 6 December; the town was dead, its streets and houses littered with corpses, and the few patriots still alive were butchered by the royalists.[55] It was now only a matter of time before Morillo conquered the rest of New Granada. Demoralization born of years of sterile civil war prepared the way for the royalist army. As it approached the provinces of Antioquia and Popayán, in March 1816, resistance crumbled: 'The people were now tired of the revolution and desired the restoration of the old government, under which they hoped to remain at peace.'[56] In May 1816 Bogotá itself was besieged, overwhelmed, and immediately subjected to an unprecedented reign of terror.

The counter-revolution, or 'pacification' as it was cynically called, was directed personally by military commandant Sámano, who introduced a new dimension of cruelty.[57] Patriots were forced to 'purify' themselves by massive fines. These were the fortunate ones. Others suffered banishment, forced labour, military conscription, imprisonment. And the patriot elite suffered death. Caldas, Lozano, Camilo Torres, Valenzuela, Frutos Gutiérrez, Pombo, García Rovira, José Ayala, Ignacio Camacho, Bernardo Alvarez, and even Baraya who had done so much of the Spaniards' work for them, were all executed. Some were hung, some were decapitated, some were shot. It was a calculated pogrom against the New Granadan upper class, and it claimed about five hundred victims. But the peasants too suffered. They were herded into public works and into road-building gangs, and forced to abandon their fields and harvests.[58] Those who were allowed to remain on the land had to work hard, as did the whole colony. For Morillo made New Granada a supply base for his army of the north; agricultural regions, the industry of Socorro, the mines of Antioquia, all had to work for the reconquest. The year 1816 was the blackest year of the American revolution, the year of the gallows in New Granada and of rampant reaction throughout the subcontinent.

Yet at the height of the counter-revolution independence was born again.[59] In New Granada there were two foci of resistance. Some of the most committed revolutionaries retreated to Casanare, and there, in that vast semi-desert, the environment itself was their best defence. Casanare became the last refuge of all the opponents of Sámano's regime and it kept the revolution alive in the darkest days of terror.[60] Nearer to royalist power the guerrillas of the interior constituted a second resistance movement. An example of guerrilla activity was the band formed in 1817 by the Almeyda brothers, José Vicente and Ambrosio, who operated in and around the Valle de Tenza, north-east of Bogotá. The Almeydas proclaimed 'Salud y libertad', 'Viva la América libre'; they called upon the people to join them 'to rid us of the shameful enslavement by the godos'; and they promised war against the enemies 'who have caused us such enormous damage'.[61] The Almeydas were a wealthy creole family whose political activities had already brought them into conflict with the Spanish authorities; having escaped from prison they were now on the run, and in addition they sought to recover the vast haciendas confiscated by the junta de secuestros in 1817.[62] The guerrillas therefore were not a popular movement: they represented creoles, whose interests had been grievously damaged by the counter-revolution. The mass of the peasantry and the Indian communities remained indifferent to their pleas for recruits, and many fled to the mountains rather than enrol in an alien cause, or, as the Almeyda put it, because 'they were not interested in the happiness of their country'.[63] The Almeydas protested that 'the cause which we uphold is not only in our own interest, but also for the public good and the benefit of the whole country'. But to swell their ranks they had to employ a mixture of force and cajolery and to rely on conscripts rounded up by friendly mayors and priests. They managed to assemble a force of two hundred and fifty, but this disintegrated after its first major defeat (21 November 1817), and many peasant guerrillas returned to their communities. The Almeydas and their sympathizers then retreated to the Llanos, to await the final victory of the revolution and the restoration of their estates. Meanwhile in Casanare the resistance movement had become a kind of happy anarchy under a series of caudillos, until the arrival of Santander introduced order and a new sense of purpose.

In 1818 Morillo was forced to withdraw some of his forces from New Granada in order to contain Bolívar in Venezuela. Now the revolution began to move again, and from the wastes of Casanare guerrilla columns penetrated into New Granada through the eastern Andes. It was to direct this renewed effort that Bolívar sent Colonel Santander into Casanare, to administer, to defend and to recruit. And the liberator himself exhorted the people to rise : 'Granadinos, the day of America has arrived. Before a year has passed the altars of liberty will have a new site in your land.'[64] In May 1819 Santander reported decisive victory over the enemy in the plains of Casanare and the final retreat of the royalist expedition.[65] Bolívar quickly decided that the time had come to invade New Granada, to make this the fulcrum on which the revolution could turn, east to Venezuela and south to Quito and Peru. After a cruel trans-Andean campaign, in which endurance, valour and the genius of Bolívar won the day, the liberating army delivered the death blow to the royalists at Boyacá (7 August 1819) and made straight for the capital. The Spanish officials, authors of terror and fearful of retribution, fled in panic to Cartagena. Viceroy Sámano departed so quickly – disguised as an Indian – that he left a bag of money

on his desk, to the great amusement of Bolívar.[66] Soon Spanish
resistance was confined to Cartagena and Cúcuta; but in the
south the republican forces could make little progress beyond
Popayán, and in the highlands up to Quito the royalists still
possessed a formidable stronghold.

Bolívar was already president of the republic. Now he
announced the kind of republic it would be – a republic of a
greater Colombia, formed from the union of New Granada and
Venezuela.[67] He began by using New Granada as Morillo had
used it, as a source of supply and revenue, not only from confiscated royalist property but also from taxes and tithes; indeed he
retained most of the Spanish taxes, as well as the municipal
government of the colony. But the liberator needed a representative in Bogotá; so he created the office of vice president for
New Granada and to it, on 11 September 1819, he appointed
General Santander, a native of Cúcuta, son of a respected if
poor creole family, and product of a legal education. Santander
was a colleague, not a friend, of Bolívar, and he was far removed
from the liberator's ideal. At twenty-seven he was a severe,
humourless and touchy man, with a strong interest in money and
a streak of vindictive cruelty, seen in his unconcealed delight
at the execution of royalists. In October 1819 he dismayed
Bolívar when he ordered the shooting of Colonel Barreiro and
thirty-eight officers imprisoned after Boyacá.[68] He owed most
of his promotion to Bolívar, partly by being in the right place at
the right time, partly because he was a superb administrator.[69]
Now his organizing talent was desperately needed : the immediate
task was to mobilize New Granada for the continental war effort;
the ultimate duty was to create a new nation.

Bolívar now returned to Venezuela to elaborate his constitutional ideas. By the Fundamental Law of 17 December 1819
the Congress of Angostura formally created the Republic of
Colombia, a permanent union of the departments of Venezuela,
New Granada and Quito, the latter still to be liberated. To endow
the new state with a constitution a congress was called, which met
at Cúcuta on the border of New Granada and Venezuela from
6 May to 14 October 1821.[70] Bolívar appointed Nariño, a known
centralist and unitarian, and recently returned from his prison
exile in Spain, as interim vice president to preside over the

congress. The anti-centralists were also represented, those who saw federalism as more democratic, more republican, a greater guarantee of liberty and a firmer restraint on the executive. These were not only provincial opinions; some interests at the centre were also federalist, unwilling as they were to carry the weight and costs of the provinces, while civilian Cundinamarca had the further fear of domination by the Venezuelan military. Bolívar's own views on these matters were well known – strong central government was the only way to win independence and the only way to constrain the social anarchy which independence released. He spoke with scorn of the 'delirium' of those who favoured federation, politicians who believed they represented the people, while in fact 'in Colombia the people are the army', those who had actually liberated the country.

These gentlemen believe that Colombia is filled with old women who sit around the firesides of Bogotá, Tunja and Pamplona. They have not troubled to notice the Caribs of the Orinoco, the cowboys of the Apure, the seamen of Maracaibo, the boatmen of the Magdalena, the bandits of Patía, the indestructible citizens of Pasto, the Guajibos of Casanare, and all the savage hordes from Africa and America who roam as untamed as wild deer in the wilderness of Colombia.[71]

Authority was needed to tame Colombians and to counteract their want of social homogeneity.

Cúcuta gave Bolívar the legal framework which he sought. The Constitution of 12 July 1821 created a strongly centralist state, a greater Colombia, comprising Venezuela, New Granada and potentially Quito, united under a single government with its capital in Bogotá, and subdivided not into three regions but into a number of departments. It was a conservative constitution: it favoured the president over the legislature, and restricted the franchise to literates who had real property valued at a hundred pesos. But it was not without liberal content: it guaranteed the classical freedoms, abolished the Indian tribute and inaugurated the abolition of slavery. On 7 September congress chose Bolívar, the victor of Carabobo and the liberator of two countries, as first president of Colombia, with Santander as vice president. But already the politicians, the lawyers and the military were sharpening their knives. As disunity reared its ugly head Bolívar was glad to leave administration of the new regime in the capable hands of Santander and to resume his career as liberator. The next battlefield was Quito, the future Ecuador.

Bolívar had originally planned to liberate Panama after Venezuela, and then move south by sea to Guayaquil. After the liberation of Cartagena, however, Panama wrought its own bloodless revolution and declared for independence on 28 November 1821. But the principal reason behind Bolívar's decision to move directly southwards was the fear that San Martín might reach Ecuador first and claim it for Peru. On 9 October 1820 Guayaquil had risen, overthrown the Spanish authorities and established a revolutionary junta. The Fundamental Law of Colombia (17 December 1819) had declared Quito part of Colombia. By the doctrine of *uti possidetis,* whereby the new states inherited the colonial administrative boundaries, this was correct, for the presidency of Quito had been subject to the viceroy of New Granada since 1740. But law was not the only weapon · 'The principal object of Bolívar was to make Guayaquil recognize the government of Colombia, by choice or by force.'[72] At the beginning of 1821 he sent General Antonio José de Sucre to Guayaquil with a thousand men to support the revolution against the royalist forces under General Aymerich and to win the rest of Ecuador for Colombia.

According to O'Leary, if Bolívar was the greatest man of the American revolution, Páez the most extraordinary, and Santander the most fortunate, Sucre was 'the most perfect by far'.[73] Son of an upper-class creole family in Cumaná, Sucre had a brilliant war record in Venezuela; a talented soldier, he was also a thoughtful, sensitive, and self-sufficient man, with a fine sense of judgment and complete loyalty to Bolívar. But in Quito Sucre was trapped in a political labyrinth, thwarted not only by the royalists, who closed the road to Quito, but also by warring factions within Guayaquil, divided as it was between those who wanted independence of Colombia as well as of Spain and those who demanded union with Peru. But if Sucre needed the insurgents of Guayaquil, these needed Sucre and Colombia; so without mention of the status of Guayaquil an alliance was signed in May 1821.[74] Sucre could now defend the coast effectively, but he still did not have the power to thrust through

the highlands to Quito, and on this front he was glad to accept
an armistice in November 1821. Protected by the cordillera on
the west, Quito was also impregnable from the north where
royalist enclaves closed the mountain passes to the revolution.

Bolívar left Bogotá on 13 December 1821 and made his way
south to penetrate this fortress.[75] Across his path lay the mountain
province of Pasto, its Catholic and conservative beliefs preserved
intact through isolation, its royalism as impenetrable as its
environment.[76] Bolívar dreaded this encounter. And after the
murderous battle of Bombona (7 April 1822) he had to abandon
the idea of taking Pasto. But his heavy losses were not in vain. He
had drawn the royalist war effort upon himself, while Sucre was
at last making progress towards Quito. Reinforced by a division
from Peru under Colonel Santa Cruz, Sucre crossed the cordillera
in April 1822 and approached Quito high in the mountains.
Instead of attacking from the south as expected, he advanced
from the north, and on the slopes of Mount Pichincha, 'its extinct
volcano covered in eternal snows', he defeated the Spaniards on
24 May 1822, the third major victory of the northern revolut-
tion.[77] While Sucre entered Quito and received the surrender
of Governor Aymerich, Bolívar accepted the grudging submission of Pasto.[78] On 16 June 1822 the liberator entered the
capital, but only to leave a reluctant Sucre as president of a
new department of Quito, while he himself concentrated on
Guayaquil, one of the most intractable problems of his career and
a cause of mounting tension between Colombia and Peru. He took
the precaution of sending troops to Guayaquil, and he went there
in person at the beginning of July.[79]

Colombia wanted Ecuador, and Ecuador needed Guayaquil;
economically the highlands had no other outlet to the sea.
Bolívar also played on the need to save Guayaquil from mob
rule: 'You alone find yourself in a false and ambiguous position.
You are threatened with anarchy. I bring you salvation.' And
on 13 July he decreed the formal incorporation of Guayaquil
into Colombia, subsequently confirmed by 'vote' of the *guayaquileños*.[80] Bolívar now awaited the arrival of San Martín, and
the two liberators met on 27 July.[81] The Bolivarian version of
the interview insisted that discussion was confined to political
matters, that San Martín did not make an issue of the status of

Guayaquil or request military aid, and that he did not procure Bolívar's agreement for a monarchy in Peru. According to San Martín's supporters, the protector needed and requested the support of Bolívar's army to complete the destruction of royalist power in Peru; and to procure this he offered to serve under Bolívar's command. The fact remained that Bolívar did not have to agree to anything. The balance was already tipped firmly in his favour. Victor of three campaigns, liberator of three countries, legal president of Colombia, *de facto* dictator of Guayaquil, Bolívar held all the cards; the future was his, in the south as well as in the north. For the next year he remained in Ecuador, waiting and resting.

(iii) COLOMBIA, ONE NATION OR THREE?

Santander, 'the man of laws', led his country in a moderate liberal revolution, in which he maintained government control against the forces of anarchy, preserved civil rights, supplied the armed forces, sustained the war effort, and attempted to apply a programme of reform.[82] He appreciated the material on which he had to work, so different from the militarists of Venezuela: 'A thousand times I bless the people of Cundinamarca, a rustic and ignorant people but endowed with great virtues and above all with a praiseworthy obedience.[83] Yet even these paragons could not resolve the new nation's financial problems, an amalgam of economic recession induced by war, reluctance of the affluent classes to pay income or property taxes, the poor quality of the fiscal bureaucracy, and above all military expenses, which accounted for 75 per cent of total expenditure. Rising deficits and failure to balance budgets sabotaged reforms, produced an ill-paid and inferior civil service, frustrated the military, and ultimately made the government vulnerable to criticism. This latent bankruptcy 'contributed more than any other one factor to the collapse of Santanderian liberalism and ultimately of the Bolivarian dictatorship as well'.[84] Foreign loans raised in London gave temporary relief, but at a heavy cost to future generations.

The regime was subject to two major pressures, conservative and federalist. These were not synonymous forces. In fact there were many political permutations. Some liberals were centralists, convinced that strong government was needed to impose liberalism. Others were federalists, because they believed that federalism was more democratic. Some conservatives wanted maximum authority at the centre. Others backed regional interests against Santanderian liberalism in Bogotá. Bolívar was at once conservative and centralist. In his absence the revolution was faltering, and Santander asked him to return to restore morale and to deal with congress. But Bolívar did not wish to be an administrator; there were still further conquests to be made for America. And the man who liberated so many people did not wish to be fettered by congress or by laws. When Santander argued that the constitution of Cúcuta was inviolable, Bolívar scorned the idea, just as he rejected the arguments of those who sought to federalize Colombia. 'I shall not keep the presidency if I am not allowed to exercise those extraordinary powers which congress voted me. I know for certain that Colombia can only be kept in order and prosperity by absolute power.... Colombia needs an army of occupation to keep it free.'[85] With each year that passed Bolívar became more conscious of the racial divisions in American society and the propensity of its people to anarchy:

I am convinced to the very marrow of my bones that America can only be ruled by an able despotism. . . . We are the vile offspring of the predatory Spaniards who came to America to bleed her white and to breed with their victims. Later the illegitimate offspring of these unions joined with the offspring of slaves transported from Africa. With such racial mixture and such a moral record, can we afford to place laws above leaders and principles above men?[86]

Eventually the call from Colombia became compelling. And in the second half of 1826 Bolívar returned from Peru to a divided nation, with Santanderian liberalism, federalism, and his own conservative Bolivian constitution all competing. The liberator reached Bogotá in November; he briefly assumed control of the administrative machine and performed some brisk repairs. He did not disguise his disapproval of what he regarded as Santander's indiscriminate liberalism and its divisive effects on the nation; and he wasted no opportunity to promote his Bolivian constitution.[87] But in the event he altered little, apart from trying 'to bring the expenditure of the country within its income'.[88]

Time was against him. He was now recalled beyond Bogotá to
Venezuela. There Páez had revolted and federalism was gaining
strength.

Venezuelan separatism had a long history. Opposition between
Venezuela and New Granada was manifest as early as 1815; it
produced resistance to Bolívar and his officers in New Granada,
and contributed to the success of the Spanish counter-revolution
in 1815–16. In 1819 national conflict was responsible for the
depositions of the New Granadan Francisco Antonio Zea as vice
president of Venezuela by the Congress of Angostura and his
replacement by the Venezuelan Juan Bautista Arismendi. Once
Colombia was constituted these tensions persisted. The great
distances separating Venezuela, Cundinamarca and Quito, the
mountain ranges, the poor communications, the heterogeneous
mass of the population, pardos of Venezuela, mestizos of New
Granada, Indians of Ecuador, all made it impossible to unite
greater Colombia or to inform it with 'national character and
national feeling'.[89] There was no impetus to economic integration; the economies of Venezuela and New Granada were
separate and independent, and while both had serious problems
these were not such as could be resolved by unification.
Venezuelans complained that they did not receive a fair share of
national expenditure. But the real discrimination was of another
kind. The relative inaccessibility of Bogotá, remote from the
periphery in time and space, deprived the Venezuelans of
adequate representation in the capital. The first freedom fighters
were now subject to new restraints, governed by a new metropolis.
Venezuelans came to regard the New Granadans as foreign
masters, a view given credence by the advantages which these
gained from the fact of being at the centre of offices and opportunities. The centralization of the republic in Cundinamarca
ushered Bogotá into a boom period, during which it became
the site of an expanding bureaucracy, new public works, fiscal
favouritism, population growth; Bogotá thus advanced from a
primitive outpost of empire to a civilized capital.[90] The
Venezuelan military were the most embittered critics of the
alleged new colonialism; they considered that while they had
fought for victory corrupt politicians in Bogotá enjoyed the
fruits. To some degree therefore relations between Venezuela and

Bogotá suffered from antagonism between military commanders and civil administrators.

José Antonio Páez, commandant-general of the department of Venezuela, expressed increasing dissatisfaction. He spoke for himself and for many Venezuelans. The llanero warrior had now acquired a huge fortune and vast landed wealth; he was an entrepreneur in commerce and agriculture, and, though his greatest passion was gambling and cock-fighting, he was trying hard to improve himself. 'As a man', noted the British consul, 'he possesses a naturally strong mind, but from being totally uneducated, is extremely diffident of himself when in the society of others endowed with the advantages of education. Feeling this inferiority, and anxious to improve, he has, within these very few years, applied himself to reading and writing; which acquirement until then he was totally ignorant of.'[91] This untutored plainsman obviously depended in some degree upon more urbane advisers – Mariño, his second-in-command, a master of intrigue and inveterate opponent of Bolívar, Dr Miguel Peña, his civil adviser, an able if unprincipled politician, and Colonel Francisco Caraboño, military colleague. These were the nucleus of a separatist or federalist faction, of which some observers believed Páez to be 'rather an instrument than a leader'.[92] Whatever the truth of this, Páez was encouraged in his inferiority complex: he came to believe that he had not received the power and recognition which he deserved. His exasperation with legislators and politicians focused especially on those in Bogotá, civilians whom he regarded as oppressors of the 'poor military'. In 1825 he urged Bolívar to take greater, even monarchical, powers, and to make himself a Napoleon of South America.[93] Bolívar was alarmed at the idea and rejected it.

In April 1826 Páez was relieved of his command and summoned to Bogotá for impeachment by congress on charges of illegal and arbitrary conduct in recruiting civilians for the militia in Caracas. The object, as Santander explained, was 'to make the first chiefs of the republic understand that their services and heroism are not a licence to abuse the citizens'.[94] But Páez resisted. Backed by the llaneros, and prompted perhaps by the Venezuelan military and the extreme federalists around him, he raised the banner of revolt on 30 April, first in Valencia, then in the department of Venezuela. The cry was raised – independence for Venezuela.[95] There was much support for Páez, though not universal support, for the sense of national identity was not sufficiently developed to appeal to everyone. The official reaction to Páez was also mixed. Santander wanted a hard line. Bolívar was more tolerant, believing that Páez and the military were victims of the excessive liberalism of civilian politicians who sought to 'destroy their liberators', and that Páez should not have been summoned by congress.[96] Bolívar sent O'Leary on a mission of pacification. The Irishman found Páez at Achaguas, capital of Apure, in a friend's house seated on a stool, playing a violin, his only audience a blind Negro. O'Leary was reminded irresistibly of Nero. Otherwise he was not impressed. After ten futile days he left with Páez's final answer ringing in his ears : 'I hope the president will not force me to be his enemy and destroy Colombia with civil war.'[97] O'Leary was convinced that the rebellion had no roots 'en el alma popular', and that Páez was an instrument of faction and swayed by those around him.[98] Bolívar himself thought differently; he appreciated that Páez stood for strong regional interests and a sense of Venezuelan identity.

From the very beginning of the revolution Bolívar's thought transcended national restraints and expressed a wider Americanism. He had long desired the creation of a great Colombia, embracing both Venezuela and New Granada. In 1813 he argued that 'union under one supreme government will give us strength and make us formidable to everyone'.[99] But his vision was not confined to Colombia : he believed that the union of Venezuela and New Granada would give strength to a greater Spanish American unity. This he hoped to forge in a congress at Panama, where plenipotentiaries of the liberated countries would coordinate American policy towards the rest of the world and simultaneously constitute an organ of conciliation among the American nations, a kind of supranational legislature. On this inspiring theme his imagination knew no bounds. In 1822 he declared : 'The great day of America has not yet dawned. We have expelled our oppressors, broken the tables of their tyrannical laws and founded legitimate institutions. But we still need to establish the basis of the social compact, which ought to form of this world a nation of republics.'[100] Whatever he meant by 'a nation of republics', he advocated supranational unity of some kind. If this were secured, he asked, 'who will resist America reunited in heart, subject to one law, and guided by the torch of liberty?' In 1826, as anarchy and infirmity appeared to consume the new states, he sought a more particular federation or union of the Andes, to include Peru, Bolivia and Colombia.

Leaving aside Bolívar's more extreme flights of fancy, it is evident that his ideas of confederation and congress assumed the existence of individual nations and simply sought to give them collective security. His ideal of a great Colombia was not a denial of national identity but an affirmation of it. He was merely trying to establish the appropriate size of a viable nation. 'If we establish two independent authorities, one in the east and the other in the west, we will create two different nations which, because of their inability to maintain themselves as such, or even more to take their place among other nations, will look ridiculous. Only a Venezuela united with New Granada could form a nation that would inspire in others the proper consideration due to her. How can we think of dividing her into two?'[101] Bolívar thus sought unity as a means to national strength and economic viability. In the first place, unity would ensure peace and well-being as opposed to the anarchy of local caudillo rule: 'I do not want these mini-governments; I am resolved to die amidst the ruins of Colombia, fighting for its fundamental law and for absolute unity.'[102] Secondly, unity would earn greater respect from other nations, from the United States and from Europe. In Bolívar's view foreign indifference and contempt for Latin American independence was a consequence of the proliferation of tiny sovereignties, squabbling among themselves: 'Sections, mere fragments, which, though large in area, possess neither population nor resources, cannot inspire interest or confidence among those who might wish to establish relations with them.'[103]

The conflict between centralism and federalism also contained a racial problem, or so Bolívar believed. He was aware that there were strong objections to the choice of Bogotá as capital, not least the fact of its remoteness. But he argued that there was no alternative, 'for though Caracas appeared to be the more natural spot, from being more populous and influential, yet the province was chiefly composed of people of colour who were jealous of and opposed to the white inhabitants, and it was desirable consequently for the general tranquility to diminish rather than augment the influence of Caracas.'[104] From the same facts the Venezuelan ruling class drew precisely the opposite conclusion. They wanted proximate power, even home rule, for Venezuela, 'a very energetic and concentrated system in consequence of its containing a great diversity of colour'.[105] Racial tension and pardo ambition required close supervision and control.

Bolívar moved into Venezuela in late 1826 to confront the Páez rebellion. Although he mobilized, he did not want violence : 'I have come from Peru to save you from the crime of civil war.'[106] Conciliation was also favoured by the majority opinion in both countries. There was little alternative. Bolívar was aware of the danger of trying to use force against Páez, 'since almost all the principal military commands throughout Colombia are filled by natives of Caracas'.[107] So he compromised. On 1 January 1827 he received Páez's submission – but at a price, namely total amnesty for all the rebels, guarantees of security in their offices and property, and promises of constitutional reform. Bolívar was privately critical of Páez, but he flattered him in public and seemed to be preparing Venezuela for separate acceptance of his Bolivian constitution and entry into the confederation of the Andes.[108] From January to June 1827 Bolívar governed Venezuela personally, but he incurred the most scathing criticism of Santander and his supporters for leniency towards Páez and for unconstitutional tendencies. The Bolivian constitution had few supporters anywhere. And political opinion in Bogotá derided the projected federation of the Andes as unrealistic and unacceptable to the component parts.[109] As Santander himself remarked, with ironic understatement, 'me parece un poco impracticable'.[110]

Yet Santander was fast losing control of events. As the political situation became more unstable, Bolívar left Venezuela to the rule of Páez and returned to Bogotá in September to assume command of the administration. Amidst the growing anarchy of 1828, when the independence of the great magnates and the restlessness of the masses threatened to destroy the young republic, the liberator spoke compulsively of the need for 'strong government'.[111] He believed that the constitution did not conform to the social structure: 'We have made the executive subordinate to the legislative, which has been given a far greater share in administration than the nation's true interests require.'[112] He himself tried to supply the deficiencies of the constitution and to give Colombia the 'strong government' which it needed. Liberals were outraged. Santander regarded the new regime as conservative and militarist, a threat to all the liberal achievements of the last six years; and he now veered towards federalism. He was not without allies, though some were an embarrassment. In March 1828 General Padilla's attempt to rally Cartagena against Bolívar in favour of Santander and the constitution of Cúcuta, a rebellion based on the coloured population of the coast, ended in failure, and this tended to have the 'effect of rallying all the people of property and influence round the person of General Bolívar, as the only one capable of now restoring tranquility in Colombia'.[113] In June Bolívar took the next logical step: he assumed dictatorship, with apparently wide support; for he alone commanded respect, and Colombia needed what O'Leary called the calming effect of 'the magic of his prestige'.[114] Yet even during the military dictatorship of 1828–30 Bolívar was never a despot; and in 1829 he rejected a project to establish a monarchy in Colombia, presented to him without previous consultation.[115]

As Colombia came apart at the seams, Bolívar struggled to repair the damage. But it was a losing battle and even Bolívar came to realize that the creation of Colombia had been premature. And as the heroic age of 'Americanism' passed, he became one of the many victims of national awareness and national rivalries, denounced as a traitor in Venezuela and a foreigner in New Granada. He could no longer ignore the forces of separatism: the immense distances, the scanty populations, the poor record of the central government, the emergence of powerful local caudillos who could express their ambition on a regional scale if not at the centre, all these were factors of division and dissension. 'However much one may wish to avoid this separation', admitted Bolívar, 'everything conspires to bring it about. It has many inherent difficulties, but who can resist the demands of passions and immediate interests? I see no way of assuaging local antagonisms or shortening enormous distances.'[116] In 1829 the Venezuelans withdrew from Colombia, arguing that 'Venezuela ought not to remain united to New Granada and Quito, because the laws which are appropriate for those countries are not suitable for ours, which is completely different in customs, climate and products; and because government applied over a great area loses its strength and energy'.[117]

Ecuador too sought its own national identity. The country's political experience was less violent than Venezuela's, whose pardos and mestizos were more ambitious than the passive and apolitical Indians of Ecuador, and whose upper classes were more active than the Quito aristocracy. But Ecuador too had its grievances. The liberal economic policy of Colombia did not give sufficient protection to Ecuador's industry, already damaged by Bourbon policy, war, and disruption of the export routes. The country had also suffered from heavy conscription and the exaction of forced loans and supplies; Ecuador sustained a substantial part of the final war effort in Peru, and Bolívar milked the Ecuadorian economy dry to pay for the Colombian army. The large agricultural estates yielded little more than subsistence production, and the only commercial output was that of cacao, together with some shipbuilding and repairing in Guayaquil.[118] These problems were neglected by the Santander regime. Bogotá provided no tax relief, no protection, and no subsidy for Ecuador. And its liberalism provoked the latent conservatism of Ecuador's ruling class, one of whose demands was for the retention of Indian tribute and Negro slavery. Ecuadoreans were under-represented in the central government and its offices, and at home they had a sense of being colonized by new imperialists. For the foreign liberators stayed on as a virtual army of occupation, and Ecuadorean civil and military institutions were staffed by soldiers and bureaucrats from other parts of Colombia. On 13 May 1830 Ecuador seceded from the union, and the former New Granada was left to bear alone the name of Colombia.

The reasons for anarchy and disintegration were many and complex. But one of the major factors was the precarious financial situation of Colombia, compounded of inefficiency in administration, corruption in the bureaucracy, and the virtual fiscal immunity of the privileged classes. For want of revenue the army was starved of pay: the consequent discontent and mutiny among the military of all ranks was a major cause of disorder and division. Yet state bankruptcy was simply a reflection of the irredeemable environment of post-revolutionary Colombia, its stagnant economy, its privileged society.

(iv) THE LIBERAL SOCIETY

War and revolution added further burdens to an already feeble economy – drift of labour, loss of animals, flight of capital. And if New Granada did not suffer such devastation as the battlefield of Venezuela, it was used for years as a supply base by both sides. The new rulers strove for economic development. Republican legislation guaranteed freedom of agriculture, industry and commerce without monopoly restrictions, and the government confined itself to providing the conditions in which private enterprise could operate. This was the theory. In practice *laissez-faire* had to be modified. The Congress of Cúcuta (1821) abolished internal customs barriers, the alcabala, and entails. But the fiscal system tended to revert to its colonial state, as more taxes were restored to finance the war effort and the postwar administration.[119] The alcabala was revived in 1826, as were many other Spanish taxes after that unhappy year. The alcohol estanco, abolished in 1826, was re-established in 1828; and the colonial tobacco monopoly continued as a major revenue until its abolition in 1850.

Foreign capital and entrepreneurs were welcomed, and soon New Granada was swarming with zealous if not always reliable adventurers.[120] Capital and enterprise were applied especially to mining, a vital industry in western New Granada.[121] Emerald mines, silver, gold, copper and platinum all attracted various forms of concessions, investments and companies, although no striking fortunes were made and no great output was achieved. In general, capital fell short of needs, technology was defective, and transport was inadequate. Before 1810 the average annual produce of the mines had been 4·5 million pesos; after 1825 it was 5·5 to 6 million.[122]

Defective communications were a basic obstacle to economic growth. Yet to transport was applied one of the few technological

innovations of the time. A monopoly concession of steam navigation on the river Magdalena was granted in July 1823 to a
German entrepreneur, Juan Bernardo Elb-rs.[123] But local
prejudice and opposition, failure to construct feeder roads and
linking canals, lack of repair facilities and fuel stations, reluctance of Colombian capital to cooperate, and the technical
deficiencies of Elbers boats, all combined to reduce operations,
and left the majority of passengers and freight at the mercy still
of journeys by canoe and *champan* (local pole-boat) in the care
of the notorious *bogas*, or boatmen.[124] Even less successful were
the attempts to introduce steam navigation on the Orinoco and
Lake Maracaibo. And the construction of roads and canals,
including a trans-Isthmus canal between the Atlantic and the
Pacific, all remained dreams, shattered by the ignorance of
Europeans and the technical incompetence of Colombians. The
fact was that the country could not absorb modern technology.
Nor could it attract foreign immigrants. There were many
colonization and land company projects, but these foundered on
the greed of entrepreneurs who sought quick profits and the
reluctance of European immigrants to come as labourers.[125]
Immigration policy contained glaring contradictions. There was
already a mass of landless peasants in Colombia, who could have
benefited themselves and the state from a distribution of land. But
these had little chance, for unused public land was either sold at
prices too high for small farmers or granted to powerful war
veterans. 'Further grants of waste lands have been made to several
individuals to the extent of another million of fanegadas. Among
these is General Montilla for a grant of two hundred thousand
fanegadas of land in this province.'[126] Republican policy, therefore, simply enhanced the hacienda system, wasteful though it
was in land and resources. The land-owning class, moreover, or
some of them, received the further advantage of agricultural loans
from the government.

Independence ended the Spanish colonial monopoly, but
foreign trade continued to be subject to restrictions, and there
was nothing approaching free trade. British observers reported
that the commercial organization of the new state was little better
than that of the colony : Colombian importers continued to shop
in Jamaica rather than direct in Europe. The tariff of 1826

imposed duties ranging from $7\frac{1}{2}$ to 36 per cent on most imports; this was primarily a revenue tariff but it also had a protective content to satisfy national economic interests; and state monopolies were protected by prohibition of the import of foreign tobacco and salt. There were also some export duties for revenue purposes, though the country's export trade was hardly flourishing enough to sustain them. Colombia's production pattern remained the same; the principal items were cacao, cotton, tobacco, dyewoods and hides, with sugar and coffee on a smaller scale. The agriculturalists of northern New Granada, like those of coastal Venezuela, demanded and received protection for their plantation products. But the weaker wheat producers of the interior were not so protected against United States flour. The manufacturing industries of New Granada and Ecuador were even more vulnerable and could offer little resistance to British competition; while the government and consumers benefited from a moderate revenue tariff, this was of little use to national producers. Independence did not destroy national industries or remove entirely the protection afforded by isolation and local preference. But industries such as textiles could not easily compete with cheaper foreign goods. So Colombian industry now entered a period of crisis: particular victims were the textiles of Socorro and the wool industry of Boyacá.[127] And the survival of the alcabala did not exactly improve the market conditions for national manufactures. The result was a great expansion of imports, while exports were confined to a moderate output of gold and silver, which continued to carry the economy, and a small trade in plantation products, chiefly cacao and coffee, all handicapped 'from a defective and expensive communication with the interior'.[128] Balance of payments difficulties were inevitable. The trade gap was bridged by illegal export of precious metals and by foreign borrowings, the latter procured in adverse conditions, badly employed and unreliably serviced. This eventually led to a limitation of imports by natural process.

The economy of Ecuador was hardly more dynamic. Exports through Guayaquil – which was also the port of exit for southern New Granada – consisted principally of cacao and bark, and amounted to an annual average of only £186,962 in the period 1821–5. As imports – English textiles and hardware, with some

United States flour – amounted to an annual average of
£230,003 in the same period, this was another trade gap which
had to be covered by foreign borrowings.[129]

In these conditions there was a marked reaction against the
early optimism of free trade opinion towards ideas of protection
and state intervention, as could be seen in the thought of Juan
García del Río and José Rafael Revenga. But protection in itself
could do little for Colombia without the growth of consumers
and the development of labour, capital and skill. And Colombian
society was not qualified to provide these factors.

The new state was conventionally liberal in its structure and
its values. Mayorazgos were abolished, though they had never
been of great consequence in Colombia. Higher, and even
primary, education was extended, but this tended to be an urban
service and hardly benefited the campesinos. Colombia remained
a seigneurial society whose structure was only marginally modified by liberal reforms.[130]

Liberal policy towards the Indians was benevolent in intent
but harmful in results. The Indians were a large minority, socially
and culturally outside the national life; they had little interest in
independence and took little part in the struggle, unless they were
coerced into the armies of one side or the other. Some Indian
groups were royalists, notably in the regions of Santa Marta and
Pasto, where they responded to Spanish prompting.[131] And
some Indian communities were reported to have wept when they
heard that the king was gone, sensing perhaps that they had lost
their ultimate protector and their guarantor of peace and
stability.[132] The white liberal view of the Indians had already
been announced by Pedro Fermín de Vargas, who really wanted
to eliminate Indians by means of mestizaje and to create a pool of
producers or wage labourers:

To expand our agriculture it would be necessary to hispanicise our
Indians. Their idleness, stupidity, and indifference towards normal
human endeavours, causes one to think that they come from a
degenerate race which deteriorates in proportion to the distance
from its origin. . . . It would be very desirable that the Indians be
extinguished, by miscegenation with the whites, declaring them free
of tribute and other charges, and giving them private property in
land.[133]

This was the voice of the American Enlightenment, and this was the policy of the new regime. The law of 11 October 1821 abolished the tribute and all unpaid labour services, though the Indians were now subject to the same taxes as other citizens. Application of the law was delayed in Ecuador, for tribute from the Indian majority was regarded by Bolívar as too important for the war effort in Peru to be relinquished. The vital issue, however, was not tribute but land.

The resguardo, or community land, protected a social organization as well as a tenurial arrangement and was basic to the Indian way of life. Already before 1810 the disintegration of the resguardos had begun.[134] From the 1750s pressure on the indigenous communities increased as land-hungry farmers prompted royal officials to herd the Indians into ever smaller areas while the vacated resguardos were auctioned off.[135] In the last two decades of the colonial regime the Indians put up a fierce struggle to defend their resguardo rights and indeed to extend them, appealing to the courts with some success.[136] But after the revolution republican legislation tipped the balance the other way. The patriot leader and scholar, Miguel de Pombo, who claimed to be a champion of the Indians, promoted an early law, passed on 24 September 1810, giving the Indians individual property rights over the resguardos and abolishing the tribute. But political instability prevented its application, and the Spanish reconquest of 1816 brought an end to the law as well as to its author. Once independence was complete the republicans returned to the issue and again sought to make the Indian an independent individualist, instead of a protected peasant. The law issued by the Congress of Cúcuta on 11 October 1821 ordered the liquidation of the resguardo system; it declared the Indians 'restored' to their rights, and assigned resguardo land hitherto held in common to individual families in full ownership; this was to be done within five years. It was hoped that the Indians would become good property-owners, agriculturalists and tax-payers. But the state did not have the technique to apply this law effectively in a way which would safeguard the Indians.[137] The lots were often minifundia, too small to be of much use or stimulus to the new owners. No subsidies or training were provided to make the peasants real farmers; in fact it was easier to sell the lots than to work them.[138] While this legislation failed to accomplish agrarian reform, it succeeded in disrupting communal work and organization which had depended on communal ownership. 'The division of resguardo land was a sublime gesture of advanced liberalism, but a tremendous error from the social and economic standpoint.'[139] Between 1821 and 1850, in the region of Boyacá, the resguardos were almost all alienated.

The Indians were rightly suspicious of republican policy. The slaves too had little cause for rejoicing.[140] The Colombian economy did not rest upon slavery as did that of Venezuela. The mining industry, it is true, used slaves and found it difficult to attract free labour. But slaves were only a marginal force in the fields. The central and eastern agricultural districts were not heavily dependent on slaves, and even the plantation sector comprised either large haciendas employing peons or smaller farmers working for themselves. Slavery was already in decline in the eighteenth century, numerically and institutionally.[141] The war provided further opportunities for escape – or for conscription. After the battle of Boyacá, Bolívar ordered a reluctant General Santander to recruit five thousand slaves in western New Granada. Santander argued that in Choco and Antioquia the slaves belonged not to the royalists but to families 'afectos al sistema', and that the mines depended on slave labour.[142] Bolívar was insistent :

What is more appropriate or just in the acquisition of liberty than to fight for it? Is it right that only free men should die for the liberation of the slaves? It is not expedient that the slaves should acquire their rights on the battlefield, and that their dangerous numbers should be reduced by a process both just and effective? In Venezuela we have seen the free population die and the slaves survive. I do not know whether this is politic, but I do know that unless we recruit slaves in Cundinamarca the same thing will happen again.[143]

Santander grudgingly complied, though there was opposition from mine-owners and agriculturalists in Cauca. In 1821 the Congress of Cúcuta issued a slave law for the whole of Colombia, but this was not a basic instrument of abolition. It only referred to those born after that date, and even then they had to serve a

master until the age of eighteen. The rest of the slaves depended
for emancipation upon compensation paid out of meagre funds
raised from death duties. This was not abolition. Nevertheless the
prevailing climate of hostility towards slavery and the passage of
time had their effect on slave discipline and expectations, and if
abolition still remained for future legislation, slavery was
increasingly a thing of the past.[144]

Liberalism was based not only on values but also on fears –
fears of social conflict and race war. The new regime sought
peace through a policy of civil rights, in the hope that Negroes
and mulattos would not resort to violence. And even immigration
was inspired in part by a desire to introduce more whites and so
reduce the relative strength of the pardos. Yet racial tension was
aggravated by the progress already made by the pardos in the
last decades of Spanish rule, a progress which now continued and
brought them into conflict with white privilege and discrimination. In principle the republican regime stood for a policy of
complete racial equality; this was the situation in law, but the mass
of the pardos were still far from enjoying real equality. The
revolution, of course, needed the pardos and the army opened its
ranks to them. And once Colombia had been liberated they were
still needed as reinforcements for the Colombian army in Peru:
'Of the 2,000 soldiers whom I saw in Carthagena going to
Peru, at least one-half were more or less of the African tinge.'[145]
So the free coloureds were an essential support of the independence movement: 'Colombia reckons among her best and bravest
officers men whom Spanish pride and tyranny deemed unworthy
to sit at a white man's table.'[146] The revolution enabled some
of the more successful pardos to acquire high military rank and
even civil office. For these independence meant real emancipation, and there was no going back. And others pressed from
behind, still frustrated by failure. Their numbers and militancy
were a matter of concern to the whites: 'the preponderance of
African blood on so very an extensive line of coast, in agitated
times like the present, cannot fail to excite serious reflection in
this country. Those now in power are by no means disposed to
disregard them.'[147] Bolívar himself did not ignore them. His
attacks on liberals in the fateful year 1826 were invariably linked
with fear of social violence: 'Where is there an army of occupa-

tion to impose order? Africa? We shall have more and more of
Africa. Seriously, anyone with a white skin who escapes will be
fortunate.'[148] These fears were exaggerated. The pardos tended to mirror
the social structure of the whites and to divide into upper and
lower classes. This worked to the advantage of the whites. In
March 1828 José Padilla, a veteran of the war against Spain,
'admiral of the nonexistent navy', proclaimed himself commandant-general and intendant of Cartagena, and sought to raise the
people of the coast against Bolívar and 'tyranny'.[149] Padilla was
a pardo, or, as O'Leary put it, a 'mulatto, ferocious and
sanguinary'; he appealed to the pardos and tried to provoke race
war.[150] But conditions were not on his side. Posada Gutiérrez,
a pro-Bolívar officer, observed:

In our coastal provinces, especially Cartagena, there are educated
and sensible pardos. As they enjoy complete equality in possession of
political and civil rights, they are well aware of their true interests.
They know that knowledge and merit are the best qualifications for
preferment, and that they can earn by lawful means due promotion
to social positions, working and living honourably. This has a
moderating influence on the rest. It is true that among the ignorant
Negroes of the fields and of the lower classes in the towns there exists
a certain hostility towards us, but this is directed more towards social
status than towards colour, for they have the same aversion to the
upper-class pardos.[151]

It was these depressed pardos whom Padilla tried to revolutionize. His enemies, of course, were indignant. Posada Gutiérrez
expressed the hope that time and goodwill would assuage these
racial tensions, 'for which we whites are not responsible'. Others
were less sanguine: 'The zambo General Padilla will meet the
same fate as Piar, because from his many declarations it is clear
that his object has been to kill all the whites and to make this
another Santo Domingo.'[152] In the event Padilla was taken and
executed. And some observers believed that the rebellion actually
strengthened the dictatorship, 'since it will have the effect of
rallying all the people of property and influence around the
person of General Bolívar, as the only one capable of restoring
tranquility in Colombia'.[153]

Colombia remained an aristocratic society, described with

great insight by Bolívar in 1828, when, in a mood of deep pessimism, he spoke of the state of slavery in which the Colombian lower class still lived, subject to local mayors and magnates, and denied the human rights to which they were entitled :

In Colombia there is an aristocracy of rank, office and wealth, equivalent by its influence, its pretensions and its pressure on the people, to the most despotic aristocracy of titles and birth in Europe. Included in the ranks of this aristocracy are the clergy, religious, professional groups, lawyers, the military and the rich. For although they speak of liberty and constitutions, they want these only for themselves, not for the people, whom they wish to see continue under their oppression. They also want equality, but by this they mean equality with the upper classes, not the lower. In spite of all their liberalism, they prefer to regard the lower classes as their perpetual serfs.[154]

The polarization of society between an oligarchy of landed proprietors and their lesser allies on the one hand and the rural masses on the other, this was the future prospect of Colombia. The rural masses and their masters were not, of course, the whole of Colombia, whose population of 1.5 million also included urban artisans, miners, and groups in the middle of society. And the rural population itself comprised tenant farmers as well as labourers, stockmen as well as peons, Indians as well as mestizos. Independence perhaps accentuated these distinctions in offering new opportunities for differentiation within existing society. But it did not offer basic mobility or decrease the divisions which Bolívar described. Nor were these divisions exclusive to Colombia. They were also to be found, in even more extreme form, in Peru.

EIGHT *The Last Viceroy, the Last Victory*

(i) PERU, RELUCTANT REPUBLIC

PERU IN 1823 was the problem child of the American revolution, repugnant to liberators and royalists alike. The creoles were committed to neither cause: seeking only to preserve their own position, they awaited the victory of the strongest. The Peruvians did not produce a great liberator. Their leaders were prone to irresolution, moved first by one impression then by another. Such was Riva Agüero, at once the pride and the shame of the creole aristocracy. In February 1823 he was appointed chief executive with the title of president of the republic and rank of grand marshal: 'Congress thus awarded political power and highest military rank to the caudillo who had provoked the military revolt against congress and who had not fought in a single campaign or a single battle.'[1] The consequences were predictable – political disorientation and military collapse.

Incapable of liberating itself, Peru was loathe to accept liberation from others. Indeed this prospect caused greater resentment than the Spanish presence had ever done, and Peruvian nationalism first expressed itself not against Spaniards but against Americans. Bolívar felt the force of Andean xenophobia before he even entered Peru. After the liberation of Ecuador he was anxious to pursue the enemy in the south and he offered aid to the Peruvian leaders; but the offer was rejected and he himself was denigrated in the Lima press. 'The members of the government', he remarked, 'are more jealous of us than they are afraid of the Spaniards.' Bolívar believed that he had a right to intervene in Peru without invitation in defence of the American revolution : 'the enemy will come here if I do not go there to forestall him; moreover, enemy territory should not be regarded as foreign territory but as conquerable territory.'[2] Yet he hesitated to go, conscious of the instability he would leave behind and the chaos that lay ahead. In March 1823 he agreed to assign six thousand troops to Peru, and in April he sent a precursor, Sucre, to establish liaison with the Peruvian government and command the Colombian advance party. But in Peru Sucre was isolated, frustrated by factionalism. In June a royalist force seized Lima. The government fled to Callao, where congress deposed Riva Agüero and appointed Sucre to supreme command. But Riva Agüero refused to accept dismissal. He withdrew to Trujillo, followed by a group of congressmen; there he raised an army and dissolved congress. The latter reconstituted itself in Lima, now evacuated by the royalists, and appointed a new president, Torre Tagle, whom Riva Agüero refused to recognize and who literally bought a following with money from the public Treasury.[3] Peru was now split into two zones, occupied in the south by Spain and divided in the north by civil war. It was the extreme inconvenience of this anarchy which drove the Peruvian ruling class to seek Bolívar's assistance. And at last, for the sake of the continental revolution, he agreed to go.

Bolívar arrived in Lima on 1 September 1823 to a frenzied welcome; he was immediately invested with supreme military and political authority. Peru was hideous to behold, the site of four separate patriot forces – Peruvian, Argentine, Chilean and Colombian – a semi-rebellious navy, and a large royalist army.[4] It had a congress, two presidents, and a dictator. The legitimate president, Torre Tagle, resented his now empty title. And the ruling class rediscovered its suspicion of foreigners. For Bolívar was forced to act as a military governor. Yet he had little to govern. Argentina and Chile were anxious to withdraw their support. In the south the Peruvian army under Santa Cruz disintegrated before it even engaged the enemy. The guerrillas of the central zone, Peruvians before all else, and torn in their allegiance between Riva Agüero and Bolívar, were reduced to a few disorganized bands.[5] And in the north, ex-President Riva Agüero, displaying more energy against Colombia than he had ever done against Spain, opened negotiations with the royalists rather than submit to Bolívar. His intentions are disputed.[6] Did he hope to establish an independent monarchy? Did he plan a joint campaign with the royalists to drive out the Colombians? Bolívar had no doubt that he was 'a usurper, rebel and traitor'.[7] Traitor or no, Riva Agüero was hopelessly wrong, for he could not negotiate successfully with Spain from a position of weakness. In any case his troops rose against him in November 1823 and submitted to Bolívar; and Riva Agüero was allowed to depart for Europe.

Bolívar was a helpless spectator as Peru tore itself apart. In January 1824 he fell seriously ill and was forced to remain in Pativilca, a small village north of Lima. 'Discord, misery, discontent and egoism reigned everywhere,' he later recalled, 'and Peru no longer existed.'[8] He complained to Torre Tagle that the Peruvian troops had no interest in the war: 'All the Peruvian troops that are not kept within a fort are sure to desert ... no sooner are they left to sleep in the open or taken on long marches than they desert to a man.'[9] Yet Torre Tagle himself was the greatest security risk. This weak and confused opportunist was preparing once more to change sides. On 5 February 1824 Argentine and Chilean troops in Callao mutinied for arrears of pay, and receiving no satisfaction from the Peruvian government they handed over the fortress to the royalists. On 29 February, with the connivance of Torre Tagle and other turncoats, the enemy occupied Lima again. Torre Tagle, the principal officials and over three hundred officers of the Peruvian army promptly went over to the royalists, as they had previously passed from the royalists to the patriots, 'for no other reason than their anxiety to be always on the strongest side'.[10] 'Peru is a chamber of horrors', exclaimed Bolívar.

Now everything depended on the liberator, and the Colombian army was the last line of defence. By decree of 10 February 1824 congress appointed Bolívar dictator and suspended the constitution. O'Leary recorded the event in a memorable passage:

The situation of Peru when this decree was issued was very different from what it was when San Martín disembarked four years previously. At that time the support for independence was general throughout Peru, and enthusiasm for the liberators matched the resources placed at their disposal. San Martín had only to come, see and conquer; he came, he saw and he could have conquered. But the task was perhaps beyond him, or at least he believed so; he hesitated and finally abandoned it. When congress entrusted to Bolívar the salvation of the republic, it handed him a corpse.[11]

O'Leary exaggerated the degree of support which Peruvians had given San Martín, but otherwise there was truth in his invidious comparison. San Martín had made the mistake of trying to win the minds and hearts of Peruvians. Bolívar perceived more acutely that Peruvians were indifferent to one cause or the other, that each sector of this highly stratified society sought only to retain its own immediate advantage, that in these circumstances only power could persuade, and only a military victory by an American army could liberate Peru. This was appreciated too by foreign observers: 'The people in general, not in military array or public official station appear to await with a quiet and patient submission, a pacific resignation, the result of the military ascendancy which is to determine their future condition.'[12]

Bolívar's friends and colleagues were convinced that it was madness to accept the dictatorship of Peru and advised him to withdraw. But Bolívar trusted his own genius and vision. After recuperating at Pativilca, he began to organize resistance, to stop the rot, to improve morale. Civil affairs he placed in the hands of a single minister, José Sánchez Carrión, an able Peruvian and known patriot. The liberator's own task was to assemble an army, to procure more troops from Colombia, more recruits from Peru, and to find money to pay for men and supplies. At the beginning of March he made his headquarters at Trujillo and in April he

moved to Huamachuco. He made northern Peru a second
Mendoza, another cradle of the revolution. He confiscated
royalist property, cajoled money out of the Church, imposed
taxes. It was now that Peruvians made their contribution to the
cause of independence with men, money and supplies.[13] Bolívar's
indispensable assistant in the task of recruiting and organizing
was the faithful Sucre, and between them they created and
trained a new army of liberation. By April 1824 it was eight
thousand strong and enjoyed two distinct assets. It possessed an
incomparable cavalry, composed of the gauchos of the pampas,
the huasos of Chile, and the llaneros of Venezuela and Colombia.
And it was paid, if not well (half a dollar a week) at least
regularly; on this Bolívar insisted.[14]

The liberators had a further advantage – the enemy's disarray.
For the Spaniards too were subverted by Peru, and they too
suffered demoralization and disunity. At the end of 1823 this was
not apparent. While Americans fought and failed each other,
the royalists consolidated their position.[15] In the north General
Canterac commanded an army almost eight thousand strong
based on Huancayo. Viceroy La Serna had a thousand men in
Cuzco. In Arequipa General Valdés' army of the south comprised some three thousand. And behind them, in Upper Peru,
General Olañeta had a force of four thousand. These formidable
armies were poised to concentrate and move on the Colombians.
It was vital that they act quickly, to anticipate Bolívar's own
build up, and to avoid the unpopularity which a parasite army of
occupation incurred in a lengthy campaign. At this point the
Spanish position was subverted from within. On 1 October 1823
Ferdinand vii, released from constitutional bondage by a
French army, abolished the constitution and restored absolutism;
provoking in Peru a royalist split between former constitutionalists La Serna, Canterac and Valdés and absolutist Olañeta.
But this was a struggle for power rather than a conflict of
principles.[16] At the end of 1823 Olañeta defected, withdrew his
military collaboration, and established in Upper Peru a crudely
conservative regime; crying out for king and religion, he ousted
the constitutional administration and packed the government
with his relations and supporters. Thus began the 'rule of General
Olañeta' in Upper Peru. The royalist hinterland, hitherto one of

the viceroy's most valuable assets, suddenly became a liability. The army of General Valdés was drawn off in a vain attempt to reduce Olañeta. And this diversion prevented the royalists from delivering a powerful blow at the Colombians in February or March, when the latter were just beginning to regroup.

Delay in acquiring this intelligence, combined with problems in his own camp prevented Bolívar from exploiting La Serna's embarrassment to the full. In May the liberator moved his army forward and upward to Pasco in one of the classical marches of the war of independence, 'over the most rugged districts, of the most mountainous country in the world, presenting at every step difficulties which in Europe would be considered perfectly insurmountable'.[17] As the troops struggled through the cordillera they were tortured by altitude sickness, hazards of the terrain, and night temperatures below freezing; infantry and cavalry had to pick their way in single file along precipitous tracks. They were followed by columns of Indians carrying supplies and equipment, and in the rear herds of cattle were driven as reserve provisions. The leadership of Bolívar and the planning of Sucre met in happy collaboration in this their most decisive campaign. By the beginning of August the liberators had assembled an army of six thousand Colombians and three thousand Peruvians high in the sierra. On 6 August they engaged Canterac on the plateau of Junín. It was a sharp and furious battle in which not a single shot was fired; the breathless silence was broken only by the clash of swords and lances and the stamping of horses. And it was the patriots' superior cavalry which won the day and forced the royalists into flight.[18]

Victory gave the liberators strategic command of the fruitful sierras of Jauja, though the Spanish army was still largely intact and its spirit still not extinguished. Leaving Sucre as commander-in-chief, with discretion to engage the enemy, Bolívar moved in October to the coast, organizing civil administration as he went; and in December he liberated Lima. Meanwhile La Serna fought back instantly. Leading the joint forces of Canterac and Valdés, an army of 9,300, he advanced on Sucre and sought to encircle him, while Sucre manoeuvred his six thousand out of distance. At last, on 8 December 1824, the two armies confronted each other at Ayacucho. Sucre's advice to his men was terse:

'Upon your efforts depends the fate of South America.' Their own fate was also at stake: royalist Indians who had already harassed the patriots now waited in the wings to cut them down in the event of their defeat and flight.[19] But it was the royalists who were defeated, as much perhaps by the hopelessness of their cause as by the tactics of Sucre, for this the last great battle of the American war was a strange anticlimax and casualties were not heavy. Viceroy La Serna was taken prisoner, and on 9 December General Canterac offered unconditional surrender. Peru was liberated, the American revolution virtually complete. The royalists could conceivably have concentrated all their remaining forces in Peru and Upper Peru and fought yet again. But what were their prospects? They had no hope of reinforcements from Spain: this perhaps was the most demoralizing knowledge of all. So after Ayacucho, Sucre's campaign of liberation took the form of accepting the surrender of one royalist garrison after another. Soon he took the war to Upper Peru. And last of all, after a lengthy and costly siege, Callao capitulated on 23 January 1826.

'These were glorious days in the life of the liberator', O'Leary remarked of the time after Ayacucho, a time marred only by the assassination of Monteagudo and an alleged plot against Bolívar's own life.[20] He spent the early part of 1825 in civil administration, reforming political, legal and economic institutions, and establishing a system of schools on the Lancaster model. In February he attempted to relinquish his dictatorship into the hands of congress, but Peruvians loved a victor and would not let him go. Yet there was one more act of liberation to which he had to attend. In mid–1825 he departed for Upper Peru, leaving Peru's own government in the hands of three ministers of state; Tomás de Heres, a Colombian, headed the war department; Hipólito Unánue, a Peruvian aristocrat, presided over foreign affairs; and José María Pando, an able *limeño* and recent convert to independence, occupied the Treasury.[21] If Bolívar had been handed a corpse, they were given a cripple.

Peru now paid the penalty for years of indecision, proof of a painful, if obvious, moral – the longer the war of independence, the greater the material damage and the slower the process of recovery. The Peruvian economy was prostrate.[22] Agriculture was one of the first victims of the wars: farms and plantations suffered from military destruction, diversion of labour, and poor American markets. The traditional prop of the economy and Peru's major exportable assets, gold and silver, were also depressed; mining production was hit by disruption of communications and by severe shortage of labour, mercury, mules and capital. Scarcity of capital affected all sectors of the economy. Between 1819 and 1825 an estimated 26·9 million dollars were shipped from Lima in British ships, representing payments for imports – consumer goods and war materials – and flight of capital to safer outlets.[23] Starved of exports and deprived of working capital, trade sank to a low level of depression, and there it was held by heavy taxes and diminished output of precious metals. Inevitably Peru could not earn enough to pay for imports of manufactured goods, at a time when excited British businessmen swarmed in to provide goods and services. Captain Basil Hall noticed the impact of recent changes when he dined in a Peruvian home in Huacho: 'A roll of English broad-cloth was resting on a French wine case, marked Medoc; on the table stood a bottle of champagne; the knives and forks were marked Sheffield, and the screen which divided the apartment was made of a piece of Glasgow printed cotton.'[24] The trade gap was temporarily bridged by foreign borrowing. A loan of £1,200,000 was contracted in London in 1822, from which the Peruvian government would receive less than £900,000.[25] A further loan for £616,000 was contracted in 1825. But the government fell into arrears the same year and suspended interest payments; in any case these loans were used for meeting previous obligations to British merchants and for financing military and naval expenditure, and there was no surplus for investment in development.

While the economic policy of the new state showed little active concern for national development, it was not on the other hand particularly partial to foreigners. The Commercial Code of 6 June 1826, though prefaced by liberal cliches, was in fact highly restrictive.[26] It suppressed internal customs and reduced alcabalas, but it placed a basic 30 per cent duty on all foreign imports; and imports such as liquor, certain textiles, sugar and other items competing with national production bore an 80 per cent protective tariff, subsequently raised to 90 per cent. Peru did not possess institutions capable of enforcing these excessive duties along her extensive coast line. The tariff, therefore, fulfilled neither its revenue nor protective functions: the Treasury suffered from contraband, the economy from stagnation, and foreign merchants from bureaucratic corruption and delay. Crude protectionism was not the way ahead for Peru. Unlike Colombia, the country had virtually no national industries to protect, and its agriculture suffered from more basic defects – including a faulty agrarian structure and lack of investment – than foreign competition. There was hope for improvement in mining, if it could attract sufficient skill and capital. But Peru lacked too many vital factors of production to create a viable industrial sector. In these circumstances, in the year 1826, the conclusions of the British consul in Lima seemed inescapable:

In Peru there is an especial call for the encouragement of commercial intercourse with foreigners; it has no manufactures of the slightest consequence; it is not likely to have any conducted by natives for many years from not possessing any of the essentials for their establishment, nor is it desirable to promote them. The introduction, therefore, of every description of foreign manufacture is particularly important; the inhabitants in general are too poor to purchase commodities at high prices; fair trade will be the sure means of their obtaining them at low rates.[27]

The allocation of scarce national resources was conducted according to the values and structures inherited from colonial society. Liberation was a sectional victory, bringing many advantages to the privileged few and few benefits to the deprived many. The social structure underwent only marginal change. Spaniards were persecuted and their properties confiscated, and many of the viceregal bureaucrats and merchants left the country. Those who remained were integrated into the Peruvian oligarchy to form an upper class of land and office, monopolists of wealth, power and privilege. The entrepreneurial function was assumed by foreigners; already by 1824 there were about two hundred and fifty British immigrants in Lima alone, representing about twenty firms, and there were others in Arequipa and major provincial towns.[28] These could not be called rivals to Peruvians, for the latter in general showed little instinct or talent for trade and industry. Those who did were frustrated by the social environment. The mestizos and free pardos of the coast were confined to the service sector and local workshops, and their prospects in the textile industry were impeded by foreign competition. Yet these were the people who were interested in social mobility and who sought to advance themselves against white resistance, especially in the professions. It was a slow process. Bolívar's experience in Peru convinced him that 'many of the higher classes had imbibed the prejudices and vices of their late Spanish rulers, and had followed their example in oppressing the lower orders'.[29]

Slavery was reduced but not abolished. San Martín did not favour universal manumission. In the early months of the war he advocated recruiting Negro slaves from royalist haciendas; and he argued that if the viceregal government continued recruiting slaves he would have to grant freedom to all the people of colour, which was not his original intention.[30] He took advantage of the protectorate to announce his more considered policy. By decree of 12 August 1821 he abolished the slave trade into Peru and declared that all children born to slaves from 28 July 1821, including those in royalist-held territory, were free and possessed the same rights as other citizens of Peru. And he ordered that each year a certain number of older slaves should be manumitted by means of state compensation to their owners.[31] Freedom was also offered to those who joined the patriot army. This was probably the only effective manumission, if manumission it was, for San Martín's other decrees were not uniformly applied. The Constitution of 1823 declared that no one could be born a slave in Peru and prohibited the slave trade into Peru.[32] But slave-owners opposed all these measures, and although the trade was discontinued slavery itself survived in coastal agriculture and domestic service. When Bolívar's constitution was adopted in Peru in 1826 the clause emancipating the slaves was omitted, the government regarding it as unrealistic.

The grounds for this belief are that the manumission of the slaves who are the only cultivators of the soil, would be followed by their desertion from the estates on which they were employed; and that the landholders would hence be exposed to have their lands left waste, as it has been found impossible heretofore to induce the natives to leave the mountainous district for the purpose of working as labourers in the low lands.[33]

It was 1855 before Peru abolished slavery.

The Indians suffered more than other Peruvians from the wars of independence. They were plundered by all the armies, and as the war swept back and forth over their heads they were seized as auxiliaries or beasts of burden, and then suffered reprisals if the other side came back.

Every military detachment that halted there unavoidably destroyed the crops of lucern, and often stole away their oxen, sheep, goats, or poultry, whenever they could lay their hands upon them. In this way hundreds of villages and thousands of individuals have been robbed of their little all; but they were poor oppressed Indians, and humble misery seldom arrests the attention or engages the sympathies of the world.[34]

Both sides treated the Indians as serfs, labourers and miners, transforming the personal services demanded of them in peacetime into military services in time of war. General Miller observed that it was the practice of both royalists and patriots 'to lay hold of the first Indian they met in the street, and compel him to clean out their barracks, to fetch wood and water, and perform the most menial offices. Habit had familiarized the officers to the custom, and they seldom corrected the evil: what, too, is most remarkable, the Indian soldiers were the most tyrannical in exacting these degrading services from their brethren.'[35] The guerrillas of central Peru relied on the cooperation of the Indians for intelligence and other services but gave them nothing in return. Thus the republicans continued to deny Indian claims, fobbing them off with promises that independence would bring them liberation from tyranny. But it was a habit of mind among the Peruvian whites to treat the Indians as inferior beings, and this could not be eradicated by legislation.

San Martín inaugurated a new policy. By decree of 27 August 1821 he abolished the tribute and declared that 'in future the aborigenes shall not be called Indians or natives; they are children and citizens of Peru, and they shall be known as Peruvians'. And a further decree (28 August 1821) abolished the mitas, encomiendas, yanaconazgos and all other kinds of personal servitude to which the Indians were subject.[36] These laws have a certain theoretical interest. They reflected a growing tendency to define the Indians in social and cultural rather than racial terms, and this was undoubtedly correct, though they failed to distinguish between the Indians of community and the more mobile cholos. Otherwise they have little significance, for they made virtually no difference to Indian conditions.

Bolívar sought to use his power in Peru from 1823 to inject further social and agrarian content into the revolution. His object was to abolish the system of community landholding and to distribute the land to the Indians in individual ownership. His first important decree, issued at Trujillo on 8 April 1824, ordered that all state lands be offered for sale at one-third of the price of their real value; these were not to include lands in the possession of Indians, who were to be declared proprietors, with right to sell or alienate their lands in any way they wished; the Indian community lands were to be distributed among the landless occupants, especially to families, who were to be entitled to full legal ownership of their portions; and it insisted that no Indian should remain without land.[37] But Bolívar's attempt to turn the Indian peasantry into independent farmers was frustrated by landlords, caciques and officials, and in the following year at Cuzco he was obliged to issue a further decree (4 July 1825), reaffirming and clarifying the first. This restored Indian land confiscated after the rebellion of 1814, ordered the distribution of community lands, regulated the methods of distribution to include irrigation rights, and declared that the right freely to alienate their lands should not be exercised until after 1850, presumably in the belief that by then the Indians would be able to read and write and be capable of defending their interests. Bolívar supplemented these decrees with other measures designed to reduce the power of caciques and to free the Indians from long-standing abuses and exaction.[38] By decree of 30 March 1824 he abolished the hated tribute, but this was not uniformly observed, opponents arguing, with some insincerity, that the Indians lost by fiscal equality. A post-Bolivarian decree of 11 August 1826 re-established the tribute on Indians under the name of *contribución de indígenas*, paralleled, it is true, by a *contribución de castas,* but the former was the larger and more assiduously applied.

The agrarian decrees of Bolívar were limited in scope and misguided in intent. They referred principally to the *comunidades,* not to the haciendas, where the peasants or colonos were annexed to the land in virtual serfdom, holding a *sayaña,* a strip of land for subsistence, on condition that they worked on the lord's estate and served in his house. As for the community lands, they had been reduced to a minimum in the course of the colonial period – by confiscations after Indian rebellions and during the wars of independence – except in the less fertile parts where there was little competition for them. As the great haciendas already occupied most of the best land in Peru, the decrees of Bolívar simply made the Indians more vulnerable, for to give them land without capital, equipment and protection was to invite them to become indebted to more powerful landowners, to surrender their land in payment, and to end up in debt peonage. And as the communities crumbled, the haciendas were waiting and ready to sweep up the fragments of Indian society: the new policy gave them an added supply of cheap labour, while the colonial labour and tenancy forms, inherited and strengthened by the republican regime, guaranteed its subordination. Bolívar's policy was not informed by deep understanding of Indian problems, only by ardent liberal ideals and passionate sympathy: 'The poor Indians are truly in a state of lamentable depression. I intend to help them all I can, first as a matter of humanity, second because it is their right, and finally because doing good costs nothing and is worth much.'[39] But doing good was not enough, or not adequately defined. To the Indians the new Peru was simply the old Peru writ large:

The Indians or Aborigenes who form the mass of the population, are much to be pitied, for their sacrifices and their sufferings have been great: ever since the revolutionary struggle commenced they have been deprived of peace, and no one event has cheered them, as they have gained nothing by the new order of things.[40]

(ii) BOLIVIA: INDEPENDENCE IN SEARCH OF A NATION

While Lower Peru was preoccupied with war and liberation,

Upper Peru was left more or less to its own fate by both sides. It was an eccentric fate. Once the guerrilla movements had been crushed there was virtually no resistance to Spanish rule.[41] A few liberal spirits, observing the course of the continental revolution, were convinced that events were moving against Spain. It was also clear that the Río de la Plata had no prospects of recovering these provinces, joined so briefly to Buenos Aires from 1776; previous failures and mistakes proved that Buenos Aires could not win Upper Peru by force and was not acceptable by choice. These considerations animated a few patriots, but they formed only a small movement, too weak to be the source of Upper Peruvian independence. The Spanish army of occupation was in a strong position, and when its peninsular leaders – Pezuela, La Serna, Valdés and Canterac – moved to Lower Peru it was left under the command of tough creole officers who supported the Spanish cause. The majority of the creole aristocracy also supported that cause, or at least did not challenge it, fearing the social consequences of subversion in this largely Indian land. When, in 1823, General Santa Cruz, a mestizo from La Paz and a former royalist himself, invaded Upper Peru, he sensed the lack of support for liberation from the north and, surrounded by royalist forces, he quickly retreated.[42]

The leader of Upper Peru's conservatives was Pedro Antonio Olañeta, a Spaniard more royalist than the viceroy, more absolutist than the king. Merchant by origin, Olañeta was now a soldier, an amateur soldier, it is true, but hard and uncompromising, and valuable to the royalists with his local knowledge and influence. He detested the post–1820 Spanish constitutionalism and distrusted the new school of Spanish commanders, La Serna, Valdés and Canterac, dangerous liberals in his view, at once unreliable and indifferent to the interests of Upper Peru. When, in 1820, these commanders were diverted northwards to confront San Martín, Olañeta was left in command of the royalist army in Upper Peru. In January 1821 the 'constitutionalist' military revolted against Pezuela: La Serna became viceroy, and he appointed General Canterac commander of the royalist army in the north and General Valdés commander in the south. This powerful, professional and liberal triumvirate now ruled Spanish Peru; their success served only to increase the frustration of

Olañeta, who also blamed them for impeding his military prospects. Spurred by a mixture of royalism and ambition, Olañeta wanted nothing less than absolute monarchy for Upper Peru, where, by 1823, he was ruler in all but name.

In October 1823 Ferdinand vii succeeded in ridding himself of constitutional restraints and restoring absolutism. By the beginning of 1824 Olañeta knew – via Buenos Aires – that the liberal cause had collapsed in Spain. He now proceeded to destroy it also in Upper Peru. In January 1824 he mutinied against La Serna and replaced the constitutional administration by an absolutist regime of his own making. General Valdés was sent to deal with the revolt, but he soon realized that force was useless against Olañeta's powerful local position. On 9 March 1824 the two commanders signed the so-called Treaty of Tarapaya, by which Olañeta was allowed to remain commander of Upper Peru; in return he agreed to recognize the authority of the viceroy, to submit to Valdés' army of the south, and to furnish such forces as the royalists required in Lower Peru. But once Valdés had gone Olañeta did none of these things; instead he assumed political as well as military command of Upper Peru and styled himself 'Commander of the Provinces of the Río de la Plata'. And he sent no troops to Lower Peru.[43] Bolívar', who saw military salvation in Olañeta's rebellion, overtly treated it as a liberation movement, though he understood its true nature. In June 1824 Olañeta rejected an ultimatum of Viceroy La Serna to submit or leave for Spain. He argued that La Serna was not the legitimate viceroy but an imposter who sought to 'destroy all principles of morality and honour'; he insisted that he himself recognized only the king of Spain; and he declared that he would die for king and religion and would fight the impious constitutionalists to the bitter end.

Olañeta's action inaugurated a civil war among royalists, the 'separatist war' of 1824, when absolutists fought liberals and the only victor could be the enemies of both. For while Olañeta appeared to be winning, in fact he deprived General Canterac of the services of the skilful Valdés and his army at the crucial battle of Junín. On news of this defeat Valdés evacuated Upper Peru and proceeded north to join the main royalist forces, leaving

Olañeta in command of the field in Upper Peru. He had powerful support.

The creole aristocracy, royalist by interest if not conviction, were forced to reappraise their position when the victories of Bolívar and the triumph of the American revolution destroyed the bases of royalism. They were prepared to abandon the sinking ship if only they could find an alternative haven, a new guarantee of their political and social predominance. Olañeta appeared to offer them an escape route. He received backing from a group of creole aristocrats, including Casimiro Olañeta, nephew of the general, Leandro Usín, José María Urcullu, José Arenales, José Mariano Serrano, Emilio Rodríguez and others, most of whom were graduates of the University of Chuquisaca. They were opportunists rather than royalists or independists. Convinced that Spain's last bastion in America was doomed, they sought an alternative regime which would preserve their interests, their landed property, their control of Indian labour; they sought a form of autonomy for Upper Peru. Did this mean independence? Not necessarily, for the independists did not yet have military superiority in Peru, and this was the only argument which the creoles appreciated. By this time most of the guerrilla leaders and their republiquetas had been wiped out by the royalists; only José Miguel Lanza and his followers remained active, and even they came to a tacit agreement with Olañeta not to continue the struggle. The field was thus left clear for the creole aristocracy, whatever decision they made.

Olañeta entered Chuquisaca on 11 February 1824, and on the following day he proclaimed absolute monarchy and the abolition of the constitutional system. The document was drawn up by José María Urcullu and Casimiro Olañeta, spokesmen of the aristocracy. Yet the creoles were still true to their own interests, not to a cause, royalist or revolutionary. They received major offices and appointments and became in effect Olañeta's ruling class. A contemporary observer noted that Olañeta 'appointed to the audiencia of Charcas judges who were his own supporters, preferring for these important offices people with marked disaffection towards the Spanish government, such as Antequera, Urcullu, his nephew Casimiro, Callejo and Cabero. In short, Olañeta behaved as though he could have been an enemy of

Spain.'⁴⁴ But a decision in favour of Olañeta could not be permanent : the creole aristocracy soon had another choice forced upon them by Bolívar and Sucre.

After Ayacucho Bolívar, President of Colombia, Dictator of Peru, assigned the liberation of Upper Peru to Sucre. The latter soon swept up the debris of Spanish rule in the sierra, entered Cuzco on 24 December 1824, and then crossed the Desaguadero to advance cautiously into Upper Peru, simultaneously negotiating with Olañeta and occupying territory. Olañeta's forces now began to desert in great numbers, responding to Sucre's call to join the liberating army. The creoles too had to make up their minds, to choose unequivocally between loyalty to a distant king and acknowledgment of the immediate power represented by Bolívar and Sucre. Olañeta decided for the king. But the majority of the creoles opted for the winning side. Thus they virtually inherited a revolution which they had not made. Cochabamba, La Paz and other towns declared their allegiance. Finally, cornered and isolated, Olañeta was mortally wounded at the battle of Tumusla (1 April 1825) and his forces defeated. This was the last battle of the American revolution, and in its wake Sucre occupied Potosí, the greatest pillar of the Spanish empire.

What was Upper Peru? A nation? A people? A province? Sucre issued at La Paz a decree (9 February 1825) proclaiming the virtual independence of Upper Peru.⁴⁵ The army, he insisted, had come to liberate, not to govern : Upper Peru could no longer continue its previous dependence on Buenos Aires, for the latter did not possess a government which represented the interior provinces; the ultimate solution would have to be based upon an understanding with Peru and Buenos Aires; meanwhile, Upper Peru would continue under the authority of the commander of the liberating army until a national congress decided the form of government. Sucre believed that this decree represented the political thinking of his leader. But Bolívar, the professional liberator, disapproved of this initiative and reminded Sucre that he was the commander of an army, not the disposer of political rights, and that in any case he had violated the principle of *uti possidetis*, by which the new states succeeded to the territorial jurisdiction of the major administrative units of the colonial period.⁴⁶

Upper Peru belongs by right to the Río de la Plata; in fact to Spain; by choice of its people, who want a separate state, to independence; and by claim to Peru, who previously owned it. To hand it over to the Río de la Plata would be to deliver it into anarchy. To give it to Peru would be to violate the international law which we have established. To create a new republic, as the Upper Peruvians demand, would be an innovation which I do not care to undertake, for only an American assembly can decide that.[47]

In fact, three months later, when he had presumably forgiven Sucre for usurping his role, he confirmed the decree of 9 February. His reasons were compelling: he knew that neither Argentina nor Peru would agree on the other procuring this territory; he himself did not want to enlarge the power of either country by awarding them a valuable mining zone; and he took account of opinion in Upper Peru itself.

A 'representative' assembly met in Chuquisaca on 10 July 1825.[48] In a country of well over one million people there were forty-eight delegates, elected by a restricted and complex franchise which included literacy and property tests; and a large province like Santa Cruz, penalized by its mass illiteracy, could send only two deputies. At least thirty of the deputies were graduates of the University of Chuquisaca, in whose halls the assembly met. And only two – guerrillas both – had actually fought in the war. Thus the creole aristocracy came into their inheritance, replacing the Spaniards in a social order – *caballeros, cholos, indios* – which endured for many generations to come. The assembly was a meeting of a local elite, men like Casimiro Olañeta, who had been first royalists, then *olañetistas*, and independists only at the last minute, and who now represented not a nation but a ruling group. For them independence meant control of policy and patronage: only in Upper Peru could they expect to rule, and they were determined that only they should rule there.[49] The assembly declared independence on 6 August, and the new republic adopted the name of Bolívar, later changed to Bolivia. The deputies also requested Bolívar to draw up a constitution for Bolivia. The liberator came in person and received a triumphant welcome on his progress through La Paz and other towns. In October he entered Potosí, where with Sucre he climbed the great silver mountain; at the summit they unfurled the flags of independence and drank to the American revolution.[50] Bolívar left Sucre to govern Bolivia and returned to Lima. There he drafted his constitution and sent it to Bolivia; it was adopted in July 1826.

In the last years of his life Bolívar was haunted by America's need for strong government, and it was in this frame of mind that he drafted the Bolivian constitution.[51] His lifelong search for a balance between tyranny and anarchy now moved unerringly towards authority. He told the British consul in Lima 'that his heart always beats in favour of liberty, but that his head leans towards aristocracy . . . if the principles of liberty are too rapidly introduced anarchy and the destruction of the white inhabitants will be the inevitable consequences'.[52] The new constitution preserved division of powers – legislative, executive and judicial – and to these he added an elective power, by which groups of citizens in each province chose an elector, and the electing body then chose representatives and nominated mayors and justices. The legislative power was divided into three bodies – tribunes, senators and censors, all elected. The tribunes initiated finance and major policy issues; the senators were guardians of law and ecclesiastical patronage; and the censors were responsible for the preservation of civil liberties, culture and the constitution – a revival of his previous notion of a 'moral power'. The president was appointed by the legislature for life and had the right to appoint his successor; this Bolívar regarded as 'the most sublime inspiration of republican ideas', the president being 'the sun which, fixed in its orbit, imparts life to the universe'.[53] The president appointed the vice president, who held the office of prime minister and would, in the absence of the president, succeed the latter in office. Thus 'elections would be avoided, which are the greatest scourge of republics and produce only anarchy'.

The rest of the constitution was not devoid of liberal details. It provided for civil rights – liberty, equality, security and property – and for a strong, independent judicial power. It abolished social privileges, and it declared the slaves free. Some observers were genuinely impressed. The British consul believed that it was 'founded apparently on the basis of the British constitution', allowing 'useful liberty' but 'obviating any mischievous excess of popular power'.[54] Bolívar himself claimed that the constitutional limitations on the president were 'the closest ever known', restricted as he was by his ministers, who in turn were responsible to the censors and scrutinized by the legislators. But this constitution was branded by its executive power, by the life president with right to choose his successor.[55] It was this which outraged many Americans, conservatives as well as liberals. No doubt the constitution can be explained by reference to Bolívar's experience of the frightening anarchy of the Perus, and of Bolivia's back+wardness and instability. But the force of this argument is reduced if account is taken of his anxiety to export the constitution to other Latin American countries. He regarded it as 'the ark of the covenant, an alliance between Europe and America, between soldier and civilian, between democracy and aristocracy, between imperialism and republicanism'.[56] And he claimed that 'in it are combined all the advantages of federalism, all the strength of centralized government, all the stability of monarchical regimes'.[57]

Bolívar considered Sucre the only man capable and worthy of exercising the life presidency. But Sucre did not want the presidency for life, and when, in 1826, he was elected to the office, he undertook to hold it only until 1828. His brief regime was a model of enlightened absolutism, a quest for economic development and social reform. Such at least was his policy, if not achievement. The obstacles to change were many and powerful. The creoles were conservative, their economic horizons bounded by stagnant haciendas, rentier values and public office; their habits indifferent to entrepreneurial activities; their social outlook wedded to a profound and immobile inequality. Warfare had dealt yet another blow to an already defective economy; and flight of Indian labour and white capital had brought mining and agriculture almost to a standstill. To construct a national economy Sucre had to lay his hands on more revenue, so his first task was to devise a more equitable and more productive tax system.[58] In 1826 congress abolished the alcabala and reduced other taxes on vital consumer goods. This was self-interest. The real test was direct taxation. Bolívar himself abolished the Indian tribute by decree of 22 December 1825.[59] It was replaced by an income tax and property tax, a revolutionary departure from the fiscal privilege long enjoyed by whites and assimilated mestizos. These interests stubbornly resisted the new policy and fought an unscrupulous campaign to revive the colonial tax system. In July 1826 the Indian tribute was restored, and the income and property taxes were abolished in December. Within a year therefore the country had returned to the colonial tax structure with all its discrimination and inequality. As Sucre pointed out, the oppressed classes were themselves divided against each other: 'The cholos do not wish to be classed as Indians, and even the Indians have distinctions among themselves.'[60]

Yet Bolivia had one asset, its silver, if only this could be realized.[61] The industry needed large injections of capital to expand operations, procure machinery and undertake drainage. For this it had to look abroad, which meant to the London money market, where the El Dorado of Potosí stirred the imagination and blunted common sense. By decree of 2 August 1825 Bolívar ordered that all abandoned and unworked mines revert to the state for renting out or auction. The British consul estimated that mines to the value of five million pesos thus became public property.[62] The new law, operating in peacetime conditions, was sufficient to produce a modest rise in silver production from 1825, and coin production also improved. General Miller, who was appointed prefect of the department of Potosí in 1825 reported that from 1810 to 1825 the mint coined an annual average of no more than half a million dollars; but during the first five months after liberation it coined upwards of a million.[63]

More spectacular results were anticipated from foreign investment. In London a mania of speculation led to the formation of twenty-six mining associations in 1824–5 for exploiting Latin American mines.[64] Of these the Potosí, La Paz and Peruvian Mining Association assembled most capital and attracted most support; it had six members of Parliament on its board and James Paroissien as its agent. The company's representatives were welcomed in Bolivia and authorized to purchase mines and associated installations, with full protection of the law and many fiscal privileges. But in London ignorant and improvident speculation was followed by a resounding crash; when, in December 1825, the money market collapsed, the vital flow of capital was cut and the company was unable to meet its obligations in South America. This brought mining operations to an abrupt halt; an official embargo was placed on machinery, equipment and supplies at the port of Arica; and the company was forced into liquidation. Many factors combined to produce disaster – the gap between inadequate capital and high costs, the ignorance and extravagance of the company's agents, lack of skilled labour, inferior draining and operating techniques. Basically the English expected too much for too little.[65] As an alternative the government attempted to assemble local capital by means of mining banks, but their resources were even further below requirements. In fact the collapse of the Potosí Mining Association ended prospects of major improvement in Bolivian silver production. The government was thus starved of revenue for investment in economic and social reforms, in roads, public works and schools. The country was desperately bankrupt.

Bolivia began life with great disadvantages. A basic requirement of a successful mining industry was quick and cheap access to overseas suppliers and markets, so that equipment could be brought in and production speeded out. But for vital ports of entry and exit Bolivia depended on other powers, on distant Buenos Aires for access to the Atlantic, and on Peru for use of Arica, its natural port on the Pacific. The government unsuccessfully tried to buy Arica from Peru. It then sought to make a viable port out of Cobija, renamed by Bolívar Puerto de La Mar. But in spite of possessing competitive tariffs, this was an unlikely outlet for overseas trade : it was five hundred miles from Potosí, on the edge of the Atacama desert, lacking roads, people and water.[66]

Like their counterparts in Peru, the Bolivian aristocracy monopolized the few assets the country possessed, and they continued to exert an inexorable control over land and labour. The Indians of Bolivia formed 80 per cent of the population at the beginning of the nineteenth century.[67] On the eve of independence they endured still the mita, repartimiento, tribute, parish charges and tithes, *pongueaje* and other personal services, and agricultural labour on the land of the whites. The Indians of the comunidades were perhaps even worse off than those of the haciendas, for they were forced to give personal services to a multiplicity of administrative authorities and officials.

Independence brought some improvement of status. The mita was abolished and, unlike the tribute, it did not reappear. In August 1825 at La Paz Bolívar proclaimed the policy which he had already attempted to apply in Peru; he abolished personal service, declaring equality among all citizens. But the creoles did not cooperate, and the Indians too were slow to respond, distrusting these measures as traps set by the cruel whites to ensnare them still more. Results were therefore negligible. 'Prejudices and timidity on their own part, and the interest of those who still keep up the delusion, in order to profit by the gratuitous labours of others, will combine to counteract the most benevolent views of the patriotic government.'[68] The Indians of Bolivia continued to be exploited by whites, contrary to the spirit of the new laws, and more and more of them became dependent on the hacendados for plots of land, the rent of which had to be paid in services on the master's estate and in his house.

Bolívar decreed a measure of agrarian reform in 1825 : the object was to distribute state land in Bolivia, preferably among 'the natives and those who have offered and suffered much for the cause of independence'.[69] But as rural misery was even worse in Bolivia than in Colombia, the scene of his first experiment, he decreed that land should be distributed to everyone in need, not simply to army veterans : 'Every individual without discrimination of age or sex shall receive a fanegada of land in the fertile areas and two fanegadas in the poorer land which lacks irrigation', the only condition being that the recipients should begin cultivation within a year.[70] But these reforms were sabotaged by the Bolivian ruling class, who regarded a free and landed peasantry as a threat to their dependent labour supply. On 20 September 1827 the Bolivian congress issued a law suspending the Bolivarian decrees concerning distribution of land to the Indians 'until the prefects of the departments concerned report on the number of Indians, and the amount of lands remaining over, in order that each one can be assigned what he needs according to the locality'. This was another way of saying no, the official word of Bolivia's rulers on agrarian reform.

Bolívar's anti-slavery policy was also unpopular. In 1825 the general assembly of Bolivia voted Bolívar a million dollars as a reward for his services; he accepted the grant 'only upon condition that the money should be employed in purchasing the liberty of about one thousand Negro slaves existing in Bolivia'.[71] The response was negative. But in 1826 he returned to the attack in his Bolivian constitution which declared that 'all those who until now have been slaves are Bolivian citizens; and they are thereby freed by the publication of this constitution; a special law shall determine the amount to be paid as indemnity to their former owners'.[72] The deputies pretended to comply, but in fact they substantially modified Bolívar's text; the new version declared former slaves free citizens 'but they cannot abandon the house of their former masters except in the form which a special law will determine'.[73] The principal objects of concern were labour and recompense, for although large-scale plantation agriculture was not practised in Bolivia slaves were used on estates and in domestic service, principally in the region of La Paz, and they represented an investment which owners were not prepared to lose. 'The only indemnity they seek', reported Sucre, 'is that slaves should be forced to work in their existing haciendas as peons.'[74] This was characteristic of abolition throughout Spanish America; slavery was replaced not by freedom but by servile labour.

The attempt of Bolívar and Sucre to transform Bolivia into a liberal, prosperous nation failed. The experiment simply proved that this new, landlocked, Andean republic could not absorb modern technology and was incapable of generating economic and social change. Bolivia's prospects were as bleak as the landscape of its windswept altiplano. But its rulers were determined to keep what little they had, and if this was nationalism then Sucre soon felt its impact.[75] The continued presence of Colombian troops brought to the surface latent passions against foreigners, passions which resentful Argentines and Peruvians did their utmost to inflame. Sucre reported to Bolívar 'the porteños and the Peruvians are very active in stirring up resentment in the country against the Colombian troops'; and Bolívar advised him : 'If I were you I would not remain in the south, because in the final analysis we suffer from the defect of being Venezuelans, just as we have been Colombians in Peru.'[76] Anxious still to re-annex these provinces, Peru lost no opportunity of exploiting anti-Colombian feelings, and in 1827–8 she combined subversion within and attack from without. In April 1828 Sucre was wounded by mutinous elements in Chuquisaca, and the government was forced to sign an agreement that all foreigners would be expelled. Sucre resigned the presidency, and in August he left for Quito, pessimistic of Bolivia's capacity to become a viable nation.

(iii) 'AMERICA IS UNGOVERNABLE'

Peruvian nationalism, so weak against Spain, so active against its republican neighbours, was a new factor of instability in Pacific South America.[77] Peruvian opposition to Chile had its origin in the colonial period when it was the hostility of a mining viceroyalty towards its provincial granary, frequently uncooperative and always resentful. It was galling now for Peruvians to witness Chileans enter their country in the guise of liberators and to observe their former satellite become an equal. Antagonism between Peru and Argentina also stemmed from intercolonial rivalry and focused on competition for the market and silver of Upper Peru. Peruvians resented the presence of Argentines in the liberating army, not least because the merchants of Buenos Aires exploited the opportunity to acquire a foothold in the market of Peru itself. Peruvian susceptibilities were also affronted by Colombian intervention. With the annexation of Guayaquil before their eyes they suspected that Bolívar had designs upon their national territory. The political tension was apparent to foreign observers: 'Although Bolívar is himself extremely popular, as popular as it is possible a Columbian should be in Peru, still there is such a jealousy, if not hatred, between the Peruvians and Columbians that there can be no real cordiality between the two people until time and intercourse may lessen the prejudice.'[78] Peruvians came to detest Bolívar's dictatorship, and they did not respond favourably to his idea of a confederation of the Andes. Peruvian nationalism, therefore, first expressed itself in rivalry with Chile, Argentina and Colombia; it was the nationalism of a formerly privileged country fighting for primacy in a new and – internationally at least – egalitarian world.

Bolívar felt the full force of Peruvian nationalism after his return from the south in 1826, though he did not give it credit for what it was, attributing opposition to selfish interests hurt by his radical reform of the administration.[79] The capitulation of Callao on 23 January 1826 completed his work as liberator and he was now free to return to Colombia with his army. Yet he stayed. The government was headed first by General La Mar, then by General Santa Cruz, but Bolívar continued to be the power behind the administration. Peruvians were increasingly restless at his presence and he became the target of conspiratorial attack, congressional opposition, and widespread criticism in the country. The conspiracy he crushed, congress he brow-beat, and his resistance to criticism had the sanction of the Colombian army.

The Peruvian ruling class were torn between resentment of Bolívar's dictatorship and fear of anarchy, social unrest and slave rebellion if he should leave. Bolívar exploited this ambiguity; he decided to impose the Bolivian constitution on Peru, in the expectation perhaps of being elected life president. Peru brought out the worst in Bolívar, at once flattering and frustrating his taste for glory and leadership; even his devoted aide noted that these were 'the days of the lost purity and innocence of his principles'.[80] It is true that Peru was not an end in itself for Bolívar. He wanted a confederation of the Andean countries, Colombia, Peru and Bolivia, and he knew that this would be more easily organized if each component had the same constitution, and if he himself exercised a powerful influence. But this too was a serious miscalculation. He was tempted to spend more time in Peru than was good for him or Peruvians. On 16 August 1826 the electoral college of Lima adopted the Bolivian constitution and nominated Bolívar president for life. A life president, backed by a foreign army, is this what Peruvians understood by liberation? It could not be. Fortunately Bolívar recovered his political sense, influenced by events in Colombia as well as in Peru. He refused to accept the presidency and prepared to return to Bogotá. The country he left was subject to unbearable tensions, torn between ambitious military and self-seeking creoles, parasites both on the oppressed Indians and frustrated castes. According to Pando, Peru was 'incapable of governing herself and unwilling to be governed'.[81] Did the future hold any hope? 'These frequent political vibrations, these internal strifes and external enmities are sadly disheartening, and create the feeling that the only hope of peace and security on this side of South America rests in the rising generation.'[82]

Peru was not alone in its instability. The insidious anarchy of Colombia and agitation in Venezuela required Bolívar's personal attention. He appreciated that he must abandon his cosmopolitanism for a more national role. He left Peru for Colombia in September 1826, and in October he wrote to General Santa Cruz an eloquent declaration of faith in national interests:

I have too many problems in my native land, which I have long neglected for other countries in America. Now that I see that the evils have gone too far and that Venezuela is the victim of my very achievements, I have no desire to incur the slur of ingratitude to the land of my birth. . . . I would advise you to relinquish American plans and pursue a purely Peruvian programme, indeed a programme designed exclusively in the interests of Peru. . . . I intend to do all the good I can for Venezuela without attempting anything further. Let you and your colleagues, therefore, do the same for Peru. Our native land must take preference above everything, as its elements have shaped our being. . . . Are there any more sacred claims upon love and devotion? Yes, General, let each serve his native land and let all other things be secondary to this duty.[83]

But national interests were in dispute, and Bolivar's native land did not want him. He had to leave Venezuela to the rule of Páez and the way of secession. In September 1827 he was again in Bogotá, President of Colombia, the last hope for stability as he strove to quench one fire after another across the length and breadth of the country. He tried for a constitutional solution but was met with factionalism and intransigence from his opponents. To preserve internal order and national security he assumed dictatorial powers in June 1828 and put a brake on liberal policies. On the night of 25 September 1828 he himself barely escaped assassination by conspirators who planned a liberal coup with Santander's connivance. Ironically he earned from this yet greater support, but he was emotionally wounded and he now entered the darkest period of his career, oppressed by what he called 'this immense disorder of America'.[84] Colombia was fast disintegrating. In 1829 rebellion in the south was compounded by war with Peru, followed in the same year by insurrection in Antioquia. And while in Colombia Bolívar was embarrassed by schemes of monarchy, in Venezuela he was vilified as a traitor and virtually declared an outlaw.

In spite of his preference for a political over a military solution, Bolívar fell back in the end on his own authority and ruled through a personal dictatorship. Every political measure, the Bolivian constitution, the life-term presidency, the constitutional regime in Colombia, received only partial or temporary support, and that because of the prestige of the Liberator. Nothing else endured. Such social mobilisation as had taken place during the war was now ended. Even political participation by the creole elite was limited, except insofar as regional caudillos ruled in collaboration with local interests. The irreducible fact remained, that the source of the dictator's legitimacy was his own personal qualities. Bolívar ruled alone, the only stable thing in a world in turmoil.

America is in chaos. Peru is on the verge of endless upheaval. Bolivia has had three presidents in five days, and two of them have been murdered. In Buenos Aires they have overthrown the president. Mexico has been convulsed by violent revolution. Guatemala and Chile have both deteriorated.[85]

In January 1830 he declared to the new Colombian congress his bitter disappointment at the achievements of the revolution: 'I am ashamed to admit it, but independence is the only benefit we have gained, at the cost of everything else.'[86] In March 1830 he resigned.

Personal tragedy completed the anguish. On 8 May he left Bogotá to make his way to the coast and exile. He was dying of tuberculosis. On 4 June his close friend and political heir, the incomparable Sucre, was assassinated on a mountain road in southern Colombia. A month before the end Bolívar professed his ultimate disillusion: 'America is ungovernable. Those who serve the revolution plough the sea. The only thing to do in America is to emigrate.'[87] He died near Santa Marta on 17 December 1830, in his forty-seventh year, 'his last moments', recalled O'Leary, 'the last embers of an expiring volcano, the dust of the Andes still on his garments'.[88]

NINE *Mexico, the Consummation of American Independence*

(i) SILVER AND SOCIETY

THE SPANISH AMERICAN revolutions were continental in
scale but not concerted in movement. They shared a common origin and a common objective, but they differed from
each other in political and military organization; prisoners of
their particular environment, they failed to synchronize their
efforts against Spain. In general Spanish American independence
had to contend with two enemies and a potential ally – the armies
of Spain, the opposition, or inertia, of the creoles, and the
embarassing demands of popular forces. None of these factors
alone could permanently impede the revolution, but in conjunction they could constitute a powerful obstacle; and when the
creoles' fear of the American populace caused them to prefer the
protection of the Spanish army, independence could not make
progress without external stimulus. Some countries like the Río
de la Plata were in a position to provide stimulus; others like Peru
depended on receiving it. But external stimulus was not always
available or acceptable. Cuba neither wanted nor received it.

Cuba's expanding sugar economy depended on slave labour, the supply of which in turn depended on the continuation of Spanish rule. The demographic strength of the Negroes, moreover, recalling as it did the black revolution in Haiti, deterred the white aristocracy from promoting change and persuaded them to place their trust in a reformed colonial administration backed by strong military force. As for outside intervention, in the absence of a local revolutionary nucleus, Cuba was more easily defended than attacked. So too was Puerto Rico, an island fortress dominated by its military establishment and virtually immune to invasion, at least to any invasion which the new states might be capable of launching. Cuba and Puerto Rico remained Spanish enclaves in an independent America.

Mexico was different and constituted yet a further challenge to the American revolution. Divided over objectives, torn by internal conflict, Mexico was a suitable case for outside intervention. Yet it could not receive it. Remote from the great centres of revolution in the south, beyond the reach of the continental liberators, Mexico fought alone and its struggle was self-generated. The Mexican revolution differed from those in South America in two vital respects: it began as a violent social protest from below; and Spain had more to lose in Mexico than anywhere else in America.

Mexico was pure colony. Spaniard ruled creole, creole used Indian, and the metropolis exploited all three. Liberation would be arduous in this the most valuable of all Spain's possessions. In the course of the eighteenth century Mexican silver production rose continuously from five million pesos in 1702, past the boom of the 1770s and an increase from twelve million to eighteen million pesos a year, to a peak of twenty-seven million in 1804. By this time Mexico accounted for 67 per cent of all silver produced in America; and the most successful zone, Guanajuato, was the leading producer of silver in the world, its annual output of over five million pesos amounting to one-sixth of all American bullion. A unique concurrence of circumstances created this great boom – excellent bonanzas, improved technology, consolidation of mines under larger ownership, lowering of production costs by government reduction of gunpowder and mercury charges and fiscal exemption.[1] Then, from the 1780s, the industry received large injections of merchant capital, a byproduct of a further development in the colonial economy.

In 1789 *comercio libre* was at last extended to Mexico, thus ending the monopoly long exerted by the consulados of Cadiz and Mexico City. New merchants entered the field with less capital but more enterprise. Competition lowered prices for the consumer; it also lowered profits. The old monopolists therefore began to withdraw their capital from trans-Atlantic trade and to seek alternative outlets which promised better returns. They reinvested in agriculture, mining and finance, with results advantageous to the economy and to themselves. Mexico contained some immense private fortunes. In Caracas a man was rich if he had a yearly income of ten thousand pesos from commercial agriculture; in Peru, with its depressed mining and stagnant agriculture, few families had more than four thousand pesos. In Mexico there were people, even outside of mining, with an annual income of two hundred thousand pesos. In some years the Valenciana mine yielded more than a million pesos profit to its owners, the Counts of Valenciana, a family which came to the colony as poor immigrants.[2] The fortunes could be as quickly lost as won; but mining, risky to individuals, was the life-blood of the colony and the life-line of the metropolis.

The other pillar of the Mexican economy was the hacienda. Many haciendas were too big to be efficient units of production. Wasteful of land and lacking the stimulus of a large market, they rarely gave a good return on investment; and they were subject to mortgages and annuities in favour of the Church, in addition to tithes and taxes. Others were essentially social investments, soaking up the capital of their creole owners. But some haciendas were highly commercial; at a time of rising land values there was an active market in land, and from about 1750 the entry of mercantile and mining capital hastened the process of land concentration, to the detriment of tenant farmers and landless labourers. On the fringe of the great estates the tiny *pegujal* offered a bare subsistence to one family. In the Bajío, where a numerous group of *rancheros* (smallholders) survived, these were squeezed into ever more reduced areas of land.[3] And below the *rancheros* peons of various kinds suffered a severe decline in their standard of living. The consequences of land monopoly were aggravated by population growth. Between 1742 (3.3 million) and 1793 (5.8 million) demographic growth reached about 33 per cent.[4] Between 1790 and 1810 the population rose from 4,483,564 to 6,122,354, evidence of rapid growth among the Indians, mestizos and other mixed groups. But there was no land for the new population, as creole and Church haciendas constantly encroached on smaller farms to remove competition and procure a dependent labour supply. The expansion of the haciendas and the growth of the rural population produced a situation in which the peasantry could not feed itself independently of the great estates. The landowners had the campesinos at their mercy, both as consumers and as labourers.

Between 1720 and 1810 Mexico suffered ten agricultural crises in which shortage of maize reached starvation level and prices far outstripped labourers' wages. The rural economy lacked a substitute for the staple maize; it endured periodic droughts and premature frosts; and it suffered from monopoly of production by the great haciendas which were able to force up prices by carefully controlling distribution. The secondary effects of famine were also savage – epidemics which devastated the people, especially the undernourished Indians and castes, and damage to other sectors of the economy.[5] The wage-price crises caused unemployment, uncontrolled flight to the towns, and social unrest which can be seen in rising urban crime statistics.[6] Impetus was given to rural banditry, the leaders of which were in some ways the true precursors of independence; such were the semi-brigand, semi-revolutionary creoles in western Michoacán who robbed Spaniards for robbing Mexico.[7] Banditry was symptomatic of a new resentment against hacendados, monopolists and speculators. Between 1778 and 1810 the masses suffered unprecedented misery from soaring maize prices, with particular crises in 1785, the year of hunger, and 1810, the year of revolution. The price of maize spiralled to 56 reales a fanega at a time when the daily wage of a labourer was $1\frac{1}{2}$ to 2 reales. It was now that the lower clergy, who were closest to the people, came to realize the desperate state of the campesinos and to appreciate the gross inequality of the agrarian structure. The Bishop of Michoacán, Fray Antonio de San Miguel, was convinced that the roots of rural distress went deeper than droughts and frosts, and that 'the maldistribution of land has been one of the principal causes of the people's misery'.[8] These views were shared by a number of enlightened creoles as the last years of the *pax hispánica* came to grief amidst the terrible droughts of 1808–9, followed by the famine years of 1810–11, when the average price of maize reached a second peak. The violence of Mexico's first revolution had its origins in the hunger and desperation of the Indian masses : 'The revolution for independence, like the French revolution, broke out in the middle of a storm of high prices.'[9]

The agrarian crises of the eighteenth century brought to the surface some of the contradictions in the colonial structure, for they occurred at a time when the economy in general was booming, and when plantation agriculture, mining and commerce were bursting with abundance. The growth of conspicuous wealth in the last decades of the old regime aggravated the inequalities of colonial society, as Humboldt noticed when he visited Mexico in 1803. The wealthy mine-owners and hacendados with their estates and mansions and ostentation, the higher clergy with their sumptuous churches and palaces, all stood in horrifying contrast to the poverty of the greater part of the population and the condition of 'barbarism, abjection and misery' to which the Indians were reduced.[10]

The social structure was rigid. In a population of six million the 1,097,928 whites formed only 18 per cent of the whole and lived in a world far removed from the Indians (60 per cent) and castes (22 per cent). The basic distinction was wealth. Manuel Abad y Queipo, Bishop Elect of Michoacán, identified two groups in late colonial society, 'those who have nothing and those who have everything. . . . There are no gradations or mean : they are all either rich or poor, noble or infamous.'[11] Humboldt, too, observed 'that monstrous inequality of rights and wealth' which characterized Mexico.[12] Spaniards and creoles shared the wealth, though not the rights. In some ways it is misleading to distinguish between the two groups, for they often belonged to the same families and possessed the same interests. But in fact they were divided. The Spaniards numbered no more than fifteen thousand in 1800; they were concentrated in the capital and central Mexico; and about half of them were soldiers.[13] Many – perhaps the majority – were poorly educated and less affluent than the creoles, who had the richest haciendas and mines, and who outnumbered the Spaniards by about seventy to one. As a successful colony Mexico attracted many immigrants, but not all who came were wealthy merchants and bureaucrats or got rich so quickly from mining as the Count of Regla. Many immigrants were poor, though this very circumstance tended to make them a dynamic group who pushed their way into commerce and mining. Commerce was always controlled by Spaniards, though once the monopoly was broken by *comercio libre* they had to be content with less profits; still, they controlled the influential consulados, and their capital financed the textile industry. And they possessed an automatic privilege. As a matter of policy the metropolis ensured that a relatively small number of Spaniards monopolized higher office in the administration and the Church and controlled the judiciary.[14] This political power counterbalanced the local strength of the creoles; but as a small minority the position of the Spaniards depended absolutely on the continuing rule of the metropolis, and this explains why they had to move quickly and decisively in 1808.

There was, nevertheless, an aristocracy of mining, commerce and land-owning dominated by peninsulares. Of the fifty new titles of nobility granted in Mexico in the eighteenth century about a half went to mining and commerce, and 60 per cent to Spaniards. In Guanajuato, for example, immigrants climbed up the social scale, getting first into trade then into mining and office, and passing inert creoles on the way.[15] It is true that a creole elite of mineowners and hacendados associated with the peninsular officials and entrepreneurs and formed with them a white ruling class.[16] But they found that there was a limit to their influence over policy. Moreover their families tended to suffer from downward mobility. Creoles were averse to business and frustrated by the shortage of professional openings; mining could be risky, and the Spaniards controlled overseas trade. They had land, the basis of creole wealth, bought by their Spanish forbears from the profits of trade and mining, but limited in its earning capacity. And once the inheritance was consumed, or divided into ever smaller units by succeeding generations, life became a battle for survival. It was easy to fall out of the elite into the social sector occupied by the majority of creoles, who were lawyers, minor officials, traders and small landowners. Here too there was great competition and creoles had to struggle to keep up with the immigrant and out of the castes. For the creoles were constantly pressed by more immigrants, who quickly got established as managers of stores, haciendas and mines, and whose sons procured positions in the militia and town councils. But they no sooner achieved hegemony than they were harassed by a new wave of peninsulares, with whom they had to share power and opportunity. So rivalry was greatest between first-generation creoles and new Spaniards, and it was from the former that many revolutionary leaders were recruited.

From the 1790s creole resentment was expressed in political agitation. In 1794 a small group of creoles plotted 'to raise the kingdom in the name of independence and liberty'. In 1799 a somewhat larger conspiratorial movement aimed at 'starting a revolution, throwing the Europeans out of the kingdom, and making the creoles masters of it'. The viceroy was worried enough to report to Madrid 'the ancient division and deep enmity between Europeans and creoles, an enmity capable of producing fatal results'.[17] The Cabildo of Mexico City had the greatest revolutionary potential. Here the creoles were a clear majority : 'The fifteen perpetual regidores were old mayorazgos, generally very deficient in learning and the majority of them with ruined fortunes.... Almost all of the perpetual regidores were Americans, having inherited their offices from their fathers, who had bought them in order to add lustre to their families; and therefore the ayuntamiento of Mexico City may be considered as the representative of that party.'[18] Among the alcaldes were a number of radical creole lawyers such as Francisco Primo de Verdad and Juan Francisco Azcárate. But torn between the elite and the radicals, the cabildo hesitated.

The Mexican Indians and Indianized mestizos comprised some 70 per cent of the population.[19] Culturally backward, brutalized, and living in physical and moral squalor, the indios were a socio-cultural group rather than an exclusively racial one. A sign of their status was the tribute, paid by community Indians, mobile Indians, and also by free Negroes and mulattos. This provided a considerable revenue, and it was therefore in the crown's interest to identify and preserve a tributary class by keeping its members separate from the whites, prohibited from wearing Spanish clothes, owning a horse, and possessing weapons. Servile to the state, they were also subject to the colonial economy and formed a cheap labour pool for use in agriculture and public works. The Indians included many mestizos, whose cultural and economic position dragged them down into the underprivileged and impoverished indios, where they were accompanied by the mulattos and Negroes (some 10 per cent of the population). These were the underdogs of this hierarchical society, the simmering mass ready to explode at the call of a leader. For Mexico, as Humboldt bluntly remarked, was 'the country of inequality'.[20] And inequality, unless remedied, would lead to Indian and caste revolution. This at least was the forecast of Antonio de San Miguel, Bishop of Michoacán, one of the few spokesmen of the oppressed whose views anticipated those of the insurgents Hidalgo and Morelos:

Let the hated exaction, the personal tribute, be abolished. Abolish also the infamous laws which brand the people of colour. Let them occupy all the civil posts which do not require a special title of nobility. Let the communal lands be distributed among the natives; let part of the royal lands be given to the Indians and castes. Let there be adopted for Mexico an agrarian law . . . whereby a poor peasant can break up the lands which the large proprietors hold and which have been uncultivated for centuries to the detriment of the national economy. Let the Indians, castes and whites be given full freedom to live together in the towns, which now belong exclusively to only one of these classes.[21]

Revolutionary change of this kind, however, would subvert a system of exploitation and dependence in which all the propertied interests were involved – the state, Spaniards and creoles. Mexico was the most beneficial to Spain of all her colonies. At the beginning of the eighteenth century Mexican revenue amounted to no more than three million pesos a year. By the end of the century this had grown to 14.7 million pesos net a year. Of this, 4.5 million was appropriated for local administration and defence, while a further four million subsidized other colonies in the Caribbean and the Philippines. The remaining six million was pure profit for the royal Treasury in Madrid.[22] Spain received from Mexico two-thirds of her entire imperial revenue, and the amount increased during the late eighteenth-century silver boom. But prosperity only intensified Mexicans' resentment of their colonial status and of the continual exit of money to the metropolis; as Mora said, material progress and 'desire for independence went together'. On 12 December 1804 Spain declared war on Britain, and immediately raised her demands on the colonies. Mexico was an obvious target. A decree of 26 December ordered the sequestration of charitable funds in Mexico and their remission to Spain.

The Mexican Church had great economic resources, a combination of real estate, income from loans and annuities, the 10 per cent tithe on agriculture, and fees for clerical services. The *juzgados,* or tribunals, of chantries and pious foundations possessed large financial reserves derived from investment loans and even more from encumbrances on private property yielding interest at 5 per cent. The Church permeated the economy, partly as a spender — on salaries, buildings, liturgy and social services — partly as a lender of capital to landowners and entrepreneurs.[23] By the end of the eighteenth century rural and urban property was encumbered with clerical charges, and Church and elite were locked into each other. The metropolis appeared to be ignorant of these facts. The Consolidation of 1804 forced the Church to move its money from Mexican creditors to the state and to accept a reduced return. It also attacked the entire propertied class in the colony. Merchants and miners, hacendados and houseowners, the powerful and the wealthy, Spaniards as well as creoles, all suddenly had to redeem the capital value of their loans and encumbrances. Protest and resistance were universal. More creoles were affected than Spaniards, though the latter made more noise, for the measure subverted their privilege and power. Perhaps the greatest hardship was suffered by a large number of medium and small proprietors, who could not assemble capital quickly enough and were forced to sell their property on highly unfavourable terms. Many substantial landowners had difficulty in repaying; a few had their estates seized and auctioned. The clergy were embittered, especially the lower clergy who often lived on the interest of loans and annuities. Bishop Abad y Queipo estimated the total value of juzgado capital at 44.5 million pesos, presumably divided between investments and annuities, and he warned the government that resistance to its redemption would be strong.[24] He went in person to Madrid to request the government to think again; Godoy gave him no satisfaction, but in due course the hated decree was in fact suspended, first on the initiative of the viceroy (August 1808), and then formally by the supreme junta in Seville (4 January 1809). Meanwhile the not insubstantial sum of twelve million pesos had been collected, and the officials who collected it, including the viceroy, shared five hundred thousand pesos in commission. The money was not actually sent to Spain until 1808–9, when she was no longer at war with Britain.[25]

The sequestration of Church wealth epitomized Spanish colonial policy in the last decade of empire. This careless and opportunist measure alerted the Church, damaged the Mexican economy, and caused one of the greatest crises of confidence in the history of the colony. In enforcing the policy Viceroy Iturrigaray broke the unity of the peninsular front in Mexico and turned many Spaniards against the administration. In reaction the viceroy became more partial towards the creoles. But these too were outraged. Mexicans saw this as the ultimate test of their dependence, the proof that they were 'colonials, born only to satisfy the insatiable greed of the Spaniards'.[26] They had to watch the spoliation of their country to subsidize a foreign policy in which they had no interest; as Fray Servando Teresa de Mier complained, 'the war is more cruel for us than for Spain, and is ultimately waged with our money. We simply need to stay neutral to be happy'.[27]

Mexico knew of the collapse of the Spanish monarchy by mid-July 1808. The news sparked off a struggle for power between creoles and peninsulares, between the ayuntamiento on the one hand and the audiencia and consulado on the other.[28] Iturrigaray, an average viceroy, appealed for unity: 'We must stay united if we wish to be dominant.'[29] On 9 August he suspended the sequestration decree. When this failed to satisfy he made further overtures to creoles, appointing many to civil and military offices and allowing public discussion of the problem of sovereignty. Liberal creoles voiced their opposition to the authority of the junta in Spain. Juan Francisco de Azcárate argued that Mexico should refuse to subordinate itself to any Spanish junta. Francisco Primo de Verdad claimed that in the absence of the king sovereignty reverted to the people; and he proposed that a national junta be elected representing the cabildos, cathedral chapters and Indian communities. Fray Melchor de Talamantes held even more radical views and really sought creole power and national independence. The Cabildo of Mexico City took the position that during Ferdinand's imprisonment sovereignty should be transferred to the viceroyalty of New Spain, to be exercised by the audiencia and cabildos. But the Spanish-dominated audiencia, indeed all Spaniards in Mexico, rejected these views, convinced that they implied a move towards independence and that the viceroy who tolerated them had become a threat to their power and privilege. They therefore planned a preemptive golpe to remove the viceroy and his creole allies in the ayuntamiento.

The conspiracy was centred on the audiencia and the consulado, with the connivance of the Church hierarchy and the principal Spanish merchants and land-owners, many of whom had suffered from sequestration. The leader was Gabriel de Yermo, a wealthy Basque sugar planter from Cuernavaca, who had married into great creole wealth and had recently been pursued by the administration for two hundred thousand pesos under the sequestrian decree.[30] The *golpistas* struck on 15 September 1808. The viceroy was seized and sent back to Spain; Primo Verdad, Azcárate and other creole radicals were imprisoned. Behind a front of compliant viceroys, the first of whom was a decrepit old soldier, Pedro Garibay, the Spaniards then imposed a hard-line administration, repressive towards creole suspects, partial towards themselves. They effected fiscal and commercial measures which favoured their own interests, eventually reaching agreement with the peninsula to pay extraordinary revenue in the form of loans, an acceptable alternative to sequestration. The military arm of the golpe was virtually a private army – the Volunteers of Ferdinand vii – a militia recruited from employees of the Spanish merchants, controlled by them, and constituting in effect an extra-constitutional guard.[31] In the provinces, too, Spanish interests made a preemptive strike after decades of frustration. In Oaxaca the Spanish merchants, alienated by the intendant system and all that it implied, seized power backed by their own militia.[32]

The Mexican revolution thus began as a Spanish reaction. The Spaniards thought it was the end; in fact it was only the beginning. The resulting creole and popular anger led directly to a new revolution in 1810. Creole conspirators, including a number of militia officers, plotted to oust the Spaniards. Popular unrest added a new dimension to the struggle, aggravated as it was by worsening conditions in the fields and the mines. A dry summer in 1809 severely reduced maize output and caused prices to quadruple. The campesinos suffered enormously, and so did other workers; the impact was felt in the mining industry, where mules could not be fed and many miners were laid off.[33] These reverses left a vivid impression in the Bajío, where the recent prosperity of mining, textiles and agriculture was brought to an abrupt halt. And it was here that violent rebellion first exploded, under a leader who came from an old but minor Mexican family, and whose captains were first-generation Mexicans.

(ii) THE INSURGENTS

Miguel Hidalgo y Costilla, son of a hacienda manager, was a creole frustrated like the rest of his class, a priest who knew at first hand the degradation of the rural masses. He resigned from a successful, if worldly, academic career in the diocesan College of San Nicolás Obispo in Valladolid to become a rural priest. In 1803, now middle-aged, 'of dark complexion, with lively green eyes, rather bald and white-haired' as Alamán described him, he became parish priest of Dolores in the Bajío.[34] He wore his personal religion lightly, lacking perhaps a true vocation and becoming the father of two children. Yet he was accessible and egalitarian, and he could speak Indian dialects. He made his parish the centre of discussions on contemporary social and economic matters, attended by poor Indians and castes as well as creoles. He organized a minor industrial programme to stimulate native manufacture for a local market – pottery, silk, tanning, weaving and viniculture – a sign of his concern for the poor and his anxiety to improve conditions. The Bajío was a relatively prosperous mining-agricultural complex, self-sufficient, having a looser social structure than elsewhere, a greater proportion of mobile, as distinct from community, Indians, and a higher percentage of free Negroes and mulattos.[35] While no one actually starved in the Bajío, there was stark contrast between the wealth of mine-owners and hacendados and the poverty of the tributary class, people who were mobile enough to find wage-work in mines and haciendas but whose progress was permanently impeded by the degrading tribute.

The Indians depended upon creole leadership for political action. But did the creoles want the Indians? From late 1809 a conspiratorial movement rallied a number of creole revolutionaries – Ignacio Allende, son of a wealthy Spanish merchant and now a militia officer, Juan de Aldama, another officer, Miguel Domínguez, an official, and other members of enlightened creole families of middle rank. They were moved by hatred of peninsulares : they wanted to depose the authorities, expel the Spaniards and establish a creole ruling junta. By mid–1810 the Querétaro conspiracy, as it came to be called, had recruited Hidalgo and he soon became its leader.[36] As a priest and a reformer he was indispensable to the conspirators; they needed someone with standing among the Indians and castes who could rally these to a cause which had few positive attractions for them. For the Indians, whatever their respect for a distant king, distrusted creoles and peninsulares alike and could not distinguish between government by one or the other. The revolutionaries, on the other hand, needed forces quickly, and they could not get these from their fellow creoles, for the latter were not united on independence. The campesinos were the only alternative, with the advantage that they might ask fewer questions. Allende early advocated the inclusion of Indians in the revolt as a kind of fighting fodder : 'As the Indians were indifferent to the word liberty', it was necessary to make them believe the insurrection was being accomplished only in order to help King Ferdinand.'[37] This was a grave miscalculation, and many of the creole revolutionaries would live to regret the tiger which they unleashed. Hildago himself had no doubts and no regrets : he believed that an appeal to the Indians was not only necessary but just. And in the course of 1810 he had his workers making crude weapons.

In September 1810 two developments forced Hildago's hand.

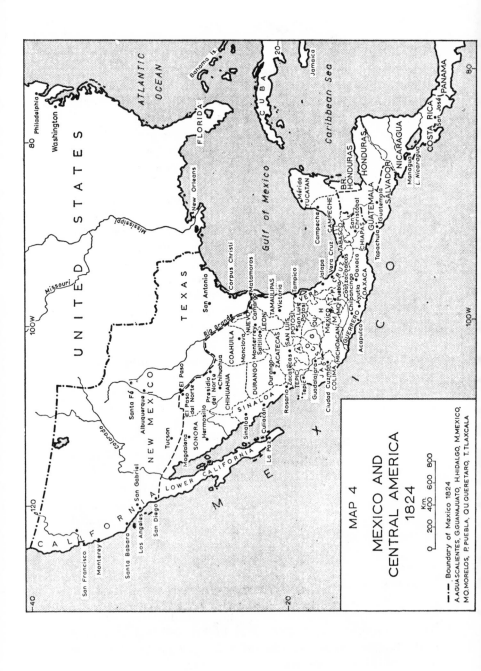

MAP 4

MEXICO AND
CENTRAL AMERICA
1824

Km
0 200 400 600 800

-·-·- Boundary of Mexico 1824
A.AGUASCALIENTES, G.GUANAJUATO, H.HIDALGO, M.MEXICO,
MO.MORELOS, P.PUEBLA, QU.QUERETARO, T.TLAXCALA

A new viceroy arrived, Francisco Javier de Venegas, veteran of the peninsular war and an uncompromising leader of the royalist cause. And the Querétaro conspiracy was discovered and destroyed. In Dolores Hidalgo now had to activate the revolution more quickly than had been planned, and as the creole revolutionaries were scattered he did not hesitate to appeal for mass support. At dawn on 16 September, taking advantage of the crowds from the surrounding country gathering in his parish for Sunday mass, he issued the *grito de Dolores*, a cry of rebellion which probably did not actually use the word independence but whose meaning was clear to succeeding generations of Mexicans. As the movement swept through the Bajío, thousands of campesinos rallied to its support; by mid-October the rebel horde numbered about sixty thousand. These recruits were chiefly Indians and castes, armed with bows and arrows, lances and machetes. After the fall of Guanajuato (28 September) they were reinforced by miners and other urban workers, but the movement never attracted more than about a hundred creole militia and a small minority of creole officers. Soon the cry was unequivocally 'independence and liberty'.

Hildago worked for popular support. His emphasis on the seizure of Europeans and their property, his abolition of Indian tribute (which forced the viceroy to do likewise by proclamation of 5 October 1810), and his invocation of the indigenous Virgin of Guadalupe, all were intended to give his movement mass appeal. Then the royalists themselves played into his hands by their defence of class interests at Guanajuato, the wealthy mining town, where Intendant Juan Antonio Riaño, an otherwise enlightened and reforming administrator, made a gross error of judgement. Convinced that the lower sectors would defect, Riaño decided to cut his losses, to assemble the local militia, all the Europeans and some creoles, together with their property and the Treasury in the Alhóndiga, and to concentrate his defences there. This merely added to the impression of class conflict. As one observer reported: 'The common people ... began to mutter openly: that the *"gachupines y señores"* wanted to defend only themselves and leave them to be turned over to the enemy, and that even the food had been taken away so that they would perish of hunger.'[38] The manoeuvre was also tactically unwise; it simply made the granary a focus of Spaniards and money, doubly attractive to rebel attack. The attack came with uncontrolled violence, making Guanajuato an unforgettable symbol. The massacre and mutilation of the defenders, the killing of prisoners, creole and European alike, the massive pillage and assault on property, the wanton destruction of mining machinery, all proclaimed the socio-racial hatred animating the revolution. The violence shocked the young Lucas Alamán; he was haunted by the 'monstrous union of religion with assassination and plunder, a cry of death and desolation', which echoed in his ears for the rest of his life.[39]

The creole-controlled Cabildo of Guanajuato issued a public statement after the massacre of three hundred peninsular Spaniards by the rebels : 'Those abominable distinctions of creoles and gachupines ... have never been made among the noble, cultivated and distinguished people of this city..... The Europeans were our relatives, they were married to our daughters or sisters, they were our good friends and we did business with them. Our interests and wealth were mixed with theirs and indeed depended upon them absolutely. In their misfortune we were all involved.'[40] But the fact remained that in Guanajuato most creoles were spared, to emphasize the distinction between the two groups. And in the west a vigorous, if untypical, force of creole rebels led by José Antonio Torres took Guadalajara and joined with the army of Hidalgo on 26 November. There followed an orgy of eating, drinking and killing; captured Spaniards were taken in groups of twenty or thirty every third night to the outskirts of the town where they were quickly decapitated.[41] Meanwhile, in Mexico City, an underground organization of about twenty creoles from the professional classes came into being after the *grito de Dolores*; known as the *Guadalupes*, it existed to serve the revolution as an intelligence network and a channel of arms, information and propaganda.[42]

Nevertheless creole participation remained on the periphery. Hildago's movement was essentially a mass movement and stood for basic revolution. He retained the allegiance of his supporters by constantly enlarging the social content of his programme.[43] He abolished the Indian tribute, the badge of an oppressed people. He also abolished slavery under pain of death. In Mexico, where slavery was a declining institution, abolition carried social rather than economic implications.[44] Land-owners had more efficient and more economical ways of working their land, preferring a peon labour force tied not by slavery but by tenure and indebtedness. So the real test of Hildago's intentions would be agrarian reform. This problem too he grasped, ordering the return of lands rightfully belonging to Indian communities :

I order the judges and justices of the district of this capital to proceed immediately to the collection of rents due up to today, by the tenants of the lands pertaining to the native communities, so that being entered in the national Treasury the lands may be delivered to the said natives for their cultivation, without being able to rent them in the future, then it is my will, that its use be only for the natives in their respective villages.[45]

The intention was to restore lands to Indians and prevent their alienation; this could not be accomplished by decree alone, and Hildago never in fact had the opportunity to establish machinery for implementing his policy. But this decree was not his last word on property. Like other commanders of the wars of independence, Hildago condoned pillage; he regarded it as a legitimate bait to attract the peasant masses to the revolution and to retain his following. So destruction and looting were endemic in the revolt. This was instant redistribution of property. Creole as well as European haciendas were robbed, and as the Indian hordes marched along they openly carried their plunder. In early November 1810 Ignacio de Aldama, one of the more timid of the creole officers, reported to Hidalgo : 'The Indians are very much out of control. On passing through the village of San Felipe I found three Europeans and a creole torn to pieces, although they held safe conducts from Your Excellency; and the Indians would not allow the priest to bury them. If these excesses are not punished our cause will suffer, and when we do try to stop them the situation will be beyond our control.' Hidalgo replied, 'No, sir, we must be careful; we have no other arms but theirs with which to defend ourselves, and if we start punishing them we shall not find them when we need them.'[46]

Outside of the Bajío, however, Hildago did not succeed in

finding even Indian supporters. The corporate and conservative Indian communities of Mexico and Puebla were less revolutionary material than the free and mobile people of the Bajío. And in general whoever reached the leaderless and apolitical Indians first could control them. The creoles worked on the masses to repudiate the revolt, and outside of the Bajío they had some success. The egalitarian doctrines and racial hatred, the attack on property and the sack of Guanajuato, the sheer size of the rebel hordes, caused a profound shock throughout the rest of Mexico and a wave of revulsion against the revolution. Hildago was condemned by the Church authorities and even by the reforming Bishop Abad y Queipo, who argued that it was creoles who suffered most in loss of property, labour and wealth, and that the revolution impeded Mexico's political progress. Among the lower clergy the movement had many sympathizers and from these it recruited officers for the peasant army and the guerrilla bands.[47] But the majority of Mexico's one million creoles opposed Hildago; his agrarian radicalism turned even anti-Spanish creoles into supporters of the colonial government. This forced him to commit himself exclusively to the peasantry and to take the revolution to further extremes, demonstrated not only by the reiteration of his earlier reforms but also by his execution of prisoners without trial, a procedure pressed upon him by his Indian followers.

Repudiated by the mass of the creoles, criticized even by his own creole officers, Hildago had little chance of military success. His eighty thousand followers were less an army than a horde, undisciplined and untrained, a positive obstacle to military operations. In the north Félix María Calleja, a professional Spanish soldier, organized the support of great land-owners and mine-owners of San Luis Potosí and Zacatecas, and created a small army officered largely by creoles. He easily prevented Hidalgo and Allende from expanding northwards and confined them to Guanajuato, Michoacán, and Guadalajara. The combination of Calleja's northern army with the regular and militia forces of the centre led by Manuel de Flon, was too much for Hidalgo. The royalist army was able to defend Mexico City, and on 17 January 1811 it routed Hidalgo's forces at the Bridge of Calderón. Hidalgo, Allende and the remnants of the rebels fled further and further north in a heroic march which ended in treachery; they were ambushed and captured on 21 March 1811, taken in chains to Chihuahua and there executed. Six of the nine-man court which tried them were creoles. This was typical. It was the royalist creoles, frightened by Hidalgo, who saved Mexico for Spain. And creoles were subsequently promoted to high civil and military office. But they still had a rebellion on their hands, not a rampaging horde but a number of guerrilla bands led by military caudillos – Ignacio Rayón, Manuel Félix Fernández (Guadalupe Victoria), Vicente Guerrero, the Matamoros, the Bravo family. And there was a new leader.

The leadership of the social revolution passed to José María Morelos, another rural priest, one indeed whose career kept him even closer to the peasantry than Hidalgo and who remained more committed to the priesthood and to religion. Morelos was born on 30 September 1765 in Valladolid, Michoacán, of a poor mestizo family, his father a carpenter, half Indian, his mother a creole.[48] In his youth he worked on an uncle's hacienda, and later as a mule driver on the Acapulco-Mexico City route. In a great effort of self-improvement he took a degree of the University of Mexico and became a priest in 1797. He was appointed first to a parish in Churumuco, one of the most miserable parts of Michoacán in the heart of the *tierra caliente,* where the climate killed his mother, and then in 1799 to nearby Carácuaro, which was hardly better. As an underprivileged mestizo, therefore, Morelos got a poor parish in the backwoods; there he laboured for eleven years, underpaid, overworked, among a sullen and impoverished Indian population; and there he became father of two illegitimate children. Stocky, coarse and swarthy in appearance, Morelos had only a brief revolutionary preparation. After the *grito de Dolores,* disturbed by the ecclesiastical censure of Hidalgo, he sought out the insurgent, was convinced by his arguments and offered his services.[49] He was commissioned as a lieutenant to raise troops on the south coast and take the revolution to Acapulco. Starting from nothing in October 1810, within a year he created a small, well equipped and highly disciplined army; this he brilliantly deployed in southern Mexico, bringing most of the coast under his control; he failed to take Puebla and thereby cut communications with Veracruz, but in November

1812 he captured wealthy Oaxaca to the great consternation of the royalists.

Morelos tried to free the revolution of the encumbrance of the Hidalgo movement, whose anarchy and violence had presented the royalists with free propaganda. He preferred an effective and swift-moving fighting force of two to three thousand trained men to be used in guerrilla tactics. He could not deny his troops booty and spoils, but he also tried to raise a legitimate revenue from reformed taxation of the areas which he held. He was merciless towards insubordination. And he preferred to use the Indian hordes in a supporting role. He reported in August 1811 : 'I place my confidence in these troops, for they have been selected with my approval. . . . Supporting our cause are the natives of fifty towns. They number several thousand and while they are not disciplined they can serve well in a subordinate capacity. I have therefore sent these men back to their fields for the purpose of sustaining the troops.'[50] While he sought to reassure public opinion by the professionalism of his forces, Morelos also projected a wide social appeal, preaching a combination of Mexican nationalism and basic reform.

Morelos was the most nationalist of all the early revolutionaries, and his nationalism seems to have been based not on careful calculation of the degree of maturity reached by Mexico but on an instinctive belief in Mexico's independence. Unlike his principal rival, Rayón, he dropped the use of Ferdinand's name either as a mask or otherwise, and spoke frankly of independence. The revolution was justified, according to Morelos, because the hated Spaniards were enemies of mankind, who for three centuries had enslaved the native population, stifled Mexico's national development, squandered its wealth and resources; and one of his basic objectives was that no Spaniard should remain in the government of Mexico. To the creoles in Calleja's army he addressed another argument: 'When kings are absent, sovereignty resides solely in the nation; and every nation is free and entitled to form the type of government which it pleases, and not to remain the slave of another.'[51] Morelos's nationalism was also inspired by the military struggle and was formed in the harsh conditions of guerrilla warfare. He strove to evoke the spirit of a national army. On the grim march to Valladolid, before a battle which was to be disastrous, he issued a moving manifesto to his troops:

The gachupines have always sought to abase the Americans to the point of regarding us as brutes, incapable of initiative or even of the waters of baptism, and therefore useless to Church and state. But I see the opposite. Americans make first-class ecclesiastics, judges, lawyers, artisans, farmers, and in the present case soldiers. In the course of three and a half years I have learned, and everyone has seen, that the Americans are soldiers by nature; and it can be truly said that in my army at least any veteran soldier could fill the office of general.[52]

Morelos's nationalism also had profound religious content. In Mexico the Virgin of Guadalupe was a national as well as a religious symbol; it demonstrated that God had shown a particular predilection for Mexico and it confirmed a sense of Mexican identity. Morelos saw independence almost as a holy war in defence of religious orthodoxy against the irreligious Bourbons and the idolotrous French. In Mexico, he asserted to the Bishop of Puebla, 'we are more religious than the Europeans', and he claimed to be fighting for 'la Religión y la Patria', and that this was 'nuestra santa revolución'.[53]

But Morelos made his greatest appeal to the masses. A royalist soldier, ex-prisoner of Morelos, reported on the insurgent army: 'None of them come from a decent family ... there are Indians, Negroes, mulattos, and delinquents, fugitives from their homelands. When anyone presents himself for service they ask him "que patria?", and he has to reply "la patria".'[54] The nationalism of Morelos had a social content which was rare at the time. In his proclamation issued at Aguacatillo in November 1810 he declared: 'All the inhabitants except Europeans will no longer be designated as Indians, mulattos or other castes, but all will be known as Americans.'[55] This was the first attempt in Mexico to abolish the legal framework of caste distinctions and to make national identity the only test of a man's status in society. Morelos also decreed the abolition of Indian tribute and of slavery. During his conquest of the south he repeated these policy statements and again proposed absolute social equality through abolition of race and caste distinctions. He also proclaimed that the lands should be owned by those who worked them, and the campesinos should receive the income from those lands. In a controversial document, the *Medidas Políticas*, he appeared to go even further, advocating the destruction, confiscation and redistribution of property belonging to the wealthy, whether lay or ecclesiastical, creole or European. But it is open to question whether Morelos was the author of the *Medidas Políticas*; in any case this was essentially a military plan of devastation, not a long-term social programme.[56]

Social liberation first required political liberation, and the immediate objective of Morelos was to destroy the colonial regime : 'To destroy the tyrannical government and its satellites, check its greed by the destruction of the means by which it wages war, and strip the rich of the funds with which the government is supported.'[57] The programme which he placed before the Congress of Chilpancingo, a small body hand-picked by Morelos to reorganize the revolution, was essentially political, providing for absolute independence, support for the Catholic religion sustained by tithes, respect for property, representative and republican institutions, separation of powers and a strong executive, with offices reserved for Americans.[58] But he also called for the abolition of slavery, of the tribute, of privileges and of all distinctions between classes. On 5 October 1813 he issued a second and definitive decree abolishing slavery, and this was endorsed by congress. The Declaration of Independence was formally made on 6 November 1813. Congress was less than enthusiastic about Morelos's social policy, though in the following year the attempt to impose a tax system graduated according to income was in his line of thought. But by now time was running out. The revival of royal power, the military reverses of Morelos, his demotion by congress, and his underground existence as a hunted guerrilla prevented the great revolutionary from further elaborating his social objectives and from producing a plan of agrarian reform before his tragic end.

The failure of Morelos can be explained to some degree in political and military terms. On 4 March 1813 Calleja replaced Venegas. The new viceroy was a tough, pulque-drinking officer who understood Mexicans, had his interests in the colony, and was determined to destroy the insurgents even if Mexico suffered 'blood and fire' in the process. He had previously had his hands tied by Spanish constitutionalism, which did not recognize the

office of viceroy, and which caused a split between the conservative and liberal wings of the royalists, and to some extent between
Spanish absolutists and creole constitutionalists.[59] In order to
keep the creoles in line Calleja ruefully applied the constitution
with the exception of freedom of the press. But in 1814 the
restoration of Ferdinand vii and of absolutism produced a new
hard line. Spaniards regarded this as a vindication of their position in the colony. And Calleja was free to make all-out war on
Morelos; as he won ground, he sent hundreds of Mexicans to the
firing squad. Morelos was now on the run. In spite of his
brilliance as a guerrilla leader he had made some elementary
strategical mistakes, one of which was to waste seven months in
1813 taking the fortress of Acapulco, leaving the royalists free to
reduce the pockets of resistance in the north and then to turn
south from a position of strength. But in the final analysis Morelos
failed because, like Hidalgo, he did not receive creole support.
Unlike Hidalgo, he earnestly sought it.

Early in the revolution Morelos made a special appeal to the
creoles and promised those who supported him not only that their
property would be respected but that high civil and military
offices would be placed in their hands. Unlike many guerrilla
chiefs, he tried to enforce strict discipline and tolerated no insubordination on socio-racial issues. From the beginning of his
campaign he saw the danger of a caste war which 'would be the
cause of our total ruin, spiritual and temporal'. He ordered that
the property of even the enemy and the guilty rich could be
confiscated only on the express orders of commanders.

The whites are the principal representatives of the kingdom, and they
were the first to take up arms in defence of the Indians and other
castes, allying with them; therefore the whites ought to be the object
of our gratitude and not of the hatred which some people are stirring
up against them. . . . It is not our system to proceed against the rich
simply because they are rich, much less against the rich creoles. Let
no one dare to attack their property, no matter how rich they are.[60]

It was only in the final stages, under the provocation of royalist
terrorism, that Morelos adopted incendiarism and war to the
death. After the defeat of Valladolid and in reaction to the royalist practice of shooting prisoners, he issued orders to kill all

military prisoners and to devastate collaborationist villages and haciendas.[61]

While Morelos had been tied down at Acapulco, Calleja had used the respite to regroup the royalist troops and incorporate reinforcements from Spain. In December 1813 the insurgent forces suffered a grievous defeat at Valladolid, followed by a further mauling at Puruarán. Congress now became a wandering body, as preoccupied with evading capture as with legislating; nevertheless it took over executive power from Morelos, while in other sectors the rebels squabbled among themselves and became easy targets for the royalist army. Congress now made a last effort to win creole support by offering them an alternative to post-restoration Spanish despotism: the Constitution of Apatzingán (22 October 1814) was a frankly liberal document which provided for an independent and republican form of government, with a plural executive and powerful legislative.[62] Morelos considered the constitution 'impracticable'; and in truth it made little impact on events. During 1815 congress was hard pressed to keep one move ahead of royalist forces. Eventually it decided to move eastwards to Tehuacan and the coast, perhaps with the intention of cutting the Veracruz-Mexico City road. The escort was entrusted to Morelos, and he was soon in action. Caught by a royalist force, he fought a brave rearguard action which enabled congress to escape, but he himself was captured and taken to the capital. He was found guilty of heresy and treason and shot on 22 December 1815, his last days sadly clouded by the demoralization he suffered from the false charge of heresy.

The creoles did not respond to Morelos: they did not want independence on his terms, involving social as well as political change. After his defeat the cause of independence receded, undermined first by bloody repression then, after 1816, by a policy of amnesty. Rebel bands continued to harrass the enemy in isolated guerrilla actions — Vicente Guerrero in the south, others in Guanajuato and Michoacán, while in the east Guadalupe Victoria had to go underground. But the mere survival of insurgency forced the royal government to provide for internal security and to place more power in the hands of the military than it had possessed before 1810. The security forces were headed by regional commanders who often turned their provinces into military fiefdoms. The counter-revolution was essentially the work of royalist creoles; the regional armies were creole armies; the administration was increasingly opened to creoles. In the period 1815-20 the creoles at last came into their own, and it was they who restored security to the haciendas and maintained social control. The creolization of power in these years indicated a shift from peninsular dominance and a widening of options open to Mexicans, or at least to the elite. And what the elite did the Church could not ignore.

(iii) THE CONSERVATIVE REVOLUTION

Spain itself was the first to disturb the delicate balance of interests which ruled Mexico. On 1 January 1820 General Rafael Riego led a liberal revolt in the peninsula; on 9 March Ferdinand VII was forced to restore the constitution of 1812 and to reconvene the cortes. News of these events reached Mexico late in April. On 27 May Viceroy Juan Ruiz de Apodaca proclaimed the constitution in the colony, and in September Mexican deputies were elected for the cortes in Spain. The new Spanish regime, in a kind of death wish, proceeded to subvert the very empire which it proclaimed. The cortes was a more radical body than its predecessor of 1812-14, and it quickly alienated the most powerful interests in Mexico. The Church was the first target. In a series of decrees issued in August and September 1820 it restricted the Church's right to own property by prohibiting the establishment of new chantries and pious foundations; it expelled the Jesuits and suppressed all monastic and hospital orders; it abolished the ecclesiastical fuero in all criminal cases; it ordered the bishops to comply, and ordered the arrest and confiscation of property of known opponents of the constitution, including the Bishop of Puebla and other prelates.[63] These anti-clerical decrees were known in Mexico, if not applied, in January 1821; naturally they provoked the Church, confirming its long held suspicion that liberals were enemies of the Church, and making it if not an agent of independence then more receptive to it.[64] The abolition of mayorazgos, repartimientos and all forms of forced labour attacked the interests of land-owners. The limitation of the jurisdiction of the audiencias and suppression of special tribunals and fueros alienated the judiciary and holders of privileges. A policy of this kind would need the backing of a loyal army. But the cortes promptly deprived itself of military support: a law of 29 September 1820 abolished the colonial militia's privilege of trial by military courts in non-military cases; and in June 1821, after many months' fanfare, the complete *fuero militar* of the colonial army was abolished. As Iturbide later declared, 'the cortes seemed determined to lose these possessions'.[65] Spanish liberalism did not in itself make nationalists out of Mexicans, but it had a destabilising effect and caused the creoles to rethink their political positions. The cortes demonstrated that liberalism was hostile to corporate privilege and withal no less imperialist than absolutism. The interest groups took notice. They found their leader in the creole Agustín de Iturbide, Catholic, land-owner, and officer.

The son of a Basque merchant in Valladolid, Iturbide was born in 1783, the same year as Bolívar. After a pious Catholic education, he began to manage a prosperous hacienda belonging to his father, and at about the same age – fifteen – he became a militia officer in his native province.[66] He was a man at harmony with his environment, and when the rebellion exploded in 1810 he immediately volunteered for the royal service, his determination confirmed when his own haciendas were occupied by the insurgents. From 1810 to 1816 he fought the insurgents without mercy, indeed without humanity; from his personal point of view the only flaw in the campaign was his failure to secure adequate reward and promotion. He later claimed that he made war not on Mexicans but on rebels who were set 'to exterminate the Europeans, to destroy property, to commit excesses, to flout the laws of war and humane customs, and even to disregard religious practices'.[67] Whatever the truth, Colonel Iturbide was a model of the creole position: he abhorred social revolution and helped to destroy it, without being completely satisfied with the Spanish regime, partly perhaps because he was a Mexican, principally because he was frustrated in his prospects.

In 1820 Iturbide was appointed commander of the royalist army of the south with a commission to defeat Guerrero and the remaining guerrillas. He went through the motions of fighting but in the course of the campaign, by December 1820, he began to elaborate a plan of independence, stressing the need to avoid bloodshed and expressing concern for the Catholic religion. By February 1821 his mind was made up, and on 24 February he published the *Plan de Iguala*, devised by himself but representing the interests of those who were threatened by Spain and whose collaboration he quickly received – the Church, the army, and the oligarchy. Independence was declared for a Catholic, united nation, in which Spaniards and Mexicans would be equal, caste distinctions abolished, and offices open to all inhabitants: 'All inhabitants of New Spain, without any distinction between Europeans, Africans and Indians, are citizens of this monarchy, with access to all positions according to their merits and virtues.'[68] The Plan called upon Spaniards to accept Mexico as their patria. And of Mexicans it asked 'Who among you can say he does not descend from Spaniards?' The answer, of course, was simple – most of the population. But the new regime was intended for acceptance by the masses, not for their benefit. The Plan guaranteed the existing social structure. The form of government would be constitutional monarchy. Church property, privileges and doctrines were preserved. Property rights and offices were assured to all those who held them, with the exception of opponents of independence. The Plan of Iguala thus created the three guarantees of 'union, religion, independence'. Independence, as Alamán pointed out with approval, was 'accomplished by the same people who until then had been opposing it'. And even creole liberals like Mora approved of Iturbide as they had disapproved of Hidalgo.[69] But the outcome was a bitter disappointment to the real revolutionaries who, after long years of struggle, had to accept independence on terms far removed from their own ideals. Guerrero ruefully signed the Plan as the best of limited options and as a means to better things. And his troops helped to swell the 'army of the three guarantees', which was the sanction behind the new regime. As for the royalist army, most of it deserted the viceroy and went over to Iturbide.

The Spanish government was not impressed; it appointed a liberal general, Juan O'Donojú as Superior Political Chief of New Spain, with orders to enforce the constitution. O'Donojú reached Mexico at the beginning of August breathing liberal sentiments, unaware that these were the last things the Mexican ruling class wanted to hear. He soon learned. He signed the Treaty of Córdoba (24 August 1821), recognizing Mexico as 'a sovereign and independent nation', and he undertook to recommend the Plan of Iguala to the Spanish government. But he died in October; and as Spanish governments, whether liberal or conservative, were all imperialist, the Treaty of Córdoba was rejected as invalid. Meanwhile on 28 September the 'trigarantine' army formally occupied Mexico City and set up a provisional government consisting of a five-man regency headed by Iturbide and a larger junta.

There could be little real unity. The majority of Mexicans were not prepared to tolerate Spaniards on these terms. So the Spanish minority, having backed Iturbide's movement, found that once they had severed connections with the metropolis, Iturbide could not protect them. They were hounded out of office, and the creoles assumed absolute control of government.[70] The masses, of course, received virtually nothing from the Plan of Iguala. Yet the popular reaction was not overtly hostile. Why should the mass of the people support the privileges of a small minority and endorse the labour and property rights of the creole oligarchy? The influence of the Church was decisive.[71] The Church's absolute adhesion to Iturbide's movement was the essential guarantee of its success, for the Church brought in the Catholic masses who might query the interests of privilege and property but did not question the message received in sermons and from priests that Iturbide was the saviour of religion against impious Spain.[72] It would be difficult to assess popular reservations. They could be seen dimly in the nostalgic sympathy for Hidalgo and Morelos, the real heroes of the masses, and in the publication of works on Morelos, the 'American martyr'.[73] The attitude of the Indians ranged from mild support, to hostility, to a more characteristic indifference.

The junta of thirty-eight men was drawn exclusively from the aristocracy of Church and state; it included no one from the early insurgent movement and no republicans. On 28 September they signed the Declaration of Independence of 'the Mexican empire'. Iturbide was confirmed as chief executive and as president of the regency, and it was agreed that he should have the title of *alteza* (highness). But once congressional elections were held dissident voices were bound to be heard. Congress met in February 1822 and almost immediately divided into three political groups: Bourbonists, who favoured a constitutional monarchy with a Bourbon as king; Iturbidists, who also wanted a monarchy but backed the candidature of Iturbide; and republicans, who opposed the designs of the army to impose a monarchy of any kind. Iturbide was in a strong position, for the Bourbons enjoyed no popularity, the republicans were leaderless, and he was a victorious military commander. In Mexico City the army, spearheaded by Iturbide's own regiment, openly pressed his claims, and a mob was whipped up shouting 'long live Agustín 1'. On 19 May congress itself, frightened by 'popular' pressure and military menace, gave majority approval to Iturbide's election as 'constitutional emperor of the Mexican empire'. He became known as Agustín 1 or, as Bolívar described him, 'emperor by the grace of God and of bayonets'.[74] In a bizarre ceremony in the cathedral Agustín 1 was annointed and crowned hereditary monarch with a crown made in Mexico.

Congress imagined it was getting a constitutional monarch. This was not Iturbide's view; he was incapable of restraint, or of remaining above parties and politics. He was a military dictator, one of the first in Latin America. And his style of government was an early model of caudillism, a series of stop-gap measures. To reassure merchants and capitalists he reduced the alcabala from 16 to 6 per cent, suppressed liquor taxes and many other duties. When revenue inevitably dropped, he began to improvise, resorting to *donativos*, forced loans, paper money, foreign loans, the consequence of which was financial confusion and weak government. The emperor had no greater success on the political front. He alienated Bourbonists and republicans alike. And his relations with congress foundered on a number of issues – how to deal with opposition (the emperor favoured jailing), his use of veto, and financial control. On 31 October 1822 Iturbide dismissed congress and replaced it with a smaller 'instituent junta'. But there was a gap in his defences. Alamán jeered that his army had more officers and musicians than private soldiers. It also had a number of enemies.

There was bound to be a military problem. Officers were

dissatisfied with promotion and pay. And Mexicans resented the continued presence of Spanish military, many of them provocative and mutinous, whom they regarded as incompatible with security and independence. The focus of trouble was Veracruz. The town was held by Mexicans but the fortress of San Juan de Ulúa was still occupied by a group of Spanish royalists, who thus controlled entry into Mexico's major port. The Mexican commander at Veracruz, Antonio López de Santa Anna, tried on his own initiative to subvert the royalist force. Insubordination combined with failure drew the angry attention of the emperor who removed Santa Anna in November 1822 and ordered him to report to the capital. Santa Anna thereupon revolted, enraged by this humiliating order which, he subsequently wrote, 'tore the bandage from my eyes. I beheld absolutism in all its power.'[75] He had been one of the first to support Agustín 1. Now he worked for a republic against a despot who misgoverned and abused congress. With the republican General Guadalupe Victoria he devised the Plan of Veracruz (6 December 1822), which demanded the deposition of Agustín 1, restoration of congress, and the three guarantees. The imperial commander, General José Antonio Echávarri, was the next to defect. He too produced a plan, the Plan of Casa Mata (1 February 1823); this called for a new congress to take power from Agustín 1, and meanwhile gave authority to provincial governments in each province. In February agreement was reached with royalists at Veracruz for a joint effort against the emperor. Thus opportunists, republicans and royalists all came together in a campaign which soon reduced Agustín 1's power to Mexico City. The emperor lost his nerve: short of revenue, allies and ideas, he abdicated on 19 March 1823. His basic mistake had been to discard the real for the image, to become an imitation king instead of a unique caudillo. The Bishop of Puebla, an admirer and supporter, always advised him 'never to dismount from his horse', in other words to rule like the military dictator he was.[76] In the end he failed to remember this. In May he sailed for Italy in an English frigate. After a stay in England, he returned to Mexico a year later, hopeful of a comeback; he was taken and shot within two days of landing.

The fall of Iturbide revealed the cracks in the union. The

division between Bourbonists and Iturbidists favoured the republicans. In 1823 the Mexican revolution reached the point
from which most of the other revolutions in Spanish America
had started. But now that the republicans had their chance, they
too were weakened by dissension. The principal division was
between centralists and federalists, conservatives and liberals.
The centralist and conservative forces in Mexican society consisted of the higher ranks of the clergy, military, merchants and
land-owners. Their most distinguished leader was Lucas Alamán.
Opposed to them were the federalists, liberals and provincials,
standing for a mixture of ideology and interests, including
regional industrial interests damaged by the economic policy of
the central government. In spite of the revolution for independence, central power was still absolute and corporate privilege
still intact. Liberal federalists wanted to reduce the power of
Mexico City, to substitute local militia for a standing army, to
restrain the sovereignty of central government by state rights.
As can be seen in the thought of José María Luis Mora,
ecclesiastic turned reformer, the heart of the liberal programme
was opposition to corporate privilege; liberals sought to free
Mexico from colonial fueros and to create a new society inspired
by the philosophy of utilitarianism and modelled on the institutions of the United States.[77] Mexican liberalism did not
involve a rejection of Hispanic values in preference for those of
France, Britain and the United States; on the contrary it derived
much of its character from the Spanish Enlightenment and from
the Cortes of Cadiz. And it operated within the existing framework of society. On many of the basic issues confronting Mexico
– social structure, landed property – the distance between liberals
and conservatives was not great. Indeed on economic development and industrialization there were no clear party attitudes,
though the Mexican most alive to entrepreneurial values and
needs, Lucas Alamán, was a pure conservative.

The forces ousting Iturbide called a constituent assembly,
which drew up a republican constitution (October 1824)
representing the major interests. On the one hand it was federal;
it created nineteen states and gave them substantial rights. But
this was not a deviation from Mexican tradition in favour of
something imported from the United States. It responded to the

latent regionalism of Mexico and provincial distrust of Mexico City; it continued the impetus given to federalism by the Spanish constitution and the cortes of 1812–20; and it reflected regional economic interests, especially the artisan industries of the provinces threatened by the competition of foreign imports.[78] In any case, after the fall of Iturbide there was no central government; therefore in coming together to create one the provinces naturally protected themselves. While the constitution was federal, it was also conservative : it established Catholicism as the official religion, abolished the most important anticlerical decrees of the cortes of 1820, and, in article 154, specifically retained the fueros of the Church and the army. As Juárez later commented, the Constitution of 1824 was 'a compromise between progress and reaction'. Guadalupe Victoria, a respected symbol of resistance to the colonial order, was elected first constitutional president with the support of the liberals of the revolution. He in turn sought to establish a consensus government, including the conservative Lucas Alamán and the liberal federalist Miguel Ramos Arizpe. With the help of loans from the London money market, he provided a kind of stability until 1827.

(iv) NEW MULE, SAME RIDER

Mexico was badly damaged by the war of independence. Perhaps as many as six hundred thousand people perished, 10 per cent of the population. Mining production fell to less than a quarter, agriculture to a half, industry to a third. Commerce with Europe and the far east was disrupted. From stagnation and recession the people suffered, and so did the government. At the end of 1823 the financial administration was declared to be in complete disorder.

Commercial emancipation quickly followed political independence. A decree of 15 December 1821 opened Mexico to trade with all nations at a uniform tariff of 25 per cent. Most of the Spanish merchants withdrew either to Spain or to Cuba and were replaced by foreigners, mainly British and Americans, who began to supply the retailers of the interior directly without intervention of middlemen. The Americans were the most successful, bypassing the capital and thus avoiding glut and poor prices, and spreading out their products directly to the northern provinces through Tampico.[79] Postwar adjustment took some time, but by 1826 customs receipts were rising and shipping was increasing (399 United States ships in Mexican ports, 95 British), signs of recovery in Mexico's overseas trade. But it was imports, not exports, that accounted for the increase. Exports still consisted of precious metals and a few agricultural products – cochineal, indigo, vanilla, cotton and hides. Output had been severely damaged by wartime destruction and flight of capital.[80] Sugar production in Cuernavaca suffered, as did the fortunes of the planters : 'Most of these were Europeans, and as such, particularly obnoxious to the insurgents', who also blocked the way to markets.[81] Mexican industry could not compete in quality or price with foreign goods. The artisan manufactures of the provinces, the cotton and woollen textiles of Puebla and Querétaro, suffered three successive blows – *comercio libre* from 1789, flight of Spanish capital during 1810–21, and postwar British competition.[82] In 1827 a new tariff was imposed, ranging between 40 per cent duty and prohibition, but it was too late to stop the rot; and the law of 1829 prohibiting foreign goods that competed with native manufactures could not compensate for the absence of factors of production. Imports, therefore, were increasing, bringing with them a worsening balance of trade, barely covered by precious metals.

The departure of Spaniards meant the departure of capital. The exodus began as early as 1814 when two convoys of peninsulares sailed from Veracruz taking with them about twelve million pesos. But most of the Spanish capitalists left prior to and immediately after independence.[83] It is impossible to quantify the amount of capital they took with them, but its withdrawal coincided with the period of greatest depression in the mines.[84] Without foreign capital, therefore, Mexico could hardly have recovered from depression. This came mainly from Britain, partly in the form of loans, partly by investments of mining companies. The first Mexican loan for £3·2 million was negotiated with Goldschmidt and Co. in 1824, the second for the same amount with Barclay, Herring and Co. in 1825; but Mexico received less than half these sums, and both companies failed, Goldschmidt in 1826, Barclay in 1828. Mining investment was also risky. By 1826 the mines had still made no returns, though the capital employed in working them produced beneficial results in adjacent agriculture, trade and employment. What was desperately needed, however, was the produce of the mines themselves.

The social revolution of 1810 caused a swift exodus of wealthy capitalists from the mining towns. The mines were abandoned and in many cases flooded; the machinery was allowed to deteriorate, and the silver raised was merely the gleanings left over from more prosperous times. But the greatest disaster was again the flight of capital, withdrawn as soon as the insurgents cut communications between Mexico City and the provinces. As the mining towns were usually surrounded by guerrillas, it was impossible for the mines to receive supplies or make remittances without the protection of a large and costly escort. So it was less the material destruction, which could have been repaired, than the loss of confidence and therefore of investment, which produced the collapse of the Mexican mining economy, and with it the depression of agriculture and trade and the dispersion of skilled labour. This was one of the most crucial problems facing the national government after 1821.

Mining policy developed under pressure from Lucas Alamán, who came from a successful mining family in colonial Guanajuato. In an attempt to reduce costs for the industry the government abolished the mercury and mint monopoly of Mexico City, and in 1821 taxes on production and export were reduced to a single 3 per cent duty on gold and silver. To attract essential capital a law of 7 October 1823 threw open the door to foreigners who were allowed to become joint proprietors with Mexicans on highly favourable terms. By 1827 there were seven British companies, one German and two American. British capital amounted to £3 million, and altogether about twelve million dollars were invested. Within a short period of time a classical story unfolded – optimism, boom and crash. At the root of the problem lay the relative meagreness of the capital invested, which amounted to no more than one-third of the previous Spanish investment, and which was cut short by the financial crisis in London in 1826. Investors were almost completely ignorant of conditions in Mexico and even of the sites of workable mines. The only source of information was Humboldt, excellent for the state of the industry twenty years previously. The English imagined that flooding and labour were the only obstacles and easily surmountable, the former by English machinery, the latter by Cornish miners. The machinery failed and the Cornishmen did not adapt, and the experience caused most of the companies to acknowledge disaster, retrace their steps and start all over again, using European management and local labour. But there was no silver boom in the 1820s. In 1826 the produce of the Mexican mines was 7·5 million dollars.[85] The oligarchy would have to rely on other sources of wealth.

Mexican society retained its immutable form, for independence had certain built-in safeguards against change. A contemporary writer described an imaginary group of people in a bar criticizing independence for giving nothing to the masses: 'Independence is only a name. Previously they ruled us from Spain, now from here. It is always the same priest on a different mule. But as for work, food and clothing, there is no difference.'[86] Privilege survived intact. The Church retained its fueros and its wealth, living to fight and to be fought another day. National governments regarded this great complex of ecclesiastical interests with a mixture of alarm and envy. The subsequent attack on Church wealth came from conservatives as well as liberals, for conservative governments represented land-owners who were frequently in debt to the Church and sought release from their liabilities. But it was the Mexican liberals who were to launch the most extensive onslaught on clerical property; and they gave the conflict a new dimension by identifying the Church as an obstacle to economic development and social change. On the eve of the great confrontation, in 1856, the maximum figure of Church property was one hundred million pesos, an immense sum, though one which represented not half the national wealth, as has usually been asserted, but perhaps a fifth or a quarter.[87]

The army also retained its fueros. But unlike the Church, with which it is often compared, it was not independent of the state, for it relied upon impoverished and sometimes liberal governments for its income. In 1821 there was a standing army of thirty-five thousand, 'if so incongruous a mass might be called an army'.[88] This was an amalgamation of patriot and viceregal forces, and to integrate them into a loyal body Iturbide was lavish with officer promotions. In promoting so many officers to very high rank he helped to create an institution which was difficult to control. The Bishop of Puebla described the national army as 'a body in itself so powerful that it might dictate whatever terms it chose'.[89] And although this army provided the sanction behind the liberating plans of Iguala and Casa Mata, it remained in fact a highly conservative force. Of the hundred and eighteen high-ranking officers – between general and colonel – listed in 1840, twenty-five had been born in Spain or in one of the Spanish colonies, eighty-one had been born in Mexico but begun their military career in the royalist army, and only twelve (born in Mexico) had served in the insurgent armies.[90] Nevertheless the army was not entirely comparable to the other two power bases in Mexico: unlike the Church and the land-owners, it did not possess an independent source of wealth; it was therefore tempted to seek short-cuts to influence and affluence by periodically seizing power in military golpes.

Hacendados felt the effects of war and depression, and many had to break up their estates and sell land to survive. Their demand for cheap labour was all the more insistent. In 1821 the latifundists urged the regency to repeal the colonial laws protecting the Indians, which they described as an obstacle to the progress of agriculture. A few days after the entry of the trigarantine army in the capital the land-owners of Puebla proclaimed: 'The greatest service the government could render to agriculture would be to observe and remedy the present disorder among the Indians, who on the pretext of their misery have been granted a protection which is harmful to themselves, to farmers and to agriculture.'[91] The agrarian system continued to be weighted in favour of monopoly land-owners, as can be seen in criticisms made by contemporary reformers: 'A rich man takes possession of all the land round a village and imposes his own law there, so that the dependent inhabitants are forced by necessity to enter into tenancies and other arrangements under highly unfavourable conditions.'[92] Campesinos were held dependent either by semi-servile rentals paid in labour or by debt peonage. Hacienda peons received only one peso a week and a small ration of maize and beans. 'This miserable wage, combined with the high cost of living, means that most of them are enslaved to the hacendado, who thus believes himself authorized to commit the greatest excesses. The peon cannot leave to work for another master, for it is asserted that the debts they have incurred can only be paid by labour. For one peso owed they get eight days in the hacienda lock-up, and if they are late for work they can get a light penalty – staked out on their backs in the open for twenty-four hours.'[93]

The defeat of Morelos ended any chance of agrarian reform. After 1821 a few tentative efforts were made towards land distribution, inspired by liberal followers of Jovellanos, the distinguished Spanish advocate of agrarian reform. In 1823 congress ordered distribution of land on the hacienda of San Lorenzo in Chachapalicingo, Puebla. In 1827 Lorenzo Zavala divided Indian lands of forty settlements in the state of Mexico. And in 1829 Francisco García, Governor of Zacatecas, created a bank to acquire land for distribution in perpetual tenancies to landless peasants, and even tried to apply a local law of disentail. But these measures only skirted the problem. And when in 1833 the liberal party issued a policy statement urging the distribution of land to the rural poor, it included the important proviso 'without invading or violating the rights of private owners'.[94]

Independence gave all Mexicans equality of rights and status. There were few slaves in Mexico; in 1821, according to the commission on slavery, there were less than three thousand, and these were concentrated in the ports of Veracuz, Acapulco and other coastal areas. Abolition was announced in the Plan of Iguala, and there was little difficulty in implementing it. On 13 September 1821 the slave trade into Mexico was prohibited, and all persons born in Mexico were declared free. These measures were confirmed and extended by the constitutional regime. The federal government prohibited the slave trade on 13 October 1824. Various state laws of abolition were passed between 1825 and 1827; and President Guerrero suppressed slavery for the whole of Mexico on 15 September 1829.[95]

Abolition completed a process of emancipation which had been accelerated in the course of the eighteenth century, when slave labour became too expensive and many ex-slaves came on the free labour market, joining those Negroes who had already gained freedom through grant, or purchase, or escape. Slavery disappeared even in the plantation sector, and many of the largest sugar estates in Cuernavaca had gone over to free labour by 1808. The high costs, uncertain supply and heavy mortality were the major inducements: 'Several of the great proprietors were induced by these circumstances, to give liberty to a certain number of their slaves annually, and by encouraging marriages between them and the Indians of the country, to propagate a race of free labourers, who might be employed when a supply of slaves was no longer to be obtained.'[96] Land-owners therefore had already insured against abolition. But what of the ex-slave? In the colonial period the emancipated Negro had to perform military service, register with the *caja de negros* and pay tribute like Indians. They remained, with the mulattos, on the margin of society, without a caste or a place, squatting on the fringes of haciendas, crowding into *palenques*, living a vagrant existence in the towns. Independence gave them at least an identity: they were now Mexicans.[97] They wanted more, of course; the mixed bloods in particular desired to advance and exploit the opportunities theoretically open to them in a liberal society. But they had to be satisfied with a declaration that classification of persons by the terms Spaniard, Indian, mulatto and other racial descriptions would not be permitted in official documents, as everyone was now Mexican.[98]

The Indians could not be abolished by decree. The tribute, the traditional mark of servitude, was now suppressed. But this still left the problem of how to define an Indian. Race was not enough: in 1826 the senate of Jalisco argued that since few 'pure-blooded Indians' remained, those whom 'public opinion' considered Indians would be regarded as such. The influence of the latifundists and the search for dependent labour conditioned the policy of the liberals towards the Indians, and behind their overtly egalitarian views lurked hacendado thinking. Immediately after independence the land-owners demanded that indebted Indians be obliged to remain on the haciendas, arguing that as free and equal citizens the Indians could make enforceable contracts. Mora argued that the new legislation replaced the old distinction between Indians and non-Indians with a new division between rich and poor, 'thereby extending to everyone the benefits of society'.[99] The liberal ideal of equality among all citizens was responsible for grave errors in the development of Indian and agrarian policy, errors which the conservatives were too complacent to correct. Carlos María Bustamante was an exception who saw the danger: 'I think I hear people say that there are no Indians any more, that we are all Mexicans. . . . This sounds like a brave illusion to me, an illusion to remedy real and serious ills. . . . No Indians exist any more but the same needs from which the Indians suffered still exist.'[100] In their own interests the creoles had to take the tension out of the colonial caste system by abolishing its legal framework and substituting social and racial equality. The new stratification by class, while introducing a modicum of mobility, maintained basic differences and preserved creole superiority. Few Indians – Benito Juárez was to be one – were able to profit from the new mobility. The protected or 'caste' status which the Indians possessed in colonial society helped to ensure the continuity of their culture. Now, in a 'free' society based not on legally defined divisions but on class, the Indians were unable to integrate themselves into the nation. They remained a separate group, concentrated in those parts of the country which offered them a place of refuge, and protected, for the moment, by their community lands. This was what they preferred. But they were not to be left alone, for the very existence of community lands was anathema to liberal individualism. So the Indians faced independence in a vulnerable position, with little faith in the whites. In 1824 a clerical member of the Veracruz congress described the Indians to an English observer as 'downright savages, who had successfully resisted every attempt to educate them. An Indian was asked whom he wished should represent him or his nation in the congress. After some thought he answered "the Holy Ghost".'[101] To the Indians God was not white.

(v)   CENTRAL AMERICA: INDEPENDENCE BY DEFAULT

Mexico assumed its national identity without the provinces to the south. These had followed a less violent way to independence. In the particular conditions prevailing in Central America — a colony of few settlers, many Indians, subsistence economies — it was imperial government which had provided the motive force to mobilise labour, impose production, organise distribution, and enclose the whole within Spanish institutions and culture. Bourbon policy injected a belief in market forces, closer central control, and greater fiscal pressure. The object was to shift the burden of taxation from the Indians to the local economy, which was now undergoing expansion. The Bourbons did not normally extract surplus remissions from Central America but kept fiscal wealth in the colony by investment in improved bureaucracy and defence, thus making it a more effective unit of a larger empire.

Central America suffered as well as gained from the attention of the Bourbons. In the late colonial period it experienced an influx of foreign goods through *comercio libre* and contraband, which tended to destroy local industry and deplete capital resources. It was also subject to excessive taxation to meet the dramatic rise of civil and military expenditure from 1793, a time of war in Europe and the Americas, when imperial revenue could not keep pace with imperial defence. While the Bourbon reforms did not achieve their major goals, least of all in fiscal matters, they increased the power of the state at the expense of local elites and undermined the traditional order of things. The creoles now displayed open resentment of peninsular Spaniards, and local opinion insisted that 'there is mortal rivalry between these two classes, each of whom seeks preponderance'.[102] In these respects Central America did not differ greatly from the rest of Spanish America. What made the situation worse was the collapse of the primary export product. The indigo trade was hit by a series of calamities, wartime dislocation, a prolonged plague of locusts, decline in quality, tax-induced higher prices, competition from Venezuela and above all from British India. Central America now found that it could not sell its dye at a profit.[103] The crisis intensified the antagonism between the producers of the interior and the export merchants, and between both these groups and the Spanish officials. For the Bourbon government, continuing its search for wartime revenue, imposed in 1804 the Consolidation of ecclesiastical funds for remittance to Spain, which drained the economy of capital and hit all rural producers who had to redeem mortgages or sell up their holdings to merchant creditors.

The collapse of the market for indigo, aggravated by inopportune tax demands, hit Guatemalan and Salvadoran dye producers. But it also damaged the subsidiary economic activities which indigo had financed, dislocating the hitherto integrated colonial economy. Cotton producers in highland Guatemala, cacao producers in Nicaragua, cattle farmers and miners in Honduras, all suffered from the depression because they were all dependent upon the export earnings of indigo. The lower classes too had little reason for rejoicing. Poor creole farmers, mestizo and mulatto labourers, and Guatemalan Indians suffered in varying degrees from rising population pressure on resources, higher food prices, and greater competition for land; and the Indians now began to lose their communal lands. These sectors had no voice. But the elites could and did make known their feelings. Creoles throughout Central America tended to blame Guatemalan merchants for their misfortunes, for paying low for exports and charging high for imports, for witholding credit, and for importing foreign goods to the detriment of local industry. They also blamed the Spanish government, whose fiscal policy, they asserted, was turning vassals into slaves.[104] This did not make revolutionaries out of creoles. But it disposed them to look for change and to take advantage of new opportunities, not least the growth of foreign trade when the Spanish monopoly collapsed during the Napoleonic wars.

While the creole elite wanted economic and fiscal reform, they were divided over political change. Some welcomed the liberal policy of the Spanish cortes of 1812 and the creation of an elected provincial deputation. The Central American representatives in Cadiz stood for constitutional reform and free trade, and a programme of this kind appealed to the local elite as a non-revolutionary alternative to the colonial regime.[105] But economic depression, the assertion of crude regionalism, and growing antagonism between Americans and Spaniards sabotaged reformism. The captain-general José de Bustamante obstructed the constitution and, from 1814, applied repressive policies.[106] This made leading Guatemalans think again, beyond reform to some form of autonomy. Others, however, reacted against change, either because they were linked to the Spanish monopoly, or because their industries were threatened by English imports, or because they disliked liberalism.

José de Bustamante, soldier and president of the audiencia of Guatemala from 1811 to 1817, represented Bourbon absolutism at its most resolute; having served in the defence of the Río de la Plata in 1806–7, he was not inclined to abandon the cause of empire in Central America. His instinct was to fight back against Mexican insurgents, Guatemalan liberals, regional revolts and British contrabandists, and to resist contagion from other revolutionary movements. But his hand was weakened, first by Spain's own policy in these years, vacillating between the liberalising measures of the cortes of 1812 and restored absolutism in 1814, then by war, depression and contraband, which reduced government revenue. Bustamante imposed forced contributions on creoles and Indian communities, an action which made it clear that there was a price to pay for Spanish power. Yet his iron hand was removed not by liberal revolution but by his own master. In 1817 Ferdinand VII tried to placate liberal merchants and removed Bustamante. The liberal cabildo of 1812–14 was reappointed and became the mouthpiece of a powerful group of Guatemalan merchants.

It was in these years that Spain began to lose control of events in Central America. First to go was the commercial monopoly. Trade with the British, officially contraband, became normal by 1818, and trade with other nations increasingly common. Pressed by the liberal cabildo, the post-Bustamante administration was forced to legitimise these practices. British textiles entered the colony, trading against indigo and silver. There was a distinct, if brief, economic boom, though this benefited only certain sectors, Guatemalan merchants, especially those who controlled indigo production, and others linked to the export economy, while artisan industries were damaged by British imports. An argument grew between protectionists and those advocating free trade, and the first economic, social and regional divisions appeared. Highland cotton farmers and artisans, Nicaraguan and other merchants from the interior, Hondurans who saw their coinage drained off, all opposed the Guatemalan merchants, free trade and liberalism, and allied themselves with Spanish monopolists and clergy to advocate return to the centralised authority of Spain.

At this point, however, Spain lost the political initiative.

Between 1819 and 1821 political authority in Central America moved more and more towards Guatemalan merchants, advocates of free trade and liberal reforms. They dominated the provincial deputation and through that competed openly for power with the audiencia and its president, now called the 'political chief', and the Spanish authorities. They were favoured first by the Spanish liberal revolution of 1820, which restored constitutionalism to Guatemala — elected town councils, provincial deputations, representation in the Spanish cortes, constitutional guarantees. This brought José del Valle to office as mayor of Guatemala City and champion of the artisans, and the creoles now sought to appoint civil judges and take over the central administration of the colony. In opposing this the Spanish authorities were not alone. They still had the support of the Church and of regional interests who opposed Guatemalan economic domination. Honduras revolted; Nicaragua rejected rule from Guatemala; Costa Rica rebuffed Nicaragua. But the Spanish administration was incapable of turning these assets to account or of leading a counter-revolution; it lacked military power and, with a virtual tax revolt on its hands, the means to finance it. Creole conservatives, therefore, could not rely on Spain, either for policy or for protection. Many thought that constitutionalism was unrealistic in a society composed largely of illiterate peasants, and their reaction to Spanish liberalism, not least its anti-clericalism, was similar to that of the Mexican elite. Political instability, they believed, unleashed social unrest, agitation among the *pueblo bajo,* rising crime rates, and Indian rebellion in 1820, all of which frightened men like Valle and caused them to believe that Spain was no longer capable of protecting them or preserving the social order.

Guatemalans, therefore, looked with interest towards Iturbide's movement and the Plan of Iguala, liberals because of its potential for autonomy, conservatives because of its political guarantees. News of Iturbide's victory reached Central America in September 1821, and cabildos began to declare their independence. The collapse of Spanish Mexico could not be ignored, and political chief Gabino Gaínza was not a man to defend a dying empire. It was clear to the elite, Spaniards and creoles alike, that if they themselves did not sieze the opportunity and impose their will, popular forces would do so. This was their fear. So independence was a case of self help; it was declared by Gainza and the provincial elites 'to prevent the consequences that would be fearful in the event that the people should proclaim it'.[107]

But what was Central America? The majority of people had only a faint sense of national identity and even the elite was divided by regions and interests. A nation did not exist. Was there even a state? Without the unity imposed by Spain there was no cohesion, and without Spanish absolutism there was no central authority. Cabildos declared their independence not only from Spain but also from each other. The drift from the centralism of the Bourbons became a stampede, as region after region declared its own independence. Moreover, individual provinces began to declare union with Mexico, thus further proclaiming the disunity of Central America. Motives for this varied. Guatemalan liberals such as Mariano Aycinena wanted union with Mexico as a means of preserving Guatemalan hegemony. Regional interest groups in Nicaragua and Honduras, on the other hand, believed that union with a distant Mexico would enable them to dominate their own regions. Iturbide was not interested in any of these things. He regarded Guatemala as part of his empire, and he sent in an army to enforce his will. Central America was defenceless, and in January 1822 a number of cabildos (less than half) voted in favour of the union.

There was still no unity. Each cabildo was its own sovereign and refused to recognise Guatemala as the capital. Soon, in the course of 1822, Central America witnessed an unprecedented sight as town opposed town, Salvador fought Guatemala, and civil war was halted only by a Mexican general. Otherwise Mexico had little to offer. Union was seen to be an illusion, for the centre was hardly more stable than the periphery; Central American representatives in the Mexican congress suffered from Iturbide's growing despotism and saw in their new metropolis Central America's problems writ large. Finally union with Mexico came to an end in March 1823 with the overthrow of Iturbide. In July 1823 a National Constituent Assembly dominated by Guatemalan and Salvadoran representatives established an executive government and declared the absolute independence of the five provinces of Costa Rica, Guatemala, Honduras, Nicaragua and El Salvador; these were joined together in the federal constitution of 1824 as the United Provinces of Central America. A federal government took office in March 1825, with the Salvadoran Manuel Arce as president. The union soon fell into anarchy and civil war, as conservatives fought liberals, the periphery fought the centre, and the provinces fought each other. The federal government did not have the resources to maintain itself and union failed through fiscal failure. Powerful regional families would not allow their resources and property to be taxed by others or see revenue leave their region for the centre. In turn interior towns would refuse to pay taxes to regional capitals. These were political positions, for the economy itself was not depressed. Indigo recovered on the world market and cochineal dye was developing. There was some investment in mining. But these developments were to the benefit not of central government but of local economic interests, Guatemalan merchants, Honduran miners.

If the central government survived in 1823–26 it was because it refrained from acting like a government, from raising an army and imposing taxes. It is true that a glimmer of reformist tradition lived on, and the influence of the constitution of Cadiz could be seen not only in the federal constitution itself but in government policy, as it sought to promote education, industry and agricultural colonisation. And on 17 April 1825 slavery was abolished in Central America.[108] But basically peace and stability depended on government inertia. As soon as the central government tried to assert its sovereignty, to raise an army and to collect revenue, it was repudiated. From 1826 to 1829 Central America erupted in riot, rebellion and conflict, and the federation vanished, as the states refused to bow to Guatemala or to agree with each other. In the colonial period the crown had been the source of political legitimacy and its agents had arbitrated disputes. Now regional family networks fought for hegemony, resources and immunity. Lower down the social scale Indians, mestizos and mulattos, hitherto docile subjects of the king, imitated their superiors and resorted to violence to improve their position. So regional caudillos gained a following and stepped into the power vacuum left by Spain. The last unity enjoyed by Central America was that imposed by the Bourbons. The collapse of absolutism ended centralisation, and Central America opted for division. By 1838 this amounted to five weak states which had still to become nations.

TEN *The Reckoning*

T HE BOURBON STATE in Spanish America was not succeeded immediately by new nation states. There was an intermediate stage in which liberating armies or caudillo bands first challenged the political and military power of Spain and then destroyed it. In some cases this was a lengthy process and involved the creation of rudimentary wartime states, capable of raising taxes and recruiting troops. But these states were not necessarily nations. Even after independence had been won the establishment of new states preceded the formation of nations. For the growth of national consciousness was slow and partial, and subject to many impediments. Yet there were new factors favouring a more positive concept of nation. The revolutionary war was itself a noble cause, for which the insurgent armies fought glorious battles, and the people made great if grudging sacrifices. Spanish Americans now had their own heroic past, their own military honour, their own revolutionary myths. They had enhanced their sense of a common past, what John Stuart Mill called an 'identity of political antecedents, the possession of a national history, and consequent community of recollections'.[1]

They were obliged, moreover, to enter into relations with other states, in Europe and in America, a process which made them more conscious of their own nationality and more exposed to national rivalries. Some of the new states — Uruguay and Bolivia — found their true identity precisely in conflict with their American neighbours.

The symbols and the language of nationalism acquired a new urgency. In the Río de la Plata the defeat of the British invaders in 1807 was celebrated as an Argentine victory in the poem of Vicente López y Planes, *El triunfo argentino*, which anticipated the use of the name Argentina, a name already hallowed in local usage but lacking 'colonial' connotations. The *Telégrafo Mercantil* further propagated the word, referring frequently to the 'ninfas argentinas', the 'sabios y ilustres argentinos', and the 'capital de la Argentina'.[2] The porteño leaders exulted in the revolution of 1810 and quickly crowned it with national symbols. 'Our liberty', observed Belgrano, 'can have as many enemies as it likes and undergo every vicissitude; for the truth is that we need these experiences to form our national character.'[3] Belgrano himself designed the blue and white flag of Argentina. López y Planes wrote the 'Patriotic March' with music by Blas Parera, which in 1813 was adopted as the national anthem. He was only one of a group of writers and poets – all of them sadly untalented – whose themes were almost exclusively patriotic. They sang of the heroes of independence, victories over the Spanish tyrants, the greatness of Argentina. When independence was complete these effusions were collected and published by authority in a volume entitled *La lira argentina* (1824), a hopeful gesture at a time when the nation was threatened at best by extreme federalism, at worst by utter anarchy.

Mexican nationalism, anticipated in the intellectual euphoria of the late colonial period, advanced a stage further during the revolutionary wars. 'Independence', wrote Alamán, 'is a natural and noble inclination in nations as in individuals, all the more when it presents a promising future and exposes great and incalculable advantages.'[4] In the early days of the revolution Mexican nationalists such as Morelos used the term 'American' to describe their country, and they referred to themselves as 'Americanos', 'la nación americana', 'los ejércitos americanos'.

To appropriate the wider name – as the United States did more decisively – was not to deny but to affirm their nationality. As Alamán remarked: 'It was very common among Mexicans to speak of the whole of America when referring to Mexico, either out of boastfulness or because they thought that America had to follow Mexico's example in everything, as Mexico was such a principal part of America.... All this proves the exaggerated ideas which Mexicans held about the importance of their country.'[5]

To what extent did Americans achieve economic independence? Economic nationalism, hostility to foreign penetration, resentment of external control, these later ingredients of Latin American nationalism were almost completely absent from contemporary attitudes. While the new nations rejected the Spanish monopoly, they welcomed foreigners who subscribed to free competition and who brought much needed capital, manufactured goods and entrepreneurial skills.[6] Latin Americans were positively deferential to Britain. 'Politically,' wrote Bolívar, 'alliance with Great Britain would be a greater victory than Ayacucho, and if we procure it you may be certain that our future happiness is assured. The advantages which will result for Colombia, if we ally ourselves with that mistress of the universe, are incalculable.'[7] These views contained a large measure of self-interest and betrayed the anxiety of young and weak states to acquire a protector – a liberal protector – against the Holy Alliance. In general, Latin American leaders overestimated the extent to which their countries needed protection: the fact was that the powers of Europe had neither the will nor the means to intervene militarily in the Americas. The Monroe Doctrine, first proclaimed in 1823, had only slight relevance at the time. It meant little to Latin Americans and indeed was not primarily directed to them: it was a unilateral statement of United States policy, warning off European incursions in the Americas, either for new colonization or for recolonizing the new states. The United States subsequently made no move to implement the doctrine unless its own interests were directly at stake. Britain too sought to pose as a protector of the new states, with no more justification but with more success. Latin Americans continued to look to British sea power and British commercial power as the best pledges of their security.

And they were prepared to invite a greater British stake in their countries than would be tolerable to later generations. 'Here [Peru], I have sold the mines for two and a half million pesos, and I expect to obtain far more from other sources. I have suggested to the Peruvian government that it sell in England all its mines, lands, properties, and other government assets to cover the national debt, which is at least twenty million pesos.'[8] This is not the language of modern nationalism. But what did it mean? Had the new states a realistic choice between autarchy and dependence, between development and underdevelopment?

Independence ended the Spanish monopoly, removed the old intermediary, and gave Spanish America direct access to the world economy. British merchants and industrialists, or their agents, promptly moved into the new markets, looking for quick sales at low prices and selling to the popular sectors as well as to the elite. Britain was not only the leading exporter to Latin America — followed at some distance by the United States, France and Germany — but also the principal market for Latin American exports. There was at first an imbalance of trade, as Spanish American agricultural and mining exports stagnated and local capital was expended on imports rather than accumulated for investment.[9] The principal owners of capital — Church and merchants — had little inducement to invest in industry in the absence of a strong and protected market. It was easier to allow British manufactures to flood the market and force out national products. Moreover, the superior supplies, credit and shipping resources of the British made it difficult for local merchants to compete and drove many of them out of business. Yet there were compensations. These were years of further industrial growth in Britain when the price of exports fell; and they fell more substantially than did the price of primary products. This seems to have given Latin America favourable terms of trade, at least until the 1850s. Meanwhile British merchants had very little political leverage in Latin America and no influence over the tariff policy of the new states; unlike Spain, the new commercial metropolis could not be accused of fiscal extortion.

Yet the Latin American economies did not respond immediately to emancipation. The wars of independence were destructive of life and property; terror and insecurity, moreover, caused flight of labour and capital, which made it difficult to organise recovery and even more difficult to diversify the economy. Lack of internal accumulation and absence, as yet, of foreign investment further impeded economic growth. Mining in particular suffered from wartime dislocation and subsequent lack of capital. Other sectors needed less capital. Cattle ranching in Argentina and Venezuela could yield profits without great investment, assisted as it was by liberalisation of trade and access to stable markets. Tropical agriculture was less buoyant, but also found ways of surviving and expanding. The different economic sectors competed for influence but the metropolis no longer arbitrated.

Policy was made by the new leaders and national economic groups. These sought to build their particular interest into a new metropolis and to reduce other regions or provinces to a kind of colonial dependence upon themselves. Capitals or ports such as Buenos Aires thus tried to monopolize the fruits of independence, interposing themselves as a controlling interest in national and overseas trade. The subregions had to insist on economic autonomy in order to protect themselves; Uruguay and Paraguay opted for complete independence; the interior provinces of Argentina chose the way of federalism. In Mexico the artisan textile industry was less successful in protecting itself against the merchants of the capital who preferred to import British manufactures; Colombian industry suffered a similar fate. The national economies, therefore, were divided originally by internal rivalry, by conflict between the centre and the regions, between free trade and protection, between agriculturalists seeking export outlets and those who favoured industry or mining, between supporters of cheap imports and defenders of national products. On the whole the promoters of primary exports and cheap imports won the argument, and the British were waiting to take advantage.

But in the final analysis the prospects of national economic development were defeated by the social structure of the new states. The polarization of Latin American society into two sectors, a privileged minority monopolizing land and office, and a mass of peasants and workers, survived independence and continued with greater momentum. Perhaps economic growth would have raised the living standards of the people and nurtured a native middle class; in some countries, such as Mexico, upward mobility was already producing a middle group. But social rigidity and false social values were a cause as well as a result of economic retardation. Many landowners regarded their property as a social rather than economic investment, and their greatest economic activity was conspicuous consumption. Even if the consumption level of the upper income groups could have been reduced, there was no guarantee that the savings would have been invested in industry. As for the peasants, they were victims of grotesque inequality – and a helpless obstacle to development. Without agrarian reform there was no prospect of raising the living standards of the mass of the people, and without this there was no possibility of industrial development. The agrarian sector was only one stage removed from a slave economy. Peasants living at subsistence level could not be consumers of manufactures; and urban workers had to spend too much on food to have anything left for consumer goods. In these circumstances there was no mass market for national industries: Latin America either took foreign imports or went without consumer goods. Meanwhile the new nations relapsed into classical export economies, producing raw materials for the world market, exploiting the area's primitive assets – land and labour.

The basic economic institution, therefore, was the hacienda, a relatively inefficient organization, producing for national consumption or for export to the world market, absorbing too much land and too little capital, and carried ultimately on the back of cheap labour, seasonal or servile. But the hacienda had more than an economic function. It was a social and political organization, a means of control, a base of the ruling oligarchy. Independence strengthened the hacienda. As the colonial state and its institutions withered, the hacienda grew more powerful; amidst the insecurity of revolution and civil war it stood firm, a bastion for its owner, a refuge for its many inhabitants. It also grew at the expense of the Church, continuing a process begun in 1767 when the vast and highly commercial estates of the Jesuits were auctioned at ridiculously low prices to neighbouring hacendados and incoming land-owners. The precedent was not lost on the new regimes. Lands of the Inquisition and of religious orders were often confiscated and sold to buyers on easy terms. And hacendados, backed by friendly governments, sometimes managed to free themselves from ecclesiastical mortgages on their property. If the war of independence was a struggle for power, it was also a dispute over resources and the creoles fought for land as well as for liberty. A new elite of landowners, rewarded from royalist property or from public land, joined the colonial proprietors and in some cases replaced them. The formation of estates went hand in hand with state building. The landowners were the new ruling class, taking over from the old colonial urban sectors of mining, trade and bureaucracy. The political ambitions of the new elite were placated by office and representation; and to satisfy their economic needs they were ready in effect to do a deal with foreigners, obtaining from the more developed nations of the northern hemisphere the credit, markets and luxury imports which Latin America itself could not provide.[10]

The new nationalism was almost entirely devoid of social content. It is true that independence was inspired by liberal and even egalitarian ideas which rejected the rigid stratification of the colonial period, legislated against the society of castes, and sought to integrate the ethnic groups into the nation. But in practice the mass of the people had little loyalty to the nations in which they found themselves; they had to be forcibly conscripted during the war and closely controlled thereafter. The absence of social cohesion caused idealists like Bolívar to despair of creating viable nations. Negro slaves and the tied peons who succeeded them, receiving few of the fruits of independence, had few reasons to feel a sense of national identity. The slave trade did not long survive independence, but slavery itself was another matter. The chronology of abolition was determined by the importance of slaves in a given economy and by the numbers available. Where there were few slaves, as in Chile, Central America and Mexico, abolition was decreed soon after independence, in the 1820s. Elsewhere, as in Argentina, Venezuela, Colombia and Peru, it survived until the 1850s, effectively barring slaves and ex-slaves from the process of nation building. The Indian population, too, remained unaware of nationality. The Indians were not intergrated into the new nations.[11] As they emerged from the colony they were an isolated and to some extent protected people, whose closest relations were with the hacienda or the Indian communities, not with the state.

The colonial caste structure, of which Indians were a part, did not survive the wars of independence. For caste society generated tensions between its components which threatened to destroy the traditional order in a holocaust of socio-racial violence. The creoles were haunted by the spectre of caste war. And to some degree the chronology of their conversion to independence depended upon two factors — the strength of popular agitation, and the capacity of the colonial government to control it. In Mexico and Peru, where viceregal authority had the nerve and the means to govern effectively, the creoles did not hasten to desert the shelter of imperial government. But where the colonial regime was thought to be weak and social explosion imminent – in northern South America – then the obsession of the creoles with law and order and their anxiety to preserve the social structure persuaded them to make a bid for power from the very beginning. In any case, popular rebellion added a new dimension to the revolution which caused the creoles moments of near panic. There was, therefore, a causal connection between the radicalism of the masses and the conservatism of independence. Spanish America retained its colonial heritage not because the masses were indifferent to the creole revolution but because they were a threat to it. During the wars of independence popular revolt, while not successful, was menacing enough to compel the creoles to tighten their grip on the revolution : they had to contain the resentment of the Indians and the ambitions of the pardos and mestizos. And after the wars they sought to ease the less tolerable tensions in society by abolishing the caste system and preparing the way for a class society, simultaneously ending discrimination against those of mixed race and maintaining their own social and economic predominance.

The Indians, however, remained a people apart, ignored by conservatives and harassed by liberals. The latter regarded the Indians as an impediment to national development, and believed that their autonomy and corporate identity must be destroyed by forcing them into the nation through political dependence and economic participation. Doctrinaire liberalism was responsible for much of the irreparable damage done to Indian society in the nineteenth century. Motives were doubtless impeccable. 'Indians,' proclaimed the Peruvian patriots, 'noble children of the sun, you are the first object of our concern. We recall your past sufferings, we work for your present and future happiness. You are going to be noble, educated, and owners of property.'[12] The final promise was the most sinister. Legislation in Peru, New Granada and Mexico sought to destroy communal and corporate entities in order to mobilize Indian lands and funds and to force the Indians out of their special status into a market economy and a national society. This involved the division of Indian communal lands among individual owners, theoretically among the Indians themselves, in practice among their more powerful white neighbours. Legislation in itself, of course, could not abolish Indian communities, which had their own mechanisms of survival. And community land was often protected in effect by the stagnation of commercial agriculture and the absence of competition for land in the decades immediately after independence. But once demographic and market pressures increased, and Spanish America became more closely integrated into the international economy, then it would be found that the Indian communities had been stripped of their defences and were open to the encroachment of the hacienda. Meanwhile, liberal policy did not integrate the Indians into the nation; it isolated them still further in hopeless poverty, their only outlet in blind and unavailing rebellion. The fruits of revolution were not all sweet and not all shared.

The history of nationalism affords examples of a further process, beyond independence and unification. This is the process of nation building, extending to the mass of the people a belief in the existence of the nation, hitherto held only by the elite, and incorporating into the nation all sectors of the population and not simply the holders of property and privilege. This objective was absent from the policy of the new leaders. The creole elite of landowners, merchants and office-holders fought not only to take power from Spain but also to determine who should receive that power. The creation of nation states was a slow and laborious process, during all stages of which the creoles retained possession of the instruments of power and refused to share them with the popular sectors.

The political systems of the new states represented the creole determination to control the Indians and Negroes, the rural labour force, and to curb the castes, the most ambitious of the lower classes. They also reacted inevitably to economic divisions and regional interests. What institutions were most appropriate to these tasks? Conservatives and liberals, products of the same elite, had different, though not consistently different, answers. A Colombian conservative remarked on the irritating self-righteousness of liberals: 'They alone tell the truth, they alone are men of honour, they alone are patriots. Those of us who do not belong to their party are dishonest, traitors, absolutists.'[13] But he conceded that at least the liberals had a coherent doctrine, whereas the conservatives stood only for personal groupings. The distinction was not entirely valid. It is true that liberals had a policy: they stood for constitutional government, the basic human freedoms, economic *laissez-faire,* opposition to military and ecclesiastical privilege. Constitutions in Mexico, Colombia, Venezuela and Chile, inspired to some degree by the Spanish constitution of 1812, embodied typical liberal values, though even among liberals there was a tendency in Spanish America to grant the president extraordinary powers and to restrict the franchise to propertied literates. Conservatives favoured a more paternalist form of government, a virtual king with the name of president. In the case of Bolívar this was the fruit not of group prejudice but of prolonged political thinking and adaptation. In Mexico Lucas Alamán also had his principles, basing his support for the Church and traditional social institutions on a profound scepticism of human perfectibility, a firm belief in law and order, and a vivid memory of the terror and anarchy of the year 1810. To some extent liberalism and conservatism represented different interests, urban versus rural groupings, entrepreneurial versus aristocratic values, province versus capital. But these interest alignments often dissolved, leaving a residue of ideas and convictions as the major factor of division. And there remained always an element of opportunism. In theory liberals favoured federalism, supposedly a decentralized and democratic form of government, while conservatives demanded a strong executive and central control. But when the opportunity occurred liberals would impose liberalism by central institutions in a unitary regime, such as that favoured by Rivadavia and Sarmiento in Argentina. And to preserve their control in particular provinces, or if they happened to be the 'outs', conservatives might well be federalists. Federalism, therefore, was not necessarily a 'progressive' force. It also tended to be an expensive form of government. The proliferation of state governments and legislatures was a means by which regional ruling classes took a firm grip of offices and patronage in their region and created jobs and sinecures for themselves. The rank growth of bureaucracies, federal and provincial, were intolerable parasites on the new states; as Bolívar complained, 'there is not a town, no matter how insignificant, that does not have a court of justice and a thousand other tribunals to devour the insubstantial revenue of the state'.[14] Moreover, the new states had expenses unknown to colonial government. Congressmen, judges, ministers, diplomats had to be paid salaries, new schools, hospitals and rudimentary social services had to be financed, all out of a revenue which the bureaucracy, sons or clients of the ruling class, regarded as fair game for plunder. One of the largest items of expenditure was the military budget. And one of the largest potential sources of revenue was the Church.

Independence weakened some of the basic structures of the Church. Many bishops deserted their dioceses and returned to Spain. Others were expelled. Others died and were not replaced. The responsibility for empty dioceses was shared between Rome, which dragged its feet over recognition of independence, and liberal governments, which would accept their own nominees or none. Shortage of bishops was inevitably accompanied by shortage of priests and religious, and many parishes were left unattended. The economic assets of the Church were also shrinking. Tithes were reduced during the wars of independence and phased out afterwards when governments withdrew official sanctions for their collection. The new rulers, conservatives and liberals alike, coveted church property and income, not to redistribute them in society but as a rightful revenue of the state; and most property owners were anxious to unburden themselves of ecclesiastical loans or liens. Yet the Church survived, and if it was temporarily weak, the state was weaker. In the aftermath of independence the Church was more stable, more popular, and apparently more wealthy than the state. Many politicians, particularly liberals, saw the Church as a rival focus of allegiance, an obstacle to state building, and they reacted by seeking to control and to tax the Church, to abolish its fueros, and to reduce its power. Some of these objectives were also extended to that other focus of interest and allegiance, the military.

The size and expense of armies were out of all proportion to their function, particularly after the last Spanish bases had been removed; for it needed little insight to appreciate that European invaders would have little chance of survival in independent Latin America. So the new states were left with virtual armies of occupation, whose function was principally the welfare of their own members.[15] To disband them was difficult because it was expensive. In the immediate aftermath of the war the Colombian army stood at twenty-five to thirty thousand, and its budget represented three-quarters of the total expenditure of Santander's government.[16] Republican armies were relatively democratic institutions : while the creole aristocracy monopolized the higher commands, men of humble origin and even pardos could work their way up to middle officer rank. But wages were inadequate and often in arrears; the inevitable results were desertion, mutiny, pillage and general delinquency. Far from providing law and order, the army was often a prime cause of violence and anarchy. From Venezuela it was reported, 'from the impoverished state of the Treasury, the troops have long been unpaid, the result of which has already begun to manifest itself in the desertion of nearly the whole of those quartered in Valencia, the dissatisfied soldiery bending their course towards the plains of Apure, committing every sort of depredation and irregularity'.[17] The great liberating armies and their successors, therefore, were regarded by civilians with mixed feelings. Liberals were positively hostile to standing armies, preferring state militias; and they tried various devices to take the menace out of the military, by prohibiting the union of civil and military commands, subordinating the army to civil government, and above all by abolishing the fuero militar. But the military clung to their fuero as a vital remnant of privilege at a time when their economic prospects were poor. Unlike the other great power groups, the hacendados and the Church, the military did not have an independent source of income. They were therefore tempted to dominate the state and control the allocation of resources. Latin America became the primeval home of the golpe and the caudillo.

During and after the wars of independence, therefore, a number of forces prevailed which were hostile to the growth of strong nation states. The hacienda was one of many rival bases of power and allegiance which challenged state institutions; peons were bound by duties to their *patrón,* whose power was immediate and whose decision was final. Corporate privilege also diminished the state. The existence of military and ecclesiastical fueros, and the survival of Indian communities as corporate entities, removed large sectors of society from the direct jurisdiction of the state. Regional separatism or autonomy, often expressing important economic interests, these too were alternative sovereignties which correspondingly weakened national development. Finally, the caudillo, who usually represented a regional power base, was one of the strongest obstacles to the development of the nation state. Yet paradoxically some caudillos could also act as defenders of national interests against outside pressure and so promote the independence and unity of their peoples and increase their national consciousness.[18]

The caudillo was a regional chieftain, deriving his power from control of local resources, especially of haciendas, which gave him access to men and supplies. Classical caudillism took the form of armed patron-client bands, held together by personal ties of dominance and submission, and by a common desire to obtain wealth by force of arms.[19] The caudillo's domain might grow from local to national dimensions. Here, too, supreme power was personal, not institutional; competition for offices and resources was violent and the achievements were rarely permanent. Caudillism was not born in colonial society. The Spanish empire was governed by an anonymous bureaucracy and maintained itself with a minimum of military sanction. The caudillo was a product of the wars of independence, when the colonial state was disrupted, institutions were destroyed, and social groups competed to fill the vacuum. Local proprietors or chieftains recruited followers who often progressed from vagrant, to bandit, to guerrilla fighter. While such bands might enlist under one political cause or another, the underlying factors were rural conditions and personal leadership. The countryside was often impoverished by destruction, and people were ruined by war taxes and plunder. As the economy reached breaking point, so men were forced into bands for subsistence under a chieftain who could lead them to booty and in the early years of the war banditry was stronger than ideology. Even when the political motivation became stronger the revolutionary armies were not professional armies, nor were the caudillos necessarily professional soldiers; the armies came together as an informal system of obedience from various interests whom the caudillos represented and could assemble. The caudillo, then, was a war leader. He was born of a perennial and universal human instinct in time of war to confer absolute power on a strong man, a single executive, who can recruit troops and commandeer resources. The process was then perpetuated by postwar conflicts, between unitarians and federalists in Argentina, between neighbouring states such as Colombia and Peru, and in the north between Mexico and the United States.

While he was originally a war leader, the caudillo also responded to civilian pressure groups of various kinds. In some cases he was representative of a large kinship elite; this was the role of Martín Güemes who was the creature of a group of powerful estancieros in Salta, made and controlled by them, and possessing no personal power outside the kinship structure.[20] More commonly the caudillo simply represented regional interests. Sometimes this was little more than the 'outs' fighting the 'ins'. But characteristically, as in Argentina, the caudillo defended regional economic interests against the policy of the centre. Again, as the centre usually employed force, the regions would commit their defence to a strong local warrior. Some caudillos – Quiroga 'the tiger of the pampas' was one – had acquired their political position as delegates of the centre rather than representatives of their own people. But it was an easy transition from delegated authority to local leadership. And many caudillos – Venezuela, as well as Argentina, provides examples – were only local until they became national, federalist until they became unitarian. On a national scale a successful golpe could bring spectacular rewards.

At this point another image of the caudillo emerged – the caudillo as benefactor, as distributor of patronage. Independence gave the creoles what they had long craved – access to all public offices. This particular fruit of independence at first went to their heads and they gorged themselves without thought of the consequences. Bolívar regarded the new bureaucracies as parasites which devoured the revolution before it was complete, using the government as a welfare service for themselves. There was no civil service, no competitive examinations, indeed little security; for appointments were made according to a spoils system, incoming governments replacing previous officials by their own clients. Caudillism, personalist as it was, fitted easily into this role. Caudillos could attract a necessary clientage by promising their followers office and other rewards when they reached power. And clients would attach themselves to a promising patron in the expectation of preferment when he reached the top. It was regarded as much safer to accept a personal promise from a caudillo than an anonymous undertaking from an institution, whether executive or legislative. So the mutual needs of patron and client were one of the mainstays of caudillism in the new states. But the reward most prized was land, and a caudillo was nothing if he could not acquire and distribute land. In spite of the spurious populism assumed by some caudillos, they were not reformers. Rosas was a demagogue who identified himself with the primitive gauchos in order to dominate and exploit them. This he did ruthlessly, seeing them as nothing more than peons or conscripts. The principal reward of revolution, land, he reserved for his elitist followers.

The disruption of the economy by the revolutionary wars, the reluctance to accumulate and invest capital, and the subsequent stagnation of production and export, left a large surplus of unemployed for recruitment into the armies of the caudillos, which gave them an illusion of participation. But the precise relationship between caudillism and economic conditions is obscure. The caudillo arose in regions dominated by the hacienda, where whole provinces were the private property of a few families, where great proprietors, whose strength lay in their estates and their retainers, disputed for power. The social environment, the economic activity, the hacienda mentality, all instilled authority, obedience, and seigneurial values. Even if the caudillo was not in fact one of the greatest land-owners, even if he came from the margin of the landed complex, he would still have to enter into contact with the system, and use the established social relations to assemble power and recruit his own clientage.[21] In the post-colonial societies of Spanish America caudillos often fulfilled an important social function on behalf of republican elites as guardians of law and order and guarantors of the existing social structure. And the reason was that their personal power was usually more effective than the theoretical protection of a constitution.

Caudillism reflected the weakness of republican institutions, which did not reassure or convince, and which could not immediately fill the gap left by the collapse of colonial government. Yet the rise and fall of caudillos, the frequent turnover of presidents, the repeated golpes, the suspension of constitutions, the constant political clamour, masked a basic stability and durability in post-independence society which made Latin America one of the least revolutionary places in the world. For these were superficial changes, struggles for power within the ruling class, factional not revolutionary conflicts, and they did not affect the mass of the people. Independence was a powerful yet finite force, which tore through Spanish America like a great storm, sweeping away the lines of attachment to Spain and the fabric of colonial government, but leaving intact the deeply rooted bases of colonial society. The Mexican peasants saw it as the same rider on a new mule, a political revolution in which one ruling class displaced another.[21] Political independence was only the beginning. Latin America still awaited those further changes in social structure and economic organization without which its independence remained incomplete and its needs unfulfilled.

Notes

ONE *The Origins of Spanish American Nationality*

1. Alexander von Humboldt, *Ensayo político sobre el reino de la Nueva España* (6th Spanish edn, 4 vols, Mexico, 1941), ii, 118; there is a more recent edition, ed, Juan A. Ortega y Medina (Mexico, 1966).
2. John Lynch, *Spain under the Habsburgs* (2nd ed., 2 vols, Oxford, 1981), ii, 212–48.
3. Quoted by Jaime Eyzaguirre, *Ideario y ruta de la emancipación chilena* (Santiago, 1957), p. 61.
4. John Leddy Phelan, *The People and the King. The Comunero Revolution in Colombia, 1781* (Madison, 1978), pp. 7–11, 30.
5. D. A. Brading, *Miners and Merchants in Bourbon Mexico 1763–1810* (Cambridge, 1971), pp. 29–30, who concludes that the Bourbons 'reconquered America'.
6. John Lynch, *Spanish Colonial Administration, 1781–1810. The Intendant System in the Viceroyalty of the Río de la Plata* (London, 1958); Luis Navarro García, *Intendencias en Indias* (Sevilla, 1959); Jacques A. Barbier, *Reform and Politics in Bourbon Chile, 1755–1796* (Ottawa, 1980); J. R. Fisher, *Government and Society in Colonial Peru. The*

Intendant System 1784–1814 (London, 1970); Brading, *Miners and Merchants in Bourbon Mexico*, pp. 33–92.

7. Guillermo Lohmann Villena, *El corregidor de indios en el Perú bajo los Austrias* (Madrid, 1957), 403–49.

8. Brian H. Hamnett, *Politics and Trade in Southern Mexico 1750–1821* (Cambridge, 1971), pp. 5–7; José Miranda, *Las ideas y las instituciones políticas mexicanas* (Mexico, 1952), pp. 191–3.

9. Concolorcorvo, *El Lazarillo de ciegos caminantes desde Buenos Aires hasta Lima* (1773) (*BAE*, 122, Madrid, 1959), p. 369.

10. Fisher, *op.cit.*, pp. 78–99.

11. Hamnett, *Politics and Trade in Southern Mexico*, pp. 55–71.

12. Concolorcorvo, *op. cit.*, p. 370.

13. Fisher, *op. cit.*, p. 91.

14. Hamnett, *Politics and Trade in Southern Mexico*, pp. 72–94, for a close scrutiny of this process; Bishop Antonio de San Miguel, *Informe* (1799), in Humboldt, *Ensayo político*, ii, 99–103.

15. Miguel Batllori, *El Abate Viscardo. Historia y mito de la intervención de los Jesuitas en la independencia de Hispano-américa* (Caracas, 1953); A. F. Pradeau, *La expulsión de los Jesuitas de las Provincias de Sonora, Ostimuri y Sinaloa en 1767* (Mexico, 1959); Magnus Mörner (ed.), The *Expulsion of the Jesuits from Latin America* (New York, 1965).

16. N. M. Farriss, *Crown and Clergy in Colonial Mexico 1759–1821. The Crisis of Ecclesiastical Privilege* (London, 1968).

17. See below, p. 314.

18. Juan Marchena Fernández, *Oficiales y soldados en el ejér-cito de América* (Seville, 1983); Allan J. Kuethe, *Military Reform and Society in New Granada, 1773–1808* (Gainesville, 1978), pp. 41–3, 170–1, 180–1, 185.

19. Leon G. Campbell, *The Military and Society in Colonial Peru 1750–1810* (Philadelphia, 1978); Christian I. Archer, *The Army in Bourbon Mexico, 1760–1810* (Albuquerque, 1977), pp. 28–31, 191–222.

20. Sergio Villalobos R., *Tradición y Reforma en 1810* (Santiago, 1961), pp. 89–100; M. Carmagnani, 'La oposición a los tributos en la segunda mitad del siglo XVIII', *Revista Chilena de Historia y Geografía*, 129 (1961), 158–95.

21. Eduardo Arcila Farías, *El siglo ilustrado en América. Reformas económicas del siglo XVIII en Nueva España* (Caracas, 1955), pp. 94–117; C. H. Haring, *The Spanish Empire in America* (New York, 1952), pp. 341–2; Sergio Villalobos R., *Comerico y*

contrabando en el Río de la Plata y Chile (Buenos Aires, 1965).

22. John Fisher, 'Imperial "Free Trade" and the Hispanic Economy, 1778–1796', *JLAS*, xiii, (1981), 21–56.

23. John Fisher, 'The Imperial Response to "Free Trade": Spanish Imports from Spanish America, 1778–1796', *JLAS*, xvii (1985), 35–78.

24. Rubén Vargas Ugarte (ed.), 'Informe del Tribunal del Consulado de Lima, 1790', *Revista Histórica* (Lima), xxii (1958), 266–310.

25. Sergio Villalobos R., *El comercio y la crisis colonial* (Santiago, 1968), pp. 99–109; Enrique de Gandía, *Buenos Aires colonial* (Buenos Aires, 1957), p. 20.

26. Pedro Santos Martínez, *Historia económica de Mendoza durante el virreinato (1776–1810)* (Madrid, 1961), pp. 122–6; E. O. Acevedo, 'Factores económicos regionales que produjeron la adhesión a la Revolución', *Revista de la Junta de Estudios Históricos de Mendoza*, segunda época, núm. 1(1961), 107–33.

27. Humboldt, *Ensayo político*, pp. 386–7, 425; Brading, *Miners and Merchants in Bourbon Mexico*, pp. 129–58.

28. Stanley J. and Barbara H. Stein, *The Colonial Heritage of Latin America* (New York, 1970), pp. 100–1.

29. Quoted by Catalina Sierra, *El nacimiento de México* (Mexico, 1960), p. 132.

30. Simón Bolívar, Jamaica Letter, 6 September 1815, Vicente Lecuna (ed.), *Cartas del Libertador* (10 vols, Caracas, 1929–30), i, 183–96.

31. E. Arcila Farías, *Economía colonial de Venezuela* (Mexico, 1946), pp. 315–19.

32. *Ibid.*, pp. 368–9.

33. Manuel José de Lavardén, *Nuevo aspecto del comercio en el Río de la Plata*, ed. Enrique Wedovoy (Buenos Aires, 1955), p. 132; Germán O. E. Tjarks and Alicia Vidaurreta de Tjarks, *El comercio inglés y el contrabando* (Buenos Aires, 1962), pp. 29–35; Susan Migden Socolow, *The Merchants of Buenos Aires 1778–1810. Family and Commerce* (Cambridge, 1978), pp. 54–70, 124–35.

34. Lavardén, *op. cit.*, pp. 130, 185.

35. Gandía, *Buenos Aires colonial*, p. 121.

36. Brading, *Miners and Merchants in Bourbon Mexico*, pp. 30, 104–14.

37. Pierre Chaunu, *L'Amérique et les Amériques* (Paris, 1964), p. 199.

38. In Guanajuato in 1792 over two-thirds of all immigrants came from northern Spain, and just over half of the total entered commerce; see Brading, *Miners and Merchants in Bourbon Mexico*, pp. 251–4.

39. Alamán, *Historia*, i, 54–5.

40. Mark A. Burkholder and D. S. Chandler, *From Impotence to Authority. The Spanish Crown and the American Audiencias 1687–1808* (Columbus, 1977), pp. 54–5.

41. *Ibid.*, pp. 134–5.

42. Humboldt, *Ensayo político*, ii, 117.

43. Alamán, *Historia*, i, 58–9.

44. The figures are from Humboldt, *Ensayo político*, ii, 28–30, with the exception of peninsulares: Indians 7,530,000 (45 per cent); mestizos, 5,328,000 (32 per cent); whites 3,276,000 (19 per cent); Negroes 776,000 (4 per cent); total 16,910,000.

45. R. A. Humphreys (ed.), *The 'Detached Recollections' of General D. F. O'Leary* (London, 1969), p. 30.

46. Humboldt, *Ensayo político*, ii, 141.

47. Brading, *Miners and Merchants in Bourbon Mexico*, pp. 259–60.

48. Magnus Mörner, *Race Mixture in the History of Latin America* (Boston, 1967), pp. 35–48; L. N. McAlister, 'Social Structure and Social Change in New Spain', *HAHR*, xliii (1963), 349–70.

49. Gonzalo Aguirre Beltrán, 'The Integration of the Negro into the National Society of Mexico', Magnus Mörner (ed.), *Race and Class in Latin America* (New York, 1970), p. 27.

50. Mörner, *Race Mixture in the History of Latin America*, pp. 60–70; Richard Konetzke, (ed.), *Colección de documentos para la formación social de Hispanoamérica 1493–1810. Vol. III* (Madrid, 1962), p. 783.

51. Bishop Illana to crown, 23 August 1768, Emiliano Endrek, *El mestizaje en Córdoba, siglo XVIII y principios del XIX* (Córdoba, 1966), p. 77; Concolorcorvo, *El Lazarillo de ciegos caminantes*, p. 301.

52. Jaime Jaramillo Uribe, 'Mestizaje y diferenciación social en el Nuevo Reino de Granada en la segunda mitad del siglo XVIII', *Anuario Colombiano de Historia Social y de la Cultura*, ii (1965), 21–48, particularly pp. 35–6.

53. 'Documentos. Los pardos en la colonia', *Boletín del Archivo General de la Nación* (Caracas), xxxv (1948), 333–51, particularly p. 336; Ildefonso Leal, 'La aristocracia criolla venezolana y el código negrero de 1789', *Revista de Historia* (Caracas), ii (1961), 61–81.

54. 'Informe que el ayuntamiento de Caracas hace al rey de España referente a la real cédula de 10 de febrero de 1795', J. F. Blanco and R. Azpurúa (eds), *Documentos para la historia de la vida pública del Libertador* (14 vols, Caracas, 1875–8), i, 267–75; cabildo of Caracas to crown, 13 October 1798, 'Los pardos en la colonia', *op. cit.*, pp. 339, 344.

55. I. Leal, 'La Universidad de Caracas y la sociedad colonial venezolana', *Revista de Historia*, iii (1962), 27–39.

56. Alamán, *Historia*, i, 67.

57. Manuel Abad y Queipo, 'Estado moral y político en que se hallaba la población del virreinato de Nueva España en 1799', in José María Luis Mora, *Obras sueltas*, (Mexico, 1963), pp. 204–5.

58. Bolívar to Páez, 4 August 1826, *Cartas*, vi, 32.

59. On the rebellion of Tupac Amaru in Peru see below, pp. 164–5; on the comuneros of New Granada, pp. 231–2.

60. Angostura Address, 15 February 1819, *Proclamas y Discursos del Libertador*, (ed.) Vicente Lecuna (Caracas, 1939), p. 205.

61. Bolívar to Sucre, 21 February 1825, *Cartas*, iv, 263.

62. Basil Hall, *Extracts from a Journal written on the coasts of Chili, Peru, and Mexico in the years 1820, 1821, 1822* (3rd ed., 2 vols, Edinburgh, 1824), ii, 9–57.

63. Sergio Villalobos R., *El comercio y la crisis colonial*, pp. 222–35; Hernán Ramírez Necochea, *Antecedentes económicos de la independencia de Chile* (2nd ed., Santiago, 1967), pp. 86–94; Guillermo Céspedes del Castillo, *Lima y Buenos Aires. Repercusiones económicas y políticas de la creación del virreinato del Plata* (Sevilla, 1947).

64. 'Reflexiones sobre rectificar la division del Virreynato del Peru', B.M. Add. 17588, f. 7v–8.

65. 'Representación de la ciudad de México a Carlos III', Juan Hernández y Dávalos (ed.), *Colección de documentos para la historia de la guerra de independencia de México* (6 vols, Mexico, 1877–82), i, 439; see also Miranda, *Las ideas y las instituciones políticas mexicanas*, p. 179.

66. M. L. Pérez Marchand, *Dos etapas ideológicas del siglo XVIII en México a través de los papeles de la Inquisición* (Mexico 1945), pp. 122–4.

67. José M. Mariluz Urquijo, *El virreinato del Río de la Plata en la época del marqués de Avilés (1799–1801)* (Buenos Aires, 1964), p. 267.

68. Charles C. Griffin, 'The Enlightenment and Latin American Independence', A. P. Whitaker (ed.), *Latin America and the Enlightenment* (2nd ed., Ithaca, N.Y., 1961), pp. 119–43,

provides the most convincing study of the political impact of the Enlightenment in Latin America. On its cultural significance see J. T. Lanning, *The Eighteenth-Century Enlightenment in the University of San Carlos de Guatemala* (Ithaca, N.Y., 1956).

69. R. Vargas Ugarte, *Historia del Perú. Virreinato (Siglo XVIII)* (Buenos Aires, 1957), p. 36.

70. Quoted by Luis González, 'El optimismo nacionalista como factor de la independencia de México', *Estudios de historiografía americana* (Mexico, 1948), pp. 155–215; see especially p. 158.

71. Quoted by Antonello Gerbi, *Viejas polémicas sobre el Nuevo Mundo. En el umbral de una conciencia americana* (3rd ed., Lima, 1946), p. 45; see also the same author's more recent *La disputa del Nuevo Mundo* (Mexico, 1960).

72. Juan Ignacio Molina, *Compendio de la historia geográfica, natural y civil del reino de Chile (CHCH*, xi, Santiago, 1878), p. 306; see also Gonzalo Vial Correa, 'La formación de nacionalidades hispano-americanas como causa de la independencia', *Boletín de la Academia Chilena de la Historia*, año xxxiii, no. 75 (1966), 110–44, and 'Historiografía de la independencia de Chile', *La Emancipación Latinoamericana. Estudios Bibliográficos* (Mexico, 1966), 83–106; Sergio Villalobos R., *Tradición y Reforma en 1810*, pp. 56–61.

73. Francisco Javier Clavijero, *Historia antigua de México* (4 vols, Mexico, 1945); see also Gloria Grajales, *Nacionalismo incipiente en los historiadores coloniales. Estudio historiográfico* (Mexico, 1961), pp. 89–117; E. J. Burrus, S. J., 'Jesuit Exiles, Precursors of Mexican Independence?', *Mid-America*, xxxvi (1954), 161–75; Gerbi, *Viejas polémicas*, pp. 118–32.

74. Clavijero, *op. cit.*, ii, 353, iv, 107–8.

75. Gabriel Méndez Plancarte, *Humanistas del siglo XVIII* (Mexico, 1941), pp. 83–111.

76. González, 'El optimismo nacionalista', *op. cit.*, pp. 158, 200, 201.

77. Gerbi, *Viejas polémicas*, p. 143.

78. Simon Collier, *Ideas and Politics of Chilean Independence 1808–1833* (Cambridge, 1967), pp. 24–7; Nestor Meza Villalobos, *La conciencia política chilena durante la monarquía* (Santiago, 1958), pp. 226–69.

79. Gerbi, *Viejas polémicas*, pp. 152–8.

80. R. J. Shafer, *The Economic Societies in the Spanish World (1763–1821)* (Syracuse, N. Y., 1958), p. 290.

81. Gerbi, *Viejas polémicas*, pp. 146–52.

82. Shafer, *op cit.*, pp. 157–68.

83. Pablo Macera, *Tres etapas en el desarrollo de la conciencia nacional* (Lima, 1955), pp. 64, 118, 120.
84. Rafael Moreno, 'La creación de la nacionalidad mexicana', *Historia Mexicana*, xii (1963), 531–51.
85. González, 'El optimismo nacionalista', *op. cit.*, passim.
86. Alamán, *Historia*, i, 156; see also José Miranda, *Humboldt y México* (Mexico, 1962).

Two   Revolution in the Río de la Plata

1. Jorge Comadrán Ruiz, *Evolución demográfica argentina durante el período hispano (1535–1810)* (Buenos Aires, 1969), pp. 77–120; Ernesto J. A. Máeder, *Evolución demográfica argentina de 1810 a 1869* (Buenos Aires, 1969), pp. 21–9.
2. Rosenblat, *La población indígena y el mestizaje en América*, ii, 155, n.1.
3. Juan Probst, in *Documentos para la historia argentina*, Facultad de Filosofía y Letras, Universidad de Buenos Aires (Buenos Aires, 1913–   ), xviii, p. xxix.
4. Santa Coloma to A. Olaguer Feliú, 22 September 1806, in Gandia, *Buenos Aires colonial*, p. 87.
5. Ricardo Zorraquín Becú, 'Los grupos sociales en la Revolución de Mayo', *Historia*, vi (1961), 40–63.
6. Bartolomé Mitre, *Historia de Belgrano y de la independencia argentina* (6th ed., 4 vols, Buenos Aires, 1927), i, 132–3.
7. *Ibid.*, i, 119; see also Julio César González and Rául Alejandro Molina, 'La "Memoria sobre la invasión de Buenos Aires por las armas inglesas" de Mariano Moreno', *Historia*, v (1960), 19–68.
8. Whitelocke to Windham, 10 July 1807, B. M., Add. 37887, ff.67–73.
9. Bartolomé Mitre, *Historia de San Martín y de la emancipación Sud-Americana* (2nd ed., 4 vols, Buenos Aires, 1890), i, 51.
10. Cornelio de Saavedra, *Memoria Autografa*, 1 January 1829, in *Biblioteca de Mayo* (17 vols, Buenos Aires, 1960–3), ii, 1040; see also Mitre, *Belgrano*, i, 155.
11. Liniers to intendants, 17 August 1808, B. M. Add. 32608, ff.32–5.
12. R. A. Humphreys, *Liberation in South America 1806–1827. The Career of James Paroissien* (London, 1952), pp. 22–32; Diego Luis Molinari, *Antecedentes de la revolución de mayo* (3 vols, Buenos Aires, 1922–6), i, 1–25, iii, 1–10; Alan K. Manchester, *British Preeminence in Brazil, its Rise and Decline* (Chapel Hill, 1933), 113–18.

13. Santa Coloma to Celedonio Villota, 16 October 1807, in Gandia, *Buenos Aires colonial*, p. 121.
14. Enrique de Gandia, *Historia de las ideas políticas en la argentina*. II. *Las ideas políticas de Martín Alzaga* (Buenos Aires, 1962), pp. 202–15.
15. Letters of Santa Coloma, 1 March, 26 August 1809, in Gandia, *Buenos Aires colonial*, pp. 157, 166.
16. Ricardo Levene, *Ensayo histórico sobre la revolución de mayo y Mariano Moreno* (4th ed., 3 vols, Buenos Aires 1960), i, 124–52.
17. *Apuntes sobre la revolución de 1809, en Buenos Aires*, in *Biblioteca de Mayo*, v, 4191.
18. Saavedra, *Memoria, Biblioteca de Mayo*, ii, 1040–7.
19. Letter of Santa Coloma, 20 January 1809, in Gandia, *Buenos Aires colonial*, pp. 155–6.
20. Enrique C. Corbellini, *La Revolución de Mayo* (2 vols, Buenos Aires, 1950), ii, 197. Viceroy Cisneros, aware of the danger, tried to reorganize and reduce the militia, which further provoked the creoles; see De Courcy to Pole, 13 August 1809, in Gerald S. Graham and R. A. Humphreys, *The Navy and South America 1807–1823. Correspondence of the Commanders-in-Chief on the South American Station* (London, 1962), pp. 40–1.
21. Zorraquín Becú, 'Los grupos sociales en la Revolución de Mayo', *Historia*, vi (1961), 40–63.
22. J. P. and W. P. Robertson, *Letters on Paraguay* (2 vols, London, 1838), i, 54–7.
23. Socolow, *Merchants of Buenos Aires*, pp. 134–5.
24. Quoted by Rodolfo Puiggros, *De la colonia a la revolución* (Buenos Aires, 1940), p. 262.
25. H. S. Ferns, *Britain and Argentina in the Nineteenth Century* (Oxford, 1960), pp. 49–51, 67–71; Ernesto J. Fitte, *Los comerciantes ingleses en vísperas de la Revolución de Mayo* (Buenos Aires, 1967); John Lynch, 'British Policy and Spanish America, 1783–1808', *Journal of Latin American Studies*, i (1969), 1–30.
26. Villalobos, *El comercio y la crisis colonial*, p. 125; see also Tjarks, *El comercio inglés y el contrabando*, pp. 11–22.
27. Humphreys, *Liberation in South America*, p. 38.
28. Cisneros, *Informe*, 22 July 1810, in Sigfrido A. Radaelli (ed.), *Memorias de los virreyes del Río de la Plata* (Buenos Aires, 1945), pp. 569–70.

29. De Courcy to Pole, 13 August 1809, *The Navy and South America*, p. 40.

30. Francisco Saguí, *Los últimos cuatro años de la dominación española en el antiguo virreinato del Río de la Plata*, in *Biblioteca de Mayo*, i, 21–195, see especially pp. 113–16.

31. *Documentos referentes a la guerra de la independencia y emancipación política de la República Argentina*, Archivo General de la Nación (3 vols, Buenos Aires, 1914–26), i, 222.

32. Diego Luis Molinari, *La Representación de los Hacendados de Mariano Moreno. Su ninguna influencia en la vida económica del país y en los sucesos de Mayo de 1810* (2nd ed., Buenos Aires, 1939), pp. 280–377.

33. *Ibid.*, p. 301.

34. See Levene, *Revolución de Mayo*, who argues that it was great, and Molinari, *Representación*, who maintains that it was slight. Tjarks, *El comercio inglés y el contrabando*, presents the thesis that the author of the *Representación* was Belgrano; see especially pp. 35–48.

35. Molinari, *Representación*, pp. 394–5 : Benjamin Keen, *David Curtis de Forest and the Revolution of Buenos Aires* (New Haven, 1947), p. 70.

36. Santa Coloma to A. Olaguer Feliú, 16 February 1810, Gandia, *Buenos Aires colonial*, p. 183.

37. De Courcy to Pole 1 December 1809, *The Navy and South America*, p. 44.

38. Humphreys, *Liberation in South America*, p. 40.

39. Lynch, *Spanish Colonial Administration*, pp. 268–73; Gabriel René-Moreno, *Ultimos días coloniales en el Alto-Perú* (Santiago, 1896–8), pp. 447–51; Manuel Pinto, *La revolución de la intendencia de La Paz en el virreinato del Río de la Plata, con la ocurrencia de Chuquisaca, 1800–1810* (La Paz, 1953).

40. Vicente Rodríguez Casado, and J. A. Calderón Quijano (eds), *Memoria de gobierno del virrey Abascal* (2 vols, Seville, 1944), ii, 60–1.

41. Levene, *Revolución de Mayo*, i, 354.

42. *Plan de gobierno*, in Carlos Ponce Sanginés and Raúl Alfonso García (eds), *Documentos para la historia de la Revolución de 1809* (3 vols, La Paz, 1954), i, pp. xxxi–xxxii.

43. *Ibid.*, p. xxxvii; Rene Danilo Arze Aguirre, *Participación popular en la independencia de Bolivia* (La Paz, 1979), pp. 108–24.

44. *Mayo Documental,* Universidad de Buenos Aires, Instituto de Historia Argentina 'Doctor Emilio Ravignani' (8 vols, Buenos Aires, 1962–4), i, pp. xi–xvii, introductory study on background of 1808–11 by Ricardo R. Caillet-Bois.
45. Levene, *Revolución de Mayo* ii, 36–72.
46. Carlos A. Pueyrredón, *1810. La Revolución de Mayo según amplia documentación de la época* (Buenos Aires, 1953), pp. 605–10; Enrique Ruiz-Guiñazú, *El Presidente Saavedra y el pueblo soberano de 1810* (Buenos Aires, 1960).
47. Corbellini, *op. cit.,* ii. 272–7; Rosenblat, *op. cit.,* i, 207–9; Roberto H. Marfany, *El Cabildo de Mayo* (Buenos Aires, 1961), p. 12.
48. Marfany, *Cabildo de Mayo,* pp. 38–42, *Episodios de la Revolución de Mayo* (Buenos Aires, 1966), and 'El pronunciamiento de Mayo', *Historia,* iii (1958), 61–126; Jorge Comadrán Ruiz, 'Algo más sobre la Semana de Mayo', *Historia,* iii (1957), 75–94.
49. Corbellini, *op. cit.,* ii, 62.
50. Marfany, *Cabildo de Mayo,* p. 52.
51. Marfany, 'Filiación política de la revolución de Buenos Aires', *Estudios Americanos,* xxi (1961), 235–53. For a balanced account of the doctrinal sources of the revolution see Ricardo Zorraquín Becú, 'La doctrina jurídica de la Revolución de Mayo', *Revista del Instituto de Historia del Derecho,* núm. 11(1960), 47–68.
52. Gandia, *Buenos Aires colonial,* p. 184.
53. Fabian to Croker, 3 June 1810, *The Navy and South America,* p. 49.
54. Marfany, 'La primera junta de gobierno de Buenos Aires (1810)', *Estudios Americanos,* xix (1960), 223–34.
55. Fabian to Croker, 3 June 1810, *The Navy and South America,* p. 50.
56. For a perceptive discussion see Tulio Halperín Donghi, *Politics, Economics and Society in Argentina in the Revolutionary Period* (Cambridge, 1975), pp. 165–8.
57. *El Censor,* 19 September 1816, in *Biblioteca de Mayo,* viii, 6870.
58. Saavedra, *Memoria, Biblioteca de Mayo,* ii, 1055.
59. Carlos S. A. Segreti, 'Mariano Moreno y la independencia, los justos títulos de la Revolución de Mayo', *Boletín del Instituto de Historia Argentina Doctor Emilio Ravignani,* v (1960), 3–30.
60. Santa Coloma, 20 November 1811, Gandia, *Buenos Aires*

colonial, p. 192; see also Emilio P. Corbiere, *El terrorismo en la Revolución de Mayo* (Buenos Aires, 1937).

61. R. R. Caillet-Bois, 'La revolución en el virreinato', *Historia de la Nación Argentina*, ed. Ricardo Levene (10 vols, Buenos Aires, 1936–42), v, ii, 160–2.

62. Ricardo Piccirilli, *Rivadavia y su tiempo* (2nd ed., 3 vols, Buenos Aires, 1960), i, 117.

63. See below, pp. 88–126.

64. Levene, *Revolución de Mayo*, ii, 116–18.

65. Piccirilli, *Rivadavia*, i, 121–3.

66. Quoted *ibid.*, i, 146.

67. *Ibid.*, 182–95.

68. Mariano de Vedia y Mitre, *La vida de Monteagudo* (3 vols, Buenos Aires, 1950), i, 211–61.

69. Jorge Comadrán Ruiz, 'Notas para un estudio sobre fidelismo, reformismo y separatismo en el Río de la Plata (1808–1816)', Academia Nacional de la Historia, *Cuarto Congreso Internacional de Historia de América* (8 vols, Buenos Aires, 1966), i, 449–99, particularly pp. 490–4.

70. Emilio Ravignani (ed.), *Asambleas constituyentes argentinas* (6 vols, Buenos Aires, 1937–9), vi, 42–5.

71. Heywood to Dixon, 13 October 1812. *The Navy and South America*, p. 80.

72. Ravignani, *Asambleas constituyentes*, vi, ii, 616–38.

73. Strangford to Castlereagh, 18 December 1813, C. K. Webster (ed.), *Britain and the Independence of Latin America 1812–1830. Select Documents from the Foreign Office Archives* (2 vols, London, 1938), i, 85–92.

74. Bowles to Croker, 26 January 1814, *The Navy and South America*, pp. 121–2.

75. Bowles to Croker, 22 September 1813, *ibid.*, p. 107.

76. Bowles to Dixon, 14 September 1813, *ibid.*, p. 110.

77. On the social base of the alternative revolutions in the provinces see Halperín Donghi, *Politics, Economics and Society in Argentina*, pp. 269–307.

78. Bowles to Croker, 3 April 1819, *The Navy and South America*, pp. 267–8.

79. Emilio Ravignani, *Historia constitucional de la República Argentina* (2nd ed., 3 vols, Buenos Aires, 1930), i, 247–50.

80. Bowles to Croker, 22 September 1816, *The Navy and South America*, p. 165; M. J. García to Strangford, 3 March 1815, Webster, *op cit.*, i, 96–8.

81. Miron Burgin, *The Economic Aspects of Argentine Federalism*,

1820–1852 (Cambridge, Mass., 1946), 15–16, 119–20.

82. 'While the colonial system existed, all manufactures and other European goods sold here at three times their present prices; while the produce of the country was given in exchange at a fourth part of what is now paid for it', Report on the trade of the River Plate, in Parish to Canning, 30 July 1824, R. A. Humphreys (ed.), *British Consular Reports on the Trade and Politics of Latin America 1824–1826* (London, 1940), p. 30; see also Ferns, *Britain and Argentina*, pp. 78–80.

83. José M. Mariluz Urquijo, 'Antecedentes sobre la política económica de las Provincias Unidas, 1810–1816', *Revista de la Facultad de Derecho y Ciencias Sociales* (Buenos Aires), vii (1952), 1313–28.

84. D. F. Sarmiento, *Facundo* (La Plata, 1938), p. 224.

85. San Martín to Bowles, 7 September 1816, *The Navy and South America*, p. 169.

86. Bowles to Croker, 22 June 1817, *ibid.*, pp. 202–3.

87. Leoncio Gianello, *Historia del Congreso de Tucumán* (Buenos Aires, 1966).

88. Facundo A. Arce, 'Aspectos de la lucha del litoral contra el centralismo de Buenos Aires. El Soberano Congreso. Misiones Pacificadores', Universidad Nacional de la Plata, Departamento de Historia, *Trabajos y Comunicaciones*, 15 (1966), 38–54.

89. Ravignani, *Asambleas constituyentes*, i, 216–18.

90. Andrés R. Allende, 'El Directorio de González Balcarce y la gestión de la Comisión Gubernativa Provincial', *Trabajos y Comunicaciones* (La Plata), 15 (1966), 11–37.

91. Ravignani, *Historia constitucional*, ii, 819; see also Leoncio Gianello *Estanislao López* (Santa Fe, 1955).

92. Halperín Donghi, *Politics, Economics and Society in Argentina*, pp. 291–4, 308–30.

93. Güemes to Aráoz, 7 February 1821, Instituto de Historia Argentina 'Doctor Emilio Ravignani', *Archivo del brigadier general Juan Facundo Quiroga* (2 vols, Buenos Aires, 1957–60), i, 298–301,

94. Circular de Francisco A. Ortiz de Ocampo, 1 March 1820, *Archivo Quiroga*, i, 131.

95. Ravignani, *Historia constitucional*, i, 321–5.

96. Hardy to Croker, 19 March 1820, *The Navy and South America*, p. 295.

97. Halperín Donghi, *Politics, Economics and Society in Argentina*, pp. 346–9.

98. Piccirilli, *Rivadavia*, ii, 12–27.

99. John Miller, *Memoirs of General Miller in the service of the Republic of Peru* (2nd ed., 2 vols, London, 1829), ii, 419.

100. *Anuncio oficial*, published in the *Gaceta Ministerial*, 7 August 1812, Piccirilli, *Rivadavia*, i, 185–6, ii, 35–6; see also Alberto Palcos, *Rivadavia, ejecutor del pensamiento de Mayo* (2 vols, La Plata, 1960).

101. Piccirilli, *Rivadavia*, ii, 38–9.

102. Guillermo Gallardo, *La política religiosa de Rivadavia* (Buenos Aires, 1962), pp. 67–78, 105–34, and, for text of law, pp. 277–80; Piccirilli, *Rivadavia*, ii, 279–89.

103. Sergio Bagú, *El plan económico del grupo Rivadaviano 1811–1827* (Rosario, 1966); José María Rosa, *Rivadavia y el imperialismo financiero* (Buenos Aires, 1964); Burgin, *op. cit.*, pp. 87–100.

104. Law of 4 September 1821, in Bagú, *op. cit.*, p. 145.

105. *Ibid.*, p. 161.

106. Decree of 19 April 1822, *ibid.*, p. 160.

107. Decree of 17 July 1823, Bagú, *op. cit.*, pp. 203–4.

108. Parish to Canning, 25 June 1824, Humphreys, *Consular Reports*, p. 23.

109. Ferns, *Britain and Argentina*, pp. 100–54.

110. British residents in Buenos Aires to Heywood, 8 July 1813, *The Navy and South America*, pp. 97–8.

111. Bowles to Croker, 28 July 1813, *ibid.*, p. 103; Rodolfo Merediz 'Comercio de frutos del país entre Buenos Aires y mercados Europeos entre 1815 y 1820', *Trabajos y Comunicaciones*, 16 (1960), 136–52.

112. Bowles to Hardy, 25 December 1819, Enclosure No. 2, *The Navy and South America*, p. 292.

113. Bowles to Croker, 21 September, 2 October, 10 October 1818, *ibid.*, pp. 243–8.

114. Parish to Canning, 25 June 1824, Humphreys, *Consular Reports*, p. 6.

115. Piccirilli, *Rivadavia*, ii, 145–58.

116. Report to Bowles by a merchant, 22 December 1819, *The Navy and South America*, p. 292.

117. R. A. Humphreys, 'British Merchants and South American Independence', *Tradition and Revolt in Latin America and other essays* (London, 1969), pp. 123–4; Ernesto J. Fitte, *Historia de un empréstito* (Buenos Aires, 1962); Ferns, *Britain and Argentina*, pp. 141–3.

118. Humphreys, *Consular Reports*, p. 24, n.4.

119. Parish to Canning, 24 October 1824, Webster, *Britain and the Independence of Latin America*, i, 118.
120. Sarmiento, *Facundo*, p. 72; see also pp. 132–5.
121. Piccirilli, *Rivadavia*, ii, 174–92.
122. See below, p. 81.
123. Ravignani, *Historia constitucional*, iii, 265–6.
124. Sarmiento, *Facundo*, p. 32.
125. Rivadavia to anon., 14 March 1830, Bagú, *op. cit.*, p. 508. See Halperín Donghi, *Politics, Economics and Society in Argentina*, pp. 211–15, 382–9.
126. *Ibid.*, pp. 72–8.
127. Tulio Halperín Donghi, 'La revolución y la crisis de la estructura mercantil colonial en el Río de la Plata', *Estudios de Historia Social*, ii (1966), 78–125.
128. Halperín, 'La expansión ganadera en la campaña de Buenos Aires (1810–1852)', *Desarrollo Económico*, iii (1963), 57–110.
129. Enrique M. Barba, 'Notas sobre la situación económica de Buenos Aires en la década de 1820', *Trabajos y Comunicaciones*, 17 (1967), 65–71.
130. Emilio A. Coni, *La verdad sobre la enfiteusis de Rivadavia* (Buenos Aires, 1927).
131. J. A. Oddone, *La burguesía terrateniente argentina* (3rd ed., Buenos Aires, 1956), pp. 76–91; Robertson, *Letters on Paraguay*, i, 54 who remarks that Saenz Valiente had twelve hundred square miles.
132. Report to Bowles by a merchant, 22 December 1819, *The Navy and South America*, p. 292; Alfredo J. Montoya, *Historia de los saladeros argentinos* (Buenos Aires, 1956).
133. Emilio A. Coni, *El Gaucho* (Buenos Aires, 1945); Ricardo Rodríguez Molas, *Historia social del gaucho* (2nd ed., Buenos Aires, 1982), pp. 64–91, 121–57.
134. Juan Manuel de Rosas, *Instrucciones a los mayordomos de estancias* (Buenos Aires, 1951); Halperín, 'La expansión ganadera', *op. cit.*, pp. 94–103.
135. Orlando Carracedo, 'El régimen de castas, el trabajo y la Revolución de Mayo', *Anuario del Instituto de Investigaciones Históricas* (Rosario), iv (1960), 157–86.
136. José Luis Masini, 'La esclavitud negra en la República Argentina: época independiente', *Revista de la Junta de Estudios Históricos de Mendoza*, segunda época, i (1961), 135–61.
137. Vieytes, *Antecedentes económicos*, pp. 403–8.
138. Decree of 9 April 1812, Bagú, *op. cit.*, p. 122.

139. *Gazeta de Buenos Aires*, 1 June 1816, No. 58.
140. Marta B. Goldberg, 'La población negra y mulata de la ciudad de Buenos Aires, 1810–1840', *Desarrollo Económico*, no. 61, vol. 16 (1976), 75–99; George Reid Andrews, *The Afro-Argentines of Buenos Aires*, 1800–1900 (Madison, 1980), pp. 44, 66.
141. Masini, *op. cit.*, pp. 157–8.
142. Goldberg, *op. cit.*, pp. 64–6.
143. Belgrano to San Martín, Jujuy, 25 December 1813, *Documentos para la historia del Libertador General San Martín* (8 vols, Buenos Aires, 1953–60), ii, 52–3.
144. Miller, *Memoirs of General Miller*, i, 271–2.
145. Emiliano Endrek, *El mestizaje en Córdoba, siglo xviii y principios del xix* (Córdoba, 1966), 12–19.
146. *Ibid.*, p. 53.
147. *Ibid.*, p. 62.
148. Mitre, *San Martín*, i, 291.

THREE   *Revolution Against the Río de la Plata*

1. J. E. Pivel Devoto, *Prólogo*, in *Archivo Artigas* (Montevideo, 1951), ii, pp. ix–x; Félix de Azara, *Memoria sobre el estado rural del Río de la Plata y otros informes* (Buenos Aires, 1943); Fernando A. Assuncão, *El Gaucho* (Montevideo, 1963).
2. Carlos Real de Azúa, *El patriciado uruguayo* (Montevideo, 1961), pp. 36–43.
3. *Ibid.*, pp. 48–51.
4. John Street, *Artigas and the Emancipation of Uruguay* (Cambridge 1959), p. 7.
5. J. E. Pivel Devoto, *Raíces coloniales de la revolución oriental de 1811* (Montevideo, 1952), pp. 100–7.
6. Street, *Artigas*, pp. 34–43.
7. Lynch, *Spanish Colonial Administration*, p. 285; Street *Artigas*, pp. 78–106.
8. Smith to de Courcy, 24 May 1809, *The Navy and South America*, p. 36.
9. J. Street, 'Lord Strangford and Río de la Plata, 1808–1815', *HAHR*, xxxiii (1953), 477–510.
10. Pablo Blanco Acevedo, *El gobierno colonial en el Uruguay y los orígenes de la nacionalidad* (3rd ed., Montevideo, 1944), pp. 239–63; Pivel Devoto, *Raíces coloniales*, pp. 227–38.
11. *Archivo Artigas*, ii, pt. 1.

12. Pivel Devoto, *Raíces coloniales*, pp. 239–52.
13. *Ibid.*, pp. 252–7.
14. Emilio Loza, 'La campaña de la Banda Oriental (1810–1813)', *H.N.A.*, V, ii, pp. 835–85.
15. De Courcy to Croker, 13 July, 15 September 1811, *The Navy and South America*, pp. 65, 67.
16. A Fernández (ed.), *Éxodo del pueblo oriental* (Montevideo, 1930).
17. Street, *Artigas*, pp. 147–52.
18. Castlereagh to Strangford, 29 May 1812, Webster, *Britain and the Independence of Latin America*, i, 168–9.
19. Pablo Blanco Acevedo, *El federalismo de Artigas y la independencia nacional* (Montevideo, 1939).
20. Published in Comisión Nacional de Homenaje a Artigas, *El Congreso de Abril de 1813, a través de los documentos* (Montevideo, 1951), pp. 37–40; see also H. Miranda, *Las instrucciones del año XIII* (2nd ed., Montevideo, 1935); Edmundo Favaro, *El Congreso de las Tres Cruces y la Asamblea del año XIII* (Montevideo, 1957), pp. 110–22.
21. M. J. García to Strangford, 3 March 1815, Strangford to Castlereagh, 14 March 1815, Webster, *Britain and the Independence of Latin America*, i, 96–100.
22. To distinguish it from independent Uruguay from 1828. For the government of Artigas in the *Patria Vieja* in 1815 see Eduardo Acevedo, *José Artigas. Su obra cívica. Alegato histórico* (3 vols, Montevideo, 1950), ii, 465–553.
23. *Ibid.*, ii, 555–656.
24. Hood to Canning, 31 January 1825, Humphreys, *Consular Reports*, p. 81.
25. Bowles to Croker, 27 July 1817, *The Navy and South America*, p. 206; Articles of a Convention, 2 August 1817, Webster, *Britain and the Independence of Latin America*, i, 187–8.
26. Bowles to Croker, 21 November 1816, *The Navy and South America*, pp. 172–3.
27. Lucía Sala de Touron, Nelson de la Torre and Julio C. Rodríguez, *Artigas y su revolución agraria 1811–1820* (Mexico, 1978), p. 267.
28. Sala de Touron, *op. cit.*, pp. 299–322; see also Halperín Donghi, *Politics, Economics and Society in Argentina*, pp. 285–7.
29. Chamberlain to Castlereagh, 20 July 1816, Webster, *Britain and the Independence of Latin America*, i, 176–8.
30. Emilio Loza, 'La invasión lusitana. Artigas y la defensa de la

Banda Oriental', *H.N.A.*, VI, ii, pp. 249–86.

31. Félix Best, *Historia de las guerras argentinas* (2 vols, Buenos Aires, 1960), i, 320–62; and see above, pp. 69–70.

32. Hardy to Croker, 24 March 1820, *The Navy and South America*, p. 296.

33. Acevedo, *José Artigas*, iii, 588–619; Street, *Artigas,* pp. 311–28.

34. Hood to Canning, 31 January 1825, Humphreys, *Consular Reports,* p. 79.

35. See above, p. 78.

36. Canning to Parish, 19 October 1825, Webster, *Britain and the Independence of Latin America,* i, 131.

37. L. A. de Herrera (ed.), *La Misión Ponsonby* (2 vols, Montevideo, 1930).

38. Canning to Ponsonby, 18 March 1826, Webster, *Britain and the Independence of Latin America,* i, 142.

39. Ponsonby to Canning, 2 October 1826, *ibid.,* i, 154.

40. Canning to Ponsonby, 27 November 1826, *ibid.,* 160.

41. L. A. de Herrera, *La Paz de 1828* (Montevideo, 1938).

42. Real de Azúa, *El patriciado uruguayo,* pp. 79–83.

43. Félix de Azara, *Descripción e historia del Paraguay y del Río de la Plata* (Buenos Aires, 1943); Efraím Cardozo, *Paraguay independiente* (*Historia de América,* ed. A. Ballesteros y Beretta, xxi, Barcelona, 1949).

44. Agustín Fernando de Pinedo, Governor of Paraguay, to crown, 29 January 1777, A. G. I., Aud. de Buenos Aires 322.

45. Fernández to Gálvez, 15 February 1783, A. G. I., Aud. de Buenos Aires 356.

46. Rivera to Saavedra, 19 May 1798, A. G. I., Aud. de Buenos Aires 322. Azara, *op. cit.,* gave the population as 97,480 in 1781–1801; see also Lynch, *Spanish Colonial Administration,* pp. 164–5.

47. Rafael Elodio Velázquez, 'La sociedad paraguaya en la época de la independencia', *Cuarto Congreso Internacional de Historia de América,* vi, 149–64; Azara, *Memoria sobre el estado rural del Río de la Plata,* p. 15.

48. Efraím Cardozo, *El Paraguay colonial. Las raíces de la nacionalidad* (Asunción, 1959), pp. 96–109, 212–22, 225–6.

49. Julio César Chaves, *Historia de las relaciones entre Buenos Ayres y el Paraguay, 1810–1813* (Buenos Aires, 1938), p. 44.

50. Manuel Belgrano, *Autobiografía,* Museo Mitre, *Documentos del Archivo de Belgrano* (7 vols, Buenos Aires, 1913–17), iii, 271.

51. Best, *Historia de la guerras argentinas,* i, 171–8.

52. Rafael Elodio Velázquez, *El Paraguay en 1811* (2nd ed., Asuncion, 1966).
53. Julio César Chaves, *El supremo dictador. Biografía de José Gaspar de Francia* (4th ed., Madrid, 1964), pp. 105–7.
54. Julio César Chaves, *La revolución del 14 y 15 de mayo* (Asunción-Buenos Aires, 1957).
55. Efraím Cardozo, *El plan federal de Dr. Francia* (Buenos Aires, 1941).
56. Chaves, *Francia*, pp. 136–7.
57. J. P. and W. P. Robertson, *Letters on Paraguay* (2 vols, London, 1838), i, 336–7.
58. Chaves, *Francia*, p. 165.
59. Bowles to Croker, 21 December 1816, *The Navy and South America*, p. 178.
60. Robertson, *Letters on Paraguay*, ii, 305.
61. *Ibid.*, ii, 23–4.
62. Chaves, *Francia*, p. 183.
63. John Hoyt Williams, *The Rise and Fall of the Paraguayan Republic, 1800–1870* (Austin, 1979), p. 41.
64. *Ibid.*, pp. 48–9.
65. *Ibid.*, pp. 87–8.
66. Robertson, *Letters on Paraguay*, ii, 279–80.
67. Peter A. Schmitt, *Paraguay und Europa* (Berlin, 1963), pp. 8–17.
68. Robertson, *Letters on Paraguay*, ii, 281.
69. *Ibid.*, 281–6.
70. Cecilio Báez, *Ensayo sobre el Doctor Francia y la dictadura en Sud-América* (Asunción, 1910), pp. 92–101.
71. Chaves, *Francia*, p. 267.
72. *Ibid.*, p. 268.
73. *Ibid.*, pp. 267–8.
74. Memorandum of 12 August 1822, *ibid.*, p. 270.
75. Rengger and Longchamps, *The Reign of Doctor Joseph Gaspard Roderick de Francia in Paraguay; being an account of a six years' residence in that republic, from July, 1819 to May, 1825* (London, 1827), pp. 47–8.
76. *Ibid.*, pp. 174–6; Williams, *op. cit.*, pp. 92–3.
77. Report on the trade of the river Plate, in Parish to Canning, 30 July 1824, Humphreys, *Consular Reports*, pp. 37, 49–50; Report to Bowles by a merchant, 25 December 1819, *The Navy and South America*, pp. 289–90.

78. V. G. Kiernan, 'Britain's First Contacts with Paraguay', *Atlante*, iii (1955), 171–91.

79. R. Antonio Ramos, *La política del Brasil en el Paraguay bajo la dictadura del Dr. Francia* (2nd ed., Buenos Aires–Asunción, 1959), pp. 45–64, 78–127; Williams, *op. cit.*, pp. 68–74.

80. Eugenio Friedmann, *Historia del azúcar en el Paraguay* (Asunción, 1966), pp. 101–3.

81. P. H. Box, *The Origins of the Paraguayan War* (Urbana, 1929); Richard Alan White, *Paraguay's Autonomous Revolution 1810–1840* (Albuquerque, 1978).

82. Robertson, *Letters on Paraguay*, ii, 34–5; Chaves, *Francia*, p. 169; Williams, *op. cit.*, p. 39.

83. Alipio Valencia Vega, *El indio en la independencia* (La Paz, 1962), pp. 190–6.

84. Charles W. Arnade, *The Emergence of the Republic of Bolivia* (Gainesville, 1957), pp. 32–56.

85. Arze Aguirre, *Participación popular en la independencia de Bolivia*, pp. 165–7, 197–203.

86. See *Antecedentes y Causa del Desaguadero*, in *Biblioteca de Mayo*, xiii, *passim*, for Castelli's Jacobin-type methods in Upper Peru.

87. Julio César Chaves, *Castelli, el adalid de mayo* (2nd ed., Buenos Aires, 1957), p. 273.

88. Best, *Historia de las guerras argentinas*, i, 195–202, 207–20, for military operations in Upper Peru, 1813–16.

89. Mitre, *Belgrano*, ii, 207.

90. See below, p. 168.

91. Mitre, *Belgrano*, ii, 331–2.

92. The Indians of Upper Peru numbered some one million in a population of 1.7 million; see Rosenblat, *La población indígena y el mestizaje en América*, i, 36–7, 199–200.

93. *Memoria de gobierno*, ii, 1–55.

94. Chaves, *Castelli*, pp. 224–7.

95. *Ibid.*, pp. 256–9.

96. Decree of Castelli, 25 May 1811, *Biblioteca de Mayo*, xiii, 11517–18.

97. Arze Aguirre, *Participación popular en la independencia de Bolivia*, pp. 160–65, 188–9; see below, pp. 165–6.

98. Valencia Vega, *op. cit.*, pp. 152–3.

99. Joaquín de la Pezuela, *Memoria de gobierno*, ed. V. Rodríguez Casado and G. Lohmann Villena (Seville, 1947), pp. xxx–xxxiii; see also *Memoria militar del General Pezuela, 1813–1815*, ed. Félix Denegri Luna (Lima, 1955).

FOUR   *Chile, Liberated and Liberator*

1. Francisco A. Encina, *Historia de Chile desde la prehistoria hasta 1891* (20 vols, Santiago, 1942–52), v, 159–69; for the census of 1813 see Raúl Silva Castro, *Egaña y la Patria Vieja 1810–1814* (Santiago, 1959), pp. 135–48.
2. Guillermo Feliú Cruz, *La abolición de la esclavitud en Chile* (Santiago, 1942), pp. 39–40.
3. Sergio Villalobos R., *El comercio y la crisis colonial. Un mito de la independencia* (Santiago, 1968), pp. 248, 258–63.
4. Hernán Ramírez Necochea, *Antecedentes económicos de la independencia de Chile* (2nd ed., Santiago, 1967), pp. 95–127.
5. Alberto Edwards Vives, *La fronda aristocrática. Historia política de Chile* (6th ed., Santiago, 1966), pp. 15–19, 22–3. For a classical, though perhaps too rigid, interpretation of Chilean society in terms of land, see G. M. McBride, *Chile: Land and Society* (New York, 1936), pp. 11–15.
6. Jean Borde and Mario Góngora, *Evolución de la propiedad rural en el Valle del Puangue* (2 vols, Santiago, 1956), i, 55–8.
7. Mario Góngora, *Origen de los "inquilinos" de Chile central* (Santiago, 1960), pp. 83–104; Borde and Góngora, *op. cit.*, pp. 74–6. On pursuit of aristocratic status see Domingo Amunátegui Solar, *La sociedad chilena del siglo XVIII. Mayorazgos y títulos de Castilla* (3 vols, Santiago, 1901–4).
8. *Representación*, 10 January 1796, Manuel de Salas, *Escritos de don Manuel de Salas y documentos relativos a el y a su familia* (3 vols, Santiago, 1910–14), i, 152.
9. Sergio Villalobos R., *Tradición y reforma en 1810* (Santiago, 1961), pp. 89–100; Jaime Eyzaguirre, *Ideario y ruta de la emancipación chilena* (Santiago, 1957), pp. 52–8.
10. Barbier, *Reform and Politics in Bourbon Chile*, p. 75.
11. Gonzalo Vial, 'La formación de nacionalidades hispano-americanas como causa de la independencia', *Boletín de la Academia Chilena de la Historia*, xxxiii (1966), 110–44; Vial, 'Historiografía de la independencia de Chile', *La Emancipación latinoamericana. Estudios bibliográficos* (Mexico, 1966), pp. 86–92; Villalobos, *Tradición y reforma*, pp. 56–71.
12. Villalobos, *El comercio y la crisis colonial*, pp. 222–35; Ramírez Necochea, *Antecedentes económicos*, pp. 86–94; Inge Wolff, 'Algunas consideraciones sobre causas económicas de la emancipación chilena', *Anuario de Estudios Americanos*, xi (1954), 169–96.

13. Simon Collier, *Ideas and Politics of Chilean Independence 1808–1833* (Cambridge, 1967), pp. 24–7.
14. Néstor Meza Villalobos, *La conciencia política chilena durante la monarquía* (Santiago, 1958), pp. 226–69.
15. Quoted by Collier, *op. cit.*, p. 207.
16. *Archivo de don Bernardo O'Higgins* (Santiago, 1946–   ), i, 251.
17. Villalobos, *Tradición y reforma*, pp. 157–60.
18. Jaime Eyzaguirre, *El conde de la Conquista* (Santiago, 1951).
19. Julio Alemparte, *El cabildo en Chile colonial* (Santiago, 1940), p. 405; Néstor Meza Villalobos, *La actividad política del reino de Chile entre 1806 y 1810* (Santiago, 1958), p. 94.
20. Villalobos, *Tradición y reforma*, p. 236.
21. Ricardo Donoso, *El Catecismo político cristiano* (Santiago, 1943), p. 100.
22. 'Memorias utiles para la historia de la revolución sud americana', *Arch. O'H*, i, 27; see also O'Higgins to Mackenna, 5 January 1811, *ibid.*, i, 63.
23. Jaime Eyzaguirre, *O'Higgins* (6th ed., Santiago, 1965), pp. 44–51. On O'Higgins see also Benjamín Vicuña Mackenna, *Vida de O'Higgins (Obras completas, v. Santiago, 1936); J. Kinsbruner, *Bernardo O'Higgins* (New York, 1968); S. Clissold, *Bernardo O'Higgins and the Independence of Chile* (London, 1968).
24. Vicuña Mackenna, *O'Higgins*, p. 129.
25. See below, pp. 149–50.
26. 'El primer congreso', *Arch. O'H*, i, 144–6; see also Julio Alemparte, *Carrera y Freire, fundadores de la República* (Santiago, 1963) pp. 96–100.
27. Alemparte, *Carrera y Freire*, pp. 39–41.
28. *Ibid.*, p. 41.
29. Eyzaguirre, *O'Higgins*, pp. 97–8.
30. On this controversial battle see Diego Barros Arana. *Historia jeneral de Chile* (16 vols, Santiago, 1884–1902), ix, 547–84.
31. Quoted by Alemparte, *Carrera y Freire*, p. 129.
32. Collier, *op. cit.*, pp. 129–78.
33. On the repressive counter-revolution and the prisoners of Juan Fernández see *Arch. O'H*, xix, *passim*; and Juan Egaña, *El Chileno consolado en los presidios, ibid.*, xx.
34. Villalobos, *Tradición y reforma*, pp. 237–41.
35. Bowles to Croker, 22 June 1817, *NSA*, pp. 202–3.
36. José P. Otero, *Historia del Libertador don José de San Martín* (4 vols, Buenos Aires, 1932), i, 234–60.

37. Mitre, *San Martín*, i, 246–94; Otero, *op. cit.*, i, 465–502.
38. Bowles to Croker, 14 February 1818, *NSA*, p. 227: Ricardo Piccirilli, *San Martín y la política de los pueblos* (Buenos Aires, 1957), pp. 219–20.
39. Mitre, *San Martín*, i, 441–98; Otero, *op. cit.*, i, 684–716.
40. Alfredo Estévez and Oscar Horacio Elía, *Aspectos económico-financieros de la campaña sanmartiniana* (Buenos Aires, 1961), pp. 97–128.
41. Miller, *Memoirs of General Miller*, i, 271–2.
42. See above, pp. 67–68.
43. Eyzaguirre, *O'Higgins*, pp. 137–52.
44. Pueyrredón to San Martín, 2 January, 18 January 1817, in Carlos A. Pueyrredón (ed.), *La Campaña de los Andes: cartas secretas e instrucciones reservadas de Pueyrredón a San Martín* (Buenos Aires, 1942), pp. 87–92; Eyzaguirre, *O'Higgins*, p. 153.
45. On the crossing of the Andes see the noble pages of Mitre, *San Martín*, i, 573–632.
46. San Martín to Castlereagh, 11 April 1818, Webster, *Britain and the Independence of Latin America*, i, 558.
47. San Martín to Bowles, 18 June 1817, *NSA*, p. 208; Piccirilli, *San Martín*, pp. 224–5.
48. O'Higgins to Chileans, 7 February 1817, *Arch. O'H*, vii, 123.
49. *Ibid.*, ii, 36.
50. José María de la Cruz, *Recuerdos de don Bernardo O'Higgins* (Santigo, 1960), p. 73.
51. John Miers, *Travels in Chile and La Plata* (2 vols, London, 1826), ii, 36–7.
52. Maria Graham, *Journal of a Residence in Chile during the year 1822* (London, 1824), p. 206.
53. Miller, *Memoirs of General Miller*, ii, 314.
54. Proclamation of the Independence of Chile, *Arch. O'H*, x, 342–4.
55. W. E. Browning, 'Joseph Lancaster, James Thomson, and the Lancasterian System of Mutual Instruction, with special reference to Hispanic America', *HAHR*, iv (1921), 49.
56. See below, pp. 150–54.
57. Robert M. Will, 'The Introduction of Classical Economics into Chile', *HAHR*, xliv (1964), 1–21, particularly p. 10.
58. O'Higgins to Terrada, 20 February 1812, *Arch. O'H*, i, 208; Eyzaguirre, *O'Higgins*, p. 78.
59. Decree of 12 November 1817, *Arch. O'H*, x, 222–3; Eyzaguirre, *O'Higgins*, pp. 170–1; Guillermo Feliú Cruz, *El pensamiento político de O'Higgins* (Santiago, 1954), pp. 25–6.

60. *Colección de historiadores y de documentos relativos a la independencia de Chile*, ed. E. Matta Vial and G. Feliú Cruz (37 vols, Santiago, 1900–54), xxv, 438.
61. Borde and Góngora, *Evolución de la propiedad rural en el Valle del Puangue*, i, 53–5, 115.
62. Jaime Eyzaguirre, 'La actitud religiosa de don Bernardo O'Higgins', *Historia*, i (1961), 7–46.
63. Maria Graham, *op. cit.*, pp. 207–8.
64. Kinsbruner, *O'Higgins*, p. 134.
65. O'Higgins to San Martín, 6 August 1821, *Arch. O'H*, viii, 137.
66. Eyzaguirre, *O'Higgins*, p. 323–33.
67. Bolívar to Santander, 14 February 1823, *Cartas*, iii, 146.
68. O'Higgins to San Martín, 12 January 1827, *Arch. O'H*, ix, 5–6.
69. Bidwell to White, 21 June 1830, Webster, *Britain and the Independence of Latin America*, i, 370.
70. Encina, *Historia de Chile*, x, 17–23.
71. Ramón Sotomayor Valdés, *Historia de Chile bajo el gobierno del General don Joaquín Prieto* (Santiago, 1962).
72. On Portales see Benjamín Vicuña Mackenna, *Don Diego Portales* (2 vols, Valparaiso, 1863); F. A. Encina, *Portales* (2 vols, Santiago, 1934); J. Kinsbruner, *Diego Portales: interpretative essays on the man and his times* (The Hague, 1967).
73. Quoted by Collier, *op. cit.*, p. 359.
74. Ricardo Donoso, *Desarrollo político y social de Chile desde la Constitución de 1833* (Santiago, 1942), pp. 9–15.
75. Kinsbruner, *Portales*, pp. 75–8.
76. See above, p. 128.
77. O'Higgins to Mackenna, 5 January 1811, *Arch. O'H*, i, 68.
78. Barros Arana, *op. cit.*, viii, 270.
79. Ramírez Necochea, *Antecedentes económicos*, pp. 126–31.
80. Decree of 21 February 1811, in Villalobos, *El comercio y la crisis colonial*, pp. 373–6.
81. Will, *op. cit.*, pp. 1–21.
82. *Gazeta Ministerial*, 12 August 1820, *Arch. O'H*, xiv, 14; Nugent to Canning, 17 March 1825, *Consular Reports*, pp. 90–1.
83. Estévez and Elía, *op. cit.*, pp. 185–6.
84. See *NSA*, pp. 211–353.
85. Report to Bowles by a merchant, 25 December 1819, *NSA*, p. 291.
86. Basil Hall, *Extracts from a Journal written on the coasts of Chili, Peru, and Mexico in the years 1820, 1821, 1822* (3rd ed., 2 vols, Edinburgh, 1824), ii, 55–7, 60–1.

87. *Gazeta Ministerial,* 29 April 1820, *Arch. O'H,* xiii, 393–4, on export of copper in English vessels.
88. Nugent to Canning, 17 March 1825, *Consular Reports,* pp. 90–106.
89. Barros Arana, *op. cit.,* xiii, 747–63.
90. *Ibid.,* xv, 69–78; Nugent to Canning, 17 March 1825, *Consular Reports,* pp. 99–101.
91. Edwards, *La fronda aristocrática,* pp. 33–6; Eyzaguirre, *O'Higgins,* p. 50.
92. Edwards, *op. cit.,* pp. 58–60.
93. Hall, *op. cit.,* i, 26–8.
94. Tomás Guevara, 'Los Araucanos en la revolución de la independencia', *Anales de la Universidad de Chile,* cxxvii (1910), 219.
95. Miller, *Memoirs of General Miller,* i, 103.
96. *Ibid.,* i, 288–9, Benavides himself was a gangster who flourished on the lawless Indian frontier until his capture and execution in 1822; see *ibid.,* i, 246–51; Hall, *op. cit.,* i, 321–75; Barros Arana, *op. cit.,* xii, 97–102, xiii, 401–38.
97. Decrees of 3 June 1818, 4 March 1819, *Arch. O'H,* xi, 81, xii, 109–10.
98. Ricketts to Canning, 27 December 1826, *Consular Reports,* p. 169.
99. Law of 11 October 1811, *Arch. O'H,* xv, 223; Feliú Cruz, *La abolición de la esclavitud en Chile,* pp. 51–3.
100. *Ibid.,* pp. 83–5.
101. O'Higgins did not personally challenge slavery: he had numerous slaves on his Peruvian sugar hacienda of Montalván; see Eyzaguirre, *O'Higgins,* pp. 414–15.
102. Feliú Cruz, *La abolición de la esclavitud en Chile,* pp. 96–102.
103. *Ibid.,* pp. 142–4.
104. *Ibid.,* p. 160.
105. Borde and Góngora, *Evolución de la propiedad rural en al Valle del Puangue,* i, 76.
106. Fredrick B. Pike, 'Aspects of Class Relations in Chile, 1850–1960', *HAHR,* xliii (1963), 14–33.

FIVE   *Peru—the Ambiguous Revolution*

1. Mitre, *Historia de San Martín,* ii, 475–7.
2. The census of 1795 gave a total of 1,115,207, broken down as follows: Spaniards (comprising a minority of *peninsulares,* a majority of creoles) 140,890; Indians 648,615; mestizos

244,313; free Negroes 41,004; slaves 40,385. See D.N. Cook, 'La población indígena en el Perú colonial', *América colonial*. *Población y economía (Anuario del Instituto de Investigaciones Históricos*, 8, Rosario, 1965), 73–110; Rosenblat, *La población indígena y el mestizaje en América*, i, 36–7; Fisher, *Government and Society in Colonial Peru*, pp. 251–3.

3. Concolorcorvo, *El Lazarillo de ciegos caminantes desde Buenos Aires hasta Lima* (1773) (*Biblioteca de autores españoles*, 122, Madrid, 1959), p. 379.

4. Heraclio Bonilla and others, *La Independencia en al Perú* (2nd ed., Lima, 1981), pp. 88–92.

5. López Aldana to Castelli, 10 March 1811, quoted in Pablo Macera, *Tres etapas en el desarrollo de la conciencia nacional* (Lima, 1955), pp. 88–9.

6. Timothy E. Anna, *The Fall of the Royal Government in Peru* (Lincoln, Nebraska, 1979), pp. 29–34; Mark A. Burkholder, *Politics of a Colonial Career: José Baquijano and the Audiencia of Lima* (Albuquerque, 1980), pp. 79–80, 84–5.

7. See above, p. 33; see also Jorge Basadre, *La promesa de la vida peruana y otros ensayos* (Lima, 1958); José A. de la Puente Candamo, *La idea de la Comunidad Peruana y el testimonio de los precursores* (Lima, 1956).

8. *El Argos Constitucional*, quoted in Macera, *Tres etapas*, p. 118.

9. John Preston Moore, *The Cabildo in Peru under the Bourbons* (Durham, N.C. 1966), pp. 200–4.

10. See Fisher, *Government and Society in Colonial Peru*, pp. 124–55.

11. Guillermo Céspedes del Castillo, 'Lima y Buenos Aires. Repercusiones económicas y políticas de la creación del virreinato del Plata', *Anuario de estudios americanos*, iii(1946), 677–874.

12. B.M., Add. 13981, ff. 24v–25, 'Noticias del comercio del Perú', 1784.

13. Francisco Gil de Taboada, *Memoria de gobierno*, M.A. Fuentes (ed.), *Memorias de los virreyes que han gobernado el Perú* (6 vols, Lima, 1859), vi, 1–353, app. 12–13, table 5.

14. John Fisher, *Minas y mineros en el Perú colonial 1776–1824* (Lima, 1977), pp. 213–33.

15. Moore, op. cit., pp. 208–9.

16. Quoted by Fisher, *Government and Society in Colonial Peru*, p. 154.

17. Hardy to Croker, 17 May 1821, *NSA*, p. 331.

18. Armando Nieto Vélez, 'Contribución a la historia del fidelismo en el Perú (1808–1810)', *Boletín del Instituto Riva-Agüero*, iv (1958–60), 9–146.

19. Fisher, *Government and Society in Colonial Peru*, pp. 203–4.

20. Fernando Díaz Venteo, *Campañas militares del virrey Abascal* (Seville, 1948), pp. 81–5.

21. José Fernando de Abascal y Sousa, *Memoria de gobierno*, ed. Vicente Rodríguez Casado and José Antonio Calderón Quijano (2 vols, Seville, 1944), i, 198.

22. *Ibid.*, ii, 82.

23. Quoted by Nieto Vélez, 'Fidelismo en el Perú, *op. cit.*, p. 139.

24. Rubén Vargas Ugarte, *Historia del Perú. Emancipación (1809–1825)* (Buenos Aires, 1958), pp. 32–8; John Fisher, 'Royalism, Regionalism, and Rebellion in Colonial Peru, 1808–1825', *HAHR*, 59, 2(1979), 250–52.

25. Fisher, *Government and Society in Colonial Peru*, p. 213.

26. Vargas Ugarte, *Emancipación*, p. 113; James F. King, 'The Colored Castes and American Representation in the Cortes of Cadiz', *HAHR*, xxxiii(1953), 33–64.

27. *Ibid.*, p. 44.

28. Moore, *op. cit.*, 213–14.

29. Abascal, *Memoria de gobierno*, i, 440, 447.

30. Scarlett O'Phelan Godoy, *Rebellions and Revolts in Eighteenth Century Peru and Upper Peru* (Cologne, 1985), pp. 284–98; Bonilla, *La Independencia en el Perú*, pp. 13–69.

31. O'Phelan, *Rebellions and Revolts*, pp. 213–42.

32. Quoted by Lewin, *La rebelión de Túpac Amaru*, pp. 402–3.

33. See 'Population of the Viceroyalty of Peru in 1795', in Fisher, *Government and Society in Colonial Peru'*, pp. 251–3.

34. L. E. Fisher, *The Last Inca Revolt, 1780–1783 (Norman, 1966)*, p. 107; Alipio Valencia Vega, *El indio en la independencia* (La Paz, 1962), pp. 36–7.

35. Jorge Cornejo Bouroncle, *Pumacahua. La revolución del Cuzco de 1814. Estudio documentado* (Cuzco, 1956), pp. 64–72; Valcarcel, *La rebelión de Túpac Amaru*, p. 50.

36. Cornejo Bouroncle, *op. cit.*, pp. 212–13, 181–6; José Manuel Valega, *La gesta emancipadora del Perú* (12 vols, Lima, 1940–3), iii; Juan José Vega, *La emancipación frente al indio peruano* (Lima, 1958).

37. Fisher, *Government and Society in Colonial Peru*, pp. 78–99.

38. B.M.,Eg. 1813, f. 571–4, Fray Hypólito, Bishop of Maynas, to minister of colonies, 1 June 1813.
39. John Fisher, 'Royalism, Regionalism, and Rebellion in Colonial Peru, 1808–1815', *HAHR*, 59, 2(1979), 232–257.
40. Manuel Pardo, Regent of the audiencia of Cuzco, 'Memoria de la insurrección del Cuzco', April 1816, Cornejo Bouroncle, *op. cit.*, 650–67.
41. M. de Odriozola (ed.), *Documentos históricos del Perú* (10 vols, Lima, 1863–79), iii, 244–6, 256–80.
42. L. A. Eguiguren, *La revolución de 1814* (Lima, 1914), pp. 47–77.
43. Abascal, *Memoria de gobierno*, ii, 210; Cornejo Bouroncle, *op. cit.*, 369–89.
44. *Ibid.*, pp. 403–34. Moscoso was a creole, a native of Arequipa.
45. *Ibid.*, p. 441.
46. Fisher, *Government and Society in Colonial Peru*, p. 230.
47. Odriozola, *op. cit.*, iii, 77.
48. Proclamation of Pío Tristán y Moscoso, Cornejo Bouroncle, *op. cit.*, pp. 479–82.
49. Pardo, 'Memoria de la insurrección del Cuzco', *ibid.*, pp. 664–5.
50. On the conservatism of the creoles see L. A. Euiguren (ed.), *Guerra separatista del Perú. Unanue, Arequipa y la historia creadora* (Lima, 1955).
51. Quoted by Vargas Ugarte, *Emancipación*, p. 127.
52. Pezuela, *Memoria de gobierno*, Rodríguez Casado and Lohmann Villena, p. xxiv.
53. Vargas Ugarte *Emancipación*, pp. 165–9.
54. Moore, *op. cit.*, p. 230; Pezuela, *Memoria de gobierno*, pp. 279–80.
55. Report of Pezuela, 13 November 1818, in J. A. de la Puente Candamo, *San Martín y el Perú* (Lima, 1948), p. 9.
56. Mitre, *Historia de San Martín*, ii, 528–97.
57. Bowles to Croker, 1 March 1817, *NSA*, p. 184; Donald E. Worcester, *Sea Power and Chilean Independence* (Gainesville, 1962), pp. 17–35.
58. Bowles to Croker, 3 April 1819, *NSA*, pp. 265–66.
59. Estévez and Elía, *Aspectos económico-financieros de la campaña sanmartiniana*, p. 155; Fritz C. Hoffman, 'The Financing of San Martín's Expeditions', *HAHR*, xxxii (1952), 634–8, who suggests that taking the two expeditions together Argentina and Chile contributed from 1.5 to 2 million pesos each; Joaquín Pérez, 'Las dificultades económicas de la

alianza argentino-chileno y sus consecuencias', *Trabajos y Comunicaciones,* 17 (1967), 153-83.

60. Estévez and Elía *op. cit.,* pp. 168-79.
61. R. A. Humphreys (ed.), 'James Paroissien's Notes on the Liberating Expedition to Peru', *HAHR,* xxxi (1951), 254-68.
62. August 1821, in Puente Candamo, *San Martín y el Perú,* p. 3.
63. Bowles to Croker, 10 June 1818, *NSA,* p. 239.
64. San Martín to Torre Tagle, 19 January 1821, Javier Ortiz de Zevallos (ed.), *Correspondencia de San Martín y Torre Tagle* (Lima, 1963), p. 34.
65. On the political thought of San Martín see Piccirilli, *San Martín y la política de los pueblos,* pp. 239-300.
66. Staples to Hamilton, 25 May 1817, Webster, *Britain and the Independence of Latin America,* i, 553.
67. San Martín to Earl of Fife, 9 December 1817, *ibid.,* i, 557.
68. Bowles to Croker, 14 February 1818, *NSA,* p. 226.
69. Bowles to Croker, 14 February 1818, *ibid.,* pp. 226-7.
70. San Martín to Torre Tagle, 13 January 1821, Ortiz de Zevallos, *op. cit.,* p. 32.
71. Puente Candamo, *San Martín y el Perú,* pp. 12-14; Vargas Ugarte, *Emancipación,* pp. 186-92.
72. Hall, *Journal,* i, 74.
73. Observers differed on the size of the royalist army but they agreed that Peruvians were in the majority: 'Out of the royal army of 6 or 7,000 men, not more than 2,500 are European'. Hardy to Croker, 22 March 1821, *NSA,* p. 326.
74. Interview with San Martín, 25 June 1821, Hall, *Journal,* i, 215-16.
75. San Martín to Torre Tagle, 20 November 1820, Ortiz de Zevallos, *op. cit.,* pp. 3-4.
76. Vargas Ugarte, *Emancipación,* pp. 239-44; on Torre Tagle see Manuel de Mendiburu, *Biografías de Generales Republicanos,* ed. Félix Denegri Luna (Lima, 1963), pp. 364-87.
77. Miller, *Memoirs of General Miller,* i, 295-7.
78. Puente Candamo, *San Martín y el Perú,* pp. 19-23, 203-12; Vargas Ugarte, *Emancipación,* pp. 273-82; César Pacheco Vélez, 'Sobre el monarquismo de San Martín', *Anuario de Estudios Americanos,* ix (1952), 457-80.
79. Miller, *op. cit.,* i, 302-3.
80. Anna, *The Fall of the Royal Government in Peru,* pp. 176-81.
81. Mitre, *Historia de San Martín,* iii, 65-92.
82. Hall, *op. cit.,* i, 222-3.

83. *Ibid.*, 226.
84. Hardy to Croker, 14 September 1821, *NSA*, pp. 347–8.
85. Hall *op. cit.*, ii, 70–2.
86. Miller, *op. cit.*, i, 372.
87. On the protectorate see Otero, *Historia del Libertador*, iii, 341–80, 512–49.
88. On the social policy of the new regime, see below pp. 275–77.
89. Miller, *op. cit.*, i, 369–70.
90. Hall, *op. cit.*, ii, 87–8: on the influence of Monteagudo in Peru see Vedia y Mitre, *La vida de Monteagudo*, iii, 61–108.
91. Puente Candamo, *San Martín y el Perú*, pp. 19–23, 34–42.
92. Humphreys, *Liberation in South America*, pp. 99–110, 116–32: Puente Candamo, *San Martín y el Perú*, pp. 73–145; Piccirilli, *San Martín y la política de los pueblos*, pp. 257–74, 283–9, 464–78.
93. Miller, *op. cit.*, i, 370–1; in 1825 congress passed a resolution abolishing the order.
94. Reproduced in Miller, *op. cit.*, i, 360–1.
95. *Ibid.*, 366.
96. Raúl Rivera Serna, *Los guerrilleros del Centro en la emancipación peruana* (Lima, 1958), pp. 20–1, 80–92, 108–13.
97. Miller, *op. cit.*, i, 377–8, ii, 138–40.
98. *Ibid.*, i, 365.
99. Humphreys, *Consular Reports*, pp. 128–9.
100. Estévez and Elía, *op. cit.*, pp. 207–10.
101. Carlos Camprubí Alcázar, *El Banco de la Emancipación* (Lima, 1960), pp. 27–31.
102. Francisco Javier Luna Pizarro, *Escritos Políticos*, ed. Alberto Tauro (Lima, 1959).
103. P.R.O., F.O. 61/2, Letter in a London Newspaper, dated Lima, 20 May 1823.
104. P.R.O., F.O. 61/1, Captain Prescott to Commodore Hardy, 23 August 1822; Miller, *op. cit.*, i, 410–11.
105. Otero, *op. cit.*, iii, 653–89.
106. On the Guayaquil interview, one of the most controversial and least documented events of the war of independence, see Ernesto de la Cruz and others, *La entrevista de Guayaquil* (Madrid, 1917); Vicente Lecuna, *La entrevista de Guayaquil* (Caracas, 1948), and 'Bolívar and San Martín at Guayaquil' *HAHR*, xxxi (1951), 369–93; Gerhard Masur, 'The Conference of Guayaquil', *HAHR*, xxxi (1951), 189–229, the most convincing interpretation; A. J. Pérez Amuchástegui, *La "carta de Lafond" y la preceptiva historiográfica* (Córdoba, 1962), and

Ideología y acción de San Martín (Buenos Aires, 1966), pp. 55–7.

107. Vedia y Mitre, *op. cit.*, iii, 111–26.
108. Mitre, *Historia de San Martín*, iii, 649–74.
109. San Martín to Guido, Brussels, 18 December 1826, Museo Mitre, *Documentos del Archivo de San Martín* (12 vols, Buenos Aires, 1910–11), vi, 503.
110. On Gamarra and Santa Cruz see Mendiburu, *op. cit.*, pp. 88–136, 328–63.
111. Miller, *op. cit.*, ii, 61.
112. *La causa de la emancipación del Perú*, pp. 419–31.

Six   *Venezuela, the Violent Revolution*

1. F. Depons, *Viaje a la parte oriental de Tierra Firme en la América meridional* (2 vols, Caracas, 1960), ii, 14–92; Federico Brito Figueroa, *Historia económica y social de Venezuela* (2 vols, Caracas, 1966), i, 63–121, 160.
2. A. von Humboldt, *Viaje a las regiones equinocciales del Nuevo Continente* (5 vols, Caracas, 1956), ii, 244.
3. John V. Lombardi, *People and Places in Colonial Venezuela* (Bloomington, 1976), p. 132; Miguel Izard, *Series estadísticas para la historia de Venezuela* (Mérida, 1970), p. 9. The remaining percentage were Indians.
4. F. Brito Figueroa, *La estructura económica de Venezuela colonial*, (Caracas, 1963), pp. 141–99.
5. *Ibid.*, p. 176.
6. Humboldt, *Viaje a las regiones equinocciales*, iii, 61.
7. Ildefonso Leal (ed.), *Documentos del Real Consulado de Caracas* (Caracas, 1964), pp. 15–23; Arcila Farías, *Economía colonial de Venezuela*, pp. 217–19.
8. Laureano Vallenilla Lanz, *Cesarismo democrático (Obras completas, 1, Caracas, 1983), p. 50.
9. See above, p. 22.
10. Representation dated 28 November 1796, in F. Brito Figueroa, *Las insurrecciones de los esclavos negros en la sociedad colonial venezolana* (Caracas, 1961), pp. 22–3.
11. F. J. Bernal, 'Las autoridades coloniales venezolanas ante la propaganda revolucionaria en 1795', *Boletín del Archivo Nacional*, xxxii (1945), 65–72.
12. Miguel Acosta Saignes, 'Los negros cimarrones de Venezuela', *El Movimiento Emancipador de Hispanoamérica*, Actas y ponencias (Madrid, 1961), iii, 351–98, and the same author's

Vida de los esclavos negros en Venezuela (Caracas, 1967).

13. I. Leal, 'La aristocracia criolla venezolana y el código negrero de 1789', *Revista de Historia*, ii (Caracas, 1961), 61-81.

14. Mariano Arcaya, city attorney of cabildo of Coro, in Brito, *Insurrecciones de los esclavos negros*, pp. 61-2.

15. Pedro M. Arcaya, *Insurrección de los negros en la serranía de Coro* (Caracas, 1949), p. 38; Brito, *Insurrecciones de los esclavos negros*, pp. 41-88.

16. For *Las Ordenanzas* see Pedro Grases, *La conspiración de Gual y España y el ideario de la independencia* (Caracas, 1949), pp. 175-6.

17. Document signed by Tovar, Blanco, Ponte, Toro, Gil and others, 4 August 1797, cited by Brito, *Ensayos de historia social venezolana* (Caracas, 1960), pp. 199-200.

18. Instituto Panamericano de Geografía e Historia, *Conjuración de 1808 en Caracas* (2 vols., Caracas, 1969), i, 55-92.

19. Instituto Panamericano de Geografía y Historia, *El 19 de Abril de 1810* (Caracas, 1957), pp. 45-7.

20. *Textos oficiales de la Primera República de Venezuela* (*Biblioteca de la Academia Nacional de la Historia*, 1-2, 2 vols, Caracas, 1959), i, 99-103.

21. Intendant Vicente Basadre, report of 4 July 1810, in *Causas de infidencia* (*BANH*, 31-2, 2 vols, Caracas, 1960), i, 128.

22. W. S. Robertson, *The Life of Miranda* (2 vols, Chapel Hill, 1929), ii, 90-92, 272; Láutico García, S. J., *Francisco de Miranda y el Antiguo Régimen español* (Caracas, 1961), pp. 395-425.

23. Simón Bolívar, *Proclamas y Discursos del Libertador*, ed. Vicente Lecuna (Caracas, 1939), p. 3.

24. Acta de la Independencia, in *La Constitución Federal de Venezuela de 1811* (*BANH*, 6, Caracas, 1959), pp. 89-96.

25. Ibid., pp. 151-211; José Gil Fortoul, *Historia constitucional de Venezuela* (2nd ed., 3 vols, Caracas, 1930), i, 217-40; C. Parra-Pérez, *Historia de la Primera República de Venezuela* (*BANH*, 19-20, 2 vols, Caracas, 1959). ii, 131.

26. *Textos oficiales de la Primera República*, ii, 95.

27. Constitution of 1811, IX, 203, *Constitución Federal*, p. 205.

28. Constitution of 1811, II, ii, 26, *ibid.*, pp. 159-60.

29. Decree of 26 June 1811, *Textos oficiales de la Primera República*, ii, 42-3.

30. Narciso Coll y Prat, *Memoriales sobre la independencia de Venezuela* (*BANH*, 23, Caracas, 1959), pp. 59-60, 63-7; Germán Carrera Damas, 'Algunos problemas relativos a la

formación del Estado en la Segunda República venezolana', *Tres temas de historia* (Caracas, 1961), pp. 96–100.

31. Manifesto to the Nations of the World, Simón Bolívar, *Obras completas*, ed. Vicente Lecuna and Esther Barret de Nazaris (3 vols, La Habana, 1950), iii, 574.

32. Parra-Pérez, *Historia de la Primera República*, ii, 77–89, 119.

33. José Domingo Díaz, *Recuerdos sobre la rebelión de Caracas* (*BANH*, 38, Caracas, 1961), pp. 98–9.

34. For a useful, if conventional, discussion of the causes of the collapse of the first republic see Parra-Pérez, *Historia de la Primera República*, ii, 465–86.

35. José Francisco Heredia, *Memorias del Regente Heredia* (Madrid, 1916).

36. On Bolívar, from a vast bibliography, see Gerhard Masur, *Simon Bolivar* (Albuquerque, 1948), a scholarly and eloquent work, but now dated; Salvador de Madariaga, *Bolívar* (reprinted, London, 1968) is an anti-Bolivarian polemic; Victor Andrés Belaunde, *Bolivar and the Political Thought of the Spanish American Revolution* (Baltimore, 1938) studies Bolívar's political ideas in the context of the whole independence movement; J. L. Salcedo-Bastardo, *Visión y revisión de Bolívar* (Caracas, 1957) specializes in the social and economic aspects of Bolívar's thought; Vicente Lecuna, *Crónica razonada de las guerras de Bolívar* (3 vols, New York, 1950) is a detailed narrative of Bolívar's campaigns; David Bushnell, *The Liberator, Simón Bolívar. Man and Image* (New York, 1970) is an expert work of reference.

37. Jamaica Letter, 6 September 1815, Simón Bolívar, *Cartas del Libertador*, ed. Vicente Lecuna (12 vols, Caracas, 1929–59), i, 183–4, 190–6.

38. R. A. Humphreys (ed.), *The 'Detached Recollections' of General D. F. O'Leary* (London, 1969), p. 28.

39. *Obras completas*, ii, 773, 1078, 1236.

40. Cartagena Manifesto, 15 December 1812, *Proclamas y Discursos*, pp. 11–22.

41. D. F. O'Leary, *Memorias del General Daniel Florencio O'Leary. Narración* (3 vols, Caracas, 1952), i, 128–9.

42. On this, the *Campaña admirable,* see Lecuna, *Crónica razonada*, i, 1–73.

43. Manifesto to the Nations of the World, 24 February 1814, *Proclamas y Discursos*, pp. 96–7.

44. Proclamation, 8 June, 1813, *Proclamas y Discursos*, p. 31.

45. O'Leary, *Narración*, i, 158–60.
46. Manifesto of Carúpano, 7 September 1814, *Proclamas y Discursos*, p. 112.
47. *Ibid.*, p. 112; O'Leary, *Narración*, i, 201–2.
48. Cristóbal Mendoza to Prior of Consulado, 29 April 1814, in Lecuna, 'Documentos de carácter político, militar y administrativo relativos al período de la Guerra a Muerte', *Boletín de la Academia Nacional de la Historia*, no. 69 (1935), 314.
49. Quoted by Carrera Damas, 'Segunda República', *Tres temas de historia*, p. 143.
50. O'Leary, *Narración*, i, 195–7, 225–36; *Detached Recollections*, pp. 34–6.
51. Lecuna, *Crónica razonada*, i, 225–85, 333.
52. For interpretations which read great social significance into the policy of Boves see Lecuna, *Crónica razonada*, i, 129–30, and Juan Uslar Pietri, *Historia de la rebelión popular de 1814* (Caracas, 1962). For a more realistic interpretation, on which the present account is based, see Germán Carrera Damas, *Materiales para el estudio de la cuestión agraria en Venezuela 1800–1830, vol. I* (Caracas, 1964), the introductory study of which has been separately published as *Boves, Aspectos socioeconómicos de su acción historica* (Caracas, 1968).
53. Carrera Damas, *Cuestión agraria*, pp. cxviii–cxix.
54. *Textos oficiales de la Primera República*, ii, 143–205.
55. Carrera Damas, *Cuestión agraria*, pp. 83–4. Compare this with developments in the Argentine pampas; see above, pp. 80–3.
56. Margaret L. Woodward, 'The Spanish Army and the Loss of America, 1810–1824', *HAHR*, xlviii (1968), 586–607.
57. Masur, *Bolívar*, p. 244.
58. José Manuel Restrepo, *Historia de la revolución de la República de Colombia* (4 vols, Besanzon, 1858), ii, 301–2.
59. Stephen K. Stoan, *Pablo Morillo and Venezuela, 1815–1820* (Columbus, 1974), p. 163; O'Leary, *Narración*, i, 297–8.
60. Jamaica Letter, 6 September 1815, *Cartas*, i, 183–4, 190–4, 195–6.
61. Paul Verna, *Pétion y Bolívar* (Caracas, 1969), pp. 157–61; Lecuna, *Crónica razonada*, i, 418; Masur, *Bolívar*, pp. 280–6.
62. Masur, *Bolívar*, pp. 293–5.
63. C. Parra-Pérez, *Mariño y la independencia de Venezuela* (5 vols, Madrid, 1954–7), ii, 141–2, 170–8, 207–27.
64. José Domingo Díaz, *Recuerdos sobre la rebelión de Caracas*, p. 336.

65. Lecuna, *Crónica razonada*, ii, 36–58.
66. O'Leary, *Narración*, i, 408, 432–9; see also Parra-Pérez, *Mariño*, ii, 385, 389–420; Masur, *Bolivar*, p. 311.
67. *Obras completas*, ii, 773, 1105.
68. Manifesto to the Peoples of Venezuela, 5 August 1817, *Proclamas y Discursos*, pp. 160–7.
69. Proclamation, 17 October 1817, *Proclamas y Discursos*, pp. 170–1.
70. Dispatch of José Ceballos, 22 July 1815, in James F. King, 'A royalist view of the colored castes in the Venezuelan War of Independence', *HAHR*, xxxiii (1953), 526–37.
71. *Obras completas*, i, 435; see Salcedo Bastardo, op. cit., pp. 105ff.
72. *Proclamas y Discursos*, pp. 148–9, 150–1; Simón Bolívar, *Decretos del Libertador* (3 vols, Caracas, 1961), i, 55–6.
73. José de Austria, *Bosquejo de la historia militar de Venezuela* (BANH, 29–30, 2 vols, Caracas, 1960), ii, 448.
74. Proclamation, 17 July 1817, *Proclamas y Discursos*, pp. 157–8.
75. O'Leary, *Narración*, i, 451–2; Lecuna, *Crónica razonada*, ii, 122–30.
76. José Antonio Páez, *Autobiografía del General Páez* (2 vols, New York, 1946), i, 139.
77. O'Leary, *Detached Recollections*, p. 20.
78. Páez, *Autobiografía*, i, 7; Correspondencia de Páez, September 1819, January 1820, in Eloy G. González, *Al margen de la epopeya* (Caracas, 1946), p. 67.
79. See below, pp. 221–2.
80. O'Leary, *Narración*, i, 461; Bolívar to Brion, 15 May 1818, *Cartas*, ii, 8.
81. O'Leary, *Detached Recollections*, p. 39; Lecuna, *Crónica razonada*, ii, 144–59.
82. Angostura Address, 15 February 1819, *Proclamas y Discursos*, pp. 202–35; O'Leary, *Narracion*, i, 495–528.
83. Gil Fourtol, *op. cit.*, i, 381–99.
84. F. Montenegro y Colón, *Historia de Venezuela* (BANH, 26–7, 2 vols, Caracas, 1959–60), ii, 9–10; O'Leary, *Narracion*, i, 545–6; Lecuna, *Crónica razonada*, ii, 300–2; Masur, *Bolivar*, pp. 366–70; J. Nucete-Sardi *et al*, *La campaña libertadora de 1819*, tomo I (Caracas, 1969), pp. 5–25.
85. Bolívar to Páez, 19 August 1818, in Lecuna, *Crónica razonada*, ii, 233–4.
86. O'Leary, *Detached Recollections*, pp. 21–2, 54.
87. O'Leary, *Narración*, i, 555; see also Alfred Hasbrouck, *Foreign*

Legionaries in the Liberation of Spanish South America (New York, 1928), pp. 190–217.

88. Lecuna, Crónica razonada, ii, 307–49; Nucete-Sardi, op. cit., pp. 75–233; on the liberation in its New Granadan context see below pp. 243–4.

89. Lecuna, Crónica razonada, ii, 463–66.

90. O'Leary, Narración, ii, 58.

91. Proclamation, 17 April 1821, Proclamas y Discursos, pp. 256–7.

92. O'Leary, Narración, ii, 79–92; Lecuna, Crónica razonada, iii, 14–52.

93. J. M. Oropeza to D. Franco, 18 June 1814, in Restrepo, Historia de la revolución, ii, 271.

94. Consulado de Caracas, sesión de 27 de mayo de 1816, Leal, Documentos del Real Consulado de Caracas, p. 184.

95. Gazeta de Caracas, 6 December 1814, in Brito, Historia económica y social de Venezuela, i, 221.

96. David Bushnell, The Santander Regime in Gran Colombia (Newark, Del., 1954), pp. 119–20, 129.

97. Carrera Damas, Cuestión agraria, pp. lix–lxxiii.

98. Sir Robert Ker Porter, Caracas Diary, ed. W. Dupouy (Caracas, 1966), pp. 69–70, 1 March 1826.

99. Tupper to Canning, 21 February 1824, Humphreys, Consular Reports, pp. 273–7.

100. José Rafael Revenga, La hacienda pública de Venezuela en 1828–1830 (Caracas, 1953), pp. 231–2, report of 22 August 1829.

101. Ker Porter, Diary, 8 December 1825, p. 34.

102. Revenga, 5 May 1829, Hacienda pública de Venezuela, pp. 95–6.

103. Revenga, 7 August 1829, ibid., p. 203.

104. Miguel Izard, El miedo a la revolución. La lucha por la libertad en Venezuela (1777–1830) (Madrid, 1979), p. 46; Consulado de Caracas, 14 January 1815, in Leal, Documentos del Real Consulado de Caracas, p. 180, estimated Caracas as 31,870 in 1810 and 11,720 in 1815.

105. Izard, Series estadísticas, pp. 9, 13, 15.

106. Salcedo-Bastardo, op. cit., pp. 185–97; Lecuna, Crónica razonada, 11, 83–4; Bushnell, Santander Regime, pp. 276–9.

107. Decretos del Libertador, i, 89–92; Carrera Damas, Cuestión agraria, pp. 204–5.

108. Bolívar to Santander, 30 May 1820, Cartas, i, 229–30.

109. Bolívar to Gual, 24 May 1821, Cartas, ii, 348–9.

110. John Lynch, 'Bolívar and the Caudillos', *HAHR*, 63, 1(1983), 3–35.
111. Ker Porter, *Diary*, 11–12 November 1832, pp. 674–89, 698.
112. Carrera Damas, *Cuestión agraria*, pp. cii–cxvi.
113. O'Leary, *Detached Recollections*, p. 51; see above, p. 212.
114. Bolívar to Santander, 30 May 1820, *Cartas*, i, 229.
115. Harold H. Bierck, 'The Struggle for Abolition in Gran Colombia', *HAHR*, xxxiii (1953), 365–86. John V. Lombardi, *The Decline and Abolition of Negro Slavery in Venezuela* 1820–1854 (Westport, 1971), pp. 48–53.
116. Bolívar to Páez, 26 November 1827, to Briceño Méndez, 7 May 1828, *Cartas*, vii, 85, 257.
117. Sutherland to Bidwell, 18 December 1827, P.R.O., F.O. 18/46.
118. Revenga, *Hacienda pública de Venezuela*, p. 106.
119. John V. Lombardi, 'Manumission, *Manumisos*, and *Aprendizaje* in Republican Venezuela', *HAHR*, xlix (1969), 656–78.
120. Lombardi, *Decline and Abolition of Negro Slavery in Venezuela*, pp. 139–41.
121. Germán Carrera Damas, 'Para un esquema sobre la participación de las clases populares en el movimiento nacional de independencia en Venezuela a comienzos del siglo xix', *Historiografía marxista venezolana y otros temas* (Caracas, 1967), p. 86.
122. Sutherland to Bidwell, 28 July 1827, Maracaibo, P.R.O., F.O. 18/46.
123. Sutherland to Canning, 11 March 1824, P.R.O., F.O. 18/8.
124. Bolívar to Santander, 7 April 1825, *Cartas*, iv, 307.
125. Revenga, 27 June 1829, *Hacienda pública de Venezuela*, p. 157.
126. Constitution of 1830, V, 14, VII, 27, Luis Mariñas Otero (ed.), *Las constituciones de Venezuela* (Madrid, 1965), pp. 225–7.
127. José Antonio Páez, *Autobiografía del General José Antonio Páez* (2 vols., Caracas, 1973), i, 416.

SEVEN *Liberation, a New Site in Colombia*

1. Anthony McFarlane, 'The Transition from Colonialism in Colombia, 1819–1876', in Christopher Abel and Colin M. Lewis, (eds.), *Latin America, Economic Imperialism and the State* (London, 1985), pp. 101–24, provides the best introduction to the period.
2. José María Ots Capdequí, *El régimen de la tierra en la América*

Española durante el período colonial (Ciudad Trujillo, 1946), pp. 119–53. Hermes Tovar Pinzón, *Grandes empresas agrícolas y ganaderas. Su desarrollo en el siglo xviii* (Bogotá, 1980), pp. 17–39.

3. Luis Ospina Vásquez, *Industria y protección en Colombia 1810–1930* (Medellín, 1955), pp. 9–13.

4. José Manuel Pérez Ayala, *Antonio Caballero y Góngora, virrey y arzobispo de Sante Fe 1723–1796* (Bogotá, 1951), *Relación*, table A; Jaime Jaramillo Uribe, 'Mestizaje y diferenciación social en el Nuevo Reino de Granada en la segunda mitad del siglo XVIII', *Anuario Colombiano de Historia Social y de la Cultura*, ii (1965), 21–48, particularly p. 25.

5. O. Fals Borda, 'Indian congregations in the New Kingdom of Granada: land tenure aspects, 1595–1850', *The Americas*, xiii (1957), 331–51, particularly pp. 342–3.

6. Manuel de Guirior, *Relación* (1776), in E. Posada y P. M. Ibáñez, *Relaciones de mando* (*Biblioteca de Historia Nacional*, 8, Bogotá, 1910), p. 149.

7. J. J. Parsons, *Antioqueño Colonization in Western Colombia* (Berkeley and Los Angeles, 1949).

8. Ospina Vásquez, *op. cit.*, pp. 37–8.

9. Henderson to Canning, 12 April 1827, Memoir on the Mines of Colombia, P.R.O., F.O. 18/43.

10. McFarlane, 'The Transition from Colonialism in Colombia', *op. cit.*, pp. 105–6, 122, n. 15.

11. For Caballero y Góngora's reference to what he called the 'Instituto de las Colonias' see *Relación del Estado del Nuevo Reino de Granada* (1789), in Pérez Ayala, *op. cit.*, p. 361.

12. Quoted by Ospina Vásquez, *op. cit.*, p. 61.

13. *Ibid.*, p. 69.

14. In 1778 the population of Ecuador was 452,890; see Pérez Ayala, *op. cit.*, table A.

15. Caballero y Góngora, *Relación*, Pérez Ayala, *op. cit.*, p. 360.

16. Humboldt, *Ensayo político*, iv, 3–4.

17. Camilo Torres and Frutos Joaquín Gutiérrez, in Ospina Vásquez, *op. cit.*, p. 54, n.106.

18. Report to crown, cited by Pérez Ayala, *op. cit.*, p. 71.

19. Fals Borda, 'Indian congregations', *op. cit.*, pp. 331–51.

20. P. E. Cárdenas Acosta, *El movimiento comunal de 1781 en el Nuevo Reino de Granada* (BHN, 96–97, 2 vols, Bogotá, 1960), i, 155–61, ii, 270–94.

21. These 'capitulations' are printed in Pérez Ayala, *op. cit.*,

pp. 74–81; see also Phelan, *The People and the King*, pp. 179–80.

22. R. M. Tisnes, *Movimientos pre-independientes grancolombianos* (Bogotá, 1962), pp. 97–217; see above, pp. 27–32.

23. Thomas Blossom, *Nariño. Hero of Colombian Independence* (Tucson, 1967), p. 31.

24. Report of Antonio de Villavicencio, 24 May 1810, in Sergio Elías Ortiz, *Génesis de la revolución del 20 de julio de 1810* (Bogotá, 1960), pp. 112–31.

25. Ospina Vásquez, *op. cit.*, pp. 81–2.

26. Pedro Fermín de Vargas, *Pensamientos políticos y Memorias sobre la población del Nuevo Reino de Granada* (Bogotá, 1953), pp. 100–15.

27. José Antonio de Torres y Peña, *Memorias* (1814) (*BHN*, 92, Bogotá, 1960), p. 32.

28. *Ibid.*, p. 49.

29. Fancisco Silvestre, cited by Jaramillo Uribe, 'Mestizaje', *op. cit.*, p. 28.

30. *Ibid.*, pp. 35–6.

31. Jaime Jaramillo Uribe, 'Esclavos y señores en la sociedad colombiana del siglo XVIII', *Anuario Colombiano de Historia Social y de la Cultura*, i (1963) 3–62, particularly p. 38.

32. Quoted *ibid.*, p. 48.

33. Restrepo, *Historia de la revolución de la república de Colombia*, i, 50–67; José Gabriel Navarro, *La revolución de Quito del 10 de agosto de 1809* (Quito, 1962), pp. 44–51; M. M. Borrero, *La revolución quiteña, 1809–1812* (Quito, 1962). The viceroyalty of New Granada comprised the captaincy-general of Venezuela and the presidency of Quito (later Ecuador) as well as New Granada itself (present Colombia) which the viceroy administered directly.

34. First manifesto of the supreme junta, in Alfredo Ponce Ribadeneira, *Quito 1809–1812, según los documentos del Archivo Nacional de Madrid* (Madrid, 1960), pp. 136–9.

35. Manifesto of the People of Quito, August 1809, *ibid.*, p. 142.

36. Report of José Fuentes González, regent of audiencia, 21 November 1809, *ibid.*, pp. 188–96.

37. Selva Alegre to Viceroy of Peru, 9 September 1809, *ibid.*, pp. 162–3.

38. Ruiz de Castilla to Governor of Popayán, 6 December 1809, *ibid.*, p. 199; Navarro, *op. cit.*, pp. 111–59, 182–7.

39. Molina to Council of Regency, 29 April 1811, Ponce, *op. cit.*, p. 236.

40. *Ibid.*, pp. 101–2; Navarro, *op. cit.*, pp. 399–400.
41. Restrepo, *Historia de la revolución de la república de Colombia*, i, 69–107.
42. Robert L. Gilmore, 'The imperial crisis, rebellion, and the viceroy: Nueva Granada in 1809', *HAHR*, xl (1960), 1–24.
43. Ortiz, *Génesis de la revolución*, pp. 36–8; Torres y Peña, *Memorias*, pp. 90–5.
44. Blossom, *op. cit.*, pp. 65–70; Ortiz, *Génesis de la revolución*, pp. 75–89.
45. 'Representación a la Suprema Junta Central de España', in M. A. Pombo and J. J. Guerra, *Constituciones de Colombia* (2 vols, Bogotá, 1911), i, 28–42; Rafael Gómez Hoyos, *Le revolución granadina de 1810: ideario de una generación y de una época, 1781–1821* (2 vols, Bogotá, 1962), ii, 18–34; Manuel José Forero, *Camilo Torres* (*BHN*, 94, Bogotá, 1960), pp. 74–94.
46. Gilmore, *op. cit.*, p. 24.
47. Luis Martínez Delgado and Sergio Elías Ortiz (eds), *El periodismo en la Nueva Granada, 1810–1811* (Bogotá, 1960), p. 40.
48. Ortiz, *Génesis de la revolución*, pp. 145–203; Acta de la Independencia, in Enrique Ortega Ricaurte (ed.), *Documentos sobre el 20 de julio de 1810* (*BHN*, 93, Bogotá, 1960), pp. 121–7; Gómez Hoyos, *op. cit.*, ii, 72–8.
49. Diario político de Santafe de Bogotá, 29 August 1810, in *El periodismo en la Nueva Granada*, p. 43.
50. Quoted by Blossom, *op. cit.*, p. 81.
51. Forero, *op. cit.*, pp. 156–74, 197–214.
52. Quoted by Blossom, *op. cit.*, p. 109.
53. O'Leary, *Narración*, i, 253–9.
54. Jamaica Letter, 6 September 1815, *Cartas*, i, 195–6.
55. O'Leary, *Narración*, i, 297–306; Francisco Montalvo, *Relación de mando* (1818), in *Los ultimos virreyes de Nueva Granada* (Madrid, n.d.), p. 88.
56. José Manuel Restrepo, *Apuntamientos sobre le emigración de 1816*, in *Autobiografía* (*Biblioteca de la Presidencia*, 30, Bogotá, 1957), p. 65.
57. Restrepo, *Historia de la revolución de la república de Colombia*, i, 388–450.
58. Oswaldo Díaz Díaz, *La reconquista española* (2 vols, Bogotá, 1964–67), i, 321–2.
59. Restrepo, *Historia de la revolución*, i, 451–71.

60. Díaz Díaz, *Reconquista*, ii, 279–92.
61. Oswaldo Díaz Díaz, *Los Almeydas* (*BHN*, 99, Bogotá, 1962), pp. 96–8.
62. *Ibid.*, pp. 34–5.
63. *Ibid.*, pp. 112, 127, 145.
64. 15 August 1818, *Proclamas y Discursos*, p. 190; O'Leary, *Narración*, i, 480–1.
65. Santander to Bolívar, 29 April, 5 May 1818, *Cartas y Mensajes del General Francisco de Paula Santander, 1812–1840*, ed. Roberto Cortázar (10 vols, Bogotá, 1953–6), i, 246–8, 252. See above, pp. 215–6.
66. Díaz Díaz, *Los Almeydas*, pp. 227–8; Sergio Elías Ortiz (ed.), *Colección de documentos para la historia de Colombia. Epoca de la independencia* (3 vols, Bogotá, 1964–6), ii, 238–41).
67. Bushnell, *Santander Regime*, pp. 10–25.
68. See Santander to Bolívar, 31 October 1819, *Cartas y Mensajes*, ii, 366–97, a long and somewhat nauseating letter justifying his act of vengeance.
69. O'Leary, *Detached Recollections*, pp. 55–7.
70. Bushnell, *Santander Regime*, pp. 14–22.
71. Bolívar to Santander, 13 June 1821, *Cartas*, ii, 354–5.
72. O'Leary, *Narración*, ii, 118.
73. O'Leary, *Detached Recollections*, pp. 12, 17–18.
74. O'Leary, *Narración*, ii, 115–16.
75. Lecuna, *Crónica razonada*, iii, 81–109.
76. For an interesting though not entirely accurate account of royalist resistance in Pasto, see History of events in Pasto, Wood to Canning, Popayán, 30 June 1825, P.R.O., F.O. 18/21.
77. O'Leary, *Narración*, ii, 143; Lecuna, *Crónica razonada*, iii, 111–80.
78. Ortiz, *Documentos para la historia de Colombia*, i, 255–302.
79. See above, pp. 184–6.
80. O'Leary, *Narración*, ii, 147–51; William H. Gray, 'Bolívar's Conquest of Guayaquil', *HAHR*, xxvii (1947), 603–22.
81. See references on p. 377, n. 106.
82. Bushnell, *Santander Regime*, pp. 40–4.
83. Santander to Bolívar, 1820, O'Leary, *Narración*, ii, 639.
84. Bushnell, *Santander Regime*, p. 76.
85. Bolívar to Santander, 6 December 1822, *Cartas*, iii, 121.
86. Bolívar to Santander, 8 July 1826, *ibid.*, vi, 11.
87. Campbell to Canning, 5 November 1826, P.R.O. F.O., 18/28.
88. Campbell to Canning, 13 December 1826, *ibid.*
89. Watts to Canning, Cartagena, 27 May 1825, *ibid.*, 18/18.

90. The balance of population in the union also favoured New Granada; Restrepo, *Historia de la revolución*, i, p. xiv, estimated New Granada 1·4 million, Venezuela 900,000, Quito 600,000; Campbell to Planta, 6 November 1824, P.R.O., F.O. 18/3, estimated 2,650,000 for greater Colombia.
91. Ker Porter, *Diary*, 19 December 1825, 1 August 1826, pp. 43, 119–20.
92. Campbell to Canning, 9 June 1826, P.R.O., F.O. 18/27.
93. Páez to Bolívar, 1 October 1825, *Cartas*, v, 243.
94. Santander to Bolívar, 6 May 1826, *Cartas y Mensajes*, vi, 316.
95. Ker Porter to Canning, 3 May 1826, P.R.O., F.O. 18/23.
96. Bolívar to Páez, 8 August 1826, *Cartas*, vi, 49–52.
97. O'Leary, *Narración*, iii, 66; *Detached Recollections*, p. 22; Manuel Pérez Vila, *Vida de Daniel Florencio O'Leary primer edecán del Libertador* (Caracas, 1957), pp. 302–4.
98. Campbell to Canning, 6 October 1826, P.R.O., F.O. 18/28.
99. Bolívar to Mariño, 16 December 1813, *Cartas*, i, 88.
100. *Obras completas*, i, 619.
101. Bolívar to Mariño, 16 December 1813, *Cartas*, i, 88.
102. *Obras completas*, i, 713.
103. Bolívar to Santander, 20 December 1819, *Cartas*, ii, 126.
104. Ricketts to Canning, Lima, 18 February 1826, Webster, *Britain and the Independence of Latin America*, i, 530.
105. Ker Porter to Canning, 9 April 1827, P.R.O., F.O. 18/47.
106. Bolívar to Páez, 23 December 1826, *Cartas*, vi, 134.
107. Watts to Bidwell, 5 August 1826, P.R.O., F.O. 18/31.
108. Bushnell, *Santander Regime* p. 346.
109. Campbell to Canning, 3 January 1827, P.R.O., F.O. 18/40.
110. Santander to Bolívar, 6 July 1826, *Cartas y Mensajes*, vi, 374.
111. Salcedo Bastardo, *Visión y revisión de Bolívar*, pp. 126–31.
112. Message to Congress of Ocuña, 29 February 1828, *Proclamas y Discursos*, p. 362.
113. Campbell to Dudley, 13 April 1828, P.R.O., F.O. 18/53.
114. O'Leary, *Narración*, ii, 601; Campbell to Dudley, 14 September 1827, P.R.O., F.O. 18/42.
115. Joaquín Posada Gutiérrez, *Memorias histórico-políticas* (BHN, 41–4, 4 vols, Bogotá, 1929), i, 283–4, 310–25.
116. Bolívar to O'Leary, 13 September 1829, *Cartas*, ix, 125–6.
117. Acta del Cantón de Valencia, 23 November 1829, Gil Fortoul, *Historia constitucional de Venezuela*, i, 653.
118. Wood to Canning, 28 February 1826, Humphreys, *Consular Reports*, pp. 228–9; Bushnell, *Santander Regime*, pp. 310–17.
119. J. M. Ots Capdequí, *Las instituciones del Nuevo Reino de*

Granada al tiempo de la Independencia (Madrid, 1958), p. 101.

120. Account of views and plans of foreigners in Colombia, Watts to Canning, 9 May 1824, Humphreys, *Consular Reports*, pp. 269–72.

121. Charles Stuart Cochrane, *Journal of a Residence and Travels in Colombia, during the years 1823 and 1824* (2 vols, London, 1825), ii, 225–8, 241–3, 379–83; *The Present State of Colombia, by an Officer late in the Colombian Service* (London, 1827), pp. 297–326; G. Mollien, *Voyage dans la République de Colombia en 1823* (2 vols, Paris, 1824), 200–31.

122. Henderson to Canning, 12 April 1827, Memoir on the Mines of Colombia, P.R.O., F.O. 18/43.

123. Watts to Canning, 9 May 1824, Humphreys, *Consular Reports*, pp. 259–60; *Present State of Colombia*, pp. 183–97; R. L. Gilmore and J. P. Harrison, 'Juan Bernardo Elbers and the Introduction of Steam Navigation on the Magdalena River', *HAHR*, xxviii (1948), 335–59.

124. For an account of such a journey, see Cochrane, *op. cit.*, i, 108–73.

125. Bushnell, *Santander Regime*, pp. 137–47, 149–50; Jesús Arango Cono, *Inmigración y colonización de la Gran Colombia* (Bogotá, 1953).

126. Watts to Bidwell, 5 August 1826, P.R.O., F.O. 18/32.

127. Ospina Vásquez, *op. cit.*, pp. 132–5.

128. Watts to Canning, 9 May 1824, Humphreys, *Consular Reports*, p. 260; *Present State of Colombia,* pp. 263–92.

129. Wood to Canning, 28 February 1826, Humphreys, *Consular Reports*, pp. 231–6, 240.

130. McFarlane, 'The Transition from Colonialism in Colombia', *op. cit.*, pp. 107–8.

131. Hamilton and Campbell, undated report on Colombia, 1824, P.R.O., F.O. 18/3.

132. José Manuel Groot, *Historia eclesiástica y civil de Nueva Granada* (2nd ed., 5 vols, Bogotá, 1889–93), i, 316–19.

133. Vargas, *Memoria sobre la población del Reino*, in Gómez Hoyos, *op. cit.*, i, 282.

134. Ots Capdequí, *El régimen de la tierra*, pp. 93–104.

135. This was the situation in Popayán as described by Fals Borda, 'Indian congregations', *op. cit.*, pp. 342–3.

136. Ots Capdequí, *Instituciones*, pp. 234–63.

137. J. M. Castillo y Roda, *Memorias de hacienda 1823, 1826, 1827* (Bogotá, 1952), pp. 95–6.

138. This was the case in Saucío; see O. Fals Borda, *Peasant Society*

in the Colombian Andes: a sociological study of Saucío (Gainesville, 1955), pp. 98–105.

139. *Ibid.*, p. 105; 'Indian congregations', *op. cit.*, pp. 349–51.
140. H. A. Bierck, Jr., 'The Struggle for Abolition in Gran Colombia', *HAHR*, xxxiii (1953), 365–86.
141. See above, p. 235.
142. Santander to Bolívar, 2 April 1820, *Cartas y Mensajes*, ii, 79.
143. Bolívar to Santander, 20 April 1820, *Cartas*, ii, 152; Santander
to Bolívar, 5 May 1820, *Cartas y Mensajes*, ii, 116.
144. Bushnell, *Santander Regime*, pp. 170–1; see above, pp. 223–4.
Colombia finally abolished slavery in 1851.
145. Hamilton, undated report on Colombia, 1824, P.R.O., F.O.
18/3.
146. Report on Colombia by Colonel Francis Hall, in Sutherland to
Canning, 11 March 1824, P.R.O., F.O. 18/8.
147. Watts to Canning, 9 May 1824, Humphreys, *Consular Reports*,
p.267; Watts to Bidwell, 5 August 1826, P.R.O., F.O. 18/32.
148. Bolívar to Santander, 8 July 1826, *Cartas*, vi, 12.
149. Posada Gutiérrez, *Memorias histórico-políticas*, i, 123.
150. O'Leary, *Detached Recollections*, p. 37; J. M. Restrepo, *Diario
político y militar* (4 vols, Bogotá, 1954), i, 375.
151. Posada Guiérrez, *Memorias histórico-políticas*, i. 127.
152. Manuel Valdés to Juan José Flores, Cartagena, 8 April 1828,
Archivo Santander (25 vols, Bogotá, 1913), xvii, 295.
153. Campbell to Dudley, Bogotá, 13 April 1828, P.R.O., F.O.
18/53.
154. L. Peru de Lacroix, *Diario de Bucaramanga* (Caracas, 1976),
pp. 112–3.

EIGHT   *The Last Viceroy, the last Victory*

1. Jorge Basadre, *Historia de la República del Perú* (5th ed., 10
vols, 1961–4), i, 32, See above, pp. 187–8.
2. Bolívar to Santander, 12–14 March 1823, *Cartas*, iii, 152–3.
3. O'Leary, *Narración*, ii, 211; Lecuna, *Crónica razonada*, iii,
307–40.
4. Miller, *Memoirs*, ii, 102–4; Lecuna, *Crónica razonada*, iii,
346–74.
5. Rivera Serna, *Los guerrilleros del Centro*, pp. 80–92.
6. For a Venezuelan view see Lecuna, *Crónica razonada*, iii,
326–40; for Peruvian interpretations see Basadre, *Historia de
la república*, i, 49–55, and Enrique Ravago Bustamante, *El
gran mariscal Riva Agüero* (Lima, 1959), pp. 177–211.

7. Proclamation, 25 December 1824, *Proclamas y discursos*, p. 298.
8. *Ibid.*
9. Bolívar to Torre Tagle, 7 January 1824, *Cartas*, iv, 6.
10. O'Leary, *Narración*, ii, 241–4; Anna, *Fall of the Royal Government in Peru*, pp. 222–5.
11. O'Leary, *Narración*, ii, 240.
12. Rowcroft to Canning, Lima, 23 September 1824, P.R.O., F.O. 61/3.
13. Vargas Ugarte, *Emancipación*, pp. 473–4, 478–81; Basadre, *Historia de la república*, i, 87–8.
14. Miller *op. cit.*, ii, 149.
15. Lecuna, *Crónica razonada*, iii, 399–401.
16. Anna, *Fall of the Royal Government in Peru*, pp. 228–31.
17. Miller, *op. cit.*, ii, 148–9.
18. Lecuna, *Crónica razonada*, iii, 412–20.
19. *Ibid.*, iii, 456–74. Lieutenant-Colonel Medina of the Colombian army was killed by the Indians of Huando on his way to Lima with Sucre's dispatch of the battle; see Miller, *op. cit.*, ii, 191–2, 200.
20. O'Leary, *Narración*, ii, 333.
21. Basadre, *Historia de la república*, i, 132–4.
22. Ricketts to Canning, 27 December 1826, Humphreys, *Consular Reports*, pp. 107–206.
23. *Ibid.*, p. 195.
24. Hall, *Journal*, i, 268.
25. Humphreys, *Liberation in South America*, pp. 122–32.
26. Printed in *Consular Reports*, pp. 198–206.
27. Ricketts to Canning, 27 December 1826, *Consular Reports*, p. 145.
28. Rowcroft to Canning, 23 September 1824, P.R.O., F.O. 61/3.
29. Ricketts to Canning, 18 February 1826, Webster, *Britain and the Independence of Latin America*, i, 533.
30. San Martín to Torre Tagle, 13 February 1821, *Correspondencia de San Martín y Torre Tagle*, p. 46.
31. Otero, *Historia del Libertador*, iii, 363–4; Museo Mitre, *Documentos del Archivo de San Martín* (12 vols, Buenos Aires, 1910–11), xi, 440. See further laws of 21 September 1821 and 8 March 1822. At the end of the eighteenth century in a population of over one million there were about forty thousand slaves.
32. Basadre, *Historia de la república*, i, 191–2.
33. Ricketts to Canning, 19 December 1826, P.R.O., F.O. 61/8.

34. Miller, *op. cit.*, ii, 93.
35. *Ibid.*, 285.
36. Otero *op cit.*, iii, 364; *Archivo de San Martín*, xi, 430.
37. Decree of 8 April 1824, *Decretos del Libertador* (3 vols., Caracas, 1961), i, 295-6.
38. Decree of 4 July 1825, *Decretos del Libertador*, i, 410-11; Salcedo-Bastardo, *Visión y revisión de Bolívar*, pp. 311-12.
39. Bolívar to Santander, 28 June 1825, *Cartas*, v, 11.
40. Ricketts to Canning, 6 February 1827, P.R.O., F.O. 61/11.
41. See above, pp. 118-26.
42. Alfonso Crespo, *Santa Cruz. El condor indio* (Mexico, 1944), pp. 30-56.
43. Arnade, *The Emergence of the Republic of Bolivia*, pp. 122-5.
44. General Jose García Camba, *Memorias*, quoted by Valencia Vega, *El indio en la independencia*, pp. 343-4.
45. Arnade, *op. cit.*, pp. 165-6.
46. O'Leary, *Narración*, ii, 366-78.
47. Bolívar to Santander, 23 February 1825, *Cartas*, iv, 270.
48. Sabino Pinilla, *La creación de Bolivia* (Madrid, n.d.), pp. 163-230.
49. Arnade, *op. cit.*, pp. 192-9.
50. O'Leary, *Narración*, ii, 388.
51. For English text see Bushnell, *The Liberator, Simón Bolívar*, pp. 48-61.
52. Ricketts to Canning, 25 April 1826, P.R.O., F.O. 61/7.
53. Message to Congress of Bolivia, 25 May 1826, Vicente Lecuna and Harold A. Bierck, Jr. (eds), *Selected Writings of Bolivar* (2 vols, New York, 1951), ii, 596-606.
54. Ricketts to Canning, 30 May 1826, P.R.O., F.O. 61/7.
55. This was not, of course, a hereditary president, as is sometimes alleged. The successor came to power by appointment, not by hereditary right.
56. Bolívar to Sucre, 12 May 1826, *Cartas*, v, 291.
57. Circular letter to Colombia, 3 August 1826, *ibid.*, vi, 30.
58. William Lofstrom, 'Attempted economic reform and innovation in Bolivia under Antonio José de Sucre, 1825-1828', *HAHR*, l (1970), 279-99.
59. O'Leary, *Narración*, ii, 420.
60. Sucre to Bolívar, 4 August 1826, *Memorias del General O'Leary* (34 vols., Caracas, 1981), i, 368.
61. Lofstrom, *op. cit.*, pp. 287-97.
62. Ricketts to Canning, 30 May 1826, Humphreys, *Consular Reports*, pp. 219-20.

63. Miller, *op. cit.*, ii, 283. According to Pentland, Potosí produced only $900,000 in 1826; the mines of all Bolivia produced in 1826 $2,619,918 in silver and $800,000 in gold; see J. B. Pentland, Report on Bolivia, 2 December 1827, P.R.O., F.O. 61/12.

64. Humphreys, *Liberation in South America*, pp. 139–44; J. F. Rippy, *British Investments in Latin America, 1822–1949* (Minneapolis, 1959), pp. 17–25.

65. Miller, op. cit., ii, 293–4; Humphreys, *Liberation in South America*, pp. 155–61; Guillermo Ovando-Sanz, 'British interests in Potosi, 1825–1826; unpublished documents from the Archivo de Potosí', *HAHR*, xlv (1965), 64–87.

66. Rickets to Canning, 30 May 1826, *Consular Reports*, pp. 217–18.

67. According to Pentland the population of Bolivia was 1,100,000, divided as follows: 200,000 whites; 800,000 Indians; 100,000 mestizos; 7,000 Negroes, of whom 4,700 were slaves. Pentland to Ricketts, 2 December 1827, P.R.O., F.O. 61/12.

68. Miller, *op. cit.*, ii, 284.

69. Vicente Lecuna (ed.), *Documentos referentes a la creación de Bolivia* (2 vols, Caracas, 1924), i, 442.

70. *Ibid.*, 442–3.

71. Miller, *op. cit.*, ii, 299.

72. Lecuna, *Documentos referentes a la creación de Bolivia*, ii, 324; see also text in Bushnell, *The Liberator, Simón Bolívar*, p. 49.

73. Lecuna, *Documentos referentes a la creación de Bolivia*, ii, 346.

74. Sucre to Bolívar, 20 August 1826, *Memorias del General O'Leary*, i, 377.

75. Agustín Iturricha, *Historia de Bolivia bajo la administración del mariscal Andrés Santa Cruz (Tomo Primero)* (Sucre, 1967), pp. 149–94.

76. Sucre to Bolívar, 20 June 1827, *Memorias del General O'Leary*, i, 436; Bolívar to Sucre, 8 June 1827, *Cartas*, vi, 305.

77. For a discussion of Peruvian nationalism see Basadre, *Historia de la república*, i, 203–16.

78. Captain Maling to Lord Melville, 18–20 March 1825, in H.W.V. Temperley, *The Foreign Policy of Canning, 1822–1827* (London, 1925), p. 560.

79. Bolívar to P. Briceño Méndez, 2 August 1826, *Memorias del General O'Leary*, xxx, 244–47.

80. O'Leary, *Detached Recollections*, p. 28.
81. Willemott to Ricketts, 31 January 1828, P.R.O., F.O. 61/15.
82. Ricketts to Canning, 16 May 1827, P.R.O., F.O. 61/11.
83. Bolívar to Santa Cruz, 26 October 1826, *Cartas*, vi, 93–4.
84. Bolívar, *Obras completas*, ii, 644.
85. Bolívar, *Cartas*, viii, 277–9.
86. *Proclamas y discursos*, p. 398.
87. Bolívar to Flores, 9 November 1830, *Cartas*, ix, 376.
88. O'Leary, *Detached Recollections*, p. 48.

NINE   *Mexico, the Consummation of American Independence*

1. D. A. Brading, *Miners and Merchants in Bourbon Mexico 1763–1810* (Cambridge, 1971), pp. 156–8, and the same author's 'La minería de la plata en el siglo XVIII : el caso Bolaños', *Historia Mexicana*, xviii (1969), 317–33, and 'Mexican Silver-Mining in the Eighteenth Century: the Revival of Zacatecas', *HAHR*, 1 (1970), 665–81.
2. Humboldt, *Ensayo político*, ii, 128–31; Brading, *Miners and Merchants*, pp. 291–3.
3. D. A. Brading, *Haciendas and Ranchos in the Mexican Bajío: León 1700–1860* (Cambridge, 1978), pp. 172–3.
4. Victoria Lerner, 'La población de la Nueva España (1793–1810', *Historia Mexicana*, xvii (1968), 327–46; Brading, *Miners and Merchants*, pp. 224–5.
5. Enrique Florescano, *Precios del maíz y crisis argícolas en México (1708–1810)* (Mexico, 1969), pp. 141–8, 190.
6. *Ibid.*, pp. 163–72.
7. Luis González, *Pueblo en vilo. Microhistoria de San José de Gracia* (Mexico, 1968), pp. 68–71.
8. Florescano, *op. cit.*, pp. 176–8.
9. *Ibid.*, p. 179.
10. Humboldt, *Ensayo político*, ii, 50–88.
11. See above, p. 23.
12. Humboldt, *Ensayo político*, ii, 149.
13. Romeo Flores Caballero, *La contra-revolución en la independencia. Los españoles en la vida política, social y económica de México (1804–1838)* (Mexico, 1969), p. 22.
14. *Ibid.*, pp. 22–4.
15. Brading, *Merchants and Miners*, pp. 208, 318–19.
16. Doris M. Ladd, *The Mexican Nobility at Independence 1780–1826* (Austin, 1976), pp. 46–52, 317–19; D. A. Brading,

'Government and Elites in Late Colonial Mexico', *HAHR*, 53 (1973), 389–414.

17. Quoted by Miranda, *Las ideas y las instituciones políticas mexicanas*, pp. 184–5.

18. Alamán, *Historia de México*, i, 93; Timothy E. Anna, *The Fall of the Royal Government in Mexico City* (Lincoln, Nebraska, 1978), pp. 31–2.

19. Delfina E. López Sarrelangue, 'Población indígena de la Nueva España en el siglo XVIII', *Historia Mexicana*, xii (1963), 516–30.

20. Humboldt, *Ensayo Político*, ii, 96; see also Catalina Sierra, *El nacimiento de México* (Mexico, 1960), pp. 61–71.

21. Informe, 1799, in Humboldt, *Ensayo político*, ii, 99–103; see also Ernesto Lemoine Villicaña (ed.), 'Un notable escrito póstumo del obispo de Michoacán', *Boletín del Archivo General de la Nación*, segunda época, v (1964), 5–66.

22. Humboldt, *Ensayo político*, 540–52; D. A. Brading, 'Facts and Figments in Bourbon Mexico', *Bulletin of Latin American Research*, 4, 1(1985), 61–64.

23. Michael P. Costeloe, *Church Wealth in Mexico. A Study of the 'Juzgado de Capellanías' in the Archbishopric of Mexico 1800–1856* (Cambridge, 1967), pp. 111–16; Brian R. Hamnett, 'The Appropriation of Mexican Church Wealth by the Spanish Bourbon Government', *JLAS*, i (1969), 85–113; Arnold J. Bauer, 'The Church in the Economy of Spanish America: *Censos* and *Depósitos* in the Eighteenth and Nineteenth Centuries', *HAHR*, 63, 4 (1983), 707–33.

24. Abad y Queipo, *Escritos*, in José María Luis Mora, *Obras sueltas* (Mexico, 1963), pp. 231–2.

25. Flores Caballero, *op. cit.*, p. 51.

26. Manifesto of the Congress of Anáhuac, 6 November 1813, Ernesto Lemoine Villicaña, *Morelos, su vida revolucionaria a través de sus escritos y de otros testimonios de la época* (Mexico, 1965), p. 427.

27. Servando Teresa de Mier, *Historia de la revolución de Nueva España* (2 vols, London, 1813), ii, 745.

28. Alamán, *Historia de México*, i, 173–245.

29. Enrique Lafuente Ferrari, *El virrey Iturrigaray y los orígenes de la independencia de Méjico* (Madrid, 1941), pp. 204–55.

30. Flores Caballero, *op. cit.*, p. 49.

31. Alamán, *Historia*, i, 262; José María Luis Mora, *México y sus revoluciones* (3 vols, Mexico, 1965), ii, 307–8.

32. Hamnett, *Politics and Trade in Southern Mexico*, pp. 122–8.

33. Florescano, *op. cit.*, pp. 150–3; Brading, *Miners and Merchants*, p. 342.
34. Hugh M. Hamill, Jr., *The Hidalgo Revolt. Prelude to Mexican Independence* (Gainesville, 1966) is the outstanding work in a large bibliography.
35. Eric B. Wolf, 'The Mexican Bajío in the Eighteenth Century', *Middle American Research Institute Publications*, xvii (1955), 177–200.
36. Hamill, *op. cit.*, pp. 109–11.
37. Quoted *ibid.*, p. 113.
38. Quoted ibid., p. 139; see also Luis Castillo Ledón, *Hidalgo, la vida del héroe* (2 vols, Mexico, 1948–9), ii, 43–58.
39. Alamán, *Historia*, i, 379.
40. Quoted by Brading, *Miners and Merchants*, p. 319.
41. González, *Pueblo en vilo*, p. 72.
42. Ernesto de la Torre Villar, *Los 'Guadalupes' y la independencia* (Mexico, 1966).
43. Alfonso García Ruiz, *Ideario de Hidalgo* (Mexico, 1955); Moisés González Navarro, 'La política social de Hidalgo', *Anales del Instituto Nacional de Antropología e Historia*, vii (1953/5), 125–38.
44. Juan Hernández y Dávalos (ed.), *Colección de documentos para la historia de la guerra de independencia de México de 1808 a 1821* (6 vols, Mexico, 1877–82), ii, 169–70, 243; Hamill, *op. cit.*, p. 136; on the social content of Hidalgo's thought see also M. S. Alperovich, *Historia de la independencia de México (1810–1824)*, trans. Adolfo Sánchez Vázquez (Mexico, 1967), pp. 114–45.
45. Guadalajara, 5 December 1810, in Hamill, *op. cit.*, p. 196.
46. Quoted in Alamán, *Historia*, i, 470.
47. Farriss, *Crown and Clergy in Colonial Mexico*, pp. 199–202, 212–24, 254–65; Karl M. Schmitt, 'The Clergy and the Independence of New Spain', *HAHR*, xxxiv (1954), 289–312.
48. Alfonso Teja Zabre, *Vida de Morelos* (3rd ed., Mexico, 1959), p. 13.
49. Wilbert H. Timmons, *Morelos of Mexico. Priest, Soldier, Statesman* (El Paso, 1963), p. 42, a good modern study.
50. Quoted *ibid.*, p. 50.
51. Morelos, 23 March 1812, Lemoine Villicaña, *Morelos*, p. 109; see also Timmons, *Morelos*, p. 51.
52. Morelos, 21 November 1813, Lemoine Villicaña, *Morelos*, pp. 439–41.
53. Morelos, 24 November 1811, 8 February *ibid.*, pp. 184–5, 190.

54. *Ibid.*, pp. 167–8.
55. Bando de Morelos, 17 November 1810, *ibid.*, p. 162.
56. Alamán alleged that Morelos was a socialist waging class war for the destruction and redistribution of property. For the fullest discussion of this problem see Timmons, *Morelos*, pp. 101–3, and 'José María Morelos – Agrarian Reformer?' *HAHR*, xlv (1965), 183–95, who emphasizes the immediate politico-military objects of the *Medidas Políticas* and attributes authorship to the *Guadalupes*, not Morelos. See also Teja Zabre, *op. cit.*, pp. 210–15.
57. Quoted by Timmons, *Morelos*, p. 102.
58. Sentimientos de la Nación, 14 September 1813, Lemoine Villicaña, *Morelos*, pp. 370–3; see also *ibid.*, pp. 399–41.
59. Nettie Lee Benson (ed.), *Mexico and the Spanish Cortes, 1810–1822* (Austin, 1966), pp. 8–9.
60. Bando de Morelos, Tecpan, 13 October 1811, Lemoine Villicaña, *Morelos*, pp. 181–3.
61. *Ibid.*, pp. 505–6.
62. Ernesto de la Torre Villar, *La Constitución de Apatzingán y los creadores del Estado Mexicano* (Mexico, 1964), pp. 380–402; see also Luis González, *El Congreso de Anáhuac de 1813* (Mexico, 1963); Ernesto Lemoine Villicaña, 'Zitácuaro, Chilpancingo y Apatzingán, tres grandes momentos de la insurgencia mexicana', *Boletín del Archivo General de la Nación*, iv (1963), 385–710.
63. Farriss, *op. cit.*, pp. 246–50; James M. Breedlove, 'Effect of the Cortes, 1810–1822, on Church Reform in Spain and Mexico', Benson, *Mexico and the Spanish Cortes*, pp. 125–31; Schmitt, 'The Clergy and the Independence of New Spain', *op. cit.*, p. 308.
64. For a different interpretation see Anna, *Fall of the Royal Government in Mexico City*, pp. 199–209, and the comment on this by Brian R. Hamnett, 'Mexico's Royalist Coalition: the Response to Revolution', *JLAS*, 12, 1(1980), 75, n. 36.
65. Neill Macaulay, 'The Army of New Spain and the Mexican Delegation to the Spanish Cortes', Benson, *Mexico and the Spanish Cortes*, p. 150.
66. W. S. Robertson, *Iturbide of Mexico* (Durham, N. C., 1952), pp. 6–8, 25.
67. *Ibid.*, p. 34.
68. Plan de Iguala, 24 February 1821, in Alamán, *Historia*, v, 740.
69. Charles A. Hale, *Mexican Liberalism in the Age of Mora 1821–1853* (New Haven, 1968), pp. 25–6.

70. Flores Caballero, *op. cit.*, pp. 88–103.
71. Farriss, *op. cit.*, p. 251.
72. Javier Ocampo, *Las ideas de un día. El pueblo mexicano ante la consumación de su Independencia* (Mexico, 1969), p. 56.
73. *Ibid.*, pp. 57–65, 165.
74. Bolívar to Toro, 23 September 1822, *Cartas*, iii, 92.
75. Robertson, *Iturbide*, p. 222; For a closer analysis of this and the other revolts against Iturbide see Timothy E. Anna, 'The Rule of Agustín de Iturbide: A Reappraisal', *JLAS*, 17, 1(1985), 79–110.
76. Morier to Canning, 19 November 1824, P.R.O., F.O. 50/6.
77. Hale, *op. cit.*, pp. 108–47, 215–89.
78. Nettie Lee Benson, *La diputación provincial y el federalismo mexicano* (Mexico, 1955).
79. Captain Rich to Commodore Owen, 30 January 1824, P.R.O., F.O. 50/8; Mackenzie to Canning, 24 July 1824, Humphreys, *Consular Reports* pp. 300–30.
80. Hamnett, *Politics and Trade in Southern Mexico*, pp. 141–4.
81. Ward to Canning, 13 March 1826, P.R.O., F.O. 50/20.
82. Jan Bazant, 'Evolución de la industria textil poblana 1544–1845', *Historia Mexicana*, xiii (1964), 473–516 : Robert A. Potash, *El Banco de Avío de México: el fomento de la industria, 1821–1846* (Mexico, 1959), pp. 10–33.
83. Flores Caballero, *op. cit.*, pp. 78–9, 153–5.
84. Mackenzie estimated 140 million pesos, *Consular Reports*, p. 303; H. G. Ward, *Mexico in 1827* (2 vols, London, 1828), i, 379–82, 36.5 million.
85. Ward, *op. cit.*, ii, 47–97.
86. Quoted by Ocampo, *op. cit.*, p. 270.
87. Jan Bazant, *Alienation of Church Wealth in Mexico. Social and Economic Aspects of the Liberal Revolution 1856–1875* (Cambridge, 1971), pp. 12–13.
88. Morier to Canning, 10 February 1825, P.R.O., F.O. 50/11.
89. Morier to Canning, 19 November 1824, P.R.O., F.O. 50/16.
90. María del Carmen Velázquez, 'Nueva estructura social en Hispanoamérica después de la independencia', *Jahrbuch für Geschichte von Staat, Wirtschaft und Gesellschaft Lateinamerikas*, 5 (1968), 264–81, especially p. 279, n.21.
91. Quoted by Ocampo, *op. cit.*, p. 275.
92. Quoted *ibid.*, p. 259.
93. Quoted *ibid.*, p. 261.
94. Jesús Reyes Heroles, *El liberalismo mexicano* (3 vols, Mexico, 1957–61), ii, 177; see also Luis González, 'El agrarismo liberal',

Historia Mexicana, vii (1958), 469–96.
95. Moisés González Navarro, *Raza y Tierra* (Mexico, 1970), pp. 50–1; Ocampo, *op. cit.*, pp. 275–6.
96. Ward to Canning, 13 March 1826, P.R.O., F.O. 50/20.
97. Gonzalo Aguirre Beltrán, 'The Integration of the Negro into the National Society of Mexico', Magnus Mörner (ed.), *Race and Class in Latin America* (New York, 1970), 11–29.
98. Constituent Congress, 27 September 1822, Moisés González Navarro, 'Instituciones indígenas en México independiente', *Métodos y resultados de la política indigenista en México* (Mexico, 1954), pp. 115–30, 143–65; Magnus Mörner, *Race Mixture in the History of Latin America* (Boston, 1967), p. 83.
99. Quoted by Moisés González Navarro, 'Mestizaje in Mexico during the national period', Mörner, *Race and Class in Latin America*, p. 147.
100. Debate, 1824, cited by Mörner, *Race Mixture in the History of Latin America*, p. 104.
101. Morier to Canning, 19 November 1824, P.R.O., F.O. 50/6.
102. Letter to *Gaceta de Guatemala*, 1797, in André Saint-Lu, *Condition coloniale et conscience créole au Guatemale (1524–1821)* (Paris, 1970), p. 118.
103. Miles L. Wortman, *Government and Society in Central America, 1680–1840* (New York, 1982), pp. 173–88.
104. *Ibid.*, p. 191.
105. Mario Rodríguez, *The Cadiz Experiment in Central America, 1808–1826* (Berkeley-Los Angeles, 1978), pp. 68–74.
106. *Ibid.*, pp. 112–23.
107. Act of Independence, 15 September 1821, *Actas de Independencia*, p. 70; Louis E. Bumgartner, *José del Valle of Central America* (Durham, N.C., 1963), p. 147.
108. Rodríguez, *Cadiz Experiment in Central America*, p. 210.

TEN *The Reckoning*

1. John Stuart Mill, *Representative Government* (London, 1926), p. 360.
2. Carlos Ibarguren, *Las sociedades literarias y la revolución argentina 1800–1825* (Buenos Aires, 1937), p. 39.
3. *HNA*, vi, 1, p. 414.
4. Quoted by González, 'El optimismo nacionalista como factor de la independencia de México', *op. cit.*, p. 188.
5. Alamán, *Historia*, i, 257.

6. For a classic study of the social and economic aspects of independence see Charles C. Griffin, *Los temas sociales y económicos en la época de la independencia* (Caracas, 1962), which is also a bibliographical guide.

7. Bolívar to Sucre, 22 January 1826, *Cartas*, v, 204.

8. Bolívar to Santander, 21 October 1825, *Cartas*, v, 142.

9. Tulio Halperín Donghi, 'Economy and society in post-Independence Spanish America', in Leslie Bethell (ed.), *The Cambridge History of Latin America, Volume III* (Cambridge, 1985), pp. 300–306.

10. Tulio Halperin Donghi, *Historia contemporánea de América Latina* (2nd edn., Madrid, 1970), pp. 142–61, 214–30.

11. Richard N. Adams, *Nationalization*, No. 60, *Offprint Series*, Institute of Latin American Studies, University of Texas (Austin, 1967), pp. 469–89.

12. Constituent Congress, Lima, to Indians of interior provinces, 10 October 1822, Cornejo Bouroncle, *Pumacahua*, pp. 532–3.

13. Posada Gutiérrez, *Memorias*, i, 158–9.

14. Bolívar, *Obras completas*, i, 1334.

15. John J. Johnson, *The Military and Society in Latin America* (Stanford, 1964), pp. 32–5.

16. The war continued in the south, of course; see Bushnell, *Santander Regime*, pp. 249–50.

17. Ker Porter to Canning, Caracas, 24 January 1827, P.R.O., F.O. 18/47.

18. John Lynch, 'Los caudillos de la Independencia: enemigos y agentes del Estado-Nación', in Inge Buisson, Günter Kahle, Hans-Joachim König y Horst Pietschmann (eds.), *Problemas de la formación del estado y de la nación en Hispanoamérica* (Bonn, 1984), pp. 197–218.

19. Eric R. Wolf and Edward C. Hansen, 'Caudillo Politics: A Structural Analysis', *Comparative Studies in Society and History*, 9(1966–67), 168–179; Robert L. Gilmore, *Caudillism and Militarism in Venezuela, 1810–1910* (Athens, Ohio, 1964), pp. 47, 69–70, 107.

20. Roger M. Haigh, *Martín Güemes: Tyrant or Tool? A Study of the Sources of Power of an Argentine Caudillo* (Fort Worth, 1968), pp. 51–2.

21. T. Halperin Donghi, 'El surgimiento de los caudillos en el marco de la sociedad rioplatense postrevolucionaria', *Estudios de Historia Social* (Buenos Aires), i (1965), 121–49.

22. Ocampo, *Las ideas de un día*, p. 270.

ABBREVIATIONS

A.G.I.	Archivo General de Indias, Seville
BAE	*Biblioteca de Autores Españoles*
BANH	*Biblioteca de la Academia Nacional de la Historia,* Venezuela
BHN	*Biblioteca de Historia Nacional,* Colombia
B.M.	British Museum, London
CHCH	*Colección de historiadores y documentos relativos a la independencia de Chile*
DHA	*Documentos para la historia argentina*
HAHR	*Hispanic American Historical Review*
HNA	*Historia de la Nación Argentina*
JLAS	*Journal of Latin American Studies*
NSA	*The Navy and South America*
P.R.O.	Public Record Office, London

Bibliographical Essay

BIBLIOGRAPHIES

Spanish American independence has a large bibliography, signposted by a number of useful guides. The latest are to be found in the bibliographical essays in Leslie Bethell (ed.), *The Cambridge History of Latin America*, Volume III (Cambridge, 1985). These update but do not entirely displace a series of earlier works: R. A. Humphreys, 'The Historiography of the Spanish American Revolutions', *HAHR*, xxxvi (1956), 81–93, and R. A. Humphreys and John Lynch, 'The Emancipation of Latin America', Instituto Panamericano de Geografía e Historia, *La Emancipación latinoamericana. Estudios bibliográficos* (Mexico, 1966), which prefaces individual studies of Gran Colombia, Mexico, Chile and Peru. A basic bibliography is to be found in Charles C. Griffin (ed.), *Latin America. A Guide to the Historical Literature* (Austin, 1971), and Francisco Morales Padrón (ed.), *Bibliografía básica sobre historia de América* (Seville, 1975). These can be supplemented by the appropriate sections of two periodical guides, *Handbook of Latin American Studies* (Gainesville, University of Florida Press), and *Historiografía y Bibliografía Americanistas* (Escuela de Estudios Hispanoamericanos, Seville). Sylvia-Lyn Hilton and Amancio Labandeira, *Bibliografía hispanoamericana y filipina* (Madrid, 1983) is a guide to bibliographies. On the role of books and the written word in the service of independence, see Pedro Grases, *Libros y libertad* (Caracas, 1974).

Sources

Spanish American historiography has served the student well, if selectively, in documentation, beginning with the classical compilations of the nineteenth century and continuing with greater abundance, and greater professionalism, in more recent decades. Argentina has been particularly prolific adding to the older editions of the Museo Mitre, *Documentos del Archivo de Belgrano* (7 vols, Buenos Aires, 1913–17) and *Documentos del Archivo de San Martín* (12 vols, Buenos Aires, 1910–11) such monumental collections as Archivo General de la Nación, *Documentos referentes a la guerra de la independencia y emancipación política de la República Argentina* (3 vols, Buenos Aires, 1914–26); Universidad de Buenos Aires, *Documentos para la historia argentina* (Buenos Aires, 1913–). And subsequently, stimulated by the hundred and fiftieth anniversary of the revolution of 1810, Argentina provided Museo Histórico Nacional, *Documentos para la historia del Libertador General San Martín* (8 vols, Buenos Aires, 1953–60); Instituto de Historia Argentina 'Doctor Emilio Ravignani', *Mayo Documental* (8 vols, Buenos Aires, 1962–64) and *Archivo del brigadier general Juan Facundo Quiroga* (2 vols, Buenos Aires, 1957–60); and the indispensable *Biblioteca de Mayo* (17 vols, Buenos Aires, 1960–63), which includes memoirs, chronicles and newspapers as well as public documents. And the archives still had more to yield, as exemplified in Academia Nacional de la Historia, *Epistolario Belgraniano,* ed. María Teresa Piragino (Buenos Aires, 1970), covering the years 1790–1820.

Venezuelan independence is also rich in documentation, beginning with classics of nineteenth-century scholarship: José Félix Blanco and Ramón Azpurúa (eds.), *Documentos para la historia de la vida pública del Libertador* (14 vols, Caracas, 1875–77); *Memorias del general O'Leary* (32 vols, Caracas, 1879–88), recently republished in facsimile edition with a two-volume Index (34 vols, Caracas, 1981); and ranging to the *Archivo del General Miranda* (24 vols, Caracas, 1929–50), now followed by a definitive edition of all the Miranda documentation in a continuing enterprise, Francisco de Mirando, *Colombeia* (Caracas, 1978–); Presidencia de la República, *Las fuerzas armadas de Venezuela en el siglo XIX; la independencia* (5 vols, Caracas, 1963) for the role of the armed forces; Pedro Grases and Manuel Pérez Vila (eds.), *Pensamiento político venezolano del siglo XIX* (15 vols, Caracas, 1960–62); and the *Biblioteca de la Academia Nacional de la Historia* (82 vols, Caracas, 1960–66), which includes a variety of source material and surpasses even the *Biblioteca de Mayo* in quantity. But Venezuelan documentation is inevitably dominated by Bolivarian texts and these in turn by Vicente Lecuna, editor: Simón Bolívar, *Cartas del Libertador* (12 vols, Caracas, 1929–59), the standard edition of the correspondence; *Proclamas y Discursos del Libertador* (Caracas, 1939); *Decretos del Libertador* (3 vols., Caracas, 1961); *La entrevista de Guayaquil* (4th ed., 2 vols, Caracas, 1962–63), the Bolivarian side of the controversy; and, with Esther Barret de Nazarís, *Obras completas* (2nd ed., 3 vols, Havana, 1950). In a final search for perfection the Comisión Editora de la Sociedad Bolivariana de Venezuela is publishing the multi-volume *Escritos del Libertador* (Caracas, 1964–   ). There is a convenient collection in English, Vicente Lecuna and Harold A. Bierck, Jr., *Selected Writings of Bolívar* (2 vols, New York, 1951). Pedro Grases has collected the basic documentation on the Constitution of Angostura in *El Libertador y la Constitución de Angostura de 1819* (Caracas, 1970). Sucre is also the subject of a grand project: Fundación Vicente Lecuna, Banco de Venezuela, *Archivo de Sucre*, Tomo I (Caracas, 1973).

If other countries have invested less in the documentation of independence, the returns are still impressive. In Colombia the older *Archivo Santander* (25 vols, Bogotá, 1913–32) was deficient in scholarship, but the researcher now has more reliable texts edited by Roberto Cortázar, *Cartas y Mensajes del General Francisco de Paula Santander*, 1812–1840 (10 vols, Bogotá, 1953–56), and *Correspondencia dirigida al General Francisco de Paula Santander* (Bogotá, 1964–   ); while the continuing *Biblioteca de Historia Nacional* (Bogotá, 1910–   ) contains many primary sources for independence. Even more useful is the complete public documentation of the government of Gran Colombia, edited by José M. de Mier, *La Gran Colombia* (7 vols, Bogotá, 1983). The Quito revolution has been documented by Alfredo Ponce Ribadeneira, *Quito: 1809–1812, según los documentos del Archivo Nacional de Madrid* (Madrid, 1960).

Peru has built upon an older tradition represented by M. de

Odriozola (ed.), *Documentos históricos del Perú* (10 vols, Lima, 1863–77) with the following compilations: José Manual Valega, *La gesta emancipadora del Perú* (12 vols, Lima, 1940–44) covering the various insurrections in Peru between 1780 and 1826; Jorge Cornejo Bouroncle, *Pumacahua. La revolución del Cuzco de 1814* (Cuzco, 1956), for revolutionary agitation in southern Peru, 1780–1814, chiefly the two great Indian rebellions. Spanish and Peruvian scholarship also provides the reports of the last viceroys: Vicente Rodríguez Casado and J. A. Calderón Quijano (eds.), *Memoria de gobierno del virrey Abascal* (2 vols, Seville, 1944); V. Rodríguez Casado and G. Lohmann Villena (eds.), *Memoria de gobierno del virrey Pezuela* (Seville, 1947); Félix Denegri Luna (ed.), *Memoria militar del General Pezuela, 1813–1815* (Lima, 1955). The 150th anniversary of the independence of Peru was the occasion of important publications: Comisión Nacional del Sesquicentenario de la Independencia del Perú, *Colección documental de la independencia del Perú* (30 vols, Lima, 1971); Rubén Vargas Ugarte, S. J., *Documentos inéditos sobre la campaña de la independencia del Perú* (1810–1824) (Lima, 1971). For Bolivian independence see M. M. Pinto, C. Ponce Sanginés and R. A. García, *Documentos para la historia de la Revolucion de 1809* (4 vols, La Paz, 1953–54); V. Lecuna, (ed.), *Documentos referentes a la creación de Bolivia* (2 vols, Caracas, 1924); D. F. O'Leary (ed.), *Cartas de Sucre al Libertador* (1826–1830) (2 vols, Madrid, 1919). The Academia Chilena de la Historia has published the *Archivo de don Bernardo O'Higgins* (28 vols, Santiago, 1946–68), a fitting companion to the older *Colección de historiadores y de documentos relativos a la independencia de Chile* (40 vols, Santiago, 1900–59), for a guide to which see Sergio Villalobos, *Indice . . .* (Santiago, 1956). Uruguay's major source is the *Archivo Artigas* (Montevideo, 1950–).

Mexican documentation began with Juan Hernández y Dávalos (ed.), *Colección de documentos para la historia de la guerra de independencia de México de 1808 a 1821* (6 vols, Mexico, 1877–82) which has remained a basic source, together with Genaro García, *Documentos históricos mexicanos* (7 vols, Mexico, 1910–12). These have been joined in more recent years by Ernesto de la Torre Villar (ed.), *La constitución de Apatzingán y los creadores del estado mexicano* (Mexico, 1964) and

Los 'Guadalupes' y la independencia, con una selección de documentos inéditos (Mexico, 1966); Ernesto Lemoïne Villicaña, *Morelos, su vida revolucionaria a través de sus escritos y de otros testimonios de la época* (Mexico, 1965); all of which can be supplemented by the continuing documentary service provided in the *Boletín del Archivo General de la Nación*. Central American independence is served by the collection edited by Carlos Meléndez, *Textos fundamentales de la independencia centroamericana* (San José, 1971). The declarations of independence of the new states have been assembled by Javier Malagón, *Las Actas de Independencia de América* (Washington, D.C., 1972).

Liberation was a great cause, which fascinated contemporaries at home and abroad and attracted a distinguished literature of memoirs and chronicles. Many of the Argentine sources of this kind are included in the *Biblioteca de Mayo*. Félix de Azara, *Descripción e historia del Paraguay y del Río de la Plata* (Buenos Aires, 1943) and *Memoria sobre el estado rural del Río de la Plata y otros informes* (Buenos Aires, 1943) are important accounts of the environment in the late colonial period by a Spanish military engineer. H. M. Brackenridge, *Voyage to South America, performed by order of the American government in the years 1817 and 1818* (2 vols, London, 1820) is the work of the secretary of the United States commission to the Río de la Plata; Woodbine Parish, *Buenos Ayres and the Provinces of the Rio de la Plata* (London, 1839; 2nd ed., enlarged, 1852) that of the first British consul. And two Scottish entrepreneurs left valuable accounts: J. P. and W. P. Robertson, *Letters on South America* (3 vols, London, 1843), and *Letters on Paraguay* (2 vols, London, 1838). For Chile and the Pacific there are a number of outstanding narratives: Captain Basil Hall, *Extracts from a Journal written on the coasts of Chili, Peru, and Mexico in the years 1820, 1821, 1822* (3rd ed., 2 vols, Edinburgh, 1824); Maria Graham, *Journal of a Residence in Chile during 1822* (London, 1824); John Miers, *Travels in Chile and La Plata* (2 vols, London, 1826). John Miller (ed.), *Memoirs of General Miller in the service of the Repbulic of Peru* (2nd ed., 2 vols, London, 1829) is a much quoted account by a British volunteer; and Edmond Temple, *Travels in Various Parts of Peru, including a year's residence in Potosi* (2 vols, London, 1830) is useful for the mining boom and its collapse. José Santos Vargas, *Diario de un Comandante de la Independencia Americana 1814–1825*, ed. Gunnar Mendoza L. (Mexico, 1982) is a vivid source for the war in Upper Peru by a guerrilla leader.

Northern South America enjoyed the attentions of the greatest observer of all, the German scientist Alexander von Humboldt, whose *Viaje a las regiones equinocciales del Nuevo Continente* (5 vols, Caracas, 1956) is a valuable piece of reporting on environment and society; it can be supplemented for Venezuela by the French observer F. Depons, *Viaje a la parte oriental de Tierra Firme en la América meridional* (2 vols, Caracas, 1960). Justice was done to Bolívar by his worthy and perceptive Irish aide, Daniel Florence O'Leary, whose *Memorias del General Daniel Florencio O'Leary*. *Narración* (3 vols, Caracas, 1952), also in volumes 27, 28 and 32 of the complete edition cited above, are the best memoirs on Bolívar and the northern revolution and exemplify the Liberator's own maxim: 'To understand revolutions and their participants we must observe them at close range and judge them at great distance'. For O'Leary's more personal observations see R. A. Humphreys (ed.), *The 'Detached Recollections' of General D. F. O'Leary* (London, 1969). There is a new, and complete, edition of L. Peru de Lacroix, *Diario de Bucaramanga* (Caracas, 1976), notable for its informal reporting on Bolívar. Páez was his own chronicler, leaving an important personal record, *Autobiografía del General José Antonio Páez* (2 vols, Caracas, 1973). Among the numerous narrative accounts of the revolution in Venezuela two stand out for their interest and perception: José Francisco Heredia, *Memorias del Regente Heredia* (Madrid, n.d.) and José de Austria, *Bosquejo de la historia militar de Venezuela* (2 vols, Madrid, 1960). For postwar conditions, Charles Stuart Cochrane, *Journal of a Residence and Travels in Colombia, during the years 1823 and 1824* (2 vols, London, 1825), and William Duane, *A Visit to Colombia in the years 1822 and 1823* (Philadelphia, 1826) are contrasting English and American impressions.

Mexico too was observed and recorded by Alexander von Humboldt, and his *Ensayo político sobre el reino de la Nueva España*, ed. Juan A. Ortega y Medina (Mexico, 1966) has, with the *Viaje*, left an indelible impression on the historiography of the late colonial period. Humboldt was a European liberal. The most distinguished native observer was a Mexican conservative, Lucas Alamán, whose *Historia de México* (5 vols, Mexico, 1883–5) was first published in 1849–52, an impressive and scholarly exercise in the writing of contemporary history. Not far behind were the Mexican liberals Carlos María de Bustamante, *Cuadro histórico de la revolución mexicana* (3 vols, Mexico, 1961); José María Luis Mora, *México y sus revoluciones* (3 vols, Mexico, 1965) and *Obras sueltas* (Mexico, 1963). The best foreign contributions are H. G. Ward, *Mexico in 1827* (2 vols, London 1828), which contains important observations on the economy by the British *chargé d'affaires;* and J. R. Poinsett, *Notes on Mexico* (Philadelphia, 1824), by the United States minister. See also G. F. Lyon, *Journal of a Residence and Tour in the Republic of Mexico in the Year 1826* (2 vols, London 1828).

The narrative sources of independence, or some of them, often throw light on a subject poorly served by the public documents, namely economic and social history; this is particularly true of foreign accounts, frequently written with an eye to investment prospects. Isolated publications in this field simply whet the appetite. From Argentina we have good editions of liberal economic writings in the pre-independence period: Manuel Belgrano, *Escritos económicos,* ed. Gregorio Weinberg (Buenos Aires, 1954); Hipólito Vieytes, *Antecedentes económicos de la revolución de mayo. Escritos publicados en el Semanario de agricultura, industria y comercio* (1802–1806), ed. Félix Weinberg (Buenos Aires, 1956); Manuel José de Lavardén, *Nuevo aspecto del comercio en el Río de la Plata,* ed. Enrique Wedovoy (Buenos Aires, 1955). These can be supplemented by Germán C. E. Tjarks, *El Consulado de Buenos Aires y sus proyecciones en la historia del Río de la Plata* (2 vols, Buenos Aires, 1962), which reproduces some of the documents. Enrique de Gandía, *Buenos Aires, 1955).* These can be supplemented by Germán O. E. quate) with comments (superfluous) from the correspondence (1787–1816) of the Spanish merchant Gaspar de Coloma. Sergio Bagú, *El plan económico del grupo Rivadaviano 1811–1827* (Rosario, 1966) gives the basic socio-economic decrees of the Rivadavia administration. For Chile and the Pacific Jaime

Eyzaguirre, *Archivo epistolar de la familia Eyzaguirre, 1747–1854* (Buenos Aires, 1960) presents a rare type of source.

Venezuela makes available exceptional documentation, with a fine introduction, on agrarian problems and policies, *Materiales para el estudio de la cuestión agraria en Venezuela* (1800–1830), *Vol. I.* Estudio preliminar por Germán Carrera Damas. José Rafael Revenga, *La hacienda pública de Venezuela en 1828–1830* (Caracas, 1953) was one of the few contemporary statesmen to warn of the consequences of foreign economic penetration. Further data on the economy can be obtained in Ildefonso Leal (ed.), *Documentos del Real Consulado de Caracas* (Caracas, 1964), and Manuel Lucena Salmoral (ed.), *La economia americana del primer cuarto del siglo XIX, vista a través de las memorias escritas por don Vicente Basadre, ultimo intendente de Venezuela (BANH,33,* Caracas, 1983). For Mexico see Enrique Florescano and Isabel Gil Sánchez (eds.), *Descripciones económicas regionales de Nueva España. Provincias del Norte, 1766–1827* (Mexico, 1976).

The documentation presented by R. A. Humphreys (ed.), *British Consular Reports on the Trade and Politics of Latin America, 1824–1826* (London, 1940) has established itself as one of the classic sources in this field, while Gerald S. Graham and R. A. Humphreys (eds.), *The Navy and South America 1807–1823. Correspondence of the Commanders-in-Chief on the South American Station* (London, 1962) has some economic content of a general kind. J. B. Pentland, 'Report on Bolivia, 1827,' ed. J. Valerie Fifer, Royal Historical Society, London, *Camden Miscellany,* 25 (1974), 169–267, is a valuable account of economic, commercial and political conditions in Bolivia in the mid-1820s based on direct observation by the private secretary of the British Consul General in Lima; there is a Spanish (and fuller) version, *Informe sobre Bolivia, 1827* (Potosí, 1975). The distinguished British compilation by Sir Charles Webster, *Britain and the Independence of Latin America, 1812–1830. Select Documents from the Foreign Office Archives* (2 vols, London, 1938), tells us more of British policy than of Latin American conditions. In the field of international relations see also W. R. Manning (ed.), *Diplomatic Correspondence of the United States concerning the Independence of the Latin American Nations* (3 vols, New York,

1925); Ernesto de la Torre Villar, *Correspondencia diplomática franco-mexicana*, 1808–1839 (Mexico, 1957); Cristóbal L. Mendoza, *Las primeras misiones diplomáticas de Venezuela* (2 vols, Caracas, 1962); C. Parra-Pérez (ed.), *Documentos de las cancillerías europeas sobre la independencia venezolana* (2 vols, Caracas, 1962); Vicente Lecuna, *Relaciones diplomáticas de Bolívar con Chile y Buenos Aires* (2 vols, Caracas, 1954). Spain has published little documentation on the loss of its colonies, in spite of its substantial archival resources. On the latter see Pedro Torres Lanzas, *Independencia de América. Fuentes para su estudio. Catálogo de los documentos conservados en el Archivo General de Indias* (6 vols, Madrid, 1912); segunda serie (2 vols, Seville, 1924–25); J. F. Guillén, *Independencia de América. Indice de los papeles de expediciones de Indias* (3 vols, Madrid, Archivo General de Marina don Alvaro de Bazán, 1953); C. Bermúdez Plata, *Catálogo de documentos de la sección novena del Archivo General de Indias*, vol. I(Seville, 1949).

GENERAL WORKS

Latin American historiography in the nineteenth century produced a number of general works on independence which have stood the test of time. The greatest classics are those of the Argentine statesman and historian, Bartolomé Mitre, *Historia de Belgrano y de la independencia argentina* (1st ed., 1857, 6th ed. 4 vols, Buenos Aires, 1927), and *Historia de San Martín y de la emancipación Sud-Americana* (1st ed., 1888–89, 2nd ed., 4 vols, Buenos Aires, 1890). The latter in particular transcends the confines of the Río de la Plata; in Mitre's own words 'the theme of both books is American independence . . . an incipient nationality, mother of other nationalities'. But this universalist tradition has been virtually abandoned. As Latin Americans have moved further from their common past, so they have paid less attention to each other's history and have made little contribution to general history. The outstanding products of Latin American historians are national histories and monographic works about their own countries. It has been left to others to write the general histories of independence. R. A. Humphreys has written a number of distinguished works, including *Liberation in South America 1806–1827. The Career of James Paroissien* (London,

1952); 'The Development of the American Communities outside British Rule', *The New Cambridge Modern History*, viii (Cambridge, 1965), 397–420; 'The Emancipation of Latin America', *ibid.*, ix (1965), 612–38; and *Tradition and Revolt in Latin America* (London, 1969). These range widely over the history of independence, combining original research and a synoptic view. Jorge I. Domínguez, *Insurrection or Loyalty. The Breakdown of the Spanish American Empire* (Cambridge, Mass., 1980) interprets known facts according to the categories of political science. Modern research culminates in Leslie Bethell (ed.), *The Cambridge History of Latin America*, Volume III (Cambridge, 1985), which presents the latest state of knowledge and has the advantage too of dealing with the economy, society and politics of Spanish America in the wake of independence.

For a Marxist interpretation of independence see Manfred Kossok, 'Revolution und Bourgeoisie in Lateinamerika. Zum Charakter der Lateinamerikanischen Unabhängigkeitsbewegung, 1810–1826', *Zeitschrift für Geschichtswissenschaft*, ix Jahrgang (Berlin, 1961), 123–43, who argues that Latin American independence was a bourgeois revolution. More recent studies by the same author include 'Di Unabhängigkeitsrevolution Spanisch-Amerikas 1810–1826', *Revolutionen Der Neuzeit* 1500–1917 (Vaduz/Liechtenstein, 1982), and 'Unidad y diversidad en la historia de la América española. El caso de la Independencia', *Acta Histórica*, 79 (Szeged, 1984), 69–81. Soviet historiography also interprets independence as an essentially bourgeois revolution, with elements of popular participation. For a guide to the extensive Soviet contribution see M. S. Alperovich, *Historiografía soviética latinoamericanista* (Caracas, 1969), pp. 18–23, the most convenient item of which is M. S. Alperovich, V. I. Ermolaiev, I. R. Lavretski, S. I. Semionov, 'Concerning the War of Independence in the Spanish Colonies in America (1810–1826)', first published in Moscow in 1956 and reproduced in David Bushnell (ed.), *The Liberator, Simón Bolívar: Man and Image* (New York, 1970), pp. 187–95.

Origins of Independence

On the Spanish background to imperial policy in the eighteenth century see Gonzalo Anes, *El antiguo régimen: los Borbones*

(5th ed., 1981), Antonio Domínguez Ortiz, *Sociedad y estado en el siglo XVIII español* (Madrid, 1981), and Josep Fontana Lázaro (ed.), *La economía española al final del antiguo régimen. III. Comercio y colonias* (Madrid, 1982). The Enlightenment can be studied in Richard Herr, *The Eighteenth-Century Revolution in Spain* (Princeton, 1958), and its impact in America in R. J. Shafer, *The Economic Societies in the Spanish World* (1763–1821) (Syracuse, 1958); see also M. L. Pérez Marchand, *Dos etapas ideológicas del siglo XVIII en México a través de los papeles de la Inquisición* (Mexico, 1945). José Carlos Chiaramonte (ed.). *Pensamiento de la Ilustración. Economía y sociedad iberoamericanas en el siglo XVIII* (Caracas, 1979) gives a selection of primary texts, prefaced by a survey of the state of the subject. The role of traditional Spanish ideology has been studied by Rafael Gómez Hoyos, *La revolución granadina de 1810: ideario de una generación y de una época, 1781–1821* (2 vols, Bogotá, 1962) and O. Carlos Stoetzer, *The Scholastic Roots of the Spanish American Revolution* (New York, 1979); for a different interpretation see Tulio Halperín Donghi, *Tradición política española e ideología revolucionario de mayo* (Buenos Aires, 1961). On the Jesuits, in particular Viscardo, see Miguel Batllori, *El Abate Viscardo. Historia y mito de la intervención de los Jesuitas en la independencia de Hispanomérica* (Caracas, 1953), and Merle E. Simmons, *Los escritos de Juan Pablo Viscardo y Guzmán* (Caracas, 1983).

Imperial reform and American responses can be studied in John Lynch, *Spanish Colonial Administration, 1782–1810. The Intendant System in the Viceroyalty of the Río de la Plata* (London, 1958); Luis Navarro Garcia, *Intendencias en Indias* (Seville, 1959); J. R. Fisher, *Government and Society in Colonial Peru. The Intendant System 1784–1814* (London, 1970); D. A. Brading, *Miners and Merchants in Bourbon Mexico 1763–1810* (Cambridge, 1971); Reinhard Liehr, *Ayuntamiento y oligarquía en Puebla, 1787–1810* (2 vols, Mexico, 1976); and Jacques A. Barbier, *Reform and Politics in Bourbon Chile, 1755–1796* (Ottawa, 1980). The attempt to reform *repartimientos* is dealt with in Brian R. Hamnett, *Politics and Trade in Southern Mexico 1750–1821* (Cambridge, 1971), and in Stanley J. Stein, 'Bureaucracy and Business in the Spanish Empire, 1759–1804: Failure of a Bourbon Reform in Mexico and Peru', *HAHR, 61,*

1 (1981), 2–28. Juan Marchena Fernández, *Oficiales y soldados en el ejército de América* (Seville, 1983) shows the increasing 'Americanization' of the Spanish army in America, while military reform is precisely defined by Christon I. Archer, *The Army in Bourbon Mexico* 1760–1810 (Albuquerque, 1977), Leon G. Campbell, *The Military and Society in Colonial Peru* 1750–1810 (Philadelphia, 1978), and Allan J. Kuethe, *Military Reform and Society in New Granada, 1773–1808* (Gainesville, 1978). Clerical immunity and its erosion by reform and revolution are studied by Nancy M. Farriss, *Crown and Clergy in Colonial Mexico* 1759–1821. *The Crisis of Ecclesiastical Privilege* (London, 1968), while the economic role of the Church and its limits are clarified by Arnold J. Bauer, 'The Church in the Economy of Spanish America: *Censos* and *Depósitos* in the Eighteenth and Nineteenth Centuries', *HAHR*, 63, 4 (1983), 707–33; and religious trends in Mexico are studied by D. A. Brading, 'Tridentine Catholicism and Enlightened Despotism in Bourbon Mexico', *JLAS*, 15, 1 (1983), 1–22. Aspects of renewed fiscal pressure are explained in Sergio Villalobos R., *Tradición y reforma en* 1810 (Santiago, 1961) for Chile, and for Mexico in D. A. Brading, 'Facts and Figments in Bourbon Mexico', *Bulletin of Latin American Research*, 4, 1 (1985), 61–64.

The violent reaction to taxation and other burdens has been studied in a number of works on the rebellions of the eighteenth century. Joseph Perez, *Los movimientos precursores de la emancipación en Hispanoamérica* (Madrid, 1977) identifies the major movements and their character. Leon G. Campbell, 'Recent research on Andean peasant revolts, 1750–1820', *Latin American Research Review*, 14, 1 (1979), 3–49, surveys primary and secondary material for the region of 'Inca nationalism'. Segundo Moreno Yáñez, *Sublevaciones indígenas en la Audiencia de Quito, desde comienzos del siglo XVIII hasta finales de la colonia* (Bonn, 1976), describes Indian protest in the region of Quito against a background of agrarian structure. Anthony McFarlane, 'Civil Disorders and Popular Protests in Late Colonial New Granada', *HAHR*, 64, 1 (1984), 17–54, classifies and interprets the numerous examples of popular protests, hitherto overshadowed by the *comunero* movement. On the latter see John Leddy Phelan, *The People and the King. The Comunero*

Revolution in Colombia, 1781 (Madison, 1978); Carlos E. Muñoz Oraá, *Los comuneros de Venezuela* (Mérida, 1971). The great Indian rebellion in Peru can be studied in Boleslao Lewin, *La rebelión de Tupac Amaru·y los orígenes de la emancipación americana* (Buenos Aires, 1957); Alberto Flores Galindo (ed.), *Tupac Amaru II* — 1780. *Antología* (Lima, 1976); and, in a larger context, Scarlett O'Phelan Godoy, *Rebellions and Revolts in Eighteenth Century Peru and Upper Peru* (Cologne, 1985). The problems of economic causation have been discussed in various contexts. Tulio Halperín Donghi (ed.), *El ocaso del orden colonial Hispanoaméricana* (Buenos Aires, 1978) is a collection of socio-economic studies of crises in the colonial order. Spanish thinking on colonial trade is the subject of Marcelo Bitar Letayf, *Economistas españoles del siglo XVIII. Sus ideas sobre la libertad del comercio con Indias* (Madrid, 1968). The trade itself is studied by Geoffrey J. Walker, *Spanish Politics and Imperial Trade*, 1700–1789 (London, 1979). Quantitative studies of *comercio libre* and its fate during the Anglo-Spanish wars are provided by Antonio García-Baquero, *Cádiz y el Atlántico* (1717–1778) (2 vols., Seville, 1976) and *Comercio colonial y guerras revolucionarias* (Seville, 1972), and by Javier Ortiz de la Tabla Ducasse, *Comercio exterior de Veracruz* 1778–1821 (Seville, 1978). John Fisher, *Commercial Relations between Spain and Spanish America in the Era of Free Trade, 1778–1796* (Liverpool, 1985) gives a precise measurement of trade between Spain and America under *comercio libre*. The role of colonial trade in Spanish economic development is discussed in Jordi Nadal and Gabriel Tortella (eds.), *Agricultura, comercio colonial y crecimiento económico en la España contemporánea* (Barcelona, 1974). Jacques A. Barbier and Allan K. Kuethe (eds.), *The North American Role in the Spanish Imperial Economy* 1760–1819 (Manchester, 1984) deals with North American trade with Spanish America in the late colonial and early independence periods.

Economic conditions in Spanish America are the subject of basic new research. The mining sector and its position in the socio-economic structure of Mexico is studied by Brading, *Miners and Merchants in Bourbon Mexico*. For mining in Peru see J. R. Fisher, *Silver Mines and Silver Miners in Colonial Peru, 1776–1824* (Liverpool, 1977), and for Upper Peru Rose Marie Buechler,

The Mining Society of Potosí 1776–1810 (Syracuse University, 1981). Enrique Tandeter, 'Forced and Free Labour in late colonial Potosí', *Past and Present,* 93 (1981), 98–136, demonstrates the importance of *mita* labour to the survival of Potosí production. Enrique Tandeter and Nathan Wachtel in *Precios y producción agraria. Potosí y Charcas en el siglo XVIII* (Buenos Aires, 1983) establish a price series for the eighteenth century and relate it to the economy of Upper Peru. Enrique Florescano, *Precios del maíz y crisis agrícolas en México* (1708–1810) (Mexico, 1969), examines rising maize prices, agrarian crisis and rural misery on the eve of the Mexican insurgency. For regional studies of the agrarian sector see D. A. Brading, *Haciendas and Ranchos in the Mexican Bajío: León* 1700–1860 (Cambridge, 1978); Eric Van Young, *Hacienda and Market in Eighteenth Century Mexico. The Rural Economy of Guadalajara,* 1675–1820 (Berkeley and Los Angeles, 1981). Humberto Tandrón, *El real consulado de Caracas y el comercio exterior de Venezuela* (Caracas, 1976), illustrates the tension between agricultural and commercial interests and the clash between Venezuelan and Spanish viewpoints, while problems of another export economy and its hinterland are studied by Michael T. Hamerly, *Historia social y económica de la antigua provincia de Guayaquil,* 1763–1842 (Guayaquil, 1973). Susan Migden Socolow, *The Merchants of Buenos Aires* 1778–1810. *Family and Commerce* (Cambridge, 1978) analyses the formation, economic role and social position of the *porteño* merchant group, while the little-known history of artisans is investigated by Lyman L. Johnson, 'The Silversmiths of Buenos Aires: A Case Study in the failure of corporate social organisation', *JLAS,* 8, 2 (1976), 181–213.

Social structure of the pre-independence period involves problems of class, creoles and race. Historians have recently tended to emphasize economic interests, social perceptions and political groupings rather than simply creole-peninsular conflict as an explanation of independence: see Luis Villoro, *El Proceso ideológico de la revolución de independencia* (Mexico, 1967), for a survey of social classes in Mexico; further refinement of analysis is provided by David A. Brading, 'Government and Elite in Late Colonial Mexico', *HAHR,* 53 (1973), 389–414, and by Doris M. Ladd, *The Mexican Nobility at Independence* 1780–1826

(Austin, 1976). Venezuelan structures are explained by Germán Carrera Damas, *La crisis de la sociedad colonial venezolano* (Caracas, 1976), and Miguel Izard, *El miedo a la revolución. La lucha por la libertad en Venezuela* (1777–1830) (Madrid, 1979). The growing tension between whites and coloureds is described by Federico Brito Figueroa, *Las insurreciones de los esclavos negros en la sociedad colonial* (Caracas, 1961), Miguel Acosta Saignes, *Vida de los esclavos negros en Venezuela* (Caracas, 1967), and I. Leal, 'La aristocracia criolla venezolana y el código negrero de 1789', *Revista de Historia* 2 (1961), 61–81, while Jaime Jaramillo Uribe, 'Esclavos y señores en la sociedad colombiana del siglo XVIII', *Anuario Colombiano de Historia Social y de la Cultura*, 1 (1963), 3–62, and 'Mestizaje y diferenciación social en el Nuevo Reino de Granada en la segunda mitad del siglo XVIII', *ibid.*, 2 (1965), 21–48, perform a similar task for New Granada. The influence of the revolution in Saint-Domingue can be studied in Eleazar Córdova-Bello, *La independencia de Haiti y su influencia en Hispanoamérica* (Mexico-Caracas, 1967). Creole demand for office and the Spanish 'reaction' are measured by Mark A. Burkholder and D. S. Chandler, *From Impotence to Authority. The Spanish Crown and the American Audiencias 1687–1808* (Columbus, 1977).

Incipient nationalism has not been systematically studied. J. A. de la Puente Candamo, *La idea de la comunidad peruana y el testimonio de los precursores* (Lima, 1956), Nestor Meza Villalobos, *La conciencia política chilena durante la monarquía* (Santiago, 1958), André Saint-Lu, *Condition coloniale et conscience créole au Guatemale* (1524–1821) (Paris, 1970), and D. A. Brading, *The Origins of Mexican Nationalism* (Cambridge, 1985), discuss various aspects of the subject. For an attempt at a synthesis see Gonzalo Vial Correa, 'La formación de nacionalidades hispanoamericanas como causa de la independencia', *Boletín de la Academia Chilena de la Historia*, xxxiii, no. 75 (1966), 110–44. On Americanism as a cultural phenomenon see the superb work of Antonello Gerbi, *La disputa del Nuevo Mundo* (Mexico, 1960). On the process of nation building at independence see the articles edited by Inge Buisson, *et al*, *Problemas de la formación del estado y de la nación en Hispanoamérica* (Bonn, 1984).

ARGENTINA, PARAGUAY, URUGUAY

The tradition of liberal historiography in Argentina found expression in a series of large-scale works on independence which are still important sources of information: Diego Molinari, *La Representación de los Hacendados de Mariano Moreno* (2nd ed., Buenos Aires, 1939) and *Antecedentes de la Revolución de Mayo* (3 vols, Buenos Aires, 1922–26); Ricardo Levene, *Ensayo histórico sobre la revolución de mayo y Mariano Moreno* (2 vols, Buenos Aires, 1920; 4th ed., 3 vols, 1960), and R. Levene (ed.), *Historia de la nación argentina* (10 vols, Buenos Aires, 1936–42; 3rd ed., 15 vols, 1963); Enrique Ruiz Guiñazú, *Epifanía de la libertad* (Buenos Aires, 1952) and *El Presidente Saavedra y el pueblo soberano de 1810* (Buenos Aires, 1960); Enrique C. Corbellini, *La revolución de mayo* (2 vols, Buenos Aires, 1950); Carlos A. Pueyrredón, 1810. *La revolución de mayo* (Buenos Aires, 1953); Ricardo Piccirilli, *San Martín y la política de los pueblos* (Buenos Aires, 1957) and *Rivadavia y su tiempo* (2nd ed., 3 vols, Buenos Aires, 1960); Mariano de Vedia y Mitre, *La vida de Monteagudo* (3 vols, Buenos Aires, 1950). Traditional historiography was challenged by a 'revisionist' school, which questioned the inevitability, representativeness, and revolutionary content of the May revolution. Some of the new research made real contributions, particularly the studies of Roberto H. Marfany, 'Dónde está el pueblo?', *Humanidades*, xxxi (1948), 253–313; 'El pronunciamiento de mayo', *Historia*, iii (1958), 61–126; 'Vísperas de mayo', *Historia*, v (1960), 87–158; *El cabildo de mayo* (Buenos Aires, 1961); *Episodios de la revolución de mayo* (Buenos Aires, 1966).

Both traditional and revisionist historiography have been largely superceded by Tulio Halperín Donghi, *Politics, Economics and Society in Argentina in the Revolutionary Period* (Cambridge, 1975) which gives a total view of the revolution and brings the subject into the mainstream of modern historical writing; see the same author's *Guerra y finanzas en los orígenes del estado argentino* (1790–1850) (Buenos Aires, 1983) for the role of the state in the war and post-war economy. David Bushnell, *Reform and Reaction in the Platine Provinces* 1810–1852 (Gainesville, 1983) studies liberalism as expressed in laws and institutions. The economic content of Argentine independence has been expertly identified by Miron Burgin, *The Economic Aspects of Argentine Federalism, 1820–1852* (Cambridge, Mass., 1946), which still stands the test of time; but for a more comprehensive study see Jonathan C. Brown, *A Socioeconomic History of Argentina, 1776–1860* (Cambridge, 1979). Foreign trade and its participants can be studied in Juan Carlos Nicolau, 'Movimiento marítimo exterior del puerto de Buenos Aires (1810–1854)', *Nuestra Historia*, 12 (1973), 351–61; H. S. Ferns, *Britain and Argentina in the Nineteenth Century* (Oxford, 1960); and Vera Blinn Reber, *British Mercantile Houses in Buenos Aires, 1810–1880* (Cambridge, Mass., 1979). Population change is measured by Susana R. Frías, César A. García Belsunce, *et al.*, *Buenos Aires: su gente, 1800–1830* (Buenos Aires, 1976), based on censuses of the city of Buenos Aires. George Reid Andrews, *The Afro-Argentines of Buenos Aires, 1800–1900* (Madison, 1980), is an important contribution to socio-racial history, and Ricardo E. Rodríguez Molas, *Historia social del gaucho* (revised ed., Buenos Aires, 1982) and Richard W. Slatta, *Gauchos and the Vanishing Frontier* (Lincoln, Nebraska, 1983) are valuable studies of the changing role of the gaucho.

Paraguayan independence can be best studied in John Hoyt Williams, *The Rise and Fall of the Paraguayan Republic, 1800–1870* (Austin, 1979), a work of research and interpretation. Richard Alan White, *Paraguay's Autonomous Revolution 1810–1840* (Albuquerque, 1978), takes a new, though partial, look at Francia. For a Paraguayan view, see Julio César Chaves, *El supremo dictador. Biografía de José Gaspar de Francia* (4th ed., Madrid, 1964); the same author has written *Historia de las relaciones entre Buenos-Ayres y el Paraguay, 1810–1813* (2nd ed., Asunción, 1959), which covers the early stages of independence in some detail. There is a comprehensive study by the distinguished Soviet historian of Latin America, M. S. Alperovich, *Revolución y dictadura en el Paraguay (1810–1840)* (Moscow, 1975). Uruguay has a large bibliography, of which the following is only a selection. Juan E. Pivel Devoto, *Raíces coloniales de la revolución oriental de 1811* (Montevideo, 1952, 3rd ed., 1957) is the best study of the colonial background of independence. The classical work on Artigas is Eduardo Acevedo, *José Artigas. Su obra cívica*. *Alegato histórico* (1909–10; 3 vols, Montevideo, 1950). The best modern work on the life and times of the liberator is John Street, *Artigas and the Emancipation of Uruguay* (Cambridge, 1959). On his federalism see Pablo Blanco Acevedo, *El federalismo de Artigas y la independencia nacional* (Montevideo, 1939). The social and agrarian policies of Artigas are the subject of original research by Lucía Sala de Touron, Nelson de la Torre and Julio C. Rodríguez in *Artigas y su revolución agraria* 1800–1820 (Mexico, 1978).

CHILE

Modern Chilean historiography inherits a long tradition of scholarship and monumentality. Francisco A. Encina, *Historia de Chile desde la prehistoria hasta* 1891 (20 vols, Santiago, 1942–52), devotes volumes 6–10 to the independence period, a collection of useful facts and independent, sometimes eccentric, theories. The student will find a more useful guide to the origins and early stages in Jaime Eyzaguirre, *Ideario y ruta de la emancipación chilena* (Santiago, 1957) and Sergio Villalobos R., *Tradición y reforma en* 1810 (Santiago, 1961). On the first political stirrings see Néstor Meza Villalobos, *La actividad política del reino de Chile entre* 1806 *y* 1810 (Santiago, 1958); on the first revolution, Raúl Silva Castro, *Egaña y la Patria Vieja* 1810–1814 (Santiago, 1959); and on further political developments, Julio Alemparte, *Carrera y Freire, fundadores de la república* (Santiago, 1963). Chilean independence is dominated by O'Higgins and Portales, a liberal and a conservative: on the first see Jaime Eyzaguirre, *O'Higgins* (6th ed., Santiago, 1965) and Luis Valencia Avaria, *Bernardo O'Higgins. El buen genio de América* (Santiago, 1980); on Portales see F. A. Encina, *Portales* (2 vols, Santiago, 1934), and J. Kinsbruner, *Diego Portales: Interpretative essays on the man and his times* (The Hague, 1967). For an interpretation of independence in terms of elite politics, see Mary L. Felstiner, 'Kinship Politics in the Chilean Independence Movement', *HAHR*, 56, 1 (1976), 58–80. On the agrarian sector see Arnold J. Bauer, *Chilean Rural Society from the Spanish Conquest to* 1830 (Cambridge, 1975). Robert M. Will, 'The Introduction of Classical Economics into Chile', *HAHR*, xliv (1964), 1–21, qualifies the traditional impression of economic liberalism. Guillermo Feliú Cruz, *La abolición de la esclavitud en Chile* (Santiago, 1942) gives the facts of abolition. The Chilean revolution was rich in political ideas; these have their historian in Simon Collier, whose *Ideas and Politics of Chilean Independence* 1808–1833 (Cambridge, 1967) analyses the ideology of independence against the background of political developments.

GREATER COLOMBIA

Venezuelan historiography has been distorted by obsession with Bolívar, as Germán Carrera Damas *(El culto a Bolívar* (Caracas, 1969)) has well understood. But at least the obsession is not devoid of high standards of scholarship. Augusto Mijares, *El Libertador* (Caracas, 1967, English version 1983) is a leading Venezuelan interpretation. The German historian Gerhard Masur, *Simon Bolivar* (Albuquerque, 1948, rev. ed., 1969) provides a dispassionate account, but the value of this book is being gradually reduced by new research and appraisals. The work by the Spanish historian Salvador de Madariaga, *Bolivar* (London, 1952, reprinted 1968), is not without scholarship and interest, but is perversely critical. Vicente Lecuna, *Crónica razonada de las guerras de Bolívar* (3 vols, New York, 1950) is a detailed account of the military and to some extent political action of Bolívar up to Ayacucho; his *Catálogo de errores y calumnias en la historia de Bolívar* (3 vols, New York, 1956–58) is a hypersensitive defence of Bolívar with some factual utility). The political and social ideas of Bolívar have been studied by J. L. Salcedo-Bastardo, *Visión y revisión de Bolívar* (Caracas, 1957) and *Bolívar, un continente y un destino* (Caracas, 1972; Eng. ed., Richmond, 1978). John Lynch examines the thought of Bolívar in a wider context in *Simón Bolívar and the Age of Revolution* (Institute of Latin American Studies, Working Papers, 10, London, 1983). On some of the property problems of Bolívar see the interesting monograph by Paul Verna, *Las minas del Libertador* (Caracas, 1977). The Bicentenary of the birth of Bolívar generated numerous congresses and a large output of writings and papers, not all of these well conceived and not all yet published. Among the latter, the papers of the Congress of the Academia Nacional de la Historia in Caracas are awaited with interest. The papers of a Congress in Hamburg and Cologne have been cited above, Inge Buisson, *et. al., Problemas de la formación del estado*. See also the articles by John Lynch, Simon Collier, David Bushnell and Germán Carrera Damas, in *HAHR*, 63, 1 (1983). And for a Marxist example mention may be made of Max Zeuske (ed.), *Interpretaciones y ensayos marxistas acerca de Simón Bolívar (Asia, Africa, Latin America*, Special Issue, 14, Berlin, 1985); these were preceded by a more substantial Soviet contribution, I. Lavretski, *Simón Bolívar* (Moscow, 1982).

The most substantial account of the first stage of independence is Caracciolo Parra-Pérez, *Historia de la primera república de Venezuela* (2 vols, Caracas, 1959), whose author has also written the history of the 'liberator of the east', *Mariño y la independencia de Venezuela* (5 vols, Madrid, 1954–57). Standing apart from these essentially political narratives is the work of Laureano Valenilla Lanz, *Cesarismo democrático (Obras completas*, 1, Caracas, 1983), an argument for the 'necessary gendarme' but also an interpretation of the revolution for independence; an early, if brief, essay in social history, Eloy G. González, *Al margen de la epopeya* (Caracas, 1946); and more recently a fine analytical study by Germán Carrera Damas, *Boves. Aspectos socio-económicos de su acción histórica* (Caracas, 1968). In other works, too, particularly *Tres temas de historia* (Caracas, 1961) and *Historiografía marxista venezolana y otros temas* (Caracas, 1967), Carrera Damas has sought to identify the social content of the Venezuelan revolution. The social limits of the revolution are also the theme of Izard, *El miedo a la revolución* (cited above, p.425). For social and economic aspects see also Federico Brito Figueroa, *Ensayos de historia social venezolana* (Caracas, 1960), and *Historia económica y social de Venezuela* (2 vols, Caracas, 1966). Slavery and abolition can be studied in John V. Lombardi, *The Decline and Abolition of Negro Slavery in Venezuela*, 1820–1854 (Westport, 1971). The commander of the Spanish expeditionary army, and the royalist position, are the subjects of Stephen K. Stoan, *Pablo Morillo and Venezuela*, 1815–1820 (Columbus, 1974).

Colombian independence has a shorter bibliography. The leading essay in contemporary history is that by José Manuel

Restrepo, *Historia de la revolución de la república de Colombia* (8 vols, Bogotá, 1942–50) by a Colombian republican. There is also a nineteenth-century classic by a Colombian conservative, José Manuel Groot, *Historia eclesiástica y civil de Nueva Granada* (5 vols, Bogotá, 1953). The early stages can be studied in José Manuel Forero, *Camilo Torres* (Bogotá, 1960). The most substantial account will be found in the relevant volumes of the *Historia extensa de Colombia* published by the Academia Colombiana de Historia: Camilo Riaño, *Historia militar: la independencia*, 1810-1815 (Bogotá, 1971); Guillermo Plazas Olarte, *Historia militar: la independencia*, 1819–1828 (Bogotá, 1971); Roberto M. Tisnes, J., *Historia eclesiástica: el clero y la independencia en Santa Fe*, 1810–1815 (Bogotá, 1971); Luis Galvis Madero, *La Gran Colombia*, 1819–1830 (Bogotá, 1970). The counter-revolution is documented by Oswaldo Díaz Díaz in *La reconquista española* (2 vols, Bogotá, 1964–67), who also gives a rare account of a creole guerrilla group, *Los Almeydas. Episodios de la resistencia patriota contra el ejército pacificador de Tierra Firme* (Bogotá, 1962). David Bushnell, *The Santander Regime in Gran Colombia* (Newark, Del., 1954) is one of the few studies of state building in the wake of independence, focusing on political, economic and social organisation. On the ideas of independence in their political context see Javier Ocampo López, *El proceso ideológico de la emancipación en Colombia* (Bogotá, 1980). For an introduction to the structure of the economy at independence see Anthony McFarlane, 'The Transition from Colonialism in Colombia, 1819–1875', in Christopher Abel and Colin M. Lewis (eds.), *Latin America, Economic Imperialism and the State* (London, 1985), pp. 101–124.

The independence of Ecuador has been studied largely in an episodic way. See, however, Demetrio Ramos Pérez, *Entre el Plata y Bogotá. Cuatro claves de la emancipación ecuatoriana* (Madrid, 1978) and, for the structural background, the monograph by Hamerley cited above (p. 424).

PERU AND BOLIVIA

The political narrative of Rubén Vargas Ugarte, *Historia del Perú. Emancipación* (1809–1825) (Buenos Aires, 1958) is still useful but has been superceded in analytical qualities by

Timothy E. Anna, *The Fall of the Royal Government in Peru* (Lincoln, Nebraska, 1979). José de la Puente Candamo, *Notas sobre la causa de la independencia del Perú* (2nd ed., Lima, 1970), is useful for the student, especially on the question of national identity. Heraclio Bonilla and others, *La independencia en el Perú* (2nd ed., Lima, 1981) is a composite work of uneven quality and varying relevance, though enhanced in the second edition by Bonilla's chapter on the popular classes. Special aspects are dealt with by Mark A. Burkholder, *Politics of a Colonial Career: José Baquíjano and the Audiencia of Lima* (Albuquerque, 1980); and John Fisher, 'Royalism, Regionalism and Rebellion in Colonial Peru, 1808–1815', *HAHR*, 59, 2 (1979), 232–57. The policy and ideas of San Martín in Peru can be studied in J. A. de la Puente Candamo, *San Martín y el Perú* (Lima, 1948); see also José P. Otero, *Historia del libertador don José de San Martín* (4 vols, Buenos Aires, 1932) and, on the creole guerrilla groups, Raúl Rivera Serna, *Los guerrilleros del centro en la emancipación peruana* (Lima, 1958). Jorge Basadre deals with the organization of the new state in vol. I of his *Historia de la república del Perú* (5th ed., 10 vols, 1961–64), while his *El azar en la historia y sus límites* (Lima, 1973) is worth reading for his reflections on the history of this period. On the Indian policy of the republic see Juan José Vega, *La emancipación frente al indio peruano (La legislación de la república, 1821–1830* (Lima, 1958).

The Guayaquil interview between San Martín and Bolívar has received disproportionate attention: G. Masur, 'The Conference of Guayaquil', *HAHR*, xxxi (1951), 189–229, provides a balanced discussion; there is a reply to this by V. Lecuna, 'Bolívar and San Martín at Guayaquil', *HAHR*, xxxi (1951), 369–93.

Bolivian historiography is less developed. Gabriel René-Moreno, *Ultimos días coloniales en el Alto-Peru* (2 vols, La Paz, 1940) is a classic, first published at the end of the nineteenth century and remarkable for the attempt to inject some social history into the narrative. Charles W. Arnade, *The Emergence of the Republic of Bolivia* (Gainesville, 1957) has performed a basic task and is indispensable. Rene Danilo Arze Aguirre, *Participación popular en la independencia de Bolivia* (La Paz, 1979) is the first serious study of the popular sectors, though it tends to fade after 1814; further aspects of social history are treated in Alberto Crespo, *et al.*, *La vida cotidiana en La Paz durante la Guerra de la Independencia* (La Paz, 1975). The policy of Sucre and the obstacles to change are researched by William L. Lofstrom, *The Promise and Problems of Reform: Attempted Social and Economic Change in the First Years of Bolivian Independence* (Cornell University, Latin American Studies Program, *Dissertation Series, 35,* 1972).

MEXICO AND CENTRAL AMERICA

Mexican independence, remarkable alike for its social violence and political debate, has attracted the attention of many historians. Modern research is summed up and further developed by Timothy E. Anna, *The Fall of the Royal Government in Mexico City* (Lincoln, Nebraska, 1978), which interprets independence in terms of enduring reformism. A Mexican synthesis, with a useful collection of documents, is provided by Ernesto de la Torre Villar, *La independencia mexicana* (3 vols, Mexico, 1982). The work by Brian R. Hamnett, *Revolución y contrarevolución en México y el Perú. Liberalismo, realeza y separatismo, 1800–1824* (Mexico, 1978), 'Mexico's Royalist Coalition: The Response to Revolution', *JLAS,* 12, 1 (1980), 55–86, and 'Royalist Counterinsurgency and the Continuity of Rebellion: Guanajuato and Michoacán, 1813–20', *HAHR,* 62, 1 (1982), 19–48, clarify many aspects of the revolution and its royalist opponents, focusing on the politics of the elites during the revolutionary decade. Of the many works on Hidalgo two are basic: Luis Castillo Ledón, *Hidalgo, la vida del héroe* (2 vols, Mexico, 1948–49), and Hugh M. Hamill, Jr., *The Hidalgo Revolt. Prelude to Mexican Independence* (Gainesville, 1966). For Morelos, too, there are two essential studies: Alfonso Teja Zabre, *Vida de Morelos* (3rd ed., Mexico, 1959), and Wilbert H. Timmons, *Morelos of Mexico. Priest, Soldier, Statesman* (El Paso, 1963). W. S. Robertson, *Iturbide of Mexico* (Durham, N.C., 1952) provides a political biography of the royalist turned liberator, which can be supplemented by Timothy E. Anna, 'The Role of Agustín de Iturbide: A Reappraisal', *JLAS,* 17, 1 (1985), 79–110, an exercise in revisionism.

The intellectual history of the period is told in detail by Jesús

Reyes Héroles, *El liberalismo mexicano* (3 vols, Mexico, 1957–61), and with great awareness by Charles A. Hale, *Mexican Liberalism in the Age of Mora 1821–1853* (New Haven, 1968); while Javier Ocampo, *Las ideas de un día. El pueblo mexicano ante la consumación de su independencia* (Mexico, 1969) tells us what Mexicans thought of independence in 1821 by reference to contemporary press, periodicals and writings. The impact of Spanish liberal policy is considered in Nettie Lee Benson (ed.), *Mexico and the Spanish Cortes, 1810–1822* (Austin, 1966); the changing fortunes of the peninsulares by Romeo Flores Caballero, *La contra-revolución en la independencia. Los españoles en la vida política, social y económica de México* (1804–1838) (Mexico, 1969); the role of the Church by Nancy M. Farriss, *Crown and Clergy in Colonial Mexico* (cited above p.   ); while Michael P. Costeloe, *Church Wealth in Mexico. A Study of the 'Juzgado de Capellanías' in the Archbishopric of Mexico 1800–1856* (Cambridge, 1967) considers the economic position of the Church. Jaime E. Rodríguez O., *The Emergence of Spanish America. Vicente Rocafuerte and Spanish Americanism 1808–1832* (Berkeley and Los Angeles, 1975) throws light on problems of nationality and international relations. Robert A. Potash, *Mexican Government and Industrial Development in the Early Republic: The Banco de Avío* (Amherst, 1983) examines the attempt to assemble capital for industrial development, while Jan Bazant, 'Evolución de la industria textil poblana (1554–1845)', *Historia Mexicana, xiii* (1964), 473–516, covers one particular industry. Hacienda changes are brought to light by John M. Tutino, 'Hacienda Social Relations in Mexico: the Chalco Region in the Era of Independence', *HAHR*, 55, 3, (1975), 496–528, and R. B. Lindley, *Haciendas and Economic Development. Guadalajara, Mexico at Independence* (Austin, 1983). The Indian problem can be studied in Moisés González Navarro, 'Instituciones indígenas en México independiente', Instituto Indigenista Nacional, *Métodos y resultados de la política indigenista en México* (Mexico, 1954), and *Raza y tierra* (Mexico, 1970). Finally for a Marxist analysis of the course and character of Mexican independence see the work of the Soviet historian, M. S. Alperovich, *Historia de la independencia de México* (1810–1824) (Mexico, 1967).

Central American independence can be approached through a study of the colonial structure and its crisis in Miles L. Wortman, *Government and Society in Central America, 1680–1840* (New York, 1982). Louis E. Bumgartner, *José del Valle of Central America* (Durham, N.C., 1963) throws much light on the essential nature of independence, while Valle can be studied in his own writings in José Cecilio del Valle, *Obra escogida*, ed. Mario García Laguardia (Biblioteca Ayacucho, 96, Caracas, 1982). Mario Rodríguez, *The Cadiz Experiment in Central America, 1808–1826* (Berkeley and Los Angeles, 1978) clarifies Spanish liberal policies and Central American responses.

ECONOMY AND SOCIETY

The historiography of independence was traditionally biased towards military, political and institutional developments, and towards the lives of the liberators. To some extent this was a natural bias, for it reflected the preoccupations of the leaders of independence, to whom it would be anachronistic to impute socio-economic objectives which they did not possess, and whose role it would be pointless to underrate. Nevertheless the new rulers represented certain interests, preserved a particular heritage, and perpetuated specific economic and social structures. Moreover, it is the task of the historian to penetrate official silence and reveal the condition and aims of all sectors of society. These problems have now begun to receive more attention from historians, especially for the pre-independence period, less systematically for subsequent decades. The pioneering work in this field was the article by Charles C. Griffin, 'Economic and Social Aspects of the Era of Spanish-American Independence', *HAHR*, xxix (1949), 170–87, amplified in *Los temas sociales y económicos en la época de la independencia* (Caracas, 1962). Important contributions are made in the previously cited works of Humphreys, García-Baquero, Fisher, Halperín Donghi, Socolow, Brown, Andrews, Buechler, Tandeter, Bauer, Arze Aguirre, Bonilla, O'Phelan, Carrera Damas, Izard, Lombardi, Florescano, Hamnett, Brading, Ladd, Van Young, Lindley, and Potash, for particular themes or countries. Special aspects, some of them in a longer chronological framework, have been studied by A. Estévez and O. H. Elía, *Aspectos económico-financieros de la campaña sanmartiniana* (Buenos Aires, 1961), on the economic problems of waging war; Luis Ospina Vásquez, *Industria y protección en Colombia 1810–1930* (Medellín, 1955), a rare study of national policy towards industry; Eduardo Arcila Farías, *Historia de un monopolio. El Estanco del Tabaco en Venezuela, 1799–1833* (Caracas, 1977), on the impact of revolution on a vital revenue; J. F. Rippy, *British Investments in Latin America, 1822–1949* (Minneapolis, 1959), and D. C. M. Platt, *Latin America and British Trade, 1806–1914* (London, 1973), on British trade and finance in Latin America in the wake of independence.

For demography general reference can be made to Nicolás Sánchez-Albornoz, *The Population of Latin America: A History* (Berkeley and Los Angeles, 1974), and Angel Rosenblat, *La población indigena y el mestizaje en América* (2 vols, Buenos Aires, 1954), while more specialised data will be found in John V. Lombardi, *People and Places in Colonial Venezuela* (Bloomington, 1976). The best guide to race relations is Magnus Mörner, *Race Mixture in the History of Latin America* (Boston, 1967) and *Race and Class in Latin America* (New York, 1970). For the survival of race discrimination in Argentina see Emiliano Endrek, *El mestizaje en Córdoba, siglo XVIII y principios del XIX* (Córdoba, 1966). On slavery and abolition see works cited under individual countries.

The abundant literature on dependence curiously contains little research on independence. An exception is the work of Stanley J. and Barbara H. Stein, *The Colonial Heritage of Latin America. Essays on Economic Dependence in Perspective* (New York, 1970), which is a sustained commentary on the endurance of colonial structures beyond the revolutions for independence.

INTERNATIONAL RELATIONS

The revolutionary movements looked abroad for recruits, materials and diplomatic support, and the new states had to enter into relations with the wider world. These relations have been expertly studied. Peggy K. Liss, *Atlantic Empires: The Network of Trade and Revolution, 1713–1826* (Baltimore, 1983) studies the Atlantic empires of Britain, Spain and Portugal within a framework of international trade and the 'age of revolution'. The role of the United States can be studied in more detail in Charles C. Griffin, *The United States and the Disruption of the Spanish Empire, 1810–1822* (New York, 1937), and in A. P. Whitaker, *The United States and the Independence of Latin America, 1800–1830* (Baltimore, 1941). On relations between Britain and Latin America see C. K. Webster, *The Foreign Policy of Castlereagh, 1812–1815* (London, 1931), and *The Foreign Policy of Castlereagh, 1815–1822* (2nd ed., London, 1934); H. W. V. Temperley, *The Foreign Policy of Canning, 1822–1827* (London, 1925); W. W. Kaufmann, *British Policy and the Independence of Latin America* (New Haven, 1951); John Street, *Gran Bretaña y la independencia del Río de la Plata* (Buenos Aires, 1967); D. A. G. Waddell, *Gran Bretaña y la independencia de Venezuela y Colombia* (Caracas, 1983); Carlos Pi Sunyer, *Patriotas americanos en Londres* (Caracas, 1978); and R. A. Humphreys, 'Anglo-American Rivalries and Spanish American Emancipation', *Tradition and Revolt In Latin America,* pp. 130–53. The policy of the European powers is covered in W. S. Robertson, *France and Latin American Independence* (Baltimore, 1939); Manfred Kossok, *Im Schatten der Heiligen Allianz. Deutschland und Lateinamerika 1815–1830* (Berlin, 1964); R. H. Bartley, *Imperial Russia and the Struggle for Latin American Independence, 1808–1828* (Austin, 1978); and relations with Rome in Pedro Leturia, *Relaciones entre la Santa Sede e Hispanoamérica* (3 vols, Rome-Caracas, 1959–60). The response of Spain to independence has been thoroughly studied: E. A. Heredia, *Planes españoles para reconquistar hispano-america, 1810–1818* (Buenos Aires, 1974); J. M. Mariluz Urquijo, *Los proyectos españoles para reconquistar el Río de la Plata (1820–1833)* (Buenos Aires, 1958); Luis Miguel Enciso Recio, *La opinión pública española y la independencia hispanoamericana 1819–1820* (Valladolid, 1967); Timothy E. Anna, *Spain and the Loss of America* (Lincoln, Nebraska, 1983); Michael P. Costeloe, 'Spain and the Latin American Wars of Independence: The Free Trade Controversy, 1810–1820', *HAHR,* 61, 2 (1981), 209–34, and 'Spain and the Spanish American Wars of Independence: The *Comisión de Reemplazos, 1811–1820*', *JLAS,* 13, 2 (1981), 223–37.

Index

Abad y Quiepo, Manuel, 23, 299, 303–4, 312
Abalos, José, 15
Abascal y Sousa, José Fernando de, xiii, 124, 125, 136–37, 161–65, 167, 169, 171, 237
Acapulco, 26, 313, 317–18, 331
agriculture, colonial, 15–16, 25
  Banda Oriental, 46, 78, 81–82, 89–90, 98, 100
  Chile, 129–30
  Mexico, 297–99
  New Granada, 228–29, 260
  Paraguay, 106–7, 115–16
  Peru, 160–61, 273–74
  post-independence, 346
  Río de la Plata, 16–17, 46–47, 59, 66–67, 78–79
  Venezuela, 190–91, 220–21
Alamán, Lucas, xiii, 17, 18–19, 23, 34, 306, 310, 321, 323, 325–26, 328, 343, 350, 417
alcabala, colonial, 11
  Bolivia, 286
  Mexico, 323
  New Granada, 232, 258
  Peru, 160
  Venezuela, 194
alcaldes mayores, 8–9
Aldama, Juan de, 307, 311
Allende, Ignacio, 307, 312
Almeyda, José Vicente and Ambrosio, 243–44
Alvarez de Arenales, Juan Antonio, 119
Alvear, Carlos de, xiii, 61, 63–65, 98
Alzaga, Martin de, xiii, 17, 41, 43–44, 47, 50, 57
Alzate Ramirez, José Antonio, 33–34

Amar y Bourbón, Antonio, 238–40
Americanism, sense of, 1, 24, 27, 30–34
  Bolívar on, 253–54
  in war, 204
  see also nationalism
Amiens, peace of, 35
Anchorena, family of, 17, 82, 103
Angostura, 214–15
  Congress of, 213, 215–16, 218, 224, 245
Antioquia, 229, 241–43, 263, 294
Apure, 214–17, 223, 253, 352
Aragua, 190, 192, 219–20, 224
Aráoz, Bernabé, 70
Aráoz de la Madrid, Gregorio, 123
Arenales, General, 176, 178, 184
Arequipa, 169, 271, 275
Argentina, 342, 347
  see also Río de la Plata
armies:
  of the Andes, 87, 138–41
  of Bolívar, 202, 212–13, 217–18
  Mexican, 320–21, 323–24, 326, 329–30
  post-independence, 352–54
  royalist, Peru, 126–27, 162–63, 171–72, 179–80, 182, 185
  royalist, Venezuela, 199, 207–9, 212–13
  of San Martín, Peru, 174–80, 185, 187–88
  of Sucre, 87, 271–73
Artigas, José Gervasio:
  agrarian reformer, 99–100, 105
  career, xiii, 93
  conflict with Buenos Aires, 69
  exile in Paraguay, 101–2, 113
  federalism, 63–64, 97–98
  independence of Banda Oriental, 65, 94–102
Asunción, 107–9, 111

Ayachucho, battle of, 87, 102, 272–73, 283, 343
Aycinena, Marino, 338
Aymerich, General, 247–48
Ayopaya, 119–20
Azara, Félix de, 18
Azcárate, Juan Francisco, 301, 304–5

Bajío, 297, 306, 311–12
Balcarce, Juan Ramón, 45, 71
Banda Oriental:
  and Brazil, 68, 95–96, 100–105
  and Buenos Aires, 26, 58
  cattle, 46, 78, 81–82, 89–91
  independence, 105, 345
  independence movement, 92–95
  rule of Artigas, 97–100
  society, 90–91
Baquijano, José, 159
Baraya, Antonio, 240–41, 243
Belgrano, Manuel:
  career, xiv, 46, 417
  consulado, 16, 48–49
  ideas, 28, 50, 68, 70, 342
  May revolution, 43, 52, 55
  Paraguay, 60, 94, 108
  Upper Peru, 63, 65, 86–87, 122–123, 126
Benavides, 155, 380 n
Bentham, Jeremy, 72
Berbeo, Juan Francisco, 232
Bermúdez, Francisco, 210, 219, 223
Beruti, Antonio Luis, 43, 53, 56
Bogotá, 218–19, 228–29, 232, 234–35, 237–42, 246, 250–51, 254, 293–94
Bolívar, Simón, xiv, 138, 141, 146
  Americanism, 25, 253–54, 256–57
  Bolivia, 286–87, 289–90
  Bolivian constitution, 250, 255, 285–86
  career, 200–201, 293–94
  death, 294
  first republic, 197–99
  Gran Colombia, 218, 245–46, 250–56, 343
  Guayaquil, 185–87
  ideas, 15, 28, 29, 30, 200–202, 210, 215–16, 266, 350, 351, 355
  land distribution, 212, 214–15, 222–23
  liberation of New Granada, 216–18, 241–42, 244–45
  liberation of Quito, 247–49
  liberation of Venezuela, 219
  Peru, 171, 187–88, 189, 268–73, 276, 278–79, 291–92
  on race, 19, 23–24, 201, 211–13, 225–26, 250, 255, 264–65, 347
  slavery, 201, 212–13, 224
  Upper Peru, 273, 281–86
  Venezuelan independence, 196–97
  war to the death, 202–5, 206–7, 210–15

Bolivia, 58
  constitution (1826), 285–86
  economy, 286–88
  independence, 89, 284, 334
  society, 288–91
  Sucre regime, 286
Bonaparte, Joseph, 36, 42
Bonaparte, Napoleon, 1, 29, 35–36, 42, 48, 52, 56
Bourbon reforms, 5–15
  and Central America, 334, 338
  and Chile, 129
  collapse of, 36
  Creole alienation from, 24
  and New Granada, 234
Boves, José Tomás, xiv, 199, 205–7, 224
Bowles, William, 99, 175
Boyacá, 231, 260, 263
  battle of, 141, 218, 244
Brazil, 43, 48, 68, 69, 78, 85, 90, 95–96, 107, 116–17
Buenos Aires, 26, 38, 40, 163
  agriculture, 81–82
  British invasions, 40–42
  and interior, 47, 49–50, 58–60, 64–71
  May revolution, 52–58
  and Montevideo, 80–104
  and Paraguay, 105–6, 107–10, 114–17
  post-independence trade, 80–81, 345
  Rivadavia regime, 71–80
  social structure, 82–88
  trade, 12, 14, 16, 17, 26, 35, 47–50
  and Upper Peru, 118, 121–26
Bustamante, Carlos Maria de, xiv, 333, 335–36

Caballero y Góngora, Antonio, xiv, 230–32
cabildo, colonial, 12
  Asunción, 107–8
  Buenos Aires, 40, 49, 55
  Caracas, 22
  Central America, 336, 338
  Guanajuato, 310
  Mexico City, 27, 301, 305
  Montevideo, 44
  New Granada, 234, 240
  Peru, 161, 164, 168, 172
  Santiago, 132
  Venezuela, 191, 196, 203
Cadiz, 12, 16, 48–49, 52, 172, 195, 208, 218, 241, 297, 335, 339
  cortes of, 36, 164, 168, 174, 325
Calabozo, 205, 213, 215
Caldas, Francisco José de, xiv, 32–33, 233, 243
Calderón, Bridge of, 312
Callao, 174, 177, 179–80, 189, 268–69, 273, 292
Calleja, Félix María, xv, 312, 314, 316–18
Cancha Rayada, battle of, 141

Canning, George, 103
Cantera, José de, 172, 183, 271–73, 280–81
Carabobo, battle of, 219, 224
Caracas:
    counterrevolution, 199, 202, 205, 207, 209, 218
    earthquake, 198–99
    junta, 195–96, 227
    society, 22–23, 191–92
Carlota Joaquina, Princess, 43
Carrera, José Miguel, xv, 135–37, 153, 156
Cartagena, 3, 26, 35, 200, 207, 210, 217, 229, 238–39, 240–42, 244–45, 247, 256, 264–65
    Manifesto, 201–202
Casanare, 213, 216–17, 239, 241, 243–44
Castelli, Juan, José:
    career, xv, 46
    May revolution, 43, 49, 52, 54–55, 60
    Upper Peru, 121–22, 124–26
Cauca, 229, 236, 263
caudillos:
    in Mexico, 313, 323
    post-independence, 339–40, 353–56
    In Río de la Plata, 64, 66, 70–71, 99, 101, 114–15
    in upper Peru, 119–20
    in Venezuela, 205–6, 211, 219, 223, 227
Cavo, Andrés, 32
Cázerez, Juan Manuel de, 51, 125
Central America, 333–40
Cepeda, battle of (1 February 1820), 70, 101
Cerro de Pasco, 184, 272
Chacabuco, battle of, 141
chapetones. see peninsulares
Charcas, 125, 282
Charles III, xv, 5, 7, 34, 35
Charles IV, xv, 35, 36, 42
Chile:
    conservatives, 148–50
    counterrevolution, 137–38
    economy, 12–13, 26, 129–30, 150–53, 347
    liberals, 146–48
    liberation, 140–41, 171–72
    liberation of Peru, 172–74, 178, 180, 185, 268–69, 291
    national identity, 30–32, 128, 130–32
    O'Higgins regime, 141–46
    Patria Vieja, 134–37
    revolution, 132–34
    social structure, 128–30, 153–57
Chilpancingo, Congress of, 316
Chirino, José Leonardo, 194
cholo, 25, 159, 172, 287
Chuquisaca, 119, 121, 282, 284, 291
Church:
    Chile, 144, 150

and Consolidation of 1804, 303, 334
and creoles, 18
fuero, 10
Mexico, 10, 303–5, 315, 319, 321, 322, 326, 329
Paraguay, 112
post-independence, 346–47, 351–52
Río de la Plata, 39–40, 73
Venezuela, 192, 198–99
Cisneros, Baltasar Hidalago de, 49–50, 53, 55, 92
Clavijero, Francisco Javier, 31, 33
Cochabamba, 119, 121, 167, 283
Cochrane, Thomas, Tenth Earl of Dundonald, xv, 142, 173–74, 176–77, 179–80
Colombia, Gran:
    disintegration, 292–94
    established, 218–19, 245–46
    Peru, 186, 268–72, 290, 291
    Quito and Ecuador, 245–49
    Santander regime, 249–50, 352
    society, 265
    Venezuela, 251–53, 255–57
Colónia do Sacramento, 90–91, 99, 102
Comercio libre, 12–16, 26, 91, 107, 129, 230, 231, 297, 300, 334
commerce; see trade
Concepción, 133–36, 146–47, 149, 152
Concolorcorvo, 8–9, 21, 159
conservativism:
    in Chile, 148–50, 153
    in Colombia, 249–50
    in Mexico, 325–26
    in Peru, 159
    post-independence, 350–51
constitutions:
    Bolivia (1826), 285–86, 290
    Central America (1824), 339
    Chile (1833), 149–50, 350
    Colombia (Cúcuta, 1821), 246, 250, 256, 350
    of 1812 in Spain, 36, 164–65, 171–72, 316–19, 350
    Mexico (1824), 325–26, 350
    Peru (1826), 276, 292
    United Provinces (1826), 79
    Uruguay (1830), 105
    Venezuela (1811), 197; (1830), 227, 350
consulado:
    of Buenos Aires, 16, 49
    of Caracas, 191–92, 220
    of Lima, 161
    of Mexico City, 297, 305
    of Santiago, 131
Coquimbo, 129, 146–47, 152
Córdoba, 38, 47, 57, 59, 65, 66, 68, 70, 86–88, 98, 121, 138
Coro, 191, 194, 198–99, 202, 219
corregidores, 8, 168, 239

Corrientes, 46, 59, 67–69, 78, 81, 98, 101, 114
cortes:
  of 1812, 36, 164, 168, 325, 345
  of 1820–21, 319–20
Costa Rica, 337, 339
creoles, 2, 295
  Banda Oriental, 93
  Bolivia, 280, 282–83, 289
  Central America, 334
  Chile, 128, 130, 135
  control of, 7
  and independence, 348, 349
  Jesuits, 9–10
  Mexico, 18, 299–301, 307, 309–310, 312–14, 317–21
  militia, 10–11
  New Granada, 233, 235–36, 238–39, 243–44
  office, 17–18
  Paraguay, 107–8
  Peru, 160–63, 167–71
  Quito, 237
  race, 19–24
  Río de la Plata, 40–52, 55, 56
  transatlantic trade, 15
  Venezuela, 194–97, 204–5, 212
Cuba, 1, 3, 295–96, 326
Cúcuta, 218, 245
  Congress of, 225, 245–46, 250, 258, 262–64
Cuernavaca, 327, 332
Cumaná, 202, 205, 214–15, 219, 247
Cundinamarca, 231, 240–42, 246, 249, 251, 263
Cuyo, 138–40
Cuzco, 159, 166, 167–70, 176, 271, 278, 283

Dolores, 306, 309
Domínguez, Miguel, 307
Dorrego, Manuel, xv, 69, 79–80

Economic Societies, 5, 33
Ecuador:
  economy, 231, 260–61
  liberation, 247–49, 268
  Negroes, 225
  separatism, 257, 293
  see also Quito
Egaña, Juan, xv, 32, 131, 133, 137, 147, 150, 157
Elío, Francisco Xavier de, xv, 44, 91–94, 95
Enlightenment, in Spanish America, 27–29
  Bolívar and, 200–201
  Chile, 142
  Mexico, 27, 325
  New Granada, 233–34, 261–62

Peru, 159
  Río de la Plata, 72
Entre Ríos, 46, 59, 67–69, 78, 81, 95, 98, 101, 111, 114
España, José María, 194
Espejo, Francisco Javier de Santa Cruz, 33, 234
estancia, estancieros:
  in Banda Oriental, 90, 94
  in Río de la Plata, 16, 68, 77–78, 80–83, 103

federalism:
  in Banda Oriental, 97–98, 99
  in Chile, 147–48
  in Colombia, 246, 249–50, 254–55
  in Mexico, 325–26
  in New Granada, 240–42
  post-independence, 350–51
  in Río de la Plata, 59–63, 66–68, 69, 79–80
  in Venezuela, 202
Ferdinand VII, xvi, 36, 42–44, 56–58, 132, 136, 138, 162, 171–72, 196, 207–9, 237, 271, 281, 305, 307, 314, 317, 319, 336
France:
  and Spain, 34–36, 42, 52, 195
  and Spanish America, 27–29, 193–94, 233, 344
Francia, José Gaspar Rodríguez de, xvi, 101, 106, 108
  dictator, 110–11
  regime, 111–15
  rise to power, 109–10
  socioeconomic policy, 115–18
Freire, Ramón, xvi, 146–47, 154
French, Domingo, 53, 56

gachupines. see peninsulares
Gaínza, Gabino, 337–38
Gálvez, José de, xvi
Gamarra, Agustín, 188
García Carrasco, Francisco Antonio, 132
García del Río, Juan, 180–81
García, Manuel J., 82
gaucho:
  in Banda Oriental, 90, 93–94, 105
  in Río de la Plata, 25, 59, 83–84, 271
Germany, 344
Gil de Taboada y Lemos, Francisco, 5
Godoy, Manuel, 35, 36, 304
Gómez de Vidaurre, Felipe, 131
Goyeneche, José Manuel de, 122, 125, 163
gracias al sacar, cédula de, 21–22
Graham, Maria, 142, 415
Great Britain, and Spanish America:
  Banda Oriental, 96, 99, 104
  Bolivia, 287–88

Central America, 335–336
Chile, 151–53, 155, 173–74
Mexico, 326–29
New Granada, 260
Paraguay, 113–14, 116–17
Peru, 183–84, 274–75
post-independence, 343–44
Río de la Plata, 40–42, 47–50, 65, 75–77, 78, 80, 81, 85, 91–92
Spain, 5, 7, 35, 48
Venezuela, 216, 218, 221
Guadalajara, 310, 312
Guadalupe Victoria (Manuel Félix Fernández), xvi, 313, 318, 324
Gual, Manuel, 194
Guanajuato, 300, 309–10, 312, 318
Guatemala, 335–38
Guatemala City, 337
Guayana, 198, 202, 210–11, 214, 222
Guayaquil, 3, 185–87, 231, 237–38, 247–49
Güemes Martin, 70, 354
Guerrero, Vicente, 313, 318, 320–21, 331
guerrillas:
  in Mexico, 312, 314, 317
  in New Granada, 243–44
  in Peru, 182–83, 269, 277
  post-independence, 353–54
  in Río de la Plata, 101
  in Upper Peru, 119–21, 126–27
  in Venezuela, 200, 207
  see also montoneros
Guirior, Manuel, 229, 232
Gutiérrez, Frutos, 241, 243

hacienda:
  in Chile, 129–30, 144
  in Mexico, 297–98, 307, 330–31
  in New Granada, 228–29, 259
  in Peru, 279
  post-independence, 346–47, 353
  in Río de la Plata, 59–60
  in Venezuela, 15, 191–92, 197, 204, 222–24
Haiti, 29, 210, 298
  see also Saint Domingue
Hall, Basil, 274, 415
Henríquez, Camilo, 131, 135–36, 137
Hidalgo y Costilla, Miguel:
  career, xvi, 306
  defeat, 312–13
  insurgent, 307–10, 313–14, 317, 321, 322
  social policy, 310–311
Honduras, 335, 336–339
Huamanga, 164, 169, 182
Huancavelica, 169
Huaquí, Battle of, 60, 122

Humboldt, Alexander von, xvii, 1, 18, 19, 34, 191–92, 299, 302, 328, 416–17

Iguala, Plan de, 321–22, 330, 331, 337
Indians:
  in Bolivia, 286–89
  in Central America, 333, 335, 339
  in Chile, 128, 140, 154–55, 157
  in Colombia, 246
  in Mexico, 7–9, 20, 298, 299, 301–2, 306–7, 309, 310–12, 314, 315–16, 321, 330, 332–33
  in New Granada, 228, 232–35, 239, 244, 261–63
  in Paraguay, 116–18
  in Peru, 8–9, 11, 20, 158–59, 164–72, 179, 181, 272–73, 277–79
  post-independence, 347–49
  in Quito, 237–38, 251, 257
  in Río de la Plata, 39, 84
  in Upper Peru, 51–52, 118–26
  in Venezuela, 194, 205
industry, colonial, 3, 5, 15
  in Mexico, 326–28, 345
  in New Granada, 230–31, 258–60, 345
  in Río de la Plata, 77–78
  in Venezuela, 221
Infante, José Miguel, 156
inquilino, 25, 130, 157
intendants:
  in Mexico and Peru, 7–9
  in Peru, 160, 161, 168
  in Río de la Plata, 40
Irisarri, José de, 152–53
Itapúa, 117
Iturbide, Agustín de:
  career, xvii, 320–21
  Central America, 337–338
  emperor, 323–24, 329
  Plan de Iguala, 321–22
Iturrigaray, José de, 304–5

Jamaica, 242, 259
Jamaica Letter, 210
Jesuits:
  and Americanism, 30–32
  in Chile, 131
  expulsion of, 9–10, 40, 319
  in Paraguay, 116, 118
Juanambú, battle of, 241
Juárez, Benito, 326, 333
Junín, 184
  battle of, 272
junta:
  in Buenos Aires, 55–58
  in Caracas, 196, 210
  in Montevideo, 92
  in Spain, 36, 43, 52, 54, 195

La Guaira, 194, 199, 200
La Mar, José de, xvii, 291
Lancaster, school system, 73, 143, 273
Lanza, Manuel Garcia, 51
Lanza, Miguel, 119, 282
La Paz, 51–52, 119, 121, 124, 125, 169,
    170, 283–84, 287, 289–90
La Rioja, 59, 70, 78
La Serna, José de, xvii, 172, 178–79, 271–
    73, 280–81
Las Muñecas, Ildefonso de, 119
Lavalleja, Juan Antonio, xv, 102–3
Lavardén, Manuel José, 16, 417
Lecór, Carlos Frederico, 100–102
liberalism:
    in Chile, 148–49, 154, 156
    in Colombia, 246, 249–50, 256–57, 261–
        64
    Indian policy, 348–49
    in Mexico, 319, 325–26, 329, 331–33
    in Peru, 160, 164–65, 168, 172, 176, 185
    post-independence, 349–51, 352
    in Río de la Plata, 60, 72–74, 79, 85
    in Spain, 36, 164, 218, 319–22
    in Uruguay, 105
Lima:
    and Chile, 131, 151
    creole elite in, 18
    enlightenment, 33
    liberation, 172, 176–80, 183, 185, 187,
        268–69, 272, 274–75, 285
    society, 158–59
    Spaniards, 162–63, 164, 179, 188
    trade, 160–61
    Upper Peru, 118
Liniers, Santiago, xvii, 41–45, 48, 52, 57,
    92
llanos, llaneros, 25, 191, 199, 201, 204–7,
    214–15, 218–19, 223–24, 252, 271
López, Estanislao, 69, 70, 101
López y Plantes, Vicente, 342
Lué y Riega, Benito de, 53–54
Luna Pizarro, Francisco Javier, xvii, 185,
    187

Magdalena River, 229, 241–42, 259
Maipo, battle of, 141, 155
Maracaibo, 190, 198, 202, 219, 259
Marcó del Pont, Francisco Casimiro, 127,
    137–38, 140, 143
Mariño, Santiago, xvi, 202, 205, 207, 210–
    11, 214, 219, 223, 252
Maturin, 203, 214
Medina, José Antonio, 51
Mendoza, 13–14, 47, 59, 65, 137–41
Mercurio Peruano, 30, 33, 159
mestizos, in the colony, 20–23
    Central America, 335, 339
    Chile, 128, 130

New Granada, 228–29, 232, 235, 251
Paraguay, 107, 118
Peru, 159, 164–65, 276
Quito, 237
Venezuela, 192
Mexico:
    and Central America, 333–34, 338
    church, 10, 303–5, 319, 321, 322, 326,
        329
    constitution of 1824, 325–26
    counterrevolution, 312, 316–19
    creole grievances, 302–6, 348
    economy, 3–4, 12–15, 296–99, 326–29,
        345–46
    independence, 321–22
    insurgency, 306–16
    Iturbide regime, 322–24
    militia, 11
    nationalism, 27, 30–34, 320, 342–43
    Society, 17, 18, 299–302, 329–33
    Spanish liberalism, 319–20
Mexico City, 301, 305, 310, 312, 313, 318,
    322, 323, 326, 328
Michoacán, 312–13, 318
Mier, Servando Teresa de, 304
militia, colonial, 10–11
    Mexico, 11, 305, 320
    Peru, 162–63
    Río de la Plata, 41–45, 52, 55, 83
    Venezuela, 191–93
Miller, William, xviii, 72, 87, 142, 178, 188,
    277, 287
mining, colonial, 2–4
    Bolivia, 287–88
    Chile, 152
    Mexico, 296–97, 327–29
    New Granada, 230, 258–59
    Peru, 161, 274–75
    Río de la Plata, 78
    Upper Peru, 161, 284
Miranda, Francisco de:
    career, xviii
    ideas, 28
    in Venezuela, 196, 199
Misiones, 101, 117
Mitre, Bartolomé, 41–42, 123, 419
Molina, Juan Ignacio, 31, 131
Mompox, 229, 236, 242
Monagas, José Tadeo, 214, 223
Monroe Doctrine, 343
Monteagudo, Bernardo de:
    career, xviii
    in Peru, 180–81, 187, 273
    in Río de la Plata, 61, 64, 124
Monteverde, Juan Domingo, xviii, 199–
    200, 203–4, 220
Montevideo:
    Artigas regime, 98–100
    and Brazil, 95–96, 102

British invasion, 41
Elío in, 44, 92–95
royalists, 63–64
trade, 48, 91
montoneros:
  in Peru, 182–83
  in Río de la Plata, 70–71, 101
  in Upper Peru, 119–20
  see also guerrillas
Mora, José María Luis, 29, 303, 321, 325, 332, 417
Morelos, José María:
  career, xviii, 313
  execution, 318
  insurgent, 10, 313–14, 322
  nationalism, 314–15, 342
  social policy, 315–17, 331
Moreno, Mariano:
  career, xix, 46
  ideas, 28
  May revolution, 55
  Representación de las haciendas, 49–50
  resignation, 60
Morillo, Pablo, xix, 138, 209–10, 212–13, 216–17, 218–19, 242–45
mulattos, in the colony, 20–22
  Banda Oriental, 88
  Bolivia, 290
  Central America, 335, 339
  Chile, 128
  Colombia, 254, 256–57
  Mexico, 301–2, 307, 315, 332
  New Granada, 235–36, 264–65
  Paraguay, 118
  Río de la Plata, 39, 41, 86–88
  Venezuela, 192–93
  see also pardos

Nariño, Antonio, xix, 28, 233, 239–41, 245–46
National Constituent Assembly, 338–39
nationalism, incipient, 24–37, 333, 342–43, 347, 349
  in Banda Oriental, 96
  in Bolivia, 290
  in Colombia, 254, 256–57
  in Peru, 159–60, 268, 291
  in Upper Peru, 120–21, 123
  in Venezuela, 200, 204
Negroes, in the colony, 19–22
  in Banda Oriental, 100
  in Chile, 128, 130
  in Cuba, 296
  in Ecuador, 257
  in Mexico, 301–2, 307, 315, 331–32
  in New Granada, 235–36, 264–65
  in Paraguay, 117–18
  in Peru, 158–59, 166, 170–71
  in Río de la Plata, 39, 41, 84–88

  in Venezuela, 191–94, 197–98, 205, 224–27
New Granada:
  Bolívar and, 200, 202, 210, 241–42, 244–45
  comuneros, 12, 232–33
  counterrevolution, 209, 242–44
  creole elite, 18, 24
  economy, 228–31, 234–35, 258–60
  Gran Colombia, 245–46, 251
  Indians and resguardos, 229, 261–63, 349
  liberation, 216–18, 238–42, 244–45
  national identity, 32–33
  race, 21–22, 235–36, 264–65
  slavery, 236, 263–64
  viceroyalty, 186
Nicaragua, 335–39
Ninavilca, Ignacio, 183

Oaxaca, 8, 305–6, 314
O'Donojú, Juan, 321–22
O'Higgins, Ambrosio, 133
O'Higgins, Bernardo:
  career, xix
  commander-in-chief, 136–37
  exile, 146
  and independence, 133–35, 150
  nationalism, 131–32
  and San Martín, 139–41, 145, 147
  supreme dictator, 141–46, 152–53, 156, 173
Olañeta, Casimiro, 282, 284
Olañeta, Pedro Antonio de, xix, 124, 271–72, 280–83
O'Leary, Daniel Florence, xx, 19, 204, 211, 253, 265, 270, 294, 416
Orinoco River, 210–11, 214, 259
Oruro, 121, 167
Osorio, Mariano, 137, 141

Padilla, José Prudencio, 225, 256, 265
Padilla, Manuel Ascensio, 119
Paéz, José Antonio, xviii, 247, 416
  property, 222–24
  rebellion, 227, 251–53, 255
  war, 214–19
Panama, 247, 253
Pando, José María, 273, 292
Paraguay:
  and Buenos Aires, 26, 58
  economic structure, 106
  Francia regime, 110–18
  independence, 89, 108–9, 345
  society, 106–7, 117
pardos:
  in New Granada, 264–65
  in Peru, 158–59, 276
  in Río de la Plata, 87–88

pardos (continued)
  in Venezuela, 191–94, 197–99, 200,
    211–13, 225–27, 251
Parish, Woodbine, 76–77, 116, 415
Paroissien, James, 181, 287
Paso, Juan José, 60
Pasto, 231, 241, 248, 261
peninsulares:
  Banda Oriental, 90
  Chile, 129
  Mexico, 301
  office, 18
  Paraguay, 107, 117–18
  Peru, 181
  Río de la Plata, 39–52, 55
Peru:
  and Chile, 26, 130–31, 134, 145, 151–
    52, 172–74, 180, 291
  Creole elite, 18, 24
  economy, 3-5, 12–13, 160–62, 183–84,
    273–76
  Guayaquil, 185–86, 247–49
  Indians, 8–9, 20, 158–59, 164–72, 179,
    181, 272–73, 277–79
  liberation (Bolívar), 267–73, 295
  liberation (San Martin), 138–39, 158,
    172–88
  nationalism, 291–93
  Pumacahua rebellion, 167–71
  royalists, 162–65
  slavery, 166, 172, 179–80, 276–77, 347
  society, 158–60, 165–66, 226, 275–79,
    348, 49
Pétion, Alexandre, 210
Pezuela, Joaquín de la, xx, 122–27, 171–
  72, 174, 176, 178, 280
Philippines, 302
Piar, Manuel, xx, 207, 210–12
Pichincha, battle of, 186, 248
Pilar, Treaty of, 71, 101
Pilar de Ñeembucú, 117
Pinto, Antonio, 147–48, 154
Pisco, 172
Pombo, Miguel de, 243, 262
Ponsonby, Lord John, 104
Popayán, 228–29, 241–42, 245
population:
  Banda Oriental, 90
  Bolivia, 288, 402 n
  Chile, 128
  Colombia, 265
  Mexico, 298–99, 326
  New Granada, 228–29
  Paraguay, 106
  Peru, 158–59, 165, 380–81 n
  Río de la Plata, 38–39
  Spanish America, 1, 19–23, 360 n
  Venezuela, 191, 221–22, 227
Portales, Diego, xx, 148–49, 153

Posada, Gutiérrez, Joaquín, 265
Posados, Gervasio Antonio, 64, 65, 138
Potosí, 26, 47, 106, 121–22, 161, 283–84,
  287
Prieto, Joaquín, 148–49
Primo de Verdad y Ramos, Francisco, 301,
  305
Puebla, 14, 312–13, 327, 331
Puerto Cabello, 199, 204, 219
Puerto Rico, 1, 199, 296
Pueyrredón, Juan Martín de, xx, 45, 60,
  68–70, 75, 140
Pumacahua, Mateo, xx, 125, 166–68
  rebellion of, 123, 124, 167–70
Puno, 169

Querétaro, 14, 307, 309, 327
Quiroga, Facundo, 70, 354
Quito, 33, 163, 186, 217, 230, 244–45, 291
  economy, 231–32, 234
  Gran Colombia, 245–49
  liberation, 247–49
  rebellion, 236–39
  separatism, 257

race, in the colony, 19–23
  Chile, 128
  Colombia, 250–51, 255
  Mexico, 22, 331–33
  New Granada, 21–22, 235–36, 264–65
  Paraguay, 118
  Peru, 158–59, 164, 165–66
  post-independence, 347–49
  Río de la Plata, 21, 84–88
  Venezuela, 22–23, 191–94, 197–98,
    205–6, 211–13, 225–27
  see also Indians, mulattos, Negroes, par-
    dos
Ramírez, Francisco, 69–71, 101, 111
Ramírez, Juan, 124, 169
Rancagua, battle of, 137–38
rancheros, 297
Rayón, Ignacio, 313, 314
Regency, Council of, 36, 108, 195
regional separatism, autonomy, 338, 353
Rengifo, Manuel, 149
repartimientos, 8–9, 160, 168
Revenga, José Rafael, 221, 261, 418
Revillagigedo, Count of, 11, 14–15
Riaño, Juan Antonio, 309
Río de la Plata:
  Banda Oriental, 89–105
  Brazil, 103–5
  British invasions, 40–42
  Buenos Aires and interior, 49–50, 58–
    60, 64–71
  Chile, 139–41, 173
  church, 39–40, 73

colonial economy, 13–16, 25–26, 39–40, 46–50
colonial society, 21, 39–40, 46–50
enlightenment, 28, 72
May revolution, 52–58
militia, 41–45, 52, 55
national identity, 32, 342
Paraguay, 105–10, 114–17
peninsulares, 39–52, 55
Peru, 173, 268–69, 291
population, 38–40
post-independence economy, 59–60, 66, 80–83
Rivadavia regime, 71–80
society, 82–88, 354–56
triumvirates, 60–63
Upper Peru, 118, 120–127, 283–84, 290
viceroyalty of, 40, 91, 107, 118
Riva Agüero, José de la, xxi, 188–89, 267–69
Rivadavia, Bernardino:
career, xxi
economic plans, 67, 73–78, 351
fall of, 79–80
government of, 71–73, 142
triumvirate, 60–61, 63
war with Brazil, 103
Rivera, José Fructuoso, xxi, 103
Robertson, John Parish, 76, 109–10, 113–14, 183–84, 415
Rodríguez Aldea, José Antonio, 144–145
Rodríguez de Mendoza, Toribio, 159
Rodríguez, Martín, 45, 71, 76, 77
Rodríguez Peña, Nicolás, 43, 52
Rojas, José Antonio de, 32, 131, 133
Rondeau, José, 70, 94, 123
Rosas, Juan Manuel de, xxi, 77, 80, 82–83
Rousseau, Jean-Jacques, 27–28, 201
Rozas, Juan Martínez de, xxi, 133–35
Ruiz de Apodaca, Juan, 319
Ruiz de Castilla, Count, 236–37

Saavedra, Cornelio, xxi, 42, 44–45, 52, 54–55, 57, 60, 61
Saenz Valiente, family of, 82, 370 n
Saint Domingue, 29, 193–94
see also Haiti
Salas, Manuel de, xxi, 32, 131, 133, 156
Salta, 38, 59, 65–66, 70, 121, 122, 354
Salvador, El, 345, 338–39
Sámano, Juan, 218, 241–45
Sánchez Carrión, José, xxii, 185, 270
San Martin, José de:
army of the Andes, 65, 68, 70, 87, 88, 127, 138–41, 171–72
army of the north, 64, 123–24
career, xxii
Guayaquil, 185–87, 247–49
liberation of Peru, 145, 158, 172–80, 270

protector, 180–84, 276–78
retirement, 187–88
revolution, 61, 63
San Miguel, antonio de, 298–99, 302
Santa Anna, Antonio López de, xxii, 324
Santa Coloma, 17, 41, 43–45, 48, 55, 82
Santa Cruz, Andrés, xxii, 186, 188, 248, 269, 280, 292–93
Santa Fe, 59, 64–65, 67–68, 70, 81, 98, 101, 106, 114
Santa Maria, 229, 241–42, 261, 294
Santander, Francisco de Paula:
and attempt to assassinate Bolívar, 293
career, xxii
liberation of New Granada, 216–18, 241, 244–45
vice president of Colombia, 246–47, 249–50, 252–53, 255–57, 263
Santiago, 18, 26, 47, 129, 133–34, 137, 141
Santiago del Estero, 70
Sanz, Francisco de Paula, 121–22
Sarmiento, Domingo Faustino, 67, 77, 80, 351
Sarratea, Manuel, 60, 63, 71
Selva Alegre, Marquis of, 237
Seville, 12, 43, 52
Sipe Sipe, battle of, 123, 126
slavery, in the colony, 20
Bolivia, 285, 289–90
Central America, 339
Chile, 130, 155–57
Colombia, 246
Mexico, 311, 315–16, 331–32
New Granada, 229, 234–36, 239, 263–64
Peru, 166, 172, 179–80, 276–77
post-independence, 347
Río de la Plata, 84–87, 105, 140
Venezuela, 29, 190–94, 197–200, 201, 204–5, 213, 224–25
Smith, Sir Sidney, 48
Sobremonte, Marquis of, 40–41
Socorro, 229, 231, 232, 234, 236, 239, 243, 260
Spain, Spaniards:
Central America, 334–38
Chile, 128, 132, 134, 135–38, 141, 143, 150
crisis of 1808, 1, 10, 35–36, 52
emigration to America, 17
imperial control, 2–17
Mexico, 17, 296, 299–306, 310, 314–15, 318–22, 326–27
Montevideo, 63–64, 90–98
New Granada, 230–32, 235, 241–45
Paraguay, 107, 117–18
Peru, 162–65, 167–68, 170–71, 172, 174, 178, 181–82, 187–88, 268–69, 271–73, 275

Spain, Spaniards (*continued*)
Quito, 238, 248
and race, 19–24
reform, 5
restoration, 207–9
Upper Peru, 68–69, 118–26
Venezuela, 194–95, 198–99, 203–4, 209, 216–19
Strangford, Viscount, 96
Sucre, Antonio José de:
assassination, 294
career, xxii
in Peru, 87, 189, 268, 271–73
in Quito, 247–48
in Upper Peru, 283–91
Suipacha, battle of, 121

Taboada y Lemus, Gil de, 5
Tacuarembó, 101, 102
Talamantes, Melchor de, 305
Telégrafo Mercantil, 32, 39, 342
Toro, Marquis of, 192, 198, 209
Toro Zambrano, Mateo de, Conde de la Conquista, 132
Torres, Camilo, xxiii, 233, 239–41, 243
Torre Tagle, Marquis of, xxiii, 177, 181, 185, 187, 268–69
trade, colonial, 2–5, 35–36
in Banda Oriental, 91–92
in Central America, 334–36, 339
in Chile, 129, 150–52
comercio libre, 12–16, 26
in Ecuador, 260–61
in Mexico, 297, 326–29
in New Granada, 259–60
in Paraguay, 106, 114–15
in Peru, 160–62, 274
post-independence, 343–45
in Río de la Plata, 59, 66–67, 75–76
in Venezuela, 192, 221
Trujillo, 177, 189, 268, 270, 278
Tucumán, 13–14, 47, 59, 65–66, 69–70, 106, 121, 123, 138
Congress of, 68–69, 140
Tumusla, battle of, 283
Tupac Amaru, xxiii, 8, 165–67

Unánue, Hipólito, 33, 159, 180, 273
United Provinces of Central America, 339
United States of America:
constitution, 63, 325
and Mexico, 326–27, 328
Monroe Doctrine, 343

and Spanish America, 29–30
trade, 152, 260, 344
University:
of Buenos Aires, 73
of Caracas, 22–23, 192
of Chuquisaca, 282
of Córdoba, 88
Upper Peru:
and Buenos Aires, 58, 63, 118, 121–26
economy, 47, 59, 161
guerrillas, 119–21, 126–27
liberation, 273
under Olañeta, 280–83
and Peru, 163, 171, 271–72
revolution of 1809, 50–52
Uruguay; *see* Banda Oriental

Valdés, Jerónimo, 172, 271–72, 280–81
Valdivia, 155, 173
Valencia, 198–199, 202, 205, 220, 252, 352
Valladolid, Michoacán, 306, 313–14, 317–18, 320
Valle, José del, 337
Valparaiso, 145, 152, 174
Varela, Juan Cruz, 56
Vargas, Pedro Fermín de, 28, 233, 261
Velasco Bernardo, 107–9
Venegas, Francisco Javier de, 309, 316
Venezuela:
counterrevolution, 199–200, 207–9
economy, 12, 13, 15, 190–92, 195, 347
first republic, 197–99
Gran Colombia, 245–46, 251–53, 255–57, 293, 352
independence, 195–97
race, 22–24, 29, 192–94, 197–98, 205–6, 211–13, 224–27
second republic, 202–7
society, 191–92, 222–24
war, 210–16
Veracruz, 35, 313, 318, 324, 331, 333
Vieytes, Hipólito, 16, 43, 46

Warnes, Ignacio, 119
Whitelocke, John, 41

yanaconazgo, 84, 165
Yegros, Fulgencio, 109–10
Yermo, Gabriel de, 305
Yucután, 8

Zacatecas, 8, 312, 331
zambos, 39, 40, 128, 205, 235